CONTEMPORARY FICTIONS
ESSAYS ON AMERICAN AND POSTCOLONIAL NARRATIVES

LEGENDA

LEGENDA is the Modern Humanities Research Association's book imprint for new research in the Humanities. Founded in 1995 by Malcolm Bowie and others within the University of Oxford, Legenda has always been a collaborative publishing enterprise, directly governed by scholars. The Modern Humanities Research Association (MHRA) joined this collaboration in 1998, became half-owner in 2004, in partnership with Maney Publishing and then Routledge, and has since 2016 been sole owner. Titles range from medieval texts to contemporary cinema and form a widely comparative view of the modern humanities, including works on Arabic, Catalan, English, French, German, Greek, Italian, Portuguese, Russian, Spanish, and Yiddish literature. Editorial boards and committees of more than 60 leading academic specialists work in collaboration with bodies such as the Society for French Studies, the British Comparative Literature Association and the Association of Hispanists of Great Britain & Ireland.

The MHRA encourages and promotes advanced study and research in the field of the modern humanities, especially modern European languages and literature, including English, and also cinema. It aims to break down the barriers between scholars working in different disciplines and to maintain the unity of humanistic scholarship. The Association fulfils this purpose through the publication of journals, bibliographies, monographs, critical editions, and the MHRA Style Guide, and by making grants in support of research. Membership is open to all who work in the Humanities, whether independent or in a University post, and the participation of younger colleagues entering the field is especially welcomed.

ALSO PUBLISHED BY THE ASSOCIATION

Critical Texts
Tudor and Stuart Translations • *New Translations* • *European Translations*
MHRA Library of Medieval Welsh Literature

MHRA Bibliographies
Publications of the Modern Humanities Research Association

The Annual Bibliography of English Language & Literature
Austrian Studies
Modern Language Review
Portuguese Studies
The Slavonic and East European Review
Working Papers in the Humanities
The Yearbook of English Studies

www.mhra.org.uk
www.legendabooks.com

SELECTED ESSAYS

Each title in *Selected Essays* presents influential, but often scattered, papers by a major scholar in the Humanities. While these essays will, we hope, offer a model of scholarly writing, and chart the development of an important thinker in the field, the aim is not retrospective but to gather a coherent body of work as a tool for future research. Each volume contains a new introduction, framing the debate and reflecting on the methods used.

Selected Essays is curated by Professor Susan Harrow (University of Bristol).

APPEARING IN THIS SERIES

1. *Enlightenment and Religion in German and Austrian Literature*, by Ritchie Robertson
2. *Perpetual Motion: Studies in French Poetry from Surrealism to the Postmodern*, by Michael Sheringham
3. *Putting it About: Popular Views of Social Rights and Wrongs in Spain in the Long Nineteenth Century*, by Alison Sinclair
4. *Perspectives on Culture and Politics in the French Antilles*, by Celia Britton
5. *Italian Rewritings: Subtexts and Reworkings in Italian literature from Dante to Calvino*, by Martin McLaughlin

Managing Editor
Dr Graham Nelson, 41 Wellington Square, Oxford OX1 2JF, UK

www.legendabooks.com

Contemporary Fictions

Essays on American and Postcolonial Narratives

JUDIE NEWMAN

LEGENDA

Selected Essays 12
Modern Humanities Research Association
2020

Published by Legenda
an imprint of the Modern Humanities Research Association
Salisbury House, Station Road, Cambridge CB1 2LA

ISBN 978-1-78188-329-7 (HB)
ISBN 978-1-78188-332-7 (PB)

First published 2020

Copy-Editor: Dr Nigel Hope

CONTENTS

	Sources	x
	Introduction	1
1	Nadine Gordimer's *The Conservationist*: "That Book of Unknown Signs"	15
2	Bellow's "Indian Givers": *Humboldt's Gift*	26
3	The Revenge of the Trance Maiden: Intertextuality and Alison Lurie	33
4	Nadine Gordimer and the Naked Southern Ape: "Something Out There"	47
5	Saul Bellow and Social Anthropology	62
6	Telling a Woman's Story: Fiction as Biography and Biography as Fiction in Mary Gordon's *Men and Angels* and Alison Lurie's *The Truth about Lorin Jones*	73
7	Postcolonial Gothic: Ruth Prawer Jhabvala and the Sobhraj Case	87
8	Solitary Sojourners in Nature: Revisionary Transcendentalism in Alison Lurie's *Love and Friendship* and Marilynne Robinson's *Housekeeping*	99
9	Bellow's Ransom Tale: The Holocaust, *The Victim* and *The Double*	116
10	Spaces In-Between: Hester Prynne as the Salem Bibi in Bharati Mukherjee's *The Holder of the World*	127
11	Rebounding Metaphors: Culture and Conquest in J. G. Farrell's *The Siege of Krishnapur*	143
12	Zapotec Man and the Torajan Granny: "Mosby's Memoirs" and the Sacrifice of the Heart	156
13	Napalm and After: The Politics of Grace Paley's Short Fiction	168
14	Jump Starts: Nadine Gordimer after Apartheid	176
15	"Dis Ain't Gimme, Florida": Zora Neale Hurston's *Their Eyes Were Watching God*	188
16	Going Global: From Danish Postcolonial Novel to World Bestseller: Peter Høeg's *Smilla's Sense of Snow*	198
17	Updike's Golden Oldies: Rabbit as Spectacular Man	225
18	Priority Narratives: Bharati Mukherjee's *Desirable Daughters*	231
19	Blowback: André Dubus III's *House of Sand and Fog*	239
20	Pictures from an Exhibition: Dalia Sofer and the Jews of Iran	253
21	Trotskyism in the Early Work of Saul Bellow	267
22	Updike's *Terrorist*: Rewriting the Domestic Myth	282
23	Saul Bellow and the Theory of Comedy	295

24 Intertextual Updike: *Gertrude and Claudius*   307
25 Presidential Politics as Sexual Politics: *Memories of the Ford Administration*   322
    Further Reading   338

    Index   340

For Chrissy Alice Revie and Ruaridh Ian Revie,
beloved grandchildren

SOURCES

The essays presented here originally appeared as follows, and are printed with the permission of the copyright holders.

1. "Nadine Gordimer's *The Conservationist*: "That Book of Unknown Signs"," *Critique: Studies in Modern Fiction*, 22, 3 (1981), 31–44. <http://www.tandfonline.com/>
2. "Bellow's "Indian Givers": *Humboldt's Gift*," *Journal of American Studies*, 15, 2 (1981), 231–38. Copyright, Cambridge University Press.
3. "The Revenge of the Trance Maiden: Intertextuality and Alison Lurie," in L. Anderson (ed.), *Plotting Change: Contemporary Women's Fiction* (London: Edward Arnold, 1990), 112–27.
4. "Nadine Gordimer and the Naked Southern Ape: 'Something Out There'," *Journal of the Short Story in English/Cahiers de la nouvelle*, 15 (1990), 55–73.
5. "Saul Bellow and Social Anthropology," in Gerhard Bach (ed.), *Saul Bellow at Seventy-five: A Collection of Critical Essays* (Tubingen: Gunter Narr Verlag, 1991), 37–149.
6. "Telling A Woman's Story: Fiction as Biography and Biography as Fiction in Mary Gordon's *Men and Angels* and Alison Lurie's *The Truth about Lorin Jones*," in Kristiaan Versluys (ed.), *Neo-Realism in Contemporary American Fiction* (Amsterdam: Rodopi; Antwerp: Restant, 1992), 171–92. Copyright Koninklijke Brill N.V.
7. "Post-Colonial Gothic: Ruth Prawer Jhabvala and the Sobhraj Case," *Modern Fiction Studies*, 40, 1 (1994), 85–100.
8. "Solitary Sojourners in Nature: Revisionary Transcendentalism in Alison Lurie's *Love and Friendship* and Marilynne Robinson's *Housekeeping*," in Kristiaan Versluys (ed.), *The Insular Dream: Obsession and Resistance* (Amsterdam: Free University Press, 1995), 303–23.
9. "Bellow's Ransom Tale: The Holocaust, *The Victim*, and *The Double*," *Saul Bellow Journal*, 14, 1 (1996), 3–18.
10. "Spaces In-Between: Hester Prynne as the Salem Bibi in Bharati Mukherjee's *The Holder of the World*," in Monika Reif-Hülser (ed.), *Borderlines: Negotiating Boundaries in Post-Colonial Writing*, ASNEL Papers, 4 (Amsterdam and Atlanta: Rodopi, 1999), 69–88. Copyright Koninklijke Brill N.V.
11. "Rebounding Metaphors: Culture and Conquest in J. G. Farrell's *The Siege of Krishnapur*," in R. J. Crane (ed.), *Critical Essays on J. G. Farrell* (Dublin: Four Courts Press, 1998), 80–96.
12. "Zapotec Man and the Torajan Granny: "Mosby's Memoirs" and the Sacrifice of the Heart," in Gerhard Bach and Gloria Cronin (eds), *Small Planets: Saul Bellow as Short Fiction Writer* (East Lansing: Michigan State University Press, 2000), 113–26.
13. "Napalm and After: The Politics of Grace Paley's Short Fiction," *Yearbook of English Studies* Special Issue on American Short Stories., 31 (2001), 2–9.
14. "Jump Starts: Nadine Gordimer after Apartheid," in Nahem Yousaf (ed.), *Apartheid Narratives: Writing South Africa* (Amsterdam and Atlanta: Rodopi, 2001), 101–14. Copyright Koninklijke Brill N.V.
15. "'Dis Ain't Gimme Florida': Zora Neale Hurston's Indian Givers, *Their Eyes Were Watching God*," *Modern Language Review*, 98, 4 (October 2003), 817–26.

16. "Going Global: From Danish Postcolonial Novel to World Bestseller: Peter Høeg's *Smilla's Sense of Snow*," *Spring: Tijdsskrift for moderne dansk litteratur* [Gaesteredaktion Postkolonialisme], 22 (2004), 9–27.

17. "Updike's Golden Oldies: Rabbit as Spectacular Man," in David Seed (ed.), *Literature and the Visual Media: Essays and Studies 2005* (Cambridge: D. S. Brewer, 2005), 123–41. *Essays and Studies* is a publication of the English Association (www.le.ac.uk/engassoc).

18. "Priority Narratives: Bharati Mukherjee's *Desirable Daughters*," *English and American Literary Studies*, 6 (2007), 130–44.

19. "Blowback: André Dubus III's *House of Sand and Fog*," *Critique: Studies in Contemporary Fiction*, 51, 4 (2010), 378–93. <http://www.tandfonline.com/>

20. "Pictures from an Exhibition: Dalia Sofer and the Jews of Iran," *Contemporary Women's Writing*, 7, 2 (2013), 152–71.

21. "Trotskyism in the Early Work of Saul Bellow," in Gloria L. Cronin and Lee Trepannier (eds), *A Political Companion to Saul Bellow* (Lexington: University Press of Kentucky, 2013), 9–27.

22. "Updike's *Terrorist*: Rewriting the Domestic Myth," in Sylvie Mathé and Sophie Vallas (eds), *European Perspectives on the Literature of 9/11* (Paris: Michel Houdiard, 2014), 33–47.

23. "Bellow and the Theory of Comedy," in *Partial Answers: Journal of Literature and History of Ideas*, Saul Bellow Special Issue, ed. Victoria Aarons and Gustavo Sánchez Canales, 14, 1 (2016), 159–73. Copyright (2016) Johns Hopkins University Press.

24. "Intertextual Updike: *Gertrude and Claudius*," in Laurence W. Mazzeno and Sue Norton (eds), *European Perspectives on John Updike* (Rochester, New York: Camden House, 2018), 166–80.

25. "Presidential Politics as Sexual Politics: *Memories of the Ford Administration*," in Scott Dill and Matthew Shipe (eds), *Updike and Politics: New Considerations* (Lanham, Maryland: Lexington Books, 2019). (All rights reserved).

INTRODUCTION

In the series to which this volume belongs authors are asked to reflect on their critical methods and approaches to literature, an implicitly autobiographical enterprise. Part of my brief here is also to discuss how the field has evolved. Not so easy when it comes to contemporary fiction. Indeed the notion of the contemporary is itself somewhat contemporary. When I began publishing, "contemporary" was scarcely even a concept. Although the term originates in the mid-seventeenth century it was mostly subsumed under "modern". In 1976 it was not significant enough to feature in Raymond Williams, *Keywords: A Vocabulary of Culture and Society*. My 1981 essay on Nadine Gordimer was published in *Critique: Studies in Modern Fiction*; nearly thirty years later I sent the editor an essay on André Dubus III (also reprinted here) which duly appeared in *Critique: Studies in Contemporary Fiction*. Same journal, different subtitle. In the 1980s "post-war fiction" was the term usually applied (meaning post-1945). It is important to note therefore from the outset that the concept of the contemporary is a cultural category, and has its own history. As Rachel Carroll has argued, it is odd in that its object is constantly receding; it does not depend on hindsight, but describes a moment, a coincidence of text and reader in an illusory perpetual present. It needs to be understood as more than a mere marker for the present. But where does the contemporary begin? When will it end? What is its value as a historicising concept? Of whom or of what are we contemporary? For Carroll (coincidentally one of my earliest postgraduate students) it involves "forging an archive of the future"; the contemporary becomes a kind of future past.[1] Peter Osborne has similarly argued that it is not just the most recent past but a new way of conceptualising the present.[2] At its worst it is in the service of legitimisation, used by cultural gatekeepers or deployed as a marketing category. The Institute of Contemporary Arts, founded in 1946, seems to have more class than it would have if named the Institute of Post-War Arts. Customers are more likely to be attracted to a restaurant with a "contemporary vibe", than one which suggests the end of food-rationing. The term is none the less usefully vague, one of those terms like "hybridity" or "globalisation" which Mieke Bal has characterised as "travelling concepts", terms which "do" rather than remaining static.[3] It allows for a large field in which there are relatively few fixed landmarks or controlling guilds, in a way which "Postmodern", "21st century" or "post 9/11" do not. This can be a problem for academics, who tend to like periodisation in the interests of institutional politics, and have broken down their fields into ever smaller and more exactly defined strip-systems, in the interests of securing a professional toehold. I was surprised when the "long nineteenth century" came into common parlance, but not when "early modern" overtook "Renaissance" to describe post-medieval writers. Though nobody seems to have promoted the short seventeenth century, even though the Restoration is a fairly discrete period. Many of these terms are hopelessly insular. As a postgraduate in American literature I remember being irritated by categorisations of Longfellow or Cooper as "Victorian", and even more annoyed by claims that Transcendentalist Thoreau was essentially just a Romantic with a pond. It was obvious too that the American Shakespeare was a rather different playwright from the English one, or indeed from the Scottish. (How we loved doughty Macbeth, in my Scottish high school, fighting to the end against wicked usurpation by Malcom and his mercenary English army.) In postcolonial literature the term can be even more difficult to define. Times can be different in different spaces. In India, unsurprisingly, the contemporary begins in 1947, with Independence.

The fuzziness of the term allows for considerable freedom in curriculum design. And yet — despite the vast numbers of contemporary novels — it is striking how many courses in contemporary fiction are focussed on a very narrow range of fiction (unlike this volume). Course leaders are often afraid that their field will look too easy, and tend to favour overtly "difficult" or enormously long novels. Postmodernists tend to benefit from this, or any novel with a hefty freight of historical detail. This volume includes an essay on Zora Neale Hurston's 1937 novel, *Their Eyes were Watching God*, which is not at all contemporary in publication date, not even post-war, but the sudden boom in Hurston studies in the 1980s and 1990s saw it became the most commonly taught novel in America. In a sense it found its own contemporaries some forty years after its first appearance, rather as Gerald Manley Hopkins became an honorary modern writer. It benefitted from the rise of feminist and African American literary analysis, and of course its engagement with history. Gordon Hutner, however, gives an amusing account of how much more common it is for a contemporary fiction course to become "eight indecipherable novels and Toni Morrison" .[4] From what I have seen, Barth, Pynchon and De Lillo are more likely to appear than Barbara Kingsolver, Kent Haruf or Anne Tyler; literature has to look complex. Though revolt is in the air. Amy Hungerford caused controversy by stoutly refusing to read David Foster Wallace's *Infinite Jest* for her postgraduate student. (It comes in at more than a thousand pages, with ninety-six pages of endnotes, one running to seventeen pages.) Even then Hungerford gave her reasons as potential misogyny, not excessive length.[5] It has to be said in mitigation that one problem for the academic in an uncanonised field is that for every novel one writes about or teaches, one has certainly read twenty others which did not make the grade. There is generally very little secondary literature; the books are expensive for students; and there are copyright questions to handle. (None of this deterred me — more on this below.)

Of late the concept of the contemporary has attracted serious attention in itself, kickstarted primarily by Giorgio Agamben's 2009 essay "What is the contemporary?" Agamben cited Nietzsche's definition in his *Untimely Meditations* (1872): "The contemporary is the untimely."[6] Nietzsche argues that those who are truly contemporary, truly of their time, are those who neither perfectly coincide with it nor adjust themselves to its demands, and who, because of this disconnection, are capable of perceiving their own time more fully. The relationship is one of disjunction and anachronism. In a sense to be of one's time one has to be out of it. The contemporary "firmly holds his gaze on his own time so as to perceive not its light, but rather its darkness'", its obscurity, its opacity.[7] "By dividing and interpolating time, the contemporary is capable of transforming it and putting it in relation with other times."[8] Being contemporary is therefore an experience of dissonance; the contemporary is not a label for a period but an existential marker. The contemporary is not the topical, though writers will tend to write about their own times, and Vietnam, the Holocaust, apartheid, the Iranian revolution, and terrorism certainly feature in my essays. Arguably therefore the most distinctive feature of the contemporary is a vexed relationship to time. In Peter Osborne's argument, where modernism tends towards a vision of a radically different future, (breaking with capitalism, say) "contemporary" suggests a vision of a more extended present, a form of the modern with a mediated, less-ruptured futurity. The new quality here is "the coming together not simply 'in' time but of times", with different but equally present temporalities in play in the present.[9]

Inevitably, therefore, intertextuality is absolutely at home in contemporaneity. Times always intersect on the page, as readers read through their previous experiences of reading other books. Indeed there is something inherently utopian about bringing together disparate discourses in a text, making them live in the reader's individual time, the time of reading, in a single historical present. Although as I muddled along through my own career I could not have theorised this position overtly (certainly not nearly as well as Carroll or Osborne) I suspect that it is no coincidence that intertextuality has been a constant thread throughout my work, or that I was drawn to the growth of utopian themes in contemporary fiction (despite the parallel growth of terrorism) for my tenth book, *Utopia and Terror in Contemporary American Fiction* (2013), or that one thread of the discussion there concerned the illusory shortening of time in a globalised world, as against the blowback from past history which often erupted murderously into it. Like Molière's Monsieur Jourdain, suddenly discovering that he'd been unwittingly speaking prose for forty years, I seem to have been operating inside a contemporary mind-set for most of my working life.

Perhaps the major advantage of the contemporary is its empowerment of readers. The chronological sweep of English Literature courses (usually kicking off in the sixteenth century and dribbling the ball towards the goalposts of the present) devalues readers' capabilities and inhibits confidence in their own powers of judgment. The conventional idea is often that students who can understand Shakespeare or Milton can manage contemporary literature with no real effort. A course like that teaches literary history, however, not literature. Readers don't actually read like that. Most of us probably begin with contemporary works, then some older "classics", before we start moving seriously backwards in time. If a course begins instead with the present (cutting out many problems of historical or linguistic understanding), teaching students how to think about narration, symbolism, rhetoric, genre, and so forth, it establishes a much firmer ground from which to venture into less familiar fields. It makes sense to me to read *Wide Sargasso Sea* before *Jane Eyre*, *Foe* before *Robinson Crusoe*. In *The Ballistic Bard* (1995) I made the case for this, in some detail, as a means of challenging cultural dominance by a self-serving canon. One consequence of the emphasis on complexity by some contemporary critics is the growth of what Kathryn Hume has termed "Aggressive Fictions", works which seem to be driven by a desire to repel the reader whether by size, complexity, narrative speed, gloom, grotesque imagery or extreme sex and violence.[10] This has opened a gulf between literary fiction and novels which , while demanding , are also rewarding to read (and are read, judging by book groups, blogs and sales figures). Although I have never engaged formally in print with reader-response theory, it has certainly been an influence on me, as has, to a lesser extent, neo-historicism, when it restores some awareness of the tension between an original and a contemporary reader of a book. Narratology is also intimately connected to the reader of a book and its social politics. I am myself a sceptical reader and tend to mutter at intervals "Says who?" Apply that question to a novel, and the results are usually interesting. Today's students, reared on television series and films, are trained up in understanding plots in ways which their predecessors could not be, and often write off plot as boring, or replace it with "the arc of the story". But narrative muscle matters, and it is often a question about a narrator which draws me towards studying a particular writer, as in the essays here on Paley and Dubus.

What drew me to this amorphous field in the first place? It's normal now for one to sketch "where one is coming from", as an index to one's influences. But when I started my student career at the University of Edinburgh I was coming from Caithness. It was a relief that my Director of Studies had actually heard of it (one of his ancestors had left it behind). I had spent a month in France beforehand where the burnt-out cars and piles of cobbles all over Paris had been a surprise. I got there in early June 1968; France was in deep shock after the events of May. But in most respects I was quite naïve. My trajectory was slightly unusual. In those days it was possible to do two degrees in six years (not a joint degree) by carrying extra subjects in both first and second years, in my case French and English, plus British History. I then spent two years studying English (keeping my hand in with French classes and a weekly written exercise), spent my fifth year as a *lectrice* at the University of Metz, and returned to complete the final year of French, generously supported by the Scottish Education Department, on condition that I gained a first in the English degree. I could not have done it otherwise; as the oldest of four I knew there was never going to be enough money for an extra year. At eighteen, unsure what career to follow, it seemed a good idea to hedge my bets by taking two degrees, although it meant a lot more work at the start. Both subjects weeded out large numbers of students after the first year, when one needed a 2.1 average to continue in the Honours class. My Director of Studies, Andrew Hook, a huge influence on my career, wondered if I could do it. So did I when I found myself one of 550 first-year English students, and I wondered even more when I realised that many of the French students had been to expensive schools abroad or were actually French. Fortunately I had won the Edinburgh bursary competition in English which gave me just enough money for the fare to France each year. I spent every summer in France as an au pair, maid, or waitress, at one point in a Michelin-starred restaurant. (Very good for one's French. There is no room in a busy kitchen for a lack of fluency.) When it came to making career decisions, however, I had no doubts that the study of contemporary fiction was where I was going; I love reading novels more than any other literature. Attempts were made to deflect me towards medieval literature — an apparently sensible idea given that I had passed exams in Latin, German and Italian, and acquired Old and Middle English, Old French, plus a smattering of old Norse and old Provençal along the way. But those benighted medievals had not managed to invent the novel, so it was not on the cards as far as I was concerned. There were real attractions to medieval literature. I had grown up in an area settled by Vikings where "norn" words were still in circulation, and I liked the Norse sagas, one of which concerns Caithness, the misnamed *Orkneyinga Saga*. They also had some fascinatingly horrible women characters, unlike the *Chanson de Roland* which featured one woman in 4,000 lines of Old French, La Belle Aude, who appeared merely to drop dead in the same stanza. The troubadour poets all seemed to be male (though I enjoyed returning to them for the penultimate essay here). I was attracted to French novels (after a course on the *nouveau roman*) and had read the whole of Proust at a great rate of knots. But at that time to teach in a university French department meant teaching French language classes and marking innumerable translations and "proses". In English one taught only literature. The die was cast.

I look back now and am somewhat astonished at how readily I headed for contemporary American fiction (American novels seemed to be better at this point than British), especially since there was never going to be much chance (I thought) of teaching it. The Edinburgh degree course finished somewhere before the Second World War, though minus Virginia Woolf (a much-appreciated lunch-hour lecture was provided by Dr Valerie Shaw). Apart from the American literature course (up to date) the only other possibility was a "Special Subject" — in my case "Evelyn Waugh and Angus Wilson". It taught me a great deal about comedy which has paid off in various essays further along the way. I wrote a dissertation on *Brideshead Revisited* and Keats (intertextuality though nobody knew the term) supervised by Kenneth Fielding. A strong strain of Dickens also ran through the course; Waugh and Wilson were both strongly influenced by Dickens, and Ken Fielding was a Dickens scholar. He was also a very sharp critic and extremely supportive. Having stupidly missed the post with my Carnegie fellowship application I asked him what to do and he personally convinced the Trust to accept it by hand. They were quite chilly when I arrived in a dishevelled state on their doorstep, but duly relented. I owe him a lot.

Essentially my choices were hedonistic. Contemporary novel was an indulgence for me (and still is). I learned to read at three and read my first adult novel at the age of seven (*Uncle Tom's Cabin*, my grandmother's Sunday school prize). It was swiftly followed by Charles Kingsley's *Hereward the Wake* and Susan Warner's *The Wide Wide World* (also from my grandmother, a major influence who later sent *Lady Chatterley's Lover* up to Caithness, thoughtfully covered in brown paper). In my first lecturing post, however, poetry and drama ruled the syllabus, and I was assigned to teach a Combined Honours course which began with Chaucer and the Gawain poet, moving on through Donne, Milton and Jacobean drama to quite a lot of eighteenth-century works. In Edinburgh those studying American literature generally skipped the eighteenth century and the Romantics. Effectively I bounced from Donne to Dickens. As a result I was usually about three weeks ahead of my students for at least the first two years. On the plus side, many of the topics were completely fresh discoveries for me, and more interesting as a result.

I was still writing about contemporary fiction of course; one area which is not represented here is my work as a reviewer, both of academic work and of fiction — an activity which took up a lot of my time early on, before University committees and departmental management took up the slack. Over forty years as an academic I published three or four book reviews or review essays every year, plus an average of three scholarly essays, and a book every three or four years. The annual *Year's Work in English Studies* chapters on Post-45 literature each ran to eighty pages. Editors tell me that it is now much more difficult to persuade academics to write reviews (which do not count in government research assessments), but I remain committed to them, partly because it enlarges my thinking, partly to keep up to date, and sometimes for light relief. Along the way I have reviewed books about John Wayne, Eoin Colfer, William Gerhardie, and a host of others. My impression today is that reviewers are more restrained than in the past; the review is often a polite summary of content. It was not thus in the past. In the 1980s I also reviewed novels for a magazine called *Words*, writing their "novel of the month" and "novels of the year" features. Some of these sparked academic work. Ruth Prawer Jhabvala's *Three Continents* (novel of the month in 1987) eventually became the topic of an essay and a book chapter; an article on Graham Greene's *The Tenth Man* in 1985 led to a journal essay on Greene and espionage. Of my choices I would still defend Irene Handl (*The Gold-Tipped Pfitzer*) and J. L. Carr (*The Battle of Pollock's Crossing*), both 1985, but others have faded from view. Who now remembers Daniel Green's *Bunter Sahib*? It offers a salutary reminder of how many novels disappear from the record along the way. About 55,000 new novels are published in America each year. Literary criticism barely scratches their surface. Nor is this a new phenomenon. Describing the slaughterhouse of fiction in the nineteenth century, Franco Moretti calculated that it would take many lifetimes to read all the books published in any one year between 1800 and 1900. Book reviews can be helpful.

One major early influence on my own work was that of my student flatmates, two of whom took a course in Social Anthropology in our first year. None of us had ever heard of it, and there were baffled discussions in the kitchen about the Nuer and the Trobriand islanders. I began to read up on it in my spare time, just for fun, and it informed my later writing much more than the works of general literary criticism listed as preparation for the dreaded Edinburgh final examination

"General Essay". William Empson's *Seven Types of Ambiguity* (Only seven? I thought he was a bit limited) and various quasi-religious works upholding literature as "improving" in some way left me cold. On the other hand I was so enthralled with H. M. Daleski's *The Forked Flame* that I corresponded with him. D. H. Lawrence remains a major enthusiasm for me, though it was surprising when I ended up teaching at Nottingham to discover that many of the details in his novels which I thought of as deeply symbolic were merely geographic. There is a river called the Papple and it does flood. So much for female symbolism in *The Virgin and the Gypsy*. In Metz I retraced the characters' steps in "The Thorn in the Flesh" using the short story as a map. As for mythic archetypes (Northrop Frye and the "myth and symbol" school of American literature) I was lukewarm. Anthropologists made myths seem more like dynamic narratives than great truths of the psyche. In short, social anthropology stuck.

It was probably no accident therefore that I gravitated towards "Saul Bellow and History" as my thesis topic. The English Literature course at Edinburgh had very little theoretical framework; it was based on close reading and the F. R. Leavis idea of literature as humanist. But the American literature course (in the hands of Andrew Hook) was altogether different, much more attentive to political history and to social context. Bellow was a student of social anthropology in the 1930s (then understood as a radical political field) and I suspect that (in the era before it was considered as imperialistic) it was still fairly radical to an eighteen-year-old from Caithness. Some of the essays here engage with Bellow's anthropological thought, with Marcel Mauss and gift exchange, Erving Goffman and frame analysis, the anthropology of the serial killer, Zapotec death practices, Mary Douglas and pollution behaviour, *inter alia*. Psychiatry reached me via the anthropological route too, and I wrote essays on Bellow and Jung, Updike and Freud, and Mukherjee and Adler. One of my central concerns is with how ideas are translated into the internal dynamic or even the formal scaffolding of a novel, gift exchange in Bellow and Hurston for example, or (very differently) Wilhelm Reich's thought in Bellow's *Henderson the Rain King* and Gordimer's *A Guest of Honour*.

Many of the literary orthodoxies of the time were deeply uninspiring, but I am of course still a product of that time, particularly in relation to formalist analysis and close reading. Nobody has ever advocated sloppy, inattentive reading, after all, and a sonnet still has fourteen lines. Cleanth Brooks and Robert Penn Warren's works (notably *Understanding Poetry* and even more so *Understanding Fiction*) still strike me as thought-provoking and, above all, useful. Part of their attraction was the practical demonstration of critical analysis. They asked very good questions of the literary work. When "theory" rampaged like Grendel's mother through departments of English literature I was less than bowled over. Having completed a second degree in French I found some of it already had a quality of *déjà vu*. But many literary people went through the equivalent of a religious conversion, loudly proclaiming the truth of (variously) Foucault, Derrida or Cixous, and there was a "born again" tendency not to give much credit to foregoing thinkers. Derrida and the Gift? Why not Mauss? I wondered. Abjection? They should go back to Mary Douglas!

Kristeva's discussion of intertextuality was a major influence on my writing, and the backbone of my fourth critical book, but her argument in *Des Chinoises* infuriated me almost as much as it appears to have annoyed Emily Prager in *A Visit from the Footbinder*. (On which I wrote an essay and a book chapter, so it does not feature here.) Writing a thesis partly on the philosophy of history also made me somewhat impatient with critics who did not seem to have investigated the origins of their own ideas. As a student I had no idea that there was a field called intellectual history. It was a shock to realise (courtesy of Dreiser's *The Financier*) just how influenced I had been as a child by Social Darwinism. The American Intellectual History Group has been a real joy over the years, not least because it meets (twice a year) only to discuss a topic one whole afternoon, with discussion continued over dinner, and all of the following morning, with no papers, publications, grants, or gatekeeping. The political and social emphasis of the American literature course at Edinburgh informed my later activities in the British Association for American Studies and as a Chair of American Studies. I also developed an abiding interest in the historical novel, and many of my essays (both contemporary and in nineteenth-century literature) pursued that. Postcolonial writing draws heavily on history of course, as I discovered in relation to Ruth Prawer Jhabvala (*Heat and Dust*), Anita Desai (*Baumgartner's Bombay*) and J. G. Farrell, as does the literature of slavery, but I am probably fairly unusual in having written a scholarly essay on Ford Madox Ford's *The Fifth Queen* (a revisionary account of Katherine Howard). The final essay in this collection deals with a novel about President James Buchanan as he stumbles into the Civil War.

After Edinburgh I went to Cambridge as a Carnegie Fellow, largely because I wanted to be supervised by Tony Tanner, whose critical work on American literature (*The Reign of Wonder* and *City of Words*) had me spellbound. He did not disappoint, though Cambridge itself did. In the second year of the fellowship, I got bored, started applying for job interviews and — third time lucky — was appointed as a lecturer at Newcastle. Employment got seriously in the way of completing the thesis (of which I had written one chapter when appointed). But I had found the Cambridge college system anathema. Clare College had not been mixed for very long (I chose it largely because it was bang opposite the University library) and was still very male in ethos. Even though Carnegie was paying for it, I objected to funding the men's boat club, sports fields and the chapel. (There was one for every college — could they not combine forces, share services and have just one vicar?) At night I slept surrounded by empty bottles, not because of wild parties, but following the official advice to have a noisy means of alerting me to any incursion by the Cambridge rapist. We carried rape alarms and all our male friends insisted on seeing us safely home and searching under beds and in wardrobes before they departed. When a demented man attempted to storm into my neighbour's room, I seized a Glenmorangie to brain him with, though not before the Clare rugby team had landed on him. There were positives, and not just the coypu I used to watch in the drainage channel near my room. The English Faculty had some interesting invited speakers (I have a warm memory of Leo Marx, whose *The Machine in the*

Garden was already a classic of American criticism). I met F. R. Leavis (bitter and ranting), and because Edward Shils was a visiting lecturer, was able to interview Bellow himself, who had a close friendship with him. I made some good friends (many as infuriated with the place as I was). There were hardly any postgraduates interested in American literature, however, and not many in the modern period. We formed a discussion group where we read papers to each other on our research, though nobody noticed. I enjoyed Simon Schama's informal seminars on Jewish history, and Allon White, also a postgraduate, made me take some literary theory more seriously. The first-ever film course (unofficial) at Cambridge, led by Stephen Heath, was also an eye-opener, though after weeks of analysis I never wanted to see *Touch of Evil* again. And of course, I began publishing, mostly reviews of contemporary fiction. Sharing a house with a Tudor historian left me with a real interest in Henry VIII and assorted heretical religious movements. (Anabaptists and Lollards seemed almost as strange as the Nuer.) Later I published several essays on novels by John Updike which engaged with witchcraft, neo-paganism and religious cults. But on the whole I was glad to depart. I signed a book contract for the thesis before the Viva, and ignored the comment from the examiner (Malcolm Bradbury) that I should overhaul the deadly boring introduction before it saw print. He was right, and I wince when I think of it, but I felt that if I saw the thesis ever again I would scream, and it stayed in a trunk, smelling strongly of Gold Leaf, for a decade before my interest rekindled in Bellow, notably in relation to his early political views and the shorter fiction.

Bellow had also been side-lined by feminist criticism, which swept through universities just as I was starting out. I have always found the relation of sexual politics to politics *per se* a natural concern for the novel, even in relation to Katherine Howard. The first essay here (on South African material) and the last two on Updike (drawing respectively on courtly love and Camille Paglia) bookend the collection with discussions of this relationship. Feminist publishing was almost as important as criticism; at last I could teach Willa Cather, Ellen Glasgow, and Edith Wharton in accessible editions. The American literature course in Edinburgh had featured one woman, Emily Dickinson (then seen as a rather peculiar recluse). Works like Sandra Gilbert and Susan Gubar's *The Madwoman in the Attic* were genuinely paradigm — shifting, and the curriculum was never the same again.[11] Though it still took a bit of fancy footwork sometimes to get women writers on courses. My first attempt to teach *Uncle Tom's Cabin*, the great bestseller of the nineteenth century, was pooh-poohed. It was "sentimental" — in other words it dealt with women and children — and of course there was also nervousness about race. I compromised on Harriet Jacobs' slave narrative instead, largely unread by my colleagues and to all appearances unobjectionably boring and loaded with history. Within two years I was teaching an entire course on American women writers plus another on the literature of slavery. Apart from Ralph Ellison I had only studied white authors as a student. Now African-American, Asian- and Native-American novels were easily available and I went on to teach a course on neo-slave narratives for almost twenty years, which included only one white author. (And published on the genre, in half a dozen book chapters and essays.) The whole field of American literature was overhauled in the 1980s (the essay on Lurie, Robinson and Transcendentalism here is an obvious product of that), much to my joy. Students also loved it, though the downside of that was the large numbers and long teaching hours. Anyone who wants to know what teaching was like in the early 1990s in a large English department should read Colin Evans, *English People* (1993), partly based on research in the department at Newcastle.[12] My identity (both as a number and as a pseudonymous character) had better remain anonymous, but given the paucity of women lecturers, is probably easily guessed.

Postcolonial literature was a later development in my career. When I wrote about Gordimer it was still Commonwealth Literature (though of course South Africa had defected). As usual I came to it via novels. Having agreed to teach an evening class at Newcastle for local adults, I had to find twenty contemporary novels that would work with a very varied group (half of whom were only there, as one informed me, because "Birds of Northumberland" was no longer on Monday nights). They had also been working all day and rushed to the class clutching a sandwich, ready to tell me just what they thought of the novel of the week. To my surprise *The Conservationist* went down a storm (it did involve some unusual birds); I wrote an essay, and then a book on Gordimer. Coetzee's *Waiting for the Barbarians* was even more of a hit (indeed it is one novel which never seems to fail to mesmerise the reader) as were works by Farrell, Rhys and Paul Scott. I taught the course for years, varying the novels and stories, and from it came a host of essays and *The Ballistic Bard*. The classes also gave me a sharp awareness of "real readers"; I remain fascinated by how people actually respond to a novel. Postcolonial writing is a particularly interesting field for reader response theory. Reading *Wide Sargasso Sea* with a group who had never read *Jane Eyre*, for example, destroyed a lot of my comfortable certainties. Indeed *The Ballistic Bard* dealt explicitly with questions of how we read, reading through other books, putting readers into the text, and the use of letters to foreground the act of reading. It was also the only one of my books to prompt my father to say that he finally saw the point of literary criticism. Quite a bit of it has been reprinted in parts (though not the chapter on *Guerrillas*, my favourite, which actually went down like a lump of lead with the evening class). When I moved to a Chair of American Studies at Nottingham my only regret was leaving postcolonial fiction largely behind (though I smuggled some into my classes). I still think Coetzee's *Dusklands* is one of the best novels about the Vietnam War, and Bharati Mukherjee had been Canadian before she became an American citizen which gave me some leeway. Neo-slave narratives, as a genre, allowed me to teach postcolonial and American writers together, Caryl Phillips and Bernardine Evaristo, as well as Sherley Anne Williams, Edward P. Jones and Charles Johnson. I realised that my two fields were not as separate as I had thought. Literature is now not so easily pigeonholed by national status, and American literature by Iranian Jews, Indian immigrants, and Afghan refugees entered the curriculum. There was a sudden cross-fertilisation of ideas. American literary specialists, in particular, learned from postcolonialists; topics like "The Global South" emerged, the transnational took shape and the "field" became much broader. In *Fictions of America* (2007) I focussed squarely on globalisation, in fiction investigating how China, India or Africa can be said to have underwritten American culture.

That openness (or fuzziness?) remains one of the pleasures of the contemporary. Nowadays it is still fairly common for an editor to ask you to introduce an essay by situating it within current debates, indicating "how you are joining the conversation". In other words, where does your work fit in? One reason I opted for contemporary fiction was that there was hardly any conversation at all and therefore not much cultural gatekeeping. I disliked having to keep kowtowing to eminent authorities before I could explore ideas. That was what was wrong with that thesis introduction, where I painfully surveyed every critic remotely relevant to the topic of Saul Bellow and history, purely so that I could cold-shoulder them for the rest of the book. Engaging with relevant arguments, debating common topics, giving credit where credit is due, is not the same as dutiful cap-doffing, and at least at the start of my career, in most other fields there seemed to be a great deal of that. There are downsides, of course. In the contemporary field you had better have something interesting to say, because there is no guarantee that anybody else is writing about these authors or wants to read about them. And they are unlikely to be teaching them. Dickens is significant; the jury is still out on most contemporaries. A nineteenth-century novel of secure canonicity (and out of copyright) can attract critical editions, journal special issues, large grants and whole collections of essays. Nobody has to make a case for writing about *Great Expectations*. While it is perfectly possible to spend most of one's career working on one major nineteenth-century writer, that would be very unwise in the contemporary field. When I started writing about Bellow he was at the height of his popularity, and went on to get the Nobel Prize. Today a seminar on his work at the American Literature Association annual conference (800 attending) will rarely reach double figures. I doubt if many students would even consider him contemporary. (He is none the less well-represented here; time will tell if that is wise.) Others have seen their star rise steadily. When I first taught Updike's *Rabbit Run* I was reported to the Dean for peddling obscenity. I went on to write my second book about him, and today the *Rabbit* tetralogy is recognised as one of the major achievements of twentieth-century literature. Many once much-lauded writers no longer feature on reading lists. Marilynne Robinson practically disappeared from view after *Housekeeping* (1981) only to have a sudden resurgence with the trilogy *Gilead* (2004), *Home* 2008) and *Lila* (2014). Though who now has read *Mother Country* (1989), her book on nuclear waste disposal in Britain which was a finalist for the National Book Award in nonfiction? (As a nuclear scientist's daughter, brought up in the shadow of a nuclear reactor, with holidays spent with his friends and fellow scientists near Sellafield, I read it with keen interest.)

One advantage of writing about older authors is also that they are dead. On several occasions the subject of my lecture popped up in the audience. The horror of expounding on Mary Gordon's father's Fascism, with her in the front row, is a vivid memory, right up there with the sudden appearance in Graz of J. M. Coetzee, five minutes into my detailed discussion of pollution anxiety in his work. (Both writers, I might say, were entirely charming, and carried me off to lunch, though even more embarrassment ensued in Graz as I gorged happily on Austrian pork products, while vegetarian Coetzee consumed two bananas.) Alison Lurie, the subject of my sixth book was immensely helpful and lent me a house while I was in Key West to interview her. Bellow (notoriously difficult) fed me chocolate cake, and explained why a squint was erotically exciting. (One of our table companions had a wandering eye.) John Updike wrote very politely to tell me that my laboured explanation of a particular scene in *Couples* was completely wrong. (The ambiguity which I had perceived was dictated by British libel laws.) Updike was so prolific a writer that he made every monograph on his work out of date within a year. Even worse he returned to a particular group of characters every ten years or so, in several novel-sequences, revising everything that had seemed obvious about them. The reader of a *Rabbit* novel reads through his or her own previous experience of reading its predecessors, as well as that of living through the events chronicled. It is a case study in the contemporary. Live novelists may also have subjects who are alive. When Charles Sobhraj, the model for the serial killer in Jhabvala's *Three Continents*, was supposedly spotted in Europe, I was rather taken aback.

Why these particular essays? The first of these essays dates from 1981 and the last is forthcoming as I write, and they cover a fairly diverse range of material. They are largely unedited apart from matters of presentation. The aim of these volumes is to bring together works which are not easily accessed, so I have largely excluded essays which have been reprinted three times or more (so no Shirley Jackson, Anita Desai, or Coetzee). Although most of my essays begin with a gleam in my eye and are written speculatively (and submitted "cold" to journals) a number of them are products of particular occasions or occurred in particular contexts, and I am grateful for those who invited them. Being asked to conduct a master class in postcolonial writing at Georg Brandes Skolen, University of Copenhagen made me look much more closely at Danish colonialism, especially in its one colony in North America, Greenland (hence the essay on Peter Høeg's *Smilla's Sense of Snow*). When the Berlin Wall was being breached and the Cold War was coming to an end, an invitation to lecture in Heidelberg on Bellow drew me to his short story "Cousins" (1984) with its focus on an earlier period of Russian-American détente, in the 1900 Jesup Expedition. When in 2014 New Perspectives Theatre Company staged the first adaptation on the stage of a short story by Saul Bellow, "Him with His Foot in His Mouth", I was asked to advise, and an essay resulted. There is an element of chance in anyone's career. Having taught English to Iranians in the 1970s (men in the Iranian navy taking courses at Leith Nautical College) I followed events in 1979 with keen interest and growing horror. A generation later the rise of American writing about Iran drew me towards novels by André Dubus III, Dalia Sofer and Gina Nahai among others. Sometimes place was more important than I had imagined. Lecturing in Shanghai to trainee teachers, on the political implications of sibling birth order in Mukherjee's *Desirable Daughters* (oldest children are conservative, in theory, the later-borns in a large sibling group more revolutionary), I realised from the suddenly rapt and motionless audience that most of them had hardly any siblings and that everything I said was gaining an extra political resonance. Stupidly I had not written the lecture specifically for the occasion. I should add in mitigation here that this was unusual. I learnt the hard way not to repeat myself. On many occasions, as I was his sole carer, my son was in the audience. On one such, giving a series of lectures in Brazil, I repeated one which I had just given elsewhere only to hear him commenting loudly to his neighbour that "this next bit is quite good". My son was a major influence on my intellectual career, as was my mother. When I found myself on my own with a two-year-old she cheerfully accompanied us to conferences all over America. The American Literature Association Conference was very family-friendly, and I went annually, making a lot of good friends as a result and learning a great deal about American literature. Without my son's experience at infant school of the "jump story" genre ("Little Foo-Foo", in his case) a whole essay on Gordimer's *Jump* would not have happened. I admit to being fond of that particular essay, which was always going to make the cut. Again it was also written partly for an occasion, the Annual Conference of Professors of English, where my illustrative pounce on my chairman (the "jump") startled the audience almost as much as "Little Foo-Foo" had startled my son.

What did I leave out? All my work on nineteenth-century American literature (a list is offered at the end of this volume for those interested), many essays which were revised and developed in my books, or are easily available there (so no Susan Choi, David Bradley, Jean Rhys, Cormac McCarthy or Chitra Divakaruni) and "paired" essays (so none on Updike's three rewritings of *The Scarlet Letter*, nor on his *The Witches of Eastwick* or *The Widows of Eastwick*), and essays on Barbara Kingsolver, Philip Roth and James McBride which are forthcoming. There is not enough space here to acknowledge debts to my colleagues and students in the American literature, American Studies and Postcolonial Literature communities, but they are many, both intellectual and other. For that reason, I was sorely tempted to include my sole piece on Shakespeare ("'Exit, pursued by a bear': *The Winter's Tale*"), which drew on contemporary understandings of carnival (and bears, of course) and was the product of a dare from a colleague.[13] In "Cousins" Bellow's hero, Ijah, laments that he "can't seem to find the contemporaries I require'", but in that respect I feel that I have been very fortunate.[14]

Notes to the Introduction

1. Rachel Carroll, "How soon is Now: Constructing the Contemporary/Gendering the Experimental," *Contemporary Women's Writing*, 9, 1 (2015), 17.
2. Peter Osborne, *Anywhere or Not at All: Philosophy of Contemporary Art* (London: Verso, 2013), 16.
3. Mieke Bal, *Travelling Concepts in the Humanities: A Rough Guide* (Toronto: University of Toronto Press, 2002), 25.
4. Gordon Hutner, "Historicising the Contemporary: A Response to Amy Hungerford," *American Literary History*, 20, 1/2 (2008), 425.
5. See Amy Hungerford, *Making Literature Now* (Stanford: Stanford University Press, 2016) and "On the Period Formerly Known as the Contemporary," *American Literary History*, 20.1/2 (2008), 420–24. The reader who wants to follow up these debates in more detail should consult Rachel

Sykes, Arin Keble, Judie Newman and Diletta De Cristofaro, "Contemporary Studies Network Roundtable," *Journal of American Studies*, 52, 4 (2018), 1122–36.

6. Giorgio Agamben, "What is the Now?," in *What is an Apparatus? and Other Essays*, trans. by David Kishik and Stefan Pedatella (Stanford: Stanford University Press, 2009), 40.

7. Ibid., 44.

8. Ibid., 53.

9. Osborne, *Anywhere or Not at All*, 17.

10. Kathryn Hume, *Aggressive Fictions: Reading the Contemporary American Novel* (Ithaca: Cornell University Press, 2012).

11. Sandra Gilbert and Susan Guhar, *The Madwoman in the Attic: The Woman Writer and the Nineteenth Century Imagination* (New Haven: Yale University Press, 1979).

12. Colin Evans, *English People: The Teaching and Learning English in British Universities* (Buckingham and Philadelphia: Open University Press, 1993).

13. Judie Newman, "'Exit, pursued by a bear': *The Winter's Tale*," *Notes and Queries*, 233, 4 (1988), 484.

14. Saul Bellow, "Cousins," in *Him with His Foot in his Mouth and Other Stories* (London: Secker and Warburg, 1984), 259.

CHAPTER 1

Nadine Gordimer's *The Conservationist*: "That Book of Unknown Signs"

Compared with Nadine Gordimer's other novels — *A Guest of Honour* (1970) and *Burger's Daughter* (1979), for example — *The Conservationist* (1974) contains little overt political comment. Gordimer has denied an overriding political purpose in her writing, maintaining that politics figures in her novels only as an element of the South African scene. In an interview she said, "Like any other writer, my allegiance is to what Proust called 'that book of unknown signs within me no one could help me read by any rule.'" This private quality of her writing, she goes on to argue, "does not mean that I think I should turn my back on 'my' Dreyfus affair in South Africa (bannings and detentions without trial) or 'my' war (against apartheid), but that their significance should be nothing less than deeply implicit in whatever I write since it is there." And she concludes: "Africa needs an articulated consciousness other than that of newspaper headlines and political speeches."[1] *The Conservationist* offers the reader precisely this other form of articulated consciousness and, in so doing, characterises the problems of South African politics and of mimetic realism as a literary technique. Gordimer maintains "that book of unknown signs," which is within the individual, and produces a reading of the signs of South Africa. To render an internal reality progressively divorced from the reality outside it, a reality of political and ontological consensus, Gordimer employs two principal strategies, the use of Zulu myth and the translation of political problems into other languages, most noticeably into sexual terms.

Although the foreground of the novel is occupied by Mehring's story, the irruption into the text of excerpts from Henry Callaway's *The Religious System of the Amazulu* introduces the language of Zulu culture.[2] The quotations are the organising points for a subtext which slowly comes into the foreground. The story appears to be that of Mehring and the white in South Africa but reveals itself as that of the blacks. Each quotation introduces or reinforces an event in the novel, surreptitiously at first, later more explicitly. The quotations begin with prayers for corn and for children and the continuation of life (61) — to be expected in what is the fourth or fifth year of drought.[3] A further series of quotations (83, 93, 113) is taken from a dream by one of Callaway's informants, in which he dreams he is awakened and ordered to go down to the river with his brother to grapple with a spirit ancestor.[4] These quotations precede the episode in the novel in which Solomon is awakened in the night by mysterious figures, at the behest of his brother, and attacked. Later quotations introduce the image of the "Amatongo" (163, 193), the ancestors who are beneath the earth (linked to the dead African buried in the third pasture), the question of material possession of Africa (213), and the bringing of rain and floods by a rainmaker (231) which precedes torrential rain and floods in modern South Africa. The final quotation widens the historical perspective to suggest the enduring occupation of the land by the blacks (247). The effect is to suggest that the events of the novel may be expressed in the rhetoric of myth.

From the black point of view the main events in the compound in the year during which the action takes place are: the drought, the discovery of the body in the pasture, the attack on Solomon, the fire, the spirit-possession of Phineas's wife with its attendant feast and dance, the flood, and finally the reburial of the dead man, as the cycle of the seasons completes itself. The subtext, buried like the black man, rises to the surface of the novel and repossesses it, obliterating the "paper" possession of Mehring and his story. The dead man is discovered in a reed bed. His body "isn't actually on the earth at all but held slightly above it on a nest of reeds it has flattened. ... The only injury he shows is a long red scratch obviously made by a sharp broken reed" (15). The situation refers explicitly to a myth of origins. Callaway points out that the cult of ancestors is connected with a bed of reeds. A father is the "uthlanga" or ancestor of his children; from him they broke off. "Uthlanga" is a reed, capable of throwing out offsets, and is, therefore, metaphorically a source of being. One of Callaway's informants, who takes "uthlanga" literally, states that man came from a bed of reeds.[5] The nest of reeds also suggests the guinea fowl, which Mehring is trying to conserve; the chapter opens with the image of the guinea fowl eggs, offered by children who have also made a nest for themselves in the grass. The fundamental questions of the novel — Who shall inherit Africa? How shall it be conserved? — are set out in terms of Zulu myth.

The cursory burial of the dead black conditions later events. The first of these is the attack on Solomon, who is discovered stripped and unconscious, on the veld. As accounts of the attack become ritualised, "the legend had already grown that he was attacked in the night by a spirit: there was something down there at the third pasture" (88). Jacobus reports the attack to Mehring in the course of a conversation primarily concerned with the interruption of irrigation on the farm by the frost. Frost also appears to have felled Solomon, whose spilt blood is frozen to the ground. In realistic terms, Solomon has been beaten up for non-payment of debts, but symbolically he has failed to pay a debt to his culture. The implication is that the "spirit" has interrupted the irrigation of the farm and that no regeneration can be expected until the "ancestor" is duly honoured. Solomon is left with a scar on his forehead, "a thick pair of puckered lips sewn together" (96). One form of communication has closed, another has been indicated.

The fire which follows centres on the third pasture: "Same thing every year but one since he has had the farm; but this time the reeds are destroyed, never before" (94). It appears to have gone through the compound, though Mehring dismisses the blackened earth as merely the ash from braziers. In Zulu practice, however, rainmakers burn the earth around their home in the belief that the god sees the black area and knows that the rainmaker is seeking rain. In Zulu myth the lightning bird brings rain, touching the grass with fire.

Rainmakers sacrifice colourful birds in the belief that, as drought takes colour away from the land, the killing of colour — the rainbow-feathered hornbill, for example — will cause the sky to weep and the god to say "Are there no colours (i.e., no rainbow) in the land?"[6] Mehring speculates as to how many birds' nests have been destroyed by the fire, and the landscape is seen as human and black: "that convict's head of stubble manged with ash" (97). When the rain comes, it is described as "taking off again with a sweep that shed, monstrous cosmic peacock, gross paillettes of hail, a dross of battering rain" (232). Drought, the dead black gangster, fire and the images of the rainbird are organised into a coherent pattern of Zulu belief.

The fire is followed by the account of the feast celebrating the initiation of Phineas's wife as a spirit medium. The account of her possession follows the pattern of Zulu possession.[7] The subject is haunted by dreams involving animals as ancestors, feels pain between the shoulder blades, rejects many different foods and fears metamorphosis into an animal. Phineas's wife experiences these symptoms and is also described as coming from Pondoland (the cult of spirit possession is believed to originate north of the Pongola river).[8] The initiation ceremony involves sacrifice of a goat and dancing, which is believed to cause the ancestral spirit to materialise; the test of the initiate is the ability to find hidden objects, here the goat. The underlying idea is that ancestors are tormenting the subject, complaining that he or she is no longer true to their culture. Interestingly, spirit possession is much more common among Zulu women than among men. Social power is gained by the possessed person who is given presents and feasts, ostensibly for the spirits: "To become diviners is for pagan Zulu women the only socially recognised way of escape from an impossible situation in family life; it is also the only way an outstanding woman can win general social prestige."[9] The phenomenon is more common among rural Zulu women to whom escape by taking a job or starting their own business is barred. It is also associated, in Lee's analysis, with sexual and family conflicts: lack of children, an engagement to marry which is resisted, or confusion of goals at the menopause. Phineas's wife "had no living children" and is "somewhere around the end of childbearing age" (164). Her fear is of turning into a lizard: "She used the name isalukazana, the lizard that is a little old woman. She is certainly becoming an old woman" (165). She is even said no longer to sleep with her husband (168). By becoming a diviner, then, the woman escapes from the pressures of her culture and her sex.

In her ravings, Phineas's wife conjures up visions of flood: "In her sleep there were also elephants and hyenas and full rivers, all coming near to kill her" (166). Her initiation precedes the flood which is seen as a female revenge: "The weather came from the Mocambique channel. Space is conceived of as trackless but there are beats about the world frequented by cyclones given female names" (232). One of these hits South Africa, washing the ground clean of the fire ashes, unearthing the body of the dead man and regenerating the burnt area. In the final scene of the novel, the conflicts appear to be resolved: "Phineas's wife's face was at peace, there was no burden of spirits on her shoulders" (267). In the background stand the female members of the sect of Zion, a breakaway from orthodox Christianity, in which Christian tenets have been adapted to indigenous patterns of thought. Zionist churches represent the old divination cult in a new form, involving sacred dancing, speaking in tongues, food taboos and possession by the Holy Spirit (often described as an ancestor).

The close of the novel, therefore, offers a quasi-resolution of white and indigenous cultures. The unconscious life of the woman shapes formally her actions in society. Through Zulu myth, Gordimer gives formal shape to the novel, articulating a different consciousness from that of the public rhetoric of South Africa. In the language of Zulu culture, possession is non-material, passive, a means of resolving social and sexual conflicts. As a cultural model, spirit possession and the ancestor cult are both enduring and flexible:

> Almost always traditional mediumistic cults are essentially conservative for they express and help to sustain the traditional standards and values of the society. Yet we have noticed that mediumship plays an important role in situations of radical and disturbing social change. The paradox is resolved if we accept that in most traditional societies change is regarded as something unwanted, even as dangerous and evil, and like other external and uncontrollable forces it is often regarded as a consequence of the activity of the spirit, in one manifestation or another. Thus the forces of radical change may be spiritualized in order that they can be accommodated and thus in some way controlled.[10]

The murdered black from the location represents change and is therefore spiritualised and controlled by the blacks, just as Christianity, a threat to their culture, is assimilated into the old divination cult. The cult offers a therapy for social deprivation, a catharsis for the Zulu woman in a subservient role. One meaning of the title, then, has been established: the blacks conserve their beliefs, and their beliefs conserve and regenerate the land and its people.

Significantly, a woman comes to express Zulu culture and to resolve its problems. The conjunction of woman and land is repeated in the events of the foreground. Phineas's wife may have achieved some independent status in her society, but the other women are visibly getting the worst of it. Dawood's Indian wife longs for Durban, Mehring's mistress is forced to flee, the Portuguese immigrant girl is molested, even the Afrikaans-speaking daughter-in-law and granddaughters of old De Beer are thoroughly cowed, described as vacant turnips. The point being made here is not, however, only a feminist one. Female exploitation and exploitation of the land are linked; sexual guilt functions as a surrogate for colonial guilts.

The fantasy-ideal form of the relationship to woman and land occurs in the incident on board the airplane. Returning from a business trip, Mehring is forced to travel tourist class and during the night engages in sexual play with his neighbour, a young Portuguese immigrant girl. The scene can be read as an example of Mehring's sexual fascism; he is a sexual colonialist — no woman is safe from his hand or eye.[11] Mehring's mind moves into the event through his perceptions of the land below him, which he sees as "soft lap after lap" of sand and desert — the opening phrase, "Golden reclining nudes of the desert" (126), refers as much to the dunes as to any sunning tourist. The body of the girl becomes the land — as Mehring locates it, explores, explicitly compares its flesh to water in the desert, experiences the "grain" of the skin, guesses his location and moves over the terrain, exploring the ridges of her anatomy. The airplane, an enclosed world outside time and place, veiled in sandstorms, allows Mehring to ignore social, sexual and class taboos. The events are "happening nowhere" (129). Moreover, Mehring's colonialism extends to the whole of reality. The closed world of the airplane communicates an impression of consciousness operating in a void, dissociated from the world beneath, annihilating reality. Beneath him the desert sand becomes "an infinite progression of petrified sound waves" (131), which he watches while caressing the girl, equally soundless, echoing back to him his own activity. Sexual activity is described as linguistic — as a monologue, as delicate phrasing, delicate questioning, and finally as entry into the "soundless o of the little mouth" (130). The relationship goes on and on in an endless night of solipsistic communication which does not advance, merely making Mehring overaware of "the bounds of himself" (130), of his confinement within his own vision of reality. The erotic quality of the experience is fundamentally autoerotic, the girl utterly passive. The method of narration is infinitely oblique. The questions — "Who spoke first? Was it at all sure that it was he?" (127) — go unanswered, even unasked. The girl's body "takes up the narrative" (127); Mehring's hand "took up the thread of communication" (128) but without actual utterance. The two collaborate in a surreptitious relationship, never fully articulated, relying on the convention that they are utterly separate while enjoying a close intimacy. Their relation is "not without tenderness, but who is ever to know that is part of the scandal" (132) — just as Mehring's relation to his land and his boys is not without tenderness but none the less a scandal. Sexual fantasy as a surrogate for colonial lusts is extended in ontological terms. As a white South African male, Mehring can have relations to women only as a form of slumming — even without crossing the race or class lines. His activity, then, can give him back only his own image. The sterile desert beneath, "echoing itself since there was no organic renewal by which life could be measured" (131), confirms this reading of the text. Solipsism prevents change and renewal of the external world. Another culture, beyond Mehring's, carries the burden of renewal and rebirth.

Mehring's activities on the airplane are presented as a flashback, framed by two images of fathers and sons — the Indians whose shop is near the farm, and the visit of Mehring's own son, Terry. The first episode takes place in an enclosed space, a circumscribed world (like Mehring's airplane). The last one leaves the closed world for a desert of space. The Indians' shop is surrounded by dogs in a ring of savagery, behind a stockade which Bismillah continually repairs, a conservationist of a more defensive kind. The image of a culture deliberately walling itself in, refusing to communicate across the lines drawn by apartheid, even collaborating with it, is also the image of a walled-off consciousness. When Dorcas's husband opens the stockade doors, the dogs do not escape, "as if for them the pattern of closed gates was still barred across their eyes" (125). Mind-forged manacles — that book of unknown signs within the mind — operate even more repressively than external restraints. Within the Indians' house Dawood and his young bride are seen crammed into one room with her dowry furniture, a further space within a space, a space which Dawood sees as paradise. His father comments, "The boy will be happy anywhere he can be touching the first woman he has all to himself. Anywhere. The room is paradise" (118). In the shop the closed world does not intersect in any meaningful way with the world of the customers. Bismillah, conversing in Gujerati with his father, enjoys total privacy. To the blacks he employs "the semantics of the trade" (119), saying one thing to mean another, cagily unwilling to say more than the absolute minimum. The rhythm of their speech is like the rhythm of Mehring's "conversation" on the plane: "Demand. Response. Counterdemand. Statement" (119). When Dorcas's husband challenges Bismillah, Bismillah deliberately distances him by communicating only through William, although Dorcas's husband is perfectly intelligible. The incident demonstrates how each closed culture mimics the one above it, absorbing and passing on the aggression. Bismillah is thinking aloud, at this point, imagining Mehring's probable reaction to his business proposition: "And go to hell, and who you bloody think you are" (122). The words are directed at Dorcas's husband, who then tears up the paper receipts of the Christmas Club, paper counters in a linguistic currency which merely exploits him. The episode dramatises the lack of consensus in South Africa, the separate existence of different codes and circumscribed worlds which communicate only crudely, underhandedly, or violently.

Mehring's separate peace is presented in the visit of his son Terry in another guise, that of exile. Terry's rucksack with its peace symbol looms large in the enclosed space of Mehring's car. The action again centres on problems of sexuality and communication. An ominous silence echoes beneath the text of the conversation. Mehring tries all the keys on the car radio, "Running down the scales of snatches of music and voices back to silence" (150). Father and son speak different languages: "Were they referring to the same things when they talked together?" (134). Neither engages with the real subject — Terry's impending military service. Indeed, the "real subject" is uncertain, existing only as a mysterious block to communication. The conversation begins beside a sign in three languages — "No thoroughfare. Geen Toegang. Akunandlela Lapha" (140) — and takes them to the point in the fields where Mehring previously tore up a letter to Terry, a dead end.

At one point Mehring considers the use of the term "Namibia": "Why that and not another invention expressive of a certain attitude towards the place?" (138). Namibia is chosen as a neutral term, one which will not suggest that the land belongs to any of the tribes occupying it and will not conjure up jealousy. Language attempts to say nothing here, to be neutral — an impossible and pointless task. Moreover, the discussion of Namibia takes place not between Terry and Mehring but in Mehring's memory between him and his white mistress. For him Namibia does conjure up jealous visions — of his mistress and, as a result of Terry's disaffection, of his wife. The rhythm of the passage is continued attempt and failure to guess the unspoken thoughts of the other and to trap him into revelation. Mehring seizes on a book published by the Campaign For Homosexual Equality as a possible answer, a reality beneath their speech: "Could this be the subject?" (151). Whether Terry is or is not homosexual remains uncertain, though in Mehring's terms he might as well be. Africa and woman are so identified that rejection of one implies rejection of the other.

A further irony is present. The book is "hidden away like the goat" (151) whose bones are to be used in Zulu divining. The method of divination is question-and-answer, slight nuances of emphasis in the answerer's response finally yielding the "correct" response.[12] Terry and his father lack even such subtlety. The book, when found, is just another inscrutable surface, a mish-mash of legal jargon and "text-book mumbo-jumbo." Mehring penetrates the neutral surface conversation only to find an even more "public," social rhetoric. Terry's withdrawal from the enclosed solipsistic world of South Africa makes him a creature in a neutralised empty world — the desert of Namibia rather than the paradise of Dawood's room or Mehring's airplane. Nothing connects subjective paradise with objective desert except the empty air. White Africa is caught in a double-bind: between Mehring, the conservationist who conserves only the mapped-out contours of his own mind, and Terry, the objective, socially conscious inhabitant of a neutral desert.

Some readers have responded to the land of Africa, sensually apprehended in Gordimer's prose, as a connecting medium, a key reality in a pastoral sense, so that Gordimer's facility for observation has been seen as a weakness: "In her desire to record accurately, to convey the exact feel, the smell, the taste of an experience, the episode itself tends to lose its outlines."[13] The main virtue of the book has been seen as its "passages of cool delicate prose that prove their author one of the ablest descriptive writers alive."[14] The natural landscape, however, is as resistant to realism as it is to rhetoric. Mehring describes it as "a landscape without theatricals … a landscape without any picture postcard features (photographs generally were unsuccessful in conveying it)" (25). The landscape is repeatedly described in terms which suggest that it exists beneath the level of conscious articulation. Sound is muffled and minimised within it: "The thudding and distant shouts are no more than a smudge on the perfect silence that stretches to the horizon" (41). Nature is not a mapped-out certainty but a process of change. Mehring contemplates a plover — "Its exquisitely neat black and white markings take his eye into visual discipline" (79), but the landscape around is tonal, softened, as a result of the fire, which leaves particles of smoke in the air. Drought has a similar effect: "Dust has the effect on the distant hills of a pencil sketch gone over with a soft rubber" (108). The cyclone, dissolving the normal landscape, is associated with a social change. When the road is washed away, Mehring is separated from the farm, and the Africans have to cope without him — as though he were dead. Jacobus opens cupboards, "as possessions must be sorted after a death, putting objects aside like words of a code, or symbols of a life that will never be understood coherently, never explained now" (238). Gordimer offers a vision of Africa without the white man — and at the same time a different form of vision. Rain dissolves the normal paths and ways of society, washing out both social domination and a way of seeing: "The sense of perspective was changed" (233).

Car tires behave as if greased, "engaging with a tangible surface only on intermittent revolutions" (233). Within the cars children shriek with joy and fear at the lack of sensation — "the impression of being carried along without any kind of familiar motion" (234). Gordimer's language conveys the same excitement engaging with a tangible surface only intermittently, carrying the reader along in a motion which operates below the level of consciousness, leaving realism and the familiar social consensus behind. At those points where the rhetoric of Zulu culture intersects with that of the "foreground" action, the perspective of the text is changed, dissolves, and the reader is uncertain which action is primary, which "background." When Mehring becomes subconsciously aware of the black corpse beneath his feet, the muddy surface of the third pasture becomes molten, almost sucking him under. He struggles to free himself from the "soft cold black hand" (228) of the mud, freeing himself less from a real threat than from his own projections. The black functions here as alter ego, so that Mehring feels "as if part of him is still buried" (227). The black as image of the subconscious is associated with the melting surface beneath him. A sexual vibration is also present in the corncob which Mehring tries, slicing through — "the tight bandage of ribbed leaves that encases it like a mummy" — to penetrate: "The white nubs so young they are not quite solid, and their white milky substance flows under the nail" (227–28). When the car is washed away in the flood, Gordimer's own account — "It was seen to float a moment and then engage with some solid surface again — just as it was about to gain the rise something burst out there" (234) — is contrasted with the public rhetoric of the newspapers, with their nine-year-old photographs of Mr. and Mrs. Loftus Coetzee, vanished "without a trace before the horrified eyes of astonished witnesses" (235). White rhetoric is washed away just as Witbooi's references from his white employers have been wiped out by the rain; the peace symbol on the water tower has been undermined and is about to collapse. The dependence of realism on materialism is undermined as matter flows and language changes. As a connecting medium the land of Africa is as unreliable as its language.

Nowhere is reality more in question than in the final pages of the novel. The reader grasps for a tangible surface in the events occurring between Mehring and the anonymous woman, his "death" which is not a death, and the mysterious figures in the background of the picnic place. Mehring's mind appears to have lost its grip on reality shortly before his "death." After he has had coffee with a friend's daughter in Johannesburg, a girl he lusts after, news reaches him that her father has been found gassed in his car, the result of a financial scandal. Mehring's reaction is obsessively guilty: "It's me. Drawn up, he has been seized, he is going to be confronted at last!" The words "It's me" are the daughter's unspoken greeting (188), the words of his arrested mistress on the telephone, and the horrid spectre of the Portuguese girl: "one immigrant girl in a city full of girls ... she is there somewhere all the time" (194). The train of associations leads Mehring to confront the colonial guilt beneath the sexual, as the coffee he has just drunk turns to poison: "Some of them take poison. A dose of cyanide, it's quicker" (195). The phrase "It's me" refers also to Mehring, equally implicated in the financial scandal of South Africa, equally guilty. Cyanide, we remember, is "the stuff that is used in the most effective and cheapest process for extricating gold from the auriferous reef. ... It is what makes yellow the waste that is piled up ... where the road first leaves the city" (195). The denouement situates Mehring in the same symbolic landscape — "a dirty place, an overgrown rubbish dump between mounds of cyanide waste" (258).

Before the denouement the last of Mehring's weapons is turned against him: his irony. Formerly, Mehring expressed his separate peace as an ability to see the "joke" in South Africa, to convert, for example, the dead African into "a story to be told over drinks" (27). Mehring's irony is continually scoring points off the white South Africans, as well as the Boers and the blacks. Towards the close of the novel, however, he is unable to maintain his ironic detachment. The girl takes his cinema invitation as a joke. Jacobus sees the invitation to see in the New Year as a joke. Mehring suffers a double rejection, by woman and black, and becomes a double prisoner, unable to communicate across the sexual and racial divide and unwilling to accept the mechanical surface communication of Johannesburg society. He is left enclosed in his room, paralyzed beside the telephone answering device, receiving its messages but unable to respond: "The machine simply stops listening. Just as he gives no answer" (200). Mehring is hiding in his room to avoid attending his friend's funeral. The psychological logic is clear. Mehring converts the dead black into a "story" to amuse white South Africa. The black is buried without honor. White South Africa then reads the newspaper story of his friend's death, and Mehring refuses to honor him. The events of the "subplot" boomerang back onto the "main" plot. Mehring's "story" is akin to the black's burial without honour. He tidies up an awkward reality, which remains just beneath the surface ready to erupt again at any point. The problem of finding a language looms large in the novel, with its images of botched contacts, failed communication and empty public rhetoric. One danger faced is the "tidying up" effect of formal narrative, which by its rhetoric interposes itself between subject and object, detaching and distancing the latter. Mehring's irony neutralises the black, but the dead man comes back to plague him from the guilty depths of his own consciousness.

What, then, of Mehring's "death" — the ambiguous closing pages of the novel? The scene reiterates and unites the themes of the novel. The car journey takes Mehring through a landscape which functions as a mental topography. He is no longer responding to normal signs and has "an awful moment looking at a green light and not knowing what it means. Jeers of horns are prodding at him. Blank" (251). He clings to familiar landmarks in an attempt to hang on to his version of reality, picking out bus stops and beer cartons — "ticking off a familiar progression of objects can be used to restore concentration" (252). Although the woman is once again a representative of the land, she is not a paradise conserved but an ecological disaster. Her face is like a cyanide dump: "The grain of the skin is gigantic, muddy and coarse. A moon surface. Grey-brown with layers of muck that don't cover the blemishes" (260). In her person she sums up all the women of the book — she babbles like a schoolgirl (254), reminds Mehring of his mistress (250), has an accent which suggests she is Afrikaans-speaking (262), and "could be Portuguese" (262). She may even be black: "That hair's been straightened and that sallowness isn't sunburn" (261). Mehring's abandonment of her prefigures abandonment of Africa:

> He's going to leave her to them ... he's going to make a dash for it, a leap, sell the place to the first offer ... He's going to run, run and leave them to rape her and rob her. She'll be all right. They survive everything. Coloured or poor-white, whichever she is, their brothers or fathers take their virginity good and early. They can have it, the whole 400 acres. (264)

As Mehring is about to possess the woman, he becomes aware "as of a feature in a landscape not noticed before" (261) of a pair of male calves in the background. Two possibilities are entertained: the man is a thug in conspiracy with the girl to beat him up and rob him, or he is a member of the police enforcing the race laws. On the level of Mehring's subconscious he is the Freudian censor, interrupting his sexual activities. On the political level he recalls the police at the start of the novel, who bury the black gangster: "These are the bastards who shovelled him in as you might fling a handful of earth on the corpse of a rat. Dispose of the body and so you dump your rubbish on somebody's private property" (263). The black man, the body, the body of woman, and the rubbish dumps form one massive image of colonial guilt. Mehring is in the reverse position to that of Phineas's wife. Her unconscious life shapes her society. His unconscious life is formally shaped and repressed by his society. The final words of the chapter are those of other people inside Mehring's head: "Come and look, they're all saying. What is it? Who is it? It's Mehring. It's Mehring down there" (265). His society is repressive, not expressive.

The problems the passage presents for the reader hinge on the questions: What is real? Which is the accepted version of events? These are precisely the problems posed by South Africa: a lack of normality, shared language, or vision. Mehring seizes on the detail of the man's comb in his sock: "If it were not for the comb — so undeniably the sort of detail that no unnerved imagination could possibly supply — there could not possibly be anyone there. But there is. Someone has been there all the time" (261). Even realistic detail functions within the nightmare, confirming its horror rather than mapping out a safe certainty. The novel ends with the reinterment of the black, the "someone" who has been there all the time and now takes final possession.

In *The Conservationist*, then, Gordimer articulates that book of hidden signs which is the individual, without translating into the language of political consensus the realism of a materialist society. Although Woman and Black Man function as symbols in the white subconscious, onto whom the conflicts of the white psyche are projected, such fantasy projection is also critically examined and set in a different perspective by the foregrounding of the black consciousness — rising from its buried position to the surface of the text. As Gordimer has said, "Politics is character — in South Africa."[15] Under her ironic title Gordimer argues that to conserve the land — to maintain it as neither the hothouse of fantasy nor the desert of neutral tones — the first task is to regenerate its language. A new rhetoric expresses rather than represses the individual, and the land possesses as much as it is possessed. The novel ends with affirmation, reconstruction of reality implying possible reconstruction of the land. *The Conservationist* is, therefore, that rarest of endangered species — a politically radical South African novel.

Notes to Chapter 1

1. Nadine Gordimer, "A Writer in South Africa," *London Magazine*, 5, No. 2 (May 1965).
2. Henry Callaway, *The Religious System of the Amazulu* (Springvale, Natal: J. A. Blair, 1878).
3. Nadine Gordimer, *The Conservationist* (London: Penguin Books, 1978), 39. Subsequent references are to this edition.
4. Passages quoted occur on the following pages of *The Conservationist* (pages in Callaway are given in parenthesis): 39, 61 (182); 83, 93, 113 (194); 163 (12–13); 193 (134, 136); 213 (77–79); 231 (391); and 247 (15–16).
5. Callaway, 3–9.
6. See Axel-Ivar Berglund, *Zulu Thought Patterns and Symbolism* (London, 1976), 56–58.
7. Callaway, passim.
8. S. G. Lee, "Spirit Possession among the Zulu," in John Beattie and John Middleton (eds), *Spirit Mediumship and Society in Africa* (London, 1969), 130.
9. Ibid., 128–58.
10. Beattie and Middleton, xxviii.
11. See, for example, rev. of *The Conservationist*, *Times Literary Supplement*, 1 November 1974, 1217.
12. Berglund.
13. Ursula Laredo, "Nadine Gordimer," in James Vinson (ed.), *Contemporary Novelists* (London, 1976), 542–46.
14. Peter Kerr-Jarrett in the *Sunday Telegraph*, quoted on the Penguin back cover.
15. Gordimer, "A Writer in South Africa."

CHAPTER 2

Bellow's "Indian Givers":
Humboldt's Gift

> He is a good man who can receive a gift well. ... Some violence, I think, is
> done, some degradation borne, when I rejoice or grieve at a gift.[1]

Emerson's essay on "Gifts" perceptively highlights the ambivalence felt in gift-giving
or receiving, an ambivalence which lies at the heart of Saul Bellow's most recent
novel, *Humboldt's Gift*. The importance of literal gift-giving has been insufficiently
recognised as a factor which governs the action of the novel, our understanding of
which is enhanced by an examination and application of the sociological analysis
of gift-exchange.[2] Gift-exchange has been most extensively studied in relation to
the North-West Coast American Indians, notably the Kwakiutl, in whose culture
the "potlatch" is a central activity. The term "potlatch" is applied to a variety of
gift-giving ceremonies, involving both the giving away of quantities of possessions
and their wilful destruction. The whole of a man's worldly goods may be dispersed
or destroyed in this fashion, in an attempt to maintain status. To eclipse a rival
chief, for example, a man may destroy all his own accumulated wealth. While
in theory the "gift" is spontaneous and disinterested, in practice it is based on
political or economic self-interest. The gift of property implies an obligation in
the recipient which, if not fulfilled, results in his loss of face. The "Indian giver"
gives in order to establish credit, since the recipient is obliged to return the gift at
a future time to the donor or his heirs, complete with interest. The destroyer forces
his rivals to destroy in their turn. As a cultural form, potlatch therefore prevents
any one individual from monopolising material goods, keeps wealth in circulation,
prevents the build-up of economic surpluses, and also subtly maintains social order.
Hierarchy is established by gifts or destruction of property, in that he who gives
away or destroys most property gains greatest status. To accept without repaying is
to invite one's own subordination.

   The Kwakiutl were well aware of the aggressive nature of gift-exchange, describing it as "fighting with property" and as a substitute for actual warfare. Interestingly, potlatch originally meant "to nourish" or "to consume" and the phenomenon has been interpreted as a sublimation of the cannibal tendency. Eli Sagan
argues that

> In more primitive times the offended man might have killed and eaten the
> offender, or merely killed him. ... Here he did none of those things, but still his
> revenge had to be fulfilled. He satisfied his aggression in the sublimated way

that was characteristic of the culture — he destroyed a valuable piece of his own property in the presence of the man who had wronged him.[3]

In Sagan's analysis such sublimation is part of the progress of civilisation as man slowly substitutes symbolic forms of aggression for naked aggression itself. In Sagan's view the two highest sublimations are art and love. Sagan's study of cannibalism examines "affectionate cannibalism", the idea that man is aggressive to those he loves, and concludes that love is the greatest gift of sexual sublimation. He further states, "Art is the other great form that is built by the sublimation of magic. The great pleasure in the experience of art is that of freely expressing one's magical desires in a controlled, sublimated way."[4]

There are interesting points of contact here with *Humboldt's Gift*, which concentrates on the love–hate relationship between Charlie Citrine, the narrator, and Von Humboldt Fleisher, the poet, and in which cannibal imagery and incidents abound.[5] Humboldt is recalled complaining that success has made him a million enemies, and that American society is inimical to poets, seeing the failure of the poetic seer as a vindication of its tough this-worldly capitalism. He continues: "I don't suppose you've read about the Cannibal society of the Kwakiutl Indians", said learned Humboldt. "The candidate when he performs his initiation dance falls into a frenzy and eats human flesh. But if he makes a ritual mistake the whole crowd tears him to pieces."[6]

In the course of the novel Humboldt and Citrine participate in a ritual of Humboldt's own making, a ritual of gift-exchange. The two men exchange blank cheques, and "take an oath as friends and brothers never to abuse this" (129). When they have each signed Humboldt comments, "This makes us blood brothers. We've entered into a covenant" (130). While Citrine loses his cheque, Humboldt cashes his. In so doing he may appear to betray Citrine, the more so in that the latter's mistress, Demmie, has just then died, flying down to a Mission for a cannibal tribe in South America.[7] Humboldt contends, however, that the betrayal is Citrine's, that Citrine is a cannibal: in writing his play *Von Trenck*, Citrine has stolen Humboldt's personality. Humboldt alleges, "I don't say he actually plagiarized, but he did steal something from me — my personality. He built my personality into his hero" (3–4). Citrine is well aware of his guilt. As a biographer he is a metaphorical "cannibal": "For I did write biographies and the deceased were my bread and butter" (116). In order to punish Citrine for his mistake, Humboldt imposes a fine, cashing the cheque not for purely economic gain but in order to reestablish his own prestige. While he appears to accept Citrine's gift, in fact he immediately destroys it, using the money to buy an enormous Oldsmobile, a sumptuous piece of property which he promptly loses, "forgetting" where he left it. Citrine failed to respect the identity of his friend, "cannibalised" him, and broke their covenant; Humboldt therefore restores his own prestige by destroying Citrine's gift. The aggression behind gift-exchange, its function as a guarantor of hierarchy and prestige, eclipses the higher forms of brotherly love and art.

Humboldt, however, is not the only character to exchange gifts with Citrine. The destruction of cars links the two plots of the novel. These two plots — low life in present-day Chicago and the past life with Humboldt in the realms of "high" culture — are played off against each other, thereby questioning the value of the higher form.[8] Rinaldo Cantabile, a small time, Chicago gangster, functions, in Bellow's own terminology, as a "contrast gainer" to Humboldt. Cantabile enters the novel in the events following a poker game. Citrine has gone slumming, to play poker with assorted "low life" characters, and loses $600 to Cantabile. The game takes place amidst discussion of Robert Ardrey, his territorial imperative, and Konrad Lorenz, suggesting a vision of the human being as fundamentally aggressive. The game, moreover, functions as a twentieth-century potlatch. In his work on gift-exchange, Marcel Mauss points out that in Kwakiutl society everything is conceived of as a war with wealth, including gambling, and he comments,

> Gambling ... even with us is not considered contractual but rather as comprised of situations in which honour is engaged and where property is surrendered although it is not absolutely necessary to do so. Gambling is a form of potlatch and a part of the gift system.[9]

When George Swiebel asserts that Cantabile has been cheating, Citrine stops his cheque, humiliating Cantabile. Cantabile's outrage has less relation to the value of the money than to the insult. In order to force Citrine to recognise him as an equal he begins by destroying Citrine's most valuable piece of property, his silver Mercedes, beating it all over with a baseball bat, so that it appears to have "suffered a kind of crystalline internal hemorrhage" (36). Citrine realises that he has lost his "protective magic" (36) in Chicago. When he offers to settle with Cantabile, Cantabile insists that the settlement be made in public, and he engineers a meeting in the Playboy Club with a gossip columnist, in front of whom Citrine hands over the cash. The meeting itself depends upon the return of obligation:

> I began to appreciate what Rinaldo had done. He had gone to great trouble to set up his encounter, pulling many strings. This Bill, a connection of his, perhaps owed the Cantabiles a favour, and had agreed to produce Mike Schneiderman the columnist. Obligations were being called in all over the place. (92)

Leaving the Playboy Club, Cantabile thrusts the money back at Citrine but compels him to hand it over once again in the apartment of a notorious jewellery fence. The act of atonement is thus carried out, both in the eyes of the press (and thus the general public) and in the presence of a high-ranking member of the criminal fraternity. Citrine has publicly reciprocated the "gift" in the eyes of both cultures. Finally, to assuage his honour decisively, Cantabile conducts Citrine to the top of a skyscraper, makes ten fifty-dollar bills into paper gliders, and sails each of them off the building. The gift has been reciprocated, property has been destroyed, and honour is satisfied. Paradoxically, Cantabile, the low-class gangster, has taught Citrine that gift-exchange is a subtle cultural form, establishing equal status between the parties to the gift. With his last two bills Cantabile feasts Citrine and over dinner asks him to provide biographical information about Humboldt to further his thesis-writing wife's career. Citrine, however, refuses to exploit his dead friend and as a result engages in the first of many meditations on Humboldt, which slowly lead him to a fuller understanding of their "blood" brotherhood.

While the gift-exchanges between Citrine and Cantabile, and between Citrine and Humboldt, are central to the action of the novel, much of its plot also revolves around the various property wars in which Citrine is engaged. Almost without exception his friends are "takers", exploiting Citrine's superior status by accepting his gifts. Citrine believes in symbolic "higher" forms and his friends pander to that belief, leaving Citrine with symbols while pocketing the cash. Szathmar owes Citrine money, and gives him Renata, a love goddess, in return. Pierre Thaxter takes Citrine's cash to produce an art magazine, defaults on the loan, and draws up an elaborate schedule of repayments:

> I could see that he entirely meant what he said. But I also knew that this elaborate plan to do right by me would be, in his mind, tantamount to doing right. These long yellow sheets from the legal pad filled with figures, these generous terms of repayment, the care for detail, the expressions of friendship settled our business fully and forever. This was magically it. (273)

For Thaxter, symbolic repayment has taken the place of real repayment. Thaxter is not, however, so indulgent to his own debtors. In order to recoup his own financial losses he attempts to threaten Stronson, the financier, with a hit-man.

Society functions as a web of obligations in which Citrine is trapped. Litigation surrounds him, lawsuits pullulate. These suits are governed less by purely economic greed than by the desire for power, vengeance and status. Denise, Citrine's ex-wife, is suing Citrine for maintenance, in a suit which is entirely governed by the desire for vengeance — not merely hers but also society's. The judge explicitly opens the case in terms which reveal the delight of Chicago society in the attack on the successful writer: "'Being on the stand is frightful for a sensitive creative person like Mr. Citrine. ...' The judge meant me to feel the ironic weight of this" (229). To the judge art is merely Citrine's capital asset; to Denise "love" is a means of financing her future. Denise's case is handled by "Cannibal Pinsker", whose method is to terrify Citrine into a settlement. As Citrine's lawyer comments, "Now you're supposed to be terrified and beg us to settle and save you from being butchered and hacked to pieces" (235). While ostensibly the court case is designed to safeguard the welfare of Citrine's daughters, in fact it is little more than a pecking ritual in which Denise, beneath the facade of the loving mother, gives free play to her aggressive instincts, and society reveals how little it values art. Events in the divorce court suggest that Bellow does not share Sagan's belief in the inevitable sublimation of aggression in the higher forms of art and love.

Although ostensibly deployed in his support, Citrine's lawyers won't hear criticism of the opposition because of their allegiance to "professional ethics." Since Charlie is effectively paying both sets of lawyers the supposed legal battle is only an empty ritual in which Charlie is bled. As he comments, "Money was a vital substance like the blood" (242). Citrine is left fighting mad, wishing that he could burst into speech like Shylock telling off the Christians, but in this court everyone except him is entitled to their pound of flesh. Citrine has become too successful and has attempted to escape his obligations to society. He can only continue to exist in Chicago by sacrificing his property. But the more Citrine gives, to Thaxter,

Szathmar and Denise, the more his higher status accrues. While in the Cantabile plot Citrine has to learn to give, his property wars teach him the limits of giving. Citrine's social position is analogous to the poker game, where he loses money as from his exalted position he discourses to his "slum" acquaintances on the social order, art, and his intellectual projects. Citrine has laid claim to superior status and in the court scene society mobilises to establish its own overriding strength. Cantabile and Denise (and the court) force Citrine out of his superior isolation, making him aware that he is part of a network of obligations and relationships.

Humboldt, as has been suggested, is another sacrificial victim to cultural norms. Yet, in terms of gift-giving Humboldt is not merely a taker. At the close of the novel Humboldt's legacies are revealed. When Citrine rejects his share of the proceeds of the scenario which Humboldt left to his wife Kathleen and to Citrine, jointly, Kathleen reveals her awareness of the ambivalence of accepting the gift. She will be under no obligations: "Because I'm a widow you won't accept your own money from me? But *I* don't want *your* share. Think of it that way" (377). In the end Citrine accepts this gift. The scenario carries a message. The hero, Corcoran, meets and falls in love with a beautiful woman and escapes with her to an idyllic island. Later, in order to write a book about it, he attempts to repeat the experience, this time with his wife. But, in order to relive the events, he is forced to bribe the natives of the island with gifts, ruining the primitive paradise with technological marvels. When mistress and wife discover his treachery, both leave him. In attempting to make literary capital out of his love he has prostituted his gifts. In an accompanying letter Humboldt makes the analogy clear: "You took my personality and exploited it in writing your *Trenck*. I have borrowed from you to create this Corcoran" (346–47). In a sense this gift is a double revenge. Firstly, it is a revenge through sublimated forms. Humboldt gets his revenge by parodying Citrine's former betrayal. He comments that "Prospero is a Hamlet who gets his revenge through art" (345).[10] Secondly, the gift is itself a revenge, a potlatch from beyond the grave. Humboldt writes, "Charles, here is my gift to you. It is worth a hundred times more than the check I put through" (346).

Humboldt's second gift is to have protected his and Citrine's rights to the *Caldofreddo* scenario, which he co-authored with Citrine, and which has now been made into a successful film. Like a play-within-a-play the film summarises and makes explicit the themes of the novel. It concerns the rivalry of two friends, Amundsen and Umberto Nobile, both explorers, and the failure of the former to rescue the latter — much as Citrine, Humboldt's friend and fellow writer, fails to rescue Humboldt from Bellevue. There is one survivor of Nobile's crew, Caldofreddo, who has turned cannibal in order to survive on an ice floe. The scenario, however, concentrates less on the cannibalism than on the aged Caldofreddo in his Sicilian village. Forced by an investigating journalist to admit his crime, Caldofreddo makes public confession to the townspeople and is forgiven — much as Citrine faces up to his "cannibalisation" of Humboldt and comes to terms with the past. Citrine uses his share of the settlement with the film producers to rebury Humboldt with fitting ceremony, and to honour him publicly. He also ensures that Humboldt's share is passed to his heir, Waldemar Wald, Humboldt's gambler uncle. In accepting the gift Citrine accepts his place in society. He is no longer the superior being who gives to all and sundry, but also a recipient, owing a debt of gratitude to the dead. In accepting Humboldt's gift he accepts that he is as much an aggressor as a victim. As a result, he is able to dismiss Cantabile and to refuse to pay up to save Thaxter from his "kidnappers." In Mauss's terms he learns the intricacy of social membership:

> Societies have progressed in the measure in which they, their sub-groups and members, have been able to stabilize their contracts, and to give, receive and repay ... to oppose one another without slaughter, and to give without sacrificing themselves to others.[11]

Humboldt's gift also restores Citrine's belief in the possibility of disinterested giving and in love. When Kathleen asks why Humboldt gave the Corcoran scenario to both of them (372), she ascribes it to his delight in wicked plotting, scheming for litigation beyond the grave. Citrine, however, sees it differently. Humboldt was a schemer, and in giving two gifts he gave of himself: "He showed us what he had most of — scheming, plotting and paranoia" (373). His gift is finally himself and, in accepting Humboldt as he was, Citrine also receives self-forgiveness: "His legacy is also his affectionate opinion of me" (351). Love allows the acceptance of the gift without threat. Humboldt's gift therefore fulfils Emerson's demand, that the giver give only of himself:

> Rings and other jewels are not gifts, but apologies for gifts. The only gift is a portion of thyself. Thou must bleed for me. Therefore the poet brings his poem. ... We wish to be self-sustained. We do not quite forgive a giver. The hand that feeds us is in some danger of being bitten. We can receive anything from love, for that is a way of receiving it from ourselves.[12]

While *Humboldt's Gift* concerns the superior artistic gifts of Humboldt and of Citrine, the gifts function also in the weltering aggression of human life. The artist cannot stand outside his society, claiming superior status and dwelling in the rarefied air of "higher" forms. If he does, society will take him at his word and exact the penalty. Like every man, the artist is not self-sustained but nourished by his fellow men. He can only repay this gift by giving of himself, freely and without condescension. While it is in the nature of gifts to be ambivalent, it is also their function to link past and present, to establish continuity of exchange, and to maintain connections between material and symbolic values. In its complex of different gift-exchanges, Bellow's novel wittily establishes the inescapability of human bonds and obligations.

Notes to Chapter 2

1. Ralph Waldo Emerson, "Gifts," *Essays* (London: Dent, 1971), 292. Bellow referred to this essay in 1963, in the context of a discussion of the disparity between "high" and "low" culture in America. Saul Bellow, "The Writer as Moralist," *The Atlantic Monthly*, 211 (March 1963), 58.
2. Bellow graduated in 1937 from Northwestern University, Chicago, with honours in anthropology and sociology. His anthropological research, in particular in African ethnography,

forms the source for many details of the Africa of *Henderson the Rain King*. See Eusebio C. Rodrigues, "Bellow's Africa," *American Literature*, 43 (1971), 242–56.

3. Eli Sagan, *Cannibalism: Human Aggression and Cultural Form* (New York: Harper and Row, 1974), 113.

4. Ibid., 123.

5. See K. E. Possler, "Cannibalism in *Humboldt's Gift*," *Gypsy Scholar: A Graduate Forum for Literary Criticism*, 5 (1978), 18–21.

6. Saul Bellow, *Humboldt's Gift* (London: Secker and Warburg, 1975), 14. Subsequent page references will be given in the text of the essay.

7. It is interesting to note that the most celebrated failure of a mission to South American Indians, in 1956, to the Auca of Ecuador, occurred because of a misinterpretation of gift-giving. The American missionaries dropped gifts from the air before landing among the Indians, to ensure a friendly reception. The Indians assumed that the missionaries were planning to eat them and therefore attacked. See David Thompson, "We're not savages — we are people," *The Listener*, 24 January 1980, 108–09.

8. See Judie Newman, "Saul Bellow: *Humboldt's Gift* — The Comedy of History," *Durham University Journal*, 72 (December 1979), 82.

9. Marcel Mauss, *The Gift* (London: Cohen and West, 1954), 101. Originally published in French as *Essai sur le Don* (Paris: Presses Universitaires de France, 1950).

10. Sagan (123) mentions Prospero as the perfect example of magical desires expressed and controlled in art.

11. Mauss, 80.

12. Emerson, 291.

CHAPTER 3

The Revenge of the Trance Maiden:
Intertextuality and Alison Lurie

As intertextuality is an extremely capacious term, some working definitions seem to be in order.[1] Most readers will be familiar with the term, as coined by Julia Kristeva, as founded upon the proposition that "every text builds itself as a mosaic of quotations, every text is absorption and transformation of another text."[2] At its narrowest, this has been taken to limit the applicability of the term to parody, mere allusion, source criticism, and casual generic resemblances. More commonly, however, the intertext of a given story may be defined as the set of plots, characters, images and conventions which it calls to mind for a given reader. In other words, it is not merely another text to which a work alludes, but to a totality, creating a general sense of a work of art which interacts with an entire tradition. The relationship obtaining between two (or more) texts is therefore between the texts as structured wholes. One can of course go one step further (following Kristeva's lead) and define a "text" as a system of signs, whether in literary works, spoken languages, non-verbal sign systems, or symbolic systems.[3] Thus, Kristeva proceeds to define intertextuality as the transposition of one or several systems of signs into another. In its furthest expansion, therefore, intertextuality may incorporate all sorts of social phenomena. We may wish to consider that paradigmatic plots abound, not just in literary culture, but also in general culture. The term "intertextuality" can describe this sense of life as repeating a previously heard story, of life predestined by the notions that shape our consciousness. In this way "real life" may be structured according to patterns familiar from literary culture — just as literary culture may be structured according to patterns familiar from "real life". It follows that the sources underlying human actions may come from other domains of reality, as much as from everyday life situations — from proverbs, folklore, fiction, music, television commercials. As Susan Stewart expresses it in her intertextual study of folklore and literature: "our neighbourhoods are full of Madame Bovarys, Cinderellas, Ebenezer Scrooges, Constantine Levins and wise fools, as much as fictions are full of people from our neighbourhoods."[4]

Intertextuality, then, offers an interactive model of art. Human experience may generate literature — but such experience has already been filtered through forms of artistic organisation. Women's writing seems particularly sensitive to the ways in which female acculturation and socialisation are promoted by such "texts" as folklore, myth, fairy tales, movies, and other sources of exemplary representations. Alison Lurie's retelling of classic fairy tales in her 1980 volume, *Clever Gretchen and Other Forgotten Folktales*, may be said to be an activity consonant with this perception of the ways in which art can affect life.[5] The tales are deliberately selected from the body of available folklore, in order to reconstitute a tradition, and to promote images of women as brave, clever and resourceful, able to defeat giants, answer riddles and outwit the devil — rather than as passively waiting for their prince to come. Lurie's semiotic expertise has also never been in doubt. Her 1981 volume, *The Language of Clothes*, a serious examination of the history and interpretation of costume, begins from the premise that one set of signs is translatable into another, that clothing may be envisaged as a sign system, and that human beings communicate in the language of dress. Importantly, Lurie emphasises here the notion of interaction between sets of signs (clothing and social context) in terms of situational participation and involvement.

According to Erving Goffman, the concept of "proper dress" is totally dependent on situation. To wear the costume considered "proper" for a situation acts as a sign of involvement in it, and the person whose clothes do not conform to these standards is likely to be more or less subtly excluded from participation. When other signs of deep involvement are present, rules about proper dress may be waived.[6]

Erving Goffman is not being invoked casually at this point. The internal evidence of *Imaginary Friends* reveals a fairly close acquaintanceship on Lurie's part with his ideas. In this connection two of Goffman's notions are of special significance, firstly that of the relation of self to role, and secondly that of "frame analysis." In the first, Goffman's most distinctive line of thought has been to adopt a dramaturgical approach to social interaction, emphasising particularly the discrepancies between the self-image which the actor presents to others in interactive process ("the presentation self") and his underlying private attitudes. Goffman's studies of such diverse groups as salesmen, hotel workers, surgical teams, games players, mental patients, argue for pervasive role playing in social situations, suggesting that the individual is always acting within a fiction, a text, which is socially evolved.[7] In this model, the autonomous bourgeois individual subject becomes more of a "holding company" for a set of not relevantly connected selves. Some roles can be independently validated (Goffman cites that of the law student), others cannot. (Goffman cites the claim to be a true believer, or a friend — two important points of contact with *Imaginary Friends*.) The reality of such claims will depend upon the establishment by group members of a shared conception of the horizon or frame of a situation, of shared symbolic systems. Thus, in Goffman's view, reality is sponsored by the team. In addition, coming on to our second point, Goffman's sociological employment of frame analysis as a metaphor for the organisation of experience has been applied to literary theory.[8] Intertextuality is the recognition of a frame, a context that allows the reader (of literature) or the actor (in a social situation) to orient him/herself, to distinguish "text" from "context", and to make sense of what would otherwise appear senseless. Just as a book offers a comprehensible *new* experience only because the reader has a framework of familiar points of contact between the self and the book, so in Goffman's analysis, everyday life depends upon the adumbration of a pattern or model, a conscious degree of role playing within the frame of situation, within the social text. Deciding what degree of involvement is required, mutually sustaining a definition of a situation — these are processes socially organised through rules of relevance and irrelevance, inclusion and exclusion, rules concerning "what counts" as the reality of the situation. Thus, almost identical actions may be transformed or transcribed by participants from one frame to another, via a systematic alteration which radically reconstitutes for participants "what is going on". An obvious example offered by Goffman is the distinction between fighting, and playing at fighting, in animal or human behaviour.

Imaginary Friends, then, draws upon Goffman's theories in order both to proceed intertextually *and* to thematise intertextuality. At first, the novel appears to be intertextual in a fairly limited literary sense. Lurie's decision to name her "trance maiden" Verena, after the inspired orator of *The Bostonians*, argues for a fairly active intertextual intention, just as the cult group, the Seekers, which Verena leads, shares its name with a similar religious group in Edith Wharton's *Hudson River Bracketed*. Nor are these merely casual allusions. Both Marius Bewley[9] and more recently Howard Kerr[10] have identified a structured intertext, a common pattern, surrounding the figure of the trance maiden in nineteenth-century American literature. Representative novels — Hawthorne's *The Blithedale Romance* (1852), Howells's *The Undiscovered Country* (1880) and Henry James's *The Bostonians* (1886) — focus upon such elements as the connection of an entranced female with some kind of Utopian social enterprise, her exploitation by a ruthless mesmerist, her romance with a sceptical male, and her eventual rescue from mediumistic servitude, through the love of a good man. This is a topos with a fairly obvious normative patriarchal content, generally involving a woman who is as passive as Sleeping Beauty in her trance, the silencing of the female, the excision of her Utopian or progressive connections, and her resocialisation within the safe categories of home and matrimony. Priscilla, the Veiled Lady of *The Blithedale Romance*, may stand as emblematic of the patriarchal view of woman — totally under male control, veiled to deny her physicality, an idol obscurely in contact with spiritual mysteries, and yet exposed to prurient commercial exploitation. Priscilla's rescue by Hollingsworth marks the end of the Utopian experiment at Blithedale, and is connected with the extinction of feminist Zenobia. Similarly, in Howells's *The Undiscovered Country*, spiritualist Dr Boynton uses his daughter Egeria as his spellbound medium, until she is liberated from his clutches by Ford, a sceptical amateur scientist. (Shakers supply the Utopian community in the novel.) Howells also implies a precise correlation between Egeria's mediumistic gifts and the repression of her sexuality. At one point, mere geographical proximity to Ford (who is simply visiting the same location) is enough to inhibit her to the extent that her powers fail her completely.

As Kerr points out, the extreme example of the passivity of the trance maiden occurs in Henry James's "Professor Fargo" (1874), an anti-spiritualist satire, in which she is actually deaf and dumb. More subtly, in *The Bostonians*, James characterises his heroine's passivity in terms of the acculturated female desire to placate and conciliate. Basil Ransom, the sceptical rough wooer of the novel, understands Verena Tarrant's gift as a speaker as simply a willingness to please, which leads her to utter the sentiments of others without compromising her own innocence. (Because they are sexually suppressed, trance maidens are always apparently innocent although they may spring from a corrupt or "low" milieu.) For Basil, the nature of these sentiments is consequent upon the person to whom Verena stands closest, at any point, in a relation of dependency. She thus passes easily from the control of her father (ex-member of the "Cayuga" Utopian experiment, now a mesmeric healer) to that of feminist Olive Chancellor, and thence after prolonged sexual and ideological warfare into the arms of Ransom. Like Howells, James also suggests that Verena's inspired self springs from a buried or displaced capacity for passion, and he indicates a sexual basis for her gifts — as well as for Olive's behaviour.

The reader who turns from James to *Imaginary Friends* will discover that all the elements of the intertext of the trance maiden are firmly in place. Verena Roberts resides appropriately on West *Hawthorne* Street, in the imaginary small town of Sophis, which is located in an area of Upper New York State which was a locus for religious fringe groups in the nineteenth century. It is close to the spot where Joseph Smith met the Angel Moroni, and where the Oneida community flourished. As the narrator comments, Verena "was right in the local tradition, only about a hundred years too late" (30).[11] Although Verena's spirit messages, received via automatic writing, emanate from extraterrestrial beings, notably Ro of the planet Varna, this is not much more than a variant on established tradition, the result of the fact that "science now dominated the culture to the point where people were sitting round a table conjuring up ectoplasmic rayguns and little green men, instead of ladies in white veils" (14). Verena also remains firmly in the tradition of American Utopianism, her cult, at least in part, a disguised attack on the affluent society. Conspicuous consumption is roundly denounced as excessive attachment to "material clingings"; Cosmic Love is invoked, and the belief system excludes evil in favour of a vision of the universe as imbued with spirit light and benevolent power. Like her predecessors, Verena is young and virginal, resides in a distinctly lower-class milieu and initially features as passively pliant, providing her interlocutors with what they want to hear, quieting anxieties, sympathising with problems, and generally providing "uplift". One cult member, Ken, figures as the sceptical young wooer, excluded from the Seekers when he denounces their beliefs, and subsequently kept at bay by Elsie Novar, Verena's aunt, who is using Verena, in a fashion not unlike Olive Chancellor, to promote her own emotional needs. In the denouement the lusty Ken elopes with Verena, who abandons the Seekers in favour of matrimony.

It would be a mistake, however, to envisage *this* Verena as sinking into passivity. *Imaginary Friends* gives us the revenge of the trance maiden in no uncertain terms. As events develop Verena progresses from passively catering to her audience, towards actively attacking their cultural norms. At the close, far from being silenced, she has expanded her career to that of radical orator. A photograph in *The New York Times* shows her protesting vigorously at a political demonstration. Two "texts" (systems of signs) are actually involved here, and it is the interaction between the two which generates the ironies of the novel. When Tom McMann and Roger Zimmern, two social scientists, set up a small group interaction study of the Seekers, they use the methods favoured by Goffman: participant observation, role-playing, and non-directive techniques. The transcription of the literary intertext into the social text (and vice versa) foregrounds the whole notion of intertextuality. In addition to their literary intertext, the Seekers are also modelled on an actual group investigated by social scientists in the 1950s and documented by Leon Festinger and others in *When Prophecy Fails*.[12] Festinger and his colleagues were studying the behaviour of individuals in groups which made specific prophesies, looking for evidence of increased commitment following disconfirmation of belief (on the model of such historical groups as the Anabaptists, Millerites, and the followers of Sabbatai Zevi and of Montanus). Alerted by press reports they investigated the activities of Marian Keech, a fifty-year-old housewife, who declared herself in contact with beings from the planet "Clarion" and prophesied the destruction of "Lake City" by flood on 21 December. (The sociologists' report omits the actual year and conceals real identities and locations beneath pseudonyms.) Mrs Keech had initially received messages by automatic writing, and then became involved with a group called "The Seekers" operating some 200 miles away. Originally a group of college students, meeting in a Protestant church to discuss religious and ethical matters, the Seekers were swayed by their pastor's enthusiasm for flying saucers, and eventually developed an eclectic belief system of their own. Some went as far as to resign from their jobs and give away all their possessions in the anticipation of imminent world cataclysm, from which they personally expected to be saved by flying saucers. If anything, Lurie's fictional text appears decidedly *less* sensational and fantastic than the events chronicled by Festinger.[13] In addition to the intertextual doubling of referents in the case of the Seekers, Lurie also thematises the operations of reading and writing involved in the production of a text, by establishing a continuing analogy between the elaboration of a fiction, and that of the belief system of a small group. Since the establishment of the "social text" itself involves interactive techniques, Lurie thus effectively sets up a *mise en abyme* or infinite regressus, in which the novel offers both a sociology of the sociologists, and a metafictional fiction. As a result, its scope expands into a discussion of the manner in which cultural norms are established and inscribed, deviance and difference defined.

The doubling of intertexts is indicated from the beginning in Verena's residence on *West* Hawthorne Street, which evokes the starting point of small group study in the United States — Elton Mayo's pioneering researches at the Hawthorne Western Electric Plant in the 1930s.[14] The methods of sociological analysis — the various conceptual frames on offer — are then themselves introduced in terms of literary genres, as texts and titles. As an empirical descriptive sociologist, Tom McMann favours the type of social diagnosis based on accumulations of case histories, known generically to the younger generation as "Nuts and Sluts". (William Foot Whyte's *Street Corner Society*, a study of street gangs in an Italian slum, is cited as a typical example of the genre.) Similarly the diagrammatic Parsonians feature as "Boxes and Arrows"; those favouring statistical analysis are involved in "The Numbers Racket". Dazzled by the prospect of collaborating as co-author with the famous McMann, Roger finds titles floating "mirage-like" before his eyes. "Anomie in a Small Town Setting" is one such; "We and It: Role Conflict in a Belief Group" is another, as Roger sets to work labelling and framing before the study has even begun. For Roger, the "real" is his career as a social scientist. The Sophis study is cut off and set apart; it does not "count" in the same way as his real life. Thus, when approaching Sophis for the first time, Roger describes the landscape of hills, barns and cows as having "all the pastoral props" (15). Putting up at Ovid's motel, he notes a paint-by-numbers picture, which "represented Art. Literature was represented by an old copy of the Post" (16), rather as if he were stepping onto a stage set. The impression is reinforced by Roger's own role play. Following good sociological principles he conceals his professional identity beneath a cover story, the fiction that he is carrying out public opinion survey work. As McMann argues, to obtain unbiased data "You had to filter your presentation" (17). In short, as the later Roger wryly remarks, "with the excuse that we were seeking truth, we were proposing to lie ourselves blind to the Truth Seekers" (18).

On first encountering the Seekers, however, Roger finds that his methods rebound upon him. Rather than settling down to observe Verena, he finds himself the focus of observation, as Verena scrutinises his "aura" and pronounces him "a complete blank" (26). This unwelcome news is compounded when she obtains a spirit message from Varna for him. The message is merely a series of interlocking loops. For Roger, this experience is profoundly disquieting: "No possible statement is as uncanny as one you can't read at all" (29). He is cheered, however, when the term "automatic writing" occurs to him. Roger is considerably more secure with a long word between him and phenomena, preferably a word which labels and positions a text within a frame of assumptions. Verena is almost as adept, however, at framing Roger within hers, as her next message suggests. Roger, attempting to suppress a fit of laughter, finds himself silently praying to the totemic deities of his brand of sociology — Max Weber, C. Wright Mills and Machiavelli. Verena promptly produces the message "Makes Favour. See Right Ills. O Make A Veil High", reinscribing his gods within her own textual system. The common-sense explanation is that Roger had unwittingly muttered the names under his breath, and that Verena, who has never heard of Max Weber, or Machiavelli, and therefore lacks the right frame to make sense of the utterance, has simply done her best with the verbal system at her disposal. Roger, however, is quite unnerved. As his previous facility with titles indicates, Roger *does* treat the world as a text, but one which he does not expect to operate on him. He believes that he can maintain distance and objectivity, observing the Seekers without being in any way affected by them.

Thus, as a participant-observer, Roger implicitly occupies a readerly role. Indeed, the Seekers' extrapolation of a system of beliefs is overtly equated with the formation of a fiction, by Lurie's concentration on messages generated by automatic writing. Verena's first message from Varna is received when words in another hand are added to a letter which she is composing, quite beyond her conscious volition. It looks like divine intervention, and very much conforms to the popular image of what an author does.[15] In this model, an author creates a narrative by some mystic alchemy or inspiration, and it is made public in a book which the reader passively enjoys, gaining private satisfactions. Similarly the traditional critical process focuses on the author as creator, and translates reader responses into statements about the work and its creator. The reader is thus able to operate without taking full responsibility for his or her own feelings, casting the self into a pseudo-objective role. The same is true of Roger, in his role as non-directive participant observer, aiming to offer as little input as possible to the group, while gaining professional satisfactions from it. As Miles Coverdale to Verena's Veiled Lady, Roger "frames" the Seekers as if they were a fiction, as if they "didn't count" as real people. Thus, in the absence of local kinship ties, the group provides an undemanding social life for all its members, which Roger labels an "imaginary kinship system". He participates in it, enjoying an evening at the Freeplatzers as "almost a social occasion" (65). Of course, for all the other participants, it is a social occasion. Only Roger has framed it as "group interaction". Roger also assumes that the Seekers' friendship for him will end with the study (254). But of course, for the Seekers, there *is* no study; they are quite unaware of the frame which Roger has placed around them. Nor is their sense of kinship unreal — whereas, as a friend, Roger is almost as imaginary as Ro of Varna.

The problem of Roger's "role distance" from the social text is particularly focused in relation to Verena. Roger originally perceives the belief system of the cult as created and authored by Verena. He describes her as "able to dream for others or to fit them into her own dreams" (45). In fact, however, Verena is co-authoring her text in close collaboration with the group. The Seekers' sessions focus upon the reception, interpretation and elucidation of spirit messages, with each member relating the messages back to his or her own personal framework (popular science in Rufus's case, spiritualism in Catherine's) and emphasising those aspects of the message which suit them best. In short, via reader input, a text is slowly extrapolated within a shaping culture, interacting with, and being modified by that culture.

Unfortunately Verena's openness to others allows her text to slip from her control, passing for a time at least to Elsie, who wrests control from Verena by enforced sexual suppression. In a hysterical, Salemesque accusatory mode, the group stigmatise Verena as a "filthy, unclean vessel" (97), polluted and spiritually weakened by proximity to Ken, who is characterised as a "negative vibrational force" (94) surrounded by a greasy, smoky aura. Verena is forced to abase herself before them, proclaiming "I am cleaned and made pure" (99) only after prolonged humiliation. Roger and Tom stand passively by, capable only of non-directive comment. On one level, the scene recognises the ethical problems posed by participant observation as a sociological method. Goffman unwittingly provides a rather good example in *Behavior in Public Places* where he discusses the different classes of involvement obligations within one situation: "I have seen patients watch passively, from a few feet away, a young male psychotic rape an old defenceless mute man."[16] Disapproving glances were apparently the most which the patients in the asylum risked. Goffman, himself, also observing, appears to have risked even less. Similarly, Roger Zimmern is uncomfortably reminded at this point in the novel of snapshots in *The New York Times* showing prisoners being tortured in Vietnam: "You couldn't help asking, why didn't the photographer do something? He was right there, wasn't he?" (104). Partly as a result of Roger's refusal to allow his objective observations to be biased by emotional involvement, Verena is now downgraded to the role of symbolic leader, while Elsie reinterprets the messages on her own terms, engineering a sharp shift in the group ethos, from its earlier Transcendental cast, towards a more Manichean, sin-oriented creed. Just as Olive Chancellor exploited Verena Tarrant's style to transmit her own convictions, so Elsie reduces Verena to mechanically rehearsing another's script. Roger describes Verena as "like a painting in reproduction", "as if she were imitating herself, or reading from a script she had memorized earlier" (105).

The death of this particular author, however, turns out to have been very much exaggerated. Verena is able to act in a consciously intertextual fashion herself, and she gains her revenge by adopting the sociologist's own methods. Earlier, when McMann was rumbled as a professor, he had adopted the strategy of over-acting, carrying more books and papers, making ostentatious notes, muttering to himself, and mislaying objects — imitating, not so much a real academic as the popular image of the absent-minded professor. Verena plays McMann at his own game, exaggerating the stereotypical role of the trance maiden into parody. In response to the repressive identification of her sexuality with sin, Verena apparently meets the group demand for purity by anorexic self-starvation. Far from internalising the prohibition against female physicality however, she externalises it, imposing her own food phobias on the group and evolving a complicated set of dietary taboos, which reduce them all to the intake of the tame rabbit. Verena also exaggerates female pliancy to the point at which her blank gaze, flat voice, and mechanical echoing of Elsie's suggestions suggest to Roger, first the "waxy flexibility" (115) of incipient schizophrenia, then an uncomfortably close mirroring of his own non-directive techniques. Both Roger and McMann subscribe to the orthodox psychological notion (initiated by William James) that the trance maiden is possessed by an ordinarily quiescent second self, emerging only in states of dissociated consciousness. In this analysis Ro of Varna is actually Verena's subconscious. Verena's revenge is to split the two investigators into fragmented selves. McMann is eventually defined as insane himself, when he becomes convinced that he is Ro of Varna. His partner's fate is also appropriate. Roger, who had constituted Verena as his object of study, finds himself subject to Varnian academic requirements, forced to take notes at meetings, copy messages, memorise prayers and generally embark on an exhaustive course of study in which he is an involuntary D student. As a result he separates himself consciously into "Clever Zimmern" (his "real" self, the objective scientist) and "Stupid Roger" (the role he plays within the group and the person who is also erotically fixated on Verena). Since fragmentation into alternate or suppressed selves is commonly the fate of women in patriarchal culture, where men are unitary characters, it is a peculiarly apt revenge.

One scene specifically emphasisaes the problems inherent in labelling behaviour as delusionary on bases of sexual norms. With Ken out of bounds, Verena makes overtures to Roger, when he consults her about the date of "The Coming", the imminent descent of Ro to earth. Erotic double entendre runs through the scene, with puns on the group's "desire for the coming" which appear to foreground the repressed sexual bases of their delusionary system. With Verena praying over him, Roger averts his eyes from her heaving breasts to take refuge in the notation of "neutral sociological details" (143) — knobs on a maple bureau, a mirror reflecting a non-existent waver in the window frame, a framed reproduction. Wavering between spiritual and sexual frames himself, it occurs to him to stop resisting. After all, "What Verena had always done with her gift was to guess what people wanted and then to give it to them" (143). Indeed, when Verena removes his shirt and jacket, on the grounds that these material clingings are preventing the Varnian vibrations from having "a chance to penetrate" (143), even Clever Zimmern collapses into Stupid Roger, and seizes her in his manly arms. Of course, on one level, if the reader accepts that Verena is deluded, Roger's scruples are entirely proper. He reflects that, but for the interruption of footsteps outside the door, "The Junior E [Experimenter] on the Sophis Project (National Institution of Mental Health Grant No. 789 etc.) would have raped his principal S [Subject]" (145). On these "objective" grounds, he should resist, as a psychiatrist is expected to resist the overtures of a disturbed patient. But who defines Verena as deluded? On less disinterested grounds, for the social study to continue, Verena must remain repressed. In Roger's theory, her dammed-up sexual energy is the source of Ro of Varna. The suspicion lingers that Roger is actively repressing Verena's as well as his own emotions, an impression strengthened by subsequent events.

At the next meeting Verena announces to the group that Ro has prohibited clothing made from natural materials. Only artificial fibres created by pure science are acceptable. Having been unwilling to remove his clothes in private, Roger finds himself forced to disrobe in public. Despite Verena's assertion that "There is no shame in the True Universe" (160), the other Seekers also show some resistance to total nudity in the front parlour, and are permitted to borrow synthetic garments from the family wardrobe. This poses no great problem for the women, who have both Elsie's and Verena's clothing to choose from, and whose apparel, in any case, tends more towards synthetics, but it is a disaster for the males. When they reappear, Ed is wearing plastic duck waders, McMann an old nylon shirt which suggests an auto salesman in the Fifties, Bill baggy paint-streaked slacks, Roger striped pyjamas, which make him look like a comic strip convict, and Rufus swimming trunks and a floral quilt. As they descend the stairs, they are framed in a wall mirror as

> some group from the Theatre of the Absurd, a tall middle-aged duck hunter, a small convict with horn-rimmed glasses, a plump comedian in baggy paint-spotted pants, and a large used car salesman, all led by a skinny lunatic in Dacron socks and a flowered quilt. (162)

By the proclamation of new sumptuary laws from Ro, Verena at a stroke deprives the males of their chosen sartorial identity. In the language of clothes, they have been effectively struck dumb. In addition they have been forced to impersonate a dramatic character, a presentation self, quite at variance with their own internal attitudes.

Up to this point Roger has been treating his involvement with the Seekers as one that "does not count" in real terms, rather as a fiction is traditionally marked off from "everyday life" on the grounds that its events are reversible, that we can "take back" their meanings by saying "it was only a story" or that we can revise their meanings by intertextual transformations and rewritings, so that (to quote Borges) "every writer creates his own precursors." Verena, however, decides not to permit this, and insists upon irreversible actions. Roger has to commit his expensive organic tweed jacket to the flames. In addition, the manner in which this occurs is carefully staged by Verena so as to re-enact and revise her own preceding humiliations. *She* may be said to be acting intertextually here; the other characters are not granted the same freedom. Thus, when the bonfire begins, the room fills with pungent smoke, exposing the whole group to the aura formerly ascribed to Ken — "as if some particularly strong and unpleasant astral force were present" (165). As the Seekers burn their garments, they proclaim "I am purified and made free" (166), a variant on the lesson Verena was forced to recite. Roger, on the sidelines, still constitutes himself as an observer. He notes, for example, that since Sissy Freeplatzer spent a long time knitting her woolly sweater, Verena was psychologically astute to leave her "to the last" (168). But Roger's turn is yet to come — *he* is actually the last to be called upon and such is the power of group consensus that he actually does burn his cherished jacket. While the Seekers have been behaving as if invisible beings (Ro and Mo) were present at their meetings, the two sociologists have been acting as if *they* were invisible, not "really there" (155), just as readers do. Verena, however, now hauls them bodily into her frame. As Roger comments, it is as if "someone else, possibly Ro of Varna, was conducting a field study on American sociologists. To him, we were the white rats" (171). Verena thus enforces the correct degree of involvement on Roger's part, by forcing him into the "proper clothes" in Goffman's terms, those which express participation in the situation. In Sophis, Roger has to kit himself out from head to toe, in inorganic clothing. The result, he realises, observing himself reframed in the motel mirror, is to transform him into "a small nondescriptly lower-middle-class young man" (174) in Dacron shirt, Orion sweater and limp slacks, a figure who now matches the motel room perfectly: "It was Stupid Roger, in his real clothes" (175). Verena's vengeance is thus both a class revenge and a sexual retaliation. The penalty for Roger's pretensions to superior detachment is to be forced into a position where he is entirely controlled. When next he is alone with Verena, he is deterred from *any* sexual responsiveness, inhibited by the knowledge that he is wearing "blue rayon undershorts decorated with beagles" (178).

It is as well to pause here to anticipate a major qualification. Although the results of Verena's actions constitute a fairly thoroughgoing revenge, Lurie fosters a productive ambiguity concerning the degree of intentionality involved. When Verena announces the new sumptuary laws, it is noteworthy that she has already donned a new, synthetic robe for the occasion. Roger catches himself thinking,

> She must have *known* what was coming ... because her old robe ... was cotton
> velvet. But of course she knew, what was the matter with me? Was I beginning
> to believe, like the Seekers, that Ro was a separate entity? (161)

But how far does the author "know" what is coming next? Verena may be scripting
the messages and pulling the plot strings without being consciously aware of her
own control. (Messages may be issuing from her subconscious.) Strong hints are also
dropped that McMann had advance knowledge of this announcement (he is clad in
synthetic trousers) and of the announcement of "The Coming." McMann wants to
test his hypothesis — that disconfirmation of the group's beliefs will not dissolve
the group — and may therefore be prompting Verena with millennial suggestions,
abetted by Elsie. Or, of course, all three may be in cahoots. When Roger finds
out that Tom has entered the date of the millennial prophecy in the records before
that prophecy was uttered, it looks like decisive evidence. Challenged, however,
Tom appeals to social norms as the explanation. Given the existence of what Roger
describes as "the ordinary Protestant delusionary system" (33), to which the Seekers
broadly adhere, an announcement of the descent to earth of a god in December is
strictly in accordance with tradition. Only Roger, who is Jewish, is surprised. In
addition, the fictional frame also conditions events. For Roger, the Varnians are
purely imaginary, mental constructs, and he therefore *knows* that no little green men
will put in an appearance. But the reader, especially if well versed in recent feminist
science fiction, for example, has no such certainty. Inside the frame of genre, little
green men are perfectly permissible. In little, therefore, the novel seems to offer a
near perfect model of the various potential theories of how a text is generated. Does
it originate in a single author? In that author's conscious or unconscious self? In
some sort of collaboration with an Ideal Reader (the reader in his presentation self)
or a Common Reader (a member of a group audience whose generic expectations
must be respected)? Or is it socially produced in accordance with a well-established
framework of group norms and assumptions?

These uncertainties are not merely matters of literary interest, as becomes
abundantly clear in the denouement. Ambiguities as to who is in control, who is
deluded, who sets the norm for the group, extend from the literary into the social
text, raising the question of the ways in which cultural hegemony is established,
how situational norms are defined, and deviance penalised. At the close of the
novel, Verena invents a happy ending for the Seekers, announcing that the Varnians
have descended to earth, that they have been incorporated into all the group
members equally, and that from now on the Seekers must go forth into the world,
to spread the word. When, however, Roger reads the last automatic message from
Ro, previously elucidated at length by Verena, he discovers that it consists only of
meaningless scrawls. Verena has deliberately engineered the dissolution of both the
group and its text, in order to be free to join Ken. For the Seekers, however, the
non-appearance of actual Varnians constitutes a fairly radical disconfirmation of
their belief system. Tom promptly intervenes, proclaiming the felt presence of spirits
within him. Reconstitution of the group is accompanied by a brisk reinterpretation

of Ro's last verbal message. "I am in Man On Earth" becomes "I am in Tom McMann On Earth." Or, in Roger's sociologese, "At approximately 2.20 a.m. on December 5, Ro of Varna was accepted by the group as being incarnated in the senior project researcher" (231).

An exceptionally non-objective reader, Tom has had a decidedly creative input into the evolution of the group text. As a result of his over-enthusiastic adoption of his new role he ends up in an insane asylum, where he is visited each week by Elsie, intent on fulfilling her desire "to make it with her god" (280). Unlike Verena, who has transformed her role as trance maiden on her own terms, Tom appears to have been entirely engulfed by his intertext; he is now fully on the inside of the "Nuts and Sluts" genre. It finally dawns on Roger that this has been threatening from the start. Two small groups have been involved throughout — the Seekers and the sociologists. Roger had been so intent on the activities of the former that he had failed to perceive that every development there was replicated in the group in which he saw himself as having primary membership. McMann's initial choice of subject — the effects of internal opposition within a small group — was occasioned by his own experience of opposition within a small group, his university department. Thus, the evolution of the study has been predestined by events which shaped McMann's own consciousness. Formerly a hero of sociology, McMann has lost out humiliatingly to younger men and is eager to revise and restore his status. The title of one of his essays, "The Sociologist — Seer or Statistician?", proves entirely proleptic of the generic options available to him. As the Seekers' seer he accrues once more the respect, reverence, even hero-worship once accorded to him within his professional group.

If Verena's escape depended on the use of her intertextual skills to redefine her role, moving out onto a larger stage, and leaving behind something of a dent in the cultural monolith, Tom's subsequent actions reveal the potential hazards of intertextual operations. Tom is also able to switch frames and to transpose systems. First he "takes back" the meaning of his incarceration, claiming that his madness was only an act, a role assumed originally in order to avoid criminal prosecution, and later perpetuated in order to allow him to undertake the ultimate participant observation study, of the asylum. (This paradigm is imported from Goffman, whose own study *Asylums* was carried out while posing as assistant to the asylum athletic director.) Having therefore established the fictionality of his own "Nuts and Sluts" intertext McMann is about to move into "The Numbers Racket" in a more sinister sense. Earlier in the novel, Roger had expressed unease with the frequency of the sociologists' non-directive repetition of group opinions on the grounds that they were offering too strong a reinforcement: "If you push quantity too hard, it becomes quality" (61). Visiting McMann, Roger is unnerved by the ordinariness of the asylum, which is reminiscent of a small college or school, perfectly standard in every way. Roger's disquiet, the product of the lack of any obvious distinction between sane and insane, will be familiar to readers acquainted with *either* the sociological literature concerning the political definition of mental illness (Goffman, R. D. Laing, Thomas Szasz), *or* the fictional intertext (*One*

Flew Over the Cuckoo's Nest, Catch 22, The Crying of Lot 49). Roger had previously experienced a similar unease when he first visited West Hawthorne Street: "The whole place made me uneasy; it was so ordinary, so average, like the mid-point on a distribution which has no positive correlative" (19). In short, in her typical frame house Verena inhabited the norm, and the norm has no real existence; it is merely sponsored by the team, socially defined by the majority. It follows for Roger that "Madness can be defined as a conception of reality that is not shared by others in your environment" (39). But McMann's conception of reality *is* shared. He has at least half a dozen followers, and is actively planning to expand the Seekers into a mass movement, with himself as their god, drawing on his own professional knowledge of leadership techniques. Nor may he be said to be pretending to be Ro of Varna. If we take the view that identity is socially defined, then McMann *is* Ro of Varna. He has been so constituted by the small group. If thousands more were to follow him, the individual delusion would be reframed, first as a mass delusion, then as a respectable religious movement, its dietary taboos as acceptable as those of any other faith, its compulsory Dacron no more surprising than, for example, obligatory headgear in places of worship. In that case, since Tom would be spending most of his time playing the role of Ro, we would have to say, with Roger, that "Ro of Varna is insane to believe he is still Thomas McMann, a professor of sociology" (286). Thus, if numbers are on his side, McMann will be able to accomplish an intertextual move himself, from "Nuts and Sluts" to "The Numbers Racket", and from statistician back to seer.

Imaginary Friends thus leaves the reader to decide for him — or herself what is the proper degree of involvement, whether in the social or the literary text, which readerly role to adopt and which reality team to sponsor. Roger's objectivity results in the loss of a woman whom he genuinely loved, passed up in favour of a small group interaction study. Tom's view, that the observer who remains external to events is not so much unbiased as incompetent (since the mental set of the group is what he needs to assume and understand), induces a degree of commitment which results in him actually being committed — to a mental asylum. In Verena's case, intertextuality may subvert literary and social ideologies to radical ends. But Verena's vacant place is swiftly filled by a male god who may prove equally adept at redefining his act, rewriting the past — and thus, potentially, controlling the future.

Notes to Chapter 3

1. For two clear theoretical accounts see Laurent Jenny, "The strategy of form," in Tzvetan Todorov (ed.), *French Literary Theory Today* (Cambridge University Press, 1982), 34–64; and Jeanine Parisier Plottel and Hanna Charney (eds), "*Intertextuality: New Perspectives in Criticism*," *New York Literary Forum*, 2 (1978). For an excellent demonstration of ways of working with intertextuality see John Hannay, *The Intertextuality of Fate* (Columbia: University of Missouri Press, 1986).
2. *New York Literary Forum*, 2 (1978), xiv, a translation of "Tout texte se construit comme mosaïque de citations, tout texte est absorption et transformation d'un autre texte." Julia Kristeva, *Sémiotike, recherches pour une semanalyse* (Paris: Seuil, 1969), 146.

3. Julia Kristeva, *La revolution du langage poétique* (Paris: Seuil, 1974).

4. Susan Stewart, *Nonsense: Aspects of Intertextuality in Folklore and Literature* (Baltimore: Johns Hopkins, 1979), 26.

5. Alison Lurie, *Clever Gretchen and Other Forgotten Folktales* (London: Heinemann, 1980).

6. Alison Lurie, *The Language of Clothes* (New York: Random House, 1981), 13. The point is made by Erving Goffman in *Encounters* (Indianapolis: Bobbs-Merrill, 1961), 145–46.

7. Erving Goffman is referred to by name in *Imaginary Friends* (London: Penguin, 1967), 275. Major works include *The Presentation of Self in Everyday Life* (1956), *Encounters* (1961), *Asylums* (1961), *Behavior in Public Places* (1963) and *Frame Analysis* (1974). Although the latter postdates *Imaginary Friends* the concept of frame is initially elaborated in *Encounters* (20, 25, 26).

8. "Claims to be a friend, a true believer, or a music-lover can be confirmed or disconfirmed only more or less." *The Presentation of Self in Everyday Life* (London: Penguin, 1967), 53.

9. Marius Bewley, *The Complex Fate* (London: Chatto & Windus, 1952).

10. Howard Kerr, *Mediums and Spirit Rappers and Roaring Radicals: Spiritualism in American Literature 1850–1900* (Urbana: University of Illinois Press, 1972).

11. Alison Lurie, *Imaginary Friends* (London: Penguin, 1967). Page references which follow quotations in parentheses refer to this edition of the novel.

12. Leon Festinger, Henry W. Riecken and Stanley Schachter, *When Prophecy Fails* (Minneapolis: University of Minnesota Press, 1956). Special thanks to Malcolm Bradbury for comments on this source made at the initial delivery of this paper at the British Association for American Studies Conference in 1988.

13. In common with Lurie's group the historical Seekers frowned on meat-eating, engaged in meetings of exceptionally long duration, during which they discussed messages received from outer space, suffered from a leadership struggle between two women, and developed a clothing taboo. (Metal on the person was suddenly forbidden, leading to the frenzied removal of trouser zippers, shoe eyelets, belts and undergarments.) When prophecy failed, Mrs Keech explained that the group had spread so much spiritual light that God had saved the world after all. Unlike Lurie's group, their story attracted national publicity and was headline news for a week in the press and media, culminating in complaints to the police about their activities, threats of incarceration in mental hospitals, and flight. Like McMann and Zimmern, the historical sociologists, posing as ordinary group members and proceeding in a non-directive fashion, found it increasingly difficult to remain neutral, and often unwittingly reinforced the group's beliefs.

14. F. J. Roethlisberger and William J. Dickson, *Management and the Worker* (Cambridge, MA: Harvard University Press, 1939). As director of the project, Elton Mayo launched the Western Electric Research Program in 1927, working with Roethlisberger and Dickson, and carrying out research at the Hawthorne Works in Chicago, which demonstrated the importance of social-psychological dynamics, operating in groups in the real world.

15. See Hugh Crago, "Cultural Categories and the Criticism of Children's Literature," *Signal*, 30 (1980), 140–50.

16. Erving Goffman, *Behavior in Public Places* (Glencoe, IL: The Free Press, 1963), 207.

CHAPTER 4

Nadine Gordimer and the Naked Southern Ape: "Something Out There"

In Nadine Gordimer's "Something Out There" two plots are interwoven, in a sequence of alternating scenes — that of a group of four terrorists, planning an attack on a power station, and that concerning another outlaw and fugitive, a mysterious escaped ape who plunders the affluent suburbs of white Johannesburg. Just as the human saboteurs go under assumed names, their identities elusive, so their animal counterpart is variously described as an ape, a chimpanzee, a vervet monkey, a baboon — even a man. The slippage between categories, the deliberate indeterminacy, is reproduced in the structure of the novella. The two plots evolve in tandem, the monkey disappearing from view at the same time as the terrorists, his attack on a white South African juxtaposed with their attack on the power station, his death reported coincidentally with the death of one of the saboteurs. At various points in the novella ape and man, particularly black man, are identified. This potentially patronising parallel represents an extremely risky narrative procedure on Gordimer's part.[1] The suggestion of similarities between ape and black is part of the standard vocabulary of racism. On 3 August 1989 black South African workers went on strike because a white foreman displayed a baboon's head with a trade union leaflet stuck in it.[2] As Salman Rushdie observed, reviewing "Something Out There", it is also commonplace for the powerful to see the powerless as animals or monsters:

> Great white sharks, killer bees, werewolves, devils, alien horrors bursting from the chests of movie spacemen: the popular culture of our fearful times has provided us with so many variations on the ancient myth of the Beast, the "something" lurking out there that hunts us and is hunted by us, as to make it one of the defining metaphors of the age.[3]

In interview, however, Gordimer argued against portraying the terrorist as a monster, even at the risk of putting writers "in a place where they are seen as supporting terrorists by portraying them as human beings. Terrorism is real, something that happens all the time. Portraying these people as humans is a more delicate and dangerous matter."[4] Paradoxically, in her attempt to demystify the twentieth-century "Beast" of the terrorist, Gordimer employs a structural parallel between these so-called monsters and an actual animal — the escaped baboon. It is a strategy deliberately designed to set up a series of questions: Is the terrorist a brute? What is the justification for terrorism? Do terrorists merely decline into the mirror image of their opponents by embracing violence? Will their projected future simply reenact the nightmares of the past? More generally, the novella places the issues of terrorism in a wider context, of the nature of man. Is man essentially only an animal, a naked ape, irremediably violent, beastly and savage? Or is there hope for his future development?

The answers to these questions — even the manner in which they are posed — depend upon an informed awareness on Gordimer's part of a series of debates in ethology, the science of animal behaviour, which have particular reference both to apes and to Africa. Primates, whether ape, monkey or chimpanzee, have been a focus of attention since the 1960s when a spate of books appeared which claimed, first to describe man's "real" or "natural" behaviour in ethological style, and secondly to explain how this behaviour evolved. Robert Ardrey's *African Genesis*, and *The Territorial Imperative*, Desmond Morris's *The Naked Ape* and *The Human Zoo*, Konrad Lorenz's *On Aggression* were all popular bestsellers; all purport to document the idea that man is an animal, that there is little we can do but accept our instinctive natures, and that we are naturally aggressive creatures. The animals most often used as models for early human behaviour are baboons, which have been exhaustively studied.[5]

Ethological ideas were given special impetus by archaeological discoveries in Africa. Until the 1920s the hunt for early man had focussed on Asia. Then, in 1924 Raymond Dart discovered the Taung skull in South Africa. Furious controversy broke out when Dart claimed to recognise features in the skull which took it out of the ape class and placed it in that of the *Hominidae*, the group which includes man and his early ancestors. Dart christened his find "Australopithecus", the Southern ape. Resistance to the idea that all human beings are descended from Africans was strong. When Dart's paper "The Predatory Transition from Ape to Man" was published, the editor of *The International Anthropological and Linguistic Review* preceded it with the disclaimer that the australopithecines were "only the ancestors of the modern Bushman and Negro and of nobody else".[6] Subsequent discoveries in the 1930s in caves near Johannesburg confirmed Dart's thesis, since when hundreds more such remains have been found on South African sites. Dart, who was Professor of Anatomy at the University of the Witwatersrand, lived to see his theories vindicated, and in 1984, coincidentally the year of publication of "Something Out There", there was a conference of world anthropologists in Johannesburg, to celebrate the fortieth anniversary of his discovery.[7]

Not all Dart's ideas, however, have proved so acceptable. Until his discovery it had been assumed that our primal ancestors resembled the shy, vegetarian ape of the forest. Observing fossilised baboon remains, with head injuries, however, Dart concluded that his "Southern ape" had killed them with an antelope humerus bone, and that the hominid hunters lived in bands, systematically killing for a living.

Essentially, therefore, Dart argued that man had emerged from the anthropoid background for one reason only — because he was a killer. As he learned to stand erect, to run in pursuit of game and to use weapons, he made new demands on the nervous system for the coordination of muscle, touch, and sight. The result was first the enlarged brain, and then man. In other words the weapon had fathered man.

It was to be a view taken up enthusiastically by Robert Ardrey in *African Genesis*, a work which popularised the "Killer Ape" theory. *African Genesis* begins as melodramatically as a horror film when the "thing" awakes:

> Not in innocence, and not in Asia, was mankind born. The home of our fathers was that African highland reaching north from the Cape to the Lakes of the Nile. Here we came about — slowly, ever so slowly — on a sky-swept savannah glowing with menace.[8]

Ardrey's final chapter is entitled "Children of Cain" and in between he paints a dismal picture of man, and an all-too-familiar one of Africa as "dark continent". In accepting that the carnivorous, predatory australopithecines were the unquestioned antecedents of man, Ardrey appeared to accept violence as the source of progress, arguing that man's best cultural efforts were spent, not on the tool or artefact, but in the perfecting of weapons. For Ardrey, the most significant of our inherited traits — territoriality, hierarchy, dominance — came from the killer apes, our forbears. He noted the popularity of Westerns and of television violence as evidence of our primitive instincts, and acclaimed *West Side Story* as a vivid portrait of the natural man. For Ardrey, juvenile delinquency was not the result of social deprivation, but was entirely normal. Untouched by cramping civilisation, the citizen of the streets found his rank and security in the gang, defending his territory and enjoying the blood and loot of the predator.

When Ardrey expanded his views in *The Territorial Imperative*, he argued that each animal society has a system of dominance and an instinct for territory which he related to the animosities of tribes and nations. Thus, if we defend our title to land, he argued, we do so for reasons no different, no less innate than those of the lower animals. For Ardrey, territory was a force older and stronger than sex in evolutionary terms. Studying the behaviour of the Ugandan kob on its stamping grounds, he concluded that males competed for "real estate" rather than females. Ardrey saw the strenuous competition of the "arena" (the place where male animals compete for territory and females come to mate with them) as speeding up the evolutionary process. Was man also an "arena" species, with prizes of property and status in the marketplace of male competition? In his view, the territory held by the pair was the prime reinforcement of the pair bond. In other words, it is territory, not sex, which holds a pair together.

Ardrey also argued that the human territorial instinct could be exploited by governments. Threats of invasion, alarms of war, the creation of "incidents" were all a means of welding a disparate society together, by appealing to territorial urges. South Africa was a classic example. Ardrey attributed the success of white South Africa to its departure from the Commonwealth, which set in motion all the paranoid paraphernalia of the territorial imperative, as the population reacted to external boycotts, embargoes, threats of war, and terrorist attacks. He concluded that: "Had the world conspired to make apartheid a permanent South African institution, it could have done no better job."[9] The point has special relevance to Gordimer's novella which considers the possibility that terrorist penetration merely adds fuel to government propaganda based on an external threat — a "something" out there — and in which the "lovely home" of Mrs Naas Klopper, wife of a real estate dealer, features prominently. Ardrey also cautioned that however superior the intruder's motives might be, morally, politically or ideologically, however contemptible the defender, the intruder would have to be capable of enormous sacrifices in order to overcome the proprietor's inherent advantage — the territorial principle. Otherwise intrusion would not only fail, but would probably accomplish only the reverse of its objectives, by reinforcing resistance. Rejecting any romantic or liberal thesis of human behaviour, Ardrey found hope for the future, not in the soul or innate goodness, but in the image of man as a bad-weather animal, designed for storm and change. In support of his ideas, he pointed out that, after man, the greatest evolutionary success among primates was the baboon:

> The student of man ... may find the baboon the most instructive of species. Among primates his aggressiveness is second only to man's. He is a born bully, a born criminal, a born candidate for the hangman's noose. As compared with the gorilla — that gentle, inoffensive, submissive creature for whom a minimum of tyranny yields a maximum of results — the baboon represents nature's most lasting challenge to the police state.[10]

Ardrey's thesis has, of course, been attacked on good scientific and moral grounds. If his "Territorial Imperative" merely revives the old "Instinct of Property" in modern dress, his emphases on competition, biological nationhood and violence as the source of progress are all deeply objectionable.[11] Ralph Holloway has described *The Territorial Imperative* as "an apology and rationalization for Imperialism, Pax Americana, Laissez Faire, Social Darwinism and that greatest of evolutionary developments, Capitalism".[12] As a result it makes a particularly apt metaphor for Gordimer to employ in the context of South Africa, a place where definitions of territory and of biological nationhood have pullulated to the point of absurdity. South Africa has been "fractured, Balkanised, scrambled into an omelette of tribal states, casinostans, white cities, black townships, grey areas, Indian reserves and Coloured suburbs".[13] The difficulties which Gordimer's whites face in classifying the escaped monkey — as ape, man, chimp, baboon, even wildcat — mirror the bizarre racial classifications of South Africans into white, black, coloured, Malay, Indian, Asian, Chinese and Griquas (with Japanese as honorary whites).

In the world at large "naked apery" remains popular, despite its flaws, perhaps because it offers absolution to its readers, a means of shifting our guilt onto "natural inheritance" or "innate aggression". Naked apery has an exculpatory function; it provides us with "attractive excuses for our unpleasant behaviour toward each other".[14] In "Something Out There" Gordimer proposes a mock-ethological study of contemporary South Africa, precisely in order to strip away all such exculpatory fantasies. The novella proceeds, in ethological fashion, by a structural comparison between man and animal, alternating its plots, which provide links and parallels between human and simian behaviour. The dominant imagery is territorial and plot events are carefully designed to set up a series of debating points with Ardrey.[15] The central tenets of "naked apery" are thus parodically enacted, the fantasy mirrored, in order to display its total absurdity.

For Gordimer,

> Books make South Africans, black and white, see themselves as they cannot from inside themselves. They get a kind of mirror image with which to compare their own feelings and motives. I think fiction raises their consciousness in this way.[16]

In "Something Out There" the language of "naked apery" is exploited for just such subversive purposes. In this connection, mirrors, reflections, mimicry and imitation become key processes. "Apeing" is central to theme, structure and language. Gordimer's white South Africans are types, satirically rendered in precise mimicry of accent, behaviour and mannerism. They themselves are members of an ersatz culture, "Europe in Africa", copying the lifestyle of the West. Thus when the Kloppers speak English they feel as if imitating television dialogue; Mrs Scholtz names her cat "Dallas". These copycat lifestyles are contrasted with the purposeful imitation, the disguises and cover stories, of the terrorists. As a result Gordimer may be said to ape and out-ape Ardrey, masking her own subversive purposes by playful imitation — just as the four terrorists imitate the norms and behaviour of white South Africa, in order to attack it from within.

First and foremost Gordimer encourages the analogy between the mysterious marauder and the "naked ape". The baboon's progress through the story recapitulates the popular account of human evolution which may be sketched as follows.[17] The early primates live in trees, eating fruit, nuts and berries. Climatic change, and hence a reduction in forests, leads to the descent from the trees to the ground where a carnivorous diet is adopted. On the ground apes become more erect, better runners; their hands are free to grasp weapons. As the hunt increases in complexity, with longer forays abroad, so a home base, a territory, becomes necessary for the dependent young and females. This development from forest ape to ground ape to carnivorous ape to killer ape to territorial ape is teasingly reproduced in "Something Out There". The first sighting of the ape is merely as "reflected between trees" (119) on the surface of a swimming pool.[18] A photograph captures only "the thrashing together of two tree tops" (118). The apparently arboreal ape is also associated with a throwback to the past. A vet recalls how elephants in the grip of their genetic homing instinct made for their former mating grounds, now flooded beneath 5,000 miles of Lake Kariba. Though their attachment to territory proved fatal, it is not always so : "nature sometimes came back, forgot time and survived eight-lane freeways, returning to ancestral haunts" (119). This sense of the creature as an ape-man or missing link is expanded in the second sighting. As two golfers search the ground for a missing ball, "Exactly where the two men were gazing, someone — something that must have been crouching — rose" (126). The arboreal ape has clearly reached the ground. The ensuing argument — was it a man, a monkey, a baboon? — sparks an interest in a journalist, who digs out from the Department of Anthropology a popular account of the anatomical differences between man, ape and baboon, together with a chart showing "the evolutionary phases of anthropoid to hominid, with man an identikit compilation of his past and present" (131). Ironically the main anatomical difference in the illustration is that the newspaper blocks out the human genitalia but leaves the anthropoid's exposed. South African evolution moves towards censorship. Later, Dr Fraser-Smith recalls that the animal's posture appeared to mimic his own, that it bent down just as he was doing, and that he recognised "someone people had been telling one another about for generations" (176). To himself he adds the secret fantasy that he had "looked back into a consciousness from which part of his own came" (176), "into the eyes of hominid evolution" (203).

The ape's next appearance reveals details of its diet. Contemplating the remains of a granadilla vine, an unnamed male comments that "Only a hungry fruit-eating animal would plunder so indiscriminately" (143). As the narrator informs us, however, "Like the human animal, it is able to adapt its eating habits to changes of environment" (188). The baboon turns carnivorous, raiding man to snatch a haunch of venison. Pet dogs and cats are hunted down, until finally it attacks its near-relation, man (in the shape of Mrs Lily Scholtz) and falls to the superior weaponry of the naked ape. Despite adopting all the evolutionary strategies which have in theory favoured man, the baboon fails to survive. "Something Out There" therefore poses the question: will the terrorists succeed (at a price) because of a willingness to make sacrifices, to subdue animal instincts in favour of a conscious choice of goals, or will their adoption of the way of aggression as challenge to the police state end in failure, like the baboon?

It is significant that, throughout its brief career, the ape has consistently maintained a territory, in the affluent suburbs: "the creature never went beyond the bounds of white Johannesburg. ... it was canny about where it was possible somehow to exist off the pickings of plenty" (181). If its precarious survival on the fringes of white South Africa mirrors the marginal existence of many black South Africans, identifying ape and black, it also holds up an ironic mirror to the affluent themselves. One such is Mrs Naas Klopper, who follows the story of the ape with interest in her "lovely home" (120 and passim) as a pleasant relief from news of boundary disputes, boycotts and censures from abroad. As naked apes go, Mrs Klopper represents the territorial imperative gone berserk. Her home pullulates with territorial markers — plants, ornaments, side-tables, pictures and plaques — and is massively over-enclosed. The eye moves to the boxed-in "en suite" bathrooms, the glassed-in sun porch, the television set hidden behind carved console doors. The entire place is financed by Mr Klopper's real estate business and it includes a stylised memorial to his hunting skills; the stools around the mini-bar are covered with the skins of impala which Naas himself has shot. Within this arena, Mrs Klopper is able to sense the presence of outsiders instinctively; she "could always feel at once, even if no sound were made, when the pine aerosol-fresh space of her lovely home was displaced by any body other than her own" (121–22). The similarity of the house to a defensive laager is suggested, however, in the design, in which a dark passage recreates "the enclosing gloom" (121) of Naas's childhood farmhouse. Despite the move from farmer to estate agent, the passage of time seems to have led Naas less far than he thinks from his past. His defences have in fact already been penetrated by the saboteurs, whom Mrs Klopper's instincts signally fail to detect.

The delusionary quality of the Kloppers' security is underlined in relation to the transitory affair of an adulterous couple. Unlike the terrorists (who have rented a safe house from Naas) the lovers have exhausted the possibilities of the local motels for their rendezvous. The man owns a huge house, set "in a lair of trees" (140) but because (even in the absence of his wife) "they are always there" (140) — his black servants — he cannot take the woman he loves onto home territory. For him, "even his room, his own bed, in a house where he paid for everything — nothing is your own, once you are married" (140). Displaced by blacks, their sex subordinate to the territorial pair bond which imposes these restrictions, the couple are condemned to make love in the emblematic locale of the mine-dumps, the refuse of the prosperity on which their wealth is founded. When a friend lends an untenanted property they rejoice: "They were secure in that cottage — for as long as they would need security" (141). This security is manifestly an illusion, however. It is appropriate that the ape at their window registers his presence only with a laugh. Although the lover denies "that someone had been laughing at them, that they could ever be something to laugh at" (142), the reader registers the sardonic comment on white pretensions to permanent tenure in South Africa. For all their real estate, their riches and their elaborate precautions, whites in South Africa have ultimately no safety and nowhere to go. In the homeless lovers Gordimer offers an ironic notation of the futility of territory, just as in the useless security devices which fail to exclude the ape from suburban gardens.

If the representation of the white South African as territorial ape serves satiric purposes, its extension into the public sphere strikes a darker note. The corollary to Mrs Klopper's "lovely home" is the police H.Q. at John Vorster Square. It, too, has been beautified: "The blue spandrel panels and glimpses of potted plants in the facade it presented to the passing city freeway, could have been those of an apartment block" (154). The cells in which detainees are interrogated are located within the core of the building, out of sight like Naas's dark passage. Here, in a break from "interrogation" duties, Sergeant Chapman reminisces fondly about his weekend hunting blesbok and shooting jackals on the land which he loves. Chapman's prisoner, a wealthy doctor, also has access to the plenty of South Africa (specifically a cottage at one of the best places for fishing on the coast) but has chosen to express his identity as a South African in community (trade union activities) rather than territory. In interview Gordimer argued that for blacks identity is with the people, as opposed to land:

> Blacks take the land for granted, it's simply there. It's theirs, although they've been conquered; they were always there. They don't have the necessity to say, "Well I love this land *because* it's beautiful."[19]

The sinister side to Chapman's lyrical nostalgia is indicated when he takes a break from work, in a Chinese restaurant. The restaurant is nameless, and has few "ethnic pretensions" (157). Ethically it has even fewer. The studied image of neutrality is belied by the off-duty policemen, seen enjoying a swordfight in a televised historical romance. This atavistic display of outdated weaponry and theatrical violence is an appropriate prelude to a broadcast from the Prime Minister, speaking from behind a prop desk, and with a ceremonial curtain as territorial marker. In South Africa there is no neutral ground. The narrator remarks that "Convenient to concentration camps there were such quiet couples, minding their own business, selling coffee and schnapps to refresh jackbooted men off duty" (157).

When Sergeant Chapman's territory is invaded and his prey — the venison haunch — stolen by the baboon, the reaction is telling. Far from recognising that not even the security forces enjoy security, his boss suggests that Chapman arm his wife: "Next time it might be more than a monkey out there in the yard" (160). The recurrence of the title phrase recalls the public exploitation by the South African security forces of the idea of "prowling subhuman invaders".[20] The Prime Minister also exploits the rhetoric of territoriality, inveighing against those who threaten "the security of your homes", those who "lurk, outside law and order, ready to strike in the dark" (149). In response, the four saboteurs smile, realising that "those being referred to as monsters are the human beings drinking a glass of water, cutting a hang nail, writing a letter, in the same room; are themselves" (150). Vusi comments that the government, unable to justify its policies, is reduced to scaring its audience with "spook people" (150) — the well-known South African tactic of "swartgevaar", black danger, of the barbarian at the gate.[21]

For black South Africans, however, the term "spook people" takes on a different application. Where Gordimer draws a parallel between ape and black, it is to mirror the exploited condition of the latter. When the baboon is seen leaving a maid's room, in a suburban backyard, the maid blazes out to the other black servants that they are unprotected, exposed: "Couldn't they see the whites always ran away and hid and left us to be hurt ?" (147). She recalls the fate of the cook's brother, a watchman at a block of flats, employed to guard tenants' cars. Attacked and outgunned, he dies "while the owners of the cars went on sleeping, stacked twelve storeys high over his dead body" (148). For the blacks, the barbarian is already within the gate. They have no need of mythical bogeymen; danger and death are all around them. For them the "something out there" is also a spook, "an urban haunter, a factory or kitchen ghost. Powerless like themselves" (148). Industrialisation and urbanisation have shattered any easy continuity with the past. The apparition is "long migrated from the remotest possibility of being a spirit of the ancestors" (148). Instead of looking back to mystificatory past fantasies they identify the spook with a specific migrant worker, found dead in the area: "Someone like that had woken up now, without his body, and was trying to find his way back to the hostel where his worker's contract, thumb-print affixed, had long ago run out" (148). The sense of the black, wandering without title to a home, an unrecognised presence in his own country, is reinforced in the white reaction to the ape's perambulations. When a representative of a suburban Residents Association demands a sweep of the area in search of the ape, the victims are all black — several illicit liquor sellers and fifteen men in breach of the Pass Laws. The animal itself evades capture:

> Like the contract labourers who had to leave their families to find work where
> work was, like the unemployed who were endorsed out to where there was no
> work and somehow kept getting back in through the barbed strands of Influx
> Control. (181)

What the suburban residents want is "for the animal to be confined in its
appropriate place, that's all, zoo or even circus" (181). The reader might substitute
the words "location" or "township" for "circus" and "zoo". Although a left-wing
writer condemns the interest in one homeless animal, when thousands of blacks are
being bulldozed out of their homemade shelters, the conservatives argue that the
monkey is "in self-imposed exile. If it had been content to stay chained in a yard
or caged in a zoo, its proper station in life, it wouldn't have had to live the life of
an outlaw" (189). The argument suggests the appeal to conservatives of the fiction
of the "homeland", by which people born and bred in Johannesburg suddenly
found themselves reclassified as citizens of a place which they had never seen
before — Bophuthatswana, Transkei or Venda, for example.[22] A circus proprietor
warns that it is unlikely that an ape which has learned to fend for itself in a hostile
environment will ever again be psychologically amenable to training. Freedom,
once gained, is not lightly abandoned. But a zoologist offers a less comforting
scenario for the future. In his opinion, apes, baboons and monkeys may survive
around Johannesburg in the summer but "when the Highveld winter comes ...
Simiadae suffer from the common cold, die of pneumonia, like people — just like
people" (182). Which people?, the reader asks. Which people die of pneumonia in
South Africa in winter? Only blacks. Sure enough, when the baboon is found dead
it proves to be "just a native species" (200), its commonplace death eclipsed by the
more newsworthy "spook people", the white saboteurs.

Although the baboon's fate appears to suggest the inevitability of white terri-
torialists maintaining domination, the terrorists offer a fragile image of a better
future, in strong contrast to the brutalist image of man. Importantly, the foursome
assumes the traits of naked apery only in order to overcome the real monstrosity of
South Africa. To survive under cover, they are forced to mimic the behaviour of
oppressor and oppressed, the whites performing a charade of "madam" and "baas",
the blacks impersonating construction workers, ostensibly building and gardening,
when their real function is to dismantle the power structures of the apartheid
state. Ironically, as would-be liberators, their first action has to be the sacking of
Kleynhans' old "boy", who accepts this as no more than the usual fate of black
servants at white hands. Beneath the ox-wagon wheel chandelier, they set up a
simulacrum of home: "a containing: a shell, a habitation" (169), in which, however,
they plot an end to the Afrikaner territorial domination which the ox-wagon
symbolises. Like the farming families around them Joy and Charles have a "combi"
van, with "housewifely curtains" (139) at its windows, but in their case the curtains
serve to hide the explosives which are being transported. One scene indicates
imagistically the revisionary intent of their imitation of the Southern naked ape. As
Charles draws up beside the Kloppers at a level crossing.

> A train shuttered past like a camera gone berserk, lens opening and closing, with each flying segment of rolling stock, on flashes of the veld behind it. The optical explosion invigorated Charles. (139)

The juxtaposition of the real estate dealer and the mobile home, against a background of a land exploding in flashes and (camera) shots, projects the very different future envisaged beneath the apparently photographic reproduction of white norms.

In similar fashion the apparent identification of the black saboteurs, Eddie and Vusi, with the ape serves subversive purposes. Like the ape they are not long content with the diet of fruit, nuts and grains which vegetarian Joy provides — though Vusi devours a bag of apricots with as much gusto as any fruit-eating animal. Like the ape they too demand fresh meat. Daringly, Gordimer turns the language of racism back upon itself. Eddie and Vusi are associated with the baboon as an endangered species. Eddie jokes that despite his fringed, Red Indian style jacket "I'm not going to be extinct" (138). When Charles (featuring as man-the-hunter) draws on his experience as a game ranger in Kruger park to identify jackal excreta, Vusi remembers that he had once infiltrated South Africa by that route, through "that vast wilderness of protected species; an endangered one on his way to become operational" (167). Less protected than the wild animals, Eddie spent his childhood "in street-gang rivalries that unknowingly rehearsed, for his generation of blacks, the awful adventure that was coming to them" (151). Paradoxically Eddie's delinquent youth prepares him for a struggle against a brutal system. Vusi's facial expression is described as buried "deep in the past of himself ... in the watergleam of his black eyes hidden in the ancient cave of skull ... in the fine gills of the nostrils" (161). The emphases — on a deep past, an ancient cave, evolutionary gills — suggest an image of Vusi as a primitive specimen — yet it is he who masterminds the entire mission. Eddie and Vusi hold up an ironic mirror to naked apery and concepts of territoriality. Both have been forced off their territory, Eddie fleeing after the Soweto Rising, Vusi forcibly relocated. Joy realises that Vusi "hadn't lived anywhere that could be called "at home" for years, and his "neighbours" had been fellow refugees in camps and military training centres" (135). The terrorists occupy *not* a physical territory, but "a habitation of resolve" (170). At the end, sheltering in a crude dugout while waiting for their chance to attack the power station, they are quite prepared to decline to a hole in the ground in order to fulfil their purposes. They too can alter their diet — toward abstinence if the situation requires it. (In the dugout they cannot smoke or cook for fear of detection, and exist on fastfood snacks.) In the torpor of a Sunday afternoon Eddie listens to reggae just like any other labourer, Charles dozes just like Naas Klopper does, ten kilometres away in his split-level lounge. But the resemblances are misleading. Theirs is a conscious mimicry. For a joke, Eddie deliberately imitates a white prosecutor mistranslating a black witness, and the group laugh in the knowledge of "the events of their world, which moved beneath the events of the world the newspapers reflected" (153).

The objection remains, none the less, that within their parallel world the saboteurs are potential killers, their mission dependent upon sophisticated weaponry. Gordimer, however, goes to some lengths to emphasise that this is essentially a distortion of their humanity. The terrorists are aiming for a "classic" mission, involving only economic damage, not loss of life. (The example of Koeberg is cited.[23]) The blacks' situation, sharing their bedroom with boxes of ammunition, is presented as entirely abnormal, not the reflection of "man the killer". The weapons are described as forming a horizon in which "the old real, terrible needs of [Vusi's] life ... were now so strangely realised" (145). "All these hungers found their shape, distorted, forged as no one could conceive they ever should have to be, in the objects packed around him" (146). Throughout the story Joy has been aware of Vusi tinkering in the back room. Hearing the clink of small tools she assumes that he is working on the weapons. In fact Vusi has been hammering beer can tabs and cartridge cases into a saxophone. *Some* of the weaponry has already been transformed into an artefact. For Charles the saxophone is depressingly reminiscent of the objects made in concentration camps, "effigies of the beautiful possibilities of a life to be lived" (163). The noise which comes from it is certainly thin and weak, "the feeble cry of something new-born" (162). Yet although Gordimer does not underestimate the vulnerability of an emergent, indigenous black culture, she does indicate that future possibilities exist, if only embryonically.

The point is made in symbolic terms in the following sequence, in which the baboon appears to a woman who is taking a bath. A reference to "pan pipes" (164) (actually the woman's toes) links back to the preceding music of the saxophone. An artefact is also introduced, a green ceramic statuette of a sacred monkey, in a local art gallery. It is described as "carved out of deep water. It lives in a cupboard behind glass" (163). In place of a mirror, the woman's bath has a glass wall, overlooking a courtyard full of greenery, where the baboon appears. The positioning of the glass sets up a parallel between the two figures. Who is on display in a glass-fronted space, ape or woman? Which is the animal, which the embodiment of culture? The imagery suggests that the woman is animalistic. In the distorted mirror of the faucet her face becomes a bulging gourd, her lower torso is foreshortened, so that

> Her legs become gangling and bowed, joined by huge feet at one end and a curved perspective that leads back to a hairy creature, crouched. There is nothing behind this voracious pudenda; it has swallowed the body and head behind it. (164)

From this image of the body as mere flesh, dominated by "animal" drives, the woman's mind moves to sex, to her monstrous stomach rising "like the Leviathan" (164), and to the fate of her ageing friends, "being brought down all around her, as a lion moves into a herd, tearing into the flesh of his victims" (164). The image of humanity as a herd of beasts at first appears to be confirmed by the statuette, a Viennese copy of an Indian piece. In India the hanuman monkey is worshipped as the guardian god of settlement.[24] The first duty of the founder of a village is to erect a statue of the monkey god. Significantly the museum, with its monkey culture, apeing Europe, has no example of the African sacred ape, "of the dog-faced ape of ancient Egyptian mythology, Cynocephalus, often depicted attendant upon the god Thoth" (164). Thoth is of course the god of writing, and in ancient Egypt the sacred baboon was considered as the scribe to the gods. When the real baboon appears, it crosses the woman's mind that he is an erotic hallucination — a man — but he is also associated with "the head of antiquity, the Egyptian basalt rigidity, twice removed — as animal and attribute of a god — from man" (165). The foreign settler ape yields therefore to an African sacred ape, indicating that the comparison of man to ape is suspect, and that man can be a creature of ideals and of culture, rather than a territorial ape. The imagery also reminds the reader that nature always wears a mask of theory — that the naked ape is only one in a succession of fantasy masks placed over the animal world.

Where this scene challenges the Ardrey thesis in symbolic terms, and in principle, emphasising transformative future possibilities, rather than an unchangeable animal nature, there remains the question of the kind of future to be realised in South Africa. When Eddie absconds from the group for a day in Johannesburg, his disappearance coincides with that of the ape. Eddie finds the city "blacker than he remembered it" with "no white centre" (174) any more, its streets full of prosperous-looking blacks. The suggestion hovers of an eventual victory for blacks in demographic terms.[25] People will eventually prove a greater force than territory. But it also raises the possibility that, as a Communist-trained revolutionary, Eddie may yet become extinct, as the creation of a black middle-class offers liberation by embourgeoisement. Eddie tours a supermarket, with "arsenals" (172) of tinned fruit on display. He learns that new clothes are coming in all the time, and admires the latest in electronic technology. There can, of course, be no guarantee that free South Africa will not be merely an apeing of Western bourgeois forms. Joy points out, however, that the apparent possibilities for blacks are in fact very firmly circumscribed. Black doctors are allowed to practise only in black areas, black lawyers are barred from taking chambers in white areas "where the courts are" (179). Territory is still demarcated. When their spending is over, the crowds in the streets "would have to go back to the places for blacks" (174). In contrast Eddie returns to his "place" in a group held together by cooperative bonds and a common purpose: "Vusi could not function without Eddie, Eddie and Vusi without Charles and Joy, Charles and Joy without Eddie and Vusi. The entity reconstituted itself irresistibly" (178). As the foursome celebrate Eddie's return, Vusi appears with the saxophone, his face emerging from the darkness like "a head from a submerged statue" (180).

As the image implies, recalling the sacred ape, Gordimer cannot go further than indicating possibilities which must, for the moment, remain concealed beneath the surface. Indeed, when Eddie and Vusi move to the temporary shelter of the "cave" (actually an old mine-working) the suggestion lingers that nothing much has changed. They carry loads of ammunition, just as "their brothers had for generations carried coal and sacks of potatoes" (191). With his unwashed clothes and earthy smell, Eddie blends in with the rural blacks, only one of the many farm labourers crowding the nearby Indian store. Digging out a pit for weapons, he jokes that he had not expected to end up "working in the mines". (191). Similarly Joy falls back into the charade of the white "madam" to see off Kleynhans' "boy"; Charles finds himself burning books. Yet despite the implications of a reassertion of past patterns, a return to the cave, a reenactment of past evils, the reader is well aware of the story which moves below the events of the surface, beyond the superficial behaviour which an ethologist might observe. Theirs is a conscious choice of strategy, not to repeat the past, but to bring to birth a different future. The point is illustrated in the final image of diminished territoriality. In his own cramped shelter, Eddie finds some lizard eggs "in a crevice of warm rock" (193). Tiny, but perfect, so small as to "scarcely contain the pulse of life" (193), the baby lizards none the less slide away "to begin to live" (193).

At the end of the novella the reader is left with a similarly tenuous and vestigial sense of the terrorists' achievement. Was the effort worthwhile merely to ensure a power cut, even if its symbolic meaning is appreciated? Was the price (Eddie's life) too high? Did the intrusion merely play into the hands of a government which is keen to use "bogeyman" scare tactics? It certainly works to the advantage of the Prime Minister. Instead of having to justify his farming policy, he is able to issue a rousing call for support "to meet the threat from beyond our borders which was always ready to strike at our country" (196). The arms cache makes good photographic propaganda; the attack provides an excuse to round up and interrogate numbers of blacks. Just as nobody ever discovered the origin of the baboon, so at the end the terrorists fade back into anonymity. Names and sketchy descriptions are provided, but "Nobody really knew what names mark the identity each has accepted within himself" (202).

At the close, however, Gordimer intervenes, to reinsert her characters into history. Dr Fraser-Smith's fantasy of having looked into the eyes of hominid evolution is revealed as just that — a fantasy — more attractive perhaps than the reality, his descent from Maisie McCulloch, the keeper of a Victorian brothel. A rotgut liquor bottle is discovered, from the first distillery in the area, Die Eerste Fabriek, founded to encourage black workers to drink, just as whites were encouraged to take prostitutes, in order to maintain them in the position of wage slaves.[26] The alternatives of real history, in all its complexity, replace the timeless myths of "naked apery". Charles may be named, patriotically, after Winston Churchill; he may also resemble a distant ancestor, a missionary, who believed in brotherhood outside the narrow biological nation of colour. Even the statue of the Indian monkey has a history. Ironically it was a gift to South Africa from a European refugee (presumably Jewish) fleeing from racial persecution at home. Gordimer makes the point here that individuals cannot know all the forces of environment, genetic endowment and cultural conditioning which make them what they are, but that they can make conscious choices, not to repeat the evils of the past but to contribute to a different future. The most significant detail is saved until last. The mine working where Eddie and Vusi hid, assumed to be only a nineteenth-century excavation, is actually much older: "It goes back further than anything in conventional or alternative history, or even oral tradition, back to the human presences who people anthropology and archaeology" (203). With Eddie and Vusi's re-occupation, history reaffirms itself over myth, for this was "an ancient mine-working *out there*, and metals precious to men were discovered, dug and smelted, for themselves, by black men" (203; my emphasis).[27] The novella therefore ends with something "out there" which is no longer a myth, a bogeyman, a monster, but an image of a past black culture, independent, in a territory all its own, which is now being reclaimed.

Notes to Chapter 4

1. Wendy Smith notes the "risky, potentially condescending parallel between the baboon and black South Africans" in "A Voice from South Africa," *Wall Street Journal*, 204 (9 July 1984), 221.
2. *The Guardian*, 4 August 1989, 10.
3. Salman Rushdie, "No One is Ever Safe," *New York Times Book Review*, 29 July 1984, 7.
4. Quoted in the *New York Times Book Review*, 29 July 1984, 7.
5. I am using the term "man" advisedly, rather than more inclusive language, to reflect the view expressed by ethologists of the male as the norm. On baboons see Irven Devore (ed.), *Primate Behavior* (New York: Holt, Rinehart. and Winston, 1965). On ethology see Robert Ardrey, *African Genesis* (London: Collins, 1961) and *The Territorial Imperative* (New York: Dell, 1966); Desmond Morris, *The Naked Ape* (London: Cape, 1967); Konrad Lorenz, *On Aggression* (London: Methuen, 1966).
6. Ardrey, *African Genesis*, 29.
7. See Michael H. Day, "Dart's Baby," *Guardian*, 25 November, 1988 (Obituary of Raymond Dart).
8. Ardrey, *African Genesis*, 9.
9. Ardrey, *The Territorial Imperative*, 292.
10. Ibid., 227.
11. For a collection of critical views see Ashley Montagu (ed.), *Man and Aggression* (Oxford: Oxford University Press, 1972).
12. Montagu, *Man and Aggression*, 181.
13. Christopher Hope, *White Boy Running* (London: Abacus, 1988), 198.
14. David Pilbeam, in Montagu, *Man and Aggression*, 113.
15. J. U. Jacobs notes that all the stories in *Something Out There* concern the idea of living space as a construct, but does not make connections to Ardrey, Morris or ethology. See J. U. Jacobs, "Living Space and Narrative Space in Nadine Gordimer's *Something Out There*," *English in Africa*, 14, 2 (1987), 31–43.
16. "A Voice from a Troubled Land," *Ontario Review*, 26 (1987), 14.
17. Morris, *The Naked Ape*.
18. Page references which follow quotations in parentheses refer to Nadine Gordimer, *Something Out There* (London: Cape, 1984).
19. Robert Boyers and others, "A Conversation with Nadine Gordimer," *Salmagundi*, 62 (Winter 1984), 6.
20. John Cooke, *The Novels of Nadine Gordimer: Private Lives/Public Landscapes* (Baton Rouge: Louisiana State University Press, 1985), 123–24.
21. Christopher Hope notes in *White Boy Running* (62–63) that "Black Danger" was a tactic in every election fought by the Nationalists.
22. Gordimer condemns the practice in interview with Robert Boyers and others, *Salmagundi*, 26.
23. Koeberg, a nuclear power station twenty miles from Cape Town, became operational in March 1984, though sabotage on 19 December 1982 delayed its completion. Nobody was injured. The ANC claimed responsibility. Gordimer has noted that in a five-year period, bombings by underground movements within South Africa have caused $432 million of damage. See Nadine Gordimer, "The Idea of Gardening," *New York Review of Books*, 2 February 1984, 3.
24. Ramona and Desmond Morris, *Men and Apes* (London: Hutchinson, 1966), ch. 1.
25. In *White Boy Running* (247) Christopher Hope implicitly supports this view, noting that in 1987 half the black population of South Africa were under fifteen.
26. See Charles van Onselen, *Studies in the Social and Economic History of the Witwatersrand 1886–1914. Volume I. New Babylon* (London: Longman, 1982).

27. The earliest mine-workings, discovered in Swaziland, date from *c.* 43000 B.C., as reported by Greg Lanning with Marti Mueller, *Africa Undermined: Mining Companies and the Underdevelopment of Africa* (London: Penguin, 1979). Vusi is seen reading this book in *Something Out There*, 160.

CHAPTER 5

Saul Bellow and Social Anthropology

In Saul Bellow's story "Cousins", Ijah Brodsky, the narrator, spends much of his time immersed in the anthropological records of Franz Boas's Jesup Expedition, of 1900, to the Siberian Chukchee and Koryak tribes. He poses the following question:

> Why were the Jews such avid anthropologists? Among the founders of the science were Durkheim, Levy-Bruhl, Marcel Mauss, Boas, Sapir, Lowie.[1]

Ijah reviews two alternative possibilities. In the orthodox explanation "They may have believed that they were demystifiers, that science was their motive and that their ultimate aim was to increase universalism" (255). Ijah, however, rejects any such liberal, humanist intention:

> I don't see it that way myself. A truer explanation is the nearness of ghettos to the sphere of Revelation, an easy move for the mind from rotting streets and rancid dishes, a direct ascent into transcendence. (255)

Ijah's offbeat interpretation of the attractions of anthropology provides the point of entry to the topic of Saul Bellow and anthropology, which has a special reference to "Cousins", a story deeply informed by Bellow's own anthropological background.

Although Bellow began his undergraduate career at the University of Chicago, studying English, he soon tired of "caesura-hunting" in literature, and transferred in 1935 to Northwestern University, graduating in 1937 with honours in anthropology and sociology.[2] One of his tutors was Melville J. Herskovits, whose studies of the cattle cultures of Africa were later to provide the material for Bellow's African tribes, the Arnewi and Wariri, in *Henderson the Rain King*.[3] Bellow went on to do graduate work at the University of Wisconsin in Madison, under Alexander Goldenweiser, but dropped out after only a few months to become a full-time writer. As he explained, "Every time I worked on my thesis, it turned out to be a story."[4] He has described his decision to study anthropology in terms which suggest a conscious identification with universalism and demystification in the cause of freedom:

> Anthropology students were the farthest out in the 1930s. They seemed to be preparing to criticise society from its roots. Radicalism was implied by the study of anthropology, especially sexual radicalism — the study of the sexual life of savages was gratifying to radicals. It indicated that human life was much broader than the present. It gave young Jews a greater sense of freedom from the surrounding restrictions.[5]

Bellow's own choice of topic for research fieldwork was not, however, designed to remove him from Midwest cold to some lush tropical paradise in the steps of Margaret Mead in Samoa or Malinowski in the Trobriand Islands. Instead, as he revealed in *To Jerusalem and Back,*

> When I was a graduate student in anthropology, it was my immature ambition to investigate bands of Eskimos who were reported to have chosen to starve rather than eat foods that were abundant but under taboo. How much, I asked myself, did people yield to culture or to their lifelong preoccupations, and at what point would the animal need to survive break through the restraints of custom and belief? I suspected then that among primitive peoples the objective facts counted for less.

In opposing "subjective" culture to "objective" facts, Bellow was none the less alive to the dangers posed by the inability to face the challenges of adaptation to meet external threats. He continued:

> But I'm not at all certain now that civilized minds are more flexible and capable of grasping reality, or that they have livelier, more intelligent reactions to the threat of extinction. I grant that as an American I am more subject to illusion than my cousins. But will the Israeli veterans of hardships, massacres and wars know how to save themselves? Has the experience of crisis taught them what to do? I have read writers on the Holocaust who made the most grave criticisms of European Jewry, arguing that they doomed themselves by their unwillingness to surrender their comfortable ways, their property, their passive habits, their acceptance of bureaucracy, and were led to slaughter unresisting.[6]

Although Bellow does not endorse this latter, tendentious argument, the development of his thought in this paragraph — from Eskimo taboos to the Holocaust — suggests that the question of cultural change and creative adaptation has a special relevance for him as a Jew. It is, of course, precisely this issue — obedience to custom versus adaptive plasticity — on which Henderson and the Arnewi part company. The Arnewi prefer to see their cows die of thirst rather than use water polluted by frogs, the taboo animal. Henderson's reaction is telling:

> Do you know why the Jews were defeated by the Romans? Because they wouldn't fight back on Saturday. And that's how it is with your water situation. Should you preserve yourself, or the cows, or the custom? I would say, yourself. Live ... to make another custom.[7]

The human cost of challenging custom is not, however, negligible. Henderson blows up custom, frogs and water-source all together in a scene of wholesale destruction.

For Bellow his immigrant status was also relevant to the choice of anthropology. Describing himself as "an exotic among other exotics" he pointed to the lack of stability available to the children of immigrants, who therefore needed to adapt as speedily as possible to their new environment. "The word for this was 'Americanization'. The masses that came from Europe in the great wave of immigration between 1870 and 1930 wanted to be as American as possible." As a result, he commented that "I don't know whether a book like *The Adventures of*

Augie March is so much a *Bildungsroman* as it is a piece of ethnography."[8] Bellow cited Augie's desire for fraternity, for example, as common to adolescent Americans of immigrant background. Augie's refusal to be conditioned by a time and place, whether as the result of his Jewish background or his American present, was also shared with his creator. In interview Bellow commented that,

> As a Middle-Westerner, the son of immigrant parents, I recognized at an early age that I was called upon to decide for myself to what extent my Jewish origins, my surroundings ... were to be allowed to determine the course of my life. ... The commonest teaching of the civilized world in our time can be stated simply: "Tell me where you come from and I will tell you what you are." ... I would not allow myself to become the product of an environment.[9]

In juxtaposing these autobiographical statements with Bellow's comments on anthropology a common thread can be discerned: a concern with the influence of, and the resistance to, environment, and with the degree to which human adaptation — in customs and in culture — is desirable, or even possible. Breaking with custom may involve the permanent loss of valuable traditions, "subjective facts" which may be more necessary than they at first appear. On the other hand, new opportunities may be generated. In the same interview Bellow expressed his belief that:

> the lamentable weakening of the older, traditional branches of civilization might open fresh opportunities, force us to reassess the judgments of culture and that we might be compelled — a concealed benefit of decline — to be independent. ... Quite simply, when the centre does not hold and great structures fall down, one has an opportunity to see some of the truths that they obstructed.[10]

In this connection Bellow's choice of anthropological research topic is particularly revealing. In selecting for study the nature of taboo among the Eskimos Bellow was consciously following in the footsteps of Franz Boas, the founding father of American anthropology. A graduate of Heidelberg, Boas did not begin as an anthropologist but as a geographer. In the 1880s Friedrich Ratzel, also a graduate of Heidelberg, had developed the doctrine that environment was the force which shaped culture. Man was a passive creature rigidly ruled by climate and geography. ("Tell me where you come from and I will tell you what you are.") When Boas travelled to the Arctic in 1883 to observe the effects of climate on its inhabitants, he discovered, however, that far from confirming his thesis of geographical determinism, Eskimo behaviour could not be explained by environment except in very shallow ways. Eskimos often did things not because of the objective facts (e.g. geographical conditions) but in spite of them. Boas had been reared by freethinking parents, and spoke of Liberalism, and the ideals of the German revolution of 1848, as a living force in his life. As a youth he had been deeply shocked when a theological friend had "declared his belief in the authority of tradition and his conviction that one had not the right to doubt what the past had transmitted to us."[11] In contrast Boas's own outlook on social life, and his motivation as an anthropologist, was dictated by one question: "How can we recognise the shackles that tradition has laid upon us? For when we recognise them, we are also able to break them."[12] Boas did not underestimate the difficulties of such demystification. In his Arctic field notebook he dwelt upon both the "beautiful customs" of the Eskimos and their "superstition", and, after noting that the fear of tradition was deeply implanted, he added the comment that it was "a difficult struggle for every individual and every people to give up tradition and follow the path to truth."[13]

Boas, of course, persisted none the less. A tireless campaigner against intolerance, he gained his student duelling scars as a result of a fracas between the anti-Semitic *Korps* and the more enlightened *Burschenschaft*, to which he belonged. He took a strong stand against Nazism from its beginnings. His books were burned in Kiel in 1933, and his work "Aryans and Non-Aryans", specially printed on tissue paper, was circulated clandestinely by the anti-Nazi underground. Influenced by Schiller (who wrote of how strong custom rends us one from another) and by Herder's idea that we live in a world which we ourselves create, Boas saw in the comparative study of cultures a means of discovering and exposing the traditional elements in thought and belief — an essential first step in the process of promoting freedom of thought. For him truth could liberate the mind from traditional error, confusion and prejudice. Man was neither dominated by biological endowment (the eugenicist theory) nor a blank slate to be written on at will. Instead Boas emphasised the plasticity of the human organism in adapting to cultural change. In opposition to the generalised image of man, propagated by the extreme diffusionists of the period, he argued that a cultural phenomenon is intelligible only from its specific past. History is therefore at the centre of his arguments. Cultural formations are not expressions of outer environment or inner biology, but are diverse historical developments, each the outcome of a prior history in which many factors have played a part.

An expert on Indian (Native-American) languages, Boas also disproved the idea that myths can be explained in terms of universal and extra-cultural symbols (e.g. the totem pole as phallus) before Bellow followed suit in "Deep Readers of the World, Beware!"[14] Among those whom Boas influenced were Alexander Goldenweiser, who also wrote about the Koryak and Chukchee, and Herskovits (who wrote the definitive account of Boas's life and works).[15] Others influenced by him included Paul Radin (whose studies of the "trickster" figure, worshipped by both Siberian and American native peoples, are an important background to *Seize the Day*), and Marcel Mauss, who went on from a study of Eskimo taboos to write *The Gift*, drawing upon Boas's study of the Kwakiutl potlatch ceremony — itself a major structural device in *Humboldt's Gift*.[16] Boas was especially interested in the "shaman" or seer, and the Jesup expedition which he organised is a major source of data on shamanism.

Fairly obviously, Boas's belief in demystifying, in breaking with tradition, aligns him unambiguously with the type of anthropologist whom Ijah Brodsky rejects. Ijah has been reading the Jesup Expedition reports, particularly the volumes concerning Siberian ethnography: *The Koryak* by Waldemar Jochelson and *The Chukchee* by Waldemar Bogoras.[17] Ijah's approach emphasises transcendence and matters of the spirit: "About this arctic desert, purified by frosts as severe as fire, I read for my relief as if I were reading the Bible" (253). Ijah's description of the world of the Chukchee — with its eternal cold and darkness, its dogs boiled alive, or crucified in sacrifice — is distinctly unenticing:

> The powers of darkness surrounded you. A Chukchee informant told Bogoras
> that there were invisible enemies who beset human beings from all sides,
> demanding spirits whose mouths were always gaping. The people cringed and
> gave ransom, buying protection from these raving ghosts. (253)

Yet for Ijah, reading about "these tribes and their spirits and shamans" (253) is
a blessed relief from Chicago. Leaving aside the obvious satirical comparison of
Chicago to a "savage Siberia" (258), the point also relates to Ijah's self-defined state
of "suspense".

In the story Ijah has two major preoccupations — his cousins (whose individual
histories are sketched, and who form the mainspring of the action) and a metaphysical
investigation of the state of human culture. In interview Bellow declared that the
impulse to write the story was not sentimental (as the memorialisation of the
cousins might suggest) but metaphysical.[18] The metaphysical theme of the story
centres upon a discussion of the possible consequences of the break with traditional
ideas. Ijah has been much exercised by Hegel's Lectures at Jena, written in the full
flush of Hegel's enthusiasm for Napoleon. In the final peroration to the lecture of
18 September 1806, from which Ijah quotes on several occasions, Hegel declared:

> We find ourselves in an important epoch, in a fermentation in which Spirit has
> made a leap forward, has gone beyond its previous concrete form and acquired
> a new one. The whole mass of ideas and concepts that have been current until
> now, the very bonds of the world are dissolving and collapsing into themselves
> like a vision in a dream. A new emergence of Spirit is at hand; philosophy
> must be the first to hail its appearance and recognize it, while others, resisting
> impotently, adhere to the past.[19]

Applying Hegel's words to what he perceives as a contemporary cultural crisis in
America, Ijah, however, doubts that *this* world is on the brink of a rebirth of Spirit
and a new stage in history. Contemplating the horrors and corruption of Chicago,
he comments that

> whether we are preparing a new birth of spirit or the agonies of final
> dissolution (and this is the suspense referred to some pages back) depends... on
> the kabbalistic skill you develop in the interpretation of these contemporary
> formations. My intuition is that the Koryak and the Chukchee lead me in the
> right direction. (253–54)

As an adviser on foreign policy, Ijah believes in his own prophetic skills. Shaman-
like, he goes "into trances" and becomes "seerlike" (254) in his office, successfully
forecasting the revolution of the mullahs in Iran, and the economic fate of Brazil.
Far from embracing change, however, he prefers to contemplate the unchanging
Chukchee, an image of fear and superstition quite alien to Hegelian optimism.
For Hegel all belief in a transcendent deity was the product of "Unhappy
Consciousness". In his view, when the individual is in a state of despair, particularly
at times of cultural crisis, he becomes divided within himself, conscious of his
own isolation, and seeks stability beyond himself in an external god. In such times,
Hegel contended, the eternal and infinite in man is "forced to take flight to the

Deity."[20] Ijah's thirst for a purified realm of transcendence, his attraction to a people mesmerised by unchanging external spirits, is carefully designed by Bellow in order to facilitate a metaphysical meditation. Ijah relates Hegel to the present by exploring a continuum of immigrant cousins, all to varying degrees representative of adaptation or resistance to major cultural change. Taking Chicago as his field location, Ijah poses the question: Will the dissolution of old ideas, bonds and traditions issue forth in a new cultural formation? Or does such dissolution merely engender anarchy, mayhem and despair?

Initially the action appears to confirm the negative hypothesis, in which change is decadence and decline, and adaptation is loss. Approached by Cousin Eunice to secure the early release from prison of Cousin Tanky (a gangster) Ijah reviews the domination of Chicago by organised crime, the involvement of another cousin (Miltie) with the underworld, and the continuous process of extortion and violence which surrounds him. Just as the Chukchee cringe and give ransom, buying protection from circumambient demons, the denizens of Chicago also pay tribute — to the mob. In Chicago "Paradise" survives only as the top floor of an Italian restaurant, itself founded on crime in the Twenties. Law has been reduced to a mere show, qualitatively indistinguishable from "Court of Law", the TV show which Ijah once hosted, and crime reaches out beyond the mob (via the Hoffa connection) to the upper echelons of the political hierarchy.[21] Cousin Eunice is the victim of more sophisticated extortion in the groves of academe, paying bribes to buy her daughter a degree (though Eunice is wily enough to declare her "integrity" so ringingly in a promissory note that she outsmarts the academics and reneges on the deal). In reaction, Eunice's other daughter has adapted to a different society, abandoning the Peace Corps to join an armed settlement on the West Bank.

Despite his reservations Ijah none the less writes two letters at Eunice's behest, on behalf of Tanky's release. He does so in order to placate his own ghosts, particularly Tanky's mother, Shana, a "primordial" woman, of a traditional Jewish type now "extinct in America" (238), who had sheltered the immigrant Brodskys. Ijah realises that, in Chicago, he is an "anachronism" (246) in continuing to honour these affective ties. Tanky is quite indifferent to the family; Eunice remains with her husband only to draw upon his health insurance. Ijah's memory of Tanky, built like a tank even as an infant, is disquietingly ominous. "A tremendous infant, strapped in, struggling with his bonds" (236), threatening to erupt at any moment from his high chair, Tanky offers a clear projection of the potential consequences of breaking through the restraints of culture and belief. A bundle of appetites and desires, he clearly needs to be held in check by every form of established bond available. Paradoxically Ijah's loyalty to past affective bonds is misplaced. It merely hastens Tanky's release upon an unsuspecting world.

The example of Cousin Seckel, who gave Ijah the books about the Jesup expedition, is even less reassuring. An expert in Indian languages, Seckel spent his weekends in Madison, Wisconsin, recording Mohican folktales from a group of survivors. In Louisiana he learnt an Indian language from its last, moribund speaker. When the latter died, the tribe and its language lived on in Seckel alone. Seckel's belief in Diffusionism ("All culture was invented *once*, and spread from a single source," 256) precludes any optimism about the future, suggesting that what is lost is gone forever, rather than being susceptible of reinvention or replacement. If Seckel is identified with obsolescence, Ijah (who reflects at one point that he "can't seem to find the contemporaries I require", 259) is also a potential "Last of the Mohicans" in Chicago. Despite his efforts to hold together the scattered remnants of his tribe (the cousins) he is forced to recognise that most of them have either died or adapted to their new savage environment. Even their language has altered towards "Hoffa language" (237) in which "integrity" means a swindle and "We Care" (227) is stencilled on supermarket walls.

Along with their language has gone the larger part of their culture. Ijah's grandfather could recite the whole Babylonian Talmud. Cousin Motty's jokes, which depend upon knowledge of Hebrew texts, proverbs and parables were once "mythic" (264) to Ijah. Now they are about as comprehensible to his fellow Americans as the Koryak tales of women hanging their sexual organs in trees, or of Raven, the Koryak trickster-hero, finding his wife transformed into a palatial underground chamber (257). As the ostensible head of the family (258) Motty is identified with Raven as the tribe's "patriarch-comedian" (266). The potential loss to culture implicit in the fate of Motty's tales is expanded in the comparison between modernist poetry and his incomprehensible jokes: "Nobody knew what he was talking about. Too much Chinese in his cantos, too much Provencal" (264).

As a youth Motty had resembled an "Indian brave" (264). Now, however, following a road accident, he has to be strapped upright in an armchair; if he reclines pneumonia will result. None the less, Ijah's first impulse is to wish to release him from his bonds. Mentally he contrasts Motty with Tanky, in his high chair, and turns back to metaphysics and the Hegelian view of dissolution.

> An original self exists or, if you prefer, an original soul. ... I believed that Motty in his silence was consulting the "original person." The distorted one could die without regrets, perhaps was already dead. The seams open, the bonds dissolve, and the untenability of existence releases you back again to the original self. Then you are free to look for real being under the debris of modern ideas. (267–68)

Where Tanky illustrated the potential horrors attendant upon the dissolution of traditional values, Motty indicates the possible advantages of freedom from con-straining bonds. Where Ijah allowed family affection to influence him with regard to Tanky's imprisonment, he recognises that the kindest thing to do for Motty would be to let him die. Ijah comments that Motty is "down to nature" (265) now. Culture and history appear to have been mere excrescences, distortions of an original self which owes more to nature than to nurture. Unsurprisingly, perhaps, Ijah, consciously seeking to "revise or rearrange myself at the core" (259), turns away from his earlier faith in affective bonds, towards the reading of Heidegger. In order to counteract old affections, to move with the times, he rehearses every negative fact known about the cousins, declaring that "Hate is perspicuous" (287) and an aid to mental clarity.

It takes one more cousin to teach Ijah that truth and freedom can transcend both nature and culture. At the close of the story Ijah learns to stop adhering to the past, impotently resisting change, in order to embrace both philosophy and his fellow men. From Motty, Ijah has news of Cousin Scholem. According to Scholem, his discoveries in biology have facilitated the first breakthrough in philosophy since Kant's *Critique of Pure Reason*, and he seeks Ijah's help in publicising his theories and therefore, implicitly, in hastening the dissolution of the old and the advance of culture. Scholem is committed to ideals of human brotherhood, exemplified in his personal experience, in the moment in the Second World War when American and Russian troops met and fraternised, on the Elbe. He has devoted his life to internationalism and is currently in the process of organising a gathering of taxi-drivers from all over the world, in Paris. Although initially sceptical about Scholem's project to "find support in Nature and History for freedom" (276), Ijah eventually rises to the occasion. He is assisted by two more cousins, the one unambiguously faithful to tradition, the other just as firmly committed to adaptation. To assist Scholem, Ijah draws upon a philanthropic fund, established by Cousin Artie, a man whose only interest was philosophy: "Modern experience had never touched him" (278). The fund is administered by his polar opposite, Mendy, a man with such a "peculiar relish for being an American of his time" (277) that he has adopted the persona of a typical middle American of the Hoover or early Roosevelt period, specialising in baseball, vaudeville, and fights with his mother-in-law. While inadaptive Artie's interest in philosophy is perpetuated in the research fund, Mendy has discovered that "the model on which he formed himself has been wiped out" (278) and that he is as hard up for comprehension as Motty was. He, too, attempts to lay claim to Ijah, now poised between the demands of three cousins, distributed at equal intervals along the curve from total cynicism (Tanky) to complete idealism (Scholem) with Mendy occupying a middle position. All are his contemporaries; each indicates a possible direction of culture towards decline, rebirth, or merely obsolescence.

Before Ijah resolves his dilemma, he interrupts his account to discuss his unrequited love for Virgie Dunton, an eight-fingered lady who none the less triumphed over her biological endowment to become a concert harpist. Ijah has been sensible all his life to her "electric binding power" (285). He compares this bond to the longed for union of sundered opposites in the love myth of Aristophanes. This apparently irrelevant episode has a crucial bearing on the resolution of the story. At the close Ijah travels to Paris to attend a conference on the rescheduling of debts and in the process reschedules some of his own affective obligations. Approached yet again to intervene on Tanky's behalf, Ijah rejects the request, proceeding instead to meet Scholem. The decision is made in the representative locale of Napoleon's tomb. Although Ijah notes that Napoleon's wish to be buried simply in the midst of the French people has been translated into monumental pomp and circumstance, the occupation of the building by the internationalist gathering of taxi-drivers bears indirect witness to the ideals of fraternity and freedom which it commemorates.

Scholem's attempt to advance beyond Kant also re-establishes a connection with Hegel. It may seem odd that Ijah's mind moves so freely between the apparently unrelated topics of anthropology (the Chukchee and Koryak) and metaphysics (Hegel and Kant). The two fields of inquiry are, however, intimately connected in the figure of the Siberian shaman. Kant had argued that the worship of powerful, invisible beings first arose from man's consciousness of his own weakness, and was extorted by fear. Hence the dread of demons lay at the origin of all religions, and there was no real difference between the Siberian shaman (Kant cites those of the Tungus and Voguls) and European prelates.[22] Both placed the worship of the deity in external rites and customs, traditional dogma and ritual. By obeying the dictates of custom rather than the law of their own reason they were therefore unable morally to amend man. As Ijah puts it, "the real challenge is to capture and tame wickedness. Without this you remain suspended" (290). Kant therefore contrasted the religion of shamans and priests unfavourably with his own "religion of reason". Hegel, however, contended that the difference between "primitive" peoples and the follower of Kant was

> not that the former made themselves slaves while the latter is free, but that the former have their lord outside themselves, while the latter carries his lord in himself, yet at the same time is his own slave.[23]

In other words, in Kant's religion, man is still divided against himself, half slave or his own slave, enslaved to reason. What Hegel posited as a force superior to reason was love, which unifies man inwardly, binding man with man and man with himself. At the end of the story Ijah discovers that the power of hate is inferior to that of love. Whereas supposedly perspicuous, seer-like Ijah fails even to recognise Scholem, the spokesman for international unity, unambiguously clear-sighted, identifies Ijah at once. "The size of his eyes was exceptional — like the eyes of a new-born infant" (293). With a pang, Ijah realises that his memories and observations of the cousins have been a means of maintaining division and separateness, and of resisting change: "I had remembered, observed, studied the cousins, and these studies seemed to fix my own essence and to keep me as I had been. I had failed to include myself among them" (294). In finally including himself, Ijah also unites with a larger human group, following Hegel in the unification of his family principles with those of civil society. Watching the motley crowd of cabbies, he has a sudden illumination:

> Then it came to me how geography had been taught in the Chicago schools when I was a kid. We were issued a series of booklets: "Our Little Japanese Cousins," "Our Little Moroccan Cousins," "Our Little Russian Cousins," "Our Little Spanish Cousins." I read all these gentle descriptions about little Ivan and tiny Conchita, and my eager heart opened to them. Why, we were close, we were one under it all. ... We were not guineas, dagos, krauts; we were cousins. (292)

This was precisely the import of the Jesup Expedition, which revealed that the Chukchee and Koryak shared most features of their culture with the native peoples of the American North West, and were in fact related to them. Bogoras's popular account is entitled "Siberian Cousins of the Eskimo".[24] When Bellow mentions a Dina Brodsky, married to Waldemar Jochelson and also Ijah's cousin, he points to a more than personal relation.[25] Bogoras and Jochelson were political radicals for whom ethnography was the path to populism and international understanding.[26] They challenged the authorities of their day and spent ten years in exile in Siberia before being released to join the Jesup Expedition; Franz Boas wrote to Moscow to ask for their assistance. Their freedom from Siberian labour camps (unlike Tanky's wished for release) was therefore intimately connected with ideals of universalism, and of human brotherhood. The Jesup Expedition, founded (like Scholem's researches) by an American philanthropist, and jointly undertaken by Russians and Americans, exemplifies fraternal "cousinhood" in both its mode of organisation and its ultimate discoveries. Ijah had used the Chukchee as examples of divisive transcendence, as opposed to the binding power of human love. Bellow, however, asserts the values of "cousinhood" not in sentimental fashion, but as founded upon anthropological and metaphysical knowledge. At the close, when Ijah chooses his "genius" cousin over the gangster, he acts upon the realisation that human beings can collaborate in pursuit of an better future, that rather than being cousins in crime, Russians and Americans can cooperate in a mutual quest for freedom and truth. It seems a peculiarly apt point on which to conclude, in the light of the later rapprochement between East and West which, shaman-like, Bellow appears in "Cousins" to have anticipated.

Notes to Chapter 5

1. Saul Bellow, "Cousins," *Him with His Foot in his Mouth and Other Stories* (London: Secker and Warburg, 1984), 255. Subsequent page references in parentheses are to this edition.
2. In response to an audience question on the occasion of the Tanner Lectures, University of Oxford, May 1981.
3. Eusebio L Rodrigues, "Bellow's Africa," *American Literature*, 43, 2 (1971), 242–56.
4. Harvey Breit, *The Writer Observed* (London: Alvin Redman, 1957), 272.
5. Nina A. Steers, "'Successor' to Faulkner? An Interview with Saul Bellow," *Show*, 4 (September 1964), 36.
6. Saul Bellow, *To Jerusalem and Back: A Personal Account* (London: Secker and Warburg, 1976), 130–31.
7. Saul Bellow, *Henderson the Rain King* (London: Penguin, 1966), 60.
8. Rockwell Gray, Harry White and Gerald Nemanic, "Interview with Saul Bellow," *TriQuarterly*, 60 (1984), 21.
9. Saul Bellow, "The Civilized Barbarian Reader," *New York Times Book Review*, 8 March 1987, 1.
10. Ibid., 38.
11. Franz Boas, "An Anthropologist's Credo," *Nation*, 147 (1938), 201. See also *The Central Eskimo* (Washington: Sixth Annual Report of the Bureau of American Ethnology 1884–5, 1888).
12. Franz Boas, "An Anthropologist's Credo," 202.
13. Derek Freeman, *Margaret Mead and Samoa* (London: Penguin, 1984), 24.
14. Saul Bellow, "Deep Readers of the World Beware!" *New York Times Book Review*, 15 February 1959, 1, 34.
15. Alexander Goldenweiser, *Anthropology* (New York: F. S. Crofts, 1937); Melville J. Herskovits, *Franz Boas* (New York: Charles Scribner's Sons, 1953).
16. See Molly S. Wieting, "Function of the Trickster in Saul Bellow's Novel," *Saul Bellow Journal*, 3, 2 (1984), 23–31; Robert Birindelli, "Tamkin's Folly: Myths Old and New in *Seize the Day* by Saul Bellow," *Saul Bellow Journal*, 7, 2 (1988), 35–48; Judie Newman, "Bellow's Indian Givers," *Journal of American Studies*, 15, 2 (1981), 231–38.
17. Franz Boas, *The Jesup North Pacific Expedition. Memoir of the American Museum of Natural History. Vol. VI and Vol. VII* (New York: American Museum of Natural History, 1908). Reprinted as

Waldemar Jochelson, *The Koryak* (New York: AMS Press, 1975) and Waldemar Bogoras, *The Chukchee* (New York: AMS Press, 1975).

18. D. J. R. Bruckner, "The Axeman Melloweth," *The Times*, 8 May 1984, 10.

19. Printed as the epigraph to Alexandre Kojève, *Introduction to the Reading of Hegel*, trans. James H. Nichols, Jr., ed. Allan Bloom (New York: Basic Books, 1969). First published as *Introduction à la lecture de Hegel* (Paris: Gallimard, 1947). See also Shlomo Avineri, *Hegel's Theory of the Modern State* (Cambridge: Cambridge University Press, 1972), and J. Hoffmeister (ed.), *Dokumente zu Hegel's Entwicklung* (Stuttgart, 1936).

20. Paul Edwards, *The Encyclopaedia of Philosophy* (London: Macmillan, 1967).

21. Bellow mentions Provenzano in "Cousins" (231), a name which occurs in connection with plots to kill Kennedy and with the Hoffa murders. See Dan E. Moldea, *The Hoffa Wars: Teamsters, Rebels, Politicians and the Mob* (New York: Paddington Press, 1978), 420.

22. Immanuel Kant, *Religion within the Boundary of True Reason*, trans. J. W. Semple (Edinburgh: Thomas Clark, 1838), 235–36.

23. G. W. F. Hegel, *Early Theological Writings*, trans. T. M. Knox. (Chicago: University of Chicago Press, 1948), 211.

24. Waldemar Bogoras, "Siberian Cousins of the Eskimo," *Asia*, 29, 4 (1929), 316.

25. See John Perkins, *To The Ends of the Earth* (New York: Pantheon, 1981), 138. A photograph of Dina Brodsky and Waldemar Jochelson appears on page 139.

26. David L. Sills (ed.), *International Encyclopaedia of the Social Sciences* (New York: Macmillan and Free Press, 1968).

❖

CHAPTER 6

Telling a Woman's Story: Fiction as Biography and Biography as Fiction in Mary Gordon's *Men and Angels* and Alison Lurie's *The Truth about Lorin Jones*

> There are four ways to write a woman's life: the woman herself may tell it, in what she chooses to call an autobiography; she may tell it in what she chooses to call fiction; a biographer, woman or man, may write the woman's life in what is called a biography; or the woman may write her own life in advance of living it, unconsciously, and without recognising or naming the process. (Carolyn Heilbrun)

Notions of realism have always been problematic for the female subject. Although it is a truth well recognised that "Realism has little to do with reality"[1] but is rather a critical construct developed in response to a particular social and ideological climate, realism none the less rests its premises on the assumption of a direct correspondence between art and life. Its attendant methods of criticism therefore involve charting the similarities and differences between experiential reality and the artist's transcript, as if "experience" were common to all. George Eliot's stated aim, however, "to give a faithful account of men and things as they have mirrored themselves in my mind" is not quite so easily realised in the case of women.[2] As Rachel Brownstein memorably puts it "Female, a Quixote is no Quixote at all; told about a woman, the tale of being caught in a fantasy becomes the story of everyday life."[3] In the feminist argument reinscriptions of experience in literature are actually organisations — or fantasies — of the dominant male culture.[4] Because women are not mirrored in culture in ways that provide us with adequate self-definition, the creation of full-blooded, substantial identities and strong female representations remains an important project for the woman writer. In contrast, in its concern to decentre humanist notions of individuality and of universal and essential selves, postmodernism has tended to fragment identity, to reveal it as a flux of differently contextualised selves, or as the product of a system of differences. Women, however, may be forgiven for considering that they are too often already portrayed as fleeting, evanescent or silenced to wish to figure as postmodernist deconstructed selves. As a result, with a few honourable exceptions, postmodernist fiction has tended to offer only games for the boys.

In Mary Gordon's *Men and Angels*, Anne Foster applies for the post of director of the college gallery — unsuccessfully.

> When the president told her she hadn't got the director's job she'd applied for, and offered her the assistant's job, he said he knew she'd be happy that they'd offered the job to a woman, as if he believed she was applying for the job only as a gesture, as a member of a class, interchangeable with any other member, and so it didn't matter that she didn't get the job herself, since it existed for her only symbolically.[5]

Reduced in this fashion to a symbol of a biological category, it is small wonder that Anne leaps at the chance to investigate the life of a neglected American painter, Caroline Watson. Caroline, a loose amalgam of Suzanne Valadon, Cecilia Beaux, Mary Cassatt and Paula Modersohn-Becker, is a figurative painter, known for her studies of women and children, flowers and landscape — a fairly typical set of subjects for the female artist. Historically women have tended to be cut off from the "high" public realm of history painting — with its grand scale and rigorous anatomical demands, and have opted instead for the still life, portrait and genre painting, and hence often for the realistic depiction of everyday life.[6] On one level therefore, Caroline's paintings are necessary representations of the lives of women, offering "a universe exclusively female" (6) and recording how women's lives have been constructed by domestic society. As such, their non-idealised iconography has a clear political value. Annette Kuhn has identified the very real benefits of realist modes of representation in dealing with women's issues, as a product of the transparency which marks all forms of realism: "Articulated within a mode of representation that does not foreground its own processes of signification, political issues can stand out clearly."[7] On the other hand Caroline's realism has tactical disadvantages, not least in the opportunities it provides for the reductive comment. The next generation coo patronisingly over her draughtsmanship: "Such attention to drapery", "Such a finely modelled ear" (178). To the unsympathetic (in this case Helene) they are as easily dismissed as Anne herself:

> She was a complete materialist. Even what she called her intellectual life was sensual. Pictures of fat mothers with fat babies. (47)

In writing about Caroline, Anne faces a dilemma. Should she ignore Caroline's personal history, to focus on the history of art?[8] Or should she yield to her intuition that it is important to represent Caroline as fully as possible: "People were hungry for details of the lives of women" (71). Anne is aware, of course, that the equation of women with the flesh, matter or nature is a stereotypical one, and has its own perils:

> The truth of the matter was that for a woman to have accomplished something, she had to get out of the way of her own body. This was the trick people wanted to know about. ... people who were interested in the achievements of women wanted the grossest facts: Whom did they sleep with? Did they have any babies? Were their fathers kind to them, cruel to them? Did they obey or go against their mothers? Infantile questions, yet one felt one had to know. It gave courage, somehow. (71–72)

Alison Lurie's biographer-heroine, Polly Alter, faces the same dilemma in *her* quest for the truth about another female painter, Lorin Jones. Jones, however, has adopted different aesthetic tactics; her paintings are vague, elusive and fragmentary. Barely representational at all, constantly revised, with blank unfinished areas, floating figures and hermetic titles, they are designed (recognisably after the school of Larry Rivers) to mystify by absences and gaps. In little, the two painters demonstrate two possibilities for the woman artist: to make statements, as Caroline does, and risk being derided as mere "flesh", or to create postmodernist selves, deconstructed, oblique and therefore vulnerable to evanescence. As analogues to the work of the writer, the artist at the centre of each novel confronts the reader with a choice of alternative models for the female subject. Lorin's paintings create no danger of stereotyping, but she is perhaps too shadowy to be a useful model; Caroline's solid representations are too easily dismissed as gross materialism.

Importantly neither Lurie nor Gordon tells the tale of the artist directly. In each case a biographer intervenes between reader and artist. Recent commentators have suggested that biography — unlike literary criticism — remains in a state of relative innocence.[9] Just as third-person narrative best produces the illusion of pure reference, so biography tends to sustain an illusory reality, as the genre most dependent upon notions of an essential self, continuous through time. For any biographer, however, there remains the awareness that (to quote Roland Barthes) biography is "a novel that dare not speak its name"[10] and that the author faces similar choices to the painter. Indeed, the metaphor of the biographer as portrait painter is one which crops up frequently in biography. Psychological realism may demand a transformative attitude to the subject. Conversely, the subject of the biography may transform the life of the author — as in the famous example of André Maurois, who saw in Shelley a mirror of his own youthful emotions and wanted to tell the story of Shelley's life in order to liberate himself. Freud had this to say of biographers:

> Frequently they take the hero as the object of study because, for reasons of their personal emotional life, they bear him a special affection from the very outset. They then devote themselves to a work of idealization which strives to enrol the great man among their infantile models, and to revive through him, as it were, the conception of the father.[11]

Freud might equally well, of course, have described the opposite case (chain-saw biography, after the school of Kitty Kelley) in which the biographer selects a subject on whom to vent his spleen and exorcise unhappy memories. Alternatively, biographers can simply be surprised by unpleasant facts — as Lawrance Thompson was by Robert Frost, or as Polly Alter is by Lorin Jones.

But what of female biographers? For the feminist — and both Gordon's Anne Foster and Lurie's Polly Alter fit the bill — there are additional problems. Bell Gale Chevigny, the biographer of Margaret Fuller, has described her own anxieties about her sense of identification, and has related them to contemporary neo-Freudian concepts of the relation of mothers and daughters. Chevigny granted that biography offered a psychological intersection between the personality of biographer and subject, and therefore accepted that "it is nearly inevitable that women writing about women will symbolically reflect their internalised relations with their mothers and in some measure recreate them".[12]

In addition, however, Chevigny recognised the danger of introducing a fresh mode of distortion, a feminist fallacy, by projecting her own fantasies onto Fuller:

> The validating stress that feminist theory has laid on the personal, the confusions about the role of the personal in our theory, the urgency and the fervour associated with a movement to redress historical and current injustice — all make feminist biographers of women more susceptible to uncritical identification.[13]

On the positive side, identification may produce a deeper understanding. Just as Margaret Fuller may have felt that her mother was elusive, so that Fuller's *Woman in the Nineteenth Century* may have been a reparative text, so Chevigny felt that in exploring Fuller, in her turn, she had created a "mirroring self":

> when I sought to explain her, especially her confusing behaviour, I was generating analogous explanations or partial sanctions for aspects of my own behaviour. At the same time I was working as such a sanctioning mirror for her. To put it another way, I had created a "mother" of sorts for myself at the same time as I was acting as one for Fuller, "mothers" of the sort that would nurture the difficult and unsteady growth of autonomous selves in us.[14]

Obviously, women who are trying to make a different life for themselves from their biological mothers can benefit from supplementary models. Chevigny needed to recreate a feminist "mother" who could sanction what she herself wanted to become. In short she needed to create a sanctioning precedent.

Although such an enterprise may involve projection, Chevigny argues that the fantasy element can be constructively experienced. In the biographical process there is a stage at which author and subject become, in effect, "surrogate" or "foster" mothers, offering maternal nurture to each other, in a relation of reciprocity. Whether foremothers are famous and their stories distorted (Virginia Woolf perhaps) or (as in the case of the fictional Caroline Watson and Lorin Jones) neglected and unknown, writing about them is likely to be, on some level, an act of retrieval which is experienced as rescue. When the work is most intensely experienced as rescue, the fantasy of reciprocal relations is likely to be activated. Thus in rescuing a forgotten or misunderstood woman, the author may be seeking, indirectly, to rescue herself. The process is therefore a double-mothering; both "mothers" nurture not an infant but a woman, and for both nurturing is a sanctioning of their autonomy. In other words, as biographers, women recreate "mothers" with whom they can integrate — *and separate* — more effectively than from their biological mothers. As they enter — and separate — from the lives which they present, so the individuality of both "foremother" and "author" may be more firmly secured.

It is against this psychoanalytic understanding of the biographer's project that *Men and Angels* and *The Truth About Lorin Jones* demand to be read. Both heroines envisage their researches as a rescue mission. The appropriately surnamed Anne Foster describes the undertaking as follows: "What she had to do was build a house for a woman she loved ... Without the house that she would build, the woman she loved, dead forty-five years, unknown to almost everyone, could not be made to live" (70). The process is one of mothering. Anne says of Caroline that "I knew her almost as I know my own children" (65). In addition it demands uncritical identification.

> Only if she lived with Caroline as a beloved presence could she come close to her in understanding. To do justice to the dead required an intimacy in which justice had no part. ... you needed to embrace them with the unquestioning love with which you embraced an infant. (96)

Similarly, Polly Alter, an unsuccessful painter, is intent on recreating Lorin Jones as the victim of the male establishment — thereby implicitly sanctioning Polly's failure — and as a child to be rescued. Polly's maternal fantasy even extends to a trip back in time to the 1960s, to find Lorin Jones alive and well in Key West:

> "God damn it", Polly would say to her, "You've got to take more care of yourself. You've got to quit smoking, get more sleep, eat better, see a doctor about that cough. You can't give up now; you're a very great painter. You're going to be in art history."[15]

Baulked in this maternal enterprise by Lorin's death, Polly resolves to find out all the facts and publish: "Then the truth would be known, and not only Lorin's life but Polly's too would be justified and made whole" (4). In the light of this fantasy of reciprocal relations, it is clearly no accident that, while writing about Lorin, Polly acquires the liberated, nurturing Jeanne as a supplementary mother and model. Or, that Anne Foster's pursuit of Caroline, carried out in order to create a nurturing foremother, and thus, in reparative fantasy, a nurtured child-self, involves the employment of Laura Post, a miserably undernurtured childminder, as surrogate mother to Anne's children. The feminist rescue mission is attended with ironies, comic in Lurie's case, tragic in Gordon's. Just as Anne sets out to save Caroline from being written off as merely "flesh", so Laura, a religious fanatic, believes that she can save Anne from the lusts of the flesh, in a dark mirroring of Anne's own activities. Separation, in Laura's case, is final. Gordon's dead female artist is lovingly investigated and recreated at the price of a living girl.

In a lighter mode, Polly Alter's pursuit of the truth about her *alter ego* is doubled by her lesbian friend Jeanne, who in less high-minded but equally committed fashion pursues Betsy, a vapid and infantile student. Lurie's two pairs of seekers and sought strike a series of variations on the central psychoanalytic thesis, culminating in the separation of Polly from both Lorin (a less rewarding subject than she had imagined) and Jeanne, and a reidentification with the male world. Both novels, therefore, set up a series of mirrorings and doublings, both in terms of character and narrative mode, in order to investigate the means by which a woman's story may best be told, the utility or otherwise of models and precedents, and the status of realism in such telling. Although the major plot strand puts foremothers and daughters first, each novel is shadowed by the ghost of a male story — an Oedipal one — which, like the backing to a mirror, sets the feminist rescue mission in sharp relief.

Initially the action of *Men and Angels* appears as a powerful demonstration of the benefits of sanctioning foremothers. As the novel opens, Anne is revealed caught in the fantasies of others as the "pretty wife" (19) in a college town: "it was a struggle for a woman in Selby to feel she had a genuine existence. Maleness shaped the town" (19). As a result, Anne rejoices in the new status accorded her by her research work, which provides her with a room of her own (formerly her husband's study), full-time childcare, and even, ultimately, a permanent job. In addition, Jane, Caroline's daughter-in-law, becomes an important supplementary model whose regard Anne prizes:

> like a brilliant shield in which she saw herself enlarged and noble. She didn't want to see the image of herself diminishing to a well-drawn miniature of the perfect couple, decorative and minor. (212)

Clearly by working on Caroline, Anne has found a mirroring self to enlarge her own. Importantly Jane and Caroline hold to a realist aesthetic. Caroline attributes her colour sense to the influence of her grandmother's garden, roundly dismissing "fancy theories of the Fauve palette" (223). Describing a painting, Jane declares confidently that "It's me and Caroline" (128). For Jane the painting is transparent; it is "about" people and lives. Anne demurs: "But was it? It was as much about Caroline's learning to move her figures off centre" (128). She concludes that, "A painting was almost never itself" (129). Anne is exceptionally slow, however, to pursue the implications as they extend to her own life. Laura, on her parallel rescue mission, entirely caught in fantasy, offers an alternative mirroring self, to which Anne is quite blind. Yet Anne and Laura are more closely identified, in many respects, than Anne and Caroline. Both have ineffectual fathers and cold mothers, who openly prefer a younger sister. Both are pale redheads with blue eyes and large feet. Both have shut down on the "flesh", Anne temporarily, in her husband's absence, Laura as a result of childhood trauma. As young women, both spent a miserable period alone in London, Anne as a student, Laura as a dismissed childminder. The one is rescued by art, in the shape of Ben, a fatherly but lover-like art historian who subsequently commissions the study of Caroline, the other by religion. Both then engage in parallel rescue missions of their own, Anne to validate Caroline against her detractors, Laura, in shadow play, to promote the salvation of Anne, whom she sees as "sinking in the flesh" (47).

As the latter image suggests, Laura's desire for idealisation is related to a succession of images of embodiment as horror. Throughout the novel the traditional Judeo-Christian identifications of woman-as-flesh, man-as-spirit, are dramatised in their damaging effects. Laura, gauche and clumsy, is contrasted with her mother's controlled "well-cared-for body" (303) and with her sister's talents for dance. In childhood Laura feels her body "pushing her down to the earth while they danced high above it, light, like stars" (305). The image is generalised in relation to Anne's daughter, Sarah, who also attends dance classes, at which the mothers pay homage to the teacher, "with a sycophantic devotion born of their sense of the inadequacy of their own slow bodies" (208). Ironically however, in the dance recital it is not Sarah's body which causes disaster, but her heavy angel's wings, which tip her over and make her a figure of fun: "Overbalanced by her wings, she couldn't get up" (209). Sarah is subsequently seen, her wings removed, but her halo still in place, being comforted on her father's knee — a small tableau clearly alluding to the novel's title. In little, the scene dramatises the paradox that giving too much weight to the angelic, seeking a total transcendence of physicality (in religion or art) makes for a more resounding and damaging fall to earth. The presence of the father is also highly suggestive, and has a proleptic relevance to Laura. Laura's desire for ideal representations is a response to her mother, who placed the brute facts of physical existence squarely before her — from bodily processes to primal scene content. In contrast, Anne, in her experience of motherhood and in her aesthetic, enjoys a sense of the flesh as vital. Posed as a conflict between an art of transcendence or of flesh, the central debate of the novel, recognisably one of the key oppositions of modernism, is also culturally gendered, opposing what turns out to be male fantasy to female realism. Laura's female subjectivity is ultimately revealed as simply the mirror of another's (masculine) desire.

In this connection narrative method enacts theme. The opposition between alternative mirroring selves is also a contest of narrative modes. The narration is divided between third-person, realist Anne, on the one hand, and Laura's stream-of-consciousness, on the other, located squarely within religious fantasy. Anne's positive representation of Caroline is re-presented by Laura's doubling narrative, which often circles back to recapitulate previous events. Major occurrences are therefore twice-told, in realism and in fantasy. On the one hand Laura's re-presentation of Anne is often "mad"; the mirroring self distorts. (Laura believes that Anne will have fond memories of a Christmas which actually confirms Anne in her dislike of the girl.) On other occasions Laura gains insights unavailable to others — that Anne suspects her husband of adultery, for example. Doubling of narrative therefore reveals dissimilarities as well as gains by identification. Appropriately, perhaps, Laura's chapters, always slighter in bulk than Anne's, abbreviate as the novel progresses. The body of the text is Anne's. Ellen Macleod Mahon has speculated that this shrinkage of Laura is the result of her embroilment in fantasy, and thus of the lack of the corrective of external reality.[16] The possibility lingers that the narrative method places her fantasy idealisation as obsessive and destructive, and that it therefore licences, in some sense, her death. Laura edits out Anne's body and with it her own. Mahon's notion of reality as "corrective", however, itself rests on realist grounds. Laura's inability to "adjust" her text to a common experiential reality raises questions about the utility of realism as a means of admitting women to a place in discourse. Realism may represent more fully than fantasy — but it may also write some women out of existence. At one point, Anne describes Laura's obsessive housekeeping to her friends. To her surprise,

> as she told the stories everyone laughed. When she described Laura's refolding all the paper bags into precisely identical shapes, the three people at the table thought it was hilarious. (257)

Relieved at the discovery that Laura can be rewritten as a funny story, Anne feels "as if her friends had introduced her to a new invention, the typewriter" (257). It is an apt comparison. Essentially Laura is written off before she dies. The narrative erodes and loses Laura, just as the world does; her gradual reduction in textual space becomes proleptic of a death which is only the most extreme form of her slow silencing in the action.[17] Laura is apparently written out of existence, as Caroline is written in.

If the reproduction of mothering fails to save Laura, it is nevertheless largely the result of the reproduction of fathering which scripts her discourse. The apparent weaknesses of female realism are negligible compared with the maleness of Laura's fantastic text which underlines the persistence of masculine fantasy, and the dangers thereof. Laura's experience is organised according to the fantasies of male culture. Her narrative attempts to reinscribe realist Anne within a masculine discourse of fathers, God the father and hatred of the body of women. Like a female Quixote she sets out to rescue Anne but eventually consigns Anne to a repetition of the past. Two points are significant here: firstly, Laura's connection with her author's biography, and secondly, the manner of her suicide, which inflicts her own preceding traumatisation on Anne and Anne's children.

To understand Laura — and her relation to the novel's puzzling title and to the tableau of father and daughter — demands an excursion from fictional metabiography to biography pure. Critical assessments of *Men and Angels* have focussed almost exclusively on its interest in mothering, maternal splitting and the dynamics of the infant–mother bond.[18] Biography, however, leads to fathers as well as foremothers. In the novel fathers are ineffectual (Anne's and Laura's) or absent (Michael, Anne's husband, in France; Michael's father unknown; Stephen Watson illegitimate). Yet the action is remarkable for a recessive plot concerned with fathers. The subordination of fantasy to realism is also the subordination of the father's story to the mother's. One point is particularly suggestive here. In Jane's memories, Caroline is carefully marked off from a fellow expatriate, Jake Golden, from Ohio, at one point a journalist in Paris who subsequently went home to New York, founded a girlie magazine, moved to the far right, converted to Roman Catholicism and supported Franco. "Caroline broke with him after that" (225). In a moving essay about her own father, Mary Gordon has described him as from Ohio, a writer and expatriate in Paris, the founder of a girlie magazine, and a convert to Catholicism who supported Franco. If Caroline is carefully positioned as his polar opposite, Laura, however, has strong affiliations with him. David Gordon was

> a right-wing Catholic of a conservatism hard now even to grasp. He once wrote an article called "Roosevelt the Antichrist." He was obsessed by the corruption brought about by modernism.[19]

He was also a biographer — drawn to a topic with which he clearly felt a strong identification. Mary Gordon has described his manuscript on the work of Claudel as either "evil" or "mad":

> it must be mad, this thing he wrote. What would one call it? He calls it a biography of Paul Claudel, but there are almost no details of Claudel's life. The piece's structure is deeply hysterical. ... It is the angriest prose I can remember having read.[20]

Much of this anger was directed at modernist aesthetics. David Gordon accused Joyce, Yeats and Swinburne of being "merely beautiful":

For this is the point, if there is a point, of the piece he is writing: the destructiveness of making a religion of art. "Make no mistake about it," my father writes, "the Religion of Art is a religion. It pretends to supplant Christianity as the solution for the deepest problems of life and for the fear of death."[21]

Laura may be Anne's physical double, but in spirit she is modelled on the father. In addition to preferring her biological father to her rejecting mother, Laura has also espoused a patriarchal god, in the belief that she is "the chosen of the Lord" and will therefore always be "sheltered in her Father's arms" (13). The moment of conversion follows immediately on a scene of rejection by the mother. Thereafter her religious evolution is all at the hands of men — from the kindly Reverend Carr, via the "indiscriminate embraces" (107) of Father Delaney, to the predatory Fletcher Voss, self-styled "Father" of the cult, the Children of Light, in which a quasi-familial structure and "love-bombing" methods find a ready prey in love-starved Laura. Simultaneously exploiting and deriding the body of woman, using Laura as both domestic and sexual slave, Delaney and Voss offer the clearest possible reflection of the dangers of phallocentric appropriation of religious experience. Laura also condemns the Religion of Art. She laments that "Anne and Jane loved paintings as they should have loved the Spirit" (160), and is equally scornful of the written word: "Books would lead no one to the Spirit" (200). Exception is of course made for the Bible. Where Anne reads and researches to create her own space, Laura reads "to keep her place" (59). The image conflates place in discourse with place in the social order. Repetitively, ritualistically, Laura reads, not to advance in text or world, but to maintain her place in society. Like David Gordon, Laura has no interest in the merely beautiful; she is as happy to embroider Minnie Mouse as the beautiful Shaker tree of life (59). And in her final behaviour — which imperils the lives of Anne's children — she is either evil or mad. Even in reparative fantasy, Laura never escapes from the father. *Men and Angels* therefore sets its investigation of feminist biography on a collision course with a patriarchal discourse — social, religious, biographical — which shadows the feminist-affirmative fiction with an awareness of the extent to which a woman's self-image may still be shaped by a male-dominant society.

In addition, the novel highlights the ease with which male organisations of experience can reassert and replicate themselves. The denouement of the novel sets the feminist rescue mission in ironic perspective, by counterpoising an actual rescue to that of fantasy, both Anne's fantasy and Laura's. When Anne learns that her children — supposedly safe in Laura's care — are playing on dangerously thin ice, a real rescue mission on behalf of real children abruptly terminates Laura's fantasy. Discovered reading behind a rock, she is sacked on the spot. In the scene, Gordon explicitly signals the dangers of repetition of an old story. Laura's activity, reading and re-reading herself into patriarchal culture, is repetitive and dangerous, to Anne's children, and ultimately to herself. Above all, it condemns her to bodily re-enactment. (Sarah comments that Laura was moving her lips while reading.) As Laura's fantasy founders, so does Anne's. At this juncture Anne's enlarged vision of herself collapses into the one-dimensional: "Like a figure of allegory she had become one quality, one vice. She had become entirely anger" (274). Representation and reality are absolutely unallied. Just as Caroline's beautiful images of maternity were belied by her neglect of her son, so Anne's fantasy of reciprocity with Caroline does not extend to Laura. As an artist Caroline's example is liberating; as a mother she authorises the neglect of yet another unmothered child. No reparations can be made to Laura for her past. Anne's rage replicates the image of Laura's angry, punishing mother and sparks the final disaster. Laura's suicide demonstrates that some damage *is* irreparable. No amount of rescue and rewriting will bring her back to life. Laura, father-identified, is too damaged for effective reparations.

Just as Anne unwittingly repeats Laura's past, so no new story is possible for Laura; she can only repeat and reinscribe. Laura's increasing attachment to Anne has advanced in tandem with Anne's growing erotic attachment to Ed Corcoran, her handyman. When Ed — the only conscientious father of the novel — rejects Anne, in a refusal tinged with a father's scornful authority, he unwittingly authorises Laura's subsequent actions. Traumatised in childhood by the "filth" of her mother's house (278–79) Laura sees Anne's home as similarly defiled by the lusts of the flesh (278) and sets out to cleanse it with blood. By slashing her wrists in the bath, however, she fills the house with the maternal stain of blood passed through water. Importantly, one of the major casualties is Anne's library; her books will never be the same.[22] In her death Laura presents Anne with the blood, nakedness and physical mess which had originally traumatised her. Just as Laura cleaned up obsessively the signs of her mother's — and later Anne's — physical existence, so Anne now finds herself scrubbing away "the physical evidence" (287) and disposing of the body. "Spiritual" Laura is now all flesh. (Emphasis is placed on the weight of her dead body.)

In this connection the notion of bodily inscription is a key emphasis. At the beginning Laura had quoted the Bible:

> Can a woman forget her sucking child, that she should have no compassion on the child of her womb? Even these may forget, yet I will not forget you. Behold, I have graven you on the palms of my hands. (9)

Earlier Laura had attempted to carve her mother's name on the palms of her hands, but had failed: "She did not have the courage for her mother's name" (9). Instead, at the close Laura chooses to follow a more illustrious precedent, and a masculine model, and by writing/engraving in her own body reinscribes herself into the role of woman as flesh. Writing herself as body, she also writes her body into Anne's life. After Laura's suicide Anne undergoes a transformation. Where before, righteous in her desire to protect her children, she had seen Laura as a neglectful surrogate mother, Laura in death becomes once more a child: "She felt that Laura's body, having met death in her house, became her child" (288). As opposed to Anne's previous fantasy of making a house for Caroline, she has actually made one for Laura. As a result, Laura also becomes a mirroring sanction for Anne. After her death Anne acknowledges that because she had won her father away from her mother, she cannot ask her mother to come to the rescue (309). She accepts the myth of her "seduction" of the father, and is prepared to accept a definitive sense of separation from her mother, while incorporating Laura permanently into her consciousness. The possibility lingers that, as a victim of patriarchy, Laura is not so much pathologised as merely positioned somewhat further along the Oedipal continuum from Anne.

Men and Angels therefore demonstrates that realism, for all its strengths, may not provide a full defence against the persistent reinscriptions of women into male fantasies. Anne and Laura's fantasies continue to produce the reverse of their intentions, a representation of woman as blood, flesh and horror which quite erases the positive images of Caroline and Anne, and a rescue mission which ends in disaster. Gordon's emphasis on the real damage done by patriarchy sounds a cautionary note to the feminist biographer.

To turn to *The Truth About Lorin Jones* is to register a remarkable set of parallels between the two novels under discussion. Lurie continues the investigation of women's relation to artistic and social structures, and like Gordon examines the fashion in which pre-existent psychological patterns shape the ways in which we order the world, but in comic terms — perhaps unsurprisingly. Lurie's career began with biography, with a memoir of her friend, the poet and dramatist V. R. Lang. Lurie had failed to find a publisher for her early work, had indeed given up writing for a period, and it was only the biography which attracted a publisher's attention and which eventually launched her career as a novelist.[23] V. R. Lang was therefore considerably more than a sanctioning precedent. Writing her biography kick-started Lurie's own stalled career. Polly Alter's biography of Lorin Jones is also, potentially, a means of restarting her career as a painter. Newly divorced and a recent convert to lesbian feminism, Polly Alter searches for the truth about her *alter ego*, and is buttressed, in practical terms, in her fantasy of reciprocity, by her friend Jeanne, an incongruously fluffy lesbian separatist, given to needlework, cooking and cats, who adopts a maternal stance to Polly. Polly's early abandonment by her father and lukewarm relation to her exceptionally unliberated mother, make her as vulnerable to Jeanne as she is to an idealisation of Lorin as sanctioning precedent. Duplicitous Jeanne, the mother figure to Lorin-as-fantasy-child, takes over Polly's life and her apartment, very nearly ousting her son in the process. As Polly pursues Lorin through a series of interviews with the latter's friends, lovers and associates, the image of her as exploited by the male establishment begins to crumble in the face of the evidence — that Lorin lived off men, sacrificing everything and everyone to the demands of art. Unwelcome revelations about Lorin are accompanied by equally unpleasant discoveries about Jeanne. In a moment of revelation Polly realises that the all-female household which she has constituted for herself masks a reinscription of the pattern of her childhood.

> And now it seemed to Polly that the scene in the apartment was like a caricature of a traditional marriage. She was the cross husband, in worn jeans and baggy sweater, owner of the house and its main economic support, working late. The tactful, charming manipulative wife, in a flowered apron was making supper and the spoilt stepdaughter was pretending to help. (279)

As Polly's idealised image of Lorin corrects itself, so she is set free from manipulative

Jeanne, and the infantile Betsy, and recognises the need to safeguard real rather than imaginary offspring, in the shape of her son Stevie. Knowledge about Lorin is accompanied by self-knowledge. In a comic and symbolic moment, her father's present of an Etch-A-Sketch toy, desired since her childhood, reveals to Polly both her father's love for her, and her own preceding failures of love for him. The revelation immediately precedes her decision to commit herself anew to men, specifically Hugh Cameron. The transparently Oedipal overtones here — Cameron is the ex-lover of Lorin, Polly's chosen foremother — are teasingly recognised and belied in the Etch-A-Sketch toy. An Etch-A-Sketch involves a magnetised screen on which drawings can be made with a wand. A shake of the screen and the drawing disappears.[24] In short it allows a picture to be both produced and erased, reproduced and corrected.

Just as Polly corrects her picture of Lorin, so the reader is actively involved in the same process. Here it is not reality which is corrective but the reader. In the novel third-person narration alternates with transcriptions of taped interviews, which reveal a woman as multifaceted as a Cubist painting, alternatively shy, spiteful, generous, unscrupulous, schizoid or grasping, according to the vested interests of the person telling Lorin's story, the interviewee.[25] These apparently perfect transcriptions from life, however, lack a vital element. Only responses are given. The reader is left to second-guess Polly's questions and therefore to take on her interrogative role. Just as Lorin's paintings left blank spaces, absences, incomplete areas, so Lurie's text replicates her mystery. As Lorin's paintings made viewers project themselves into the vision, as Polly has projected herself into Lorin's life, so the reader becomes an active presence within the novel and must struggle to maintain an independent view. Narrative method therefore dramatises the uneasy relation of nurturance and autonomy which is its subject. Lorin is less a "real" female subject than a discursive construct, co-produced by author and readers, a process which clearly privileges the construction of meaning over the raw event. As a minor character puts it: "Events happen to you, sure but it's up to you to decide what they mean" (189).

Polly is left with a dilemma. Should she write an orthodox analytic biography, aimed at the art world? Or a feminist exposé? Should she draw a flattering portrait, or one with "warts and all"? And what kind of life and career will she choose *for herself* by the kind of book which she composes? In her mind's eye Polly envisages a series of visions of her future self, a figure of power and importance in the art world, or alternatively as an impoverished feminist, in full awareness that she was "about to choose, not only a version of Lorin Jones' past, but also her own unattractive future" (290). At the end, just as Lurie employs a postmodernist method in which the truth about Lorin becomes many different truths, so Polly opts for a metabiography in which all her findings, contradictory or otherwise, will be pluralistically presented.[26] In so doing she also opts for Hugh Cameron and a renewed career as a painter. Lorin's ambiguity is in the end more fruitful for her biographer than Caroline Watson's solid representations. Because Lorin's life is almost as mysterious as her paintings, Polly has to choose her own life story and authorise herself. Lorin can be at best only a partial model, and paradoxically that is the source of Polly's freedom. As Polly corrects a fantasy of Lorin-as-innocent-victim, so the novel invites the reader to participate in — and separate from — the fantasy, to form the picture and to correct it. In consequence, as Lurie privileges a postmodernist or metafictional discourse over transcriptions of "reality", so she privileges fiction over biography, and story over lives. Where Laura's case demonstrated how access to discourse may involve submission to phallocentricity, the masculine and the symbolic, where Anne found only a partial and unreliable sanctioning foremother in Caroline, Polly finds in Lorin — because fragmented, because a construction — a means to script her own life and take control of her own plot. Lurie therefore moves away from biography and towards fiction as the preferred enhancer of a woman's autonomy, and she is in good feminist company. To quote Carolyn Heilbrun:

> What matters is that lives do not serve as models; only stories do that. And it is a hard thing to make up stories to live by. We can only retell and live life by the stories that we have read or heard. We live our lives through texts.[27]

Where Laura's life may not be rewritten, Lurie argues for a sense of alternative destinies, that to choose a story is to choose a life. Fiction becomes biography — and biography fiction. Polly's biography of Lorin will be metafictional but it will script Polly's life thereafter. As lives become stories, so stories become lives. Polly Alter therefore sets out to construct both a new life for Lorin Jones and for herself. Whether she can do so without the kinds of cost indicated by Gordon is a problem passed on to the reader.

Notes to Chapter 6

1. Alison Lee, *Realism and Power: Postmodern British Fiction* (London: Routledge, 1990), 3. Lee's succinct discussion of realism deserves to be more widely known. On the relation of women to postmodernism see Patricia Waugh, *Feminine Fictions: Revisiting the Postmodern* (New York and London: Routledge and Kegan Paul, 1989).
2. George Eliot, *Adam Bede* (London: Penguin 1980), 221.
3. Rachel Brownstein, *Becoming a Heroine* (New York: Viking, 1982). Quoted in Carolyn Heilbrun, *Writing a Woman's Life* (London and New York: W. W. Norton, 1988), 76.
4. Nancy K. Miller, *Subject to Change: Reading Feminist Writing* (New York: Columbia University Press, 1988), 43.
5. Mary Gordon, *Men and Angels* (London: Penguin, 1986), 20. Subsequent references follow quotations in parentheses.
6. Linda Nochlin, *Women, Art, and Power, and Other Essays* (London: Thames and Hudson, 1989), 86.
7. Annette Kuhn, "Real Women," in Judith Newton and Deborah Rosenfelt (eds), *Feminist Criticism and Social Change: Sex, Class, and Race in Literature and Culture* (London: Methuen, 1985), 270.
8. Recent feminist art-historians have argued that the individual biographies of women artists have been overemphasised to the detriment of serious consideration of their art. See Rozsika Parker and Griselda Pollock, *Old Mistresses* (London: Routledge and Kegan Paul, 1981), xix.
9. Stephen Logan, "Uncluttered by cloisters," *Observer*, 14 April 1991, 63; Ira Bruce Nadel, *Biography, Fiction, Fact and Form* (London: Macmillan, 1984).
10. Heilbrun, 28.

11. Sigmund Freud, *Leonardo da Vinci: A Psychosexual Study of an Infantile Reminiscence* (London: Routledge and Kegan Paul, 1948), 115–16. Interestingly Freud's discussion centres on Leonardo as marked by the absence of a father but doubly mothered by a biological mother and a stepmother.

12. Bell Gale Chevigny, "Daughters Writing: Toward a Theory of Women's Biography," *Feminist Studies*, 9 (1983), 80.

13. Ibid., 81.

14. Chevigny, 94.

15. Alison Lurie, *The Truth about Lorin Jones* (London: Michael Joseph, 1988), 4. Subsequent references follow quotations in parentheses.

16. Ellen Macleod Mahon, "The Displaced Balance: Mary Gordon's *Men and Angels*," in Mickey Pearlman (ed.), *Mother Puzzles: Daughters and Mothers in Contemporary American Literature* (Westport, CT: Greenwood Press, 1989), 91–99.

17. I have learned here from Paula Le Gallez, *The Rhys Woman* (London: Macmillan, 1990), 9–21, a discussion of the process of textual reduction of an alter ego in Jean Rhys, "La Grosse Fifi".

18. See Ellen Macleod Mahon (as above); Susan Rubin Suleiman," "On Maternal Splitting: A Propos of Mary *Gordon's Men and Angels*," *Signs: Journal of Women in Culture and Society*, 14 (1988), 25–41; Ann Janine Morey, "Beyond Updike: Incarnated Love in the Novels of Mary Gordon," *Christian Century*, 20 November 1985, 1059–63. Mahon highlights the role of Jane as Caroline's foster daughter, and parallel to Laura; Suleiman discusses the impulse to split the maternal figure into "good" and "bad" mothers, as in psychoanalytic readings of fairy tales, and examines Anne, Laura and Caroline as doubles; Morey considers the theme of incarnation and embodiment in relation to the theological identification of woman with the body. The emphasis on motherhood was reinforced by Gordon in "On Mothership and Authorhood," *New York Times Book Review*, 10 February 1985, 1, 34–35.

19. Mary Gordon, "My Father's Daughter," *Mademoiselle*, May 1985, 250.

20. Ibid.

21. Ibid., 252.

22. Gordon says of Anne's books, "I'm obsessed by the objective correlative, of the emotional damage being physical damage." in M. Deiter Keyishian, "Radical Damage: An Interview with Mary Gordon," *The Literary Review*, 32, 1 (1988), 71.

23. Alison Lurie, *V. R. Lang: A Memoir*, privately printed, 1959; and in *V. R. Lang: Poems and Plays* (New York: Random House, 1975). Like Lorin Jones, V. R. Lang was a woman of many different personae. Like Lorin and Polly she visited Key West, where she met her husband. Lurie describes her own early publishing difficulties in "No One Asked Me to Write as Novel," *New York Times Book Review*, 87 (6 June 1982), 13, 46–48.

24. As described by Alison Lurie. Personal interview, Key West, 19 February 1991. I am grateful to the British Academy and the Research Committee of the University of Newcastle Upon Tyne for grants to enable me to visit the United States in February 1991.

25. Since most of Polly's interviewees are "carry-over" characters from Lurie's other novels, the reader has *their* fictional biographies as available information, often ironising or undercutting their accounts of Lorin.

26. A suggestive example exists in the biography of Edie Sedgwick, Sixties pop star, which juxtaposes comments quoted without linking narrative from various sources who speak with — and against — each other through quoted transcripts. The narrator is almost entirely removed from the text. See Jean Stein, *Edie: An American Biography* (London: Cape, 1982).

27. Heilbrun, 37.

CHAPTER 7

Postcolonial Gothic:
Ruth Prawer Jhabvala and the
Sobhraj Case

Gothic motifs are exceptionally prevalent in postcolonial fiction, even from very different locations. Classic postcolonial transformations of Gothic emanate from the Caribbean (Jean Rhys's *Wide Sargasso Sea*), Africa (Bessie Head's *A Question of Power*) and India (Ruth Prawer Jhabvala's *Heat and Dust*). In Canada, Gothic is almost the norm, whether in Margaret Atwood's comic *Lady Oracle*, or Anne Hébert's *Héloise* (the Québécois tale of a vampire who haunts the Paris Metro), or Bharati Mukherjee's Asian-Canadian *Jasmine*. Not surprisingly, when the heroine of Alice Munro's *Lives of Girls and Women* thinks of writing about Jubilee, Ontario, she promptly chooses to begin a Gothic novel. Nearer home, ghosts wander the pages of Paul Scott's *Raj Quartet*, and J. G. Farrell begins his *Empire Trilogy* in a decaying Great House, complete with mysteriously fading heroine, demonic cats, and an ever-widening crack in the external wall. Further afield, what is Isak Dinesen doing on a coffee farm in Kenya in 1931 but writing *Seven Gothic Tales*?

It is Dinesen's activity which first raises the question of the ideological consequences of the transfer of a European genre to a colonial environment. Gothic does not always travel well. As Eric O. Johannesson was swift to note, Dinesen creates a fictional Africa which is the counterpart of the eighteenth-century European feudal world of her tales.[1] Setting out into an African forest, she writes: "You ride out into the depths of an old tapestry, in places faded and in others darkened with age, but marvellously rich in green shades").[2] One suspects the Kikuyu did not share her view of a leopard as "a tapestry animal".[3] (Dinesen exemplifies here the tendency of the West to textualise the colonial, to transform the Other into a set of codes and discourses which can be recuperated into its own system of recognition, as hegemonic discourse accomplishes its project of endlessly replicating itself.) The consequences of generic transfer suggest, then, the difficulty implicit in any counter-discourse — the danger of reinscribing the norms of the dominant discourse within its own apparent contestation, as (to quote Richard Terdiman), "the contesters discover that the authority they sought to undermine is reinforced by the very fact of its having been chosen, as dominant discourse, for opposition". [4]

Rewritings, counter-texts, run the risk of slippage from oppositional to surreptitiously collusive positions. Postcolonial Gothic is therefore Janus-faced. At its heart lies the unresolved conflict between the imperial power and the former colony, which the mystery at the centre of its plot both figures and conceals. Its discourse therefore establishes a dynamic between the unspoken and the "spoken for" — on the one hand the silenced colonial subject rendered inadmissible to discourse, on the other that discourse itself which keeps telling the story again and again on its own terms. As a European genre, Gothic cannot unbind all its historical ties to the West. Conversely, its ability to retrace the unseen and unsaid of culture renders it peculiarly well-adapted to articulating the untold stories of the colonial experience. Eve Kosofsky Sedgwick has analysed the Gothic emphasis on the "unspeakable", both in the intensificatory sense of "nameless horrors" and in the play of the narrative structure itself, with its illegible manuscripts, stories within stories, secret confessions, and general difficulty in getting the story told at all. As Sedgwick puts it, Gothic novels are "like Watergate transcripts. The story does get through, but in a muffled form, with a distorted time sense, and accompanied by a kind of despair about any direct use of language."[5]

In her analysis a central privation of Gothic is that of language. When the linguistic safety valve between inside and outside is closed off, all knowledge becomes solitary, furtive and explosive. As a result, dire knowledge may be shared, but it cannot be acknowledged to be shared, and is therefore "shared separately", as the barrier of unspeakableness separates those who know the same thing. This Gothic apartheid is almost a classic definition of Imperialism's hidden discourse — the collaboration in a surreptitious relationship, never openly articulated, which is that of coloniser and colonised.

It is possible, however, for a novel to exploit both strategies — to politicise Gothic by overcoming the taboo on speaking, without slipping into the dominant discourse. A symptomatic reading of Ruth Prawer Jhabvala's *Three Continents* is instructive. *Three Continents* is situated at the sharp end of the Gothic generic transfer, both because of its Indian subject matter, and because of its relation to one of the West's more recent horror stories: the Sobhraj case. Jhabvala indicates the relationship of the "unspoken" of Gothic with the activity of "speaking for" of culture by firmly connecting the "unspeakable" nature of events (dark hints, half-told stories) to a story which has already been told so often as to be recognisably a product of Western hegemonic discourse. In modelling her central protagonist, Crishi, upon Charles Sobhraj, the Asian serial killer, Jhabvala contests a dominant cultural narrative while she avoids buying into the cultural stereotype of the exotic Gothic villain. Rather than shifting the problem of violence onto universal grounds (Gothic evil), Jhabvala emphasises the mutual implication of literary, cultural and political texts in its production. Social dislocation and socioeconomic dispossession in the wake of the end of Empire become determining factors in the representation of the Gothic protagonist.

A strong strain of Gothic has been identified in the works of Jhabvala, which feature demon lovers, mysterious Indian palaces with intricately concealed secrets, ruined forts, poison, willing victims, and the eroticisation of spirituality, with gurus standing in for sinister monks and ashrams for convents.[6] Jhabvala is, of course, influenced by eighteenth-century European literature. Her London University MA thesis concerned "The Short-Story in England 1700–1753", and among other topics discussed are the Oriental tale and the falseness of its "East", which was based on preconceived literary notions. Jhabvala also lamented the prevalence of the tale of the "unfortunate maiden fallen into the hands of a dusky seducer".[7] This is nonetheless precisely the plot of *Three Continents,* in which Harriet Wishwell, the scion of a wealthy, if now declining, American clan, stands to inherit a fortune with her twin, Michael, on their twenty-first birthday. When the pair fall under the spell of the mysterious Rawul, one of Jhabvala's ambivalent guru figures, the possibility looms that their legacy will pass swiftly through his hands and into those of his charismatic second-in-command Crishi, Harriet's husband, whose sexual favours she shares with homosexual Michael and the Rawul's mistress, Rani. In the novel Jhabvala conflates historical Gothic with the plot of modern Gothic. As defined by Joanna Russ, the latter involves a young, shy, passive heroine, with absent or ineffectual parents and a friend or ally in the pale, bloodless "Shadow Male".[8] She travels to exotic settings, forms a connection with a dark, magnetic "Supermale", finds herself up against "Another Woman", and has to solve a "Buried Ominous Secret", usually in modern Gothic a criminal activity centred on money. The plot generally ends in attempted murder. In *Three Continents* the exotic area is India; the persecuted Harriet is totally passive and after an initial ambivalence towards dark, super-phallic Crishi, becomes his sexual slave, disregarding sinister rumours. (There was, of course, a first wife with a nameless fate.) Rani features as the other woman. Harriet's family includes a conventionally vapid mother and a pathologically spendthrift father, neither of whom is much help to her. The pallid Michael fulfils the textbook role of the Shadow Male, apparently representing the security of childhood, but actually inducting Harriet into the Rawul's "Sixth World" movement. The Buried Ominous Secret turns out to be an international smuggling ring, masterminded by Crishi, who transports jewels and *objets d'art* across borders under cover of the movement. Throughout the novel the reader is afforded glimpses of the real situation, with recurrent dark hints and a veritable anthology of half-told stories and half-heard conversations in the wings, creating an atmosphere of sustained menace. Elements of historical Gothic are self-consciously introduced, often in a fashion which suggests the conditioning force of the literary genre on Harriet. Her first encounter with Crishi in her brother's room is presented as an erotic shock, "as of a live wire suddenly coming in contact with an innermost part of one's being", though the demon-lover has appeared only to borrow some shaving cream.[9] Later he succeeds in binding Harriet to him, forcing her body to move in unison with his "as if my body obeyed him more than it did me" (59) until she makes good her escape and flees, in true Gothic heroine mode: "I didn't stop running till I was in the house" (60). The scene is somewhat undercut by the fact that what Crishi was enjoying was a three-legged race at a Fourth of July party. Nonetheless, Harriet soon awakens in the night "suddenly as if someone had called me" (111). As a matter of fact, somebody has — Crishi — who is standing by her bed (no Jane Eyre long-distance telepathy here). The couple repair to the emblematic locale of the ruined Linton house, where, after peering through the windows at its ruined splendours (Cathy and Heathcliff), Crishi seduces Harriet. Later, exulting in passion, Harriet describes herself as "a woman savage running to her mate" (115) when in fact she has been dispatched to fetch Crishi's trousers. Quite clearly Jhabvala is consciously exploiting Gothic conventions while underlining the distinction between the conditioning force of literary genre and the resistant fact of Crishi. A group of "bhais", the Rawul's henchmen, rival any eighteenth-century group of banditti, and Rani takes to haunting Harriet's bedroom by night, "her reflection ghostlike in the mirror" (304), like some madwoman in the attic. After a journey through "uncharted regions" (366) sealed in a small chamber lit by a ghostly blue light (the sleeping coupe of an Indian train — an interesting variation on the Gothic image of live burial), the novel ends with the ascent of a winding stair to a crenellated roof terrace, reminiscent of Thornfield Hall, where all is revealed by the villain. The twist in the tale lies in Harriet's transition from victimhood to complicity. At the close, Harriet joins with her demon-lover to conceal Michael's murder and to forge the suicide note which will ensure that his fortune passes to them.

As a smuggler of art objects, Crishi is explicitly connected to the cynical and exploitative transfer of art from one culture to another, in his case via the plundering of the East to the benefit of the West. The questions raised by generic transfer are therefore thematised within the action itself. Artistic transfer is nonetheless a two-way traffic, as Jhabvala's exploitation of European conventions in a postcolonial environment demonstrates. Is this use of "Asian Gothic" merely a Eurocentric, Orientalist strategy, to adopt Edward Said's terminology? Or does it offer the postcolonial writer opportunities to criticise European textual and ideological practices by strategies unavailable to the realist novel? Does it merely contribute to the already abundant literature of India as horror story? Or can it illuminate the roots of violence in the postcolonial situation?

The answer to these questions depends upon an informed awareness of the other story within the novel. Sobhraj's early life stands as emblematic of all those who have been displaced, whether by war, the redrawing of territorial boundaries, changes in cultural sovereignty, political oppression or economic dispossession: all are factors which interact in the production of his story. As the illegitimate offspring of a Vietnamese mother and an Indian father, born in Saigon when it was under Japanese occupation administered by the Vichy French regime, Sobhraj's early experiences included capture by the Vietminh, rescue by the British, abandonment by his mother who married a French lieutenant, and life on the streets of Saigon. When French defensive activity reintensified and the lieutenant returned, his mother reclaimed him, only to move to Dhakar, French West Africa, then France. Sobhraj ran away by ship to Saigon, only to be promptly sent to Bombay by his father in a vain attempt to gain Indian citizenship. Stateless, institutionalised at various points, Sobhraj shuttled between countries until adulthood, excluded from the dream of nationality, economic security or family identity.

In the 1970s Sobhraj left a trail of bodies across India, Thailand and Nepal; he specialised in smuggling gems for which he needed a constant supply of fresh passports, bought or stolen from overlanders on the hippie trail. He then graduated to the *modus operandi* of a "drug and rob" man, first surreptitiously administering laxatives and other drugs, then "medicines" which reduced his victims to helplessness. Many of his targets, like Harriet and Michael, were seeking mystic enlightenment in the East. While planning to rob the jewellery store in Delhi's Imperial Hotel in 1976, Sobhraj was finally caught when he drugged an entire package tour of sixty French graduate engineers, whose instantaneous and simultaneous collapses in their hotel lobby finally aroused suspicion. Sobhraj was at various points arrested and jailed in Kabul, Teheran, Greece and Paris, and made several daring escapes, notably following an unnecessary appendectomy, from which he bore identifying scars. A man of considerable charisma, he often gained the sympathy of his victims and accomplices by tales of his awful youth (as Crishi does with Harriet). His main female accomplice, a young Canadian, appears to have been kept in total sexual thrall to him. Other parallels with the fictitious Crishi are legion. Both men spend part of their youth in Bombay (110), live by jewel smuggling and participate in murder. The hotel jewellery shop is the locus of mystery in *Three Continents*. Crishi goes in for martial exercises (for Sobhraj, it was karate), has abdominal scars, prison sentences in Teheran and elsewhere (139) and has carried out jailbreaks (176). Both Sobhraj and Crishi relish media exposure, the former after his arrest, the latter in connection with the "Sixth World" movement. For both, mobility is all. Harriet tends to assume that Crishi is somewhere around the house, only to receive phone calls from New York or Zurich. (Sobhraj once walked out saying that he would be back in an hour, then sent a telegram from Iran.) At the close, when Harriet is looking for Michael, she encounters Paul, one of the Westerners, who is clearly very unwell. Like others in the group, he has given Crishi his passport and is begging for its return. It is an exact replication of the means by which Sobhraj surrounded himself with couriers, targets and accomplices. Paul came to India "to get away from home, from his family, from himself ... not to be bound by anything" (353). Boundless freedom has left him, however, without the means to move on, in a position of statelessness.

Charles Sobhraj's story has already been told several times, in two works of "faction", one since revised and updated, in a TV mini-series, and in various newspapers and magazines, quite sufficient to suggest that the Sobhraj case is one of those "Orientalist" horror stories which the West likes to repeat.[10] From the first, the story served ideological purposes. In India it broke at an opportune moment during the Emergency Rule powers of Indira Gandhi, when the Maintenance of Internal Security Act meant that anyone suspected of "subversion" could be jailed indefinitely. In India the international dimension of the story was insisted upon: "India's newspapers, subdued and fearful under Indira Gandhi's dictatorial powers, relished a story that had no political overtones. The 'notorious gang' and 'international killers' were profiled endlessly, mug shots decorating Sunday feature pages."[11]

In the West the evolution of the story was classically hegemonic, its political complexities steadily watered down in favour of a stereotypically Orientalist tale. One of the first in the field, Thomas Thompson, in his "faction", *Serpentine*, drew explicit parallels between the events of Sobhraj's life and the dismantling of the French colonial empire. Thompson's portrayal of him as a casualty of colonialism, lacking roots, security and identity, ends on a note that appears to have offered Jhabvala the cue for the American opening of her novel. In jail in India Sobhraj was apparently considering his future:

> He required a country in which he was neither known nor wanted by police, one in which riches abounded, one whose boundaries were easy to traverse illegally, one whose residents were generous with attention and applause. At last report, the serpentine roads of destiny — he believed — would lead him to the United States.[12]

Thompson's implicit recourse, here, to the "invasion scare" model of Gothic is very much the emphasis of other works, which have tended to minimise the postcolonial background. In *Bad Blood* Richard Neville and Julie Clarke read Sobhraj in terms of a paradigm of early deprivation. Neville went to Delhi to interview Sobhraj with a theory "of Charles as a child of colonialism, revenging himself on the counterculture".[13] He concluded, however, that Sobhraj's claims to anti-Imperialist motivation were groundless, and read his story in terms of individual psychological rejection. Updating the book ten years later for a television mini-series, Neville revealed that his relationship with his co-author had been severely threatened by his involvement in the case, and that the pair had come close to being polarised into victim and accomplice. Julie Clarke's sympathies had remained with the killer's victims; Neville however admitted that when interviewing Sobhraj he came to feel "like a conspirator".[14] The mini-series, *Shadow of the Cobra*, developed the hint, focusing its plot on the threat to one romantic relationship (two young journalists) and transforming Sobhraj from child of colonialism to diabolical villain.[15] In an artistic trajectory which says much for the extent to which the rage for the Raj has been transformed into the redemonisation of the East, the role of Sobhraj was taken by Art Malik, veteran of *The Jewel in the Crown*, *The Far Pavilions* and *Passage to India*. The blurb to the reissued tie-in said it all: "An audience with psychopathic mass murderer Charles Sobhraj. It was like having supper with the devil." Reviewers concurred that Sobhraj was a "plausible, Bruce Lee style, Asian fiend"[16] operating in the "dangerous jungle" of Asia.[17] There, this "diabolically charismatic"[18] villain took his victim on a "descent into hell".[19] The evolution of the various accounts shows the West writing and rewriting Sobhraj into the norms of the snaky Oriental villain, with socio-economic readings excised in favour of (at best) popular psychoanalysis, and (at worst) elements of *Vathek*, Milton's Satan and Fu Man Chu.

In contrast, Jhabvala's understanding of the socio-economic dimension of the story is already evident in her first attempt at the theme. In her short story "Expiation", the plot centres upon a nouveau riche Indian family who have made a fortune in textiles, and their son's fatal involvement with Sachu, a criminal from a deprived background. Sachu's target for kidnap, ransom and murder is the child of an Indian military family, described as light-skinned educated gentry who speak Hindi with an accent "like Sahibs".[20] Arrested, Sachu boasts of his philosophy to the press, much as Sobhraj did. In "Expiation", the crime is less the product of a fiendish Oriental torturer than a revenge across both class and race, against the preceding Imperial norms (the Sahibs) and their replication in a newly industrialised India.

The account chimes with recent research on the serial killer, which contextualises his motivation in socio-economic terms. Anthropologist Elliott Leyton has argued that serial killers are intensely class conscious and obsessed with status.[21] The majority are adopted, illegitimate or institutionalised in youth, and seek a sense of identity in international celebrity. Typically, their victims are drawn from a social category above that of the killer, and the prime mission is to wreak revenge on the established order. (Ted Bundy, for example, took the most valuable "possessions" of the American middle class, their beautiful and talented university women.) In "Expiation" the fictitious Sachu wreaks revenge simultaneously on the Eurocentric army officers *and* the new entrepreneurial class via the deaths of both their offspring. For Leyton, as for Jhabvala, serial killers are the dark consequences of the social and economic formations that pattern our lives. Killings of this nature are a protest against a perceived exclusion from social discourse, and constitute a form of utterance on the part of those who have looked at their lives and pronounced them unliveable:

> The killings are thus also a form of suicide note (literally so with most mass murderers, who expect to die before the day or week is out; metaphorically so for most serial murderers, who sacrifice the remainder of their lives to the "cause"), in which the killer states clearly which social category has excluded him.[22]

The act itself is therefore the "note", an unspeakable crime which is nonetheless a message that society must learn to read. Unlike mass murderers, serial killers tend to want to live to tell their stories and bask in fame. Once society has read the message, the story will be retold by press and media, and become a means to identity. Two other factors cited by Leyton in the formation of the serial killer have a bearing on *Three Continents*: firstly, the inculcation of a dream or ambition which society betrays, and secondly the necessary existence of cultural forms that can mediate killer and victim in a special sense, ridding victims of humanity and killer of responsibility. (Leyton cites the social validation of violent identity in modern films, television and fiction. Jhabvala employs a totalitarian political movement.)

In recasting events in the Gothic mould Jhabvala is able to repoliticise the story, revealing its horrors without stereotypical demonisation by insisting on the interrelationship of the Gothic "unspeakable" and the "spoken for" of culture, the discourse from which the postcolonial is excluded, the discourse into which the Other can break only by violence.

Where the Sobhraj case was used in India as a diversion from the increasingly dictatorial nature of the political settlement, Jhabvala supplies a public political dimension by the introduction of the Rawul's militaristic "Sixth World" movement, which dehumanises its followers and legitimises brutality on the basis of a vaguely transcendental cult. Ostensibly devoted to the unification of the globe by "Transcendental Internationalism", the Rawul plans its transformation into a "stateless, casteless, countryless" (201) world by transcending not so much spiritual as national and political bounds, and with them "the tiny concepts, geographical or other, of an earlier humanity" (241). Linda Bayer-Berenbaum has connected the resurgence of twentieth-century Gothic with the waning of Sixties cults, arguing that both movements were motivated by the search for an expanded and intensified consciousness. She therefore likened the Gothic revival to "a variety of religious cults that have grown in popularity, be they Christian fundamentalist, Hari Krishna, the Sufis, or most recently, the Moonies. Unlike these movements though, Gothicism asserts that transcendence is primarily evil."[23]

In *Three Continents* the Gothic "secret" provides an ironic revelation of the real import of the Rawul's transcendental activities in the political world and the extent to which they operate as a legitimising cover for Crishi, the excluded. Natural and political boundaries *are* crossed, but for criminal reasons. The movement towards being citizens of the world depends heavily for its day-to-day activities upon stolen passports. The plan to unite the best of all civilisations translates into the pillaging of material artefacts. Harriet and Michael throw off Western materialism, only for it to come back to haunt them from the Third World. Mobility is the mark of both the Western truthseeker — and the serial killer. Just as the latter links the culturally spoken and the unspeakable, so Crishi reveals in his actions the revenge of the excluded. Sobhraj, the stateless exile, killed those whose wilful deracination parodied his own state, just as Crishi, who has had disinheritance forced upon him, sees to it that his condition is shared.

In addition to reflecting the Rawul's project in a dark mirror, so the Gothic structure dramatises Harriet's surreptitious slippage from a countercultural to a collusive position, from victim to accomplice, and implicitly from a readerly to a writerly role. At the beginning of the novel Harriet's stunned silence as the Rawul takes over is such as to make her almost a voyeur, watching her story unfold and guessing its outcome from the same hints available to the reader. Again and again the text tells us that Harriet can get no explanations from the men: "What was it all about? Who were they, and why had they come? I waited for Michael to tell me, but he had no time to tell me anything. 'You'll find out,' was all he said'" (15). The reader is thus brought into close affective proximity to events, while being simultaneously warned off from any uncritical suspension of disbelief. Originally Harriet and Michael communicate wordlessly, the one often completing the other's thoughts (14). Crishi, however, appropriates their private language (specifically the term "neti" meaning "phony") and deprives them of it. Though each is enjoying Crishi's sexual favours, neither feels able to discuss the matter, converting their former spiritual communion into a shared secret, separately held. When Harriet shares her bed with Rani as well as Crishi, she feels Michael "willing me not to speak" so that the act remains "unmentioned, rather than unmentionable" (215).

The prohibition on speech even extends to Crishi's marriage proposal. He manages to propose by proxy, through Rani, so that Harriet becomes "spoken for" without ever being spoken to.

The secret engagement and muffling of events is in strong contrast to the ever more publicity-conscious Movement, which develops to the point at which "interviews became the central activity of the house" (133). The Rawul has a tendency to convert all his utterances into speeches for public consumption, even those delivered to his small daughters (268). Linguistic and political structures evolve together. A chat with the Rawul becomes "more in the nature of an audience. Everything around the Rawul was taking on more formality" (119). The movement to transcend all boundaries begins to use security guards and checkpoints and to beat up intruders. Even Michael's speech patterns change so that instead of groping for thoughts he becomes brisk and unreflective: "he no longer had to think. ... It was all there, all formulated" (223). Where Gothic mystery preserves the possibility of unvoiced stories, the Sixth World movement accretes everything to one public formulation, assisted by Anna Sultan, a journalist who provides their first "major media exposure" (182). Harriet's difficulty in getting at her story contrasts with Anna's ease. Harriet notes that "Everything I had only guessed at Anna seemed to know for sure" (138). Anna's account nonetheless includes a highly fanciful tale of the Rawul's initial encounter with Crishi, first in his dreams, then promptly discovered asleep in a poet's tomb. Over the others' protests, Rani and Crishi endorse the story: "'It's what the common reader wants,' Crishi said. 'Ask Harriet. ... Harriet liked it and she's a very common reader. You have to give them these sort of stories'" (184). The incident provides an explicit comment on the way in which cultural formations function to legitimise exploitation. Anna Sultan herself turns the personal into the public, making her reputation with a daring profile of a Lebanese leader: "daring because she had recorded his private along with his public activities, and had not drawn back from chronicling her own affair with him" (133).

For Anna any assignment involves a love affair, which is speedily terminated when her story is finished. In Crishi, however, she meets her match, as the postcolonial subject refuses textualisation except on his own terms. Crishi's only interest is the book which will publicise, authenticate and create his identity, whereas Anna becomes personally attached and exploited in her turn — the fate which threatened Richard Neville at Sobhraj's hands. It is a telling image of the revenge of the excluded subject, who turns his own exploitation against his exploiters to write his own social message.

It is not for nothing that the group is compared to a movie company (40); their lives are being swallowed up by public performance. The Rawul even stages appropriate public ceremonies to authenticate the movement. Harriet's wedding is briskly converted into a symbol of the synthesis of East and West, so symbolic that Crishi spends the wedding night with Rani. From perceiving herself with Michael as "blank pages no one had ever written on" (259), Harriet is being steadily scripted into a public role. A second ceremony which involves the public weighing of the Rawul against a pile of books, supposedly representing the wisdom of the ages, reveals both the totalising project of the movement, and its amorality. Like Crishi, the Rawul intends to textualise himself on his own terms. Michael had wanted to buy bound sets of volumes as counterweights, but Crishi exercises a financial veto so that the Rawul is actually outweighed by a motley collection of tattered second-hand copies of the Bible, Plato, *The Tibetan Book of the Dead*, Carlos Castaneda and Kierkegaard. The form of this attempt to appropriate all cultures to one universal meaning is ludicrously parodic; several volumes have to be removed from the scales to balance the Rawul. Significantly "it was at Kierkegaard that the Rawul started to swing up" (279) — appropriately, given Kierkegaard's separation of the religious and the ethical spheres. The twins, however, react uncritically. For Michael the event is a summation of "everything he had thought and read and experienced. ... It was all summed up for him in the pile of books on the one hand ... and the Rawul on the other" (279). Meanwhile Harriet uses the mythologising process in order to put a high gloss on Crishi's activities, reflecting that "it doesn't seem to matter that sometimes these gods don't behave too well, Venus running off with Mars, Krishna cheating on Radha — they still remain gods" (277–78).

Once on Indian soil however, Crishi lives up to Krishna, his trickily elusive namesake, and naked power emerges from behind the myths and legends as the Rawul's movement swiftly modulates into a conventional political party. Harriet and Michael are now linguistically isolated — they speak no Indian languages. Michael's death is the direct result of the clash between the spoken and the unspoken. Impatiently he demands that the Rawul make a religious oration, rather than merely entertaining influential politicos: "'When's he going to speak? He's got to speak,' he insists" (331). Michael is slow to realise that: "everyone knows that real power, whether political, economic, social, psychological or even mystical, functions silently and has no need of the semblance of speech, even though it never ceases to use that semblance to persuade that we participate".[24] Secure in his power base, the Rawul dispenses with the mediating forms which had previously legitimised him. Instead, his wife speaks, giving secret instructions in her own language to her henchmen who promptly remove Michael. The power to which Michael contributed by his rhetorical formulations is unleashed to silence him, and to consign him to the unspoken of Gothic.

In contrast, Harriet's movement into collusion with crime is rendered as a progression from the unspoken to the fully discursive, as Jhabvala demonstrates that the final horror is equally located in the process of "speaking for". Harriet's collusion is dramatised at the close in the suicide note which she co-authors with the presumed killer. Harriet knows very well that Crishi's account of Michael's suicide is a lie (the supposed suicide note is too badly spelled to be his). She collaborates nonetheless in rewriting the note in more convincing fashion, revising a visibly false story to make it more believable. Revision becomes replication-as-falsity. Harriet would have been truer to the facts of murder if she had allowed the gaps and absences in the original to speak for themselves. No longer a common reader, Harriet has progressed to writing as complicity and betrayal. She writes "with ease" (383), almost with enjoyment, as if becoming Michael, speaking for him, constructing a fiction of defeated dreams as his motive:

> I said that I — that is, I, Michael — was going away because there was nothing in this world that was good enough for me. ... I said that if once you have these expectations — that is, of Beauty, Truth, and Justice — then you feel cheated by everything that falls short of them; and everything here — that is, here, in this world — does fall short of them. It is all neti, neti. (383)

As that last word indicates, Harriet uses their private language to authenticate a public document. Spiritual communion has become the unspeakable. Framed to meet legal requirements, the note is multiply authored — ostensibly by Michael, actually by Harriet, partly at Crishi's dictation. It is the product of multiple silencing: that of the postcolonial subject, of the woman excluded from knowledge and, fatally, of the representative of the society which excluded them. At the close Crishi has carried out the action which communicates a social message of defeated hopes, while Harriet, writing as a male and at the same time "writing off" a male, has produced a socially legitimising text. The note therefore conceals — and sanctions — an act of violence.

This essay began with a question — whether the Gothic novel is an accomplice in the process of Eurocentric textualisation of the East, or whether it may serve to reveal the sources of violence in the colonial encounter. In countercultural Harriet, who slips into the position of accomplice, Jhabvala provides a searching investigation of the psychopathology of power, the process of domination and its relation to mediating cultural forms. The complicity of the writer in generic manipulation and transfer may indeed amount to collusion in violence and exploitation, but may also reveal the bases of such violence in silencing and exclusion. The duplicity of Gothic — its propensity for crossing boundaries, violating taboos, transgressing limits, together with its sense of blockage, privation and prohibition against utterance — makes it the perfect means to dramatise the horrors of the relationship between the social group which sanctions its actions by cultural forms, and the excluded from discourse who speak by deeds. The Gothic undermines the Rawul's pretensions to one-ness and totalisation at the same time as it preserves the unspeakable quality of the killer's actions. By its intertextual nature, its ability to translate from one text to another and back, it prevents the univocal from holding sway. At the close, therefore, Jhabvala offers a multiple text, a piece of writing which conceals a secret and reveals a silenced story, which demonstrates the writer's complicity and — by highlighting issues of fictionality — separates the reader from affective collusion. As the original suicide note showed, truth for the postcolonial writer may be measured as much by its failure to represent itself as by its social production. What the Gothic does not say, its half-told stories, constitute the evidence of a contrary project undermining public formulations. By preserving the unspoken within the text, Jhabvala remains true to the events of both political and social history.

Notes to Chapter 7

1. Eric O Johannesson, *The World of Karen Blixen* (Seattle: University of Washington Press, 1961), 129.
2. Karen Blixen, [Isak Dinesen], *Out of Africa* (London: Putnam, 1937), 64.
3. Blixen, 65.
4. Richard Terdiman, *Discourse/Counter-Discourse: The Theory and Practice of Symbolic Resistance in Nineteenth Century France* (Ithaca: Cornell University Press, 1985), 65.
5. Eve Kosofsky Sedgwick, *The Coherence of Gothic Conventions* (London: Methuen, 1986), 13.
6. Laurie Sucher, *The Fiction of Ruth Prawer Jhabvala: The Politics of Passion* (London: Macmillan, 1989), 61–66.
7. Ruth Prawer Jhabvala, "The Short-Story in England: 1700–1753" (Master's thesis. London University, 1950), 42. I am grateful to Ruth Prawer Jhabvala for permission to quote this passage.
8. Joanna Russ, "'Somebody's Trying To Kill Me And I Think It's My Husband': The Modern Gothic," in Juliann E. Fleenor (ed.), *The Female Gothic* (Montreal: Eden Press, 1983), 31–56.
9. Ruth Prawer Jhabvala, *Three Continents* (London: John Murray, 1987), 16. Subsequent page references follow citations in parentheses.
10. One is reminded here of the 1830s revelations about thuggee, the murder of unsuspecting travellers by Hindu religious assassins, which provided a sensationalist focus for British reformist writing, and the first best-selling Anglo-Indian novel, Philip Meadows Taylor's *Confessions of a Thug* (1839). See Patrick Brantlinger, *Rule of Darkness: British Literature and Imperialism, 1830–1914* (Ithaca: Cornell University Press, 1988), ch. 3.
11. Thomas Thompson, *Serpentine* (London: MacDonald 1980), 565–66.
12. Ibid., 659.
13. Richard Neville and Julie Clarke, *Shadow of the Cobra: The Life and Crimes of Charles Sobhraj* (London: Penguin, 1989). Originally published as *Bad Blood: The Life and Crimes of Charles Sobhraj* (London: Pan, 1979), 343.
14. Ibid.
15. For an account of the mini-series see Rosalie Horner, "Art of Darkness," *Radio Times*, 15–21 July 1989, 4–5 and Bill Pannifer, "Watching Week," *The Listener*, 13 July 1989, 33.
16. Patrick Marnham, "Sobhraj's Slow Poison," *Books and Bookmen*, Feb. 1980, 11.
17. Norman Peagam, "The Trail of the Holiday Killers," *Far Eastern Economic Review*, 13 (August 1976), 10.
18. Marnham, 11.
19. Gerry Clarke, "Rev. of *Serpentine*, by Thomas Thompson," *Bestsellers*, January 1980, 383.
20. Ruth Prawer Jhabvala, "Expiation," *New Yorker*, 10 October 1982, 49.
21. Elliott Leyton, *Hunting Humans: The Rise of the Modern Multiple Murderer* (London: Penguin, 1989). First published as *Compulsive Killers* (New York: New York University Press, 1986).
22. Ibid., 26–27.
23. Linda Bayer-Berenbaum, *The Gothic Imagination* (Toronto: Associated University Press, 1982), 12–13.
24. Christine Brooke-Rose, *A Rhetoric of the Unreal: Studies in Narrative and Structure, Especially of the Fantastic* (Cambridge: Cambridge University Press, 1983), 389.

CHAPTER 8

Solitary Sojourners in Nature: Revisionary Transcendentalism in Alison Lurie's *Love and Friendship* and Marilynne Robinson's *Housekeeping*

The very simplicity and nakedness of man's life in the primitive ages imply this advantage that they left him still but a sojourner in nature. (Thoreau, *Walden*)

It is something of a truism that American cultural myth validates the retreat into isolation, with the consequent rejection of the restricting forces of civilization, the latter often female-identified (Aunt Sally, Dame Van Winkle). Whether Huck is lighting out for the territory, Natty Bumppo for the prairie, or Thoreau for Walden Pond, the myth is overwhelmingly that of the male as solitary sojourner in nature, entering the wilderness to gain access to truth. Isolation is a key emphasis — whether the male is actually alone, as in the Emersonian or Thoreauvian versions, or in the major variant, in which he has as his companion a "buddy", who, generally by virtue of race, is deemed uncultured, outside of, or marginal to the symbolic order, almost himself a part of nature.[1] Huck and Jim, Natty Bumppo and Chingachgook, McMurphy and Chief Bromden: it is a story which we all know so well that it hardly bears rehearsal. Feminist critics have argued, in response, that American literature offers particular difficulties for women. Judith Fetterley contends that the female reader is continually asked to identify with men and against herself.[2] The title of Nina Baym's influential essay speaks for itself: "Melodramas of Beset Manhood: How Theories of American Fiction Exclude Women Authors."[3] Carolyn Heilbrun describes *Deliverance* as "the latest in a series of fictional escapes into the 'territory' where women do not go, where civilization cannot reach, where men hunt one another like animals, and hunt animals for sport".[4] In what follows the concern is not to analyse the myth itself, but to take it to some extent as read, and to offer a reading of two novels by contemporary women which investigate what happens when women engage with the myth. Both Emmy Turner (in Alison Lurie's *Love and Friendship*) and Ruth Stone (in Marilynne Robinson's *Housekeeping*) follow in the footsteps of Emerson and Thoreau as solitary sojourners in nature; in both novels variations are struck on the "buddy" motif; both examine the myth of the New Eden — that divinely appointed second chance represented by America.

The relationship of women to the myth is complicated. As outsiders in patriarchal culture, women have also been held in relative isolation from each other and from any sense of social consensus.[5] In a culture which validates isolation as a means to truth, women are therefore doubly disadvantaged: they are, in a sense, isolated from isolation, understood as a transcendent virtue. They are positioned as the old story of culture from which the new story must distinguish itself, to form a new cultural myth. In the European cultural paradigm woman is nature, not culture. But when nature becomes culture, she is briskly redefined, repositioned and consigned to repetition. Huck Finn, after all, lights out not once, but twice. Aunt Sally is an old story as well as a female story. As he says, "I been there before."[6]

In the figure of the solitary sojourner in nature, the reader is of course confronting what has been variously described as a master narrative, grand narrative or metanarrative, towards which postmodernity has displayed considerable incredulity — whether voiced through Foucault's localism, new historicism's anecdote, or any other opposition to totalizing claims. Jean-François Lyotard's is the clearest exposition available. For Lyotard "the grand narratives of legitimation" (historical or religious), which have claimed access to the true nature of things, are open to question and to temporary replacement by "petits récits" (little stories) with more modest, local ambitions.[7] The question of legitimation remains, of course, insistent. If we accept that the grand narratives have collapsed, we are in a position where the social subject dissolves in a dissemination of language games. Lyotard evinces the proliferation of new languages available to us — machine languages, matrices of game theory, new systems of musical notation, the language of the genetic code. Since nobody is fluent in all these languages, the possibility of a universal metalanguage recedes — grounds for pessimism in some quarters. On the other hand, the delegitimation of the masternarrative results in a reaffirmation of narrative itself, as a central instance of the human mind, and a mode of thinking fully as legitimate as that of abstract knowledge. In this argument then, narrative is no longer in retreat in the face of abstract denotative, logical or cognitive procedures. If, as Lyotard affirms, "Narrative is the quintessential form of customary knowledge", the work of the novel becomes of central cultural importance.[8]

In support of his vision of the centrality of narrative Lyotard makes three important points. Firstly, he notes that popular stories recount positive or negative apprenticeships: the successes or failures of the hero bestow legitimacy upon social institutions or role models. Secondly, narrative form lends itself to a great variety of language games, allowing all sorts of other statements to slip in. And lastly the transmission itself of narratives, involving sender, addressee and hero, communicates what one must say in order to be heard (sender), what one must listen to in order to speak (addressee) and what role one must play in order to be the object of narrative (hero). In short, a narrative tradition is intimately involved with a community's relation to itself and its environment; the set of rules that constitute the social bond is transmitted through narrative. Postmodernity therefore becomes a condition in which no single instance of narrative can exert a claim to dominate narration by standing beyond it. There is no single or originary speaker; we are all, to some extent, addressees of immemorial previous narratives. Where grand narratives link little narratives, either around a referent (classicism) or an original sender (modernism), the serial disposition of little narratives (one after another) means that no one narrative can become the masternarrative, organizing the field of language elements. To quote Bill Readings:

> Crudely, each little narrative does not aim to tell *the* story, to put an end to narrative; rather a little narrative evokes new stories by the manner in which, in its turn, it has displaced preceding narratives in telling a story.[9]

Art is not, therefore, in the service of cultural transformation; it is cultural transformation. Feminist critics have also, quite independently, highlighted the centrality of narrative in relation to cultural change. Carol Christ, for example, draws an explicit parallel between telling stories and living lives.

> In a very real sense there is no experience without stories. Stories give shape to experience, experience gives rise to stories ... for those who have had the freedom to tell their own stories ... but this has not usually been the case for women. Indeed there is a very real sense in which the seemingly paradoxical statement, "Women have not experienced their own experience" is true.[10]

Instead, women may live out inauthentic stories provided by a culture which they did not create — conventional stories of love, courtship and marriage, for example. Woman is often neither sender, nor addressee, nor hero of narrative. The creation of new literary traditions may therefore offer a prime means to cultural change. As Joanne Frye puts it,

> because the novel as form resists fixity and responds to its social context through interaction rather than simple ideological miming, its literary resources are peculiarly responsive to women's needs for alternative resolutions.[11]

As an active participant in the processes of change the woman reader may claim personal agency, setting aside cultural determinisms, to make sense of experience in different ways. Frye again: "as novelistic narrative is an agent of interpretation, it becomes as well a possible agent of reinterpretation, not only giving form but also altering accepted forms".[12]

    How far, however, is it possible for the masternarrative to be completely challenged? As Frederic Jameson's concept of the political unconscious indicates, the possibility remains of the return of the grand narrative. Robert Kiely puts it in a nutshell:

> Story patterns of social coercion and victimization, of education and political responsibility cannot be purged any more than language can be. Dislocated, dishevelled, deprived of respectability these patterns remain in the mind of the reader.[13]

Moreover, if the masternarrative could be completely challenged, would that be a desirable state of affairs? How is the writer to avoid the reinscription of the notion of dominance in the replacement narrative? The problem presents itself in acute form for the American woman writer — who may wish to make it new, *without* invoking the Adamic myth, to develop autonomy *without* "self-reliance", to be *in* nature without being *of* nature, and to cultivate relationality outside the buddy relationship. Alison Lurie and Marilynne Robinson employ different tactics, with varying degrees of success.

In *Love and Friendship*, Emmy Turner, transplanted to the isolated New England campus of Convers College, envisages herself communing with nature in the steps of Emerson and Thoreau. Emmy's family, though not physically New Englanders,

> had the tradition of being spiritually so. They believed that in their four years at Convers the sons of the family breathed in the air of a higher spiritual state.[14]

Hitherto excluded from this all-male enclave, Emmy (a female Emerson) finds the very silence and chill of Convers inviting. "It suggested revelations in deserts and forests, Thoreau and Descartes" (18). Even amidst the rigors of the New England winter Emmy's enthusiasm continues unabated:

> after all, the heroes and philosophers of New England, all the founders of the Convers tradition had lived through winters like this. Here one could still practice self-reliance; ... one could listen through the long, cold, black evenings for the inner voice. (5)

What Emmy listens to, initially, is her husband Holman preparing his classes. Convers specializes in a compulsory freshman course entitled "Hum C", which explicitly encodes its public values. A lightly fictionalized version of the famous innovative Amherst course, English 1–2, Hum C is loosely based on logical positivist principles, in which the teacher goes on asking questions and the student answering until the latter learns to use words accurately.[15] The object is to wipe the mental slate clean, so that each student can create his own moral universe anew, thinking for himself. Lurie gives a typical example:

ASSIGNMENT II

Here is a photograph, an airview of Convers College.

(a) Let us assume you are now somewhere in the middle of the area contained in the photograph and you recognize this as a photograph of the spot you are now on. What do you do to recognize this?

(b) Define in the context of (a) "the spot you are now on."

(c) What difference do you see between this spot and the one in the map in Assignment No. 10? (24)

The aim of the exercise is to prompt the student to recognize his ability to make orders of various complex kinds. As a language game, Hum C implies that all final questions concerning truth are outmoded. It breaks up preconceptions and makes the individual abandon older beliefs. Significantly the Amherst course had an empowering aim. Originally designed for non-literary students who lacked confidence in their writerly abilities and had had little access to canonical texts, the underlying assumption of the program was that the student does know something, and that he can be enabled to communicate that knowledge, drawing on his own (unlegitimated) experience. Students were likely to be asked to write about maps, photographs, sports. In addition, the course had an operationalist basis. One assignment set out to establish that the length of an object (a line in a visual illusion) was merely the sum of the operations performed in its measurement. To extrapolate: a word means what it means to the individual. He is the operator of its meanings.

Although debarred from her husband's lectures, Emmy Turner sets to work to take the course by proxy, eager to participate in a language game, which, as she is swift to recognize, has distinctly American assumptions, potentially providing a point of access to the masternarrative. The point is made explicitly in a conversation between Holman and Emmy.

> "They keep asking questions simply to clear away all the rubbish that everyone takes for granted and what's left is what you really believe; what you really see, I mean, the way *you* see it and nobody else. Like Emerson."
> "Emerson?" Holman raised his head,
> "Yes, like Self-Reliance. ... Convers now probably looks a lot like Concord used to ... when they were all thinking about the same things as in Hum C." (66)

Holman is less than appreciative, however, of his wife's new-found interest in Transcendentalism, though he keeps his thoughts to himself. "She would always want to see every idea from an emotional point of view. ... He did not mind — women should be that way" (67). Ironically bearing out his thoughts, Emmy contemplates him in sour silence. "I am more isolated than anybody ever was in Concord, she thought. ... they had friends to talk to. I bet Emerson talked to his wife" (67). Appropriately, perhaps the result of the ensuing conversation is that she does see Holman afresh; she sees him as decidedly unattractive and falls out of love with him. Far from Convers producing a higher spiritual state, Emmy finds that the converse is true as she ends up communing with nature in the arms of an appropriately named lover, Will Thomas. Just as Hum C's refusal of metaphysics delivers its students to sense experience, so Emmy's idealism lapses into sexuality. As she reflects, "When I listen to my inner voices they only say things like: 'I think I will call up Will,' or 'Let's give Emmy the largest piece of pie'" (201). Most of the love affair is carried on in the great outdoors, and in emblematic locations. Emmy and Will are observed at one point by a stranger:

> a couple making love right out in the snow. ... In spite of the weather, the woman was apparently naked to the waist; and quite brown — I imagine there must still be a good deal of Indian blood hereabouts. Beyond them ... were the fields which were lush with corn and squash and tobacco ... last fall. (180)

In point of fact Emmy is tanned from a recent holiday in Bermuda. The comment, however, returns Will and Emmy to a scene imbued with origins, in references to indigenous peoples and crops. Making love in the great outdoors, however, exposes Emmy first to poison ivy and then to the full savagery which civilized society turns upon instinctual pleasures. Emmy's return to ethical origins takes place in a narrow and precisely calibrated society in which the social self triumphs over the impulse to nonconformity.[16]

As this false Eden reveals its true colours, so Hum C comes in for reappraisal. When Holman is alerted to Emmy's adultery he finds his suspicions revolving through his mind as if part of an assignment.

> The mid-term exam, which he had just finished correcting, was as clear in his mind as a map, but now it seemed all to refer to him. This is an Optical Illusion. What do you do to see these lines not only as lines but as an Optical Illusion? What other kinds of Illusions have you come across in your experience? (261)

In addition, when Holman follows the method of Hum C, relentlessly cross-questioning Emmy, the results are neither personally nor ethically satisfying. By these means Holman transforms the prints of the cleaning lady's galoshes in the snow into evidence of adultery with three different people — none of them Will Thomas. Having by this stage already abandoned Will, Emmy speaks nothing but the truth when she denies Holman's accusations. The precise linguistic truth, in this case, wipes the slate clean in a less than moral sense. Lurie's novel, therefore, exposes the male language game, with its pretensions to privileged truth, and idealistic moral content, to experience — and finds it decidedly wanting. Hum C is, in Emmy's description, nothing but a "stupid word game" (26).

Not all language games remain, however, as local and unlegitimated as Hum C. Slowly the possibility emerges that there is a second story underlying the masternarrative of Transcendental idealism — a story organized upon corporate, economic and distinctly male principles. Rather like *Who's Afraid of Virginia Woolf?*, the novel emphasizes the mythic substructures and archaic practices of the academic community, and by extension of society at large. In its cyclical movement from autumn to the following summer, in the presence of Will as mock fertility god (impregnating the Dean's wife) and in satiric references to rites of passage and initiation, animism and magic, the novel sets in motion a parodic transformation of Walden into Wasteland. One interpolated language game is particularly significant. At a dinner party, Julian Fenn reveals just how little Convers actually acts on its stated aims. When teaching *Walden* Julian takes it seriously enough to spend a weekend living rough in the woods with his students. The result is censure by the Dean who informs him that "it's not the part of a teacher to suggest actions to the students" but to "deal exclusively in ideas" (138). Hum C remains a language game, not a narrative implicated in cultural change. Holman agrees that Convers is false to its stated ideals: "right here in town they're running pagan rituals ... at the fraternities" (42). In the story of his own fraternity initiation which he goes on to tell, animal worship looms large. The pledges are sent out to buy a terrier, which is christened "James Dawg" and confined in squalor with the pledges for the whole of "Hell Week". At the end of the week the animal is supposedly slaughtered, and the festivities conclude with the "great Dog-Eating Ceremony" as the pledges, blindfolded, are passed parts of the unfortunate animal's insides to eat. (It is in fact raw calf's liver.) The initiation rite includes two elements of especial narrative interest. It is preceded by a ceremony of inquisition in which (rather as in Hum C) the pledges are interrogated about their sexual practices. Telling the right story is crucial: "If you had no heterosexual stories to tell... it was best to make some up, or else you would be questioned on still more embarrassing matters" (43).

As anthropological study indicates, fraternities are both overtly homophobic and implicitly homoerotic — rather like classic American literature.[17] Fraternity initiations cleanse young men of the despised "feminine" or "effeminate" self, bounded to mothers, humiliating them and exposing them to various forms of mock death in order to wipe out the past, break pre-existent bonds and rebond to the brotherhood. At one point in the novel Holman worries about the choice between supporting his mother financially, or paying his fraternity dues (123). Given that sexual expression is communicated and learned through discourse, the discourse associated with fraternity practices operates as a strategy of knowledge which sanctions the deployment of male power in acts of sexual aggression. Peggy Reeves Sanday has investigated the incidence of fraternity gang rape, for example, in which the woman (often unconscious) is a surrogate victim in a drama in which the main agents are males interacting with each other. In group activity of this nature homoerotic desire is "simultaneously indulged, degraded, and extruded from the group".[18] What the ritual says is that women "ask for it". (Participants are often shocked by the charge of rape.) By defining women as "wanting it" the men simultaneously convince themselves of their heterosexual prowess and bond to each other by co-participation in a forbidden act. Holman expounds further on his fraternity activities, describing "Pig Night":

> Everybody brought in the easiest lays they could find, **see... God, what a collection... Pigs. But turn out the lights and you couldn't** see them... Girls like that will do anything. They enjoy it actually. (290)

As Holman's stories indicate, the "right story" is a narrative that excludes or degrades women, while paradoxically functioning as a guarantor of heterosexual "normality". Importantly Holman's account of his fraternity ritual is based on fact (an individual fraternity)[19] and describes practices which are still current.[20] As rites of initiation and passage, fraternity rituals share common characteristics with many of the classic American cultural myths of virgin land, new beginnings, and regeneration through violence. Fraternity initiates, then, act as addressees of an immemorial narrative, a well-established social script.

The point is made explicit in the remainder of Holman's account of the initiation ceremony. As well as themselves telling the right story, the initiates also form the audience to a story. The ceremonies culminate as the president of the fraternity reads aloud the traditional *Tale of Wooglin*. "It was not brief, but briefly the story described the famous hunter Wooglin and his march through the great desert with his faithful companion James Dawg" (45). In this Disneyesque parody of the buddy relationship, the starving hunter is about to collapse when Dawg rolls over on his back and looks up at him touchingly: "a voice speaks out of the sky: 'Rip Open the Dawg and Eat!' At this point all the frat brothers repeated in chorus: 'Eat! Eat! Eat!'" (46). Blindfolded, lying on their backs, the pledges ingest the raw liver. As a communal male ritual the story perpetuates the real values of Convers society, and highlights the masculine exclusivity of such key American *topoi* as the errand in the wilderness, isolation in nature and the buddy relationship, here underpinned both by the approving chorus of the social group, and by the voice of God. Teleological and social sanction combine. The fraternity ritual, then, teaches how to tell the right story (what one must say in order to be heard), how to react as a member of a community (how to listen in order to speak), and (in the pledges' dramatic imitation of Dawg's position) what role one must play in order to be the object of narrative.

As opposed to the idealism of Hum C, the fraternity story legitimizes a dog-eat-dog mentality. Julian comments that "It must have been cannibalism originally. After all, that christening ceremony; the dog became the 25th pledge. You were actually eating a freshman" (46). Holman demurs. "Nobody really dies. The dog was our scapegoat" (46). Scapegoats do not remain, however, comfortably enclosed within Holman's little narrative. Where Hum C is not legitimated by the community, fraternity discursive practice extends into the frame tale of the novel, expanding from local anecdote to masternarrative. In feminist analysis fraternity rituals have been described as a "sexual subculture".[21] Arguably, however, the ritual inscribes the majority culture, the dominant narrative, within the ostensibly oppositional culture — the converse culture — of the university. Commenting on the Amherst fraternities Gail Kennedy argues that

> The fraternities represent an entrenchment of the world without inside the college community. They are the centre of a kind of social education that reinforces the conventional values of our society in an environment where those values are being analyzed.[22]

When Holman tells his anecdote, he does so in order to reaffirm his membership of an elite group. But, *by* telling it he betrays the vow of secrecy taken at his initiation; he breaks the bond which guaranteed his status, the compact which dictated what role one must play to be an object of narrative. When asked why he was prepared to undergo ritual humiliation, Holman replied that he looked forward, in the future, to watching others being victimized in their turn. Fraternity members resort to abusing others (women, new pledges) in order to renew their sense of the social power of the brotherhood. In fact, however, they have become (in Sanday's analysis) "subjected beings who submit to fraternal authority and mold their identity to fit the mythologies of masculinity".[23] To put it another way, the initiates may associate themselves with the great hunter, Wooglin, but are in fact playing the role of James Dawg.

In the plot of Lurie's novel the apparent subtext usurps the public discourse, expanding from anecdote to action as mock death becomes real injury and a succession of scapegoats fulfil the community's darker needs. Julian Fenn is disgraced and ousted; Will is tolerated as a legitimate scapegoat, only because he is an artist; finally, real damage is done. In the course of the novel Dicky Smith, a tiresomely doggy student who hounds the staff with his bundle of dog-eared manuscripts (252) is rechristened "Fido". In a concluding disaster, during student unrest, Holman is implicated in pushing Fido into the burning foundation pit of the new Religion building, where he is semi-incinerated. Significantly Fido's heterosexual identity is suspect. Holman describes him as a "pansy bastard" (323), and speculates that in expelling Smith and his two fellow ringleaders the college is "glad of the opportunity to get rid of those three queers" (324). Holman may not actually have pushed Fido in, but he is a willing spectator, just as in the fraternity ritual. Lurie makes Holman's guilt unambiguous. He confesses to Emmy: "'I stood there and watched him burn. And I liked it... Guilty,' he said finally" (342). Just as it is guilt and scapegoating which hold the fraternity together, along with its macrocosmic society, so Holman's admission mends the Turners' marriage. They reunite in shared guilt, Emmy assuring Holman that her money will pay Fido's medical bills and wipe the slate clean, Holman looking forward to a long residence in Convers. Two fraternities have asked him to become their advisor (326).

Throughout the novel Emmy's actions are placed in ironic perspective by a technical device. Lurie ends each chapter with a letter from a visiting novelist, Allen Ingram, whose own novel advances in tandem with Lurie's, and finishes at its close. While the plot of Lurie's novel concerns heterosexual love, Ingram's plot is not described in his letters to his friend: Ingram is homosexual. Emmy's story, therefore, remains enclosed in a male narrative of love and friendship. Ingram's letters are clearly indicative of male letters in the broader sense, as *belles lettres*. In the final analysis she is unable to resist objectification in a male culture text — a text which conjoins overt homophobia and covert homoeroticism. In Ingram's last letter he describes meeting Emmy at the kennels where he is leaving his puppy, Beowulf. Emmy assures him that he should not worry about abandoning his faithful companion. If he wants another dog, she says, he can always buy one (just as the fraternity does, just as Holman pays off Fido). Prior to this, Emmy had had a revelation: "I belong to myself" (343), she announces. Emmy *has* found herself at Convers, but the self in question is not, perhaps, very much worth finding. She has entered a male masternarrative — but not the one she anticipated. Remembering how her brothers had returned from Convers boasting of their sexual exploits, she realizes that

> Not only did these things apparently not cancel out the spiritual gain ... from attending the college, they seemed somehow to be necessary to it. Emmy reflected that she also could claim to have sown her wild oats at Convers. (338)

Emmy's attempts to break into male traditions have been ironically rewarded. At the close of the novel she watches Miranda's children playing blind man's buff:

> Something was wrong with the game, though. "But they're all blindfolded!" Emmy objected. "Yes", Miranda replied, "They like it better that way." (350)

The tableau of the blindfolded group, an image crossing over from fraternity ritual into the main narrative, recalls Emerson's comment in "Self-Reliance":

> what a blind man's buff is this game of conformity ... most men have bound their eyes with one or another handkerchief, and attached themselves to some one of these communities of opinion.[24]

While Lurie's swingeing satire exposes the illusions at the centre of the master-narrative, the question of cultural change remains unanswered. In the portrayal of Convers, *Love and Friendship* therefore suggests the difficulty implicit in any counter-discourse, the danger of reinscribing the norms of the dominant discourse within its apparent contestation, as (to quote Richard Terdiman) "the contesters discover that the authority they sought to undermine is reinforced by the very fact of its having been chosen, as dominant discourse, for opposition".[25] Rewritings, counter-texts run the risk of slippage from oppositional to surreptitiously collusive positions. Revising the masternarrative may see its return in subtextual form.

Where Lurie displays a woman attempting to enter a male world, Robinson adopts the reverse strategy and simply excises the male. In *Housekeeping* there are no living male characters at all. The only males to have speaking, if cameo, parts are essentially reduced to functions of social authority: a teacher enforcing the rules, a sheriff enforcing the law.[26] Rather than storming the gates of male culture she opts for a feminized world. Does this all-female world succeed in its contestatory project? From its opening line — "My name is Ruth" (7) — with its echoes of "Call me Ishmael" and "My name is Arthur Gordon Pym" — *Housekeeping* sounds an intertextual note.[27] The action — the slow dilapidation of the house of the family patriarch, the admission of nature into culture, the divestment of the trappings of domesticity — clearly relates to Thoreau's concept of minimal housekeeping. Robinson herself commented that "I used to say to myself that *Walden* could have been called *Housekeeping*."[28] The denouement of the novel, as Ruth burns down the house and escapes, carries suggestions of Poe and Twain, though in this case the protagonist leaves a socially conformist sister behind, and goes on the road with her aunt. In interview Robinson described *The Narrative of Arthur Gordon Pym* as having that characteristic pattern of so much American literature, where people go through a journey that leads to a kind of realization that is just at the limits of their ability to comprehend, or articulate, and after that, there's an openness where earlier experience becomes impossible.[29]

Robinson's intertextual references frame more than one wilderness scene reminiscent of the forest scenes of Cooper or Hawthorne which offer moments of renewal of contact with primary sources of value in nature. In short, the ghosts of Emerson, Thoreau, Dickinson, Hawthorne and Poe haunt a novel which is actively related to the classic narratives of America, those stories which the culture continues to repeat. Robinson herself has heralded Poe's awareness of the dream quality of popular forms. "If something is repeated and repeated as a formula, it's because it's a kind of dream the culture can't stop dreaming."[30]

One such recurring American dream comes in for particular scrutiny. Writing in 1985, Robinson inveighed against the domination of American culture by a mythic version of the past.

> We are enchanted by a myth of history, a truly venerable fable which goes like this. Once the world was as it ought to be, then came the Catastrophe, after which we have toiled in twilight, lost and downcast. No one knows how old that story is, but it has never been more passionately believed.[31]

In her view, the idea of a breach, before and after with some catastrophe in between to account for a grand-scale qualitative decline, represents a paradigmatic structure which dominates American thinking. Whether the catastrophe is represented as the Biblical Fall, the advent of industrialism, the decline of an old regime, the Civil War, the end of the frontier, is irrelevant. The Golden Age can be prehistorical, classical, third world or "American in any previous era."[32] The story remains the same. The myth of the fresh start, the New Eden, depends upon that of preceding catastrophe. No Fall, no New Eden. Where *Love and Friendship* moves from mock deaths in fraternity rituals to real disaster, *Housekeeping* traces a reverse route, pullulating with images of catastrophe, of floods and fires, accidents and mishaps, from its opening image of mass death in a train accident to the final fate of Ruth and Sylvie, supposedly drowned in the lake which had earlier claimed their mother and grandfather.

The notion of housekeeping obviously also has special resonances for women, in the sense of symbolizing all the cultural practices which support patriarchy.[33] A problem exists therefore in the juxtaposition of the women's story and the transcendental story. In the course of the novel sisterhood is defeated. Lucille chooses order, social conformity, dressmaking and home economics, abandoning Ruth whose close relationship with Sylvie Foster, repeatedly presented as a surrogate or foster mother, is uncomfortably close to regression to an earlier mother–child dyad. Is Ruth's choice a positive affirmation of a life outside the feminine-acculturated norm? Or has she merely exchanged one conventional story for another, in which merging with nature leads to being swamped by sylvan Sylvie and a consequent loss of autonomy? Robinson may be reconstructing the "buddy" relationship in terms of a neo-feminist paradigm of relationality as strength.[34] None the less at the close of the novel Ruth has escaped with Sylvie into freedom only because, like Huck Finn, she has been presumed drowned. Is Ruth lighting out into nature, in rebellion? Or is she an enactment of what literature has already done to women, unhousing them, making them storyless, nameless, without a place in culture? Does taking over a male paradigm erase the female once again? — as, for example, when Thelma and Louise go on the road the only autonomy available to them involves the replication of male violence, the only territory which they can light out for is that of death, the end of the road for all those heroines who opt out of the conventional female plot: Edna Pontellier, Lily Bart, Hawthorne's Zenobia. The answer depends once again on the status of other language games within the frame narrative.

The discrepancy between the male story as placed in culture, the female as occluded, is highlighted in the contrasting stories of Ruth's grandparents. In the initial scene a train on which the grandfather is traveling crashes into Fingerbone Lake and is lost, the ice reforming in a fresh new surface as if the machine had never entered the garden. Nobody sees the accident, nobody locates the train: it is a catastrophe which is almost immediately erased by a new beginning. None the less the event is extensively reported in the papers. Importantly, catastrophe gives the male a place in culture which is denied the female. Ruth's grandmother had always looked forward to the moment when "her simple private destiny would intersect with the great public processes of law and finance — that is to her death".[35] But when, much later, she dies, the papers merely feature "photos of the train ... and of workers hanging the bridge with crepe and wreaths, and of, in a row of gentlemen, a man identified as my grandfather" (38). Among all these men there is no photograph of the grandmother. Indeed, the family realize that, were the pages to cross Sylvie's transient path, she would remain unaware that her mother's death was the occasion for resuscitating the male story. In contrast Ruth and Sylvie's "deaths" do gain access to the public sphere. Sylvie carries everywhere a newspaper clipping with the headline "LAKE CLAIMS TWO" (182). The townspeople have no doubt that the pair are dead. Mention is made of their mother's drowning in the lake, "also an apparent suicide" (182). In short, the story, which has always been waiting to claim them, now does so. This time, however, it is not legitimated. Ruth and Sylvie survive. Robinson's is a conscious restaging of the myth of catastrophe which marks itself off from the old story without replacing it with a masternarrative of newness.

In general, critics have read the intercalated stories of the novel as designed to reject traditional expectations about female narrative, offering Ruth different ways of being a woman, alternative role models of transience and unhousing.[36] What the stories also offer, in less essentialist fashion, I would argue, is a different way of being American — a way of making it new without invoking the violence of catastrophe. The first story told to Ruth strikes the keynote. Ettie, an old lady of imperfect mind, suddenly tells Ruth of a Catholic lady in San Francisco with a parrot on her balcony. When the cathedral bells rang, the lady would pray and the parrot pray with her: "the woman's voice and the parrot's voice, on and on, between clamor and clangor" (24). When the lady falls ill, she turns out to be dispensable: the parrot goes on praying just as well without her. The display of orthodox religion as parroted piety, of woman's voice as senseless repetition, ends however with the San Francisco Fire. "The fire took the church and its bells and no doubt the parrot, too, and quite possibly the Catholic lady" (25). Superficially the story is a random tale, which appears comically contingent to the action of the novel. Yet Ruth learns from this juxtaposition of woman, catastrophe and presumed death. At the end she stages her own fire, her own mock-catastrophe as an escape from conventional structures. The story is not as contingent as it looks.

Similarly, Sylvie's stories launch a two-pronged attack on conventional stories of women and of America. In content the tales are entirely oriented towards the revision of female roles. One story tells of a woman unhealthily obsessed with her child, another of a woman so lonely that she has four children in five years "and none of it helped at all" (61). The overall effect is to argue that marriage and motherhood — however absorbing — are not enough.[37] The circumstances of transmission, however, are unusual. The setting is catastrophe — a flood which cuts the threesome off from their neighbours. Lucille, unable to bear isolation, becomes intent on reconnecting to the social group. When she asks "What happened to the children?" (61), Sylvie replies "The usual things ... If there really were any children" (61). As Sylvie warns, there are currently only two possibilities for these children; either "the usual things" will happen to them, or they won't exist at all. The setting, however, also emphasizes games. By questioning the veracity of her story, Sylvie draws attention to its status as unconfirmed language game. Indeed, she tends to transmit her stories in the context of games-playing — Monopoly, Crazy Eights, Solitaire. In their conjunction of catastrophe with play, Sylvie's stories offer examples of local "petits récits" evolving out of the failure of the masternarrative. The stories do not "add up" to a new paradigm. Nor do they quite strike out the old. A second pair of stories concerns the relationship of woman to nature. One describes a transient woman freezing to death, alone, in winter. The other concerns Sylvie's experience of sunrise one Sunday with her friend Alma. Again, nature appears in threatening guise. Sylvie describes the dawn chorus as the birds' cries of alarm as they sense the wind "as rank as a hunter" and "smelling of blood" (79). There is no transcendent epiphany; when dawn breaks Alma and Sylvie eat hotdogs companionably in the sun. Although the story has a contingent, pointless feel, it celebrates female relationship as opposed to the vision of nature as a place of death in isolation, bloody hunters and violence.

The tales are immediately followed by Ruth's description of the furniture of Sylvie's room, on which the grandfather had long ago painted images — cherubs, a peacock, a hunting scene.

> Each of these designs had been thought better of and painted out, but over years the white paint had absorbed them, floated them up just beneath the surface. (80)

In registering these palimpsestic male artefacts, Ruth recognizes that the slate cannot be wiped entirely clean.[38] The culture of the patriarch, however deeply buried, is always likely to return to being, still identifiable and loaded with iconographic meaning. Women's stories, then, may best promote cultural change by means of a second creation rather than an entirely new creation. The erasure of the past would merely re-enact the story of the new Eden.

The transmission of Sylvie's last two stories foregrounds the question of cultural change. The first concerns a woman who rode the rods from South Dakota to Portland to see her cousin hanged. For Lucille Sylvie's involvement with such "trashy" people is an embarrassment. Sylvie, on the other hand, comments that "She's his only relative, except for his father, and he's the one that was strangled ... *She* didn't strangle anyone" (92). Lucille is overridingly concerned with the wider interpretive community: "How could people of reasonableness and solidity respond to such tales?" (2). Sylvie goes on to describe a woman in Oklahoma who lost an arm in an aircraft factory, but who still manages to support six children by giving piano lessons. (93). Both tales stretch credulity; their "truth" is open to question. Both celebrate traditionally female virtues in unfamiliar ways. It is, after all, praiseworthy to rush to the deathbed of a relative; or to support six children single-handed (metaphorically speaking). Society does not usually conjoin these images of normal female behaviour with a hobo at a hanging or an amputee Rosie the Riveter. For Lucille the significant point is once again not content but the manner of transmission. Sylvie relates her story while recumbent on a park bench where she has been sleeping in full public view. Lucille cannot tolerate the expansion of the story from language game to public discourse, even if local and unauthenticated. Instead, like Jay Gatsby before her, she reads herself back into culture via *"Ivanhoe and The Light that Failed and Wuthering Heights and Little Men and National Geographic* and anything else she took to be improving" (116). Lucille never tells a story — she is only a reader, in a sense *the* reader. When she leaves home, Sylvie's stories stop. Without Lucille "she had no stories at all to tell" (120). Sylvie's silence suggests the degree to which the audience has constitutive function. Without Lucille, Sylvie has no purpose in narration, for Ruth has served her apprenticeship as addressee and now becomes the storyteller in her turn, moving the narrative onto a wider stage.

Ruth's first independent act of narration takes place as an isolate in nature in an emblematic locale — a ruined house in the woods. As Martha Ravits has pointed out, the scene echoes with cultural memory, with Thoreau, Cather, Lincoln's log cabin, *The Little House on the Prairie*.[39] Contemplating the ruins, Ruth supplies a tale of catastrophe and fall. "The ridgepole had snapped, no doubt under the weight of snow. That was probably the beginning of the catastrophe" (135). She relates a story of a family in similar circumstances who had survived by such desperate measures as eating their shoes and fingernails. "The woods were full of such stories" (136) as if there had been a massive "exodus" or "wholesale obliteration" (136). Puzzlingly, however, abandoned homesteads are actually rare, "so perhaps all the tales of perished settlers were at root one tale, carried off in every direction" (136). Ruth's storytelling registers catastrophe narrative as a tall tale, rare and exaggerated, but sufficiently powerful to be carried in all directions, to fulfil the endless replication that is the function of hegemonic discourse. Ruth has learned from the stories of solitary transients:

> in every case they will tell you that they were abandoned, disappointed, or betrayed ... that only remarkable events, of the kind one reads in books, could have made their condition so extreme. (137)

The manner of their narration, however, their gestures and eye movements, convicts them of lying. For Ruth then, isolation breeds lies, and exceptionalism is catastrophe.

In contrast, where Ruth's own experience of isolation in the woods allows her entry into the cultural story, but also marks a critical distance, the sheriff of Fingerbone is entirely at one with his interpretive community. Fingerbone is an area much given to sudden death:

> what with the lake and the railroads, and what with blizzards and floods and barn fires and forest fires and the general availability of shotguns and bear traps and homemade liquor (152–53)

violence is inevitable.

> There were any number of fierce old stories, one like another, varying only in the details ... For decades this same sheriff had been summoned like a midwife to preside over the beginnings of these stories, their births in ditches and dark places out of the bloody loins of circumstance. (153)

These violent acts are the true creations of the community, the offspring of the catastrophe myth — their births presided over by the male as guarantor of origins. In policing beginnings the sheriff also rules over endings; to have a legitimate, authorized point of origin is to be on track for a predestined ending, to be addressed by a story that must be told in a certain way.[40] When the sheriff intervenes to remove Ruth from Sylvie, Ruth therefore responds appropriately. Refusing to re-enter the family home she takes refuge at night in the orchard where she tells her last story.

> Once there was a young girl strolling at night in an orchard. She came to a
> house she had never seen before... A door stood open so she walked inside.
> It would be that kind of story, a very melancholy story. ... She would be
> transformed by the gross light into a mortal child. And when she stood at the
> bright window, she would find that the world was gone, the orchard was gone,
> her mother and grandmother and aunts were gone. Like Noah's wife on the
> tenth or fifteenth night of rain, she would stand in the window and realize that
> the world was really lost. (174)

Ruth's story is now a means to rewriting her own life and preventing her
reintegration into the dominant cultural paradigm. She *is* the girl, but in refusing
to re-enter the house she leaves the old catastrophe story behind her. As the orchard
location suggests, on a teleological level she refuses to re-enact the myth of the Fall
from spirit into flesh; on a social level she refuses the conventional construction of
femininity. Sylvie's stories modelled alternative possibilities for women on the road;
now Ruth will live them out, turning story into life.

At the close of the novel seven years have passed, Sylvie and Ruth are still drifters,
still outside society, still officially dead. But the ending centres upon Lucille. With
the instruction "imagine Lucille in Boston" (186) Robinson passes on the work
of producing the next story to the reader. Ruth and Sylvie feature as absences,
negatives who are none the less powerfully present to Lucille, the figure of the
reader.

> No one watching [Lucille] ... could know how her thoughts are thronged by
> our absence, or know how she does not watch, does not listen, does not wait,
> does not hope, and always for me and Sylvie. (186)

In conjuring the reader to construct a speaking presence in absence, a positive in a
negative, an existence in terms of nonexistence, Robinson leaves the women poised
outside both endings and beginnings.[41] They are "dead" in terms of catastrophe
narrative, but very much alive in their own space. As Ernesto Laclau has commented
(in another context) "insofar as something ends, something radically different must
commence. In such a case it is impossible to avoid the category of the 'new.'"[42]

Where Lurie's heroine remains in claustrophobic isolation within the enclosure
of the male masternarrative, Robinson emphasizes continuity, as the sequential
serial narrative opens out, potentially, to the next *petit récit*. In her ending that is not
an ending, in her revisionings which do not quite destroy the old story, Robinson
is therefore alive to one last possibility, that the myth of Catastrophe may persist in
the postmodernist masternarrative itself — the masternarrative of the collapse of
the masternarratives. But that — since essays must end — would be another story.[43]

Notes to Chapter 8

1. Classically stated in Leslie Fiedler, *Love and Death in the American Novel* (New York: Criterion
   Books, 1960).
2. Judith Fetterley, *The Resisting Reader: A Feminist Approach to American Fiction* (Bloomington:
   Indiana University Press, 1978).
3. Nina Baym, "Melodramas of Beset Manhood How Theories of American Fiction Exclude
   Women Authors," *American Quarterly*, 33, 2 (1981), 123–39.

4. Carolyn Heilbrun, "The Masculine Wilderness of the American novel," *Saturday Review*, 29 January 1972, 41.

5. Joanne S. Frye, *Living Stories, Telling Lives: Women and the Novel in Contemporary Experience* (Ann Arbor: University of Michigan Press, 1986), 26.

6. Mark Twain, *The Adventures of Huckleberry Finn* (London: Penguin, 1966), 369.

7. Jean-François Lyotard, *The Postmodern Condition*, trans. Geoff Bennington and Brian Massumi (Minneapolis: University of Minnesota Press, 1984), 51.

8. Ibid., 19.

9. Bill Readings, *Introducing Lyotard: Art and Politics* (London: Routledge, 1991), 69.

10. Carol P. Christ, *Diving Deep and Surfacing: Women Writers on Spiritual Quest* (Boston: Beacon Press, 1980), 4–5.

11. Frye, 6.

12. Ibid., 21.

13. Robert Kiely, *Postmodern fictions and the Nineteenth Century Novel* (Cambridge, MA: Harvard University Press, 1993), 34.

14. Alison Lurie, *Love and Friendship* (New York: Macmillan, 1962; London: Penguin, 1977), 11. All page references are to the Penguin edition.

15. See Theodore Baird, "The Freshman English Course," *Amherst Alumni News*, 5 (1952), 194–96; James H. Broderick, "A Study of the Freshman Composition Course at Amherst: Action, Order, and Language," *Harvard Educational Review*, 28, 1 (1958), 44–57; Gail Kennedy, *Education At Amherst: The New Program* (New York: Harper and Brothers, 1955).

16. See Amanda Lohrey, "The Liberated Heroine: New Varieties of Defeat," *Meanjin*, 38 (1979), 294–304.

17. See Peggy Reeves Sanday, *Fraternity Gang Rape: Sex, Brotherhood and Privilege on Campus* (New York: New York University Press, 1990) for a definitive discussion and a comprehensive bibliography.

18. Sanday, 12.

19. An account of fraternity initiation by a contemporary male writer. Alison Lurie, personal interview, Key West, Florida, 18 February 1991.

20. See Sanday. Richard Ford, "Rules of the House," *Esquire*, 105 (1986), 231–34 describes initiation in the 1960s. Mark C. Carnes, *Secret Ritual and Manhood in Victorian America* (New Haven: Yale University Press, 1989) describes the earlier period, discussing all types of fraternal organizations. In 1883 70,000 men belonged to college fraternities.

21. Sanday, "Introduction".

22. Kennedy, 130.

23. Sanday, 175.

24. Ralph Waldo Emerson, *Essays* (London: Dent, 1971), 35.

25. Richard Terdiman, *Discourse/Counterdiscourse: The Theory and Practice of Resistance in Nineteenth Century France* (Ithaca: Cornell University Press, 1985), 6.

26. See Thomas Foster, "History, Critical Theory and Women's Social Practices; 'Women's Time' and *Housekeeping*," *Signs*, 14, 1 (1988), 73–99.

27. See Maureen Ryan, "Marilynne Robinson's *Housekeeping*: The Subversive Narrative and the New American Eve," *South Atlantic Review*, 56, 1 (1991), 79–86; Martha Ravits, "Extending the American Range: Marilynne Robinson's *Housekeeping*," *American Literature*, 61, 4 (1989), 644–66; Marilyn R. Chandler, *Dwelling in the Text* (Berkeley: University of California Press, 1991); Joan Kirkby, "Is There Life After Art? The Metaphysics of Marilynne Robinson's *Housekeeping*," *Tulsa Studies in Women's Literature* 5, 1 (1986), 91–109; Gunilla Florby, "Escaping This World: Marilynne Robinson's Variation on an Old American Motif," *Moderna Sprak*, 78 (1984), 211–16; Marcia Aldrich, "The Poetics of Transience: Marilynne Robinson's *Housekeeping*," *Essays in Literature*, 16, 1 (1989), 127–40.

28. Tace Hedrick and others, "Interviews with Marilynne Robinson," *Iowa Review*, 22, 1 (1992), 4.

29. *Iowa Review*, 6.

30. *Iowa Review*, 5–6.

31. Marilynne Robinson, "Writers and the Nostalgic Fallacy," *New York Times Book Review*, 13 October 1985, 1.

32. Ibid.
33. See Rosaria Champagne, "Women's History: *Housekeeping*: Memory, Representation and Reinscription," *Women's Studies*, 20, 3–4 (1992), 321–29; Paula E. Geyh, "Burning Down the House? Domestic Space and Feminine Subjectivity in Marilynne Robinson's *Housekeeping*," *Contemporary Literature*, 34, 1 (1993), 103–22; William M. Burke, "Border Crossings in Marilynne Robinson's *Housekeeping*," *Modern Fiction Studies*, 37, 4 (1991), 716–24.
34. See Nancy Chodorow, *The Reproduction of Mothering* (Berkeley: University of California Press, 1978); Carol Gilligan, *In A Different Voice: Psychological Theory and Women's Development* (Cambridge, MA: Harvard University Press, 1982); Jean Baker Miller, *Towards A New Psychology of Women* (London: Allen Lane, 1978).
35. Marilynne Robinson, *Housekeeping* (New York: Straus, Giroux, 1981 and London, Penguin, 1982), 27. All further page references are to the Penguin edition.
36. See Ryan; Aldrich; Elizabeth A. Meese, *Crossing the Double Cross: The Practice c: Feminist Criticism* (Chapel Hill: University of North Carolina Press, 1986).
37. Ryan, 84.
38. See Allyson Booth, "To Caption Absent Bodies: Marilynne Robinson's *Housekeeping*," *Essays in Literature*, 19, 2 (1992), 79–90.
39. Ravits.
40. "The beginning is the first step in the intentional production of meaning." Edward Said, *Beginnings* (Baltimore: Johns Hopkins University Press, 1975), 5.
41. Geyh, 119.
42. Ernesto Laclau, "Politics and the Limits of Modernity," in Thomas Docherty (ed.), *Postmodernism: A Reader* (London: Harvester, 1993), 330.
43. I am grateful to the Research Committee of the University of Newcastle Upon Tyne and to the British Academy for grants which enabled me to interview Alison Lurie on 18 February 1991 and to attend the European Association for American Studies Conference in March 1994, at which this essay was originally delivered.

CHAPTER 9

Bellow's Ransom Tale:
The Holocaust, *The Victim*
and *The Double*

Although critics have differed on the relationship of *The Victim* to the Holocaust there is a general consensus that its presence is essentially muffled, if not insignificant. For Mark Schechner it is

> deeply buried, yet tightly woven into the fabric of the narrative, rarely explicit but always there, like a symptom.[1]

L. H. Goldman notes the curious silence on the topic of Bellow's normally loquacious characters.[2] Peter Hyland argues that despite a focus on anti-Semitism, the novel does not treat the Holocaust directly, though he feels that it is "haunted" by it.[3] One of the most recent critics to discuss the novel, Michael Glenday, even rejects the importance of anti-Semitism to the novel:

> I cannot follow the argument of those critics who regard this novel as centrally concerned with anti-Semitism.[4]

Glenday proceeds to a thoroughgoing revision of Allbee, who rises in the critical scale in proportion as Leventhal sinks. For Glenday, Leventhal is "a Jew without any of the fine Jewish qualities"[5] who suffers from "touchiness about anti-Semitism"[6] (in 1947!) and who appears as "Caliban" to Allbee's Prospero, an "infirma species" inhabiting a debased reality.[7] Glenday's view stands in strong contrast to Malcolm Bradbury's "the repulsive Allbee",[8] Tony Tanner's "anti-Semitic degenerate failure",[9] and Ihab Hassan's refreshingly robust "insufferable creep".[10] Apart from the discussion of anti-Semitism only one critic (S. Lilian Kremer) has drawn attention to specific Holocaust material in the novel, in its pervasive images of asphyxiation, the colour yellow (the badge) and closely packed trains.[11]

Arguably, however, the Holocaust provides the occasion and the major structural principle of the novel, in particular in relation to its double plot. Various commentators have noted the motif of Allbee as the double in *The Victim*, with the influence of Dostoevsky particularly cited.[12] In addition, the novel alternates between two plots, Leventhal's persecution by anti-Semitic Allbee, and the sickness and death of Mickey, Leventhal's brother's child, a plot which is often seen as subordinate to the Allbee story. A precise correlation none the less exists between the death of the child and the emergence of Allbee as persecuting double, a connection which draws upon psychoanalytic theorisations, specifically the work of Otto Rank.

First, however, a brief excursus into Bellow's autobiography. In interview in 1990 Bellow was asked about the relative absence of the Holocaust in his writing. He agreed that

> There were lots of things I hadn't been able to incorporate.
> Things that got away from me. The Holocaust for one. ... I may even have been partly sealed off from it.[13]

According to Bellow, it was only in 1959, when he visited Auschwitz, that the Holocaust "landed its whole weight on me". He admitted to finding it odd that he had not been moved to write about it. "I can't interpret it creditably to myself. I'm still wondering at it. I lost close relatives."[14] Bellow's reluctance to confront the topic — understandable as it is — becomes potentially more comprehensible in the description offered, in the same interview, of his childhood. At the age of eight, Bellow spent six months in hospital with T.B. Already a good reader he could read his chart at the end of the bed and knew, even at that age, that it was very unpromising. In the ward he was constantly exposed to the death of children:

> This happened regularly. A lot of fussing in the night and a screen around the kid's bed and nurses running back and forth with flashlights. And in the morning an empty bed. You just saw the bed made up for another kid. Before long there was a kid in it. You understood very well what had happened, but it wasn't discussed or explained.[15]

As a result, Bellow felt forever after that he had been in some fashion "excused from death, that it was a triumph, that I had gotten away with it".[16] There was, he concluded, "a duty that came with survival", he owed something "to some entity for the privilege of surviving."[17] Bellow, in short, was already possessed — at a very early age — of that complex of emotions which William G. Niederland has termed the "survivor syndrome".[18] In his childish narcissism, Bellow describes his survival as a triumph. In the most provocative analysis of the survivor, Elias Canetti argues that

> The moment of survival is the moment of power. Horror at the sight of death turns into satisfaction that it is someone else who is dead. ... Whether the survivor is confronted by one dead man or by many, the essence of the situation is that he feels unique. ... All men's designs on immortality contain something of this desire for survival.[19]

Bellow also describes himself as having got away with it — as if he had escaped a deserved punishment. Robert J. Lifton (who studied survivors of Hiroshima and the Holocaust) found "survival guilt" a common phenomenon, a magnification of the guilt that is present in every bereaved person: Why am I — unworthy that I am — alive when better people are not?[20]

In *The Victim* Leventhal, recalling his narrow escape from indigence in the Thirties, often says that "I was lucky. I got away with it."[21] He never forgets the hotel on Lower Broadway, and

> the part that did not get away with it — the lost, the outcast, theovercome, the effaced, the ruined. (23)

Leventhal's imagery here draws upon the notion of economic disaster, but his guilt is clearly that of a survivor, who did not particularly deserve to survive, but was luckier than the rest. The slippage here between economic and historical frames of reference has a special relevance to Bellow's reaction to the Holocaust. In interview, Bellow was asked about the intellectual impact of the Second World War. He replied that he had completely misunderstood the war because he was under the influence of Marxism. Although Kristallnacht gave him pause, Bellow, as a Trotskyist, stood by the belief that a workers' state, however degenerate, could not wage an imperialist war.

> I was still at that time officially sold on Marxism and revolution, but I sobered up when France fell.[22]

In short, Bellow's initial understanding of the events in Europe in terms of the primacy of economic forces in history was impelled to yield to a sharper awareness of the nature of anti-Semitism. He promptly joined up:

> I had recognized Hitler for "what he was". I knew most of the story, and not only did I feel that my Jewish Marxist friends were wrong in theory, but I was horrified by the positions they — we — had taken.[23]

The Victim is Bellow's examination of both the guilt and the responsibilities of the survivor. It is, in a sense, about the Holocaust, because it is not, ostensibly, about the Holocaust.

The epigraphs to the novel strike the appropriate note. The first, in which a merchant accidentally kills the child of an Ifrit, and is promptly faced with massive and apparently undeserved retribution, could hardly offer a more telling example of undeserved guilt. The accidental nature of the death (the Ifrit's child is killed by a discarded date stone) corresponds to that of Mickey, an innocent killed by an extremely rare bronchial infection, a death for which nobody — certainly not Leventhal — can be blamed. The second epigraph offers a more disquieting image of a multiplication of the individual as frightening, connecting to the double motif:

> Be that as it may, now it was that upon the rocking waters of the ocean the human face began to reveal itself; the sea appeared paved with innumerable faces, upturned to the heavens; faces, imploring, wrathful, despairing faces that surged upward by thousands, by myriads, by generations ...

In *The Pains of Opium* De Quincey precedes this image of a mob of persecutors concealed behind one face with lines which emphasise the presence in his dreams of "the tyranny of the human face", with its "tormenting" powers.[24] De Quincey's mental disturbances have been traced, persuasively, to the death of a child, his young sister, whose bandaged head created in De Quincey a morbid fear of turbans and thus of the East.[25] His nightmares were full of Oriental and Asian images and he was particularly tormented by the figure of a Malay, who had visited him at

Wordsworth's cottage in Grasmere, and who, in his opium addiction, assumed the role of demonic double. De Quincey gave the Malay enough opium to kill him on the spot, but the double survived to haunt him in his dreams. After the passage which Bellow quotes, De Quincey continues

> The Malay has been a fearful enemy for months. I have been every night through his means, transported into Asiatic scenes.[26]

The reader turns the page to find that Bellow's novel begins, "On some nights New York is as hot as Bangkok" (9), going on to evoke a composite Orientalist scene of tropical heat and foliage and "barbaric fellahin" (9). The two epigraphs initiate a novel in which death, responsibility, guilt, racial prejudice, the emergence of a persecuting double, all combine.

It is important to note here that it is only after the onset of Mickey's serious illness that Allbee puts in an appearance. Indeed, according to Elena, Mickey has died and revived. When Leventhal is called to his sickbed, Elena tells him that Mickey had stopped breathing for a period. Leventhal corrects her: "He was breathing all the time. How could he stop and start again?" (14), but she insists that he did. Leventhal's reaction is extreme:

> Leventhal's composure was not perfect; it was tinged with fear. He thought ... "What superstition! Just like in the old country. The dead can come back to life, too, I suppose, and all the rest of it." (14)

Writing about the uncanny, Freud explicitly connected it with

> that class of the frightening which leads back to what is known of old and long familiar.[27]

Freud draws upon the work of Otto Rank whose study, *The Double*, understands the double as originally an insurance against the destruction of the ego, an energetic denial of the power of death.[28] In this argument the "immortal soul" may be considered as the first double of the body. Doubling is therefore originally a preservation against extinction on the part of the self, in its narcissistic self-love. Rank noted, however, that the initially reassuring figure is also capable of reversing its aspect at a later stage of development, and from being an assurance of immortality becomes the uncanny harbinger of death. (In folklore, to see one's double is rarely good news.) In this connection Freud comments on the fear of ghosts, arguing that modern men "still think as savages do on this topic", with our apprehension based upon the fear that the dead person becomes the enemy of the survivor and seeks to carry him off to share his new life with him.[29] Rank draws especially upon literary examples and on modern film (*The Student of Prague*) on the grounds that "cinematography, which in numerous ways reminds us of the dream-work," can express psychological material clearly.[30] He remarks that dreams are particularly interesting in connection with doubles: "It should not be forgotten that one sees oneself in dreams."[31] "From the experience of dreaming, man may have taken the proof for his belief that the viable ego might exist even after death."[32] He notes that the offensive double also pursues his other in dreams, in which, fleeing from the double, he finds himself surrounded by a large crowd of self-replicas from whom escape is impossible (the situation of De Quincey).[33] Rank notes that a double may be identical or antithetical, a means of avoiding guilt by projecting responsibility for one's actions away from one's own ego; that the impulse to rid oneself of a double by violence is an essential feature of the motif — though yielding to the impulse is often fatal; and that the motif may be linked to fear of ageing, with signs of sin and age transferred to the double (points exemplified in *The Picture of Dorian Gray*.) The pursuer is often also identified with a brother. He gives examples of works in which a wife protects against a double. (In Maupassant's *He*, the *preliminary* sketch for *The Horla*, the hero decides to marry purely to rid himself of a double.) Rank also draws attention to the fact that in most double motifs the final catastrophe is the result of a relationship with a woman, often ending in the suicide of the hero by way of the death intended for the irksome persecutor. The apparent paradox of cases in which the fear of death actually leads to suicide, and the frequency with which the double is slain, suggest that man's horror of death is not purely because of his natural attachment to life (which can, after all, be less than enticing) but from love of the personality peculiar to him, his own unique self. Apart from death the other major threat to such primary narcissism is erotic; narcissism resists the dissolution of the ego in sexual love as much as its immolation in death. The double may appear in order to prevent dissolution by interrupting sexual activity, or thwarting relationships. (In *The Student of Prague* he interrupts the lovers' every tryst.) Rank therefore concludes that, because of the narcissistic esteem of our own egos, the fear of the destruction of the self, the individual creates an image as close as possible to the self in the double; the thought of death is rendered supportable by assuring oneself of a second life, after this one, as the soul.

> As in the threat to narcissism by sexual love, so in the threat of death does the idea of death (originally averted by the double) recur in the figure who, according to general superstition, announces death.[34]

As a result the double may become a rival in sexual love, and a persecuting messenger of death.

Now, it is obvious that Bellow's novel offers a multiplicity of points of contact with Rank's analysis. Mickey's death hangs over the action, filling Leventhal with fear. Allbee returns to haunt him after years of absence — Leventhal has repressed all memory of him. His uncanny nature is dramatised in his mysterious appearance. Leventhal hears a bell ring — but there is nobody at the door, nor has the super seen anyone enter or leave. Yet Allbee's letter is in Leventhal's box. Against a background featuring a revivalist band (24) Allbee appears in a line next to a chorus girl, a heavily painted lady whose significance is connected to commodified replication (the identical members of a chorus line). The ensuing conversation is distinctly odd. Allbee remarks, "Now that you've found out I exist..." and Leventhal instantly counters "Why should I doubt that you exist? Is there any reason why you shouldn't?" (28). When he tries to grip his arm he feels "no resistance" (30), as if his arm were going through Allbee as easily as Allbee apparently goes through doors. When he denies having arranged to meet Allbee, the latter brushes his objections aside with the comment "it's immaterial" (30). Leventhal dismisses Allbee, recalling him only when Mickey's condition worsens: "what a time it was to have thought of him!" he reacts (46). But as later events demonstrate, it is absolutely the right time to have thought of him. Allbee appears as a ghastly harbinger of death and a persecuting double in direct response to the threat to Mickey. Just as the Holocaust reactivated Bellow's childhood experience, reviving repressed material in sharpened, guilty form, so in the novel, a Jewish child is threatened by death, and in guilt and fear Leventhal allows a double to emerge to persecute him. Other elements of the plot — Allbee's diabolical and Faustian connections (the threatened soul), the decisive break with Allbee over the woman whom he installs in Leventhal's bed, and the apparent suicide attempt which almost kills them both, are readily comprehensible in the light of Rank's analysis.

The connections to the Holocaust emerge most clearly in relation to two structural elements common to Bellow and Rank: acting and dreams. Acting offers an exceptionally good metaphor for the narcissistic splitting and reduplication of the ego. Allbee is repeatedly characterised by Leventhal as a bad actor, a poor imitation of the genuine article, himself. The horror film which Leventhal attends in the novel also highlights the uncanny double:

> an old scientist was seen haunting the dressing room of a theatre where he had murdered his mistress many years ago. He had hallucinations about a young star who resembled her and he attempted to strangle the girl. (88)

The movie is *The Climax* (1944), lavishly filmed in the Paris Opera and marking Boris Karloff's return to Hollywood, after his rejection of monster roles in favour of more "dignified" ones.[35] Karloff plays a physician who has killed a singer, and now finds that the new star is the double of her predecessor. Leventhal finds himself unable to watch the film, which takes place in a deathly environment, a stifling airless cinema with "nebulous" lamps, in "dust-eaten" shades (88). When he goes out for air, however, he is confronted by an old man who describes Karloff as understanding "what a mastermind is, a law unto himself" (89). The old man's description of total narcissistic involvement irresistibly recalls the Nazi glorification of the Superman or Übermensch. Jung, indeed, argued that the appeal of Hitler rested on his ability to function as the shadow (Jung's term for the *alter ego*) to the entire German people.[36]

If the film connects acting, doubles and the Holocaust, the subsequent cafeteria discussion of what constitutes good acting is no less relevant, as a group of Jews argue about anti-Semitism, and acting (in the double senses of role play and moral behaviour). Schlossberg's test for a good actor is the appropriate response to death. His examples involve the bereaved Nazimova, as one of Chekhov's *Three Sisters*, and Livia Hall (close homophone of Leventhal) as the murderess of her "other half". The group speculate about acting as duplication, wondering, for example, why there are "so many Victorias" (111). Later in the novel Schlossberg reappears, still discussing death, in this case the modern inability to face it, as opposed to an older generation. Conversation ranges over insurance against death (in the economic not the psychological sense), the sewing of one's own shroud, and survival guilt. (Mrs Harkavy feels "wicked still to be here at my age while the children die." 200).

Schlossberg draws the moral:

> I have to be myself in full. Which is somebody who dies, isn't it? ... I'm not
> three people, four people. I was born once and I will die once. You want to
> be two people? More than human? Maybe it's because you don't know how to
> be one. (208)

Schlossberg goes on to lament the transformation of modern man into a whole corporation of selves, replicating the division of labour. Most critics have read the image of the crowd in *The Victim* in similarly economic terms as representing the pressures of urban life and the masses.[37] As Bellow's De Quincey epigraph suggests, however, and as the pushing, stifling crowds in the novel confirm, the crowd also features as an image of a number of replica selves, hostile and competitive, an image of destruction by and in the mass. When Leventhal takes the ferry from Mickey's sickbed back to New York, for example, he finds himself amidst a "crowd of souls" (57).

The images of crowds, acting and the Holocaust come together in two dreams. The first of them occurs when Leventhal has finally allowed Allbee into his home. This is despite the fact that Allbee is clearly bent on persecuting him and has wrung from him the only overt reference to the Holocaust in the novel: "Millions of us have been killed" (123). Beginning as a response to the fear of death Allbee has become the double who punishes Leventhal for surviving, making him relive the experience of anti-Semitic persecution. In the dream Leventhal is quite overtly split into two selves:

> He had an unclear dream in which he held himself off like an unwilling
> spectator; yet it was he that did everything. (138)

The situation, a railway station hung with flags, in which crowds controlled by guards are being loaded onto trains, is instantly recognisable as an image of the Holocaust.[38] Leventhal, however, is eager to board the train, running in an attempt to catch it. A surge of the crowd displaces him into a freshly paved and plastered corridor, a new installation, but before he can reach the tracks, he is halted by two men. The one, a working man, appears sympathetic but "he was an employee and couldn't interfere" (139). (He is only following orders.) The other, in a business suit, pushes Leventhal out into an alley. Leventhal's face is covered with tears. The dream suggests that Leventhal has made every effort — in his double dream self — to get on the train, to share the fate of the crowd around him, but has been thwarted despite himself. Waking, Leventhal has "a sense of marvellous relief ... a rare pure feeling of happiness" (139). His dream double has assuaged his guilt, sought out his own destruction, and been excused from death by a mysterious authority figure. Leventhal has a sudden insight:

> it was supremely plain to him that everything, everything without exception
> took place as if within a single soul or person. (139)

Fragmentation yields to unity here, in the reverse of the opening epigraph, as the self comes back together and the threatening mass becomes a single soul. One is reminded of the American motto "E Pluribus Unum", one out of many. Leventhal, of course, escaped the fate of European Jewry because he was in America.

After Mickey's death, as Leventhal accepts that he is one person, a person who dies, his relation to the crowd changes. In the park after Mickey's funeral, he hears the revivalist band and remembers a story he had once read about "Hell cracking open ... and all the souls, crammed together, looking out" (151). Eying the crowd around him, however, he continues: "But these were alive, this young couple ... this woman late in pregnancy" (151). Despite his sorrow, Leventhal is now able to accept death, and to turn towards life and love. In allowing Allbee to persecute him he has largely exorcised his excessive guilts and surrendered his narcissistic defences. Now, "Max and the family had replaced Allbee in his mind" (154), and he sends for his wife.

It should come as no surprise therefore that Leventhal's ensuing dream, which also has a bearing on the Holocaust, should include a double — but a double firmly feminised. The dream also returns to the business representative of the first dream, not as a saviour but as complicit in the horror. In the dream a salesgirl in a store demonstrates shades of rouge to Leventhal by drawing spots on her face, wiping each off on a soiled hand towel, dyed red as a result, and then bending back to the mirror to repeat the process. The salesgirl recalls the painted ladies of Freud's essay on the uncanny (to whom he was repeatedly drawn back), the chorus girl of the earlier scene, and (via the image of stage make-up) the notion of acting. In making herself up the woman is "putting on a face" — many faces, multiplied in the mirror. Leventhal, however, is brought to semi-consciousness by the smell of the red soiled towel. (The female symbolism here does not need to be belaboured.) The battle is between a woman and an uncanny double.

> The odour of the towel had from the beginning seemed *familiar*. (228; my emphasis)

The return of the familiar, the repressed, marks the return of the Holocaust to consciousness. Leventhal's mind, semi-conscious, moves from the towel to the bathroom, and to an uneasy awareness that though he can hear steam hissing in the pipes, the room is cold. He rouses himself to the smell of hissing gas: Allbee is attempting to gas them both. "Gas was pouring from the oven" (229). The reference to Nazi "showers" could hardly be more explicit. Where Leventhal's first dream potentially suggested the saving force of capitalist America (the businessman) the second dream indicts big business, recalling its crucial role in the Holocaust. Bellow's Marxism was not lightly abandoned. The colours (German "Farben") of the woman' s paint recall I. G. Farben, the German business conglomerate which began by making dyestuffs, then went on to build both its own new plant and a private concentration camp at Auschwitz, and manufactured Zyklon B, the gas for its extermination block (a gas deliberately manufactured without the "indicator" of its familiar smell). Leventhal's dream began with an image of cars in rapid motion. I.G. Farben made the synthetic gas and rubber on which Nazi Germany depended for its mobility.[39] In the dream the familiar links to the source of horror; Leventhal's life, however, is saved by his ability to bring the repressed matter to the surface, to consciousness, a consciousness assisted here by the female presence in the dream. The dream expresses Leventhal's renewed — if fearful — openness to sexual love and the disappearance of the deathly double. Allbee is now firmly ejected.

At the close of the novel, several years later, the reader learns that Leventhal looks years younger and has "lost the feeling that he had, as he used to say, 'got away with it'" (230). When Allbee reappears at the theatre he looks older, unhealthy, with a decayed appearance and deepened wrinkles about his eyes which have "a fabric quality, crumpled and blank" (236) — very much the image of the ageing or decaying portrait. Appropriately he is in the company of an actress, Yvonne Crane, whose professional existence depends upon defying the ageing process, and on playing many roles. Mary, who has seen her picture "a hundred times" (134), comments "How do they stay looking so young?" (234). Leventhal, on the other hand, has accepted a more natural means to immortality. Eyeing the pregnant Mary, Allbee comments that Leventhal is clearly following the injunction to "Increase and Multiply" (236). It is in some ways an inconclusive ending, leaving the reader poised between the hero and the double, and ending on a question. It may make more sense if we return to the initial epigraph.

Discussing the motif of the double in literature, Rank took an essentially pathological view, noting how many writers were mentally disturbed, given to paranoia, drink, drugs, self-abuse and hallucination. The example of De Quincey supports the view of double literature as at best therapeutic, at worst the record of delusion. Arguably *The Victim* was therapeutic for Bellow, who himself noted a change after it from gloom to holiday.[40] Critics have also been swift to see the subsequent novel — *The Adventures of Augie March* — as marking a breakthrough. Bellow's first epigraph is taken from "The Tale of the Trader and the Jinni". The story is an example of the "ransom frame" in which the act of story telling serves to redeem a human life.[41] In the story the merchant is saved by the intervention of two other storytellers whose stories distract the Jinni, much as Scheherazade distracts Shahriar in the frame-tale from his intention to kill her. In other words the merchant is saved from suffering as a result of a death which he did not intend, by the very process of storytelling. As Paul Coates puts it:

> Works of fiction exist in a space between the Double and the Other. To enter into a work of fiction is in a sense to transform the Other into a Double: to discover in the apparent foreignness of another person the lineaments of one's own aspirations and hopes.[42]

As the multiple plot structures of the *Thousand and One Nights* demonstrate, storytelling is a better defence against the powers of death than any other, for it doubles reader, author and character, by sympathetic identification — a form of love. *The Victim* is a narrative of trauma which becomes a narrative of reparation, the first of a long, reparative career.

Arguably, it is also highly suggestive in the paradigm offered for the importance of the theme of death in Bellow's novels, and for the treatment thereof. Double plots are a common feature of Bellow's writing, with one half of the pair, as in De Quincey, often associated with the "Other": America and Mexico in *The Adventures of Augie March*, America and Africa in *Henderson the Rain King*, America and Eastern Europe in The *Dean's December*, Dr Lal in *Mr Sammler's Planet*, Dahfu in *Henderson the Rain King*, the pickpocket in *Mr Sammler's Planet*. In *Humboldt's Gift* Cantabile emerges as persecuting double when Citrine learns of the death of Humboldt; Henderson sets off for Africa in immediate response to the death of Miss Lenox; the death of Valeria haunts *The Dean's December*; *Seize the Day* ends with Tommy Wilhelm absorbed into the crowd at a funeral. Herzog writes letters to the dead but is brought back to emotional health after watching the trial of a woman accused of causing the death of a small child. Even more suggestively, in the light of Bellow's ambivalence to his Trotskyite past, when Augie encounters Trotsky in Mexico he identifies him with the power of death:

> Death discredits. Survival is the whole success. The voice of the dead goes away. There isn't any memory. The power that's established fills the earth and destiny is whatever survives.[43]

More generally, *The Victim* offers an illuminating comparative perspective on other novels of trauma and mass death. Toni Morrison's *Beloved*, for example, with its epigraph

> *Sixty million*
> *and more*

focusses on the uncanny tale of a murdered child returning as a ghostly double to haunt and persecute the guilty mother, coming between mother and lover and finally being ejected only after threatening her life. Louise Erdrich's *Tracks* moves from an opening evocation of genocide to the rescue of a dying child and a narrative which alternates between two trickster figures, Nanapush and Pauline. As an aged Chippewa trickster figure, Nanapush may seem to have little connection to Saul Bellow's urban heroes, yet faced with the threat of death he uses the same tactic of storytelling as survival mechanism:

> During the year of sickness when I was the last one left, I saved myself by starting a story. ... I could hardly keep moving my lips. But I did continue and recovered. I got well by talking. Death could not get a word in edgewise, grew discouraged, and traveled on.[44]

Notes to Chapter 9

1. Mark Schechner, *After the Revolution: Studies in the Contemporary Jewish American Imagination* (Bloomington and Indianapolis: Indiana University Press, 1982), 127.
2. L. H. Goldman, "The Jewish Perspective of Saul Bellow," in L. H. Goldman, Gloria Cronin and Ada Aharoni, *Saul Bellow: A Mosaic* (New York: Peter Lang, 1992), 3–19.
3. Peter Hyland, *Saul Bellow* (London: Macmillan, 1992), 23.
4. Michael Glenday, *Saul Bellow and the Decline of Humanism* (London: Macmillan, 1990), 28.
5. Ibid., 27.
6. Ibid., 29.
7. Ibid., 34.
8. Malcolm Bradbury, *Saul Bellow* (London: Methuen, 1982), 29.
9. Tony Tanner, *Saul Bellow* (London: Oliver and Boyd, 1965), 27.
10. Ihab Hassan, *Radical Innocence: Studies in the Contemporary American Novel* (Princeton: Princeton University Press, 1961), 299–300.
11. S. Lillian Kremer, "The Holocaust in *The Victim*," *Saul Bellow Journal*, 2 (1983), 15–23.
12. Daniel Fuchs, *Saul Bellow: Vision and Revision* (Durham, NC: Duke University Press, 1984), 43–49.

13. Saul Bellow, *It All Adds Up: From the Dim Past to the Uncertain Future: A Non-Fiction Collection* (London: Secker and Warburg, 1994), 312.

14. Ibid., 313.

15. Ibid., 290.

16. Ibid., 289

17. Ibid.

18. Helen Epstein, *Children of the Holocaust* (New York: G. P. Putnam's Sons, 1979), 100–03.

19. Elias Canetti, *Crowds and Power* (London: Penguin, 1962), 227.

20. Epstein, 107.

21. Saul Bellow, *The Victim* (London: Penguin, 1966; first published New York: Vanguard, 1947). Subsequent page references follow quotations in parentheses.

22. Bellow, *It All Adds Up*, 307.

23. Ibid., 310.

24. Thomas De Quincey, *Confessions of an English Opium-Eater*, ed. Richard Garnett (London: Kegan Paul, Trench, Trübner, 1891), 137.

25. John Barrell, *The Infection of Thomas De Quincey: A Psychopathology of Imperialism* (New Haven and London: Yale University Press, 1991).

26. De Quincey, 137.

27. Sigmund Freud, "The Uncanny," *The Standard Edition of the Complete Psychological Works of Sigmund Freud. Vol. XVII*, ed. James Strachey (London: Hogarth Press, 1955), 242.

28. Otto Rank, *The Double: A Psychoanalytic Study*, trans. and ed. Harry Tucker, Jr. (Chapel Hill: University of North Carolina Press, 1971). The publishing history of *The Double* is complex. It was published in several versions in German (1914, 1919, 1925), French (1932), and English (1941) before the publication of *The Victim*. Harry Tucker provides a clear account of the various versions.

29. Freud, 242.

30. Rank, 4.

31. Ibid., 82.

32. Ibid., 83.

33. Rank attributes the example to Jerome K. Jerome, but his translator notes that this is inaccurate. I suspect De Quincey is the intended example.

34. Rank, 85.

35. Paul M. Jensen, *Boris Karloff and His Films* (South Brunswick and New York: A. S. Barnes, 1974).

36. Carl Gustav Jung, *Essays on Contemporary Events: Reflections on Nazi Germany* (London: Ark, 1988), 6.

37. Bradbury, 40–47.

38. Kremer.

39. Joseph Borkin, *The Crime and Punishment of I. G. Farben: The Birth, Growth and Corruption of a Giant Corporation* (London: André Deutsch, 1979); Peter Hayes, *Industry and Ideology: I. G. Farben in the Nazi Era* (Cambridge: Cambridge University Press, 1987). The relation of private capital to the Nazi regime has received many different interpretations. The story of I.G. Farben (I.G. = "Interessengemeinschaft") has been told several times. The account by Joseph Borkin is clear and readable. Peter Hayes provides a list of American and other accounts, including two works published like *The Victim* in 1947 (in New York): Howard Ambruster, *Treason's Peace* and Richard Sasuly, *I G Farben*. I.G. Farben's directors were tried at Nuremburg, though their sentences were comparatively light.

40. Bellow, *It All Adds Up*, 41.

41. Peter L. Caracciolo (ed.), *The Arabian Nights in English Literature: Studies in the Reception of The Thousand and One Nights into British Culture* (London: Macmillan, 1988).

42. Paul Coates, *The Double and the Other: Identity as Ideology in Post-Romantic Fiction* (London: Macmillan, 1988), 1.

43. Saul Bellow, *The Adventures of Augie March* (London: Penguin, 1966), 482.

44. Louise Erdrich, *Tracks* (London: Picador, 1989), 46.

CHAPTER 10

Spaces In-Between:
Hester Prynne as the Salem Bibi in
Bharati Mukherjee's
The Holder of the World

Bharati Mukherjee is a writer who has never seen her "country", Bangladesh, the ancestral home of her father; born and brought up in Calcutta, she moved successively to Iowa, to a long residence in Canada, and finally back to the United States, where, in 1988, she became an American citizen.[1] Her novel *The Holder of the World* sketches a similar transnational trajectory — only in reverse. In its frame-tale, the American narrator, Beigh Masters, a twentieth-century asset-hunter, is engaged in a quest for a lost Mughal diamond, the Emperor's Tear, and in the process excavates links between seventeenth-century Massachusetts and pre-colonial India. In the inset tale, Indians (Native Americans) are replaced by Indians (from the subcontinent) as the heroine, Hannah Easton, moves from Puritan New England to the Coromandel Coast, and the court of the Emperor Aurengzebe. (The title is the translated form of Alamgir, another name for Aurengzebe.) Along the way there is a torrid affair with an Indian lover, a Rajah, and Hannah returns to America with his child, Pearl Singh. Mukherjee was inspired to write by a pre-auction viewing at Sotheby's in New York of a seventeenth-century Indian miniature of a woman in elaborate Mughal court dress — a woman who was Caucasian and blonde:

> I thought, "Who is this very confident-looking 17th-century woman, who sailed in some clumsy wooden boat across dangerous seas and then stayed there? She had transplanted herself in what must have been a traumatically different culture. How did she survive?"[2]

Transactions between cultures are therefore at the heart of the novel, which reveals in its closing pages that Hannah Easton, the "Salem bibi" — the white mistress from Salem — was the original for Hester Prynne, the heroine of that most canonical of American novels, Nathaniel Hawthorne's *The Scarlet Letter*. Mukherjee's novel therefore takes its place in a well-established tradition of rewritings or "revisionings" of the classics of the past, from *Wide Sargasso Sea* to *Foe* or *Water with Berries*.[3] In most cases the "pre-text" is an emblematically colonial discourse, which almost singles itself out for contestation whether it involves a Caribbean madwoman in Jane Eyre's attic, Caliban or Friday on their islands, or Turtons and Burtons in Forster's India.

But why rewrite *The Scarlet Letter*? More than one reader failed to see the relevance or necessity of this pre-text to Mukherjee's novel — the connection looks like "a highly arbitrary explanation for one of the most mysterious figures in American Literature. She might just as easily have turned out to be the governess in *Anna and the King of Siam* as Hester Prynne."[4]

Indeed, although there are clues for the alert reader, the connection only becomes overt in the closing pages when the reader is informed that Hannah knew one of Hawthorne's ancestors, who passed on the story that became "his morbid introspection into guilt and repression that many call our greatest work" (286), a work which bears little relation to Mukherjee's version of historical "truth": "Who can blame Nathaniel Hawthorne for shying away from the real story of the brave Salem woman and her illegitimate daughter?" (284).[5]

Readers will recall that in Hawthorne's novel, set in 1642–49 in Puritan New England, Hester Prynne is condemned to wear a scarlet letter on her chest as a badge of shame. Her husband, Roger Prynne, who adopts the name of Chillingworth, has been missing, presumed drowned, though he is actually held in captivity by the Indians. In his prolonged absence Hester has yielded to temptation with Dimmesdale, the local vicar, by whom she bears a child, Pearl. Rather as in *The French Lieutenant's Woman* (which also owes a debt to Hawthorne), social ostracism sets her free from the narrow constraints of Puritan ideology and she transmogrifies to some extent into a freethinker and an emblem of passion and rebellion. As far as American criticism is concerned, the jury is still out on the degree to which Hawthorne endorses Hester's views. As Philip Rahv put it, "The dark lady is a rebel and an emancipator; but precisely for this reason Hawthorne feels the compulsion to destroy her."[6] In the novel's outcome, Chillingworth succeeds in defeating Hester's attempt to escape with her lover by sea, Dimmesdale confesses and his guilty flame is promptly extinguished by death, Pearl returns to the Old World, and Hester eventually ends her days in gloomy Boston, still something of a walking sandwich-board against sin. As this thumbnail plot-summary indicates, the connection between Mukherjee's Hannah and Hawthorne's Hester is considerably less obvious than that between, say, Bertha Mason and Rhys's Antoinette Cosway.

Mukherjee's novel also raises other questions, transgressing the institutional and nationalist boundaries within which most literary critics still operate. To put it baldly, should it be the topic of an essay on "New Literatures in English" or on American Studies? Is Mukherjee a postcolonial writer or, as she has claimed, an American immigrant? For many reviewers, Mukherjee's apparently tenuous linkage of Hannah/Hester represents a means of self-aggrandisement, of laying claim herself to a place in the American canon. Fakrul Alam describes it as a novel which has been "designed to secure for herself a place in the great tradition of American fiction".[7] It is a view which also gains support from Mukherjee's own robust declaration of her identity as immigrant:

> I am an American. I am an American writer, in the American mainstream, trying to extend it ... I am not an Indian writer, not an exile, not an expatriate. I am an immigrant.[8]

In this sense, rewriting *The Scarlet Letter* is not so much an act of counter-discursive contestation as a claim to a place at the table with the canonical elite. It none the less breaks what seems to have almost become a taboo — the rigid distinction between American and postcolonial literature. Even the most recent overviews of postcolonial writing largely ignore America,[9] and in American institutions the teaching of postcolonial writing risks breaking connections with American literature, particularly African-American writing, rather than strengthening them. Postcolonial "browns" are easier for the academy to handle — out there in some remote exotic space — than American blacks on the doorstep. Mukherjee's self-identification as immigrant may get her out of the ghetto of "minority" writing, but it also suggests the adoption of a conventional American alibi-identity. One thinks of Oscar Handlin's comment that the history of immigration *is* the history of America, and of the persistent American Puritan myth of origins as that of a beleaguered band fleeing persecution for freedom (as opposed to the first permanent American settlement, further south in Jamestown, which was a straightforward colony). Mukherjee's novel apparently exploits the Puritan myth in its opening description of Hannah's life as an immigrant's daughter in Massachusetts, the survivor of a notorious Indian massacre in King Philip's War, a traumatised orphan who is adopted and brought up in Salem until marriage to Gabriel Legge transports her overseas. Strikingly, Mukherjee advances the clock from Hawthorne's 1640s to Hannah's birth in 1670, to allow Indian (Nipmuc) savagery to occupy centre-stage (scalpings, killings, a game of football with a decapitated head) and to re-create the sense of beleaguerment in a hostile environment.

Geographical manipulation is also a factor here. Hester Prynne is disgraced in Boston. In shifting the scene to Salem, Mukherjee could hardly have selected a more emblematically Puritan locale. Perhaps largely courtesy of Arthur Miller, the town is almost synonymous with Puritans and conjures up immediate images of gloomy divines fanatically expunging all evil from their midst. Indeed, in the manufacture of the American past, Salem has a privileged status as an ur-location. The tourist who visits Salem today will find the town pandering wholesale to its reputation as "the witch city". The town fire-brigade, for example, has this title embossed on its engines, together with a rather nippy image of a hag on a broomstick. In the centre of town, the Salem Witch Museum commemorates the 1692 witchcraze with a full multimedia program, sound- and light-show, tour of a re-created dungeon, and live re-enactment of a witch trial. ("Children love this macabre exhibit", according to the guidebook.) Farther afield, a second historic site offers "The Pioneer Village", one of the earliest historical theme parks built in America. No sound- and light-show here, but thatched cottages, wigwams and dugouts, as built by the early settlers, an insect-infested pond with ducking-stool, and periodic displays by pikemen, sweating to death in full costume. It is a more primitive experience in more ways than one. There is, however, a third site in Salem, or, rather, a whole complex of buildings: the Salem Maritime National Historic Site, which commemorates a different Salem — the town whose material prosperity was entirely founded on trade with the East. Here, along with Hawthorne's birthplace, the "House of the Seven Gables", which supposedly inspired his novel of that name, and the Custom House where he worked, is the Peabody Museum with its enormous collections of Asian art, porcelain, textiles, and precious objects from India, China and Japan, its maritime collections, and a mass of souvenirs of the East. In the days of its prosperity, Salem was not "the witch city". Its city seal bore a palm-tree, a Parsee, and a ship, with the motto *"Divitis indiae usque ad ultimum sinum"* (To the farthest port of the rich East).[10] Between the 1780s and 1830s, Salem was a major international port for the East Indies and China trade — silk, tea, chinaware, textiles, and above all the pepper trade, of which Salem had a virtual monopoly. By 1799, forty-one Salem vessels had called at Calcutta, Madras and Bombay; twenty-one at Batavia and Sumatra and the Dutch East Indies; and five at Canton. Salem ships bore such names as the *Arab, Bengal, Borneo, Ganges, Grand Turk, Hindoo, Malay, Tigris* and *Zenobia*. So extensive were Salem's contacts in India and the East Indies that some traders actually believed "Salem" to be the name of a sovereign nation. It was probably the richest American city per capita in 1790. One ship, the Eliza, brought in over a million pounds. Trade was so profitable that there was no need to rely on making a profit on the outward voyage; ships were often simply sent out in ballast. In "Old News" (1835), Hawthorne himself noted the luxury of the Salem merchants' town houses, their silk beds and hangings, damask tablecloths, Turkish carpets, ivory, china and cashmere shawls. Indians also visited Salem, from the "Lascars" of ship's crews to the bearded Sikh who is recorded in much the same terms as a museum exhibit, and inspired almost as much astonishment as the famous elephant imported from Bengal in 1796.[11] A Salem pastor wrote that "No young man of Hawthorne's time considered his education finished before he had visited India, China or the Malay archipelago."[12] If this was something of an exaggeration, it is none the less true that the young men's social life revolved around the Salem East India Maritime Society with its exhibition hall and meetings. On festive occasions such as the annual dinner, its members dressed as Mandarins, Rajahs or Sultans and paraded through the streets. Salem's subsequent decline, the result in part of Jefferson's embargo, was hastened by the development of new deep-draft clipper ships which could only be outfitted in deepwater ports such as Baltimore, Boston, or New York. By the 1830s the golden age of Salem trade was waning, and in 1846 the last pepper ship from Sumatra entered the port. In the intervening years, however, Salem had made a fortune out of the East.

It was also a trade with which Hawthorne had intimate connections, as Luther S. Luedtke has emphasised. Hawthorne was born in Salem, the son of an East India captain who died in Surinam in 1808, leaving the three-year-old Hawthorne to be brought up by the family of his mother, Elizabeth Manning. His father had sailed to the East half a dozen times, and left behind logbooks and journals, including that of a trip to Bengal in 1796, and to Madras, on the Coromandel Coast, in 1800. Nathaniel was brought up in the Manning household on Herbert Street, close to the wharves. He himself found employment in the Boston Custom House, 1834–41, and then as Surveyor for the district of Salem and Beverley, 1846–49, losing his job as a result of Zachary Taylor's election and the manoeuvrings of pork-barrel politics. Hawthorne's paternal ancestry included William Hathorne, 1607–81, a persecutor of Quakers, and John Hathorne, 1641–1717, notorious for his presence at the 1692 witch-trials — both Puritans in the gloomiest stereotypical mould. (Hawthorne hid the shame of his ancestry behind a letter — inserting the letter W into his own surname.) All five of John Hathorne's sons, including Hawthorne's grandfather Joseph, went to sea. The Mannings were a mercantile family with extensive business interests. As Gloria Erlich notes, however, most biographers of Hawthorne have been much more interested in his Puritan forebears than in the tradesmen and sea-captains who actually dominate the family history.[13] Mukherjee's project, then, of restoring connections between Hawthorne and India takes its place in an honourable tradition of filling in the gaps in history, correcting and amplifying the record, and curing that amnesia which is America's second name.

Curiously, although the canon of American literature has been extensively revised, expanded and rewritten in recent years, particularly by New-Historicist critics, there has been an echoing silence on the topic of Hawthorne and the East — with one very honourable exception. The attempts of a generation of "New Americanists" to restore the unacknowledged agency of the historically marginalised in shaping a dominant tradition have tended to focus on the role of African-Americans, women, and, to a lesser extent, Native Americans.[14] Historicist attempts on *The Scarlet Letter* have gone through various manoeuvres, emphasising the historicity of Hawthorne's novel (originally one of the planks in the ahistorical romance theory of American literature) either in its setting or as relating to the moment of its composition. Walter Benn Michaels, for example, translates economic forces into generic structures, examining how Hawthorne's anxieties about the fluctuation in value of American real estate relate to his deployment of the romance genre, opposing radical fictionality to the socially implicated forms of the novel. In his introduction to his recent volume, *New Essays on the Scarlet Letter*, Michael J. Colacurcio describes all the new essays as "significantly historical" in their approach.[15] His own is devoted squarely to the history of the Puritans and its presence in the novel in references to the works of Winthrop and Mather. Increasingly desperate attempts have been made to establish a connection with anxieties over slavery, despite (or perhaps because of) the fact that Hawthorne was famously dismissive of abolitionism and supported the Compromise of 1850. Attention has focused on issues of vexed paternity and miscegenation ("A is for Abolition"), the frequent references to blackness as evil, and the concern with psychological slavery in the characters. Jean Fagan Yellin skilfully detects the iconography of abolitionism, used against itself. In addition, the novel has been read as a response to fear of red revolution (1848) or, in its civil-war setting, as engaging with the American sense of impending civil division.[16] Even at high-school level, the most determined attempts are being undertaken to make Hawthorne historically "relevant" and to drag his novel towards political engagement. A very recent textbook for high-school students devotes chapters to such issues as illegitimacy, single mothers, corporal punishment, child custody, witchcraft, and the adultery of TV evangelists, and includes in its topic lists such questions as "Compare and contrast the cases and characters of Dimmesdale and Jimmy Swaggart", "Do a campy stage production of Wigglesworth's Day of Doom" and "Stage a witch trial".[17] There is nothing in any of this about the East.

In creative writing there is a silence almost as deafening as the critical elision of the imperial space. Maryse Condé's *I Tituba* sees the black slave Tituba's story as part of Hester's imaginative inspiration, though her Hester, pregnant in prison, hangs herself, and the story is that of the slave.[18] Christopher Bigsby's *Hester* and its sequel *Pearl* are squarely focused on the seventeenth century, establishing connections with Civil-War England in texts fairly bristling with information on Norfolk emigration history. John Updike rewrites *The Scarlet Letter* three times, in *A Month of Sundays, Roger's Version* and *S.*, telling the story successively from the viewpoint of the adulterous minister, the wronged husband and the heroine. Although in modern dress, the Puritan heritage is very much to the fore in the trilogy's interest in conflicts between sexual passion and religious repression. Only the third volume, *S.*, re-orientalises its heroine and makes an Indian connection — and that is to a dubious ashram in Arizona, whose "Indian" guru turns out to be Jewish.[19] Popular film focuses on the Puritans but picks up politically correct cues from the cultural climate — particularly slavery, Native Americans and the persecution of women. Those who have undergone the ordeal of watching Demi Moore in *The Scarlet Letter* (1995) will have noted that the film is knee-deep in Indians (Native Americans), to whom Dimmesdale is pastor, includes a witch-scare, and has a well-endowed black female slave featuring prominently in a bath. In the denouement, it is rather as if *The Last of the Mohicans* had been crossed with *The Crucible*, as Hester is rescued from the scaffold itself by the Indians, led by Dimmesdale on a charger. In other words, in both critical and creative work, where Indians do feature it is as Native Americans; where the Other is invoked it is as African-American or as woman. The splendid exception to this consensus is Luther S. Luedtke, who in 1985 (just as Mukherjee was observing her Indian miniature) published *Nathaniel Hawthorne and the Romance of the Orient*, which discusses the history of Salem, the seafaring background, and the presence of "Oriental" material in Hawthorne's works. Luedtke concentrates his attention on the dark "Oriental" heroines — Zenobia in *The Blithedale Romance*, who bears the name of that Syrian queen who was vanquished by Aurelian in AD 272, Miriam in *The Marble Faun*, and Hester, described by Hawthorne in *The Scarlet Letter* as having "a rich, voluptuous, Oriental characteristic, — a taste for the gorgeously beautiful".[20] He also traces the source-material of "Rappaccini's Daughter" to the poison damsel tales of Indian mythology, catalogues Hawthorne's extensive reading of first-hand accounts of the East (whether tales of seraglios or more respectable travelogues), his essays on Eastern topics, and the influence on him of the "Oriental tale" (in Voltaire's version particularly). He concludes that traditional moral, historical and symbolist readings of *The Scarlet Letter* have not fully realised the cultural dialectic of the Puritan pastor and his "Oriental" other, or their failure to make a universe of their separate "spheres" (to use one of Hawthorne's dominant metaphors). Hawthorne describes Hester's letter as "her passport into regions where other women dared not tread", for it has accustomed her to a "latitude of speculation" altogether "foreign" to her compatriots (199). The journey of exploration is figured nonetheless as a pointless "wandering ... in the dark labyrinth of mind; now turned aside by an insurmountable precipice, now starting back from a deep chasm. There was wild and ghastly scenery all around her" (166). The connections between known/unknown, native/outlandish, New England/the East remain essentially unforged. For Luedtke, "what we experience as the genius of *The Scarlet Letter* is not the rich domestic life of 17th century New England alone, but the counterweight which that culture provided to Hawthorne's Oriental flights of imagination".[21] It is, in short, the tension between foreign and domestic which gives the novel its power. For all the strength and originality of this argument (which has been quite passed over by most critics), it does pose problems, in that it concentrates on the East as "Orient", as an imaginative stimulus, and remains thin on actual connections to the Eastern trade. It might readily be objected that Hester is Oriental only in the stereotypical sense (dark and sexy) and that she could as easily come from Italy like Beatrice Rappaccini, or from the Azores like the lady of "Drowne's Wooden Image". Luedtke strains the argument in places in order to demonstrate an Oriental connection which may appear simply not to be there. The more interesting question — and the one addressed by Mukherjee — is *why* it is not there. Why, when Salem was steeped in the Indies, when Hawthorne himself worked in the Custom House, when his whole family were connected to the trade with the East, did Hawthorne choose to concentrate almost entirely in his novel on the Puritan moment?

That "almost" needs glossing. It is well here to call attention to the structure of Hawthorne's novel, in which the tale of Hester is preceded by an introductory sketch or preamble entitled "The Custom House" — a sketch which many readers still skim over. As Christopher Bigsby puts it, the sketch "is different in tone from the rest of the book and has its pleasures but, if it should pall, stay with it for ahead lies a remarkable story".[22] Writing in 1850 in "The Custom House", Hawthorne puts the emphasis squarely on decline and degeneration. He alludes briefly to the fact that Salem was once a prosperous port, but what he describes, in some detail, is a scene of decay, of dilapidated warehouses and grassy overgrown pavements. The past vigour of Salem trade is relentlessly downplayed. In his account, the merchants feature only as geriatrics: "old King Derby", "old Billy Gray" and "old Simon Forrester" (28); their empire is a mere temporary aberration in the historical record. Simon Forrester's head is described as scarcely in the tomb "before his mountain-pile of wealth began to dwindle" (28). When Hawthorne includes an account of his own ancestry, he ignores the Mannings and seafarers in favour of an account of William and John Hathorne, noting that, after these stern Puritan divines, the rest of the family sank from public view: "From father to son, for above a hundred years, they followed the sea" (10–11), he comments dismissively. He then describes his research as poking about in the pointless rubbish of history, "reading the names of vessels that had long since foundered at sea" (29), and of merchants whose names were already fading off their tombstones. According to Hawthorne, he has made a decent effort to reanimate that past: "to raise up from these dry bones an image of the old town's brighter aspect, when India was a new region, and only Salem knew the way thither" (29). But the material turns out to be quite unrewarding. What he does find, however — the one piece of the past to quicken his curiosity and set off his imagination — is the small piece of mouldering cloth, the scarlet letter, which is the catalyst for the tale that follows. In his preamble, therefore, Hawthorne deliberately distances himself from the mercantile trade of Salem and effaces his commercial background in order to leapfrog the reader over the years of India trade to a tale of Puritans. The evidence of real history is left behind in favour of a fictional pre-Revolutionary artefact, and a myth of origins. As a result, Hawthorne leaves a conspicuous space between the Puritan beginnings in the mid-seventeenth century and the era of decline in the nineteenth — a "space in-between" which Mukherjee sets out to fill. Hannah Easton returns to America in 1701, lives on until 1750, and, together with her daughter, becomes an inspiration for the American Revolution. What I want to suggest here is that Mukherjee spots the gap in the story, the space in-between the Puritan tale of origins and the decline which Hawthorne describes — the space of imperial expansion and Eastern plunder which was the foundation of New England fortunes, the sphere of activity of Hawthorne's own family, and (as the development of this argument will indicate) a major contributor to specific forms of cultural authority in America. Where Hawthorne refuses to make connections, Mukherjee's novel reveals, in the words of its narrator, "a hunger for connectedness, a belief that with sufficient passion and intelligence we can deconstruct the barriers of time and geography" (11).

It is important to recognise that Mukherjee's novel does not merely offer the Salem trade as a latent context, or Hawthorne's novel as a belated afterthought, but as literal articulation. In rewriting the letter, Mukherjee establishes specific parallels and connections in which reinscription is a dominant focus. In *The Scarlet Letter*, Hester is noted for her embroidery and transforms the badge of shame into an ornate sign of defiance. Hannah is similarly skilled with her needle, and both women are reputed for their nursing skills. Mukherjee combines the two: Hannah goes in for an early form of skin-grafting, a violent suturing together which is an apt image for the method of Mukherjee's novel, making reparative connections to remedy past violence — whether the scalpings of the Indian wars or the injury sustained in the final battles of the novel between Muslim and Hindu. Hannah's husband's actions are, by contrast, the reverse in intention. Where she pieces together, he inscribes violence. Hannah is tempted to adultery when Gabriel is reported lost at sea — he is actually in "savage" captivity, like his original. She, however, does not succumb, and Gabriel returns to beat up the hapless suitor. Where Hester was forced to wear an "A", Gabriel carves a blood-red "F" for fornication on the suitor's forehead — a scarlet letter of a different type. Later, when Gabriel in his turn is sent off on business by his superior, Cephus Prynne, who has designs on Hannah (shades of David and Bathsheba), Gabriel murders him, carving "H" on the corpse's forehead (for Hannah, presumably). Both erotic guilt and textual violence are ascribed to men. After the murder, social ostracism sets Hannah free (165), much as it did Hester.

Mukherjee also takes pains to invoke the Manning past. Hannah's best friend is Hester Manning, who lives on Herbert Street and drowns in mysterious circumstances when jilted by Gabriel Legge. The description of her corpse, fished out by Gabriel with a hooked pole, centres on the lips "twisted into a bitter, gaping O" (66) and on the rigid, outstretched arms. The scene refers explicitly to the death, in *The Blithedale Romance*, of Zenobia, hooked out and impaled by Hawthorne's narrator (in some readings, her destroyer). Rigidity, violence and the inscription of that violence in letters are the province of Gabriel Legge, as opposed to Hannah's embroidery, which is imaginative and reparative. Hannah herself has a reputation for "spells" or fits, and is kept as something of a recluse by her adoptive parents, who keep young men at bay. Hawthorne's mother, Elizabeth Manning, was given to similar fits of illness, and was also reclusive. Though a young widow, she never remarried. Hannah's mother is discovered at the close of the novel also wearing a letter, "a shameful I boldly sewn in red to her sleeve. It meant 'Indian Lover'" (284). When the Nipmuc attack Brookfield, Rebecca takes the opportunity to stage her own death to escape with her lover, by whom she has not one but five illegitimate children. Hawthorne's Manning ancestors also wore a letter I, but for a different reason. Gloria Erlich notes that in 1680 the wife of Nicholas Manning accused him of incest with his sisters, who were convicted, whipped, and exposed in church with their sin writ large in capitals on their heads. Mukherjee's narrator playfully notes the extent to which Hannah is sequestered by her family, and comments: "Incestuous, obviously ... wanted her to themselves" (61). Again, Mukherjee's reinscription of the letter associates a guilty past with the Manning name. In contrast, Rebecca has taught Hannah an alternative alphabet of revolt which substitutes for the gloomy Puritan hornbook ("A is for Adam's Fall") a rewriting that alters all the signs: "A is for Act, B is for Boldness, C is for Character, D is for Dissent, E is for Ecstasy" (54), an alphabet which Hannah completes to herself: "I is for Independence." Other connections between the two novels are more obvious — both Hannah and Hester have black-eyed illegitimate daughters called Pearl; both are associated with physicians, Hannah with Dr Aubry in London and the Venetian Antonio Carreri in India, Hester with her husband, also a doctor. Hester plans to escape from Salem on a rather dubious privateer, potentially a pirate ship; Hannah escapes by marrying Gabriel, who eventually trades in his job as an East India Company factor for an equivalent career in plunder, as a pirate. Hannah's story comes to light in a parody of Hester's, when Beigh Masters finds, in a dusty box in a museum of maritime trade near Salem, a set of Indian miniatures of the Salem bibi. The links between the two novels criss-cross in a tissue of connections, complicated by name changes and transfers. Hannah, for example, is renamed Mukta or Pearl by her servant Bhagmati. She renames Bhagmati Hester, after the friend she has lost. The Salemites rechristen her "White Pearl" and her daughter "Black Pearl". Elleke Boehmer has commented on the transferability of Empire's organising metaphors, citing as her example the name "Indian" used for native peoples from the Maoris to the Caribs.[23] Mukherjee's achievement is to send the name ricocheting back, from America to India, from one Bay Colony (Massachusetts) to another (the Bay of Bengal), one group of Indians to another, and even, in the examples of the Puritans and Aurengzebe, one ascetic religious group to another. In the process, all names become bundles of relationships, forcing the reader to think always in terms of multiple rather than monolithic referents. Every letter has its alternative meaning, or meanings; reinscription is embedded at every level of the novel.

Mukherjee also generalises the case of the canonical text as cultural authority, by her frame-tale, which extends the connection from the single classic text and writer to the institutions which create canonicity. It is no accident that the frame-narrator, Beigh Masters, is a Yale graduate, that Mukherjee's Fort Saint Sebastian is located on the outskirts of present-day Madras, or that the plot involves the early years of the East India Company and the pursuit of a famous diamond. Gauri Viswanathan has noted that the founding history of at least one major university in the United States — Yale — has its roots in the mercantile activities and imperial politics of the East India Company. Elihu Yale (to whom Mukherjee refers in the novel, 129), made his vast fortune as a nabob in Madras by a combination of legitimate trade and more questionable activities. He was responsible for the financing of Yale College in its early years, primarily by a gift of a shipment of textiles — muslins, poplins, silks, calicos and other merchandise which was turned into hard cash on the Boston market. As soon as this arrived in 1718, the trustees changed the name of their college to honour Yale. The goods netted them £800, the largest private donation to Yale for at least a hundred years, and thus

> established the closest links between Yale College and the spoils of British imperialism, the plundering careers of East India Company men merging ... with the pragmatic aspirations of colonial America's new brood of educators and theologians.[24]

The American colonists had approached Yale directly in terms which exploit the interchangeability of India and America in order to extract cash, and yoke together the two as similar areas of colonial exploitation. Cotton Mather wrote obsequiously:

> There are those in these parts of Western India, who have had the satisfaction to know something of what you have done and gained in the Eastern, and they take delight in the story.[25]

What Yale had been doing in "Eastern India", as Viswanathan establishes, was to create a personal fortune by any means at his disposal, including the acquisition of a private fort, trade on his own behalf independent of the Company, extortion of taxes from the indigenous inhabitants of "Black Town", ruthless repression of the townspeople's revolt, the hanging of English "pirates" in public as a warning to his competitors, and a great deal of experience as a diamond merchant. (Yale sold the King of Siam false rubies at one point and swindled him out of a considerable sum.)[26] Gabriel Legge, we may note, is involved in local repression, executes offenders, and eventually sets up on his own account, with his own private fort. He sends his plunder to New York. Viswanathan highlights two major issues implicit in Yale's career — the way in which one cultural authority (Yale's in India) translates into a new form of cultural authority in America (Yale College), and the economic transformation from British mercantilism to full-blown imperialism and the circulation of wealth in a global economy. These are issues vital to any consideration of canon-formation (as cultural authority) and its economic connections (in transnational, global, institutional practices). Just as the exploitation of India establishes the fortunes of Yale College, so it is implicated in the creation of America's canonical classic *The Scarlet Letter*. Mukherjee's novel deliberately brings the two "spheres" together — postcolonial and American literature — upsetting institutional authorities in the process, crossing boundaries and renegotiating the spaces of cultural authority. As the example of Yale indicates, canonicity is not the property of the work alone, but of the processes of its transmission, in educational and economic institutions.

But here it is worth pausing for a moment. Up to this point, my argument has been proceeding (in good New-Historicist fashion) to argue that Mukherjee restores our awareness of the gaps and absences in the official record, the absences in history that (if we are to believe Pierre Macherey) are what the text is all about. In doing this, Mukherjee is in good company. Anthony Ilona, for example, has noted a spate of historical novels of late, including, in 1994 alone, David Dabydeen's *Turner*, Abdulrazak Gurnah's *Paradise* and Fred D'Aguiar's *The Longest Memory*. Ilona poses the question: Is this quest for roots and history a backlash against notions of dislocation, fragmentation of identity, ambivalence and mimicry? Or are these merely warts on the commercial face of publishing, with issues of imperial history fostered by publishing establishments keen to retain the rules of division, of then and now, here and there, them and us? Like Hawthorne in his custom house, it may be tempting to consign postcolonial matters to some distant misty past, to write of slaves and trade, the Indian Mutiny or convicts at Botany Bay, rather than race riots and forced deportations. New-Historicist writing offers a potential solution to the problem, in its determined crossing of temporal borders, its circulation and exchange of different time-frames, tracing the commerce between past and present. Mukherjee, for example, presents Hannah's story through the present-day narrator, who draws explicit parallels between the boom on the Coromandel Coast in the 1680s and that on Wall Street in the 1980s. Mukherjee's brief sketch of the economics of the Coromandel establishes strong connections between India and America. Following the abrogation of the East India Company monopoly in 1688, the period of the 1690s was one of deregulation, a form of "late-stage capitalism such as America saw in the 1890s or the 1920s, or ... the late 1980s" (101).[27] The Coromandel is described as like Manhattan in the 1980s, with every "interloper" (independent trader) the equivalent of a real-estate agent, art dealer, arbitrageur, stockbroker, corporate lawyer and investment banker, all of them in the middle of the biggest real-estate boom, jewel auction and drug emporium of the last five hundred years (107). Dutch, Portuguese, Danish, French and English trading-posts stretch up the shore "like Condos on the Florida coast" (102). Far from escaping from her own time and place, Mukherjee offers in this respect an example of how a culture thinks about itself in a particular historical moment, highlighting the cultural interplays and mergers that take place in America, its polyethnicity and syncretism, whether in the seventeenth century or in the twentieth.

But problems remain. Patrick O'Donnell has commented that the desire for the concrete, material, factual and artifactual pervades contemporary literary studies and that New Historicism partakes of this amalgamatory desire. In this sense we are all, in a way, seeking the Emperor's Tear. The novel risks ceding its imaginative power to the attractions of history — just as *The Holder of the World* closes with its narrator enjoying (courtesy of virtual-reality techniques) total immersion in the sensations and images of that last Indian battle. O'Donnell takes as his example Walter Benn Michaels' discussion of Hawthorne, noting the inordinate amount of fact referred to by this New Historicist. There is, he argues,

> the implicit assumption that an increase in information will lead to an increase in the determinacy of meaning ... [Michaels'] method is a piecing-together of material from, seemingly, randomly-selected realms of being, as if to prove the overwhelming presence of the forces moving behind land speculation wherever one looks merely because bits of information can be gathered and juxtaposed in a certain way. Such an arrangement creates the illusion of inevitability that foregrounds a version of the will to meaning, a desire to get "at" the material and the supposed reflective relation between social force, authorial intention, and the signs projected within discursive structures.[28]

In piecing together her novel from a mass of material — East India Company records, the history of Salem, Hawthorne's biography, tales of pirates, the history of the Puritans, the development of medical knowledge, Indian wars, to name but a few of the sources which she researched for eleven years — Mukherjee similarly brings together a mass of historical data; but does an aesthetic pattern emerge? Susan Koshy, for one, complains of the "fatal clutter" of the novel, of its having too many props.[29] If amnesia is one problem, so is hypermemorialisation; a novel is not a museum.

It is in this respect that the full originality of Mukherjee's novel becomes evident. Mukherjee's strategy is to guard against the danger of overhistoricising by using a frame-tale that explicitly cautions against the New-Historicist belief in the primacy of information. In the frame-tale, a computer programmer, Venn Iyer, is engaged with the problem of creating an interactive model of historical reality, inputting a mass of data to re-create the experience of one particular day. Venn is as deterministic as a manic New Historicist. For him, design is all; there are no accidents: "everything in history is as tightly woven as a Kashmiri shawl" (189). In its opening pages, the novel sets out the dichotomy between restoring history and drowning meaning in data. Venn "animates information" (5), intent on reconstituting historical density and texture: "The past presents itself to us, always, somehow simplified. He wants to end that fatal unclutteredness" (6).

The process involves a randomly chosen date, 29 October 1989, for which the research team are supposedly ingesting all the world's papers, weather patterns, phone directories, satellite passes, arrests, TV shows, political debates, airline schedules, cheques written and credit-card purchases so that — when the database is complete — interaction with a personality will be possible, enabling "any of us to insert ourselves anywhere and anytime on the time-space continuum" (6). In theory, this restoration of clutter looks highly desirable. Venn's method fuses history and cultural studies. Beigh's profession in asset-retrieval reveals a similarly cultural-materialist bent. She describes her job as "Uniting people and possessions; it's like matching orphaned socks, through time" (5). A warning note is struck, however, by the congruence of their two fields, both implicitly materialistic. Venn's metaphors are commercial: "History's a big savings bank ... we can all make infinite reality withdrawals" (6). It appears, however, that restoring the density of experience may not be so easy for postcolonial locales. "Because of information overload, a five-minute American reality will be denser, more 'lifelike,' than five minutes in Africa. But the African reality may be more elemental, dreamlike, mythic" (7).

Just in case the reader has missed the ironies of which Venn seems blissfully unaware, Mukherjee underlines the implicit exoticism by presenting the potential time-travellers as historical tourists: "Time will become as famous as place. There will be time tourists sitting around saying 'Yeah, but have you ever been to April fourth? Man!'" (7). (The phraseology irresistibly suggests the overlander on the hippie trail, outdoing his interlocutor in his access to exotic locations.) The subjectivity of the process is also emphasised. Because it is interactive, no two time-travellers will access the same reality. What we withdraw will depend upon what we invest. Every time-traveller will answer a thousand personal questions, from which a "personality genome" will be created:

> By changing even one of the thousand answers, you can create a different personality and therefore elicit a different experience. Saying you're brown-eyed instead of blue will alter the withdrawal. Do blonds really have more fun? Stay tuned. (7)

The point connects explicitly to Mukherjee's rewriting. By altering one or two elements in the "original" story of Hester Prynne, Hawthorne creates a very different personality. At the close of the novel, when Venn's team input the data from Coromandel and allow Beigh an immersive experience of virtual history, Hannah turns out to be blonde. Mukherjee's rewriting certainly allows her more "fun" than Hawthorne allows his dark lady.

The virtual-reality experience therefore establishes a vital difference between Mukherjee's novel — also a reanimation and connection of historical data — and history. And it also looks to the future. Cyberspace is also a space in-between, a somewhere which is nowhere, with its doubtful freedoms and new forms of imperialism. It is frequently described as a "new world" in which we "navigate" and "explore" — in theory, a world without boundaries.[30] Implicitly, Mukherjee's rewriting of *The Scarlet Letter* poses the question of the future of this new world, a successor to America — as potential liberation or as a new space of global domination. Venn has been described as looking for an information formula that will organise facts into pattern; "He wants to grow a crystal garden" (259). Beigh's mind jumps to the most perfect crystal in the world, the Emperor's Tear, and Venn organises her virtual time-trip as a quest for the diamond. Beigh's first trip is disappointing; for some reason she intercepts a lady in a yellow jacket demonstrating faucets in Kansas City. She comments that "data are not neutral ... To treat all information as data and to process it in the same way is to guarantee an endless parade of faucets in Kansas city" (279). When Venn's technology is perfected, however, Beigh finds herself transported back to the Coromandel, herself becoming Bhagmati. Hannah steals the stone and passes it to Bhagmati, who, mortally wounded, thrusts it into her body: "I feel the organs, feel the flesh, the bowels of history and with my dying breath I plunge the diamond into the deepest part of me" (283).

In this final scene, Aurengzebe's diamond, the emblem of totalising power, is discarded, its fabulous wealth wholly unrealised: Beigh is content to leave it in Bhagmati's presumed grave in Madras. Although she has found the truth of Hannah's life, it is a truth that is no longer identified with an object. In its reflective, prismatic qualities, the diamond has stood as an image of the ways in which history can be reflected, refracted, retrieved or revised. It is also, however, an object of monetary value, and that (it is suggested) is what will really organise the data. Once Venn and his team have refined their technology, "MIT will prosper on the patent and maybe buy out Harvard, and the rest belongs to the heirs of the Coromandel factors, the franchisers and marketers jockeying for market share" (278). Essentially, the team are the heirs to the East India Company, the new imperialists of cyberspace, where, as potentially in our own canon-forming institutional practices — at Yale, Harvard, or MIT, at Konstanz or Newcastle — the danger looms of allowing economic pressure to efface life-giving connections. Mukherjee's novel uniquely celebrates imagination over fact, restoring a history by deconstructing New Historicism, and warning against the transformation of postcolonial discursive practices into a new form of cultural authority.[31]

Notes to Chapter 10

1. Bharati Mukherjee, "A Four-Hundred-Year-Old Woman," *American Studies Newsletter*, 29 (1993), 52.
2. Joseph A. Cincotti, "Same Trip, Opposite Direction," *New York Times Book Review*, 98 (10 October, 1993), 7.
3. See Judie Newman, *The Ballistic Bard: Postcolonial Fictions* (London: Arnold, 1995).
4. Vivian Gornick, "Playing Games with History," *Women's Review of Books*, 11, 3 (1993), 15.
5. Bharati Mukherjee, *The Holder of the World* (London: Chatto & Windus, 1993). Subsequent references follow quotations in parentheses.
6. Philip Rahv, "The Dark Lady of Salem," in *Literature and the Sixth Sense* (London: Faber & Faber, 1970), 55–75.
7. Fakrul Alam, *Bharati Mukherjee* (Twayne's US Authors 653; New York: Twayne: 1996), 11.
8. Mukherjee, "A Four-Hundred-Year-Old Woman," 53.
9. For example, Elleke Boehmer, *Colonial and Postcolonial Literature: Migrant Metaphors* (Oxford: Oxford University Press, 1995).
10. On the history of Salem see Luther S. Luedtke, *Nathaniel Hawthorne and the Romance of the Orient* (Bloomington: Indiana University Press, 1989) and James Duncan Phillips, *Salem and the Indies* (Boston, MA: Houghton Mifflin, 1947).
11. Phillips, 364.
12. Luedtke, 23.
13. *See* Gloria C. Erlich, *Family Themes and Hawthorne's Fiction: The Tenacious Web* (New Brunswick, NJ: Rutgers University Press, 1984).
14. See Jonathan Arac, "The Politics of *The Scarlet Letter*," in Sacvan Bercovitch and Myra Jehlen (ed.), *Ideology and Classic American Literature* (Cambridge: Cambridge University Press, 1986), 247–66; Walter Benn Michaels, "Romance and Real Estate," *Raritan*, 2 (1983), 66–87; Sacvan Bercovitch, *The Office of "The Scarlet Letter"* (Baltimore: Johns Hopkins University Press, 1991); Lauren Berlant, *The Anatomy of National Fantasy: Hawthorne, Utopia and Everyday Life* (Chicago:

University of Chicago Press, 1991); Richard H. Brodhead, *The School of Hawthorne* (Oxford: Oxford University Press, 1986); Eric Cheyfitz, "The Irresistibleness of Great Literature: Reconstructing Hawthorne's Politics," *American Literary History*, 6, 3 (1994), 539–58; Michael J. Colarcurcio, *New Essays on "The Scarlet Letter"* (Cambridge: Cambridge University Press, 1985); Louise DeSalvo, *Nathaniel Hawthorne* (London: Harvester, 1987); Charles Lewis, "The Ironic Romance of New Historicism: *The Scarlet Letter* and *Beloved* Standing in Side by Side," *Arizona Quarterly*, 51, 1 (1995), 33–60; Toni Morrison, *Playing in the Dark: Whiteness and the Literary Imagination* (Cambridge, MA: Harvard University Press, 1990); and Jean Fagan Yellin, *Women and Sisters: The Antislavery Feminists in American Culture* (New Haven: Yale University Press, 1989).

15. Colarcurcio, 22.

16. Bercovitch, *The Office of "The Scarlet Letter"*.

17. Claudia Durst Johnson, *Understanding "The Scarlet Letter": A Student Casebook to Issues, Sources, and Historical Documents* (Westport: Greenwood, 1995).

18. Mara L. Dukats, "The Hybrid Terrain of Literary Imagination: Maryse Condé's Black Witch of Salem, Nathaniel Hawthorne's Hester Prynne, and Aimé Césaire's Heroic Poetic Voice," *College Literature*, 22, 1 (1995), 51–61.

19. See Judie Newman, *John Updike* (London: Macmillan, 1988) and James A. Schiff, *Updike's Version: Rewriting The Scarlet Letter* (Columbia: University of Missouri Press, 1992).

20. Nathaniel Hawthorne, *The Scarlet Letter*, ed. Brian Harding (Oxford: Oxford University Press, 1990), 83. Subsequent references follow quotations in parentheses.

21. Luedtke, 220.

22. Christopher Bigsby, *Hester: A Romance* (London: Weidenfeld & Nicolson, 1994), 189.

23. Boehmer, 53.

24. Gauri Viswanathan, "The Naming of Yale College: British Imperialism and American Higher Education," in Amy Kaplan and Donald E. Pease (eds), *Cultures of United States Imperialism* (Durham, NC: Duke University Press, 1993), 93.

25. Ibid., 87.

26. See Fanny Penny, *Diamonds* (London: Hodder & Stoughton, 1906), for an earlier novelist's treatment of Yale. Penny also provides useful material, in her other books, on the Coromandel. Mukherjee's narrator also shares her name with that of John Masters, author of *Coromandel!* (New York: Viking, 1955), which offers interesting points of contact with *The Holder of the World*.

27. For the accuracy of Mukherjee's portrayal of the Coromandel in the seventeenth century, see: Sinappah Arasaratnam, *Merchants, Companies and Commerce on the Coromandel Coast 1650–1740* (Delhi: Oxford University Press, 1986); K. N. Chaudhuri, *Asia Before Europe: Economy and Civilisation of the Indian Ocean from the Rise of Islam to 1750* (Cambridge: Cambridge University Press, 1990); and Tapan Raychaudhuri, *Jan Company in Coromandel 1605–1690* (Verhandelingen van het Koninklijk Instituut voor Taal-, Land-, en Volkenkunde, Deel 38; The Hague: Martinus Nijhoff, 1962).

28. Patrick O'Donnell, "History without Theory: Re-Covering American Literature," *Genre*, 22 (1989), 387. See also Peter Carifiol, "The Constraints of History: Revision and Revolution in American Literary Studies," *College English*, 50 (1988), 605–22; Anthony Ilona, "Crossing the River: A Chronicle of the Black Diaspora," *Wasafiri*, 22 (Autumn 1995), 3–9.

29. Susan Koshy, review of *The Holder of the World*, *Amerasia Journal*, 20.1 (1994), 189.

30. For examples of colonialist discourse as applied to virtual reality, see Howard Rheingold, *Virtual Reality* (New York: Summit, 1991), 116, 183, and Barrie Sherman and Phil Judkins, *Glimpses of Heaven, Visions of Hell: Virtual Reality and its Implications* (London: Hodder & Stoughton, 1992), 172. Greek *"cyber"* means "steersman". Interestingly, commentators observe that for the experience to be successful it is a mistake to provide too much data (Sherman and Judkins, *Glimpses of Heaven*, 125). Photorealism is a false grail: a virtual world needs to be not quite real or it will lose its pull on the imagination. Or, as Keats put it (quoted by Mukherjee in the series of epigraphs to the novel's subsections): "Heard Melodies are sweet, but those unheard | Are sweeter."

31. I should like to express my gratitude to Monica Reif-Huelser, University of Konstanz, for the invitation to address the Annual Conference for the Study of the New Literatures in English, 13 September 1996, at which a first version of this essay was delivered, and for assistance with travel costs from the British Council and the University of Newcastle Upon Tyne. A longer version of the essay appears as Judie Newman, "Spaces in Between: Hester Prynne as the Salem Bibi in Bharati Mukherjee's *The Holder of the World*," *Journal of Literary Studies*, Special Issue: Politics and the Novel, 13, 1/2 (1997), 62–91.

CHAPTER 11

Rebounding Metaphors:
Culture and Conquest in
J. G. Farrell's *The Siege of Krishnapur*

J. G. Farrell's *The Siege of Krishnapur* (1973) has come under attack from more than one direction. As an historical novel it has inevitably drawn critical fire. On the one hand readers have objected to the documentary clutter of the novel which draws heavily upon Farrell's reading in historical source material concerning the Indian Mutiny and the Victorians. Russell Davies, reviewing the novel in the *Observer*, complained that "Farrell seems to have fallen victim to his own capacity (which must be prodigious) for research; this account of a siege in Hindustan is utterly clogged with what Farrell has found out about mid-Victorian India."[1] Margaret Drabble noted the pervasive impression that objects had a life of their own even at the expense of people.[2] The reader is regaled with excerpts from the catalogue of the Great Exhibition, the contents of Fleury's luggage, debates over cholera, and the minutiae of Seidlitz powders, spine pads, Tweedside lounging jackets and mutton pies. Farrell himself defended this approach to history in terms which align him with that school of history writers who are less concerned with kings and concepts than with "breakfast and washing".[3]

> The most important things, for the very reason that they are trivial, are unsuitable for digestion by historians, who are only able to nourish themselves on the signing of treaties, battle strategies, the formation of Shadow cabinets and so forth. These matters are quite alien to the life most people lead which consists of catching colds, falling in love, or falling off bicycles. It is this real life which is the novelist's concern.[4]

Alternately, in the other critical camp, the accusation levelled is that Farrell is *too* imaginative, ahistorical in terms of the Indian location; that he takes no firm political position on the Mutiny or by extension, on imperialism. For Ronald Binns, "[t]he politics of the Empire Trilogy seem elusive and ambiguous".[5] The complaint is made that the Indians themselves scarcely figure in the novel: "the sepoys are never shown as people at all, but merely as cannon fodder, and comic fodder at that".[6] The critical consensus is that the novel is less concerned with the effects of imperialism, than with the illusions of Victorian "civilisation mongers".[7] Similarly, Allen Greenberger understands the book as less about what the British did to India than about what ruling India did to the British; David Rubin sees the Mutiny as an occasion for a meditation on the fragility of Victorian civilisation, and more broadly, of all civilisation.[8] In general, within their different readings, most critics have responded to the sense in which the British regard the Indians as mere metaphors, experimental subjects whose reactions test or validate the British civilising mission. India is thus not an historical location, but a stage, greenhouse, or laboratory in which to experiment with Victorian ideas of progress, medicine, technology, religion and culture. Even when the novel is read with an eye to its political extension, it is interpreted not as history but as metaphor. Neil McEwan argues that each volume of the Empire trilogy essentially concerns a siege, in which a small group of embattled British defenders are threatened by the encroachment of the "foreign" or indigenous, and that the siege is a metaphor for today's world rather than the past: "British civilisation is besieged in the modern world ... Siege mentality in each book offers a metaphor for modern British thinking."[9] In short, although critics have differed on what the metaphor "stands for" — a Victorian defeat, a modern defensiveness, the universal fragility of culture — all have identified a metaphorical quality inherent in the structure of Farrell's work.

Where the opponents of clutter clearly find Farrell too historical and insufficiently literary, the metaphorical emphasis inevitably raises the kinds of objections which have been made to the neo-historicist work of Hayden White — that it produces a version of history which elides or obscures the truth of events, allowing a fictional vision to foster voluntaristic or relativist interpretations of the past.[10] As Gesa Mackenthun remarks, at its most extreme this vision of history is represented by Paul de Man's comment that history is "purely a linguistic complication".[11]

As Mackenthun further observes, although it would be foolish to say that deconstructionists, semioticians and tropologists are the handymen of neocolonial aggression, the claim that some poststructuralist theory is quietly complicit with such politics cannot be easily dismissed.[12] Gene Bell-Villada complains that the only response of the American critical establishment to political oppression in Latin America, for example, consists in "its elaborate paraliterary schemes, its wars on referentiality, and its preachments that 'history is Fiction, Trope and Discourse'".[13] The power to make history is not equally distributed. Farrell, for example, ends the story before the British atrocities which marked the resumption of imperial control. No sepoys are blasted from cannon mouths; no Indian civilians raped or butchered. The novel appears to privilege every last detail of the British in India while consigning the Indians to the status of figurative or metaphorical existence. The purpose of this essay, however, is to outline an alternative possibility: that metaphor is not merely Farrell's method, but also, in quite striking fashion, his anti-imperialist theme. It is in the exposure and reversal of the process of metaphor-making that Farrell's politics lie.

Interestingly, one of the most compelling responses to Hayden White's new historicism offers a vision of imperial history which focuses upon metaphor. In *The Poetics of Imperialism* Eric Cheyfitz counters the assertion that history is always linguistically constructed with the rejoinder that language is itself *historically* constructed. Cheyfitz offers a suggestive perspective on Farrell, in his concentration on the ways in which European colonisers "mapped" their New World (in the specific example of America) according to the opposition between the metaphoric and the proper (or as we would now call it the literal). For Cheyfitz the proper must be understood in terms of the relation to European notions of property and identity; there is a distinct correlation between the translation of colonial reality into European texts and the translation of commonly held land into European property. In support of his thesis Cheyfitz cites Aristotle's basic definition of metaphor as transporting a term from a familiar to a foreign place, from its "proper" signification to a figurative sense, with the idea of resemblance or similitude determining the decorous limits of such transportation. "Metaphora" derives from the verb "metaphero" — to carry across. ("Translation" is an alternative rendering of the term.) In the *Poetics* Aristotle tells us that metaphor is "the application of an alien name by transference either from genus to species, or from species to genus, or from species to species, or by analogy, that is proportion."[14] Cheyfitz glosses the definition as follows:

> as Aristotle's definition of metaphor suggests with its notion of the "transference" of an "alien name" into a familiar context, the very idea of metaphor seems to find its ground in a kind of territorial imperative, in a division, that is, between the domestic and the foreign.[15]

In the poetics of imperialism, therefore, the figurative becomes the foreign or strange, the proper becomes the natural or normal. (Cheyfitz argues that it is no coincidence that the colonisation of America coincides with the formulation of a modern poetics in terms of national self-definition, by Elizabethan literary theorists.) The theory of metaphor is therefore inseparable from ideas of place, and of the frontier between the domestic and the foreign:

> From its theoretical beginnings, then, metaphor comes under suspicion as the foreign, that which is opposed to the "proper", defined inescapably as ... the natural, the domestic, the familiar, the authoritative, the legitimate.[16]

Improper use of metaphor may violate the decorum of class- or race-distinctions. Proper usage maintains decorum in civil speech, clothing the impropriety of naked words. "Far-fetched" comparisons are the frontier of metaphor, dubiously acceptable. Rhetorical decorum demands that in the name of propriety, the domestic should dominate the alien, the different must be sacrificed to similitude.

Cheyfitz is not, of course, alone in highlighting the phenomenon of metaphor in the imperial context. Gesa Mackenthun's analysis of the fashion in which imperial prose, from the sixteenth century onwards, has embraced a series of discursive processes which served to translate the enterprise of Empire into acceptable history is entitled *Metaphors of Dispossession*. In this connection, Mackenthun's introduction calls attention to the work of Cheyfitz and others. Bernard Vincent, for example, has examined the synchronicity of the discovery of America, the expulsion of the Jews and Moors, and the production of the first Castilian grammar. As its producer Antonio de Nebrija, remarked, "language is the perfect instrument of Empire".[17] In *Marvellous Possessions* Stephen Greenblatt similarly examines the relationship between language and colonialism, emphasising the discourse of the marvellous as a salvific supplement to rituals of appropriation. Greenblatt has defined metaphor as a simultaneous perception of likeness and difference, potentially providing a positive model for intercultural communication.[18] Greenblatt's metaphor therefore occupies something of a privileged space beyond the imperial politics of language.[19]

Like Greenblatt, Cheyfitz allows the possibility that metaphor can open up a space for interpretation: "metaphor is duplicitous, playing the part of a double agent in a foreign intrigue" operating on the frontier between the domestic and the foreign.[20] Unlike Greenblatt, he includes it nevertheless within the politics of imperial poetics, on grounds of differing degrees of agency and non-agency. For Cheyfitz there remains a gulf between words and deeds. In *The Tempest*, for example, Caliban's curses may ring out, but they remain un-enforceable words, mere figures of speech. Prospero's figures have the power to literalise themselves, to act immediately as engines of torture on Caliban's flesh (1.2.370–73). Caliban may know how to curse but he has no power to turn language into proper deeds. For Cheyfitz, therefore, the image of a "rack" of language on which Prospero threatens to torture Caliban is expressive of the belief in an absolutely persuasive efficient machine of eloquence which convinces the other to be a slave, to cede his "property" in his self, but to do so willingly. It is an argument which draws, in its essentials, upon the Gramscian notion that cultural hegemony can be best established and maintained through the consent of the dominated.

In *The Siege of Krishnapur* Farrell exposes the process of concealing material domination beneath the veneer of figurative culture to comprehensive scrutiny. As Ronald Binns notes, the early chapters of the novel offer an image of a highly domesticated India.[21] For the Collector, it is "hard to believe that one was in India at all".[22] At a ball, as the dancers execute a galoppe, they are described in terms which completely remove their military-style performance from any literal significance, "charging and wheeling rhythmically as if all this were taking place not in India but in some temperate land far away" (45). The aptly named Collector (actually of taxes) has turned the British Residency into a display case for his collection of objects which stand for the triumphs of British civilisation. The fact that many of them are linked to the Great Exhibition accentuates their metaphoric role. A gorse-bruiser, for example, completely useless in India, is none the less proudly displayed as evidence of the ingenuity of British technological design. Statues tend to be heavily symbolic — *The Spirit of Science Conquers Ignorance and Prejudice* and *Fame Scattering Rose Petals on Shakespeare's Grave*. At the culmination of the siege, however, the sepoys force the state of property onto the metaphors of British greatness in scenes which explicitly connect culture with conquest. The artefacts which have previously represented the high tide of Victorian civilisation — pianos, statues, books — go to shore up the fragile siege defences, as the rains begin to wash away the earthen ramparts. Translated from the domestic arena (the Residency) to the frontiers of the foreign, their role as metaphors of civilisation collapses. Victorian culture is exposed as merely the icing on the cake of conquest. The domestic metaphor is appropriate. Short of ammunition the British load their cannon with every available projectile — from marbles and false teeth to cutlery.

The results are devastating. One sepoy is discovered with a silver fork projecting from a lung; another's spine has been shattered by *The Spirit of Science Conquers Ignorance and Prejudice*. Others have been struck down by teaspoons and fish knives, and "an unfortunate subadar had been plucked from this world by the silver sugar-tongs embedded in his brain" (319). The domestic is now the deadly. The connection between cultural hegemony and straightforward military domination is dramatised in the conversion of the electroplated heads of British poets into cannonballs. Predictably Shakespeare proves particularly fatal:

> Without a doubt the most effective missiles in this matter of improvised ammunition had been the heads of his electrometal figures. ... And of the heads ... the most effective of all had been Shakespeare's; it had scythed its way through a whole astonished platoon of sepoys advancing in single file through the jungle. The Collector suspected that the Bard's success in this respect might have a great deal to do with the ballistic advantages stemming from his baldness. The head of Keats, for example, wildly festooned with metal locks ... had flown very erratically indeed, killing only a fat money-lender and a camel standing at some distance from the field of action. (335)

Figurative language, once embodied in these decidedly canonical, rhetorical representatives of English culture, becomes a deadly weapon. The imperialists' words are enforceable, capable of backing themselves up with proper power — or, indeed, with the power of property. Busts of Plato and Socrates provide handy wings for the cannon emplacement. Even when the Cutcherry is blown up the resultant snowstorm of paper bewilders the attackers and gives the British the chance to regroup (239). In this connection the selection by Farrell of the siege of a domestic location as the central action is peculiarly appropriate. Although the British flag flies over it, the target is not a fort or a military encampment but a residence, replete with library, dining room, nurseries, marble staircase, kitchen, verandah and croquet lawn. Though it begins as a metaphor for the ways in which the Victorian mind is furnished (14) it is also quite heavily provided with actual furniture. The location allows the "domestic" to be as much under attack as the national — the two concepts coincide.

The physical transportation of the furnishings from the domestic sphere to the borders of the foreign is accompanied by a series of literary strategies designed to display the fashion in which in the Mutiny the process of cultural metaphorising rebounds upon the British. If transferring and translating objects is what metaphor is all about, the sepoys, in a sense, take the British at their word and force them to transport their metaphors into the realm of the literal. The imperialists lose their ability to cloak domination with metaphor and do not much like it. Many of Farrell's comic effects are the result of metaphors being taken literally, or of objects becoming agentive. Animated objects are one of the classic mechanisms of comedy, as are objects in the wrong place (Lieutenant Cutter's horse in the drawing room, a cow inside a palace). As the latter example demonstrates, the "right place" is also heavily culturally determined. The Hindus do not find the cow remotely comic or out of place, for example. Movement from the metaphoric to the proper often has bathetic results, deflating imperial pretensions. At other points Farrell relies for his startling effects on the breach of decorum, as metaphors are over-extended, "fetched" too far. In short, whether deflating high-flown metaphors, making a metaphor incongruously literal, inflating a metaphor beyond the limits of decorum, or transferring the metaphoric into the proper, Farrell displays an intense sensitivity to metaphor as part of an imperial poetics.

The examination of imperialist poetics, however, is not merely implicit in Farrell's style. The opposition between the figurative and the literal is quite overtly thematised in the opening pages of the novel, in a scene which offers something of a *prise de position* on Farrell's part — a poetry reading. The reading itself is thoroughly contaminated with the language of domination. The Collector attends only in order to defend the ladies against the attacks of the hypercritical Magistrate. In previous days every poem had been well received. Each had "glutted itself with praise like a jackal" (16). The comparison offers a proleptic image of the deflation from the metaphoric to the literal which is to come, when actual jackals will feast upon the British dead. Unsurprisingly, the Magistrate's attacks censure the poetic in favour of the "proper". His scorn for the figurative is swiftly established in his reaction to Mrs Worseley's poetic offering, "I consider that we've had far too many erl-kings in recent weeks, though I can assure you that even one erl-king would be more than enough for me" (17). So much for Goethe.[23] Erl-kings are decidedly not English, domestic or proper. Mrs Adams does not fare much better with an effusion which appears to involve nature, serpents and the Fall of Troy. The Collector, already uneasily aware that there may be trouble brewing, finds his mind moving unconsciously from the poetic siege to the actual. If he has to defend the ladies against real, rather than verbal attacks, has he the means? His eyes rest approvingly upon the Residency walls "thickly armoured with paintings" (17). Miss Carpenter's verses in praise of the Great Exhibition recall his attention from the military to the figurative:

> Power like the trunk of Afric's wondrous brute,
> Had, on that stage, its double triumph found,
> To lift the forest monarch by the root,
> Or pick a quivering needle from the ground. (18)

Importantly, the poem is heavily metaphoric: it needs considerable explication to make its comparisons comprehensible and bring its meaning back to earth. Miss Carpenter proceeds to explain her metaphors: "this image of the Exhibition was a reference to the versatile talent of Edmund Burke" (18). The ensuing bafflement demands a farther explanation: "this talent of Burke's had been compared to an elephant's trunk, which could uproot an oak or pick up a needle" (18). In taking a property (Burke's talent), the metaphor for that property (an elephant's trunk) and developing it into a full-fledged figure (the poem), itself glorifying the broader cultural discourse of imperialism (the Exhibition), Miss Carpenter has opened up a space for interpretation while remaining (if only narrowly) within the bounds of decorum. After a second stanza extolling the dutiful masses, however, she proceeds to a third:

> Pebbles and shells which little children find
> Of rainbow-tinted hues, on ocean's shore;
> Though full of learning to the thoughtful mind,
> Themselves how vain, how shortly seen no more! (19)

The lines are based upon Newton's description of himself as "only a child picking up pebbles on the shore of the great ocean of truth" (19). In extending her imagery to these further shores, however, Miss Carpenter has gone too far — from the glorification of power to its deflation as nought but vanity in the longer, universal view. The Magistrate promptly launches a frontal attack, dashing Miss Carpenter back to the "proper" level, by invoking regulatory notions of decorum:

> It's entirely beyond my understanding why you should feel you have to say "Afric's wondrous brute" instead of "elephant" like everyone else, and "forest monarch" instead of "tree". Nobody in his right mind goes about calling trees "forest monarchs" ... I've really never heard such nonsense! (19)

Miss Carpenter has glorified the foreign, the exotic and the marvellous, extending her metaphors beyond the domestic to an image which, in the empowering of the alien (the elephant) and natural sovereignty (the forest monarch) raises the imperial hackles. In the Magistrate's view her metaphors are too far-fetched, both in territorial and in figurative terms. Nor is the Magistrate unrepresentative; the reference to Burke may not be accidental. The Magistrate has an illustrious predecessor in the shape of James Mill, who famously attacked Burke's rhetoric. Mill's distrust of the imagination was accompanied by a demand for simple language. In his history of India, having complained that Sanskrit had too many words for the same thing, he stated baldly that "The highest merit of language would consist in having one name for everything which requires a name and no more than one."[24]

As Javed Majeed has commented, "Mill's world is the world of measurable concrete objects, and language has to be held down in this world".[25] Even within the pages of the novel itself Miss Carpenter is not alone in coming under suspicion for her breach of imperial poetic decorum. Fleury, a would-be quasi-Romantic poet, creates considerable alarm by his behaviour, so much so that Dr Dunstaple, learning that Fleury had been given to playing the violin by moonlight in a ruined pagoda in his ancestral home (25) jumps to the same conclusions as the Magistrate: "Perhaps George was insane?" (25). Fleury's taste is for sad things — "death, ruins and unhappy love affairs" (29) — of which he later gets a literal fill in the course of the siege. Tellingly, Fleury's self-identification as lovelorn, pining poet swiftly fades once in India, in favour of a more down-to-earth, "broad-shouldered" military role.

If the poetry reading is largely focussed upon the farther shores of the figurative, it is framed between two discussions of bafflingly literal objects — the chapatis, the circulation of which is generally taken to be the first sign of the impending mutiny. The chapatis sweep the countryside "like an epidemic" (11), a proleptic image of later ills which beset the British community — from boils to cholera. The chapatis gain their disquieting power from the fact that they have been moved from their proper (Indian) place. They turn up in a British dispatch box, on the front steps of the Residency, neatly arranged on a desk. They remain entirely resistant to explanation — as they do to this day. The untranslatability of the chapatis is vital. Nobody knows what they are a metaphor for. They are physically carried from one place to another without gaining metaphoric status. Indeed, they are not metaphoric at all; they are "proper" objects which cannot be incorporated or translated by the Europeans. If the Indians have featured only as a metaphor, a figure in the imperialists' eyes, the chapatis signal their non-metaphoric status, stubbornly refusing to be interpreted according to any imperial scheme of meaning. They exist only in the realm of the literal or proper — and they have now been moved into the little England of the residency, threatening an exchange of tenor and vehicle, and violating the domestic illusion. Arguably, by *not* giving the Indians a voice in the novel Farrell *increases* their access to agency rather than diminishing it. Silence may be a source of resistance and challenge, a refusal to enter metropolitan discourse.

The point is supported by the portrayal of General Jackson who visits the residency shortly before the outbreak of hostilities. The beginnings of the Mutiny are signalled by the loss of meaning occasioned by the substitution of one object for another. The general, now rather forgetful, arrives carrying a cricket bat as an aide-memoire. He is paying no attention to the chapatis, or to the possibility of unrest; he has come to discuss a cricket match. In the course of conversation, however, he absentmindedly puts the bat down and picks up a book, promptly losing all sense of the purpose of his visit. The mnemonic technique relies upon the physical object which can have only one meaning — just like the chapatis. A book contains too many possibilities for meaning to be kept under control; anything figurative leaves the general completely at sea: "He had taken a surreptitious look at the title, which was *Missionary Heroes* and told him nothing" (73). When the general puts in his next appearance, fatally wounded in the revolt, the description is highly indecorous. The sowars try to stop the flow of blood by turning the general first one way then the other "as someone eating toast and honey might try, by vigilance and dexterity, to prevent it dripping" (100). Ronald Binns has noted the frequency of such wildly incongruous comparisons, including, for example, the comparison between sepoys and flies on a treacle pudding, or a mutineer and a trout in a restaurant tank.[26] Arguably, however, this stylistic device owes less to European influences (Surrealism or Lewis Carroll in Binns's suggestion) than to Farrell's anti-imperial tactics. The overextension of metaphor beyond the bounds of decorum drives vehicle and tenor apart, and reveals the intractable nature of the object, transgressing regulatory poetics. Objects in their proper place are non-threatening, an aid to self-possession or to possession *tout court*. Out of context — the chapatis, the missionary book in the hands of the general, the blood on the domestic toast — they become dangerous, menacing, an image of individual and national lack. Seen in resistance to classification (as opposed to properly displayed, classified, positioned) objects draw attention to the artifices which we employ to gather a world around us. Without the cricket bat the General can neither collect himself for action nor recollect his mission. As James Clifford notes (in a discussion of ethnographic collections):

Some sort of "gathering" around the self and the group — the assemblage of a mutual "world", the marking off of a subjective domain that is not "other" is probably universal. All such collections embody hierarchies of value, exclusions, rule-governed territories of the self. But the notion that this gathering involves the accumulation of possessions, the idea that identity is a kind of wealth (of objects, knowledge, memories, experience) is surely not universal. ... In the West, collecting has long been a strategy for the deployment of a possessive self, culture and authenticity.[27]

John McLeod has analysed *The Siege of Krishnapur* persuasively in terms of the trope of collecting. In his argument the Great Exhibition is not merely a source for Farrell's novel, but also parodies the ways in which material objects and possessions were collected to demonstrate British greatness, to negotiate a sense of sameness from multifarious artefacts. By constructing a rhetoric of objects, "the collection is a metaphor for the production of discourse".[28] As Farrell's metaphoric method demonstrates, it is also a discourse designed for the production of metaphor. Farrell's thematisation of imperial poetics is therefore appropriately embodied in the mega-metaphor of the Great Exhibition.

In this connection Farrell cunningly sets up a series of scenes of display in which objects transgress or affront imperial notions of decorum, failing to gather together into a meaningful uniformity. James Clifford has noted both the way in which Western culture accentuates property and its tendency to classify objects in an edifying or pedagogical fashion. A collector is expected to have a rationale for the collection, and information about it. In Western culture private fascination with a single object (as opposed to an ennobling collection) is negatively marked as fixation, obsession, or idolatry. A postcolonial collector, as Clifford suggests, would need to return to the object its status as fetish (our fetishes, not those of some exotic "Other"); we need to accord to objects in collections the power to fixate rather than simply to edify and inform, as a reflection of a totalising conception. The erotic is clearly a potential ally of the anti-imperialist in this respect.

The courtship manoeuvres of Fleury and Harry are a case in point. Critics have tended to assume a misogynistic attitude to women in Farrell's novels, in which women often feature as bizarre or excessively physical objects. Farrell's portrayal of Louise and Lucy, however, brings the metaphoric back to the literal and explodes the notion of a hegemonic collection, precisely by highlighting the gulf between the literal body and the metaphors which are used to cloak it. In the early courtship scenes the wholeness of the community is established in scenes of display in which the women are mere adjuncts to the imperial-military mission; what threats there are to British domination are merely metaphoric. The proleptic quality of the imagery looks ahead to the literal. Louise and Fleury attend a picnic in a green glade in the botanical gardens, compared by Fleury (in full poetic flow) to "a ruined church made by Nature" (32). To his horror the British set to work to glut themselves on ham, mutton pies, oysters, tongue, chicken and duck, while the younger officers make "dashing assaults on their own hamper" (33) watched by an audience of ragged, hungry natives. Later, the starving Fleury will find himself wishing he had glutted more and poeticised less as he finds himself fighting for his life in the residency (built in the shape of a church 13), incongruously clad in forest green (a coat fashioned from the covering of the billiard table), observing in his turn a group of Indians, picnicking at a distance while enjoying the progress of the siege. The tables have been turned as the British exhibit their misery rather than their triumphs, metamorphosing into natives — ragged, starving and covered in boils.[29] Similarly the ball at which Fleury and Louise wheel and turn in a military style galoppe involves punkahs flapping over them "like wounded birds" (41) while pallid English ladies long for the arrival of the guest of honour, General Hearsey. Fleury comments that the matrons are not exactly enticing: "How true that English ladies do not prosper in the Indian climate! The flesh subsides and melts away, leaving only strings and fibres and wrinkles" (43). In a few months his beloved will be even more thin and pale, overshadowed by vultures and also longing desperately for the arrival of a general, preferably at the head of a relief column. When Lieutenant Stapleton (one of Louise's admirers) finally arrives to relieve the defenders he recoils in horror: "He had never seen Englishmen get themselves into such a state before; they looked more like untouchables" (340). Indeed, as far as Lieutenant Stapleton is concerned Louise *is* untouchable. When he goes to embrace her he is stopped in his tracks: "she stank" (340). Fleury, equally malodorous, has a distinct erotic advantage.

Louise herself takes some time to abandon her habitual metaphors, especially as far as Lucy is concerned. In the midst of the siege, squatting in the lee of a shattered grand piano, Louise is obsessed by the dangers posed to her brother, Harry, not as might be expected by musket balls and cannon fire, but by Lucy whom she envisages as "making mincemeat" (213) of Harry's affections and as capturing his heart. Despite the fact that she is nursing an ugly boil on her own neck, Louise "could only put an ugly complexion" (213) on Lucy's actions — she makes no connections between her metaphors and the actual physical condition in which she finds herself. The dynamic of the novel continually reverses the direction of "transport" as the metaphors rebound upon the British. Normally Lucy's behaviour would not perturb Louise: "to have their hearts besieged and conquered, was, after all, at least one of the things that men were here for" (213). But Lucy is a "fallen" woman. In Louise's inimitable phrase, a man had "been permitted to view that sacred collection of bulges, gaps, tufts of hair and rounded fleshy slopes which ... signalled their own message: 'Womanhood'" (213).

In some respects, Lucy functions here as a surrogate Other. She has been beyond the bounds of decorum since the beginning of the novel, isolated beyond the domestic pale in the dak bungalow, which is situated in the native town. Her readmission to the residency is part and parcel of the threats to decorum — linguistic and social — posed by the siege. In Louise's view Lucy has displayed her "collection" inappropriately. The description of Lucy's bulges, gaps and tufts dismembers the hegemonic, collective concept "Womanhood" in favour of the erotic fetish. This technique of fragmentation of whole into fragmented parts or objects is general in the novel, which is rife with images of dismemberment, beyond what might merely be motivated by the military situation. Sepoys fill their breeches with stolen rupees and carry them off on their shoulders like "heavy, trunkless men" (134). Fleury steps on an object which he takes to be an eye (it is actually a grape 156). A sepoy is blasted to pieces, leaving only a pair of legs standing (325). Amputation features prominently (189). The Magistrate, obsessed with phrenology, fixates upon the skulls of the defenders, particularly Lucy's which should offer decisive evidence of the prominence of the Amative in her personality. (In the event it disappoints him.) The padre, equally obsessed with the argument from Design, actually reduces his argument to a list of disconnected bodily parts, from the eel's eye to the hog's tusks, the proboscis of the bee, the middle claw of the heron and the hump of the camel (166–68). Mrs Scott undergoes a Caesarean (201), the description of which (like many of Dr McNab's notations) reduces the person to a collection of bodily symptoms, including (shockingly to Dr Dunstable's notions of domestic propriety) the late Mrs McNab. Peterson is eaten by jackals, except for his hands which remain fleshed, and look like gloves on a skeleton (216). The boundaries of human and animal are also transgressed. Chloë, a lapdog whose coat is repeatedly compared to Louise's tresses, eats a sepoy's face. Louise, starving, eats the poultice on her own face. A pariah dog, formerly a mass of sores, flourishes on the richer diet offered by the siege, and fawns on Fleury. Lucy, also a pariah, is reintegrated into the domestic circle and fawns similarly on Harry. The movement from the metaphoric to the proper — or from the proper to the metaphoric — involves an exchange of positions between the foreign and the domestic, the human and the animal, the whole and the part.

One scene in particular undermines the notion of British homogeneity. Louise's worst fears are realised when Lucy, beset by a plague of cockchafers, rips off all her clothes in plain view of Fleury and Harry, revealing her entire "collection". Because of the insects, however, only parts of Lucy appear, a breast emerging at one point from the black mass, a knee cap at another: "But hardly had a white part been exposed before blackness covered it again" (255). Just as Louise became "untouchable", Lucy has crossed the racial divide. She is "as black and glistening as an African slave-girl" (255). In ceding her property in herself she appears to have yielded to slave status. Yet she has also escaped from hegemonic definition. All the men's efforts to restore her to a state of whiteness are defeated by the number and mass of insects. Even when they discover a useful technology (ironically it involves designing a tool from the boards of a Bible to shave off the insects — so much for the argument which justifies the biblical message on grounds of design) Lucy's body never quite returns to a state of wholeness. The men proceed piecemeal: "When they had done her back, they turned her over and set to work on her front" (256). Fleury attempts to transform Lucy from object to metaphor once again, envisaging himself as a sculptor "in his efforts to carve an object of beauty out of the primeval rock" (256) and comparing her to the Collector's plaster cast of *Andromeda Exposed to the Monster*. But, following in Ruskin's footsteps, his attempts to treat a woman as a metaphor, to aestheticise her and reintegrate her into the status of collectable whole, founder on Lucy's pubic hair:

> "D'you think this is *supposed* to be here?" asked Harry, who had spent a moment or two scraping at it ineffectually with his board. Because the hair, too, was black it was hard to be sure that it was not simply matted and dried insects.

> "That's odd", said Fleury, peering at it with interest; he had never seen anything like it on a statue. "Better leave it, anyway, for the time being. We can always come back to it later when we've done the rest." (256)

Lucy is definitively displayed as Other, as woman and as black. She had capitulated previously to an erotic siege. Now she has progressed from the metaphoric to the literal, as the cultural concept "Womanhood" is reduced to a collection of objects no longer under hegemonic domination. The power of the erotic object to disrupt the homogenising classification could hardly be more clearly demonstrated. Indeed, the siege is something of a liberating experience for women (those who survive). Miriam expresses herself tired of womanhood (241); Louise progresses from the insipid creature of the opening to "a young woman of inflexible will-power" (333). As for Lucy, "[a] wonderful change had come over her since the episode with the cockchafers" (264). All her petulance has disappeared, leaving her placid and cheerful. The attention paid by Fleury and Harry to Lucy's actual rather than metaphoric Amative bumps has clearly had a highly beneficial effect.

A coda remains. At the close of the novel, the Indians have failed to take the Residency, largely because they have never *collected* themselves sufficiently to launch a concerted attack (224). The survivors disperse. Many years later the Collector encounters Fleury in London. The two men have now exchanged ideological positions. Poetic Fleury has been completely integrated into the Victorian hegemony, and roundly declares his faith in its culture; the Collector sees things differently: "Culture is a sham", he said simply. "It's a cosmetic painted on life by rich people to conceal its ugliness" (345). The Collector has sold all his *objets d'art* — whereas Fleury now has "a large collection of artistic objects of which he was very proud" (345). Fleury's beliefs are undercut, however, by his real mission in Pall Mall, which confirms the importance of the physical beneath the veneer; he cuts short his peroration on the glories of ideas because he has an adulterous appointment with "a young lady of passionate disposition" (345), an appointment which he keeps firmly concealed from the Collector. The latter has given up all attempts to gather a coherent world around him. He paces the streets of London observing everything, indiscriminately, and reads newspapers endlessly, scanning the items in the order in which they are printed, without attempting to hierarchise, or to add up the vast amount of entirely random detail which he thus absorbs into some coherent whole. When he thinks of India he recollects only one image — that of two villagers drawing water from a well. It is the image with which Farrell's novel opens, as an unnamed traveller crosses the "bald earth" (9) of the plain and thinks for a moment that he has glimpsed a town in the distance. On closer inspection, however, the image of civilisation is revealed to be one of the ancient cemeteries known as "Cities of the Silent" (10). In the past Krishnapur, a centre for civil administration, had offered an image of a dominant culture, its bungalows built on a lavish scale (10), its residents living in "magnificent style" (10). Now deserted and in ruins, it offers a mournful picture: "a visitor might well find himself reminded of the 'City of the Silent' he had passed on his way to Krishnapur" (10–11). It is an image which encapsulates Farrell's message, in a novel in which the reader, like the traveller, advances towards the distant, elaborate and culturally styled only to recoil, as metaphor boomerangs back to the bald, the literal and the silent. Readers expect to be transported into a different world in the pages of a novel, especially in a historical novel, always something of a process of recollection and display. It is Farrell's achievement that he combines such transport with a continual reminder of its perils.

Notes to Chapter 11

1. Russell Davies, "Rev. of *The Siege of Krishnapur,* by J. G. Farrell," *Observer,* 2 Sept. 1973, 74.
2. Margaret Drabble, "Things Fall Apart," in J. G. Farrell, *The Hill Station: An Unfinished Novel and an Indian Diary,* ed. John Spurling (London: Fontana, 1982), 182.
3. Caroline Moorehead, "Writing in the dark and not a detail missed," *The Times,* 9 September, 1978, 12.
4. J. G. Farrell, "J. G. Farrell Commented," in D. L. Kirkpatrick (ed.), *Contemporary Novelists* (London: St James Press, 1986), 920.
5. Ronald Binns, *J. G. Farrell* (London: Methuen, 1986), 35.
6. Drabble, 189.
7. Aijaz Ahmad, *In Theory: Classes, Nations, Literatures* (London: Verso, 1992), 229.
8. Allen J. Greenberger and Edith L. Piness. "The Legacy of the Raj: J. G. Farrell's *The Siege of Krishnapur,*" *Indo-British Review: A Journal of History,* 11, 1 (1984), 112–17; David Rubin, *After the Raj: British novels of India since 1947* (Hanover, NH and London: University Press of New England, 1986).
9. Neil McEwan, *Perspective in British Historical Fiction Today* (London: Macmillan, 1987), 131.
10. Hayden White, "'Figuring the Nature of the Times Deceased': Literary Theory and Historical Writing," in Ralph Cohen (ed.), *The Future of Literary Theory* (London: Routledge 1989), 20.
11. Gesa Mackenthun, *Metaphors of Dispossession: American Beginnings and the Translation of Empire, 1492–1637* (Norman and London: University of Oklahoma Press, 1997), 299.
12. Mackenthun, 301.
13. White, 30.
14. Eric Cheyfitz, *The Poetics of Imperialism: Translation and Colonization from* The Tempest *to* Tarzan (Oxford: Oxford University Press, 1991), 35.
15. Cheyfitz, 36.
16. Ibid., 90.
17. Bernard Vincent, *1492: L'Année Admirable* (Paris: Aubier: 1991). Quoted in Mackenthun, 318.
18. Stephen J. Greenblatt, "Learning to Curse: Aspects of Linguistic Colonialism in the Sixteenth Century," in Fredi Chiappelli, (ed.), *First Images of America: The Impact of the New World on the Old,* vol. 2 (Berkeley: University of California Press, 1976).
19. Cheyfitz, 106.
20. Ibid., 92.
21. Binns, 69.
22. J. G. Farrell, *The Siege of Krishnapur* (London: Penguin, 1973), 17. Subsequent page references follow citations in parentheses.
23. Goethe's poem "Der Erlkönig" concerns a malevolent goblin who lures people to destruction. Appropriately, given Farrell's theme, its title (king of the alders) is the result of a mistranslation of the Danish term for King of the Elves. It is both far-fetched in terms of its mythological content and in terms of its transference of a foreign concept into a different context.
24. Javed Majeed, *Ungoverned Imaginings: James Mill's* The History of British India *and Orientalism* (Oxford: Clarendon Press, 1992), 164.
25. Ibid., 164.
26. Binns, 77.
27. James Clifford, *The Predicament of Culture: Twentieth-Century Ethnography, Literature and Art* (Cambridge, MA: Harvard University Press, 1988), 218.
28. John McLeod, "Exhibiting Empire in J. G. Farrell's *The Siege of Krishnapur,*" *Journal of Commonwealth Literature,* 29, 2 (1994), 126.
29. Binns, 79.

CHAPTER 12

Zapotec Man and the Torajan Granny: "Mosby's Memoirs" and the Sacrifice of the Heart

"Do you know what that is?" my host reached out and patted a large bundle in one corner of his living room. It looked like the bundle of old clothes you pick out for the charity shop. ... "It's my grandmother."

Before the advent of television, no Western house was complete without a granny to sit with the children and spout idiotic wisdoms at them. Many Torajan houses still have one, but she may be dead. The body is wrapped in vast amounts of absorbent cloth to soak up the juices of putrefaction. Quite quickly, the whole bundle becomes relatively inoffensive . ...

"Aren't you going to greet her?"

"Pleased to meet you granny." A gesture was difficult: a handshake was impossible, but it would have been overly familiar to pat the bundle.

"Wah, that's good."

"How long has she been dead?"

He looked at me appalled. "We don't say that. She's 'sleeping' or 'has a headache'. She won't die until she leaves the house. She's been sleeping for three years now." He reached over and took down a huge cassette player to offer musical entertainment. The tapes, I noticed, were stored in alphabetical order on the body which made a handy shelf.

"You'll miss her when she dies," I said.[1]

Nigel Barley's account of his encounter with a Torajan grandmother offers a convenient point of entry to Saul Bellow's "Mosby's Memoirs", a tale in which the imaginative remapping of the border between life and death is a key operation. As Barley demonstrates (in the longer anthropological study of death customs, from which the above is extracted) death may be seen in the West as a precise point in time, but in many cultures it is a continuing process, even, indeed, a process capable of going into reverse. Any reader who has contemplated the enormous variety of mortuary practices and concepts chronicled by anthropology will concur that "it is striking how little other people's views on the borders of death coincide with our own."[2] The geography of death is not universal: the Styx has a pronounced tendency to wander in its course. Chinese who die abroad and are brought home for burial, for example, are treated as alive and welcomed as such; they will officially die only much later. In Hindu ritual the deceased dies only at the moment when the skull is split on the funeral pyre. Conversely, an ascetic who has renounced the world through symbolic death needs no further rites and is slid into the Ganges without further ado. His social death has preceded the arrival of the biological Grim Reaper. Among the African Dowayos a person who faints has "died", even if revival immediately follows. This is not (unlike say, Western orgasmic imagery) a metaphor. The Dowayos insist that such people did die. But then they simply stopped being dead.[3]

As several commentators have argued, the decline of the belief in Purgatory in the West after the Reformation has encouraged the tendency to assume that we have no social relation with previous generations, that those on this side of the frontier can no longer affect those on the other — and vice versa. Each individual henceforth keeps his own balance sheet and the next world withers away.[4] In much of the world, however, as the Torajan granny demonstrates, the dead remain an important part of society. Even in the West, vestiges of the concept of residual death persist, in such beliefs as the bleeding of the wounds of the murder victim in the presence of the killer, or in our uncertainties concerning the status of the brain dead, the aborted foetus, or the "heart-beating cadaver" necessary for successful kidney transplants. Western culture feels the need to pin down the precise moment and cause of death. (How often does a death certificate ascribe death to "old age"?) Other cultures are less "rational" and meet different social needs in different ways. In the Solomons there are no precise equivalents for the English terms "dead" or "alive"; one term includes the dead, the very old and the very sick.[5] Memorial practices may deny death — or anticipate it. Amongst the Dogon of Mali, when funerary rites have been performed for a person who is "missing presumed dead", there is no possibility of accepting him as alive again, even if he returns in robust good health. In other cultures the anticipation of death finds its clearest application in the entombment of the living — the live burial of wives or servants with the deceased, or the walling up of saintly recluses. In the West the segregation of the living from the dead is rigidly observed. No photographs are taken of the dead, for example, whereas in Java (as in many other cultures) it is normal to photograph the corpse with the family (who imitate the "tenseless" expression on the face of the dead.[6] As Barley comments, our photographs are forgeries of memory in which everyone is always smiling. "In the Western album, the last scene, the funeral, is always missing."[7] Memoirs are, for obvious reasons, a similar case in point. Although ostensibly anticipating death which is implicitly acknowledged as imminent, they also deny it. When Willis Mosby sets out to memorialise himself, his intention is to defeat death rather than to acknowledge it, to keep his reputation alive and to prolong his social existence by assuring himself a place in the historical record. The ambiguity of the borders of life and death is powerfully asserted in the tale, in a fantasy which obsesses Mosby. As he tours the ruins of Mitla,

> Mosby was going once more through an odd and complex fantasy. It was that he was dead. He had died. He continued however to live. His doom was to live life to the end as Mosby. In the fantasy he considered this his purgatory. And when had death occurred? In a collision years ago. He had thought it a near thing then. The cars were demolished. The actual Mosby was killed. But another Mosby was pulled from the car.[8]

It is particularly appropriate that Mosby's fantasy of self-impersonation, doubling and death as an open frontier should occur in Mitla, near Oaxaca in Mexico. The Oaxaca valley is an area which has attracted anthropologists in droves — among them Bronislaw Malinowski, and Elsie Clews Parsons whose *magnum opus, Mitla: Town of the Souls, is* referred to by Mosby.[9] Interest in the area and scholarly work shows a marked increase from 1965 onwards.[10] Susan Drucker-Brown notes that an anthropological bibliography of Oaxaca lists 1,002 items between 1974 and 1979.[11] As Bellow would have known from his anthropological background, and from personal visits to Oaxaca, Mitla was the focus for the mortuary cults of the Zapotecs.[12] According to local tradition Mitla was the centre of the world of the dead.[13] In Mitla the Spanish term for hell was translated into Zapotec as "gabihl" — a realm of the dead coexistent with this world, where souls lived much as in their own lifetime. Heaven was not a dwelling place of souls, but a vague, faraway place where God and the saints lived. People who died lived on in the "gabihl", close to their living relatives. Tombs in the area have been exhaustively studied. (To vary an old joke, the typical Mitlan family appears to consist of parents, children, an anthropologist and an archaeologist.) The monuments reveal powerful images of both denied and anticipated death. According to tradition the more fanatical Zapotecs practised a form of self-sacrifice by being voluntarily cast into the subterranean charnel house, there to wander amidst festering corpses until they also died.[14] One of the most recent commentators on the tombs, Arthur G. Miller, notes that in pre-Hispanic history Mitla (the name derives from Nahuatl "Miquitla" — land of the many dead) was primarily a place for the interaction of the dead with the living.[15] In the pre-Hispanic past the Zapotecs, like the Torajan, literally lived with their dead in houses which included tombs beneath the living quarters. These residential tombs were not sealed up for eternity but periodically reentered and rearranged, the walls repainted, as the death of a family member necessitated a social reorganisation of the tomb. The walls were painted with red hematite pigment, as was the corpse, perhaps as an image of life-giving blood. In short, "the Zapotec response to mortality was to live with it and to make it part of everyday and ritual life."[16] As a result whole generations of the dead were incorporated into the family unit:

> For the Zapotec, death was a particularly powerful social bond that literally cemented the present with the past. They lived with death.[17]

Importantly, however, although Bellow's frame tale situates his memorialist in Mitla, Mosby's memories centre upon Europe in the immediate aftermath of the Second World War, and upon a Jewish character, Lustgarten, who is repeatedly characterised as "Zapotec" because of his squat, black-haired look and the shape of his nose (155). Lustgarten is introduced into the memoirs as comic relief and essentially takes over the tale. The conjunction of Mitla with post-Holocaust Europe suggests that the topic at the heart of the story concerns other images of mass death, of families dead together, and of combined anticipation and denial of death. Mexico provides a substitute place of death — an area which may be envisaged either as a place where there are many dead — or no dead at all; a place where nobody is dead because people remain in close contact across the boundary between life and death, a place where a fantasy of dying-but-not-dying can be fully staged. Staginess is a particularly appropriate term. Bellow stages the act of writing within the tale, as Mosby writes memoirs which we read over his shoulder, in order to distance himself protectively from the material and to accentuate the impression of a stagy, self-conscious dramatisation, a ritual.

Let us return for a moment to the Torajan granny. While the tale makes serious points about liminality and death, it is also a funny story. Indeed the "blurb" for Barley's study describes the whole volume as "blackly comic". Barley himself notes that

> comedy and indulgence too have their place at death. Madness and pantomime, the slapstick flinging of excrement and insults, attempts to copulate with one's grandmother or the deceased, heavy sexual trading, gluttony and drunkenness are all well documented as part of regular, obligatory funeral arrangements.[18]

In Britain few funeral games survived the liturgical controversies of the sixteenth century (though an Irish wake may offer some degree of counterexample). The "joke slot" in the western funeral has been largely reduced to the variety of ways in which cremated ashes can be disposed.[19] The Mexican Day of the Dead, however, involves a joking relationship to the dead, even today, with much jollity, dancing, excess, and the mass consumption of skulls made of chocolate or sugar paste. Essentially the dead are being welcomed back to the land of the living and royally entertained. Joking, however, need not simply represent an affirmation of life. It may function less as an image of irrepressible vitality than as a counter-irritant. Ritual jokes may be quite aggressive in content, using dirt, insult and ambiguity to express the nature of a dangerous and marginal event, with a very thin line between solace and aggression. (Shakespearean fools are a case in point.) Ritual joking, then, may not involve "real" amusement any more than ritual mourning involves real grief.[20] In some cultures smiles and laughter are not necessarily signs of joy. One of Barley's colleagues who worked in West Africa after the war could never explain why, when she showed local people the first pictures coming out of the concentration camps, they laughed. If she had witnessed a funeral among the Nyakusa, who have formal joking partners whose function is to continually exasperate both dead and bereaved, or the Betsilea of Madagascar (who have fights between men and bulls, drink themselves into unconsciousness, and cover their faces with the shroud-cloths in order to engage in blind, orgiastic and incestuous sex) she might have understood that there is more than one "right response" to death.[21] Her experience has a particular relevance to "Mosby's Memoirs" in which Bellow performs his own comic mourning ritual, as a means to confront the deaths of millions in the Holocaust, and as a reflexive investigation of his own writerly activity. Published in 1968, immediately before *Mr Sammler's Planet* in which the Holocaust is finally treated directly (albeit in the memories of Sammler, an intellectual as sure of his own self-importance as Mosby and similarly scornful of those who fail to meet his high standards), "Mosby's Memoirs" approaches its buried topic circumspectly, through layers of indirection, surrogate characters and substitute geographies, until at its close the narrator is finally able to enter the tomb.

This is not the first time that Bellow has used an oblique strategy to approach material of this sort. Bellow's treatment of the Holocaust in his fiction has been characterised by indirection. In interview in 1990 Bellow was asked about the relative absence of the Holocaust in his writing. He agreed that

> There were lots of things I hadn't been able to incorporate. Things that got away from me. The Holocaust for one. ... I may even have been partly sealed off from it.[22]

According to Bellow, it was only in 1959, when he visited Auschwitz, that the Holocaust "landed its whole weight on me".[23] He admitted to finding it odd that he had not been moved to write about it. "I can't interpret it creditably to myself. I'm still wondering at it. I lost close relatives."[24] Bellow's reluctance to confront the topic — understandable as it is — becomes potentially more comprehensible in the description offered, in the same interview, of his childhood. At the age of eight, Bellow spent six months in hospital with T.B. Already a good reader, he could read his chart at the end of the bed and knew, even at that age, that it was very unpromising. In the ward he was constantly exposed to the death of children. As a result, Bellow felt forever after that he had been in some fashion "excused from death", "that it was a triumph that I had gotten away with it".[25] Survival guilt therefore marks Bellow's fiction from an early age. As an American Jew, of course, Bellow escaped the fate of European Jewry. In interview, Bellow was asked about the intellectual impact of the Second World War. He replied that he had completely misunderstood the war because he was under the influence of Marxism. Although Kristallnacht gave him pause, Bellow, as a Trotskyist, stood by the belief that a workers' state, however degenerate, could not wage an Imperialist war. Bellow was indeed such a committed Trotskyist that he arranged to meet the great man in Mexico. Unfortunately, death got there first. On the morning of their scheduled meeting Trotsky was assassinated; Bellow saw him only in the emergency room of the hospital, just after he had died.[26] Later he drew the moral, commenting that as a result he understood

> what a far-reaching power could do with us; how easy it was for a despot to order a death; how little it took to kill us; how slight a hold we, with our historical philosophies, our ideas, programs, purposes, wills, had on the matter we were made of.[27]

After France fell, Bellow came to his senses :"not only did I feel that my Jewish Marxist friends were wrong in theory, but I was horrified by the positions they — we — had taken".[28] Later Bellow looked back on his political views as comically naive.

> Our own movement ... was often foolish, even comically absurd. During the Spanish civil war, the issue of material aid for the Spanish republic was furiously debated by comrades who didn't have a dime to contribute.[29]

In *The Victim*, as I have argued elsewhere, Bellow constructs in Allbee an anti-Semitic double for his hero, Leventhal.[30] In allowing Allbee to persecute him, Leventhal finally exorcises his own guilt at surviving and confronts the degree of responsibility which he owes to the past. As an alter ego, Allbee is drawn very much in terms of Otto Rank's analysis of the figure of the Double. Originally an insurance against death (as in the first double, the immortal soul), the double is also a figure which may reverse its aspect, becoming a harbinger of death and the enemy of the survivor. In Rank's analysis the double appears as a defence against the dissolution of the ego — whether in death or in sexual love (hence the frequency with which doubles interrupt sexual activity or thwart relationships). In "Mosby's Memoirs" death hangs over the action, Mosby is old (he describes himself as a ruin, 154), and writing his memoirs. It is therefore unsurprising that a double appears in the shape of Lustgarten. Importantly Jewish Lustgarten suffers from the same political naivety as the younger Bellow. Mosby chronicles the recondite examination which he and his friends made of the same issues:

> Whether the American working class should give *material* aid to the Loyalist government of Spain. ... There was, of course, no material aid to give. But *had* there been any, *should* it have been given. (155)

Lustgarten also displays an agonised ability to split hairs over the issue of Finland.

> Here the painful point of doctrine to be resolved was whether a Workers' State like the Soviet Union ... could wage an Imperialistic War. (156)

Jewish Lustgarten remains in America throughout the war "just sitting around" (163), but arrives in Europe immediately after its end, intent on making a fortune. Mosby's comments foreground the Holocaust:

> Lustgarten may have felt, *qua* Jew, that he had a right to grow rich in the German boom. That all Jews had natural claims beyond the Rhine. On land enriched by Jewish ashes. And you never could be sure, seated on a sofa, that it was not stuffed or upholstered with Jewish hair. And he would not use German soap. (159)

If Lustgarten is a double to Mosby he is also an emblematic figure of the Jew who has survived unscathed. The evocation of the ubiquity of Jewish remains recalls the description of Mitla as a place of death. Mosby, in poetic mode, registers the mountains

> Whose fat laps are rolling
> On the skulls of whole families. (170)

Mitla offers a seductive locale for Bellow's imaginative response to the Holocaust, a place marked by sacrifice and expiation, where death is emphasised as a negotiable frontier, where one's family dead can be maintained in close social proximity, where the relationship between the generations and the community of human beings is insisted upon. "Mosby's Memoirs" evolves in response to the questions posed by mass death: how can the dead be accepted as dead and properly mourned? Does a less "rational", non-western belief system offer the right way to carry out the process of mourning?

"Mosby's Memoirs" shares many features with *The Victim* — doubles, Holocaust material, a near-death experience. The startling difference is that of tone. In *The Victim* the mode is largely tragic. In the denouement Allbee almost succeeds in gassing Leventhal. The later tale is comic — though it is a comedy which has a very black edge. More than one reader has, indeed, found that the unstable mixture of comedy, irony, farce and horror creates a problem in reading the tale. Robert F. Kiernan describes it perceptively as "a scenario which owes more to the Marx brothers than to Marx",[31] whereas others have emphasised Mosby's guilt (Hyland), the purgatorial nature of the experience (Dutton) and the satire on Mosby's intellectualism. (Fuchs).[32] If, however, the tale is read within the context of ritual mourning comedy, much becomes more comprehensible.

The characteristic note is struck from the beginning, in the association of comedy and aggression.

> The birds chirped away. Fweet, Fweet, Bootchee-Fweet. Doing all the things naturalists say they do. Expressing abysmal depths of aggression, which only man — Stupid Man — heard as innocent. (149)

The nonsense language foregrounds the conventional association of fools with birdsong as noted by Willeford in his study of fools in culture, and exemplified in the fool's coxcomb. Fools are associated also with death (death as jester, death who makes fools of us all) and are therefore unkillable — because already liminal. (The obvious example is that of the circus clown who jumps to his feet after being hit over the head with a sledgehammer.) Forms of duality also run through the range of clowns and fools, as in the ventriloquist and his dummy, the comedy "team" of straight man and comic, mirrors in a funhouse, and the device of the foolpair (Lear and Fool, Don Quixote and Sancho Panza, Don Giovanni and Leporello.)

> Often when we recognize someone as a fool we do so partly because we sense that he is somehow double, even if he is alone.[33]

Although Mosby is emphatically alone in Oaxaca his activity as a memoir writer effectively doubles him. The narration oscillates between Mosby as first person narrator and Mosby as third person character: "Mosby speaking of himself in the third person as Henry Adams had done in *The Education of Henry Adams*." (156). Doubling himself in his memoirs as a defence against death effectively delivers him, however, into the hands of another double, Lustgarten. Initially Lustgarten also has a defensive role. Mosby is concerned that his memoirs are not very funny. His own wit has more in common with death than with life. His jokes are killing. One example is indicative: "Willis Mosby, who was in Toledo with me when the Alcázar fell, made me die laughing" (150). As in "Him with His Foot in His Mouth", Mosby's satirical sallies are deadly: "He was like the Guerrilla Mosby of the Civil War. When he galloped in, all were slaughtered" (166). In order to inject some comic relief into his account (and thus keep the reader reading and Mosby's name alive) Mosby recreates Lustgarten, as a foil, a comic figure to his own straight man. If Lustgarten's political pretensions are absurd, his later attempts to storm the bastions of capitalism are even more laughable. Swindled by his business partner, betrayed by his wife, he is comprehensively fooled by all and sundry. He, too, has connections with death, however. When Mosby first meets him in Paris, he is recalled in the blood red interior of a bank, identical in colour to Napoleon's sarcophagus in Les Invalides. Lustgarten is employed at this point by the U.S. Army in graves registration, much occupied with cemeteries and monuments. Lustgarten also survives a car crash, an event which associates him with Mosby's fantasy self and with survival guilt. Prosaically, Lustgarten laments his survival (163) because his life insurance would at least have covered the financial losses of his mother, uncle and brother — all ruined by the crash. Survival here is more reminiscent of the unkillable clown than of some sinister ghostly double.

If Bellow ascribes his own political errors satirically to Lustgarten, it is none the less striking that Lustgarten is allowed to expiate them. After his fiasco as would-be capitalist Lustgarten gives Marxism one more chance and departs for Yugoslavia, "a candidate for resurrection" (165) for what he assumes is a "V.I.P. deal" (165) as a foreign observer, with seminars in dialectics to boot. "I really believe Tito may redeem Marxism by actually transforming the dictatorship of the proletariat" (165), he proclaims. He returns emaciated, sun-blackened, sick and embittered from what has turned out to be a forced labour brigade. Lustgarten may not have experienced the actual horrors of the Holocaust, but as a member of a chain gang in Dalmatia he has been thoroughly punished for his errors. Abused by fate, battered and ragged, Lustgarten remains a clown in the Chaplinesque mode. Tellingly his wife shares his clownishness — they are a fool pair — and it entails an image of doubleness:

> Trudy too was funny, however. What a large belly she had. Since individuals are sometimes born from a twin impregnation, the organism carrying the underdeveloped brother or sister in vestigial form ... Mosby often thought that Trudy had a little sister inside her. And to him she was a clown. (172)

Even Trudy's face registers self-division — the left eye wanders (159). For all his amusement, Mosby is now, however, reminded of several uncomfortable facts — his own adultery with Trudy for example. Like any good double, Mosby had come between Lustgarten and the object of his affections, with disastrous consequences:

> his vision of Lustgarten as a funny man was transmitted to Trudy. She could not be the wife of such a funny man. (172)

If Lustgarten fulfils one comic purpose, that of the fool who survives everything and the expiatory comedian, Mosby (who makes fun of Lustgarten in his misery) fulfils that of the joking partner, the counter-irritant.

Up to this point it may appear that Mosby's strategy has worked rather well. The tale of the Lustgartens, undeniably comic, holds the reader's attention and (as Mosby remarks) has a certain symmetry. "There was a coda: The thing had quite good form" (168). Lustgarten is glimpsed once more on his way to the offices of *Fortune* magazine, prosperous, remarried and happy. Predictably, he is on the wrong elevator for *Fortune*, the story of his life as opposed to Mosby's secure place in the public eye. At the close of the tale, however, as the reader leaves the joking partner behind to return to the frame tale in Mexico, the story reverses its aspect and turns back upon itself. ("There was a coda: The thing had quite good form.") By allowing Lustgarten to take over the story, Mosby allows him to become a threat to his identity rather than a means of defence. Essentially Lustgarten's counterexample reveals the extent of Mosby's social death. Unmarried, friendless, childless, Mosby has suppressed all human ties — unlike Lustgarten, a keen father and uxorious husband. Ruled by his intellect, Mosby's concern with rationality and objectivity has been absolute. Mosby had declared during the war that the Germans were winning because their managerial revolution had come first (151). He went on to assert that:

> however deplorable the concentration camps had been, they showed at least the rationality of German political ideas. (151–52)

To adopt Mosby's cold rationality would be akin to killing the dead all over again. Mosby scorns Lustgarten's tears ("Such unmastered emotion was abhorrent", 163) and restricts his comment on Lustgarten's passionate fatherhood to the supercilious statement that "For Plato, this childbreeding is the lowest level of creativity" (169). For all his clever political-historical pronouncements, Mosby has no actual connection to society at all.

At the close of the tale, Mosby sets off to tour the monuments of Mitla. The tour begins with the tree of Tule, an image of continuity in community between the living and the dead:

> A world in itself! It could contain communities... [recalling] a primal tree, occupied by early ancestors. (170)

Mosby's fantasy of death-in-life recurs at this point, immediately before he enters the final tomb. His own self-division has now become overt, as the language of the story becomes that of Beckettian clowning. A textual double act is staged in his memories.

> At this time, Mosby had been making fun of people.
> "Why?"
> "Because he had needed to."
> "Why?"
> "Because." (172–73)

Entering the tomb, dyed red, Mosby contemplates the horrors of human sacrifice — an image of the loss of the heart which has made him a Zapotec man in a way in which Lustgarten never was. Around him he admires the precision of the cut stone, the geometrical masses and the mathematical perfection of the masonry. As Dan Fuchs has argued, the precision, calculation and sacrifice of the human all align Mosby with the tomb.[34] H. Porter Abbott comments that the Mexican sepulchre is an image of the tomb which Mosby has constructed for himself — and called his life.[35] Contemplating the tomb, he reflects on the contrast between foolish Lustgarten "who didn't have to happen" (173) and historically important Mosby, a complete and finished product.

> He had completed himself in this cogitating, unlaughing, stone, iron, non-sensical form. (173)

Nonsensical, but unlaughing, Mosby is a fool, but not an unkillable one. Mosby had intended the Lustgarten digression as "the correction of pride by laughter" (167), a means of maintaining human interest in an inhuman story. Where kings have jesters for purposes of ritual insult and self-revelation, Mosby has Lustgarten. But Lustgarten is the jester who betrays Mosby into a real confrontation with death. By creating a third-person self Mosby dehumanises and depersonalises himself to the point of extinction; Lustgarten steps into the character vacuum. All Mosby's efforts to defer death, to fantasise it away, now founder on the logic of his own belief in precision, objectivity and reason. In the tomb he is seized with horror.

> His heart was paralysed. His lungs would not draw. Jesus! I cannot catch my breath! To be shut in here! To be dead here! Suppose one were! Not as in accidents which ended but did not quite end existence. *Dead*-dead. (174)

In the last scene the typical forgery of memory in the memoirs is corrected. As in Bellow's encounter with death in Mexico (Trotsky) the scene registers the fact that death is inevitable, for all Mosby's intellectual historicising. The reader will also note that in the face of the finality of death Mosby reverses from third to first person ("His heart ... his lungs ... I cannot"), no longer split between his two selves. Stooping, he emerges from the tomb, at last a penitent survivor.

If "Mosby's Memoirs" allows Lustgarten to expiate previous errors, Mosby (the writer, the wit, the thinker about history) does not get off so lightly. And nor, perhaps, does Bellow's audience. For if Mosby is doubled, so are we. As an audience to "Mosby's Memoirs" we read of the imaginary audience for which Mosby is providing the comic relief which we are enjoying, comic relief which also takes us to the edge of the tomb. Like Mosby in Mitla we are placed in an ambiguously liminal position, simultaneously within two tales, two audiences and two locations. The form of "Mosby's Memoirs" thus duplicates its theme. In the face of death Bellow multiplies the number of characters and readers, establishing a convergence between story theme and narrative environment, as inset tale and frame tale coalesce into one. At the end Mosby is restored to his individual self and comes back from the death-in-life which has been his. As Kiernan notes, "to his surprise the reader ends up respecting a man he suspects he should loathe".[36] Arguably the reader's empathy results from the uneasy sense that he too has been doubled and fooled. Reading "Mosby's Memoirs" is uncomfortable, offering an experience of both solace and aggression. If Lustgarten's expiation reassures, Mosby's fate offers no such relief. The tale also constitutes a thorough investigation of the writer's activity. It is a mark of the seriousness of Bellow's exploration of the issues posed by the Holocaust that, as a comic writer, he implicitly interrogates his own practice. Is comedy a form of denial of death, an evasion? Alternatively, is the comic writer a "guerrilla" whose comedy merely enlarges the field of slaughter? Arguably, Bellow's comedy — dark as it is — provides a necessary counter-irritant in an extended ritual of mourning, insisting upon the vital role of the imagination in maintaining the social relation to the dead.

Notes to Chapter 12

1. Nigel Barley, *Dancing On The Grave: Encounters with Death* (London: John Murray, 1995), 54–55.
2. Ibid., 55.
3. Ibid., 47.
4. Ibid., 79.
5. Ibid., 54–57.
6. Ibid., 72.
7. Ibid.
8. Saul Bellow, *Mosby's Memoirs and Other Stories* (London: Penguin, 1971), 171 (first published New York: Viking, 1968). Page references to the Penguin edition follow quotations in parentheses.
9. Elsie Clews Parsons' work on the sacred clowns of American native peoples, and among the Zapotecs in Mitla, is also relevant to the tale. See Elsie Clews Parsons, *Mitla: Town of the Souls and other Zapoteco-Speaking Pueblos of Oaxaca, Mexico* (Chicago: University of Chicago Press, 1936) and "The Sacred Clowns of the Pueblo and Mayo-Yaqui Indians," *American Anthropologist*, 36, 4 (1934), 491–514.
10. Joseph W. Whitecotton, *The Zapotecs: Princes, Priests and Peasants* (Norman: University of Oklahoma Press, 1978), vii.
11. Bronislaw Malinowski and Julio de la Fuente, *Malinowski in Mexico: The Economics of a Mexican Market System*, ed. Susan Drucker-Brown (Boston and London: Routledge and Kegan Paul, 1985), 43.
12. Judie Newman, "Saul Bellow and Social Anthropology," in Gerhard Bach (ed.), *Saul Bellow at Seventy-five: A Collection of Critical Essays* (Tübingen: Gunter Narr Verlag, 1991), 137–49.
13. Charles M. Leslie, *Now We Are Civilized: A Study of the World View of the Zapotec Indians of Mitla, Oaxaca* (Detroit: Wayne State University Press, 1960).
14. Hyatt and Ruth Verrill, *America's Ancient Civilizations* (New York: G. P. Putnam's Sons, 1953).
15. Arthur G. Miller, *The Painted Tombs of Oaxaca, Mexico: Living With the Dead* (Cambridge: Cambridge University Press, 1995), 221.
16. Ibid., xix.
17. Ibid., 31.
18. Barley, 34.
19. Ibid., 39.
20. Ibid., 40.
21. Ibid., 34.
22. Saul Bellow, *It All Adds Up. From the Dim Past to the Uncertain Future: A Non-Fiction Collection* (London: Secker and Warburg, 1994), 312.
23. Ibid., 313.
24. Ibid.
25. Ibid., 289.
26. Bellow's story, "The Mexican General," *Partisan Review* 9 (May–June 1942), 178–94, draws upon this experience. See Judie Newman, "Saul Bellow and Trotsky," *Saul Bellow Journal*, 1, 1 (1981), 26–31 (Chapter 21 in this volume).
27. Bellow, *It All Adds Up*, 101.
28. Ibid., 310.
29. Ibid., 100–01.
30. Saul Bellow, *The Victim* (New York: Vanguard, 1947). See Judie Newman, "Bellow's Ransom Tale: The Holocaust, *The Victim*, and *The Double*," *Saul Bellow Journal*, 14, 1 (1996), 3–18 (Chapter 9 in this volume).
31. Robert F. Kiernan, *Saul Bellow* (New York: Frederick Ungar, 1989), 132.
32. Peter Hyland, *Saul Bellow* (London: Macmillan, 1992); Robert R. Dutton, *Saul Bellow* (New York: Twayne, 1971); Daniel Fuchs, *Saul Bellow: Vision and Revision* (Durham, NC: Duke University Press, 1984), 43–49.
33. William Willeford, *The Fool and His Sceptre* (Northwestern University Press, 1969), 42.
34. Fuchs.

35. H. Porter Abbott, "Saul Bellow and the 'Lost Cause' of Character," in *Saul Bellow in the 1980s: A Collection of Critical Essays*, ed. Gloria L. Cronin and L. H. Goldman (East Lansing, MI: Michigan State University Press, 1989), 113–36.

36. Kiernan, 135.

CHAPTER 13

Napalm and After:
The Politics of
Grace Paley's Short Fiction

I object not to facts but to people sitting in trees talking senselessly, voices from
who knows where. ("A Conversation with my Father") [1]

Grace Paley's commitment to political radicalism has never been in much doubt.
Comparatively few contemporary writers have accompanied American POWs
home from Hanoi, been arrested on the White House Lawn, or been dragged off
in shackles to serve time in the Greenwich Village Women's House of Detention.
Paley's pacifist, socialist politics are also deeply rooted in a family past where
memories were still fresh of Tsarist oppression — one uncle shot dead carrying the
red flag, and parents who reached America only because the Tsar had a son and
amnestied all political prisoners under the age of twenty-one. At this point, Paley's
father (imprisoned in Archangel) and her mother (in exile) took their chances (and
all their surviving relatives) and very sensibly ran for their lives. Her grandmother
recalled family arguments around the table between Paley's father (Socialist), Uncle
Grisha (Communist), Aunt Luba (Zionist) and Aunt Mira (also Communist). Paley's
own street-wise adolescence involved the usual teenage gang fights — between
adherents of the Third and Fourth Internationals.

Until recently, critics of Paley's work have tended to focus upon gender politics,
and upon the feminist form of her writing, with its communal narration, revisions
of conventional genre and restoration of women's unwritten experience.[2] The 1998
publication of *Just As I Thought*, a collection of Paley's autobiographical pieces,
has drawn attention back, however, to politics in the newspaper sense of the
term.[3] Reviews were, at best, mixed. For Alan Wolfe (in the *New Republic*) Paley
exemplified an idealistic, romantic, impractical Leftism, complacently convinced of
its own righteousness, and demonstrating how the Left in America

> has happily chosen the easy path of political sentimentover the difficult business
> of moral reckoning.[4]

In his view Paley's sentimentality had converted radicalism into "little more than a
story itself", in which America is always bad, and all the countries which challenge
it, implicitly good.

Only a storyteller could write in Paley's gushing terms about the idyll of North Vietnam. "Water spinach," she exclaims, "is a wonderful vegetable." And only a fabulist could write about her fellow writer Christa Wolf and never discuss her work for the East German secret police.[5]

Carol Iannone, in *Commentary*, was (predictably) even more scathing, accusing Paley of having been seduced by a Potemkin-style display in Vietnam, and reminding her of the North Vietnamese "re-education" camps, and the fate of Vice Admiral James Stockdale. [6] In her account Paley insists that American POWs were always very well-treated, quoting in support the Vietnamese proverb:

The man in the sky is a killer, bring him down; but the man on the ground is a helpless human being.[7]

Even without stampeding quite as far to the right as Iannone, it does seem faintly unlikely that the North Vietnamese had evolved such a perfect form of human nature that nobody ever revenged their napalmed children by taking a pitchfork to a captured airman.

Be that as it may, Paley has none the less defended the political impetus behind her stories. Interviewed in *Index on Censorship*, she complained that

there's some kind of inhibition in this country about writing about people who live and think politically. But I don't feel like I'm writing about seven people in the world. It's not so pathetic a minority as they want us to think.[8]

While some of her readers were entirely sympathetic, she recorded hostile reactions from others.

I get people saying, what's all this politics in here? What's interesting is that in almost any other country in the world, nobody would ever dare to think of saying, what's all this politics in here?[9]

Even worse, the reading public does not always get a choice in the matter. Publishers have certainly abetted a wholesale depoliticisation of Paley's writing. The last three stories of *Later The Same Day* were published in *Mother Jones* (a progressive political journal) after being rejected everywhere else.[10] In addition, though some of Paley's stories are frequently anthologised, they are the less overtly political tales.

I meet people who think the only story I ever wrote was "Goodbye and Good Luck."[11]

So is it possible to be a storyteller and yet remain politically and morally responsible? Or does Paley convert politics into story — and, perhaps more worryingly for the literary critic, story into politics? In the space available here, one story must serve as something of a test case. In "Faith in a Tree", Faith sits in a sycamore tree, freely discoursing upon the other mothers in the park around her, descending only when drawn to earth by the sight of a handsome male. When a group of war-protesters are ejected from the park by the police, Faith does not intervene, to the fury of her son Richard who promptly chalks their slogans on the blacktop, converting his mother to political involvement. The story marks a political turning point, a major change of life-direction.

Then I met women and men in different lines of work, whose minds were made up and directed out of that sexy playground by my children's heartfelt brains, I thought more and more about the world.[12]

Paley visited Vietnam in 1969, with six others, three of them filmmakers (the film was impounded on their return), the others charged with the job of accompanying POWs home. Importantly the first version of the story (published in *New American Review* in 1967, before Paley visited Vietnam) leaves Faith unconverted, ending as she climbs back into her tree, when she realises that the dashing Phillip is attracted to another woman. [13] The collected version (*Enormous Changes at the Last Minute*, 1974) adds the sudden interruption of the protesters. The story is very much two colliding stories — an initial story which is gender-political, representing the unseen lives of women, their voices interwoven with Faith's, looking after children in the local park, and a second macro-political story which introduces global politics in a fairly obvious fashion. The two are ostensibly linked by the concern for children — the protesters carry a sequence of posters, one of which portrays a napalmed child. The posters are identical to those which Paley herself remembers carrying.

> Years ago — 1966 or 1967 — people in the peace movement carried a poster of a well-dressed young man holding a cigarette against the arm of a child. On the poster a question was asked: *Would you burn a child?* In the next poster, the man applied the burning cigarette and the answer was given: *When necessary.* The third poster showed a child burned and crippled by American napalm[14]

From one point of view, however, it may be argued that the story deteriorates as story, as a result of the Vietnam material, ceasing to be a free-floating, digressive celebration of women's language and experience, to become conventional, a story with a "twist" at the end, a sudden point which appears completely unmotivated by what precedes it. Richard's role as child-conscience (shades of Little Eva) is also ambiguous. He is after all a proponent, even in his childish way, of violent intervention. He punches his mother and argues that Faith should have slugged the cop, to allow the peace demonstration to proceed. On the other hand, if the whole point of the story is the conversion of Faith to political action as a result of the demonstration, the preceding twenty pages, in which a woman sits in a tree apparently babbling nonsensically, merely delay the getting of the political message. In a sense they obscure confrontation with the facts of American violence — the implicit criticism of the fictional father, commenting intertextually on his offspring's story in "Conversation With My Father". The brokenbacked form of the tale brings into sharp focus the potential mismatch between form and message. Indeed it is arguable that this is part of Paley's intention. The protesters, with their violent images, are swiftly dismissed by one witness: "They'll only turn people against them" (98). The form of their action — a noisy parade — recalls the inherent problem of finding an appropriate form for political protest — in life as in story. When people form lines, hold up banners and advance in serried ranks, to "march" against war, they may not look very different from their militaristic opponents lined up opposite them. The images on the flags may be different, but both groups behave like armies. The form itself carries a message of aggression, despite its surface intentions. And the short story form has to address the same problem. When a short story suddenly delivers a shocking moral in a heart-stopping twist, there is a degree of textual aggression towards the reader, impaled on its point.

So what is the connection between anti-war protest and a woman babbling in a tree? Two points are significant here — Faith's bird's eye view, and the tree itself. The story establishes an implicit contrast between narratorial omniscience and womanly limitation, drawing attention to an illustrious narrative forefather. Like some latter day surveyor of "The American Scene" Faith looks down upon the park and notes its pool, "in which, when Henry James could see, he saw lilies floating" (78). It is, of course, Washington Square Park. This is the park where, famously, in the novel *Washington Square*, Catherine Sloper chose not to meet her lover, Morris Townsend, in favour of accepting his advances in a respectably furnished parlour. James described the area in 1880 as having "a kind of established repose which is not of frequent occurrence in other quarters of the long, shrill city".[15] Grace Paley was active in the movement to preserve this park from real-estate interests, and from the plan (subsequently defeated) to drive a road through it. Unlike James, Faith enjoys a view which is less tranquil, more feral, offering an image of city-as-jungle. Over the tree tops, beyond dangerous Central Park, "Far north, the deer-eyed eland and kudu survive, grazing the open pits of the Bronx Zoo" (78). Faith may not enjoy godly omniscience — she distinguishes carefully between the god who looks down from "Holy Headquarters" (77) and sees everything, and herself, "the creation of His soft second thought" (78) — but her position allows for a degree of superiority none the less. Like a Foucauldian surveillant in a panopticon, Faith enjoys a panoramic view of her fellow "prisoners", confined to the park by childcare. Although the story can be read as a celebration of womankind, her position suggests that she has the other women in her sights as much as in her sight. She comments freely, for example, on Mrs Wilson's pretentiousness, Anna's bad character, Mrs Finn's dogmaticism, Lynn's self-absorption. Both Adam Meyer and Minako Baba have drawn attention to the implicit condescension of her position, literally looking down on the others from superior heights.[16] As the imagery establishes, she enjoys the full empire of the gaze, in her description of the playground, expanding it from micro- to macrocosm by her nautical metaphors (metaphors which, with their suggestions of the image of the large woman as a ship in full sail, are not necessarily complimentary). Mrs Lewis, like a large liner manoeuvring slowly into position, "swings within the seconds of her latitude" (78); Mrs Finn becomes a "broad barge", with "cabooses dragged by clothesline at her stern" (78) with one child, her "roaring captain" (79), clinging to her ample "upper deck" (78), as she goes puffing towards the "sandy harbor" (79) of the playground. Sexy Lynn Ballard, tilting like a delicate sailboat, a toy for boys, floats along the same channel to "drop light anchor" (79) on a bench. The suggestion is of aerial reconnaissance, a view from a crow's nest or look-out post. Faith's irony may preserve the story from sentimentality (a charge to which any writer who celebrates the experiences of mothers and children will always be exposed) but distance is also potentially a form of attack. In the story Paley plays with notions of distance in order to collapse them, to bring the potentially aggressive "man in the sky" (even a woman merely half way up a tree) to the ground and humanise them. Faith may see herself as a victimised woman, stuck with unremitting childcare, but she is none the less an American, looking down from a height.

Although the narrative appears to digress and meander in a decentred way, idling from anecdote to unrelated anecdote, there is a subtextual logic to its movement, which centres upon notions of distance. Distance undercuts feeling and responsibility in several examples. On the one hand, distance allows Mrs Finn to pass judgment. Faith comments that Mrs Finn is "more in charge of word meanings than I am. She is especially in charge of Good and Bad" (85). Mrs Finn's child, Junior, is actually at some physical distance, imprisoned upstate for theft. The family, however, have managed to disclaim responsibility: "It was Adam's Fall not Junior that was responsible" (85), distancing from the specific local crime (the desire for a ten-speed Italian racer) to the global conviction of Sin. Lofty definitions of Good and Evil can be a useful means of abdicating from any real moral involvement. In her childhood, Faith herself was celebrated in the press for travelling long distances as "the third commercial air-flight baby passenger in the entire world" (80). In her account her mother unsentimentally sent the baby off alone to prove that in some sensible socialist future, "she wasn't the sort to hang on ... she wouldn't cry at my wedding" (80). More mundanely, fathers in the story are both physically and emotionally distant, as in the case of Phillip, unsure what age his own son is, now the boy has moved to Chicago, or Ricardo, Faith's absent husband, exploring equatorial regions, and leaving his children to Faith to bring up. Although Faith envies Ricardo his adventurous freedom, his letter to her comprehensively deflates the charms of distance, in favour of the attractions of the local:

> I am not well. I hope I never see another rainforest. I am sick. Are you working? Have you seen Ed Snead? He owes me $180. (82)

In contrast, Faith comically inflates the tiny world of his son, Richard, the "prince" of the day care centre for the deprived children of working mothers, "Lord of the West Side loading zone" whenever it rains on Sundays, "chief of the dark forest of four ginkgo trees" (87). Unlike his father's, Richard's jungle experiences are emphatically local. A small world suddenly expands here, to the horizon; the "larger" world shrinks into bathos. Playfully, Faith extols the virtues of the local in a digression describing a plan to make one month of public-school attendance part of the private school curriculum, to demonstrate

> the value of exposing children who had read about the horror at Ilium to ordinary street fights, so they could understand the *Iliad* better. (90)

The anecdote offers a tongue-in-cheek version of the argument that involvement in local issues and political conflicts can inform the understanding of global war.

Importantly this play with distance is not limited to theme, metaphor or imagery. In terms of narrative form manipulations of distance are what make the story politically effective. In the tale (as Jacqueline Taylor has demonstrated in a sophisticated formal analysis) it is often quite difficult to distinguish between Faith's unspoken thoughts, expressed only to the reader, and her direct utterances.[17] When she wonders to herself "How can you answer that boy?" (84), it is a surprise to the reader when Mrs Junius Finn, "some distance away" (85) on the other side of the park, actually replies. Faith's empire of the eye is violated by the unpredictable ability of sound — words — to cross long distances. The ironic inflation and deflation of the scene upsets the reader's ability to maintain a safe distance. It is rather as if we had the wrong reading glasses on. The scene jumps suddenly at us. We are not securely outside the story (in our tree), nor are we snugly inviolable, sharing the headspace of a narrator. Other characters, who seemed to be some way away, can suddenly get up close and personal. What seemed like a private monologue for the reader alone, for example, is suddenly dismissed by Richard: "That's a typical yak yak out of you, Faith" (84). If a reader can be said to have a "body space" within a story, this story would violate it — perhaps a suggestive metaphor in the context of Vietnam.

As a result the story insists upon physical closeness rather than aesthetic distance, with a series of incidents in which space expands or contracts according to the dictates of the senses. At times it is as if we were in a whispering gallery, where sound can travel a long way to be audible right beside us, at times it is as if deafness struck at six inches, such is the domination of the visual. Paley had fought to preserve this particular park from developers. Importantly she had also been part of the movement to permit music in the park, seen by city authorities as a threat to civil order:

> they wouldn't allow any guitars or singing, flutes or oboes, anything. And we finally simply sat down together in the fountain circle with the children, and we just sat and played guitars and recorders and fiddles. [The police] went after us, knocking people around a little.[18]

Paley's group won, though she comments ruefully that "Now it's so noisy you can hardly stand it."[19] In the story the subjective limitations of both eye and ear are insisted upon. Mrs Finn is "deaf to passion" (85); Phillip's offended eyes are described in minute close-up. Richard's teacher is deaf to the attractions of his nonsense verse. The narrator registers one group of upwardly mobile fathers only as the whistlers; her absent husband is portrayed as a ball of spit in her ear. Faith comments that it takes most men two years to appreciate Anna's bad character ("to see how bad she was", 97) but "it takes the average passer, answerer, or asker about thirty seconds to see how beautiful she is" (97). In contrast, when two music lovers traverse the park, they pay absolutely no attention to the women. Their mental space is entirely filled by a radio playing the Chromatic Fantasy. They are up close — close enough for Anna to hear their comments on the music — but as personally distant as the contemporary user of a personal stereo on a crowded train. Another passer-by, a representational artist, spots Kitty and Antonia and "squared them off with a filmmaker's viewfinder and said, 'Ah, what a picture!', then left" (88). He treats the women as if they were deaf, or some distance away — as if they were merely objects offered to the gaze of the passing male. There are many such males, characterised by Kitty as "squint-eyed speculators" (88). One such sits down beside Lynn and "speaks softly to her left ear while she maintains her profile" (86), completely avoiding his eyes. Kitty assumes he is offering her a dramatic role; Faith sees it as obvious that he is a "weekend queer" suggesting a "neighborhood threesome" (86). For the reader it is irritating not to know what the unspecified temptation actually was. Successively we crave the omniscience which Paley here denies us — just as we crave the safety of the inviolable narrator, and don't expect her characters to interrupt or criticise her. We are, in readerly terms, in the sky, rather than on the ground. Faith draws a tentative moral

> I don't believe civilization can do a lot more than educate a person's senses. If it's truth and honor you want to refine, I think the Jews have some insight. Make no images, imitate no God. After all, in His field, the graphic arts, He is pre-eminent. [Let God] be in charge of Beauty. ... and ... let man be in charge of Good. (89)

The comment connects the story with a familiar strand of anti-ocular discourse in Western culture, particularly in the contrast between lived, temporally meaningful experience, immediacy of speech (the word) and collective activity, *and*, on the other hand, dead spatialised images, the distancing effect, and potential violence, of the gaze, and the passivity of individual contemplation. Paley's argument against the dehumanising effects of the hegemony of the eye draws on a long tradition, from the validation of the Word of God over the graven image, to Foucault's analysis of vision as complicitous in the apparatuses of surveillance, central to the maintenance of repressive power in the modern world.[20]

In descending from her tree Faith abandons the distant view in favour of the conversation at ground level, the local rather than the global. Paradoxically it is this movement which broadens her moral field of action. Paley has commented in interview on the way in which her involvement in local issues connected to more global action.[21] The original title of the story was "Faith: In A Tree". In the story's second creation, however, the colon was omitted, allowing the pun on faith/belief in a tree. Paley preserved the trees in a small local arena; her character now commits herself to the same action on a global scale. In her accounts of Vietnam Paley dwells, at several reprises, upon the greenness of the landscape, a "mist of greenness", "our green Hanoi".[22] Oddly, no commentator appears to have drawn the obvious connection between a tree and the Vietnam war. Napalm, as nobody needs to be reminded, is a defoliant. The subtle politics of the story operates subtextually, as opposed to the graphic imagery of the protesters, to translate the local into the global, with the New York park standing as an image of another despoiled area, struggling to preserve its green spaces for its children. When the women, longing for exotic travel, admire Phillip's French, it appears to be merely a digression. "'Cambodge...' Phillip said. He said this softly as though the wars in Indochina might be the next subject for discussion" (95). The reader assumes that they won't be, that Phillip is merely playing with sound. But like a half audible undertone, the sound comes to our attention, culminating in the noise of the anti-war parade. Backing away, circling around, the story closes in on its real topic, catching the reader by surprise. Paley has remarked that she often needs two stories in order to make one:

It's these two stories working against each other and in connection with each other that make it happen.[23]

By its indirection, the story reverses the proverbial phrase, suggesting that rather than not being able to see the wood for the trees, most of us cannot see the tree for the wood — our views are too global, too distanced, too visual to pick up the message of the word on the ground.

Notes to Chapter 13

1. Grace Paley, *Enormous Changes at the Last Minute* (London: Virago, 1979), 162. The collection was first published in New York by Farrar, Straus, Giroux in 1974.
2. See for example Jacqueline Taylor, *Grace Paley: Illuminating the Dark Lives* (Austin: University of Texas Press, 1990); Gloria Cronin, "Melodramas of Beset Womanhood: Resistance, Subversion and Survival in the Fiction of Grace Paley," *Studies in American-Jewish Literature*, 11, 2 (1992), 140–49. A discussion of Paley's work which undertakes a political analysis in terms of conversation as both form and political model is Adam Sorkin (ed.), *Politics and the Muse: Studies in the Politics of Recent American Literature* (Bowling Green: Bowling Green State University Popular Press, 1989).
3. Grace Paley, *Just As I Thought* (New York: Farrar, Straus, Giroux, 1998).
4. Alan Wolfe, "The Saint," *New Republic*, 218, 26 (29 June 1998), 38.
5. Ibid., 36.
6. Carol Iannone, "A Dissent on Grace Paley," *Commentary*, 80 (August 1985), 54–58.
7. Paley, *Just as I Thought*, 79.
8. Grace Paley, "We don't say a lot of what we think," *Index on Censorship*, 19, 1 (1990), 13.
9. Ibid.
10. Grace Paley, *Later the Same Day* (New York: Farrar, Straus, Giroux, 1985).
11. Paley, *Index on Censorship*, 13.
12. Grace Paley, *Enormous Changes at the Last Minute* (London: Virago, 1979), 100. Subsequent page references, given parenthetically in the text, are to this edition of the story.
13. Grace Paley, "Faith: In a Tree," *New American Review*, 1, 3 (1967), 51–67.
14. Paley, *Just As I Thought*, 115.
15. Henry James, *Washington Square* (London: Penguin, 1963), 16.
16. Minako Baba, "Faith Darwin as Writer-Heroine: A Study of Grace Paley's Short Stories," *Studies in American-Jewish Literature*, 7, 1 (1988), 40–54; Adam Meyer, "Faith and the 'Black Thing': Political Action and Self-Questioning in Grace Paley's Short Fiction," *Studies in Short Fiction*, 31 (1994), 79–89.
17. Taylor.
18. Paley, *Just As I Thought*, 157.
19. Ibid., 158.
20. See Martin Jay, *Downcast Eyes: The Denigration of Vision in Twentieth-Century French Thought* (Berkeley: University of California Press, 1994).
21. Wendy Smith, "*PW* Interviews Grace Paley," in Gerhard Bach and Blaine H. Hall (ed.), *Conversations With Grace Paley* (Jackson: University Press of Mississippi, 1997), 126–30.
22. Paley, *Just As I Thought*, 62–64.
23. "Grace Paley Interviewed by Ruth Perry," in Janet Todd (ed.), *Women Writers Talking* (New York, Holmes and Meier, 1983), 39.

CHAPTER 14

Jump Starts:
Nadine Gordimer after Apartheid

As apartheid has crumbled, the question which has presented itself repeatedly is whether the South African novelist has lost his or her essential subject. Can the white novelist survive the end of apartheid — or has the artist's inspiration disappeared, together with the tools previously employed? The question betrays an assumption — common, I would argue to both postcolonial and post-apartheid writing — that it can engage only with representational, realistic portrayals of an essentially political subject matter — that without Empire — or, in this particular case, without Afrikaner Nationalism — it has no independent existence of its own. The question of use value as opposed to aesthetic value is therefore a question which lies at the heart of postcolonial writing: South African literature simply presents an example at the sharp end of the spectrum.

Recent debates in South African literary criticism have centred upon the problem of the artist's role in relation to society, specifically in what has become known as the Albie Sachs debate, and in the response to the writings of Njabulo Ndebele. During forty years of opposition to apartheid the avowed aim of literary practitioners was "solidarity criticism", placing a strong emphasis on social realism and the evaluation of writing in relation to its adherence to a materialist dialectic.[1] Writing was seen as a "cultural weapon" and was supposed to concentrate upon expressing collective rather than individual experiences in a mode of popular realism. In 1989 Albie Sachs made a speech, "Preparing Ourselves for Freedom", a paper prepared for an ANC in-house seminar on culture.[2] Sachs (somewhat teasingly) proposed banning the phrase "culture is a weapon of struggle"; he described solidarity criticism and the instrumental view of culture in general as impoverishing artistic production and as merely a means of appearing politically correct. Above all he argued that the result of solidarity criticism was simply to ensure that all South African literature was about the oppressor. In his description of recent South African writing, he lamented the narrow range of themes, the closing off of ambiguity and contradiction, and the stereotypical nature of character. For Sachs the power of art lay in the capacity to expose contradictions and reveal hidden tensions. The concentration on the struggle had closed off whole areas of human activity. "And what about love?" asked Sachs, rhetorically:

> Can it be that when we join the ANC we do not make love any more, that
> when the comrades go to bed they discuss the role of the white working class?[3]

Sachs' light-hearted, teasing tone was part of his point; the medium was also the
message. For Sachs the editing out of everything but the political, the filling up of
novels with oppressors, trauma, misery, risked a further reduction of the individual
already threatened by apartheid:

> What are we fighting for, if not the right to express our humanity in all its
> forms, including our sense of fun and capacity for love and tenderness and our
> appreciation of the beauty of the world?[4]

A better strategy was to allow art to bypass, overwhelm and ignore apartheid
by establishing its own space. Sachs' paper was punchy, if somewhat lacking in
nuance, and it stirred up a hornet's nest of debate. Doubts were expressed on the
pronouncements of an exile (even such an honoured exile as Sachs), who might be
seen as out of touch with South African reality, and the risks of depoliticisation
were repeatedly invoked. The spectre of a return to the autonomy of the text, in
liberal-formalist terms, was raised. The implicit suggestion that the Movement
saw the freedom of artists as within its gift, envisaging a donor relation to culture,
also rankled. Others simply saw Sachs' comments as premature. Indeed, one of
the debates concerning Sachs' paper had to be cut suddenly short. The Umlazi
participants in the Natal COSAW debate left early "because barricades were already
being set up in anticipation of a major attack".[5] The struggle wasn't exactly over.

In contrast to Sachs (who was, after all, simply producing a short position paper)
Njabulo Ndebele's was a more measured and deeply thought response, expressed
in a series of essays collected in *Rediscovery of the Ordinary*. Ndebele highlighted
the dangers of a quasi-journalistic literature of indictment characterised by the
psychology of the slogan and by intellectual powerlessness. Such literature may
inform but it cannot transform. Indeed Ndebele cautioned against an over-reliance
on information, which could itself mirror the tactics of the opposition with its
concern with information manipulation. Strongly influenced by listening to
African oral storytellers (on trains and buses, on their way to work) he noted that
their tales were not at all political: "When they talked politics, they talked politics.
When they told stories, they told stories."[6] For him such storytellers were the
makers of culture. Even when their stories were not centred on resistance, they
had a social purpose. Similarly for Ndebele richness of character was not simply the
product of bourgeois escapism into an ethos of individualism. Interiority could be
a way in which the individual steps out of the network of exchange relations and
values, away from the performance principle and the profit motive and towards
passion, imagination, conscience. It is against this background of ongoing debate
that Gordimer negotiates her own strategy for post-apartheid writing, a strategy
which both recognises the necessary connection between art and its social or
political objectives, and also offers a critique of art as merely a weapon of struggle.

Nadine Gordimer's collection *Jump* spans the period in which apartheid was
dismantled, beginning with stories centred on defensive structures, whether external
(the destabilisation of neighbouring states), or internal (portrayals of the laager).

Along the way individual stories cast side glances at the 1986 repeal of the Mixed Marriages Act ("The Moment"), detainees ("Spoils", "Home"), the underground ("Safe Houses"), township violence ("Keeping Fit"), the growth of "revolutionary tourism" ("What Were You Dreaming?") until the collection closes with a final tale, "Amnesty", centred on the release of political prisoners, presumably in 1990, when the ANC, PAC and SACP were unbanned and a general release of prisoners took place. Several stories are based on or allude to news items or real events: the secretion of a terrorist bomb in a pregnant sweetheart's hand luggage, for example, or the conditions on the Mozambique/South African border which Gordimer reported on for a television documentary.[7] In its reception, the collection tended to be approached by reviewers in terms of its historicity and representation of the real world, with Gordimer cast firmly in the role of the artist as a political figure dealing with the representational. Although Gordimer was actually on a lecture tour promoting *Jump* when she received news of the award of the Nobel Prize for Literature, the prize didn't do much for the reviews of the volume. The collection was received as something of a disappointment, more the product perhaps of a "cultural worker" than of a Nobel-winning artist. Reviewers tended to detect an overemphatic tone, an excess of political gesture or humourless parable, and in particular a tendency to unbalance a tale by final sentences which spelled out a moral or added an O. Henry "twist".[8] Firdaus Kanga complained that "Gordimer writes a hectoring sentence, underlines a phrase that unbalances a whole story with its weight".[9] In "The Moment Before the Gun Went Off", for example, the last sentence reveals that the young black accidentally shot by the Afrikaner was not his "boy" but his illicitly conceived son. James Wood felt that this revelation produced the effect of a sudden bump in the last sentence which grounded and spoiled the story, drawing it into brute statement.[10] "Some Are Born to Sweet Delight" concludes as a terrorist bomb blows a plane, the heroine and her unborn child to smithereens. "Once Upon a Time" ends as a white child is ripped to shreds on the razor wire designed to safeguard his fairytale home. Conversely, however, critics noted a reflexive subtext in these apparently too obvious stories — a narrator-as-character, candidly admitting to the invented nature of the tale ("Once Upon a Time", "A Journey") or emphasising the deceptive nature of the facts presented ("My Father Leaves Home"). The presence of the narrator continually reminds the reader that this is story, as she intervenes to annul the action and send it back into the realm of fiction. In several stories ("A Journey", "The Ultimate Safari") Gordimer herself appears as a grey-haired lady, watching on the sidelines.[11] For some readers the multivocal form demonstrated a laudable attempt to end cultural monopoly by a full representation of the Other in a variety of perspectives and narrators, so that the voice of the white bourgeoisie no longer fills up the artistic space of fiction.[12] For others, however, the volume simply failed to cohere.

Gordimer's critics, however, had missed a vital dimension of the collection — and one which makes it one of the most interesting of Gordimer's formal experiments — the explicit connection between story and bodily action indicated in its title. Reviewers were less in touch with the genre of the short story than the author herself. In *Jump*, Gordimer plays with one particular genre of the folktale

— the "jump story". One example will suffice to indicate the major features of the genre. This one is from Tennessee:

> A woman went out on the porch of her lonely farmhouse and cried, "Come on my handsome lover." A deep voice answered from the forest, "I'm coming."
> The woman returned to the house. In a few minutes she went out again and called, "Come on, my handsome lover." The deep voice answered from the pasture, "I'm coming." Again she went inside. And again she returned to the porch to call, "Come on, my handsome lover." The deep voice answered from the garden gate, "I'm coming." Finally the woman made her last call and received her answer. "Come on my handsome lover." "I'm HERE", said the voice — and a big black bear *ate her up.*[13]

The story is designed to make the audience jump, quite literally. It is worth noting that this is a slightly unusual example, since it has an erotic element. More normally jump stories are scary in their subject matter; they are grotesque or involve the supernatural: a dismembered hairy toe seeking revenge upon the child who severed it from a giant, a ghost slowly climbing the stairs: "I'm at the bottom of the stairs." "I'm at the landing." "I'm outside the door." "I'm at the foot of the bed." This example usefully highlights the elasticity of the folk form, which depends more on performance, structure and audience, than upon static content. The Florida Public Library Youth Program, for example, promoting oral tale-telling as a route to increased literacy, included several jump stories of a traditional nature in its program, but also suggested the incorporation of various types of community involvement: "Have parachutists explain their equipment and talk about their experiences."[14] (In America, airborne firefighters are smoke-jumpers.) The form is not, of course, limited to one social or national group: it figures in the folk traditions of the Arab world, for example, as well as the African-American.[15] Folklore scholars will recognise it as a Formula tale: Motif Z13.1 ("Tale-teller frightens listener: yells "Boo!" at exciting point").

Typically, however, the tale ends abruptly in physical contact with and consequences for the audience, usually as the storyteller tickles, grabs or pounces upon a listener. "Jump stories" tend to be macabre, orally performed by a storyteller, often in a group situation (hence Gordimer foregrounds the storyteller as deceptive performer, and offers the sense of a multivocal group or collective narration). Today they are probably most easily recognised in animal stories told to children (who are a dominant presence in Gordimer's tales). In group narration the teller often pounces upon the child who looks most scared. "Little Foo-Foo", in which a fairy turns a rabbit into a field mouse, is a common playgroup example, told to the under-fives.[16]

Why tell jump stories? Firstly, there is an obvious aggressive element here. That "pounce" is reminiscent of the learning experience of the puppy or kitten, a play device which teaches lessons about the hunt. The story usually involves something or someone slowly creeping up on you, stalking before pouncing, and in selecting the most scared person present, picking off the weakest member of the group. We experience being the prey — the pounced upon — but the story also offers a script for predation, and in some stories (that bear, for example) it is the formerly hunted which pounces in its turn. The return of a dead animal or person, reclaiming bodily parts, also suggests links to the hunt, and to the guilty conscience of the hunter, with connections to taboo animals and totems. The story thus emphasises the interchangeability of predator and prey, with the tables turned as victimiser becomes victim. It may be "only a game", but it nonetheless offers a rehearsal of violence and victimisation, in a secure context.

That context also calls out for comment. Despite the scariness, it is arguable that there is an element of reassurance in the telling of the tale (as opposed to the content) in that it ends in bodily contact with a safe adult. Imagination leads into physical action in the baldest possible sense — but it is circumscribed within the frame of a secure situation. The story gives us a playful enactment of fear and pain, fright and tickle, say, but it is only play, and the pounce is often also the embrace of the family tale-teller. Above all, then, the jump story is irremediably physical. It involves the body, both in performance and often in content. "Cadaver Claims its Cannibalized Organs" is a representative Arab example.[17] A Virginian recounts a tale in which a child is asked to retrieve bones from a graveyard, with the bones returning to frightening effect.[18] Indeed it may not be stretching it too far to see Gordimer's 1974 novel, *The Conservationist*, as an extended jump story, involving the return of a dead body to plague the protagonist, who is actually "jumped" (ambushed) at the close in a hallucinatory moment of horror.[19] Certainly the submerged or repressed body which comes back to haunt the white imagination is generally recognised as a common motif in Gordimer's work.[20] One of her earliest published stories, "Is There Nowhere Else Where We Can Meet?" (1953), in which a black man pounces upon a white girl, is based on "Little Red Riding Hood", itself a jump story, though in this case the black man is arguably more the victim than he is the wolf.[21] The genre, then, offers a demonstration of an artistic creation extending suddenly into the "real" world, with real physical effects produced on the body of the listener. It is therefore a perfect example of a story written with an eye to functioning as a weapon of struggle. It is a form which we might almost expect to have been adopted by the South African writer. It draws on oral tradition so is "of the people" in a way which more rarefied modernist or postmodernist writing is not. (Gordimer cheerfully published one of these stories, "A Journey", in *Playboy*.) The macabre content allows a satiric purpose — the jump story exposes horrors — and the structure (evident in the overall arrangement of Gordimer's collection as well as within individual stories) dramatises the post-apartheid reversal of roles from victimiser to victim as the setting of the tales comes steadily closer to home.

It is worth pausing for a moment to establish that the case for seeing the collection as based upon the genre of the jump story depends on more evidence than its title alone. In the tales, the O. Henry twists are often extended into an almost physical pounce, as if the reader were seized and physically inscribed in the action narrated. In this respect it is striking how many of the reviewers speak in terms of a sudden bump or start; of "the moment when the political and the personal connect to deliver a blow to the heart",[22] or of the endings which "strike at the gut."[23] In broad terms the collection emphasises predation with its repeated images of the hunt ("Spoils", "Teraloyna") or the sexual chase ("A Find"), of children caught, seized or abducted ("Jump", "Once Upon a Time") or vulnerable to wild beasts. In "The Ultimate Safari" children fleeing a Renamo raid cross the Kruger Park in almost equal terror of white police, bandits and prowling beasts, huddling together by night in a squirming mass lest a lion *"jump* right into the middle of us."[24] Physical activity is thematically important — trekking to safety, parachute jumps, jogging, journeys — as is the suggestion that children's games have suddenly turned to brutal reality — jogging to desperate flight, parachute jumping for fun leading to military activity, a "safari" to a struggle for survival, a child's toy becomes a cache of plastic explosive. By demonstrating how a story can turn into an event, Gordimer implicitly thematises the connection between fiction and action. Hunters and hunted also cross over at several points. In "My Father Leaves Home", the father as a child of thirteen flees pogroms in Europe only to become a member of an oppressive racist regime in South Africa. The narrator, on a pheasant shoot in her father's original country, recognises that in his treatment of blacks her Jewish father had turned from prey to predator. Watching the shoot the narrator stands aloof: "only a spectator, only a spectator please" (66) she begs, but the shoot merges with the image of past pogroms, Cossacks on horseback riding down human beings, and her father shouting at his black labourer. As she comments, "I did not know that I would find, here in the wood, the beaters advancing, advancing across the world" (66).

So are these stories essentially propaganda or parable, tales designed to pounce upon the reader to make one point with maximum force? As we might expect, things are a little more complicated than that. The dangers of too easy a continuum between fiction and action are dramatised in "Once Upon a Time." The narrator has been asked to contribute to an anthology of stories for children, and refuses, despite the argument made to her that "every writer ought to write at least one story for children" (23). Like Ndebele and Sachs, the unnamed writer declares "I don't accept that I 'ought' to write anything" (23). Awakened in the night by what sound like footsteps stealthily approaching, "moving from room to room, coming up the passage — to my door" (23) the narrator finally recognises that the sounds are merely the creaking of a house built on undermined ground. Nobody is about to pounce on her. Yet unable to sleep she begins "to tell myself a story; a bedtime story" (25). Satiric in intention, the tale opens with a family "living happily ever after" (25) in an affluent South African suburb, their home surrounded by security devices and razor wire. When the mother reads the young son the tale of Sleeping Beauty, however, the little boy acts it out. He pretends to be the Prince, who braves the thicket of roses, and impales himself upon the shining "razor thorns" of the security fence. The story has impelled the child to action — but with fatal results. The child has been "jumped" not by an outside bogeyman but by the very measures which were designed to protect him. The story which the narrator tells demonstrates the risks of storytelling — as well as its power. In little, the tale dramatises the central issue of the collection — the extent to which the writer should write certain types of story, the risks of too straightforward a connection between story and action, and conversely the costs of storytelling which is cut off from its social context. It is, of course, the European fairy story of white South Africa which has actually killed the child.

If "Once Upon a Time" engages (perhaps too obviously) with the oral tale and the norms of the jump story, the title story adopts a more complex approach. In "Jump" a "turned" Renamo prisoner, is forced to relate his story again and again to his interrogators.[25] The tale which he tells is a jump story, in several senses. His parents had complained when their son took up parachute jumping, "enjoying yourself frightening us to death" (12), but the real military activities are infinitely more scary and involve the abduction of young children, brought in as rewards for the military. Jumped on and imprisoned by newly independent blacks for taking an illicit photograph, promptly politicised, the man had used his contacts in a parachute club to become a counterrevolutionary mercenary, changing sides only when he saw the fate of black children, abducted and raped. The soldier told his story (going over to the enemy to do so) in order to end this other jump story. One pounce upon him has impelled counterrevolutionary action; the sight of others who have been seized impels him to its opposite. The protagonist is discovered at the start of the tale as in a tracking shot through the hotel lobby, the halls, elevator, corridor, apartment door, the room:

> he is aware of being finally reached within all this as in a film a series of dissolves passes the camera through walls to find a single figure, the hero, the criminal. Himself. (3)

The camera jumps him; he is prey to the press. The tale speaks directly to Ndebele's concern with the lack of ambiguity in South African characters. As a "turned" figure, the protagonist is both hero and villain. In addition he has been previously identified with the documentary (his initial arrest was for taking a photograph) and with the manipulation of information. It is only when he sees an abducted child, however, that he is transformed; he reaches the point where "someone begins really to know. Instead of having intelligence by fax and satellite" (17). Importantly the young man has had to tell his story repeatedly into a tape recorder, and the tale reaches us, as readers, with frequent reminders of this oral performance, from interruptions from his interviewers to asides which comment on the narration: "He would explain to his audience", "at this point in the telling" (8). His story has an obvious use-value, as propaganda for the revolutionary side, and he is, as a result, paraded before the television crews of BBC, CBS, Antenne 2, Zweites Deutsches Fernsehen:

> he told his story. For the first few months he told his story again and again in performance. Everyone has heard it now. (6)

Now that he has contributed his particular story as a weapon of the struggle he has no further role to play: "Once he's told everything, once he's been displayed, what use is he to them?" (18). In contrast Gordimer's story moves into the contradictions and ambiguities of the young man's role, focusing on interiority. The story extends further, focusing upon the whole person, the person who continues after the propaganda story has been told. At the close, the young man looks forward to one final jump, suicide from his upper storey window:

> Jump. The stunning blow of the earth as it came up to flexed knees, the parachute sinking silken.
> He stands, and then backs into the room.
> Not now; not yet. (20)

No final jump is offered to the reader, to wrap up the events in an easy conclusion. Gordimer's story avoids the spectacular or sensational; the story will go on, into the realm of the ordinary.

The role of the body in these stories also raises larger questions concerning social control and the ideal of the "civil" society. In "What Were You Dreaming?" a black hitchhiker picked up by a revolutionary tourist, doing the rounds of the South African political theme park, caters very carefully for his audience in his tale of woe (eviction, illness, seven fatherless children). This is the story they want to hear — not the real details of drink, assault and grievous bodily harm. The white liberal, sensitive to questions of delicacy, colludes with him, to obscure the truth from the tourist. When he notices the African's missing front teeth she coyly allows him to see it as merely a fabled sign of sexual attractiveness. In fact, the teeth have been deliberately removed as an advertisement for the African's prowess at male-on-male oral sex. In the interests of telling the right story the woman is unable to pronounce the term "cocksucking." The tourist is allowed to dismiss it as "just another sexual myth" (223). Myth is what conditions his approach to South Africa, which sidesteps ambiguities and unpleasant realities in a fable of the noble oppressed. The body tells a different story.

Several of the stories are even less coy. "Spoils", another staging of the scene of predation, opens with the narrator commenting on the smell of his meat-eater's wind. On a visit to a private game reserve, he is sickened by his own appetite for meat, and by extension, repelled by his participation in a predatory society. "I want no part of it" (161) he declares, no part of the meat, the hunt, nor the global violence brought to him in the morning news bulletin. In direct contrast a fellow guest figures as his polar opposite — a young man who has been in political detention. The latter shows no squeamishness at the terrorist bombs in streets, cars and supermarkets:

> these don't confuse *him*, make carrion of brotherhood. He's brave enough to swallow it. No gagging. (168)

When the group are invited to see lions at a recent zebra kill, however, "Everybody is game" (170), game for the excursion, but also in imagistic terms, part of the cycle of predation. In the truck they become an undifferentiated mass "pressed together, swaying, congealed, breathing in contact" (171). Nobody can opt out of this bodily contact — it would be far too dangerous to leave the vehicle so close to the lions. Later the guests settle down to fresh paw-paw and bacon, boerewors and eggs. Back at the kill the dung beetles are already carrying off the zebra's stomach contents. There seems to be no way out of the prey–predator continuum and its violence. In its metaphors the story draws explicitly on Norbert Elias' account of the development of civil society, as exemplified in the slow development of manners.[26] Meat-eating is a particular focus. Elias argues that whereas in medieval society whole carcasses were carved at table, with knives freely flourished, the threshold of repugnance steadily advances until reminders that the meat dish is connected with the killing of an animal are avoided. The meat is carved elsewhere; strong taboos on the use of knives are developed. More generally the distastefully physical is removed behind the scenes of social life, whether it concerns reminders of the dead animal or of the human animal, in physical processes such as sexual and eliminatory functions, bodily secretions, nakedness or aggressive drives. At the close of the story the guide Siza is spotted with a knife. To the white observer it is "the knife that is everywhere" (178) — on the news, on dark street corners, in the gaols. But Siza carves out only a small, skilfully butchered portion of zebra, just enough for his family, leaving the major part of the slaughtered beast behind:

> The lions, they know I must take a piece for me ... It's all right. But if I take too much, they know it also. Then they take one of my children. (179)

Ironically it is Siza who fulfils the earlier medieval injunction that a well-bred man should be capable of skilful carving, should give away the best portion of the meat and should keep only a small portion for himself. As opposed to the lack of true civility of his guests, Siza operates in a different cultural economy, in which it is not merely a case of "to the victor the spoils", but in which some degree of sharing, of reciprocity, is implied, an ability to take part, to play one's part, without either withdrawing completely (and ineffectually) or swallowing everything whole as one of an unthinking mass. Somewhere between predator (lion) and prey (zebra) Siza negotiates a safe part for himself, a part which relies on the folk lesson of the jump story. The jump story, we will recall, involves both fear and playful pleasure. The return of the animal (bear, lion, social embarrassment) may represent a threat, or a pleasure, in the freedom from bodily repression and from the hegemonial net.

This ambivalence of the body features prominently in "The Moment before the Gun Went Off", another treatment of the disjunction between the public story and the internal story. As reported in the press the story of the Afrikaner farmer, regional Party leader and Commandant of the local security commando, who accidentally shoots one of his black workers, will go all over the world. It is in fact an ordinary story of an accident, "there are accidents with guns every day of the week" (111) but in the South African context it becomes spectacular, sensational, and enormously useful to the opponents of the regime:

> the story ... will fit exactly their version of South Africa, it's made for them. They'll be able to use it in their boycott and divestment campaigns, it'll be another piece of evidence in their truth about the country. (111).

As Marais realises, he and the black man will become "those crudely-drawn figures on anti-apartheid banners, units in statistics of white brutality" (111). The moment before the gun went off was actually a moment of childish excitement, sharing features with the jump story. Marais had picked up his twenty-year-old unacknowledged son Lucas to go hunting, with Lucas riding on the back of the truck, the better to spot the kudu. The farmer had a rifle beside him, and when the truck went over a pothole the sudden jolt fired the rifle, killing Lucas, who was leaning over the cab roof. At first the farmer thought Lucas' fall was a joke, assuming that Lucas had toppled off the cab "in fright." The farmer "was almost laughing with relief, ready to tease" (117) as he opened the door of the cab, but "the young man did not laugh with him at his own fright" (117). This time the joke of "Bam! Gotcha!" has ended in death. To the unwary reader the sudden revelation of Lucas' paternity is one more example of white South African hypocrisy, another plank in a propaganda platform. But what Gordimer's story also shows us is Marais' reaction after the gun went off, a reaction observed but hushed up by the local police captain. "He sobbed, snot running onto his hands, like a dirty kid. The Captain was ashamed, for him, and walked out" (113). Marais' bodily processes have escaped from his control, as they did when he was a "dirty kid" (113) fathering Lucas. The revelation of bodily closeness and connection here opens up a fragile Utopian possibility implicit in the jump story's physicality, the possibility of communication and connection between black and white in the body, in an era beyond the prohibitions of the apartheid state. The police Captain and his laws define Marais as a "dirty kid" for the physical expression of emotion, sexual in the past, remorseful in the present. Bodily shame is located in the police state, not in the father–son relationship. Gordimer has repeatedly envisaged the body (sensuality) as a potential means to political liberation, looking ahead (to borrow a phrase from J. M. Coetzee) to a future when "bodies are their own signs", as opposed to being caught in the signifying systems of a state which considered the individual to be completely classifiable by bodily features.[27] In a jump story bodies are merged — if only momentarily — in a relationship of danger and reassurance, fear and pleasure. There is an escape from social control. Although inevitably fragile and unrealised, physical contact provides a potentially Utopian element in the jump story. In a nation divided according to the body, physicality is fundamental to resistance against oppression.

If the collection demonstrates the importance of action in the pursuit of justice, it also constitutes a searching inquiry into the ethics — and the aesthetics — of such action. In *Spring Is Rebellious*, Ari Sitas argued that:

> In Natal ... grassroots creators have known how fragile their bodies were and how they got broken in gaol; how they got pierced real easy by spears; ... they knew all along that their only "aesthetic weapons" have been their bodies and what their brains remembered or remade into stories.[28]

Gordimer takes the commentator at his word. In its bodily emphasis, in its foregrounding of the oral tale, in its reminders to us of the primacy of story and of the risks of story — Gordimer amply fulfils the role of the storyteller as maker of culture and — to return to our opening question — demonstrates that there is plenty of life in white writing, even after apartheid.

Notes to Chapter 14

1. See Graham Pechey, "Post-Apartheid narratives," in Francis Barker, Peter Hulme and Margaret Iverson (ed.), *Colonial Discourse/Postcolonial Theory* (Manchester: Manchester University Press, 1994); Susan Van Zanten Gallagher, "The Backward Glance: History and the Novel in Post-Apartheid South Africa," *Studies in the Novel*, 29, 3 (1997), 376–393.

2. Albie Sachs, "Preparing Ourselves for Freedom," paper prepared for an ANC in-house seminar on culture, in Ingrid de Kok and Karen Press (eds), *Spring Is Rebellious: Arguments about Cultural Freedom* (Cape Town: Buchu Books, 1990).

3. Sachs, 21.

4. Sachs, 21.

5. *Spring Is Rebellious*, 17.

6. Njabulo Ndebele, *South African Literature and Culture: Rediscovery of the Ordinary* (Manchester: Manchester University Press, 1991), 37.

7. Nadine Gordimer, "The Ingot and the Stick, the Ingot and the Gun: Mozambique–South Africa," in George Carey (ed.), *Frontiers* (London: BBC Books, 1990), 50–77.

8. Andrew V. Ettin, *Betrayals of the Body Politic: The Literary Commitments of Nadine Gordimer* (Charlottesville and London: University of Virginia Press, 1993).

9. Firdaus Kanga, "Jump and Other Stories," *Times Literary Supplement*, 11 October 1991, 14.

10. James Wood, "Lyrical Analyst of a Nation," *The Guardian*, 10 October 1991, 27.

11. Karen Lazar, "Nadine Gordimer," in Eva Hunter and Craig Mackenzie (eds), *Between the Lines II* (Grahamstown: National English Literary Museum, 1993), 21–37.

12. See, for example, Jeanne Colleran, "Archive of Apartheid: Nadine Gordimer's Short Fiction at the End of the Interregnum," in Bruce King (ed.), *The Later Fiction of Nadine Gordimer* (London: Macmillan, 1993), 237–43; Karen Lazar, "'Jump' and Other Stories: Gordimer's Leap into the 1990s: Gender and Politics in her Latest Short Fiction," *Journal of Southern African Studies*, 18, 4 (1992), 783–802.

13. Olivia Murray Nichols, "'The Handsome Lover': A Romantic Example of the Jump Story," *Tennessee Folklore Society Bulletin*, 57, 3 (1981), 124. On Jump stories I am grateful to my informants Gloria Cronin (Brigham Young University), Hasan El-Shamy (Indiana University), Trudier Harris (University of North Carolina), Andrew Hook (University of Glasgow), J. D. A. Widdowson (National Centre for English Cultural Tradition, University of Sheffield) and William A. Wilson. See also E. Martin Pederson, "Folklore in ESL/EFL Curriculum Materials," paper presented at the Annual Meeting of the Teachers of English to Speakers of Other Languages, Atlanta, Georgia, 13–17 April 1993.

14. Carolann Palm Abramoff, *Once Upon a Tale* (Tallahassee: Florida Library Services, 1995). See also Robert S. McCarl, "Jump Story: An Examination of an Occupational Experience Narrative," *Folklore Forum*, 11 (1978), 1–17.

15. See Hasan El-Shamy, *Folk Traditions of the Arab World: A Guide to Motif Classification* (Bloomington: Indiana University Press, 1995). For a discussion of the African American tale, "The Golden Arm," told by Joel Chandler Harris to Mark Twain, who subsequently performed it repeatedly on stage, see Andrew Hook, "Reporting Reality: Mark Twain's Short Stories," in A. Robert Lee (ed.), *The Nineteenth Century American Short Story* (London: Vision, 1985), 103–19.

16. Thanks to Mrs Lilian Harris and Class 3, Archibald First School, Gosforth, Newcastle Upon Tyne, 1998.

17. Hasan El-Shamy, personal communication.

18. Trudier Harris, personal communication.

19. Nadine Gordimer, *The Conservationist* (London: Cape, 1974).

20. Judie Newman, *Nadine Gordimer* (New York and London: Routledge, 1988).

21. Nadine Gordimer, "Is There Nowhere Else Where We Can Meet?" in *The Soft Voice of the Serpent* (London: Gollancz 1953).

22. Firdaus Kanga.

23. Rita Ciresi, "Review of Nadine Gordimer's *Jump*," *Library Journal*, 116 (August 1991), 149.

24. Nadine Gordimer, *Jump and Other Stories* (London: Bloomsbury 1991), 39. Subsequent page references are to this edition.

25. The story does not specify his political allegiance, but the source for the tale (*Frontiers*) so describes him.
26. Norbert Elias, *The Civilizing Process*, trans. Edmund Jephcott (Oxford: Blackwell, 1994). (First published as *Über den Prozess der Zivilisation* (Basel: Haus zum Falken, 1939).)
27. J. M. Coetzee, *Foe* (London: Penguin, 1987), 157.
28. *Spring Is Rebellious*, 94.

CHAPTER 15

"Dis Ain't Gimme, Florida":
Zora Neale Hurston's
Their Eyes Were Watching God

Who owns Zora Neale Hurston? That was the question asked in 1990 by Michele Wallace, in an analysis of the ways in which Hurston has been appropriated by later scholars. Wallace's pungent comparison of later critics to so many "groupies descending on Elvis Presley's estate" in their haste to turn Hurston to their own purposes strikes a cautionary note for any subsequent writer.[1] As she notes, the risk of canonisation is that the work will be misused to derail the future of black women in literature and literary criticism. For Wallace, Harold Bloom's introduction to his *Modern Critical Views* anthology of 1986 is a case in point. Bloom prefaces a collection of African Americanist and feminist essays with an introduction which essentially erases them, in which, ignoring race almost entirely, he concentrates on the novel as a story of sexual repression, compares Hurston's protagonist successively to Richardson's Clarissa, Dreiser's Carrie, Lawrence's Ursula, and finally moves from character to author to propose Hurston as The Wife of Bath. Writing anything further about Hurston must strike one as a dubious proposition, for if any one novel has been commodified and fully incorporated into the new canon of American literature, it is *Their Eyes Were Watching God*. As Hazel Carby argues, the boom in Hurston studies which has produced a snowstorm of books, papers and dissertations, ever since Alice Walker rediscovered her in the 1970s, is the result of a variety of factors: MLA support, the book trade, special courses on women's and on black writing, Afrocentric strategies of analysis, nostalgia for happy rural blacks (as opposed to innercity violence), political activism of different types, and the quest for literary ancestors.[2] Gloria Cronin observes, however, that amidst all this variety of motive, the criticism has none the less been largely dominated by one type of essay — reading the novel as a feminist triumph tale, unshaded by any less than affirmative vision of the heroine. "Readings of the book have been overdetermined by feminist, multi-cultural and Africanist political imperatives of the last twenty years."[3]

What has escaped attention in this debate is the degree to which Hurston herself focussed on these very questions of ownership and appropriation in *Their Eyes Were Watching God*, in the backbone structure and plot of her novel, in the characterisation of the heroine's three lovers, in the frame tale, and in such incidents as the "mule story", Teacake's gambling activities and the rabid dog. *Their Eyes Were Watching God* represents a creative appropriation by a black woman, of an anthropological discourse, first analysed by a white Jewish male, Franz Boas, and associated with a Native American people — the discourse of gift exchange. Hurston studied with Boas, one of her principal mentors, whose major work *The Social Organisation and Secret Societies of the Kwakiutl Indians* concerned Kwakiutl "potlatch", a form of gift exchange which became famous as the exemplification of the theory of conspicuous consumption advanced by Thorstein Veblen.[4] The Kwakiutl had a variety of gift-giving ceremonies involving the giving away of quantities of possessions or their wilful destruction. A man might destroy or disperse all his worldly goods in an attempt to maintain status, or to eclipse a rival. While in theory the gift was spontaneous, in practice it was based on political or economic self-interest: the gift of property implies an obligation on the recipient — which, if not fulfilled, results in loss of face. The "Indian giver" gives in order to establish credit, since the recipient must return the gift at a future time, with interest. The destroyer forces his rivals to destroy in their turn. As a cultural form therefore, potlatch prevents any one individual from monopolising material goods, prevents the build-up of economic surpluses and subtly maintains social order. Potlatch is none the less fundamentally aggressive (described by the Kwakiutl as "fighting with property"). Originally potlatch meant "to nourish" or "to consume", and it has been seen as a sublimation of cannibal rites.[5]

Gift exchange as aggression is of course a cultural phenomenon as old as the War of Troy. The idea of the fatal gift (e.g. the Rheingold, Scott Fitzgerald's "The Cut-Glass Bowl") survives even in etymology. As Marcel Mauss noted, the semantic history of the German word "Gift" contains the idea of the present or possession that turns to poison. "Gift" in German now means poison. Modern survivals of gift exchange include gambling, which is commonly considered not as contractual but as involving honour and the surrender of property, even when it is not absolutely necessary to do so; philanthropic giving (e.g. the rivalry and competition of a pledge dinner); and intellectual property, where the donor retains an interest in the object given. (Artistic ownership is often considered to survive beyond the sale of the actual work of art.) Academics preserve gift exchange in the form of the scholarly offprint.

As a collector of folk material, over which proprietary rights remained with her patron, Mrs Rufus Osgood Mason, Zora Neale Hurston was intensely aware of the ambiguous nature of such ownership. Indeed her relationship with her patrons — those who gave her gifts — was clearly an uneasy one, as more than one critic has noted. Robert Hemenway sums it up: "What Hurston possessed during the Renaissance decade was a career in patronage."[6] Essentially Hurston had major financial support from three white women (Annie Nathan Meyer, Fannie Hurst and Mrs Mason) beginning in 1925, and spanning the years while she graduated from Barnard and conducted fieldwork in African-American folk culture. She met Mrs Mason in 1927 and signed a contract for $200 a month, a motion picture camera and a car, in order to collect folklore in the South for two years. The folklore collected was to be Mrs Mason's property. Mrs Mason finally cut off funds in September 1932, having reduced the stipend by half in 1931. Hemenway notes that Hurston was unable to write creatively while under the influence of personal patronage and suggests that "Hurston sensed, later in the patronage period, that something about the gift-giving had inhibited her talent."[7] Mrs Mason gave Hurston the money to carry out her work, but in return she had to give back to a white donor (and culture) the materials of her own people. Instead of beginning studies in general ethnology in 1935 Hurston used the time instead to write her novel. In *Their Eyes Were Watching God* she gives without being passive, placing those who "take" (the readers) under obligation to repay, in what amounts to a meta-anthropology, turning the anthropologist's tools on himself.

How does this work? As Sherley Anne Williams has noted, by the end of the novel,

> Janie has come *down*, that paradoxical place in Afro-American literature that is both a physical bottom and the setting for the character's attainment of a penultimate self knowledge.[8]

In outline the story is that of a woman who swaps status and prestige of an empty material kind (running a store as the wife of the town mayor) for erotic happiness "on the muck", picking beans in a booming farming area of Florida, at her lover's side. From an initial loveless marriage, arranged by a grandmother (Nanny) whose sole motivation is to preserve Janie from being like other African-American women ("De nigger woman is de mule uh de world"[9]) Janie becomes a field labourer, a participant in a world which originally seemed beneath her, willingly working at her man's side and finally at one with her community. As Williams argues, the differences between the image of the mule and its final reversal are obvious. On the muck, Janie is working only in name; she converts hard toil into play. Teacake has asked, not ordered:

> his request stems from a desire to be with Janie, to share every aspect of his life with her, rather than from a desire to coerce her into some mindless submission. It isn't the white man's burden that Janie carries; it is the gift of her own love. (297)

One might wonder, however, how this romantic vision squares with the Teacake who steals Janie's money and spends it on a party; beats her; and attempts, in a rabid frenzy, to kill her. Williams's unconscious use of the term "gift" is telling. In Hurston's world the gift is always also a threat, a potential act of aggression, and the structure of her novel draws out all the tragic ambiguities involved in the safeguarding — and the voluntary loss — of prestige.

Janie's story (profoundly economic in emphasis as Houston Baker has argued) focuses on three representative husbands. The first, Logan Killicks, is selected by Nanny, purely in order to safeguard the budding Janie's honour and security. As Baker comments, Nanny's history under slavery dictates her strategic manoeuvres in the wars of property and propriety:

> Having been denied a say in her own fate because she was property, she assumes that only property enables expression.[10]

The African-American community bear silent witness to their own awareness that Janie has been given in marriage, rather than choosing her own fate. Nobody gives any wedding gifts to the couple (39) and they depart empty-handed from the feast. By not giving presents, the community demonstrate solidarity with Janie, and a fundamental distrust of her commodification as a bride. To Janie's protests that she wanted a husband to love and to be loved by, Nanny can argue only that she should be glad of the organ in his parlour, his house and his sixty acres. Nanny assumes that Janey is hankering after "some dressed-up dude dat got to look at de sole of his shoe everytime he cross de street tuh see if he got enough leather dere tuh make it across" (42). For Nanny, Janie's property is much more important than her feelings, as assuring her status and security:

> "You can buy and sell such as dem wid what you got. In fact you can buy 'em and give 'em away." (42)

In the mouth of an ex-slave, the comment on the commodification of a person as property to be bought or disposed of at will is particularly chilling. It takes Janie only a short while to realise that she owes nothing to Killicks as her final words to him reveal. "You ain't done me no favor by marryin' me. And if dat's what you call yo'self doin', Ah don't thank yuh for it" (53).

In contrast, Janie's second husband, Joe Starks, apparently establishes at the outset that she is a gift all in herself, and recognises the fact by showering her with presents: "he bought her the best things the butcher had, like apples and a glass lantern full of candies" (56). Yet, as his dealings with the townspeople reveal, Joe Starks gives only to establish credit and "take". Eatonville has been founded as a town by the gift of land from Captain Eaton, a gift which Starks derides as far too small in size to assure economic prosperity. By buying 200 acres from Eaton, Starks "gives" the people of Eatonville a town — though it is a town which they then buy from him with their own money. To celebrate the town's foundation he offers a "treat" of crackers and cheese, followed up by a barbecue. (They provide most of the food.) He uses their labour to cut drains and streets, and establishes Janie as a conspicuous object of display, dressed up to the nines in his store. Whenever Joe gives, it is for the purpose of assuring his own prestige and status, and ultimately seeing the gift come back tenfold. In the famous mule story, for example, Joe establishes his prestige by the destruction of property. He buys Matt Bonner's bony, cussed, yellow mule for five dollars, to Matt's astonished delight. Joe, however, humiliates Bonner by destroying the mule as an object of economic value. He sets it free.

> "Beat yuh tradin' dat time, Starks! Dat mule is liable tuh be dead befo' de week is out. You won't git no work outa him."
> "Didn't buy 'im fuh no work. I god, Ah bought dat varmint tuh let 'im rest. You didn't have gumption enough tuh do it." (91)

While Starks gains the respect of the townspeople Janie, sensing the potential parallel between woman and mule, is more pointed in her comments:

> Freein' dat mule makes uh mighty big man outa you. Something like George Washington and Lincoln. Abraham Lincoln, he had de whole United Sates to rule so he freed de Negroes. You got a town so you freed a mule. (92)

In a capitalist economy, freedom becomes an ambiguous gift. Just as the original gift of land for the town was too small to assure its prosperity, so the gift of freedom without economic equality becomes ambivalent. Like the vultures later seen feeding on the mule's carcass, like Starks feeding off the townspeople, the gift lays obligations on the recipient, and nourishes the giver. Janey is displayed by Starks as a "lady" — just as he displays the retired mule. Above all, Jody's gifts — like the salt pork he apparently donates to Mrs Tony — are carefully calibrated. After Mrs Tony has begged for a piece of meat for her starving children, after she has poured scorn on the tiny piece which he cuts for her, and flounced out of the store, Starks comes back to his seat on the porch, after a moment's pause. "He had to stop and add the meat to Tony's account" (116). Mrs Tony has shamed her husband by accepting the gift; Starks has maintained his own prestige at no cost whatsoever. As Houston Baker argues, Starks is intent on imitating the economics of Anglo-America.[11] He clearly represents an aggressive, white-identified capitalism, consuming Janie. As textual evidence makes explicit, Hurston evidently understood the dynamics of the relationship in terms of gift exchange. When Starks slaps Janie (over a ruined dinner) the text in manuscript reads "she began to fold in on herself and to take without giving."[12] Janie has become emotionally dead. When she retaliates, destroying Joe with an emasculatory insult, she realises that the fatal blow has been to separate the man from his possessions.

> When he paraded his possessions hereafter, they would not consider the two together. They'd look with envy at the things and pity the man that owned them. (123)

When Joe sickens (kidney disease) the rumour immediately runs that Janie is responsible. Poison is suspected. The accusation is symbolically appropriate. As the only person to see through his gifts, Janie has understood how gifts can turn to poison, property to a source of pity and danger. Meanwhile the townspeople bring gifts of broth and sick-room dishes to replace Janie's suspect cooking. They nourish Starks without recognising the extent to which he has made them consumers and consumed them. When Joe dies, the system lives on. He is replaced by Hezekiah, seen refusing credit with the ringing phrase, "dis ain't Gimme, Florida, dis is Eatonville" (142). But in a sense the town is "Gimme, Florida", founded on and entrapped within the economics of the gift.

In contrast Teacake appears to be a subtler manipulator of gift exchange. From the beginning of their relationship Teacake is established as a games player prepared to take Janie's king (147) at checkers, a taker on equal terms with her. For the townspeople his gifts to her are motivated by the inheritance which she possesses from Joe. "Dey figger he's spendin' on her now in order tuh make her spend on him later" (168). The community, for whom an older woman can only lose prestige when in erotic association with a younger man, foresees a fate for Janie similar to that of Annie Tyler, who lost her pride and all she possessed to her younger lover, Who Flung (179). Although Janie may argue that "Dis ain't no business proposition, and no race after property and titles. Dis is uh love game" (171) the reader may feel similarly uneasy when the pair marry and Teacake promptly disappears with the

$200 which Janie had secretly pinned inside her shirt. Janie has imbibed enough of Joe Starks's views to conceal the existence of the cash from Teacake, as well as the twelve hundred dollars which she has in the bank. In order to demonstrate his lack of interest in material things, Teacake takes Janie's money and gambles it away, in the context of a stupendous feast, a ritual destruction of property. At the feast he gives ugly women money to stay away, a form of gift giving which destroys female status. Janie is also excluded. Ostensibly Teacake is motivated by his perception of the crowd at the party as of lower class than Janie. "Dem wuzn't no high muckty mucks" (186). In reality he uses her money to teach her her place in his community, destroying her assumed class prestige in the process. Appropriately, Teacake gets the money back — with interest — in the course of a gambling game. He is careful to let the losers have a chance to win back their losses — etiquette even today in gambling. The men grumble, but with one exception, agree that the game was fair. But the aggression just below the surface culminates none the less in a furious fight, in which Teacake gets knifed. Teacake's involvement with money is as dangerous to him as it was to Joe Starks.

On the surface it may appear that Teacake is able to provide Janie with a better place in a more authentic, less money-driven world than Joe Starks, offering her an open, giving form of love and treating her as an equal. Indeed the workers on the muck are distinguished by the celebratory nature of their existence, replete with parties, dances, games and music, without apparent reference to the world of commerce.

> They made good money ... So they spent good money. Next month and next year were other times. (197)

When one woman does attempt to establish her own separate prestige (based on intra-community colorism), arguing that she and Janie, both "light-skinned" should "class off" from the darker members of the race (210) Janie is unpersuaded by Mrs Turner's arguments.

> "Us can't do it. We're uh mingled people and all of us got black kinfolks as well as yaller kinfolks." (210)

Mrs Turner pays no attention to her protests. She is quite content to live off the workers' money (profits from her restaurant business) while deriding them in private. (She consumes as she apparently nourishes.) Teacake promptly takes a hand, arranging to "rescue" Mrs Turner from a disturbance in her restaurant. While loudly proclaiming that Mrs Turner deserves respect, Teacake succeeds in orchestrating a riot which entirely destroys all her property. To add insult to injury, the prime movers appear the next day and make Mrs Turner a ceremonial present of five dollars apiece.

Yet for all his apparent openhandedness, his lack of interest in prestige on white terms, and his ability to function on a footing of equality with Janie, Teacake is still mired in the world of money. The process of destruction of property culminates when the idyll on "de muck" terminates in a hurricane which lays waste the whole area. The hurricane functions as a great leveller, reducing animals and men to one common society. In their flight Teacake and Janie pass a dead man entirely surrounded by snakes and other animals.

> Common danger made common friends. Nothing sought a conquest over the other. (243)

Significantly Teacake's tragic mistake had been to ignore Indian folk knowledge. He discounts the warnings of the local Seminoles that there is a hurricane on the way, in the first place because they are not property-owners ("Indians don't know much uh nothin' ... Else they'd own this country still." 231) and secondly because of the lure of money.

> Beans running fine and prices good, so the Indians could be, *must* be wrong. You couldn't have a hurricane when you're making seven and eight dollars a day picking beans. (229)

As the dyke bursts, he sees his error:

> he saw that the wind and water had **given** life to lots of things that folks think of as dead and **given** death to so much that had been living things. (236; my emphasis)

The gift comes also to Teacake, and is fatal. Teacake's death by rabies offers a horrendously appropriate image of the consumption of the human being, his identity eaten away by the saliva of the rabid animal until he can no longer consume, eat or drink. The image of contagion by saliva is significant. Nanny arranged Janie's marriage so that she would not become "a spit cup" (37) to others. Starks provided her with a luxury spit cup, painted with sprigs of flowers, but a spit cup none the less. Teacake becomes the cup himself, catching the disease from canine spit. Rabies appears to present the spectacle of a man turning into a dog, becoming possessed by the animal, until he snarls and bites — just as in totemic possession. It is as if the totemic animal is eating the man. In addition Teacake's paranoid jealousy when rabid transforms him into a mirror image of Jody, the arch capitalist, devotee of consumer exploitation, and finally himself consumed.[13] More specifically (and an answer perhaps to critics such as Peter Messent who have found the mad dog plot melodramatic and forced) rabies associates Teacake with the Kwakiutl cannibal dance in which the initiate bites a piece of flesh from an enemy's arm, identifying with the totemic animal. Teacake's last action, falling from Janie's bullet, is to sink his teeth in her arm. The position of the snarling dog, standing on a cow's back, above the floodwaters heaving with fish, snakes and people, recalls the animal hierarchy of the totem. Kwakiutl totems often depict animals biting a "copper". As the imagery suggests, gift exchange thus goes some way to account for the difficulties posed for modern critics by the character of Teacake. Teacake's last gift to Janie was a packet of garden seeds. She gives away all their other possessions, keeping only the seeds to plant back home, for a living remembrance. Teacake remains a giver, seeding the future with a promise of growth, rather than leaving a legacy of material objects. But Teacake is also a warning to the future, his fate admonitory. As the gift exchange structure demonstrates, Hurston did take account of an Indian warning, not least in the fashion in which she frames her tale.

At the close of the tale, prestige and hierarchy are reasserted. The black victims of the hurricane are tipped into a mass grave, carefully sorted from the whites for whom all the coffins are reserved. Janie's love affair with Teacake has been underwritten by the store and she can go home again. As Baker comments, Janie's freedom with Teacake was enabled by Starks's property. "Her position derives from the petit bourgeois enterprises she has shared with her deceased husband."[14] For Baker, therefore,

> *Their Eyes Were Watching God* is, ultimately, a novel that inscribes, in its very form, the mercantile economics that conditioned a "commercial deportation".[15]

The comment, however, applies at best only to Janie's story and not to Hurston's. In Janie, Hurston focuses upon the possibility that her own work (fiction, folklore, anthropology) could allow others to "buy safely in" to African-American culture, to appropriate and own its material without considering the fundamental institutional and economic structures which inscribe it as valuable material rather than as ongoing, living process. If the themes of the novel underline the dangers of the donor-as-taker, the frame of the story is equally strategic. The story is framed by a gift — Pheoby's nourishing (and appropriately creole) dish of "mulatto rice" — a sly, ambivalent gift which makes reference to Janie's white blood. It is in return for this gift that Janie tells her story. The process of story telling, the manner and occasion of the story's delivery, is as significant as the content. Hurston goes to some lengths to underline the nature of the story-telling as a form of gift exchange. When Pheoby offers the gift, Janie is swift to underline the impossibility of repaying in terms of material exchange. "You must think Ah brought yuh somethin'. When Ah ain't brought home a thing but mahself" (14). Pheoby's comment, "Dat's a gracious plenty," is met by teasing denigration of the gift of food,

> "Ain't you never goin' tuh gimme dat lil rations you brought me? ... Give it here and have a seat." (15)

This is followed, once the plate has been well and truly cleaned, by the instruction to "take yo' ole plate. Ah ain't got a bit of use for a empty dish" (15). In the distance the people of the community remain on the porch, clearly discussing Janie's return as if *she* were a meal to be feasted upon. "Ah reckon they got me up in they mouth now" (16). Janie refuses to satisfy their appetite for her story directly, on the grounds that they will not understand. They are "puttin' they mouf on things they don't know nothin' about" and "so long as they get a name to gnaw on they don't care whose it is, and what about, 'specially if they can make it sound like evil" (17). Instead, to avoid her gift becoming poison, she tells the story to Pheoby on the grounds that when the latter repeats it, it will remain Janie's story.

> You can tell 'em what Ah say if you wants to. Dat's just de same as me 'cause mah tongue is in mah friend's mouf. (17)

As she tells Pheoby, "you got tuh *go* there to *know* there" (285). A story is not simply transferable from one teller to another, context-free, like an object in a collection of folklore. It needs a reader with understanding, knowledge of its meanings. Janie warns Pheoby that "tain't no use in me telling you somethin' unless Ah *give* you de understandin' to go long wid it" (19; my emphasis). And what she gives is an awareness of the nature of the donor relation.

Hurston's story is designed both to nourish the folk and to liberate it from the property wars of capitalism. The exchange between Pheoby and Janie establishes the story as a gift — but a gift which lays obligations on both the black community and the reader. The frame tale transforms the gift into a moral transaction, maintaining human relationships rather than exchange relations, and preventing the treatment of authenticity as a marketable product. Folk elements in the novel — verbal contests, the buzzards dancing a call-and-response over the mule's carcass, folktales and games — are carefully positioned inside a frame which establishes the importance of context and highlights folk culture as a dynamic relation and process rather than a reified object. By employing African-American, Native American and white (Jewish) sources, Hurston provides the reader with very creole rice indeed. In its implicitly hybrid form *Their Eyes Were Watching God* defends a "mingled" culture as against essentialist "authenticity". In a postcolonial context Trinh T. Minh-ha has remarked on the dangers posed by authenticity as opposed to hybridity.[16] Just as anthropologists want to study "primitive" (non-state, non-class) societies, so the Third World representative whom the modern sophisticated public ideally seeks is the "unspoiled" African or Asian, thus remaining preoccupied with the image of the "real" native, the truly different, rather than with issues of economic hegemony, racism, feminism and social change. Similarly, in the African-American context there is a risk that "authenticity" becomes a product to be marketed, bought and sold, displayed in a museum, or, worse, on an academic's bookshelves. Anachronistically Hurston had recognised the possibility of functioning as an "otherness machine manufacturing alterity for the postmodern trade in difference".[17] Janie only "goes folk" once she has made her money, rather as a modern-day millionaire may choose to collect art objects from the oppressed past of his ancestors. But her story is framed and structured in such a way as to prevent the reader functioning in any naïve fashion as a mere consumer of another culture. An increased awareness of the novel's insistent language of commodity and exchange implicitly combats romanticised readings of it as a feminist triumph tale. Triumphalism has itself been located within a dubious rhetoric of status. As a result, *Their Eyes Were Watching God*, a creole mixture drawing syncretically upon the cultural work of White-, Jewish-, African- and Native-American, constitutes a literary gift which makes the nature of cultural appropriation problematic.[18]

Notes to Chapter 15

1. Michele Wallace, "Who Owns Zora Neale Hurston? Critics Carve Up the Legend," in her *Invisibility Blues: From Pop to Theory* (New York: Verso, 1990), 172–87. Quoted p. 174. Wallace refers to Harold Bloom (ed.), *Modern Critical Views: Zora Neale Hurston* (New York: Chelsea House, 1986).
2. Hazel Carby, "The Politics of Fiction, Anthropology and the Folk: Zora Neale Hurston," in Michael Awkward (ed.), *New Essays on "Their Eyes Were Watching God"* (Cambridge: Cambridge University Press, 1990), 71–94.
3. Gloria Cronin, *"Their Eyes Were Watching God,"* Unpublished paper, ALA Conference, San Diego, May 1998, p. 4.

4. Franz Boas, *The Social Organisation and Secret Societies of the Kwakiutl Indians* (Washington, D.C.: 1897). Robert Hemenway, *Zora Neale Hurston: A Literary Biography* (Urbana: University of Illinois Press, 1977), 63, gives an account of Hurston's relationship to Boas, whom she idolised. He notes that Boas had already discovered that Indians, presumed to be savages, maintained a highly complex, sophisticated belief system, and that the evidence suggested the same was true for illiterate black people. It would therefore be quite logical for Hurston to make connections between Indian and black folklore. On Boas, see Melville Herskovits, *Franz Boas* (New York: Charles Scribner's Sons, 1953). Boas was such a notable foe of racism that his 1933 essay "Aryans and Non-Aryans" was circulated clandestinely, printed on tissue paper, by the Anti-Nazi underground. Hurston also studied with Melville Herskovits at Northwestern University in 1935–36 but gave up her doctorate and used her Guggenheim money to write the novel. It is worth noting that Saul Bellow graduated from Northwestern in 1937 with honours in anthropology and sociology, and that he went on to graduate study with Herskovits. Bellow's *Humboldt's Gift* (London: Secker and Warburg, 1975) is also structurally based upon gift-exchange. See Judie Newman, "Bellow's 'Indian Givers': *Humboldt's Gift*," *Journal of American Studies*, 15, 2 (1981), 231–38. Hurston's 1933 short story, "The Gilded Six-Bits," *Story*, 3 (August 1933), 60–70, also involves a poisonous gift, a gold coin which Hurston's 1933 short story "The Gilded Six-Bits" also involves a gift which turns out to be merely gilded. Missie May is seduced by a travelling man in exchange for the coin, but discovered by her husband, who forgives her and uses the coin to buy candy in the store.

5. For a later, but comprehensive account see Eli Sagan, *Cannibalism: Human Aggression and Cultural Form* (New York: Harper and Row, 1974). See also Marcel Mauss, *The Gift* (London: Cohen and West, 1954). Originally published as *Essai sur le Don* (Paris: Presses Universitaires de France, 1950).

6. Robert Hemenway, "The Personal Dimension in *Their Eyes Were Watching God*," in Awkward (ed.), *New Essays on "Their Eyes Were Watching God,"* 32.

7. Ibid.

8. Zora Neale Hurston, *Their Eyes Were Watching God* (London: Virago, 1986). ("Afterword" by Sherley Anne Williams, 297.)

9. Ibid., 29. All subsequent citations follow quotations in parentheses.

10. Houston A. Baker, "Ideology and Narrative Form," in *Blues, Ideology and Afro-American Literature: A Vernacular Theory* (Chicago: Chicago University Press, 1984), 57.

11. Ibid., 58.

12. John Lowe, *Jump At The Sun: Zora Neale Hurston's Cosmic Comedy* (Urbana: University of Illinois Press, 1997), 174.

13. Peter Messent, *New Readings of the American Novel* (London: Macmillan 1990), 243–88.

14. Baker, 58.

15. Ibid., 58.

16. Trinh T. Minh-ha, *Woman, Nature, Other: Writing Postcoloniality and Feminism* (Bloomington: Indiana University Press, 1989), 89.

17. Gail Ching-Liang Low, "In A Free State: Post-Colonialism and Postmodernism in Bharati Mukherjee's Fiction," *Women: A Cultural Review*, 4, 1 (1993), 17.

18. The initial version of this essay was given as part of a round table discussion of Hurston at the American Literature Association Conference in San Diego in 1998. I am grateful to Professor Gloria Cronin for inviting me to participate, and for her enormously helpful comments on Hurston.

CHAPTER 16

Going Global:
From Danish Postcolonial Novel
to World Bestseller:
Peter Høeg's *Smilla's Sense of Snow*

Reviewing for the *Toronto Star*, John North asked:

> What are the odds of a translated novel by a relatively obscure Danish author and featuring a part Inuit female scientist/detective living in Copenhagen succeeding in the overcrowded North American book market?[1]

The question was rhetorical. The novel under review was Peter Høeg's *Smilla's Sense of Snow*, first published in Danish in 1992, and by 1997 a blockbuster U.S. and world bestseller in translation. The novel's success was even more surprising given its focus on the history and afterlife of Danish colonialism, not an immediately topical theme. With the exception perhaps of the Caribbean islands of St. Thomas, St. John and St. Croix, a Danish colony sold to the United States in 1917 (now the United States Virgin Islands), American awareness of Danish imperialism has not been noticeably acute. A roster of Danish colonies would add some holdings in India (passed to the British in the nineteenth century), 200 km of the Guinea Coast of Africa (ditto) and a few trading posts. Without wishing to underestimate Danish colonial activity (which included involvement in the slave trade) the international general reader is unlikely to have been drawn to the novel by fascination with the topic. And yet, Denmark has one territory which is still part of North America: Greenland. Situated geologically as part of the Canadian Shield, Greenland became a Danish colony in the eighteenth century, a province of Denmark in 1953, and gained Home Rule in 1979, remaining part of Denmark (though not, now, of the European Union). It is also host to an American settlement. When Germany invaded Denmark in 1940 the United States invoked the Monroe Doctrine and made an agreement with Denmark allowing the establishment of American military bases. Thule (massively expanded during the Cold War) remains the United States' most northerly base, hosting a unit of the Ballistic Missile early warning system. In Høeg's novel, the plot turns upon the existence of this US presence, a colony within a colony, and its relation to its hosts, in a narrative foregrounding metaphors of pollution and parasitism, in relation to translation.

Smilla's Sense of Snow offers a fascinating case study of the ways in which translation functions to create a world literature; the extent to which it fosters domination of minority language cultures by more powerful linguistic communities; and the degree to which translation may erase local differences, homogenising culture or pandering to the demand for the exotic while safely domesticating it. In its rapid spread across world publishing markets, the novel appears to exemplify that flexibility and adaptation which characterise the global, serving the interests of the trade in ethnic differences while revealing the various degrees of complicity between local oppositional discourses and a global system. Translation may be said to lie at the heart of any transnational system which moves across cultures and languages. In literary critical terms, working with a translation is suspect, impure. Atwood's Professor Pieixoto, translating the handmaid across time and space, into the assumptions of his own culture, and getting her altogether wrong, offers an object lesson to the current writer, not a Danish speaker and dealing with work in translation, with all which that implies of interference and disruption of cultural messages. Translation, however good, is never an innocent activity.

The relation between translation and postcoloniality has become a focus for contemporary critics, kick-started by the appearance of Eric Cheyfitz's *The Poetics of Imperialism* (1991), Vicente Rafael's *Contracting Colonialism* (1988) and Tejaswini Niranjana's *Siting Translation* (1992).[2] Douglas Robinson's *Translation and Empire* (1997) offers a succinct and discerning introduction to the ways in which translation has been understood: as a channel of Empire, assisting in the colonisation of subject peoples; as a lightning rod for cultural inequalities after the collapse of colonisation; and as a potential channel of decolonisation, primarily as a means to decolonise the mind.[3] Robinson draws attention to the power differentials which control what gets translated and how. As Lawrence Venuti argues

> Translation is uniquely revealing of the asymmetries that have structured international affairs for centuries.[4]

Translation is deeply implicated in relations of domination and dependence, a powerful tool in the formation of cultural identities, and in the creation of representations of foreign cultures which simultaneously construct a domestic subjectivity. Venuti notes the dominance of English-language cultures. English is the most translated language worldwide, but one of the least translated into. In 1987, he points out, only 1,700 books were translated from Italian into English, 5,000 from German, while 32,000 were translated from English into other languages. Translation thus occupies a marginal place in Anglo-American cultures. A great deal of money is made translating from English; very little is invested in translating into it. In addition, translations are expensive and tend to be designed to serve domestic interests.

> A best-selling translation tends to reveal much more about the domestic culture for which it was produced, than the foreign culture which it is taken to represent.[5]

In a special issue of *Public Culture* (2001) devoted to translation in a global market, Emily Apter highlights the role of translation in globalising the canon, to create "global Lit". In her view the increased motility of global culture may foretell a time when national labels will become obsolete as an international aesthetic emerges in which location has become increasingly meaningless. For Apter,

> "Global" signifies not so much the conglomeration of world cultures arrayed side by side in their difference but, rather, a problem-based monocultural aesthetic agenda that elicits transnational engagement.[6]

In this connection, the drive towards a transnationally translatable monoculture reveals itself in the ways in which linguistic superpowers call the shots, marginalising former healthy cultures. Translation elides the situatedness of texts, dehistoricising and depoliticising them. As Venuti argues, the result may be that translation

> makes ideas and forms appear to be free-floating, unmoored from history, transcending the linguistic and cultural differences that required ... their translation in the first place.[7]

Conversely, of course, improved translatability may be a good thing, improving connections between nations and unbordering zones of cultural production.

How then can a writer in a relatively powerless language community create a novel which both crosses borders and communicates beyond his own specific location, while embodying resistance to dominant cultural hegemonies? In Høeg's case, as the development of this argument will establish, translation may imply interference with the message, but that interference may also be part of the message, and not necessarily an accessory to commodification. Although Høeg's novel is steeped in history, its major strategy is inscribed within its aesthetic and formal structures, in plot, character, imagery and language. Previous criticism has highlighted the thematic and historical freight which the novel carries, in accordance with the overriding tendency of postcolonial theory — even when broadly understood as signalling a critical stance towards forms of Empire rather than a concern with a narrow historical period — to analyse novels in terms of cultural and political themes and preoccupations, or contemporary issues. It would be relatively easy to take a thematic approach to Smilla, to note that she is a hybrid figure, part-Danish, part Greenlandic; that she acts on behalf of an oppressed Greenlandic child, used as a guinea pig by representatives of established scientific power; that her pursuit of the truth about his murder confronts readers with some unpalatable facts concerning Danish treatment of Greenlanders in the past, their transformation into "Northern Danes", in "Denmark's Northernmost county"; [8] the history of mineral exploitation and so-called "scientific" racism; and the uneasy contemporary relations between modern Europeans and their immigrant communities. More critically — but still essentially thematically — the critic might contrast Smilla's hybridity with her nostalgia for a constructed Greenlandic innocence, symbolised by the child Isaiah, who represents also her own past, a childhood spent hunting seals with her Greenlandic mother. Or, indeed, the novel might be interpreted as an exercise in exotic nostalgia, as a work that, for all its good intentions, never introduces its readers to any contemporary resident of Greenland, treating the Arctic territories as a land of fantasy and alien life. Reviewers commented that the novel began well but that its second half transformed it into a conventional thriller in which Smilla discovers that in Greenland a strange meteor (an energy source and apparently alive) has brought back to life a presumed-extinct Arctic worm, another alien life-form which Isaiah had carried with him to Denmark, and which was the focus of the scientists' plots and counterplots. Alien life forms thus appear to be located in the immigrant, the minority and the "Other". From this point of view the novel can be approached not as a rigorous confrontation with colonial guilt, but as an implicitly racist parable, involving the death of the dangerous infected — a very politically incorrect novel. Since the worm kills most of its hosts, these "aliens" pose a severe threat not just to the Danes but also to all mankind. Dangerous imagery.

Like the fictitious worm, the novel displayed a capacity to spread rapidly, moving swiftly from Denmark onto a world stage. From its appearance in 1992 it had been published in 24 countries, from Brazil to South Korea, by 1997; at least ten more countries had bought translation rights. As Eva Hemmungs Wirten notes, it epitomises the status of the book as global commodity. Early expectations for the book were for a modest print-run of 5,000–7,000 copies, which swiftly rose to 40,000 with the mass-market version expected to hit 2 million. Reviews hailed the book — but also applauded the quality of its translation, by Tina Nunnelly, of the Fjord Press in Seattle.[9] The book was assisted by a massive advertising campaign in the US of $50,000 dollars, a Book of the Month Club selection in 1993, and when it came out in paperback, promotional paraphernalia which included "Think Snow" baseball caps and pillows, and a reader's companion. TIME voted *Smilla* "Book of the Year". Then the film appeared: *Smilla* had gone global.

The film, *Miss Smilla's Feeling for Snow*, directed by Bille August, in 1997 in English, cost 35 million dollars, and stars an international cast — Julia Ormond, Gabriel Byrne, Richard Harris and Vanessa Redgrave, among others. Isaiah was played by a seven-year-old Canadian, who was already a veteran of the Toronto production of *Miss Saigon* — as if ethnicities were interchangeably performative. The only major role played by a Greenlander was that of Juliane, the stereotypically feckless "drunk native", played by Agga Olsen. Predictably the film omits much of the novel's social criticism (no references to *Das Kapital* or to Smilla's political education with the Greenland Marxist Society), and in place of the original open ending, substitutes a conventional resolution, closing with an explosion which blows up villains, worms and meteorite in one blast and leaves only the romantic leads (Ormond and Byrne) alive. Greenlanders apparently welcomed the film, in the belief that it might increase tourism. August, however, wanted a bleak atmosphere and was annoyed by the strength of the Greenlandic sun. He therefore shot at dawn and dusk. Where the novel attacks the idea that Greenlanders are "primitive" or timeless, as if at some earlier stage of development than Europeans, the film opens with an image described in the Screenplay as "a fur-clad Inuit hunter poised above a small opening in the ice — so still he seems as frozen as the landscape. A timeless image; this could be the present day — or a thousand years ago."[10] Seconds later the meteor hurtles through the air and an avalanche engulfs him. He is frozen, timeless, and then disappears in a flurry of snow as the screen turns to white. Høeg had disassociated himself from the view of indigenous people as unspoiled; but Bille August described Greenland in terms which emphasise a lack of culture, as "a landscape totally untouched by the hand of man".[11] Strikingly, then, the opening of the film erases the human presence, in favour of a vast whiteness, and the ending restores the landscape to the same emptiness as the wheel turns full circle. At this point we might say that any resistant content had been emptied from the novel, which had become a fully commodified product. The story has been translated from Danish to English to the screen, and in its content no longer carries any postcolonial charge. As a result, it appears to exemplify that flexibility and adaptation which characterises the global — a flexibility of form which serves the interests of the trade in ethnic differences, and which informs the various degrees of complicity between local oppositional discourses and a global late-capitalist system. As Graham Huggan explains it, keeping the margins exotic is the objective of the mainstream — policing its boundaries, and keeping the margins available to the mainstream, but on the mainstream's own terms.[12]

But can this flexibility and adaptation also be subversive? E. San Juan Jr. would maintain that it cannot, that postcolonial discourse merely mystifies the political and ideological effects of Western hegemony by its linguistic and textual emphasis, ignoring the real resistance of the Third World to domination. For him, Homi Bhabha's emphasis on contingency and indeterminacy simply legitimises a new master narrative.[13] Bill Ashcroft, in contrast, argues that postcolonial cultures develop in ways which reveal remarkable capacities for change and adaptation, and for local engagements with global culture, using imperial culture for their own purposes, just as Smilla uses the system's own scientific records to outwit the system. For Ashcroft the experience of the postcolonial world demonstrates that change won't come by attempts to establish fortress societies or to abolish globalisation, but by strategies to transform it, by appropriation and adaptation.[14] In this connection Peter Høeg's use of the rhetoric of pollution, the trope of the parasite, and global interchanges and contrasting situated knowledge, creates a nexus of images informed by the work of Michel Serres, which offers a counterargument, establishing the novel as not merely a critique of colonial and neo-colonial domination, but also of the globalising impulse.

The image of the infected immigrant draws very obviously upon the rhetoric of pollution. One example is instructive. In J. M. Coetzee's novel *Waiting for the Barbarians* a magistrate occupies a fort on the frontiers of an unnamed Empire.[15] A visiting Colonel, Joll, has been torturing the native inhabitants, a group of fisher people whose condition is thoroughly wretched. They are dirty, diseased and disliked. When Joll departs the magistrate announces, "I want everything cleaned up! Soap and water! I want everything as it was before".[16] In his desire to erase the dirty story of Empire, he is tempted to resort to the type of purification which today would be termed "ethnic cleansing". He considers making a fresh start by marching the smelly diseased prisoners into the desert and simply burying them there. But he does not do so.

> That will not be my way. The new men of Empire are the ones who believe in fresh starts, new chapters, clean pages; I struggle on with the old story, hoping that before it is finished it will reveal to me why it was that I thought it worth the trouble.[17]

As the magistrate has discovered, there can be no clean pages in human history without some sort of violence. The lure of the "purified" clean empty space, the new beginning, the neatly bounded territory, is a dangerous one, in culture at large, as in literature. As Rey Chow argues, defilement and sanctification — the clean and the unclean — belong to the same symbolic order, and modernity (in trying to be new) "must incessantly deal with its connection to what precedes it in the form of destruction", citing Paul de Man's comments on the "desire to wipe out whatever came earlier".[18] Cultures like to impose systems — scientific or everyday — on inherently untidy experience. As Mary Douglas puts it

> It is only by exaggerating the difference between within and without, above and below, male and female, with and against, that a semblance of order is created. [19]

Douglas argues that human beings are likely to condemn as "dirty" or "polluted" any object, person or idea which is likely to confuse our cherished classifications. Culture will always evolve rules for avoiding anomalous things, in order to strengthen the definitions which they challenge. In Biblical dietary taboos (her example) the principle of cleanness in animals is that they should conform fully to their class, occupy their right place. Birds fly and are clean. Four-footed animals that fly (flying squirrels) are unclean. Almost anything that creeps, crawls or swims, that moves between land and sea, is unclean because its place or movement is of an indeterminate nature. Margins are dangerous. People in a marginal state, placeless, left out of the social patterning, become "dirty", sources of pollution and danger, because their status is indefinable. This can include social outsiders, or offenders against the bounded wholeness of the human body: the racial minority, the physically disabled, the sexually ambiguous, the parasite which penetrates the bodily boundaries. The body is a model which can stand for any bounded system. Its boundaries can represent any boundaries which are threatened or precarious. Danger also lies in marginal states because transition is neither one state nor the other, but indefinable. To have been at the margins — in the disordered regions of the mind, say, or in "unexplored" areas of the globe — is to have been in danger — and at the sources of power. Works of art may be understood in terms of their function of enabling us to go beyond the explicit structures of our normal experience, into areas of formlessness, indefinability, which can be credited with powers, some dangerous, some good. In ordinary society, however, any transgressor of a social boundary is treated as a dangerous polluter. The transgressor has crossed some line which should not be crossed, and society mobilises to reinforce the boundaries. Purity — the clean and bounded space — is the object and it is the enemy of change, ambiguity or compromise. Colonial enterprises frequently depict the space into which they are expanding as empty, a "new world", a fresh start, an open prairie, on which clear lines and boundaries can be drawn. At the same time the native or marginal is characterised as dirty, unclean or corrupt — the drunken Juliane and her dirty child Isaiah spring to mind.

Two images are crucial to the action of *Smilla*: the white empty space, and the polluted unclean body, and they come together in the event which initiates the action, Isaiah's death, falling from a roof. When Smilla reaches the roof she finds an empty, snow-covered place, shining with reflected light. Only Isaiah's tracks show in the snow, leading to the edge where he jumped to his death. There are no other footprints except Isaiah's. "No one has been across the surface of the snow except him" (9). For the Danish police the verdict can only be accidental death. Dr Loyen tells Smilla, "It was quite clear from the footprints that he was alone on the roof when it happened" (22). The roof was empty. This is an emblematic image of unmarked, clearly defined space. It conjures up the one familiar image of Greenland in the popular mind. What everyone "knows" about Greenland is that successive waves of settlers arrived — and died. The Norsemen came — and died. The Danes who went to look for them found nobody there. Greenland is empty; the pages of its history are blank. And that timeless emptiness is uncorrupted. "The ethnographers have cast a dream of innocence over North Greenland" (76). But Smilla can read the tracks. As a Greenlander she has "a sense of snow" (72). Because of the precise pattern of acceleration she can see that Isaiah, terrified of a pursuer, went back nine feet to the centre of the roof to get a running start, to try to jump to the next roof. Smilla benefits from situated knowledge. The Greenlandic eye can translate the markings and "read" the page, even when it is meaningless, blank, to the Danes. Snow is not actually white smoothness; it is read in many different ways, throughout the novel. It is almost as if Høeg set out to dramatise that cliché of all linguistic study, that "the Eskimos have many words for snow". For Elsa Lübing, snow is a symbol of inconstancy (drawing on the *Book of Job*); for Smilla it is a symbol of truth (drawing on *Revelation*). Smilla finds Elsa because Mrs Lübing wrote a note in the margins of the official letter awarding Juliane a pension — she left an illicit track on the page, a second message which interfered with the official one. When Smilla approaches Elsa for help the marginal writer turns out to occupy a place at the heart of power, the Cryolite corporation. Elsa collaborates with Smilla because she opens her Bible at random at the very phrase quoted by Smilla. Elsa's reading is textual, docile to authority, bound to power; Smilla's is bodily and depends upon operating across disciplinary categories.

> Reading snow is like listening to music. To describe what you've read is like explaining music in writing. (43)

In literary terms Smilla's reading is a model for the postcolonial reader. We tend to expect place to be bounded; we guard the boundaries of our own knowledge domains; we expect novels also to stay in their places — nationalistic or generic, Danish or postcolonial, social novel or thriller. But art crosses boundaries and exceeds our limited definitions. These include generic definitions. Høeg uses the detective genre to parody the mode of the "expert investigator", the skull-measuring anthropologist of the past, pursuing the truth about the native. Smilla therefore risks contamination herself by taking on the role of investigator. She tracks Isaiah's killers, just as they tracked Isaiah. She is prepared to get her hands dirty in the cause of truth, just as she was prepared to take in Isaiah, a decidedly grubby, smelly child, deafened by recurrent ear infections and already a victim of the worm.

Let's go on from reading the blank space to reading the worm. Inscriptions *of* the body (tracks in snow) are easier to decipher than those on the body. When Lagermann shows Smilla X-rays of the victims of another "accident" in Greenland, the images are "a chaos of black and gray nuances" (243), almost unreadable. "Do you notice anything?" he asks. Smilla peers. "Even when he points it out I don't understand." He tracks it for her. "It's a needle-thin, whitish line, uneven, crooked. It wanders up along the smashed vertebrae, disappears up the ribs, reappears at the tip of one lung, vanishes and shows up again near the heart, outside and partly inside of it, in the long ventricle." Moritz explains the line by showing a second photograph of a man infected by Dracunculus, the Guinea worm. "A truly nasty parasite. Up to three feet long. Works its way through the body with a speed of up to half an inch a day. Finally sticks its head out through the thigh" (244). The reader may, at this point, share the comment of Moritz's trophy child-bride, Benja, "That's gross" (244). The scene provokes visceral, bodily disgust in the reader; it displays what is inside the body, breaching its boundaries. The X-ray image is, in itself, penetrative, a violation of bodily limits. At the same time it reveals a prior penetration and pollution by an alien life-form, the unclean parasite. In the case of Isaiah and his father, the parasite is Dracunculus borealis, the Arctic worm, a parasite which, unlike all others, kills its host, and given enough hosts, could expand to cover the globe. As such the image appears to play into the rhetoric of pollution as opposed to the clean white space, an image, drawn from the stock of anti-immigrant rhetoric, of the primitive alien life-form which expands from its proper place and destroys the cultures it penetrates.

But the genesis of this parasite enforces a counter-reading. In this case it is the colonial parasite which takes root in the indigenous host and exploits it. The Arctic worm is prehistoric, an image of the "primitive" or "timeless" just like the racist image of the Greenlanders as "a transitional form of ape" (18). When the scientists graft the worm larvae onto living human tissue, they potentially unleash a parasite on all humanity. Propagating the timeless turns out to be a potentially deadly enterprise. The post-mortem reveals that Isaiah's body bears a puncture mark. It has been recently penetrated, not by the worm, but by the needles of the scientists, monitoring the worm's progress by regular muscle biopsies. The real parasites penetrating Isaiah's body are the Danish scientists. The villains are financing their planned expedition to Greenland by the manufacture of hard drugs. Smilla's ally, Jakkelson, also bears puncture marks on his body, those of the addict to heroin, another substance which takes over the body and coexists with it. As we are told, "A good parasite does not kill its host" (453). The scientists' drug-financed power base was on the borders of Laos, Burma and Cambodia, where they encountered the Guinea worm, which comes essentially from dirt. It lives anywhere where people depend upon surface, polluted water. The scientists have carried out their grafts in "empty" Greenland where they will not be discovered. Up to now the worm has lived in balance with its hosts. Now it is going global, adapting and mutating from a parasite which feeds on its host, to a killer. The worm is linked to Africa (the Guinea worm), and to the East, to those borders where the scientists found themselves at war "with support from the US" (457), and to the Arctic territories where Isaiah's father dies. Empire is mutating here from a local, Danish power-system to a world-wide killing machine. In its plot and imagery, therefore, the novel constructs a postcolonial critique of the imperial rhetoric of purity.

What of characterisation? Importantly the killer worm is female. Verlaine explains that "women are vermin" (456) (i.e. parasites), thus placing women in a super-category of the unclean and polluting. The female worm is bigger than the male; when it penetrates the skin "it pushes its womb out and emits a white fluid full of millions of larvae" (457). (Disgust contorts the scientist's face.) Several critics have commented on the sexual indeterminacy and gender reversals of Smilla and her lover, the Mechanic.[20] Just as the female worm penetrates and emits its fluid, so Smilla takes the male role in sexual activities. She defies easy gender categorisation. She loves clothes and mothers Isaiah — but she can't cook, is skilled at hand-to-hand combat, and keeps a screwdriver in her pants to stab/penetrate others. In contrast, the Mechanic loves cooking, weeps readily, blushes furiously and is passive to her suggestions. Traditionally, in Greenland a woman may hunt, but only if she renounces family life and dresses as a man. (The Greenlanders are also category bound.) "The collective could tolerate a change of sex but not a fluid transition stage" (33). Smilla's mother hunts like a man, but she plays both gender roles; while hunting she breastfeeds Smilla. The characterisations of the novel, therefore, continue the emphasis on resisting fixed categories. Danger — and power — come from these boundary crossings, whether political borders (Africa, United States, Laos, Denmark, Greenland); gender categories; or bodily boundaries. The reader is left perpetually unsure of any firmly bounded place. Smilla, for example, remembers at one point walking with a group across a hot plain, surrounded by flat, lifeless spaces, the only living creatures in an empty world, through saltpans, dunes and a sandstorm. When and where was this? "The time was 11.30 at night, the burning light was the midnight sun" (311) and the location was north-east Greenland, an Arctic desert. Both place and time are out of joint for the European reader. Smilla understands the attraction of imposing order on contingency. She contemplates the oil platform at Nuuk and says, "What they want is to coerce the other, the vastness, that which surrounds human beings" (360). She herself is drawn to the clearly delineated spaces and forms of Euclidean mathematics, and when she realises that her own frozen, empty existence is threatened by her love for the Mechanic, she resists change as long as she can, trying to keep him out of her space. As she notes,

> People perish during transitional phases. ... It's not difficult to coast along when things are going well, when a balance has been established. What's difficult is the new... The new feelings. (346)

Importantly Smilla makes this observation from the constricted space of a kitchen dumbwaiter in which she is crouching, using its lift shaft to travel surreptitiously between the decks of the Arctic ship. Like the worm, Smilla travels through a food-channel, moving through the bowels of the ship to enter the spaces which are supposedly off-limits, impenetrable, in order to reach the truth. To outwit the parasite, she has parasitised herself.

Which brings me to Høeg's irresolute ending. At the end of the novel, we return to formlessness, an Arctic space in which fog obscures the outlines of objects. Smilla does not need to pursue Tørk onto the new, thin ice and kill him. The Arctic will do it for her, that very emptiness which Tørk sought to dominate, the emptiness which colonial fantasy projects onto the places which it plans to exploit. The surface of the ice is "thin as a membrane, a fetal membrane. Underneath the sea is dark and salty like blood, and a face is pressing up against the icy membrane from below; it's Isaiah's face, the as-yet-unborn Isaiah" (468). This is an image of death as penetrating a body boundary, but also as a passage toward birth. It is an image of a new beginning which is also a death, bloody and interstitial. Tørk is not yet dead but in a space between life and death; the unborn child is in a similar interstitial space, separated by only a slight barrier from the realm of life. The novel closes ambiguously.

> Tell us, they'll say to me. So we will understand and be able to resolve things. They'll be mistaken. It's only the things you don't understand that you can resolve. There will be no resolution. (469)

If you understand, in other words, you will understand the need to remain in the area of interstitiality.

In interview Høeg commented that he wanted at the end to have the realistic plane of the novel crack, to leave the reader uncertain: "Are we inside the mind of the author? Is this simply a psyche making its presence felt, the characters merely slivers of this psyche? What's going on?"[21] In short, we don't know where we are, inside or outside, and the page is suddenly just that, a page on which the author is writing, not a realistic landscape. Although the crime has been solved the death has been deferred, the final meaning postponed. Homi Bhabha has argued that the deferred or postponed meanings in cultural translation are a guarantee that the postcolonial is not bound to any one fixed referent; contingency and indeterminacy are guarantees of freedom. E. San Juan Jr. contests this view, arguing that Bhabha ignores the fact that "utterance addressed to a specific listener in a specific situation is concretely determinate".[22] Just as the ending seems indeterminate, the reader may feel that Høeg's novel is ambiguous, that the symbolism of the worm can slip from host to parasite, imperialist to imperialised. But in this case there is the possibility of a third term, resistance, which focuses upon language, my final aesthetic focus. Throughout the novel there is a series of images of balked communication, or messages which meet with interference. The Mechanic stutters; Isaiah is deaf; Andreas Licht, already blind, is deafened by his assailants (penetrating his ear with a live electric wire); phone calls are cut off or overheard by different listeners from those intended; Miss Lübing's entry phone drowns out Smilla's voice in static crackle. A similar phenomenon involves the presence of an interloper or third party in major scenes: Benja interrupting redundantly, Smilla commenting satirically on events; Miss Lübing's neighbour admitting Smilla, taking her for a florist; Lagermann's wife mistaking Smilla for the babysitter with a series of utterances at cross-purposes. One scene is particularly striking. Smilla discovers a cassette tape hidden by Isaiah and can't make it out at all. The recorded voice is in East

Greenlandic, a southern dialect incomprehensible to Smilla. The tape is interrupted by noises, the sound of an engine, electric noise from the cassette player, the palimpsestic hiss of a previous recording which has not been fully erased. The tape ends suddenly with jazz, described by Smilla as having "a strange precision ... What takes the greatest precision is that it is supposed to sound like total chaos" (121). When the acoustic expert deciphers the tape, the spoken message appears to be a description of a journey. But the significant sounds are located in the interference behind the voice — a motor, a prop plane, a jet, a clatter of dishes, a waiter speaking Danish and American English, and a jazz pianist. The expert wonders where in the world you can have an East Greenlandic hunter sitting and talking in a restaurant where tables are being set, a Dane is yelling in American English, you can hear an airport in the background, and a famous jazz pianist is playing in the restaurant. The answer is Thule American Air Base, specifically its club. This is the evidence which provides the story of the original accident in Greenland. This evidence is what Isaiah was killed for. The interference, the noise, is the message itself. The chaos is actually precision, identifying a precise location.

The scene opens the way to a more positive reading of the parasite. The truth about the parasite and the interference in the message come together here and return to the original starting point of this chapter, concerning the role of translation. In his book *The Parasite*, Michel Serres, the philosopher of science, has pointed out that in French the term "le parasite" also means noise.[23] A parasite is a noise in a channel. Noise is part of communication. It cannot be eliminated from the system. The speech utterance is not "determinate". In any communication we have three elements, a message, a channel for transmitting it, and noise or interference which accompanies the transmission. Noise makes a reading of the message more difficult. But it is always there. There is therefore no message without resistance, no space without the parasite. Ideally noise is what is not communicated, a kind of chaos or third element to the message, the part of difference that is excluded. Every formalism (mathematics, say) is founded on the exclusion of the third element of noise, to keep one area of knowledge separate from another. But in fact, different knowledge domains interpenetrate — postcolonialism and Danish literature, for example. The noise is the interesting part of the communication. The speaker or sender may see it as an obstacle, but for the reader it has its own informational value. The parasite is therefore a catalyst for complexity and interest.

> Whether it produces a fever, or just hot air, the parasite is a thermal exciter. And as such it is both the atom of a relation and the product of a change in this relation.[24]

The meteor, a foreign body and heat source from outer space, is almost too obvious a dramatisation of the notion of the thermal exciter. Serres himself uses the vocabulary of table manners and hospitality in his account, drawing on Horace and the fables of La Fontaine (who, he notes, uses rats as his examples of the parasites, as opposed to "worms in the intestines").[25] The parasite feeds on another but also brings charm and interest to the table, information, energy and even (if the guest is a god) danger. Guest and host are conflated in the French term *l'hôte*, with the implicit recognition that the parasite is its own *pharmakon*, both the disease and the cure. (The novel's emphasis on food, drugs, and the joys or hostilities of the table, picks up the argument subliminally.) Above all, Serres makes the point that there is no exchange without the parasite, the third party who appears to be redundant noise.

Serres goes on to ask if there is a space outside parasitism, a pure or clean space, and his answer is that all culture depends upon the parasite, in its different meanings. In a conflation of economics and culture, he argues that to grow crops demands a cleared space, and therefore boundaries. Inside is empty; outside are weeds, bugs, interference. But something always comes in. There is always a hole in the fence. Thus, the real origin [of culture] is "the making of a blank space and its simultaneous parasitism".[26] The image is highly suggestive as a description of the scene of crime in the novel — an empty space which has been parasitised by Isaiah, his own space already parasitised by the worm, which provides the interference with emptiness, and offers the clues to all the revelations which follow. History begins with the parasitism of space, with deviation and diversification, so that the parasite, the boundary-crosser, the interfering noise, is also the motor of change and history.

> History hides the fact that man is the universal parasite, that everything and everyone around him is a hospitable space. Plants and animals are always his hosts; man is always necessarily their guest.[27]

Or as the villain puts it in the novel: "Human beings are the parasite. The worm is an instrument of the gods" (457).

Without multiplying examples redundantly, it is important to note that in other significant ways the work of Michel Serres informs the novel. Bounded spaces are a constant focus. The novel opens with maps of Greenland and Copenhagen, spaces of fact which are parasitised by fiction, most obviously in the fictitious island of Gela Alta. Smilla is fascinated by Euclidean geometry, a frequent point of reference for Serres. A series of scenes feature Smilla breaching territorial defences, climbing the fence of the Cryolite factory (81), passing through the hole in her father's hedge, escaping from her father's house past the police guard, escaping from the Casino, gaining access to the forbidden deck of the *Kronos* by dumb-waiter, entering Tørk's sleeping quarters by subterfuge. External phenomena penetrate internal spaces. Smilla is surprised to find that it is snowing in Lagermann's living room. (A flour bag has burst.) Serres's attention to the "thirds" in any apparent binary is comically enacted, as Smilla (hiding in the shower) witnesses a sado-masochistic erotic encounter between two of the villains. In similarly voyeuristic fashion, the existence of the meteor was only discovered through the intervention of a third party, Benedicte Clahn, who was charged with reading mail going in and out of postwar Germany, as part of Allied surveillance, intercepting messages as a third party. Smilla figures in police records as having previously been denied access to Northern Greenland, following violation of Canadian territorial boundaries. (The polar bears which she was tagging showed even less respect for boundaries than Smilla.) Smilla is intensely claustrophobic, and when threatened with imprisonment at police HQ, caves in. "The Greenlandic hell is the locked room" (103). The police building is entirely featureless and empty, described through a succession of negatives — no sign on the door, no typewriters tapping, no nameplates, nobody in the corridors, nothing on the walls, tables, or windowsills, and in the interview room, no coffee, cigarettes, or tape recorder (98). Yet when Smilla and Ravn enter the office she is surprised to find a third party already there, sitting in the dark. When Smilla herself responds to the threat by retiring in fright from the investigation, her own first reaction is to create a private fortress, walling herself off from her neighbours, disconnecting her telephone and her doorbell. Her space is none the less invaded by successive interlopers, including Juliane at the back door, the window cleaner at the window, and finally the mechanic pushing a note through the letterbox, "the last entrance that the world hadn't tried to force its way through" (111).

Recognising that withdrawal behind fortifications is not a useful strategy, Smilla evolves from the fiercely independent, uncommunicative, anti-parasite to willingly parasitising herself. She takes a five-figure sum from her father, preying on "his vital organs: His wallet and his checkbook" (40). She accepts hospitality (she becomes the "guest") from various hosts, enjoying the Mechanic's fish soup, Miss Lübing's spiced cookies, the delights of the Brioche d'Or (156). She herself acts as a somewhat less elegant host to Isaiah (eating mackerel off newspaper on her floor) and serves food to the villains on the *Kronos*. She realises that an invisible hand "has pushed me forth into a network of sewer pipes", running beneath the landscape of Denmark (137). Penetrating the law offices of Hammer and Ving, joining the crew of the *Kronos*, she disguises herself in both cases as a cleaner, exploiting the desire for the clean space in order to further her own strategic pollution. Cleaners enter dirty spaces by right. On board ship she is able to interfere with the plotters' activities by repeatedly running noisy loads of laundry; the crew assume that Smilla is where the noise is. To gain access to the ship Smilla has to draw upon Birgo Lander, a ship's broker who describes himself as inhabiting a world of parasitic interchanges: "a ship's broker lives off other ship's brokers who live off other ship's brokers" (201). Lander owns part of the Casino Øresund, a fortress space. "All the walls are decorated with rivets and the door frames are three feet thick and finished with bolts. The whole thing is designed to resemble a safe" (220). A wall of glass, "like a black barrier" (220), faces the water outside. Officiously regulated, with an inspector for every two tables, the Casino actually propagates the gambling bug, "one of the most voracious creatures in the world" (221). As Lander describes it, "The moment you buy your chips a little animal takes up residence inside you, a little parasite" (221). Legalisation has merely increased the Casino's potential client base, "like an infectious disease which was once under control but has now been let loose" (224). Lander has also realised that the poison is the *pharmakon*. After losing everything several times he bought a share in the casino deliberately. Owners are not allowed to gamble in their own casinos. The tables are turned as, to quote Serres, "The host counter-parasites his guest."[28] Captain Lukas is not such a lucky gambler:

> a parasite ... has eaten him up from the inside and now takes up more room than he does (222)

which is why he takes up the captaincy of the *Kronos*.

In the image of the ship, Høeg constructs an extreme example of the opposition between bounded space and external threat. On a ship "private space must be subjected to the severest discipline if it is to withstand the dissolution, destruction, and pressure to yield coming from all sides" (277). The *Kronos* is "ice-class", double-hulled to resist external pressure. Outside it, the sea represents Smilla's fear of formlessness and disorientation, a confusion that

> will work its way into the chambers of my inner ear and destroy my sense of orientation; it will fight its way into my cells and displace their salt concentrations ... leaving me deaf, blind, and helpless. (264)

Within the ship, however, every space includes a potential interloper; every room has an intercom from which orders crackle; spaces are penetrated by fire alarms and the sprinkler system, and the crew form different interest groups. As Verlaine notes, the ship may have rules (the Captain's and Tørk's) but "They're dependent on us; we're just the rats" (298).

In the denouement, Tørk is defeated by a combination of Smilla, the Mechanic and Lukas. In a scene of poetic justice, the latter takes revenge on Verlaine, using a harpoon gun to penetrate him in the same spot where Verlaine stabbed his brother to death. The Mechanic attacks Tørk when the latter tells a lie, saying that he shouted out to Isaiah to warn him away from the edge, and that Isaiah turned around but chose to ignore him. Isaiah was deaf; he could not have heard Tørk's cry, even if he made it. Smilla comments that: "The most important information always comes at the end. As if in passing. In a side letter. In the margin" (382). Tørk's casual lie is enough to propel the Mechanic onto him and send him out onto the ice. Like Elsa Lübing's marginal annotation, it is a small phrase which provides entry to the truth and changes the dynamics of the situation. Isaiah died because noise was eliminated from his hearing channels. "Interference", the parasite as noise, might have saved him.

As, indeed, it provides a means for Smilla and the Mechanic to raise the alarm and get help. Laying out his theory, Serres's example of noise as a parasite concerns a telephone ringing at a feast, interrupting conversation at table, "the noise interrupting the messages". Once he answers the phone, "the sounds of the banquet become noise for the new 'us'. The system has shifted." Moving back to the table, the noise slowly becomes the diners' conversation once again. In the system noise and message exchange roles according to the position of the observer and the action of the actor. What is mere noise to those at table is a message for the recipient of the call; their conversation is merely noise to him.[29] When the mechanic uses the ship's radio to call for help, it at first looks as if interference will get in the way. He picks up a Canadian classical music station, for example, not the station he wants. The conversation with Ravn is interrupted by "the crackling of empty space" (431); it fades, returns, clarifies, then is "carried away through a tunnel of noise and vanishes" (435). The Mechanic is perilously positioned between two conversations; he has the headset pulled away from him to listen for any noises in the corridor. When Smilla hears interference in the phone conversation, she assumes the noise is coming from the Mechanic, but in fact the sounds of distress are from Ravn, confronting the fact that Tørk murdered his daughter in Singapore. As Smilla comments, "In some ways it has become easier to orientate ourselves in the modern world. Every phenomenon has become international" (123) and "There's nothing local left any more. Something happens in Greenland, it's connected to something else in Singapore" (230). But where globalisation may be seen in terms of a Euclidean notion of space, defined by Serres as a homogenous plane to be overcome, divided up and approached by calibration,[30] the Mechanic has constructed the space of his message topologically, as a distribution of points in a complex spatial arrangement. He is able to use interference to relay his message beyond the tracking devices of the criminals, hopping from the ship's location in the Northwest Passage, to Sisimiut, on to Reykjavik, to Torshavn, and to Lyngby, creating a smokescreen which hides his position. Interference is used as a means to resistance. Where the villains attempt to dominate space, the Mechanic is able to use its tangled relations to his advantage, in short local hops and deviations which outwit the global system of surveillance. What this suggests is that patterns of communication cannot in themselves be understood globally, without following the series of displacements and transformations that occur between the points. Serres understands knowledge as an endless distribution of intricate shores connected by innumerable passages, using the example of the Northwest Passage

> with shores, islands and fractal ice floes. Between the hard sciences and the so-called human sciences the passage resembles a jagged shore, sprinkled with ice and variable. ... Less a juncture under control than an adventure to be had.[31]

Smilla and the Mechanic are, of course, sending their message from the beginning of the Northwest Passage.

As Ruth Mayer has argued, in a time of globalisation it is unsurprising that the image of the parasite should be so widespread.[32] Popular films and novels are full of images of viruses and parasites, notions of infection, contagion, infiltration and contact. Today, she argues, people, goods, ideologies, patterns of consumption travel around the globe, and areas not yet in touch (empty areas) seem like a challenge to the smooth machinery of global translation and transformation. Mayer demonstrates that the parasite theme tends to be enacted in conjunction with images of global interaction, communication and contact, as in this novel in the contacts between Africa, America, the Arctic, Indochina and Denmark. The buzzword of our time is flexibility, through which we escape the confines of local culture, but our adaptive capacities are also those of unpredictable infection, "the flip side of global contact scenarios".[33] What Høeg does differently to such films as *Alien* or *Outbreak* is to embed the notion of resistance into the parasite plot. Crossing boundaries is both danger and power. The notion of the parasite, of interference with the message, exemplifies Mayer's description of the redesigning of cultural contact "by messing up the poles of confrontation and forcing our attention toward the very channels between these poles",[34] making the parasite a "mediate, a middle, an intermediary" as Serres describes it.[35] As a result Høeg's novel, centred upon the opposition of empty space and its simultaneous parasitism, offers a potentially revealing paradigm for postcolonial studies in the age of globalisation.

Notes to Chapter 16

1. John North, "The Snow Must Go On," *Toronto Star*, (16 October 1993), J19.
2. See Eric Cheyfitz, *The Poetics of Imperialism: Translation and Colonization from the Tempest to Tarzan* (New York: Oxford University Press, 1991); Vicente L. Rafael *Contracting Colonialism: Translation and Christian Conversion in Tagalog Society Under Early Spanish Rule* (Durham, N.C.: Duke University Press, 1988); Tejaswini Niranjana *Siting Translation: History, Post-structuralism and the Colonial Context* (Berkeley: University of California Press, 1992). Given the real problems of discussing a translated text, I am grateful to the participants in my master class at the Georg Brandes Skolen, University of Copenhagen, 2004, for the opportunity to test my own reading of *Smilla's Sense of Snow*, and to the editors of *Spring* and the translators (Morten Gaustad and Sara Koch) who subsequently transformed my lecture into Danish. See Judie Newman, "Postkoloniale Parasitter. Peter Høeg's *Frøken Smillas fornemmelse for sne*," *Spring: Tijdsskrift for moderne dansk litteratur*, 22 (2004), 9–27.
3. Douglas Robinson *Translation and Empire: Postcolonial Theories Explained* (Manchester: St. Jerome Publishing, 1997).
4. Lawrence Venuti, *The Scandals of Translation: Towards an Ethics of Difference* (Routledge: London and New York, 1998), 58.
5. Venuti, 125.
6. Emily Apter, "On Translation in a Global Market," *Public Culture*, 13, 1 (2001), 3.
7. Venuti, 93.
8. Peter Høeg, *Smilla's Sense of Snow* (New York: Dell, 1995), 119. First published as *Frøken Smillas fornemmelse for sne* (Copenhagen: Munksgaard/Rosinante, 1992). Subsequent references follow quotations in parentheses.
9. Eva Hemmungs Wirten, "Smilla Rules: Exploring Translation Studies and Book History," *SHARP News*, 10, 1 (2000/01), 1–4. Wirten provides an excellent discussion of the details of the novel's translation. The British version is attributed to F. David, a pseudonym for Høeg and his Danish editor.
10. Karin Trolle (ed.), *Miss Smilla's Feeling for Snow: The Making of a Film by Bille August Adapted from the Novel by Peter Hoeg* (London: Harvill, 1997), 82.
11. Ibid., 25.
12. Graham Huggan, *The Postcolonial Exotic: Marketing the Margins* (London: Routledge, 2001), 22.
13. E. San Juan Jr., "Establishment Postcolonialism and Its Alter/Native Others: Deciding to be Accountable in a World of Permanent Emergency," in C. Richard King (ed.), *Post-Colonial America* (Urbana and Chicago: University of Illinois Press, 2000) 171–97. For a reading more receptive to Bhabha's concept of hybridity, see Prem Poddar and Cheralyn Mealor, "Danish Imperial Fantasies: Peter Høeg's *Miss Smilla's Feeling for Snow*," in Prem Poddar (ed.), *Translating Nations* (Aarhus: Aarhus University Press, 1999), 161–202.
14. Bill Ashcroft, *Post-Colonial Transformation* (London: Routledge, 2001).
15. J. M. Coetzee, *Waiting for the Barbarians* (London: Penguin, 1982).
16. Ibid., 24.
17. Ibid., 25.
18. Rey Chow, "Where Have all the Natives Gone?", in Padmini Mongia (ed.), *Contemporary Postcolonial Theory: A Reader* (London: Arnold, 1996), 132.
19. Mary Douglas, *Purity and Danger: An Analysis of Concepts of Pollution and Taboo* (London: Routledge and Kegan Paul, 1966), 4. See also Judie Newman, *The Ballistic Bard: Postcolonial Fictions* (London: Arnold, 1995), ch. 6.
20. See Rachel Schaffer, "Smilla's Sense of Gender Identity," *Clues*, 19.1 (1998), 47–60; Annelies Van Hees, "Fiction and Reality in *Smilla's Sense of Snow*," *European Studies*, 18 (2002), 215–26.
21. Trolle, 15.
22. E. San Juan, Jr., 176.
23. Michel Serres, *The Parasite*, trans. Laurence R. Schehr (Baltimore: Johns Hopkins University Press, 1982). See also "Michel Serres," abstracted from John Lechte, *Fifty Key Contemporary Thinkers* (London: Routledge, 1994). <http://uvpress.uv.es/Acosotextual/serresbio.html>. [Accessed 17 February 2004].

24. Serres, *The Parasite*, Translator's introduction, x.

25. Ibid., 7.

26. Ibid., 179 ff. Steven D. Brown, "Parasite Logic," Paper for Cultures of Information 2, Keele University, 25 November 2001, 8. <http://devpsy.lboro.ac.uk/psygroup/sb/parasite.htm> [accessed 17 February 2004].

27. Serres, *The Parasite*, 24. Serres makes a careful distinction between predation and parasitism, seeing the former as merely a first stage in human history (10). In his view, human beings live off animals as parasites, eating them, wearing their skins. Smilla may begin as a hunter, but in Denmark, in her silk-lined kidskin pants, she is already a parasite.

28. Serres, *The Parasite*, 52.

29. Serres, *The Parasite*, 66.

30. Steven D. Brown, "Michel Serres: Myth, Mediation and the Logic of the Parasite," 3. <http://devpsy.lboro.ac.uk/psygroup/sb/Serres.htm> [accessed 17 February 2004]. See also Steven D. Brown, "Michel Serres: Science, Translation and the Logic of the Parasite," *Theory, Culture and Society*, 19, 3 (2002), 1–28.

31. Michel Serres, with B. Latour, *Conversations on Science, Culture and Time*, trans. R. Lapidus (Ann Arbor: University of Michigan Press, 1995), 70.

32. I am enormously indebted here to Ruth Mayer, *Artificial Africas: Colonial Images in the Times of Globalization* (Hanover and London: University Press of New England, 2002), ch. 7. Although she does not discuss Høeg, Mayer examines films, novels and comic depictions of parasitism in relation to Africa, and draws illuminatingly on the work of Serres.

33. Mayer, 290.

34. Ibid., 260.

35. Serres, *The Parasite*, 63.

CHAPTER 17

Updike's Golden Oldies:
Rabbit as Spectacular Man

In the opening scene of Updike's *In the Beauty of the Lilies* D. W. Griffith is filming a medieval costume drama in 1910, in which Mary Pickford gallops across a castle lawn in pageboy tights, supposedly bearing a momentous message, "Sire, the king bids the troops to attack the Saracen infidels!"[1] Overcome by the weight of her costume and the torrid heat of Paterson, New Jersey, Pickford faints as the camera comes in for a close up — and simultaneously, in his rectory, Updike's pastor hero, Clarence Wilmot, loses his faith. It is an emblematic moment, as the crusading Pickford takes over the role of religious inspiration from Clarence, and as the visual image replaces the spoken word. Since *The Call to Arms* is a silent film, Pickford's message will be spelled out on the screen in white on black, ornately framed. Coincidentally Clarence develops a throat problem and becomes unable to preach, trading in his vocation for a job as an encyclopaedia salesman, and regular movie attendance. Clarence's granddaughter Essie Wilmot becomes a film star, Alma DeMott (the soul of the demotic) who ministers to far larger masses than Clarence ever did. The novel explicitly engages with the notion that churches have been replaced by movie houses as locations of mystery, passion and spiritual renewal, with "larger-than-life gods and goddesses, emanating as images of light moving across and conquering the darkness."[2] As Jack de Bellis, almost the only critic of Updike to consider the role of cinema in his work, argues, Essie's vocation as a screen goddess connects with yearnings for perfection and immortality, and the escape from a flawed and meaningless reality.[3] In the words of one reviewer

> The cinematic close up marked a moment in history when the face of God was put in the shade by other divine faces who had the added advantage of being able to offer worshippers a signed photo.[4]

Updike's works have of course multiple points of contact with the cinema, including intertextual references and allusions in his novels, the construction of novels using cinematic devices (montage in *The Poorhouse Fair*, the present tense in *Rabbit, Run: A Movie*, that novel's original title), poems ("Movie House"), movie reviews, essays (on Doris Day, Gene Kelly and Lana Turner) and reminiscences. A lifelong fan of Disney cartoons, Updike has rarely missed a Disney animation since he saw *Snow White and the Seven Dwarfs* in 1937. As a child Updike wanted to be an animator because "To create motion, frame by frame, appeared Godlike."[5] Recalling the old movie houses of his youth, he described them as lifting men and women "from their ordinary lives onto a supernatural level. ... No wonder so many of the vacant theatres are now churches. We worshipped in those spaces."[6] What is most significant, however, about the interface between film and Updike's fiction is not the various techniques or references drawn from individual films and deployed in specific novels, but the place of cinema in Updike's consideration of the overall relationship between American society and the visual. Updike, a would-be cartoonist, a trained artist, the author of *Just Looking*, a book of art reviews, and an authority on Vermeer, might be expected to be interested in our society's fascination with the eye. Indeed, his most recent novel, *Seek My Face* forms an extended homage to American art, with its characters constructed as amalgams of key figures: Rauschenberg, Johns, Lichtenstein, Pollock, Warhol and Indiana. Above all, it is the social impact of visual domination which most concerns him; cinema is only one strand in a wide-ranging exploration of the role of the spectacular in contemporary life. In focussing upon the opposition of cinema and church, in *In the Beauty of the Lilies*, Updike draws upon a long tradition of anti-ocular discourse, and a general ambivalence towards the spectacular in the West, as related to the fear of idolatry in the three major Western religions: the idea that what is "real" is somehow not capable of representation. It is not for nothing that Judeo-Christian prophets, for example, tend to hear the voice of God without visible manifestation.[7] The opposition between word and image, voice and vision is particularly acute in *Rabbit at Rest* and its sequel "Rabbit Remembered".

In contrast to the usual understanding of the neorealist as a policeman of the emotions and a disciplinary overseer engaged in ideological control, Updike is deeply concerned with the role of the instincts in American society.[8] Updike's *Rabbit* tetralogy draws quite clearly, though not naively, on Freud's analysis of society as founded upon repression, the idea that, because the lasting interpersonal relationships on which society depends presuppose that the sex instincts are inhibited, there is a high personal price to pay for the benefits of civilised life and technological progress, and a fundamental opposition between sensual gratification and social utility.[9] Updike introduces this conflict between work and play explicitly in *Rabbit, Run*; he proceeds in *Rabbit Redux* to examine the potential MacLuhanite sensual liberation of the individual, set free by new technology from the visual slavery of Gutenberg man; and in *Rabbit is Rich*, analyses the ways in which society may deform and exploit the instincts by the creation of mass fantasy. In *Rabbit, Run*, Harry's indulgent holiday from virtue with Ruth is ended by the death of his daughter, and a return to family and repression. In *Redux* the excursion with Jill and Skeeter again closes with death, a return to the family, and a job in the family business. In *Rabbit is Rich* an actual excursion (to the Caribbean) brings Harry into metaphoric contact with death and returns him to the fold. So far, so disciplinary. But in *Rabbit at Rest,* Updike changes direction. The novel begins on holiday (retirement in Florida), then makes a brief return to the world of work, only for Harry to restage his original "run" once more, this time definitively, returning to die in Florida as the circle of the tetralogy closes upon him. In *Rabbit at Rest* desire is over-indulged, actively encouraged by a society more interested in consumption than production. Notions of play, games, leisure and holiday occupy centre stage, together with their commodification in the leisure industries, whether official (Harry's golf and watersports, various films) or unofficial (Nelson's permanent holiday of crack addiction which triggers Harry's return to the world of work). The family business comes under threat from Harry's own indulgence (overeating and adultery), Nelson's addiction, women (Harry's feminist wife), gays (Nelson's associates in embezzlement are AIDS sufferers trying to buy miracle drugs) and finally other races (the Japanese reassert the work ethic and pull the plug on the Toyota franchise). It is easy to see a case for reading the novel as racist, homophobic and sexist. Dilvo Ristoff, for example, sees Rabbit as "a prisoner of a nostalgic pull that brings to his mind images of a world that is grander and better, more glorious and more desirable than the drudgery and turmoil he now faces."[10] Even worse, Updike inscribes this particular discourse of indulgence in global, political terms, as the Cold War — the ultimate image of repression at home and abroad — comes to an end and America finds itself liberated into insignificance, consigned to the sidelines "like a big Canada".[11] For Harry, "Without the Cold War, what's the point of being American?" a suggestion reinforced by the plot.[12] When his adultery with his daughter-in law is discovered, Harry could make peace with his family. In choosing to flee to Florida instead, Harry creates his own personal Cold War, an icy, hostile stand-off. The problem posed by Harry's identification with an older ideal is the extent to which Updike is guilty of a similar nostalgia for the repressive Cold War certainties of an older America — a time when the family business — and by extension the American economy — was less vulnerable to the threats of women, gays and racial "Others". Importantly Harry's final run has a soundtrack — a long sequence of golden oldies played on the radio which Harry listens to as he heads South to death. Superficially a nostalgic celebration of an earlier America, both in the songs themselves and in the nostalgic associations with radio (as an older medium than, for example, an in-car sound system), the sequence is crucial to Updike's engagement with techniques of demystification of the spectacle and of resistance to visual domination.

At the risk of digression, an example from contemporary film forms a useful jumping-off point for discussion of these songs and their relationship to the politics of *Rabbit at Rest*. In *Reservoir Dogs*, in one of the nastier images of violence in recent film, the Michael Madsen character (Mr Blonde) becomes nostalgic about a golden oldie and plays it while torturing a young cop and cutting off his ear.[13] The song is "Stuck in the middle with you", performed by Stealer's Wheel in 1974 and including the lines:

> Clowns to the left of me, jokers to the right,
> Here I am, stuck in the middle with you.[14]

It is a scene which exposes the evocation of a supposed past middle ground as a killer nostalgia, a surface celebration which overlays and obscures the violence beneath. It is an image which highlights one of the major issues in approaching *Rabbit at Rest* — the opposition between a story of middling, average Americans, and the damage caused by their unrepressed gratifications. Above all it is a scene of such sickening violence that it calls our spectatorship into question. The viewer becomes uneasy with the fact of viewing, precisely because the scene separates the visual spectacle — torture — from the soundtrack in a fashion designed to create a disjunction between the two, undermining the seamless nature of what Guy Debord has termed the "society of the spectacle".[15] In what follows I shall argue that Updike proceeds to a similar analysis and demystification of the spectacle, in surprising agreement with one of the more radical thinkers of the French left, particularly in his employment of nostalgic popular song in opposition to the dominance of the visual.

In *Rabbit at Rest* leisure has become society's tool. Play and work have been collapsed into each other. The image presented here is entirely consonant with that presented by Debord in *The Society of the Spectacle*: the analysis of a society which has been turned into a gigantic spectacle, in which the visible form of the commodity totally occupies everyday life, uniting production and consumption in one monstrous system. Critics have made a similar point about the world of the Rabbit novels, brimming with brandnames and products. (For the curious it is worth noting that there are 871 brandname mentions in *Rabbit at Rest*.) As Martin Jay has argued, Debord's critique employs familiar motifs from other anti-ocular discourses. In particular it builds upon the opposition between (on the one hand) lived, temporally meaningful experience, immediacy of speech (the word) and collective participation, and (on the other hand) dead spatialised images, the distancing effect of the gaze, and the passivity of individuated contemplation. In Debord's words,

> The whole life of those societies in which modern conditions of production prevail presents itself as an immense accumulation of spectacles. All that once was directly lived has become mere representation.[16]

Debord particularly homes in on notions of play, as opposed to modern "leisure" practices which are in fact penetrated by and subordinated to the world of work. In the view of Debord and his fellow Situationists, what is referred to as liberation from work, increased leisure time, is a liberation neither within labour itself nor from the world labour has brought into being.[17] (In a description which chimes uncannily with Nelson's addiction and Harry's final morphine heaven, the spectacle has become "a permanent opium war waged to make it impossible to distinguish goods from commodities, or true satisfaction from ... survival."[18]

Debord is, of course, merely one of a whole series of modern thinkers who have homed in on the dominance of Western culture by the visual. As Michel de Certeau puts it,

> from TV to newspapers, from advertising to all sorts of mercantile epiphanies, our society is characterized by a cancerous growth of vision measuring everything by its ability to show or be shown and transmuting communication into a visual journey.[19]

Vision has been understood as implicated in the surveillance central to repressive power in the modern world, as Michel Foucault argues in *Discipline and Punish* (1975).[20] Foucault's argument that the eighteenth-century focus on visible surfaces gave way to a penetrating gaze into the body itself (notably in the dissection of corpses) with the result of more visual penetration being a focus not on life but on death, on the body as a dominated object, is exemplified in the novel in Harry's angioplasty, a heart operation under local anaesthetic which he is able to watch on a monitor, during which he has a heart attack on screen. Film critics have been much exercised by the power of the gaze, particularly as it positions the male as the gazer, the woman as the object of the gaze, with predictable sexist consequences. Whereas most thinkers, however, focus on the disciplinary and repressive effect of being the object of the gaze, Debord stressed the dangers of being its subject — of being the person who does the gazing, rather than the person gazed at. In his view seduction by the spectacle of modern life was more nefarious than Big Brother's omnipresent watchfulness. Orwell envisaged the TV screen in the corner of the room as watching us. Updike follows Debord in being more alert to the dangers of us watching the screen, and, as in the case of Harry's angioplasty, of us watching our lives rather than living them.

Debord's term "spectacle" implies in French a theatrical presentation of commodities, in which commodities are like idols worshipped in lieu of gods. Debord understood alienation not as rooted in production (as in the nineteenth century) but in consumption. As a left-wing theorist, Debord was intent on creating a movement which would help the masses unmask the illusions which enslave them.[21] Like most radical movements, the Situationists' heyday was brief, flourishing from 1966 to 1968, and then declining, though their influence has been detected in the punk movement, in which deliberate ugliness and ripped clothing undercut the seamless illusion of the consumer dream. Stavros comments in the novel on the politicisation of consumption by punks: "Pain is where it's at for punks ... For these kids today, ugly is beautiful. That's their way of saying what a lousy world we're giving them."[22] *Rabbit at Rest* is notable for its interest in passive spectatorship, and the fashion in which human beings become subordinate to images. Harry, in the hospital, lives only through the TV screen, quite literally. A machine is doing the living for him — he is watching *The Harry Angstrom Show*, his own heart. Judy, possessed by a gluttony for images, channel-surfs continually, offering an image of technological short-circuiting of emotional affect as whole families become interchangeable on screen:

> Faces, black in *The Jeffersons*, white in *Family Ties*, imploringly pop into visibility and then vanish.[23]

Pru orchestrates a seduction from television scripts, Janice becomes a business woman after watching *Working Girl*. Harry's obsession with the Lockerbie bombing focusses on an event which appeared to watchers as the disappearance of a dot from a screen. When Harry scares his family by getting lost, Nelson emphasises invisibility as death. "Suddenly we looked around and you weren't there. Like Pan-Am 103 on the radar screen."[24] Harry is later drawn to the image of the Challenger space rocket disaster, in which the death of the astronauts is a national spectacle, watched live on TV. When Nelson hits Pru, he feels as if he was "standing outside watching and felt no connection with myself. Like it was all on television.[25] When

Harry watches a football game on TV the game is almost invisible as the result of a sudden fog. Television coverage has been reduced to the sideline cameras; nobody knows what is really going on; there is an unbridgeable gap between real action and media image. The crowd "rumbles and groans in poor sync with the television action, trying to read the game off the electronic scoreboard."[26] The crowd are actually present, but their understanding and reaction is attuned only to the visual media. As an image of American politics, it could hardly be more telling.

For Debord, "The spectacle is capital accumulated to the point where it becomes image."[27] The commodity takes over social life. Similarly, Updike's characters don't dominate the products — the products dominate them. Even when he is lusting after Pru in a bathing costume, Harry registers a brandname — it is her "Spandex crotch" which fills his eye. Nelson does not run his habit; cocaine runs him. This is a novel in which we are bombarded with images through the mass media, with advertising invading everything. Reality has become nothing more than a simulation. When Harry marches in a Fourth of July parade as Uncle Sam, liberty is converted into the spectacle of liberty. Some are excluded from the celebration. Judy's Girl Scout troop mounts a display in which one girl features as the Statue of Liberty, surrounded by others whose faces are painted brown, black, red or yellow to represent the races of mankind. Representation is all. The girls have to be painted, since there are no Asian or black girls in the troop. The parade itself clearly represents an older America replete with nostalgic sound track, a medley of half-heard snatches of music, incongruously mixing a pipe band wailing forth "Highland killing songs" and a local rock singer impersonating Presley, Lennon and Orbison, together with "American Patrol" and "Yesterday".[28] Leading the parade, Harry finds the main street (cleared for the event) eerily empty. Normal life has been put on hold, replaced by the spectacle. The scene is followed by the funeral of Harry's lover, Thelma Harrison. Looking for her "no-brand-name church",[29] Harry and Janice get lost and end up instead in a shopping mall with six-screen Cineplex. Nobody there has any idea where the church might be. The real priorities of American society are not in much doubt here.

Debord, of course, wrote without reference to Disneyland. But it is not coincidental that Updike sets his novel in Florida, surrounded by spectacle-worlds, theme-parks and pseudo-realities — spectacles which hardly seem any different from the world surrounding them. Leisure time tends to be considered as our "real" life, those authentic moments away from work. But in Florida the leisure is completely commodified by tourism. Wherever they are, the Angstroms are effectively tourists on their own lives, watching rather than living, taken over by the images and the commercial brandnames. In Valhalla Village, family dinner is dominated by bingo numbers blaring from a loudspeaker. Harry can see Judy speak, and Pru's mouth move in response, but the sound track is that of the bingo caller, in a commercial game. The Angstroms' words have been lost. When Harry is fighting for his life having a heart attack, he encourages Judy to sing, to keep him conscious and to keep her occupied. Judy runs out of nursery rhymes and can only sing snatches of television commercials, McDonalds, American Airlines, "like switching channels back and forth" and "Coke is it!" followed by jingles from the movies.[30] A cheerful Disney soundtrack accompanies Harry's agonising pain — a disjunction between sound and image akin to that in *Reservoir Dogs*.

In what precedes Harry's final run, therefore, the novel foregrounds the passivity of a spectacular society, implicitly contrasting it with Harry's nostalgia for the Cold War world of an older America. Importantly the Florida to which he returns (in the off season) is no longer the world of permanent holiday, but a nostalgic time warp. On his daily walks Harry moves away from the mass vacation locale to an older community. The main sound coming from the houses is that of scratchy radio music mixed with human voices. This area of town, with its old-fashioned wooden houses, chicken coops and general stores, reminds him of the town of his childhood

> in the days of the Depression and distant war, when people still sat on their porches and there were vacant lots and odd-shaped cornfields.[31]

In "Reflections on Radio" Updike noted that "In my childhood and youth, radio was everywhere"[32] and applauded its appeal to the imagination. "Freed from the tyranny of visual mimesis" radio liberated its hearers, as opposed to the "image-saturated modern consciousness which has pre-experienced everything".[33] The nostalgia, however, is shadowed by the fact that this is a black community. The scene offers an implicit critique of nostalgia by displaying the economic underpinnings, the labour for the hotels, theme parks and condos, which make the permanent holiday possible. In *Rabbit, Run* Harry had begun a similar trip, also listening to songs on the radio.[34] When he tries to reenact this journey, however, he finds the original country garage, bathed in nostalgia in his own mind, now engulfed in "sulfurous illumination".[35] On the radio Harry hears a news item concerning Jim Bakker, a disgraced TV evangelist, the embodiment of the Word as dominated by the visual medium. Further South news comes of preachers declaiming prayers to sports crowds through bullhorns, the Word writ large, in protest against the attempt to remove organised prayers before football games.[36] Harry is not religious, however, and turns off the Bible stations in favour of a long sequence of songs on the radio. Superficially the songs (and the fact that they are in the "older" medium of radio) suggest a nostalgia for the past. They are golden oldies, "the music of your life" in the presenter's phrase,[37] heavy on crooners and songs of love, "the sweet old tunes, the tunes he grew up by".[38] Many of the songs apparently evoke personal events. Johnny Ray's "Cry" recalls the moment when Harry's sweetheart did send him a letter of goodbye, for example. Dean Martin's "That's Amore" recalls early sexual experiences. "It's a rare song that doesn't light up some of his memory cells."[39] In symbolic terms also the songs tend to have relevance to Harry's own life. "A-Tisket, A-Tasket" with its second line "I've lost my yellow basket", evokes Harry's decline from his former stardom as a basketball hero. Ella Fitzgerald's heart attacks may also be relevant. "Love me Tender" recalls Presley's death from overindulgence; Frankie Laine ("Mule Train") had bypass surgery for the second time in 1990. Several songs make explicit reference to impending death: the black bordered letter in "Mule Train", "Vaya Con Dios" and "Just a Gigolo", which closes "Life goes on without me".[40] "The Wayward Wind", "On the Road Again" and "Rambling Rose" remind us that Harry has wandered off the straight and narrow, in erotic terms, and is now literally on the move away from his wife and family. It is tempting to read this as irresponsible flight, the nostalgic staging of a personal Cold War. Certainly the song "Wheel of Fortune" suggests that Harry is in some way coming full circle.

On the car journey, however, Harry is entirely alone, free, and above all invisible. Nobody knows where he is, nobody is watching. He is not under surveillance. Invisibility, like the dot disappearing on the screen, is either death or freedom. Potentially, then, the songs offer access to a non-homogenised, individualised history beyond the realm of the spectacular, a space where the whole texture of Harry's personal history overlays "Love Me Tender". Most readers will be familiar with the experience of suddenly hearing a song which recalls emotional scenes from earlier periods of our lives. Musical references of this type are essentially intertextual, with specific but transmutable memories, both private and public, attached to them by time. We can attempt to hang on to the original context and meaning of the song (nostalgically) or transmute it by adding other memories or placing the song in a new context. In general, we tend to resent it if a popular song is transferred from our own private memories to a commercial frame, as for example Marvin Gaye's "I heard it on the grapevine" suddenly became the soundtrack for a scene involving Levi jeans in a laundrette. Ad agencies have been quick to realise the added value a great rock song can add to their products, by conjuring up a particular mood and time. Can one now hear "Search for the hero" without thinking of a Peugeot 406 commercial, or "He ain't heavy, he's my brother", independently of Miller Lite beer? Subconsciously we think of these songs as part of our individual lives, as if we are having the emotions, not having them supplied by a commercial song. But is this the case? Harry comments bitterly (on Connie Francis's "Where the boys are"), that it came out in the "beach-party era", when the songs celebrated a leisure funtime of barbecues and parties. Harry, however, was working as a linotyper by then, "no more parties for him".[41]

So "whose life are these songs?"[42] The songs selected also glorify a cheerful ethnic mix in a schmaltz of emotion which papers over political dissent — invoking an earlier American ideal of the "melting pot". They include Latin-American, Israeli, African-American, Italian and other immigrant groups, featuring Sinatra, Dean Martin, the Three Caballeros, Nat "King" Cole, Ella Fitzgerald, and "Oh My Papa!". Some of these songs are "classics". But the tenuousness of this political harmony may be indicated by the inclusion of "Tzena, Tzena", an Israeli hora issued in 1950 as the B side to the Weavers' first big hit, "Goodnight Irene". It is not an obvious candidate for inclusion in a roll call of golden greats, though it is a song which remains popular at Jewish weddings, and might well feature on the radio in Florida. Harry, however, has not heard it in years. As he comments, "The music doesn't come ethnic any more."[43] As a folksong (if a somewhat packaged one) it was part of the agenda of a group which performed political and union songs, and was blacklisted and put out of business in 1952, as part of the McCarthy witch-hunts. The cheerful dance music ("Tzena, Tzena, can't you hear the music playing?") and Utopian lyrics ("Pioneering all together, come and lend a hand, Tzena, Tzena, building a new nation") are thus out of sync with an era of political oppression.

Ethnic or racially "other" performers were tolerated — and exploited — in the entertainment business only as long as they did not rock the political boat. To a lesser extent the songs also call into question authoritative gender constructs. Neither racial nor gender categories are really as stable as an earlier America would have had it. Sound allows a freedom which scopic discipline does not. It is not an accident that Harry listens to Orbison's falsetto and to Johnny Ray. Ray was billed as the next Sinatra but assumed by some listeners to be black and/or female.[44] In the Fifties people could not necessarily see the singer on screen. Sound was more important than the visual message. Connee Boswell ("Say It Isn't So") was crippled by polio and usually appeared seated in an elevated wheelchair with a gown designed to make it look as if she was standing. Few of her fans knew that she was wheelchair-bound.

In its bricolage of song excerpts, memories and titles the sequence asks whether there is a free space for the individual — a space in which authentic personal experience can take precedence over media substitutes — or whether the individual's life is scripted and programmed by the media, the emotions exploited and the personality "scored" for the right performance in the spectacle. In this respect it is striking that Updike indicates the sounds of the songs, not just the words: Patti Page's "Never let me gooooo, I love you sooooo", Kay Starr's "Puleazzze let it be now" and Ray Charles "yesterdayssss" are spelled out quasi-phonetically. Although readers may have their own memories of these songs, we remain programmed to perform in only one way — just as the performers themselves were tolerated as ethnic performers, only within the bounds of commercial culture, contributors to the spectacle which holds them captive. The text thus confronts its readers with the constraints upon our freedom. We will all remember or ignore the songs to different degrees, connect them to different experiences and be informed to varying degrees about the fate of the Weavers or the gender and race of Johnny Ray. We have a degree of reader-freedom in how we remember these songs, connected to our own individual histories. On the other hand, the songs can only be performed in one way. The reader is firmly "cued" into the correct performance, by a medium which cuts every 30 minutes to news bulletins, in the usual "infotainment" sequence of international, national and local items, reinforcing the sense of human experience as firmly under the control of dominant cultural programming. Even if we do not know the songs at all we will be forced to recognise that their very alien quality in itself suggests that the same will be true of today's songs in forty years' time. As Harry recognises,

> the songs of his life were as moronic as the rock the brainless kids now feed on
> ... it's all disposable, cooked up to turn a quick profit.[45]

Yet the songs have a politically effective result none the less. The long musical excursus takes place in almost complete absence of any external visual scene. The reader has almost no visual cues at all to the outside world. Instead Harry focusses on visual images from his childhood — Kroll's department store with its "otherworldly displays" of goods.[46] In his youth Harry had been an ardent believer in capitalism, as represented by Kroll's. When Kroll's closes, he realises that "the world was not solid and benign, it was a shabby set of temporary arrangements rigged up for the time being, all for the sake of money."[47] The immersion in sound and the separation from the visual scene has led Harry to the perception that the political landscape is not geology, an unchanging background against which life takes place, but stage scenery, "spectacle", painted hardboard.[48] When he does focus once more on his surroundings he finds that he is approaching Disney world. For miles a succession of amusement and theme parks go rolling by — Wax Works, Circus World, Sea World — as the spectacular nature of his society is finally revealed to him, without its illusory mystifications. In this technique of setting the spectacle against itself Updike invites comparison with the strategies of the Situationists in their critical separation of word and image. Debord, for example, made a film (*Hurlements en faveur de Sade*) in which the sound dominated vision and for four-fifths of the film the screen was completely blank.[49] The film caused riots among spectators, forced to endure twenty minutes of final silence to boot. Later Debord realised that the refunctioning of the image could serve political ends better than its obliteration — visual material was ironically undercut by sound commentary, or hijacked for illicit purposes to strip away enslaving illusion. He proposed that rather than censoring *Birth of a Nation* for its racism, for example, a sound track should be added, denouncing the horrors of American Imperialism. Characters from *True Romance* were given different cartoon balloons and made to declaim revolutionary sentiments. In this way it was possible to confront the spectacle with its own effluvia and to reverse the usual ideological format, in order to disrupt a society organised as appearance on the field of appearance itself. Similarly Updike mounts a spirited resistance to the hegemony of the visual, and deploys the word in favour of a penetrating critique of American society. What the novel demonstrates is that seduction by the spectacle may be resisted without surrendering to punishment from the panopticon.

On his deathbed, Harry had tried to tell Nelson the secret which he has kept up to this point — that Nelson has an illegitimate sister, Annabelle Byer, the product of one of Harry's liaisons. But his voice has failed. The existence of the sister is "an old story, going on and on, like a radio nobody's listening to" — a secret personal story which has never been part of the social script.[50] The radio is silent. It appears that Nelson will now never know of her existence. As readers, of course, we do — we have access to a personal, individual history outside the norms of the social spectacle. The ending of the novel, therefore, confronts us again with the disjunction between authentic, lived experience — a personal history — and the loss of that experience along with the loss of the voice. As Maurice Blanchot put it,

> the everyday loses any power to reach us; it is no longer what is lived, but what can be seen or what shows itself, spectacle and description, without any active relation whatsoever. The whole world is offered to us, but by way of a look.[51]

Yet there is a postscript to *Rabbit at Rest*, the novella "Rabbit Remembered", in which Annabelle Byer, Harry's daughter, plays a leading role. The years have passed and Nelson can hardly remember his father, though his description of him reminds the reader of Harry's immersion in the norms of his society:

>   Time has turned the *spectacular man* to powder in just ten years. (my emphasis)[52]

At first it appears that Harry's life remains framed in irony and loss, and that his own late-gained understandings have simply disappeared with him. On his run south, Harry had, if only fleetingly, located a site of potential resistance to the domination of the visual, but the next time the reader encounters him in his car, he is going in reverse direction, as Nelson and Janice re-enact his journey, carrying his cremated remains back to Pennsylvania for the funeral. When Judy weeps in a motel at the thought of Grandpa's ashes, alone in the trunk of the car, the family place the urn reverently on top of the television set, as if Harry were part of the picture gazed at. Even worse, at the following stop, they manage to forget the urn in the bathroom of a Comfort Inn. Nelson understands this "unconscious vengeance in their leaving Dad behind, as he had more than once left them behind."[53] When Annabelle contacts the family, she apparently offers a chance for Nelson to reconnect with his father. At Thanksgiving, however, she inadvertently triggers an orgy of revenge on Harry by proxy. While Georgie Harrison enthuses about Broadway shows and offers free tickets, the family put on a show of their own. Ostensibly discussing President Clinton, the assembled relatives overlay the public figure with their own lived experiences. Annabelle defends Clinton for his love of people, his gambler's nerve and the inability to hold a grudge, but the appeal of a reckless, greedy charmer is lost on the others. Ronnie Harrison, now married to Janice, takes revenge on the man who slept with both his wives, and his mistress (Annabelle's mother), describing Annabelle as the daughter of "a hooer and a bum".[54] Nelson's stepbrothers join in the fray, avenging their seduced mother by describing Clinton in terms which are wincingly apposite to Harry ("He's dead meat. He's a leftover going fuzzy at the back of the fridge"[55]) and take an implicit sideswipe at Janice via the First Lady: "She's been enabling his affairs for years."[56] An infuriated Nelson defends his father against the loathsome Ronnie, demanding of his mother "Why did you marry him? How could you do that to us?" The "us", he realises, must include his dead father.[57]

A final car journey establishes the extent to which Harry's influence lives on. At the close of the novella Nelson, his wife Pru, Annabelle and Billy Fosnacht go to see the film *American Beauty*, on the millennium eve. As in the car trip in *Rabbit at Rest*, external visuals are muted. Leaving Instant Classics, the aptly named second-run, cut-price cinema, Nelson loses his way and ends up heading for outer darkness, missing the dazzling displays of millennial fireworks, and narrowly avoiding a fatal car crash right beside the site of Kroll's department store, as a computer glitch extinguishes the lights of Brewer. Despite the millennial date, the scene could not be less spectacular. The disjunction between lived temporally-meaningful experience and the illusory satisfactions of a spectacular society is highlighted in the general sense of anti-climax, of people staying home with their families, and in Ronnie's observation that the millennium has already dawned in Fiji, Australia and Japan. "For most of the world the millennium is already history! Time is relative."[58] Similarly *American Beauty* is relayed to the reader only through the words of the characters, collectively discussing it in the car. Just as their personal histories dominated the public story of Clinton, reinterpreted through their own hostilities, so the film is subordinated to the Angstroms' personal concerns. Significantly *American Beauty* is a film about perception, exploring the disjunction between projecting an image and being true to oneself.[59] Much of the action of the film is seen through a window or a camera lens, allowing the reader to step back and watch without quite surrendering to the image. At one point a character, Jane, accuses the video-wielding Ricky, of being "like any other dweeb who worships Quentin Tarantino for the same reason you can't let go of that camera: because you don't know how to be a real person in a real life." Ricky, however, uses the camera to reveal real beauty in the everyday, as in girl-next-door Jane for example, as opposed to the commercially perfect Angela, a nubile would-be starlet. Ricky, a former drug addict and mental patient, uses the camera therapeutically to help set everyone in the film free from their old selves, and to allow them to face death, a constant fascination in the film, in which a car wreck allows a teenager to stare into the eyes of a corpse and claim to have seen God. The overall moral is that if we "look closer" (a tag in the film) there is beauty and joy in ordinary things, as opposed to the artificial images of perfection cultivated on screen and in a spectacular, consumerist society.

Ricky's experience clearly chimes with that of Nelson, himself a former drug addict, now a therapeutic counsellor, who understands very clearly the problems of the "perfect" image. One of his clients, Michael DiLorenzo, son and heir to the firm of "Perfect Cleaners" has recently killed himself, unable to live up to his parents' expectations that he would become Mr Perfect. Michael's schizophrenia is described as a fatal disjunction between word and image. While voices hammer inside his head urging him to kill, "Things up close look far away; there is no clear depth in which to locate himself."[60] If Nelson is Ricky, Janice corresponds to Carolyn Burnham, a failed mother, adulteress and real estate agent, and Harry is Lester Burnham, whose midlife crisis and flight from his job plunge the family into chaos. Lester's fresh start ends in death, illustrating for Nelson that there can be "No fresh start, no mercy." For Nelson, death is just a "freeze-frame", an arrest, a final stop light.[61] *American Beauty*, however, is narrated by Lester from beyond death, most memorably at the close when he recalls the magic of the stars and of his grandmother's hands. The Angstroms' reactions are mixed, displaying some desire to believe in the film's transcendent message, combined with a healthy scepticism for its more transcendent excesses. The film certainly assists Billy Fosnacht in feeling less afraid of mortality ("Didn't Kevin Spacey look happy dead?"[62]) but he is upset by the gay subplot. (As a dentist he is afraid of contracting AIDS from his gay patients.) Pru is dismissive: "that guy never acted like a man who had ever noticed his grandmother's hands or anything else except his own selfish itches and threatened ego".[63] The alert reader will remember at this point Harry's frequent memories of his mother's large hands as opposed to his son's "little Springer hands", recreated in Judy and will qualify Pru's dismissal.[64] Unlike Annabelle, who applauds Lester, Pru also dismisses the scene in which Lester, propositioned by Angela, refrains from taking sexual advantage of her: "I think that was unrealistic, too. Most men would have just screwed her anyway. I mean, he'd been dreaming about nothing else."[65] Ten years ago Pru had propositioned Harry, who had not resisted temptation. In the novella alternative constructions of Harry are offered — vilified as Clinton, idealised as Lester.

Nelson, however, finally conjures up and exorcises the loved-but-abusing father, in a scene which privileges voice, immediacy of speech and collective participation over the spatialised images which the foursome have just contemplated on screen. At Thanksgiving Annabelle had identified with Clinton as "poor in a crummy town with an abusive stepfather" a comment which gains full relevance only in the final scene of the novel.[66] Remembering Pru's adultery with her father-in-law, Nelson skilfully opens Annabelle up, forcing her to confront the sexual abuse she had suffered at the hands of her stepfather. In *American Beauty* Lester's daughter, Jane, hates her father and asks Ricky to kill him. ("Kill my father. Do it."[67]) Indeed the film plays with the spectator's assumptions, suggesting at various points that Jane, Ricky, Carolyn, or Ricky's rebuffed gay father may have shot Lester. Annabelle does not endorse Jane. "I didn't like her. I identified with the other one, the pretty one who acted like a tramp but turned out to be a virgin."[68] Annabelle is desperate to hang onto innocence, to rewrite a painful history (mother as "Savvy old tramp",[69] father as abuser), but Nelson will have none of it. "What do you think, Annabelle? How far would the older man have gone? The father figure? ... How far did Mr Byer go with you?"[70] (It is Nelson's "inner ear" as a counsellor which had previously alerted him to the falsity of Annabelle's glowing descriptions of Frank Byer.)[71] In the car he is alert to the tone of Annabelle's "childishly trusting" voice, and picks up her emphasis on innocence and youth in her delight in the schoolkids' routine as cheerleaders.[72] Brutally, he forces her to admit that her stepfather's death was a relief: "I felt I'd killed him! Good for me!"[73] It is at this point that Harry becomes an almost palpable presence in the car. Nelson dare not turn his head to look at the backseat, where his sister is being comforted by Billy: "his sensation of a fifth person in the car is so strong he needs to strengthen his grip on the steering wheel."[74] For the reader the sense of impending disaster, engineered from beyond the grave, is teasingly evoked. Moving forward Nelson refuses to yield at the intersection to a larger vehicle, and narrowly avoids a fatal accident. As he squeaks past the other car, Christian rock-music bursts upon him from a concert, and he feels as if "a contentious spirit is leaving him".[75] Death is no longer a freeze-frame. As Billy says, "It's funny about death. When you actually face it, it's kind of a rush."[76] The implication is that the characters have now integrated a realistic image of Harry into their lives, recalled him and exorcised him. Nelson recommits to Pru. Ronny and Janice move to Florida. Annabelle and Nelson enjoy a final telephone conversation in which he assures her that "The very motion of our life is towards happiness" and she reminds him that nobody is perfect.[77] In the final lines Annabelle reveals her intention to marry Billy in church, and Nelson agrees to give her away. The collective discussion in the car, the primacy of the word, the rejection of the perfect, transcendent image, have delivered the Angstroms back, if not into the arms of religion, at least into the arms of each other.

Notes to Chapter 17

1. John Updike, *In the Beauty of the Lilies* (London: Hamish Hamilton, 1996), 4.
2. James A. Schiff, "The Pocket Nothing Else Will Fill: Updike's Domestic God," in James Yerkes (ed.), *John Updike and Religion: The Sense of the Sacred and the Motions of Grace* (Grand Rapids, MI: William B. Eerdmans, 1999), 62.
3. Jack DeBellis, "'It Captivates ... It Hypnotizes.' Updike Goes to the Movies," *Literature/Film Quarterly*, 23, 3 (1995), 169–87.
4. Allison Pearson, "Honest John," *Observer*, 5 May 1996, 14.
5. John Updike, *More Matter: Essays and Criticism* (London: Hamish Hamilton, 1999), 642.
6. Ibid., 643.
7. Martin Jay, *Downcast Eyes: The Denigration of Vision in Twentieth Century French Thought* (Berkeley: University of California Press, 1993).
8. For an excellent account of the relationship between realism and surveillance see Mark Seltzer, "The Princess Casamassima: Realism and the Fantasy of Surveillance," in Eric J. Sundquist (ed.), *American Realism: New Essays* (Baltimore: Johns Hopkins Press, 1982), 95–119.
9. See Judie Newman, *John Updike* (London: Macmillan and New York: St Martin's Press 1988), and "*Rabbit at Rest*: The Return of the Work Ethic," in Lawrence R. Broer (ed.), *Rabbit Tales: Poetry and Politics in Updike's* Rabbit *Tetralogy* (Bowling Green: Bowling Green State University Popular Press, 1998), 189–206.
10. Dilvo I. Ristoff, *John Updike's* Rabbit at Rest: *Appropriating History* (New York: Peter Lang, 1990), 5.
11. John Updike, *Rabbit at Rest* (London: André Deutsch, 1990), 352.
12. Ibid., 436.
13. *Reservoir Dogs*, dir. Quentin Tarantino (Dog Eat Dogs Productions, 1991).
14. The song was written by Gerry Rafferty and Joe Egan (EMI Music Publishing Company, 1974).
15. See Tom McDonough (ed.), *Guy Debord and the Situationist International: Texts and Documents* (Cambridge, MA: MIT Press, 2002), particularly Greil Marcus, "The Long Walk of the Situationist International," 1–20; Thomas Y. Levin, "Dismantling the Spectacle: The Cinema of Guy Debord," 321–454; and Jonathan Crary, "Spectacle, Attention, Countermemory," 455–66. Levin's account of Debord's films is invaluable, given that Debord withdrew them all from exhibition after the murder of his friend Gérard Lebovici in 1984.
16. Guy Debord, *The Society of the Spectacle*, trans. Donald Nicholson-Smith (New York: Zone Books, 1995). First published as *La société du spectacle* (Paris: Buchet-Castel, 1967), 12.
17. Debord, 22.
18. Ibid., 30.
19. Michel de Certeau, *The Practice of Everyday Life*, trans. Steven F. Rendall (Berkeley: University of California Press, 1984), xxi.
20. Michel Foucault, *Surveiller et punir: naissance de la prison* (Paris: Gallimard, 1975).
21. McDonough, *Guy Debord and the Situationist International: Texts and Documents* (Cambridge, MA: MIT Press, 2002.).
22. Updike, *Rabbit at Rest*, 237.
23. Ibid., 77.
24. Ibid., 25.
25. Ibid., 258.
26. Ibid., 161.
27. Debord, 24.
28. Updike, *Rabbit at Rest*, 365.
29. Ibid., 366.
30. Ibid., 138.
31. Ibid., 471.
32. Updike, *More Matter*, 803.
33. Ibid., 804.
34. John Updike, *Rabbit, Run* (London: Penguin, 1964), 26.

35. Updike, *Rabbit at Rest*, 431.
36. Ibid., 442.
37. Ibid., 452.
38. Ibid., 430.
39. Ibid., 452.
40. Louis Prima, the singer, starred as the voice of King Louie in Disney's *The Jungle Book*, before spending years in a coma after a major operation. I am grateful to Jon Bennett, Hugh Brogan and Warren Chernaik for assistance in identifying and commenting on particular songs. Other details are drawn from the individual singers' websites and from the following websites: <http://www.songlyrics4u.com>; <http://www.lyricsfreak.com>; <http://www.oldies.com> [all accessed 26 June 2004].
41. Updike, *Rabbit at Rest*, 453.
42. Ibid.
43. Ibid., 452.
44. Ray was billed as the next Sinatra but assumed by some listeners to be black and/or female. (See David Chappell, University of Arkansas, Fayetteville, "Hip Like Me: Racial Cross-Dressing in Popular Music before the Advent of Elvis," Paper presented on 9th May 1998 at the Martin Luther King Memorial Conference, University of Newcastle Upon Tyne.)
45. Updike, *Rabbit at Rest*, 454.
46. Ibid., 455.
47. Ibid.
48. Neal Ascherson, "Comment," *The Observer*, 3 May, 1998, makes this point about the Situationist legacy.
49. Jay, 423.
50. Updike, *Rabbit at Rest*, 275.
51. Maurice Blanchot, "Everyday Speech," *Yale French Studies*, 73 (1987), 14.
52. John Updike, "Rabbit Remembered," in *Licks of Love* (New York: Knopf, 2000), 297.
53. Ibid., 271.
54. Ibid., 300.
55. Ibid., 297.
56. Ibid., 293.
57. Ibid., 301.
58. Ibid., 340.
59. *American Beauty* (1999) was directed by Sam Mendes and written by Alan Ball. Ball's screenplay, available at <http://scifiscripts.name2host.com/msol/A_B.html> [accessed 26 June 2004], is much less sentimental than the finished film. Jane and Ricky are convicted erroneously of murder and jailed; Carolyn marries her lover after Lester's death, and Angela becomes a film actress.
60. Updike, "Rabbit Remembered," 232.
61. Ibid., 343.
62. Ibid..
63. Ibid..
64. Ibid., 356.
65. Ibid., 346.
66. Ibid., 295.
67. Ibid., 344.
68. Ibid.
69. Ibid., 346.
70. Ibid..
71. Ibid., 252.
72. Ibid., 345.
73. Ibid., 347.
74. Ibid.
75. Ibid., 353.

76. Ibid.
77. Ibid., 357.

CHAPTER 18

Priority Narratives:
Bharati Mukherjee's *Desirable Daughters*

Nobody will deny that this is an age of connectedness, in horizontal terms, with simultaneity of time and the borders of space erased. How do we establish meaningful connections in the general soup of signs in which the modern individual swims? In an Internet world, story links to story, windows open on new stories, and no overall authority establishes priority. James Lull poses the question succinctly:

> The challenge for people today is to navigate and combine an unprecedented range of cultural territories and resources, ranging from relatively unfamiliar terrains imported to the self through technological mediations and human migrations of various types, to territory that is far more familiar and stable, such as that offered by religion, nation and family, in order to invent combinations that satisfy individuals' changing needs and preferences.[1]

One temptation in such a world of rapid change is for people to group "around primary identities: religious, ethnic, territorial, national."[2] In the absence, however, of a dominant code or master-narrative, Lull argues that culture is becoming an individualistic enterprise, in which people create their own supercultures or cultural matrices, becoming in a sense their own "cultural programmers",[3] not merely as consumers or as members of an audience but by actively fusing near and far, traditional and modern, in order to create material and discursive worlds which transform life-experience and reconfigure the meaning of cultural space. Lull's comments are highly suggestive in relation to Bharati Mukherjee's *Desirable Daughters*, and especially to its narrator Tara, whose attempts to centre the story upon her individual experience are repeatedly frustrated by a whirling centrifuge of other stories, alternative models, involving different territories, migrations and mediations.

Mukherjee's novel ranges widely across time and space, with a murder plot which links India, the Indian community in America, and the narrator, Tara Chatterjee, from Calcutta, living, in San Francisco with her lover, a Hungarian refugee, ex-Hells Angel, and now "Zen Master of the Retrofit", proofing Californian homes against the threat of earthquake. As Tara comments,

> I saw my life on a broad spectrum, with Calcutta not at the centre, but just another station on the dial.[4]

Tara's ex-husband Bish made a fortune in computer bandwidth routing technology with his Stanford friend Chet Yee. Bish's story, fairly obviously, recalls that of Sabeer Bhatia, inventor with his Stanford friend Jack Smith, of Hotmail, subsequently sold to Microsoft for $400 million. Bish's globally operating connections threaten to dwarf Tara's individual existence. She writes the novel in order to place herself centre stage, arranging the materials around herself.

As Amitava Kumar comments,

> It is the software writers from India rather than the fiction writers who are wired to the circuits of global production.[5]

One mark of the effect of globalisation upon the novel is the resurgence of interest in theories of the novel which might be termed "Darwinist", "evolutionary" or "sociobiological". Edward O. Wilson argues that literature has a profoundly adaptive function, part of the human urge to create scenarios, reading ahead into distant places or times.[6] Stories thus enable human beings to survive and reproduce better in their environment. In Wilson's example, myths of serpents improve people's chances of vigilance and survival in societies where snakebite is an important cause of mortality.

Wilson also highlights the fashion in which stories frequently focus upon "cheater detection". Contractual agreement pervades human social behaviour and as a result the capacity to detect cheating has developed to exceptional levels. Both points are suggestive in relation to a novel which explores the consequences of snakebite across the centuries, and focuses upon true and false claimants. Wilson's points are of course in some ways blindingly obvious. In *Beyond Ethnicity* Werner Sollors makes a more specific case for considering the function of American stories in relation to family and migration.[7] Sollors emphasises the complicated fashion in which narratives of descent (inherited family ties) intersect with narratives of consent (chosen identities, imagined communities) in the making of an American self. In the American national character, notions of legitimacy and privilege based upon descent are repeatedly denied in favour of the newcomer's rebirth into a forward-looking culture of consent.

What kinds of story are adaptive therefore in a broadband world? What are the "right" stories for globalised citizens? Mukherjee explores the oppositions of tradition and modernity, descent versus consent, through the microcosm of a sibship, as its members adapt to different environments, as "family" stories and "global" plots jockey for position as priority narratives. Mukherjee uses the dynamics of a group of sisters to explore the way a story is claimed, transmitted or denied, how even in the apparent homogeneity of three almost identical sisters divergent roles are created, and what the political consequences are of a place in a sibship, envisaged as a literary model largely replacing "vertical" lines of descent. The desirable daughters, Padma (Didi), Parvati and Tara, are part of an apparently doomed social group, teasingly described in Darwinian terminology, as "homo bengalensis, subspecies Hindu Calcutta, subbreed Ballygunge"[8] a middle-class, conservative, Calcutta-bred clan, "already extinct in our native habitat" (245). The plot turns upon a case of attempted identity theft when Tara finds a stranger, "Chris Dey", claiming to be her nephew. "Chris Dey" addresses Tara in terms which emphasise family intimacy and sisterly kinship, as "Tara-mashi" (34): maternal aunt — referring to a lateral branch of the family. Unknown to her sisters, Didi had given birth to an illegitimate son. As the illegitimate offspring of a Bengali Brahmin's eldest daughter, Chris Dey's existence goes unrecognised. His descent is utterly denied. Before he can claim his heritage, his place is usurped by an interloper who kills him and steals his name and attempts to take his place in the family. By the time Tara establishes the existence of the illegitimate child, the real son is already at the bottom of the sea. The claims of descent are false. The point of the novel is not to re-establish contact with a denied male line, but to focus on a sibship.

The novel begins with the story of the Tree Bride. In its opening epigraph Mukherjee evokes tradition — both as impossible to follow, and as a felt necessity.

> No one behind, no one ahead.
> The path the ancients cleared has closed.
> And the other path, everyone's path,
> Easy and wide, goes nowhere.
> I am alone and find my way.

Mukherjee commented that this Sanskrit verse, adapted by Octavio Paz, translated by Eliot Weinberger, and passed to her by a Bolivian graduate student in Berkeley, embodied "the globalisation that we really want to prize ... that we can take from each other's heritages what we need and sew it together into our heritage".[9]

The opposition between the narrow traditional path and the broad, pathless present is embodied in the contrast between the opening scene of the novel and its broadband present. The novel opens onto a path disappearing into darkness and fog. To any modern reader the action — the arranged marriage of a five-year-old girl — is likely to evoke unease. Everything suggests the horrors of past "darkness" and absence of consent. Such enlightenment as there is, is European and modern. The procession is preceded by servants holding naphtha lamps. "No one has seen such brilliant European light, too strong to stare into" (4). But in a plot device which suspends lines of descent in favour of sibship connection, Tara Lata, the bride, is not about to be transferred to a human bridegroom to continue an ancestral line. She is headed deep into the forest to marry a tree. Her family tree is just that — a large hardwood. Indian lack of light is apparently the cause; the groom has died of snakebite in the dark, and Tara Lata has been transformed into an unmarriageable girl, who brings ill fortune. For a solution her father turns to Hindu custom. In marrying her to a proxy-husband, a tree, and burying her dowry gold beneath it, he permits her to occupy the respected position of married woman, within the family home. What appears to be a bizarre practice is in fact a highly efficient adaptive strategy. The apparent return to tradition is also a revolt against modernity. Tara Lata becomes famous for acts of rebellion and she becomes a freedom fighter and martyr.

Paradoxically, therefore, in pursuing Indian tradition and confining his daughter to a life without the distractions of husband, children and mother-in-law, the father transforms her into a rebel. Faced with rapid change, he has opted for an apparently "primary" identity, potentially validating a nationalist past against the diminished claims of the modern present. "Enlightenment" is apparently discredited; the inventive traditionalist secures his daughter's place in the world by a fiction of marriage which returns her unscathed to her sisters.

But why has Tara chosen to tell this story? Tara's own story is ostensibly that of an entirely untraditional Bengali-American who has rebelled against the life of an Indian wife, and set up home with a lover in a multi-ethnic neighbourhood almost synonymous with revolt: the Haight. Hers is emphatically a broadband world. As students at Stanford her husband Bish discovered a process for allowing computers to create their own time, instantaneously routing information to the least congested lines (24). Bish is part of the process of globalisation, the process by which people become increasingly interconnected across natural borders and continents. His mobile phone routing devices connect the whole world. Bish's discovery was prompted by a football game in which the players exploited the "West coast offense", a tactic in which short passing plays replace the running game, to control the ball. The lateral throws have the effect of stopping the clock and buying time. The bandwidth system, called CHATTY, is about width "using the whole field, connecting in the flat, no interference, a billion short passes linked together" (24). It is also the method of Mukherjee's novel. In interview Mukherjee said that

> The aesthetic strategy of the book was using the width of the field — of history, geography, diaspora, gender, ethnicity, language — rather than the old-fashioned long, clean throw.[10]

So, what happens in the novel is that the reader is passed from story to story across a broad geographical and historical sweep; the narrative passes from one controller to another, with the story moving forward through changes of direction, and side-passes. The straight trajectory of a story based on descent is replaced by a model which involves side connections, sibships and lateral moves. Arguably, through the connectedness of information, and the shrinking of space and time, all our histories intersect in the modern world. We can no longer move back onto the traditional narrow path; we are in the same time with interconnecting histories, and an awareness of time as space. Bish's discovery underlines the sense in the novel of a complex network of connections in which people are both receivers and senders across a very broad field, where routers are as important as roots. Tara is faced with a variety of shared histories and has to reconfigure her own cultural space, becoming to some extent a cultural programmer, navigating a range of cultural territories. In a metaphor drawn from anti-earthquake technology the story concerns the problems of how, given the seismic shifts in people's lives, we can "retrofit", making for a secure structure, without embracing either rickety traditions or a simplistic fundamentalism, how we relate tradition and modernity in the new networked world.

Tara's connection to the Tree Bride is not, therefore, a connection back to a secure, primordial identity, steeped in religious tradition, but to a rebel. She feels a profound connection to the Tree Bride, as a member of a sibship; both had two sisters.

To an external eye, Tara's sisters are very alike. All share a birthday; all have played the same roles in the same operettas at the same convent school; all are docile to parental expectations. But the apparent homogeneity is an illusion. The novel excavates their histories in explicit relation to theories — not of descent through the generations — but of sibship and birth order, to place the emphasis on rebellion rather than conformity. It is not for nothing that the father, the Tree Bride, and Tara Chatterjee are all third children.

What I want to suggest is that Mukherjee deliberately casts her discussion of the relation of tradition to modernity in the context not of vertical lines of descent and consent but in terms of sibships and lateral familial connections, a model which is suggestively related to a networked world. Alfred Adler argued that a major determinant of personality is birth order.[11] However apparently alike, siblings are not actually born into the same family. By birth order children will hold different positions, and their quest for identity, power and attention is influenced by their sequential positions as siblings. Each child is born onto a different "stage" in the family home and learns to perform a script with the help of parents who try to direct the play. The firstborn is born into a small family and receives a great deal of attention; laterborns have to find different ways to earn centre stage. Because they are not so strongly watched and disciplined by parents, the laterborn may have more freedom to create an individual personality. Firstborns tend to be conservative and rule-bound. They arrive first and then use their superior power to defend the status quo. Firstborns understand power precisely because they have been "dethroned" and have lost it. For laterborns the rules are less rigid and they have to look within themselves for latent talents that can be identified through systematic experimentation, in order to find a niche.

Although Adler did not spell out the political implications, Frank J. Sulloway's bestseller, *Born to Rebel*, advanced the argument that during socially radical revolutions, laterborns have been much more likely than firstborns to adapt revolutionary alternatives. In his hypothesis, laterborns opt for radical rebellion; firstborns try to preserve a waning orthodoxy or at best opt for reform. During the Protestant Reformation, for example, laterborns were nine times more likely than firstborns to suffer martyrdom for the new faith; firstborns five times more likely to die for the old. Democratic presidents show a consistent tendency to nominate laterborns to the Supreme Court. All appointments made by Kennedy and Johnson were laterborn. "At the level of the US Supreme Court, sibling differences determine the laws of the land."[12] Firstborns are more likely to be involved in war: Roosevelt, Mussolini, Churchill, Stalin. Middle children, who cannot resist older siblings and cannot be aggressive to the "baby" below, are flexible and favour compromise, coalitions and non-violence: Martin Luther King, the second of three. Trotsky, Castro, Danton, Lenin and Yasser Arafat are all laterborns.

Siblings are thus very different politically and philosophically despite similar backgrounds. Birth order theory is a Darwinian story. Tara's son Rabi is completing a school science project, to "illustrate a panel of Galápagos finches" (55), an explicit reference to Darwin's study of the finches which demonstrates the principle that diversity is a useful strategy. Different species find different spaces and avoid competing for food. Similarly, children develop different interests and abilities to minimise direct competition. The three sisters occupy different places on the family stage. Didi, the eldest, earns her living as a traditional Indian performance artist. Parvati shares her family space with a constantly changing cast of extended family members and consequently lives in a world of compromise. As the third child, Tara repeatedly finds herself displaced, her own story spiked in favour of somebody else's more compelling narrative. Like a sibling being pushed aside, her story of Chris Dey is repeatedly dismissed. Every time that Tara is about to take hold of the story she is upstaged, or recast by more powerful directors who briskly absorb her into *their* cultural plots. In the quest for truth she is continually deflected by a more able cultural programmer, making sense of the world by telling a different story, or (in a repeated metaphor) running a different movie. The novel thus replaces an Oedipal narrative in which the yoke of parents, colonial history or tradition, has to be thrown off, in favour of a sibling story, less vertical and more horizontal. Siblings are like broadband, occupying different positions in the field.

In India Tara's identity was fixed by family identity. In America Tara enjoys the ability to invent and reinvent herself, as a "border-crashing claimant of all people's legacies" (79). But the arrival of "Chris Dey", another border-crashing self-inventor, destroys Tara's certainties. Tara's reaction is not to challenge her big sister directly but to first seek an ally in her middle sister. But when Tara telephones to describe the invading Chris Dey, she finds Parvati in the midst of a real invasion. Robbers have broken into the building and beaten a neighbour to death. Suddenly the story is really about Parvati and her burglar. When Tara visits Jack Singh Sidhu, to get police help, she is infuriated to realise that he sees her use of her maiden name as an attempt to conceal her real identity. For Singh, the story is about Bish. The global story is the priority story. Millionaire Bish is the real target. Or is the story about Rabi? In a letter he makes it clear that while Tara has seen "Chris Dey" as the interloper at the heart of the family, Rabi sees things differently. "This is not about him, either the real one or the fake. It is about me, another kind of fake" (163). The title of Rabi's school play says it all ("Ma, I am gay", 165). Rabi's story takes priority over that of Chris Dey, just as Bish had displaced Tara in Jack's version of the plot, just as Parvati's story of robbery and murder eclipsed Tara's story of the nephew. Tara has been competing ineffectually in the family sphere, waved into the wings by others whose stories are always centre stage.

So should Tara opt instead for a return to Didi and tradition? Just as her role as a child was to act out the parental script, so Didi has adopted even more traditional roles, staging Indian mythological evenings. She appears to have found an individual place on the stage which successfully unites family and nation. When she invites Tara to a party, she provides her with a new hairstyle, manicure, "museum quality" designer sari and traditional gold jewellery. Failed rebellion gives way, apparently, to museumised tradition. What Tara does not realise is that Didi has actually inserted her into quite a different script. The party has its own economy. The sari which Didi loans Tara is actually for sale, as is the twenty-four-carat gold jewellery. As the star of a TV shopping channel, Didi is an icon to the Indian community and her parties are "a kind of home shopping service for upscale Indians" (231). Tara's hair was cut, the better to display the earrings to busy businessmen and their normally stay-at-home wives; the sari is designed to expose sufficient cleavage to show off the necklace. It dawns on Tara that she is performing in an advertising stunt, with tradition exploited to consumerist ends. Ironically, she is at her most "traditional" when most commodified.

When her own phone rings, Tara is reconnected to Bish (in a hot tub in Brisbane). Bish appears omnipotent, better-protected than half the world heads of state with "no end to the technical and human networks he commanded" (256). He has an assembly plant in Bangalore, a marketing arm in Bombay, and a start-up in Bangladesh. His connections create an empire which overrides national boundaries and hostilities. Indeed, he is about to evade the limits of time and space. Flying back from Australia to San Francisco, he will be "back some time before we leave" (256). The modern world appears to offer a straight connection to truth, courtesy of the efficiency and directness of modern communications technology. Jack confirms via cell phone that Chris Dey is a member of the Dawood gang, a criminal cartel controlling crime in Bombay, with major interests in Bollywood movies. Tara may be "in a movie" in a more sinister sense than she imagines. Ruefully Tara registers "the joys of globalization" (223). Modern connectivity has its darker side. Manuel Castells has highlighted the emergence of global crime, the networking of powerful criminal organisations across the planet, as a relatively new phenomenon; in his argument criminal penetration of financial markets constitutes a critical element in a fragile global economy, and an essential feature of the information Age.[13] Mukherjee herself has good reason to be aware of the transnationality of crime. In *The Sorrow and the Terror* (on the 1985 Air India bombing) she drew attention to world-wide Sikh fundraising and cyberterrorism, and to the laxness of airport security.[14] As a result she found herself stalked and under death threat for two years. Globalisation connects the Indian Dawood gang across the globe, threatening security and destroying identities. Fundamentalism can exploit the same networks and synergies. If traditionalism can be transposed into radical revolt (like the Tree Bride), modern globalisation can do the reverse, hand in glove with the forces of coercive and fundamentalist tradition.

At the close of the novel Bish is seriously injured by a bomb, triggered by a reconfigured cellphone. CHATTY's stock value plunges, upsetting the world economy. The reader ends the novel convinced that the target was Bish, that the bomber was part of an international globalised criminal network, and that the aim was financial. The false Chris is the product of a world in which it is easy to make global connections, communications are swift, and no border is impenetrable, a post-9/11 world. Modernity is to blame, and it appears as if the father at the start was right to resist the modern world.

But there is a catch. This is volume one of a projected trilogy, in which volume two, *The Tree Bride*, is in some sense the heir to volume one, inheriting its characters and history. In this case many of the conclusions of the first volume (concerning the motivations for a bombing) are reversed or negated in the second. And the third volume — potentially altering the story again — has yet to appear. In this respect the novel sequence is peculiarly contemporary. In the putative trilogy, the second story takes over the stage from the first, dethroning its authority as priority narrative, but is itself (as the reader is well aware) vulnerable to the appearance of a third story. The parallel is explicitly to the three daughters of the title, and their lateral broadband connections.

Notes to Chapter 18

1. James Lull, "Superculture for the Communication Age," in James Lull (ed.), *Culture in the Communication Age* (New York and London: Routledge, 2001), 138.
2. Manuel Castells, *The Rise of Network Society* (Oxford: Blackwell, 1996), 3.
3. Lull, 136.
4. Bharati Mukherjee, *The Tree Bride* (New York: Hyperion, 2004), 20.
5. Amitava Kumar, "Passages to India," *Nation*, 24 April 2000, 39.
6. Edward O. Wilson, *Consilience: The Unity of Knowledge* (New York: Little, Brown, 1998), 77ff.
7. Werner Sollors, *Beyond Ethnicity: Consent and Descent in American Culture* (New York: Oxford University Press, 1986).
8. Bharati Mukherjee, *Desirable Daughters* (New York: Hyperion, 2002), 245. Subsequent page references follow quotations in parentheses.
9. "Bharati Mukherjee in Conversation with Barbara Lane". www.commonwealthclub.org/ archive/02/02–05mukherjee-speech.html (accessed 9 May 2002), 2.
10. Dave Welch, "Bharati Mukherjee Runs the West Coast Offense," <http//www/powells.com/ authors/mukherjee/html> (accessed 13 October 2004).
11. In what follows I draw upon and paraphrase, Frank J. Sulloway, "Sibling-Order Birth Effects," 14059, at <http://www.sulloway.org/sibling-orderEffects 1200D.pdf> (accessed 28 October 2005); "Forum and Debate on Birth Order," <http://inst.santafe.cc.fl.us?~mwehr/gepsyc/ FMBirord.html> (accessed 29 October 2005); Alfred Adler, *Understanding Human Nature* (Greenberg: New York, 1927). Adler recognised, of course, the importance of other factors such as sex order, parental age, cultural, religious and social beliefs, but none the less saw birth order as a very important factor.
12. Sulloway, 295.
13. Manuel Castells, *End of Millennium* (Oxford: Blackwell, 2000), 210.
14. Clark Blaise and Bharati Mukherjee, *The Sorrow and the Terror: The Haunting Legacy of the Air India Tragedy* (New York: Viking 1987). See also "Bill Moyers Interviews Bharati Mukherjee," Transcript. PBS, 20 May 2003.

CHAPTER 19

Blowback: André Dubus III's
House of Sand and Fog

Since Seymour Hersh published an article in the *New Yorker* in April 2006, exposing an apparent Pentagon plan to attack Iran, an attack in which for the first time since Hiroshima the use of nuclear weapons was contemplated, Iran has become a focus of American attention.[1] It was not always thus. As Gary Sick observes, before the Iranian hostage crisis, Iran hardly even evoked a stereotype for the United States citizen, not even in the way China, Egypt or India did.[2] At best, as Persia, it might suggest cats, carpets and caviar. American awareness of Iran was characterised by a combination of ignorance and wholesale amnesia. For Hamid Dabashi the invasion plan raised the question "of hegemony and Empire — one with or without the other." Did the American empire have a hegemonic project or ideological agenda? Or was it just making a mess all over the world?[3] Recent debates have focussed keenly on this question of the degree to which the American state knows what it is doing and consciously pursues imperialist aims. For Niall Ferguson it is an empire which dare not speak its name, an "imperialism of anti-imperialism", posing as liberationist.[4] Hardt and Negri simply portray American domination as corresponding with economic domination.[5] In his Empire trilogy (*Blowback*, *Nemesis* and *The Sorrows of Empire*) Chalmers Johnson equates empire with militarism, based upon American armed forces stationed in foreign countries, whether in an advisory and support capacity, or in the 737 US bases in some 130 countries which he counted in 2006, and described as "a planet-spanning baseworld" of foreign enclaves which function as parasitical neocolonies completely beyond the jurisdiction of the occupied nation.[6] For Johnson, most US imperialism operates as a "stealth imperialism" well below the sightlines of the American public.[7] Americans' ignorance about their country's operations also explains why attacks on Americans are greeted with cries of shock and outrage. In his analysis Johnson adopts the term "blowback", first invented by officials of the CIA to refer to

> the unintended consequences of policies that were kept secret from the American people. What the daily press report as the malign acts of "terrorists" or "drug lords" or "rogue states" or "illegal arms merchants" often turn out to be blowback from earlier American operations.[8]

Examples would include the 1988 Lockerbie bombing, blowback from the 1986

Reagan administration's raid on Libya which killed Gaddafi's stepdaughter; or the epidemic of cocaine use in US cities fuelled by Central and Southern Americans whom the CIA or the Pentagon had supported in Nicaragua. (The Contras made deals to sell cocaine in the US to buy arms and supplies.) Because we live in an increasingly interconnected, globalised system, we are all living in a blowback world, though the time lags between events, and the distancing effects of geographical displacements, tend to erase the causative links. "The unintended consequences of American policies and acts in country X are a bomb at an American embassy in country Y or a dead American in country Z."[9] In these circumstances it is easy for memory to falter — or to be erased. Dabashi argues that the US propaganda machinery is contingent on a systematic loss of collective memory, as if America really had moved, in Francis Fukuyama's formulation, beyond history.[10]

In this connection Iran brings the issue of what Americans know into sharp focus, as the recent controversy over Azar Nafisi's memoir, *Reading Lolita in Tehran*, indicates. Memoirs by and about Iranian women have become exceptionally popular in America, with at least eight mass-market titles published in the last seven years.[11] For Gillian Whitlock such memoirs are "soft weapons", used to buttress aggressive Western intervention in other countries. Life narratives of this type, emphasising the oppression of Muslim women, play to Western traditions of benevolence, masking privilege, reifying dominant social relations, and naturalising the neoliberal discourse of the free circulation of ideas, goods and peoples in global networks of exchange.[12] (Whitlock gleefully notes the participation of Nafisi in a marketing campaign for Audi automobiles. For the promoters, Nafisi was fashionably cool: "Azar is to literature what Audi is to cars."[13]) An Iranian commentator similarly argues that memoir-writers are deeply enmeshed in the politics of rendering Iran from a transnational perspective, making Iranians "Other" in a neo-Orientalist discourse, authored by American-identified women.[14] Hamid Dabashi portrays Nafisi as a comprador intellectual, functioning as a feigned "native observer", claiming a fake authority and authenticity.[15] In his view, her book supports the US agenda for Iran, particularly by propagating a view of Islam as violent and abusive to women. Fighting against Islamic terrorism becomes a means of saving Muslim women from the evil of their men: Laura Bush famously justified the US invasion of Afghanistan as an opportunity to liberate Afghani women from the gender hierarchies of the Taliban.[16] This is a tactic which is a continuation of a similar strategy employed by the British in India (the campaign against sati) and China (the campaign against footbinding) and memorably characterised by Gayatri Spivak as "white men saving brown women from brown men".[17] The Empire intervenes in a mode of "human rights imperialism", justifying intervention by its humanitarian and liberationist mission. This is not the place to discuss in detail the controversy over Nafisi's portrayal of Iran, ably tackled by Fatehmeh Keshavarz and John Carlos Rowe, respectively.[18] It is worth noting, however, that Nafisi's own text is amnesiac. In a lengthy, and largely pro-American, discussion of the modern history of Iran she never mentions the CIA coup of 1953, which reinstated the Shah in power.

André Dubus's novel *House of Sand and Fog* (1999) makes an important counterbalance to Nafisi and her fellow memorialists, engaging with the issues for which "blowback" will serve as shorthand, exploring how the forgotten past returns to plague an ignorant American and how "human rights imperialism", particularly the use of gendered horrors to legitimate Western domination, manages to compound the damage. Where memoirs risk functioning as a means of making Iran other to America, *House of Sand and Fog* pursues a narrative strategy which makes Iranians into Americans — and Americans into Iranians. In its themes and techniques the novel establishes the intersection of distance and knowledge as its key concern. *House of Sand and Fog* is the first American bestseller centred on a Muslim protagonist; it was a finalist for the National Book Award, enthusiastically adopted by Oprah Winfrey, made into a major film, and has some 2 million copies in print. As Donna Seaman commented, it depicts "a microcosmic conflict of profound cultural implications".[19] The novel imports a wealthy Iranian refugee family to California to do battle with a working class Italian-American woman over their rival claims to their own place in America, a house. Kathy Lazaro, a recovering cocaine addict, with no connections to, or understanding of, American oil-politics in the Middle East, loses her house through a bureaucratic error to Massood Behrani, formerly a colonel in the Shah's Iran. Behrani and his traditional Muslim wife are pitted against the sexy, self-indulgent Kathy, and her policeman lover, Lester. The city has sent a tax bill to the wrong place, evicts Kathy for non-payment and auctions the house at a knockdown price. When the error is discovered the Colonel agrees to sell the house back, but only at full market value. Fairly obviously there are sizable issues at play in the fight to the death which follows, as a downwardly mobile "old" immigrant confronts the upward mobility of the new immigrant. Kathy, a domestic cleaner who inherited the house from her father, is only a slip away from the underclass, living in a recognisably blue-collar America of truck stops, diners, cheap motels, and country-and-western music. The Colonel almost appears to be living in a different country entirely, in a city made up of recent immigrants, as he drives through Japan Town, past Spanish-speaking areas, and Iraqi and Nicaraguan businesses.

Kathy's Kafkaesque nightmare seems entirely undeserved. She thought the mistake had been rectified, has ignored the letters from the tax officials, and doesn't know that her house is about to be repossessed. Throughout, she is characterised by ignorance. She repeatedly describes the Behranis as "Arabs", talking "Arabic or Israeli" (73), and names them variously as Bahroony, Behmini and Barmeeny.[20] She has about as much awareness of Iran as she has of the origins of her cocaine supply. It is beyond her to envisage that her life as an ordinary American might be affected because America supported a corrupt and torturing regime. The Colonel, however, sees himself as a victim of events; he buys the house in all innocence as an opportunity to follow American ideals and climb up the property ladder. Confronted by Kathy, he feels "accused of a crime I did not commit" (135). The suspicion lingers, however, that as a member of the Iranian military, he may have been complicit in other crimes which were committed. The novel takes considerable risks in the way it sets up this conflict. Does a rapacious Oriental dispossess an American of her lawful inheritance? Or has Kathy a false sense of her entitlement? Is the Colonel (hardworking, disciplined and a firm believer in the American dream) the true heir to America? Is Kathy an unfortunate victim? Or a messy, self-indulgent woman, dissipating everything her father worked for in a cokestorm, a representative of the soft underbelly of a decadent America? Or was that cokestorm itself also the result of American support of corrupt foreign regimes? To what extent are the protagonists innocent — or ignorant? And is their absence of knowledge culpable and in some senses intentional?

Dubus's plot is carefully designed to emphasise the long history of American involvement in Iran. The Behranis flee Iran one week after the fall of the Shah (January 1979) and reach America with $280,000. The Iranian Islamic Revolution of 1979 came as a complete surprise to Americans. It was only in November 1978 that US foreign policy experts began to see that the Shah was faltering.[21] (It is usually seen as one of the CIA's greatest predictive failures.)[22] The violent Anti-Americanism which followed, the storming of the US embassy with fifty-two Americans held hostage for fourteen months, was an even greater shock to a public which thought they were rather well liked in Iran. What Americans did not "know" was the long-term effect of the 1953 CIA-sponsored coup which removed Mossadeq, an elected leader, to protect US access to Iranian oil. Most analysts agree that America intervened in 1953 largely out of ignorance, in the mistaken belief, fed to them by the British, that Mossadeq, a conservative, was turning towards Communism. Effectively Eisenhower removed a moderately democratic government to install a repressive dictatorship. In 1953 the Shah fled at the first sign of trouble, and returned only with US support. In 1979 the Shah entered America on 22 October and as a result on 4 November the Tehran embassy was overrun. Iranians remembered that the US had previously returned the Shah to his throne and they feared a repetition. The 1979 revolution was, in many respects, blowback from the 1953 coup.

It is no accident that the Colonel is in the airforce, and previously bought F-16s from the Americans, nor that he retains the trappings of wealth, nor that he has gravitated to San Francisco, home of Lockheed and Boeing. As an airforce officer he has benefited disproportionately from American largesse. The Shah's reign was characterised by militarism and excess. In the period between 1953 and 1957 alone, the US provided $500 million to Iran, one quarter of it earmarked for the military.[23] The Shah's defence budget was never less that 23% of the general budget. American aid and technological assistance also established the secret police, SAVAK, answering directly to the Shah, run by men with military backgrounds and regulated only by military tribunals. Interrogation, torture and imprisonment without trial were so commonplace that in 1974 Amnesty International described Iran as having the worst human rights record in the world.[24] The Shah's principal aide for military procurement was an air force general; the Shah took a keen interest in the airforce, even in the appointment of middle-ranking officers. (The Colonel is pictured with the Shah in a photograph prominently displayed in the living room.) Writing before the revolution, Robert Graham noted that

By virtue of their role as defenders of the throne — not of the realm — the Officer corps has become a privileged class. Their pay and fringe benefits put NATO to shame, including the provision of villas, domestic personnel, low taxes on luxury goods and holiday compounds.[25]

Effectively Iran was a US military base, policing the Persian Gulf for America. Successive Presidents allowed an enormous arms build-up and sent in technical personnel to support sophisticated weaponry. Modernisation on the Western model was marked by excess, memorably condemned by Khomeini as "Westoxification". The Persepolis celebrations of 2,500 years of monarchy, in October 1971, cost $100 million, with French chefs from Maxims serving up dishes of Breast of Peacock on Limoges porcelain. (At this point Tehran still lacked a sewage system.) In *House of Sand and Fog* Kathy does not lose her house to an invading "Other" but to an American citizen, the product of American past policies. Behrani buys the house with money which can only be American in origin.

Given Dubus's Marxist training it is tempting to see Behrani's refusal to sell the house back at less than its full market value as a neat demonstration that "property is theft", and that capitalist economics underwrite the final disaster. But Kathy's outrage is also reminiscent of the Western reaction to the Iranians when Mossadeq nationalised the Anglo-Iranian oil company, and demanded a fair market price from the West, instead of the notional 16 per cent which had previously been paid.[26] The Colonel wants a fair price for his assets and a legal profit. He has shored up American access to cheap oil, and in some respects has a claim to a rightful share in the economy. At the risk of making a banal observation, Dubus continually emphasises the American reliance on cheap gasoline. The novel opens with an emblematic scene in which the Colonel, along with Panamanian, Vietnamese and Chinese workers, toils in the hot sun on the southbound lanes of Route 101. The Colonel has become one of the "garbage soldiers" (17), spearing refuse for the Highways department, a soldier of lesser rank but still part of the infrastructure of an oil-based economy. On the way home he admires the mansions of Pacific Heights with their Porsches, Jaguars and Lamborghinis, "the cars of the old Tehran" (20) where he had himself enjoyed the use of a huge Mercedes equipped with TV, telephone and bar. Even now he drives a Buick Regal, carefully stowed in the garage of a luxury hotel, to conceal his servile day job from his fellow exiles. Four nights a week he works in a convenience store, attached to a gas station. Kathy never connects the Colonel to her own home. Yet when she loses it she tells Lester wryly that she is "staying at the Bonneville" (85), in other words living in her car, one of the larger gas-guzzlers, given to her by her brother, an auto-dealer. (When she tells him that her husband has left her, he merely asks, "Did he take the Pontiac?", 197.) Kathy's father bought the house from the profits of a delivery business; she remembers long hours in his van. Dispossessed, she relies on gas station restrooms and spends her time in aimless driving. Later, as her sense of dispossession becomes more acute, she acquires some hardware (Lester carelessly supplies her with his gun) and drunkenly holds up a gas station to get fuel to attack and burn out the Behranis — a violent American stealing someone else's oil.

If both Kathy and the Colonel embody the operation of American petropolicies, the role of shoring up a dictatorship by force falls to Lester, a field-training officer in the local police. Earlier in the novel the Colonel remembered an encounter with a young Iranian policeman, a Savaki, who told him that the way to interrogate "subversives" was to focus on their children. "Make a subversive watch his little one lose a hand or arm and they will tell you everything" (61). In an attempt to make the Colonel give the house back, Lester (minus his badge but in uniform) visits the Colonel and tells him, "You have a family. I'd be thinking more about them if I were you" (168). Behrani makes the connection immediately to the possibility that "America has its officials who operate over the law" (170), "dark men in suits, Savakis" (170). Effectively the apparent "Others" have swapped places. Formerly American power was masked behind Savak; now the masks are removed. Lester is a Savaki; the American steals oil by force; the Colonel's rank and power are stripped away to reveal a dirty soldier, keeping Americans on the road.

Narrative method enforces the underlying connections between the apparently oppositional characters. Dubus divides the novel into two parts. In the first, events centre upon responsibility; "Not knowing" drives the plot, and becomes an effect of the narrative method, which confronts the reader with a corrective perspective. Part One is alternately narrated by the Colonel in first person and present tense, and Kathy, also in first person, but in the past. The sequential arrangement of events (first the Colonel, then Kathy, with her narrative looping back over events which the reader has already witnessed first hand) places Kathy in the position of the unaware American. In section 16, for example, covering Wednesday and Thursday, Kathy celebrates what she believes is the imminent return of her house.[27] But the reader has already reached Friday with the Colonel, and knows that following the lawyer's advice on Thursday, he is not going to give it back. Kathy is the person who does not know, whereas the reader is often superior in knowledge and watches a naïve American who is clearly about to come to grief. Kathy's use of the past tense suggests a desire to distance herself from involvement in events, which she narrates as fixed in time and unchangeable. In contrast the Colonel's present places reader and character "in" events simultaneously. We share his narrative space, without any of the distancing effects of a time lag, whereas we look back on Kathy as if in a past arena. Temporal distance reverses spatial distance. Iran is right in our lap; the American is operating at a distance. The two individual narratives at first encourage an oppositional reading — as if the reader were weighing up a balance sheet of rights and wrongs, Kathy versus the Colonel. Kathy's brother believes in resolving a problem by the balance-sheet method: "On one side of the page you got your costs and on the other side your benefits. All you do is mark which one is which, then you weigh one side against the other and you get your decision" (84). Kathy, however, is not very good at telling a plus from a minus, a benefit from a cost. Nor is her opposition to the Colonel so clear-cut. Slowly parallelism operates to bring them closer together, and to make sense of the one through reference to the other. The novel thus demonstrates that the "I" has no story of its own which is not also the story of a relation or set of relations. As Judith Butler puts it, "When the I seeks to give an account of itself, it can start with itself, but it will find that this self is already implicated in a social temporality that exceeds its own capacities for narration."[28]

Throughout the first part of the novel a series of parallel events remind the reader that responsibility is shared, that ignorance is not innocence, and that "not knowing" causes disaster. Americans become Iranians imagistically, just as Iranians became Americans. The plot erases the distance between the two by bringing the results of foreign policies into the domestic sphere. Evicted, Kathy is advised to keep her distance and avoid returning to her former home. As Gerald Turkel notes, when the law takes control of a dispute, procedural and spatial boundaries are established to control and direct the conflict in ways that limit the direct expression of animosity.[29] Not here, however: Kathy steadily breaks down the distance, accosting the Colonel's workmen, haranguing potential buyers, entering the house to plead with his wife, and finally staging a suicide attempt on the doorstep, until she is back in her own bedroom. She invades the house to force an awareness of his error on the Colonel, and to demand reparation. Throughout, she is motivated by the desire to conceal the truth from her family. They do not know that her husband has left her, or that she has lost the family inheritance. Similarly, the Colonel's children do not know that he is slaving in menial jobs, to keep up appearances so that his daughter Soraya can make a suitable marriage. He withholds the true situation from his wife, Nadi, who does not know that the house was auctioned in error. "Not knowing" is the engine of the plot, and of the novel's exploration of individual responsibility.

The parallels also establish that it is not difference which unleashes violence but sameness under the skin. Parallel events occur in successive units of narration with events in the Colonel's life mirrored in Kathy's account. In the fifth section, for example, Behrani recalls Nadi's accusation that they were forced to flee (and are now on a death list) "because of you, you and your SAVAK friends" (57). Behrani denies any responsibility for SAVAK: "I purchased fighter jets. I was not with SAVAK" (58). Recalling, however, the encounter with the torturer (American-trained), he becomes uncomfortable. He "did not like to be reminded of the secret police", the role of America, or that "this was the manner in which our king retained his throne and our way of life" (62). The Colonel met the torturer at his friend General Pourat's house, at a highly ceremonialised drinking party where the oldest man ritually serves the vodka to the younger ones, regulating their consumption and implicitly keeping their excesses under control. The traditional way of life depends, however, upon more sinister controls; the authority of the older man is only a politer version of a repressive dictatorship. From the account of this group meeting, the novel moves immediately to Kathy recalling her inability to control her drinking and drug use. She attends the group meetings of a rehabilitation programme, Rational Recovery, which emphasises that irrational behaviour and beliefs can be overcome by the use of our reason.[30] In Rational Recovery the addict creates a personification of the compulsive thoughts tempting him to drink: the Beast (65). The Beast is actually seductive and internal, but Kathy is encouraged by the programme to see it as an occupying force, an "Other" and alien threat, rather than the result of her own weakness. Once externalised, it can be attacked. Kathy actually prefers Alcoholics Anonymous, which is based on the idea that our behaviour is caused by circumstances over which we have no control. RR insists on personal accountability; AA on surrendering all responsibility to a higher power. Predictably, Kathy loves it, especially the group meetings with everyone "telling their stories and backing each other up, nobody any wiser and more together than anyone else" (65). In telling her own story, Kathy presents herself as a powerless victim, pushed around by the state authorities and under alien occupation. As the Colonel takes over her house, so the Beast takes over Kathy. The Colonel on the other hand sees through the apparently benign controls of the Iranian male hierarchy to the punitive reality at its centre. The parallel memories offer an oblique comment on the novel itself, as the reader switches between the disciplined Colonel and the powerless Kathy, giving their rival accounts of themselves.

From drink to sex: the following sequence expands the parallelism between the two, through parallel erotic encounters. Nadi invites the Colonel to her room (a fairly rare occurrence for him); Kathy makes love with Lester. Earlier the Colonel had reproached his wife for her hypocrisy over SAVAK. "She never complained of the maids and soldiers she used for the upkeep of our home ... or of our bungalow there overlooking the Caspian" (58). Nor did she object when they were automatically taken to the front of the cinema line, despite the fear visible in the manager's eyes. Now, freed from the need to keep up appearances, "free of our own masquerade, our own lies" (81), the Colonel feels once again like the young man on his wedding night. Sex eliminates time and distance, restoring an innocent past. Similarly, Kathy, in bed with Lester, feels "sixteen all over again" (94). In the patrol car with Lester, however, she notices the fear of the other drivers, all of them moderating their speed and avoiding eye contact — just like the cinema manager in Iran. Two formal social occasions follow: Kathy and Lester go out on a proper date, for dinner at the Hyatt. The Behranis host a party for Soraya on her return from her honeymoon. Both situations appear to offer a clearer view through the previous fog of lies: the Behranis entertain on their "Widow's walk" with a vista to the ocean; the Hyatt features a revolving restaurant with a clear view of the landscape in the round. The Colonel explains the situation with the house to his son; Lester decides to tell his wife everything and end "this masquerade ball I've been at for years" (121). But their disclosures are only partial. Kathy tells Lester that drinking was her husband's problem, not hers, and promptly falls off the wagon. Lester's "not knowing" that she has real problems with alcohol is a major contributory factor to the final disaster. Kathy also edits her past to focus only on herself as a young girl, to avoid mentioning her first husband, divorce, rehab and suicide attempts. Similarly, Soraya, horrified at finding her parents in a small bungalow and desperate to keep up appearances in front of her mother-in-law, spends the party reminiscing about her life as a young girl in Tehran, enjoying parties and calls from the Shah. The Colonel has not told Nadi his problems because he wants her cheerful and innocent as a child, and has maintained "this mask for my children" (164), never explaining their difficult financial situation. Assuming a false responsibility for his women, treating them as irresponsible children, is ultimately destructive. His lack of candour with Soraya poisons their relationship. Nadi retreats from him into the music of Googoosh, a music "of romantics ignorant of any history but their own" (213).[31] Kathy is so unwilling to reveal the truth to her mother that all communication between them breaks down.

The parallels establish a resemblance between the apparent opposites and draw them together across their narrative separations, before the plot erupts into the violence of Part Two. At the mid-point of the novel a tenuous resolution is reached with Kathy once more back in her own bedroom, sheltered by the Behranis who have saved her life. Implicitly the novel makes the point that the recognition of guilty responsibility is more likely to produce a solution than forcible intervention and the re-occupation of the moral high ground. The reader absorbs both narratives, sees the parallels and erases the apparent distance between them to establish a shared position. In the words of one reviewer, "the hope for a home that is free of the stranger, a home that is all mine, and not also partly yours, is an illusion built on the most unsteady ground".[32]

The tragedy of the novel is initiated with a change in narrative focalisation. In Part Two Lester suddenly emerges as the focaliser of the story, in third person and past tense, a third party erupting into the narrative, upsetting a precarious balance and taking charge of events. Feeling neglected by Kathy and "shut out" (268), not knowing about her drinking problems, he smashes into the kitchen, in the mistaken belief that she needs rescuing, and goes on to hold the Behranis hostage to force the return of the house. Lester's intervention, motivated by his desire to protect Kathy against "brown men", triggers comprehensive disaster. By the close of the novel the Colonel, his wife and son are dead, Lester's family has broken apart, and he and Kathy are facing lengthy jail terms. Part One sets up an initial opposition over the disputed territory, but eventually associates Kathy and the Colonel, both American citizens, both complicit, both learning to recognise a degree of responsibility. Part Two demonstrates the dangers of premature intervention on the basis of situational ignorance. Whatever the difficulties of resolving the dispute over the house, it is Lester's intervention which seals everyone's doom. He is the logical extension of the Colonel's desire to protect women, viewed as innocent children who are not fully responsible for their actions. In political terms he is the outsider who interferes in the domestic affairs of others, out of mistaken idealism. Ironically, he is an American naïve idealist, who becomes an Iranian-hostage taker (as opposed to an Iranian hostage-taker). The sudden access to Lester's thoughts is a surprise to the reader and in narrative terms plays with notions of "inside" and "outside", domestic and foreign. As readers we listen to the voices of Kathy and the Colonel, but in Lester's case an authority is in charge of our access to him, in the shape of an omniscient narrator. With Lester, authority enters the text.

In the novel, Dubus uses the image of domestic violence to draw the political moral, substituting the domestic microcosm for the political macrocosm. A classic image of the kind of "barbarity" that the West deplores is offered by the fate of the Colonel's cousin, Jasmeen. When she has an affair with a married American oil executive, her father locks her up and beats her repeatedly (also beating her mother for good measure). When his son hears market talk of "the Behrani family, of the shame their *kaseef* [dirty] daughter had brought upon their heads" (151) he forces his father to act to avenge their disgrace. The father drags Jasmeen out by the hair, barefoot, bruised and in her nightdress, and shoots her dead. Everything in this anecdote conspires to present the dangers of brown men to their women. The target is not the American seducer but the woman. The killer is not just the father but the family males in collaboration. Afterwards, "None of her brothers or uncles would take revenge on Jasmeen's killer" (152). The abuse is collective, serial (repeated beatings) and involves more than one woman. The Colonel, however, dissociates himself from the event. "I hated my uncle ... The hurting of women I have not approved of" (153). Though he drags Kathy away from the house, bruising her, he rejects further violence. "I am not my uncle from Tabriz" (186). When he discovers Kathy (now also having an affair with a married man) in a suicide attempt, he suddenly remembers "my long dead cousin, Jasmeen" (214) and, overcome by tenderness, takes her into the house. Watching Kathy sleep, he wonders if now, perhaps, she will be able to acknowledge "who her real enemy has become" (218). The sequence of events establishes the Colonel as a flawed individual but in the end a man who is a rescuer, not someone to be rescued from. As he remembers Jasmeen, he recalls again the Savaki torturer and acknowledges that he had not made a sufficient moral stand (218).

In the final analysis the enemy is not the Beast within Kathy, or the apparent alien "Other", now inside her house, but Lester. Lester's very first intervention provokes domestic violence. When Lester originally threatens the family, a panicky Nadi upbraids the Colonel who slaps her. Contemplating the moment, he feels as if "it belongs not to my family but another" (169). Lester would not have gone to visit the Colonel, if not for his own family problems. Just as Kathy waited in her car to shout at the Colonel, so Lester's wife Carol waited outside police headquarters in her car, "shouting and crying. Hitting me" (155). Earlier in the novel Lester discussed the inadequacies of the domestic violence laws. In California, no matter which spouse initiates the violence, the police have to take both in (161). Responsibility is shared. However large the husband or slight the wife, if she defends herself she will be arrested (162). One husband repeatedly beats his wife, who dares not bring charges; they appear in public, arm in arm, "like it was nobody's business" (111). In response Lester takes the law into his own hands, planting drugs on the erring husband, to give the wife the opportunity to escape. Kathy's response is telling. She questions Lester's right to do this, wondering if the wife liked being the powerless victim. And why, she wonders, does Lester need "to wear this cape and mask" (113)? Lester's illegal intervention in an affair which was not his business is part and parcel of his American idealism.

Lester does know something of Iran, and he uses that knowledge to threaten the Colonel. Lester's wife has volunteered at different points for a variety of causes, Palestinians for Self-Rule, South African Alliance to end Apartheid, the Coalition against Intervention and Oppression. Lester met her when she was working a political leaflet table, protesting against multinational corporate interventionism. She immediately lectures Lester at length on Nicaragua, El Salvador, and (in a garbled soundbite) "the CIA killing the elected leader of Iran in 1953 for oil fields for the Rockefellers" (238). She goes on and on, until suddenly "she began to run out of gas" (238) and they head for a hamburger joint. Carol's dream is to travel to the battle zones of the world "to capture the truth of American imperialism" (238) — to intervene against intervention. Lester was attracted to her all-purpose mall radicalism: "it was her conviction he had proposed to" (237). Like her, he "had no idea what he wanted to do, but whatever it was, he wanted it to be good, he wanted to do good" (238). Thwarted by his young family from entering a larger political arena, he carries on the crusade at home. He joins the police because he sees a poster of a young cop standing between a man and a woman with the slogan "World Peace begins at Home", beside the hotline number for victims of domestic abuse. Lester is motivated by fear of his own weakness, in a newly transnational world. In his adolescence he had been repeatedly bullied as the only Anglo in a Texas school. Lester's girlfriend, Charita, was Latina, and he recalls how her brother Pablo had pushed Lester away from her, grabbing her by the hair and hauling her off. Lester did nothing to stop him. The incident is a mirror image of the Jasmeen story — though here brown men are protecting brown women against white men. For Lester it is one of many events in his life in which he fears that "one day someone would see just how unfit and weak he really was" (229). In his worst dreams he is surrounded by crowds of those he has arrested, ganging up on him as all his actions come home to roost. Just as Lester adopts the role of crusader, without realising that it is internal weakness which is the real problem, so America is prepared to go to war on behalf of its idealistic self-image.

   In Lester, Dubus satirises the American need to be clean, innocent, to act as the self-appointed moral policeman of the world, and as the guardian of other nations' women. Lester wants "not only to clean up everybody else's act, but to make the world safe again by doing so" (235), to set the world to rights once and for all. Homeless, Kathy and Lester retire briefly to an isolated cabin on a lake, a neglected fish camp, where they immediately engage in an absolute orgy of cleaning and scrubbing. The suggestion is of a return to an earlier, pure America, of poverty without power. The lake is fed by an underground spring and evokes Lester's wonder at being back at "the source of something" (139). Kathy bathes in the Purisima River and feels "cleansed to the bone" (157). For a moment the cabin suggests an uncompromised America without oil or empire: the cabin is at some distance from the road, inaccessible to cars and has no electricity or mains drainage. The idyll is shortlived, however. Surfacing with a hangover, Kathy longs for mango juice, a shower, air-conditioning and an aspirin. She goes off to get drunk and steal gas, and Lester pursues her to the house.

   The road to hell is paved with good intentions. The final disaster is caused by Lester's "protective" interventionism, accelerated by the characters "not knowing" the true facts of their situation, and concealing weakness behind a show of strength. The Colonel's young son Esmail, used as "human collateral" (310) by Lester, is shot dead because Lester concealed from him the fact that the gun he seized was not loaded. Lester recognises that Esmail would have put the gun down had he known, "But Lester had denied him the truth" (347) out of fear. Nadi dies because the Colonel wants to protect her from knowing that her son is dead; he suffocates her. He also does not want her to know that he had ordered Esmail to keep the gun pointed at Lester. Since he gave that order in Farsi, he takes that fact to his grave. He does face the truth about his past, "For our excess we lost everything" (329), but can't resist leaving a last message for Soraya telling her not to take less than $100,000 for the house. The Colonel dies by his own hand but only after he has reassumed the external trappings of power, donning his air force uniform before putting a plastic bag over his head. As he dies, hearing the roaring of F-16s in his ears, "the plastic becomes iron" (339) against his face; he is once more a man behind a mask. Lester, as a policeman in jail, is an outsider on the inside and once his time in protective custody expires, his fate at the hands of the inmates can be imagined.

But what of the woman at the centre of the story? Kathy, half strangled by the Colonel, survives, temporarily voiceless from her injuries. Because she is mute, her fellow inmates christen her "Remote". Kathy uses silence to maintain the distance between herself and everyone else; she is glad to have a glass screen between her and her family when they visit. She is "safely out of their reach in every way" (362). Even when her voice recovers, she remains silent, "relieved I didn't have a voice" (361). She has become a parodic version of one of the voiceless, brutalised, silenced women on behalf of whom so much rhetoric has been expended in the discourse of human rights. For the reader, however, who does have access to her voice, she cannot be an innocent victim. In jail she rejects her lawyer's plan to plead diminished responsibility in the aftermath of her suicide attempt, reiterating that she does not want to look as if she were not responsible for the kidnapping (360). Significantly it is at this point that Kathy abandons the past tense and moves into the present (357) placing the reader right beside her.

House of Sand and Fog was published in 1999, before the enormous "blowback" of the 9/11 attacks. Four years later it was adapted for the cinema.[33] Just how far the average American was envisaged as capable of accepting the savage irony of the novel's ending may be gauged from the treatment of the two central characters. In the movie, the scales are weighted heavily against the Colonel. In the novel the opening scene introduces him as a hardworking labourer for the American dream, toiling with other immigrants on the highway. On screen he first appears as the father of the bride at Soraya's extravagantly staged wedding. Later it is strongly implied that he has Savaki connections. On the other hand, Kathy's cocaine use is suppressed; she does not hold up a gas station; she goes to the rescue and attempts to save the Behranis by artificial resuscitation; and at the close she gets off scot-free. As a result, the film protects its American audience against a full recognition of the damage done in their name. The reason may of course be partly the result of the 9/11 attacks. Feelings were raw when the film was made, and a terrible knowledge had been forced upon the nation. In the light of later events, *House of Sand and Fog* has assumed a prophetic quality. Dubus's next novel, *The Garden of Last Days*, focuses upon the reported encounter between one of the 9/11 hijackers and a Florida stripper, on the eve of his deadly mission. Gender politics are again the central focus as American and Islamic rescue missions collide. A drunken wife-beater abducts the stripper's little girl in the belief that he is protecting her, while the hijacker tries to save the stripper from her degenerate Western life as a commodified sex object. In this novel, however, not knowing has become an excess of knowledge. This time we know only too well how the terrorist plot will end.

Notes to Chapter 19

1. Seymour Hersh, "The Iran Plans," *New Yorker*, 17 April 2006, <http://www.newyorker.com/archive/206/04/17/060417fa_fact> [accessed 20 April 2008].
2. Gary Sick, *All Fall Down: America's Tragic Encounter with Iran* (New York: Random House, 1985).
3. Hamid Dabashi, "Native Informers and the Making of the American Empire," *Al-Ahram Weekly Online*. <http://weekly.ahram.org.eg/2006/797/special.htm> [accessed 10t July 2007].
4. Niall Ferguson, *Colossus: The Rise and Fall of the American Empire* (London: Allen Lane, 2004).
5. Michael Hardt and Antonio Negri, *Empire* (Cambridge, MA: Harvard University Press, 2000).
6. Chalmers Johnson, *Nemesis: The Last Days of the American Republic* (New York: Henry Holt, 2006), 6. See also Chalmers Johnson, *Blowback: The Costs and Consequences of American Empire* (New York: Henry Holt, 2000) and *The Sorrows of Empire* (London: Verso, 2004).
7. Johnson, *Blowback*, 65.
8. Ibid., 8.
9. Ibid., 17.
10. Hamid Dabashi, *Iran: A People Interrupted* (New York and London: The New Press, 2007).
11. Azar Nafisi, *Reading Lolita in Tehran: A Memoir in Books* (London: I. B. Tauris, 2003) is the most notorious. See Jennifer Worth, "Unveiling *Persepolis* as Embodied Performance," *Theatre Research International*, 32, 2 (2007), 143–60, who also lists *Lipstick Jihad* by Azadeh Moaveni (2005), *Even After All this Time: A Story of Love, Revolution, and Leaving Iran* by Afschineh Latifi (2005), *Journey from the Land of No: A Girlhood Caught in Revolutionary Iran* by Roya Hakakian (2004), *Funny in Farsi: A Memoir of Growing up Iranian in America* by Firoozeh Dumas (2004), *Saffron Sky: A Life between Iran and America* by Gelareh Asayesh (2000), *To See and See Again: A Life in Iran and America* by Tara Bahrampour (2000) and *Foreigner* by Nahid Rachlin (1999).
12. Gillian Whitlock, *Soft Weapons: Autobiography in Transit* (Chicago and London: University of Chicago Press, 2007), 13.
13. Ibid., 22.
14. Seyed Mohammed Marandi, "Reading Azar Nafisi in Tehran," *Comparative American Studies*, 6, 2 (2008), 179–89.
15. Dabashi, "Native Informers".
16. Sally Kitch, "Gendered National 'Identity Politics': The US and Afghanistan." Paper presented at the annual meeting of the American Studies Association, 2008. <http://www.allacademic.com/meta/p113693_index.html> [abstract accessed 21 April 2008].
17. Gayatri Chakravorty Spivak, "Can the Subaltern Speak?," in Cary Nelson and Lawrence Grossberg (eds), *Marxism and the Interpretation of Culture* (London: Macmillan, 1988), 299.
18. Fatemeh Keshavarz, *Jasmine and Stars: Reading More than Lolita in Tehran* (Chapel Hill: University of North Carolina Press, 2007); John Carlos Rowe, "Reading *Reading Lolita in Tehran* in Idaho," *American Quarterly*, 59, 2 (2007), 253–75.
19. Donna Seaman, "Review of *House of Sand and Fog*," *Booklist*, 95, 11 (1999), 961.
20. André Dubus III, *House of Sand and Fog* (New York: Vintage 1999). Page references follow quotations in parentheses.
21. Stephen Kinzer, *All the Shah's Men: An American Coup and the Roots of Middle East Terror* (Hoboken, NJ: John Wiley, 2003), x: "Almost no one in the United States knew what the CIA did there in 1953."

22. Michael Donovan, "National Intelligence and the Iranian Revolution," in R. Jeffreys-Jones and Christopher Andrew (eds), *Eternal Vigilance? Fifty years of the CIA* (London: Frank Cass, 1997). I am grateful to Rhodri Jeffreys–Jones for his suggestions for readings in the history of Iran.

23. See Robert Graham, *Iran: The Illusion of Power* (London: Croom Helm, 1978) for an account of US aid.

24. Graham (ibid.) provides a good account of SAVAK.

25. Ibid., 181.

26. Stephen Kinzer, *Overthrow: America's Century of Regime Change from Hawaii to Iraq* (New York: Henry Holt, 2006). Kinzer notes the consistent pattern in which American regime change tends to install repressive regimes which it then cannot control, weakening American security and producing generations of militants.

27. The action covers three weeks in August 1993, with a day-by-day chronology carefully indicated, followed by a final section covering a few weeks after the deaths, and ending with Kathy's mother's visit on Labor Day (the first Monday in September).

28. Judith Butler, *Giving an Account of Oneself* (New York: Fordham University Press, 2005), 7.

29. Gerald Turkel, "Property, Law and Violence: A Thematic Analysis of *House of Sand and Fog,*" *Humanity and Society*, 30, 4 (2006), 384.

30. Marc Galanter, Susan Egelko and Helen Edwards, "Rational Recovery: Alternative to AA for Addiction?" *American Journal of Drug and Alcohol Abuse*, 19, 4 (1993), 499–510.

31. Googoosh, the most popular Iranian singer in the 1970s, did not record or perform from 1979 to 2000, as a result of the ban on female solo singers, envisaged as temptresses. She was briefly jailed and then lived under virtual house arrest.

32. Cyril Jones-Kellett, "The Home Builder: A Try for the American Dream," *San Diego Union-Tribune*, 14 February 1999, BOOKS 3.

33. *House of Sand and Fog*; produced by Michael London and Vadim Perelman, directed by Vadim Perelman, written by Vadim Perelman and Shawn Lawrence Otto (DVD DreamWorks, 2003).

CHAPTER 20

Pictures from an Exhibition:
Dalia Sofer and the Jews of Iran

Dalia Sofer's novel *The Septembers of Shiraz* opens with a striking juxtaposition. In September 1981 Isaac Amin, a wealthy Jewish gemmologist, is arrested by revolutionary guards at his desk in Tehran, where his calendar stands open at a glossy photograph of the tomb of Hāfez in Shiraz, subtitled "City of Poets and Roses."[1] Shortly afterwards, blindfolded, he is transferred to the notorious Evin prison. With his eyes "submerged in blackness" (8), he is embarrassed by the comments of passers-by in the street. "Deprived of his vision, he has forgotten that others can still see" (9). The juxtaposition of colour and poetry on the one hand, darkness and deprivation on the other is emblematic of the dynamic set up in the novel between a colourful past world of cultural glory, and the contemporary Islamic republic, depicted in terms of greyness and brutality.

Isaac is a highly representative figure. Under the Qajar dynasty (1797–1925) the Jews of Iran had faced a variety of discriminatory measures, but under the Pahlavi regime they prospered, and Isaac is no exception, rising from poverty to riches. The reigns of the two Pahlavi Shahs were a golden age for Iranian Jews, as discriminatory laws were repealed, Jews were able to serve in the military, attend state schools and live outside the Jewish quarter. Rapid modernisation during the Shah's White Revolution (1963–79) created enormous opportunities, and the urban Jewish community participated fully in a booming economy. The Pahlavis projected an image of continuity between the present and the pre-Islamic past, emphasising secular and nationalist pursuits, values and symbols, such as Persian art and music. While retaining Jewish identity, the Jews wanted to be perceived as Iranian and assimilated to this culture, identifying with nationalist aspirations and values. They saw themselves, after all, as denizens of Iranian territories for 2,700 years since the Assyrian exile. Judaism is the oldest minority religion in Iran. Many Iranian Jews thus emphasised the majestic distant past as an integral part of Jewish history.[2] Isaac is the only child in his family to bear a Jewish name; his younger siblings' names are Iranian, Shahla and Javad. This new national identity based on the Aryan race of ancient Iran posed some problems in the Nazi period, with newspaper propaganda trumpeting the supposed common Aryan origin of Germans and Persians, but effectively the Jews moved from the ghetto to the upper middle class in one generation. In 1968 the Iranian Jewish community was the wealthiest such community in Asia and Africa. In 1976, they numbered some 62,000, the largest Jewish community in Asia and Africa (with the exception of South Africa). In 1979 it all ended. The Islamic Revolution triggered a mass exodus of some two million Iranians to the United States, with the result that there are now more Iranian Jews in Los Angeles (popularly known as "Tehrangeles") than in Iran (35,000 and 25,000 respectively). About 85% of Iran's Jews have fled since 1979. In one neighbourhood in Tehran the Jewish population fell from 7,000 in 1979 to 70 in 1999.[3] Sofer remembers lining up at school to chant "Death to America. Death to Israel."[4] As Roya Hakakian notes, "The Islamic republic undid an ancient history and made us extinct."[5]

A generation later, the result is an outpouring of American-Iranian memoirs and novels, many by women. Perhaps unsurprisingly, almost all of these writers are possessed by an overwhelming urge to memorialise the lost past. Gina Nahai's work is representative. Nahai immigrated to America aged sixteen and has published four novels, three on Iranian themes. To her surprise, when she began to research her first novel she found that there was almost no written historical record of the Jews of Iran; the only history (three volumes in Farsi) was out of print.[6] As a result she spent seven years interviewing Iranians in America, where there is now an impressive archive collected under the aegis of the American Jewish Oral History Project in Los Angeles, and a modern history.[7] The archival impulse is particularly strong in Nahai's fiction. *Cry of the Peacock* (1991) sets the story of a Jewish woman in twentieth-century Iran against a backdrop of Iranian history from 1796 to 1982. *Moonlight on the Avenue of Faith* (1999) adopts fairy tales and magic in order to explore the political transition from the Jewish ghetto in Tehran in 1938 to city life in 1956, exile in America and, in a flight of feathered fantasy, a bird's eye view of Iran in the 1980s, torn apart by war. Moonlight, a light that is only seen in darkness, becomes a metaphor for a fragile hope. In the novel the attempt to break the curse of the past (a line of doomed women) clashes with the realisation that escape will also mean the end of family history.[8] The characters in the house on the Avenue of Faith are beset by robber ghosts, stealing the treasures of the past, who eventually turn out to be the owner herself, liquidating her assets to secure her financial future. *Caspian Rain* (2007) focuses on a Jewish family during the Shah's last years, confronted by an avenging ghost from the ghetto past which they are attempting to deny in their upward social ascent. Situated somewhere between magic and history, Nahai's fiction interrogates the history and politics of a lost world, at times revelling in the past, at times attempting to escape its haunting presence.

Memoirs by and about Iranian women have become exceptionally popular in America, with some twenty mass-market titles published in the last seven years.[9] They include Jewish American memoirs: *Journey from the Land of No: A Girlhood Caught in Revolutionary Iran* by Roya Hakakian (2004), and Ferideh Goldin, *Wedding Song* (2003). For Gillian Whitlock such memoirs are "soft weapons", used to buttress aggressive Western intervention in other countries. Life narratives of this type, emphasising the oppression of women, play to Western traditions of benevolence, masking privilege, reifying dominant social relations, and naturalising the neoliberal discourse of the free circulation of ideas, goods and peoples in global networks of exchange.[10] An Iranian commentator similarly argues that memoir-writers are deeply enmeshed in the politics of rendering Iran from a transnational perspective, making Iranians "Other" in a neo-Orientalist discourse, authored by American-identified women.[11] The past can serve the present in many, often ambiguous, ways. The position is even more complex when the women involved are not oppressed Muslims but Iranian Jews in exile.

The Jewish experience of modern Iran is fundamentally ambivalent. If the Pahlavis were good for the Jews, they were not so good for everybody else. The glories of the Ḥāfez mausoleum may resonate with the Shah's encouragement of pride in a pre-Islamic past as part of the nationalist agenda, but Isaac's blindfold is also emblematic. In order to prosper, as he comes to realise, he had to turn a blind eye to the abuses of the regime. The Shah's reign was characterised by militarism and excess. In the period between 1953 and 1957 alone, the US provided $500 million to Iran, one quarter of it earmarked for the military. American aid and technological assistance also established the secret police, SAVAK, answering directly to the Shah, and regulated only by military tribunals. Interrogation, torture and imprisonment without trial were so commonplace that in 1974 Amnesty International described Iran as having the worst human rights record in the world.[12] Modernisation on the Western model was marked by lavish extravagance. The Persepolis celebrations of 2,500 years of the Peacock Throne, in October 1971, cost $100 million, with French chefs from Maxims serving up dishes of Breast of Peacock on Limoges porcelain. (At this point Tehran still lacked a sewerage system.) In contrast, in 1981 Isaac's daughter Shirin sees Tehran as "the black city" (243), "black and permeable, filled with holes through which people fall and disappear" (241). To his family Isaac has simply disappeared into a black hole. The reader, however, is not spared the details of his torture, merely for being a Jew with a rich lifestyle and family in Israel. Judaism and Zionism tend to be conflated in Iranian political rhetoric.[13] The novel was carefully researched, drawing on Sofer's father's imprisonment, prison memoirs, and her family's own escape, sixteen hours on horseback and six on foot to cross the Turkish border.[14] Sofer even obtained an audio recording of an interrogation and torture session.[15]

Despite this meticulous historicity, the novel paints a picture of the Jews of Iran, which offers a critique of the archival and memorial. Sofer interrogates the relation between art and terror, through the method of ekphrasis — the evocation in the verbal text of a series of visual images. Primarily she sets up a dialectic between images of the colourful past and those of a darker present, though the opposition is not in any sense simplistic. Firstly, Sofer depicts the Shah's emphasis on pre-Islamic art as a reaction against a colonial past. Isaac's sister Shahla has married Keyvan, whose father, a minister under the Shah, has already fled. Shahla, however, cannot bear to leave behind her collection of rococo furniture and a home crammed with priceless antiques. Keyvan's grandfather was a court painter to the Qajar king, Nasir al-Din Shah, whose portrait, painted by the grandfather in 1892, looks down from the wall as Shahla is served tea and cakes on a fine European porcelain service, also a gift from the Shah. For Isaac's wife, Farnaz, the French madeleines trigger a political rather than a Proustian insight, as an image of the country's aspirations, its desire for cosmopolitanism, and its delusions of grandeur. Nasir al-Din was thoroughly

Europeanised, the first Iranian to be photographed, and himself a noted painter and photographer. For Shahla, "This painting alone is reason enough to stay" (55). She can't let go of a cultural capital which will be worthless elsewhere. Keyvan's career as a professor of art history is heavily dependent on his lineage; nobody would care for his opinions on art if it were not for his last name. Keyvan, however, is now less certain of the value of art; he fears arrest. "How will this painting — and all the pages I've written about it in all those useless art magazines — help me in jail?" (55). The scene is immediately followed by a description of Isaac in jail, cigarette-burned and suffering, watching his cellmate Mehdi carving in wood. Mehdi is attempting to make a clog for his daughter, without much success. He throws it down, exasperated, "Enough artistic expression for today" (64). Though the clog is poorly executed and of no commercial value, Isaac sees in the wooden shape the clean intentions of its maker, and his hope for reunion with his child. The clog is some sort of argument for the intrinsic value of the artistic impulse, even in times of terror. Isaac's mind moves to Farnaz, as attached to her possessions as Shahla, and similarly refusing to leave Iran. For him, a certain warmth has gone out of her, "leaving her face beautiful but flat, like one of her prized paintings" (67). Sofer's novel appears to make no bones here of the way in which the materialism of the Jews has overtaken their culture. Isaac works with valuable jewels but has not put enough value on his family; Farnaz and Shahla are slaves to their possessions.

Where the Qajar painting appears to indict materialism and Eurocentrism, pre-Islamic art offers a different perspective. Isaac's family is eventually torn apart by the revolution and Shahla and Javad escape ahead of him. In order to launder the cash paid to the people-smugglers, Farnaz has to pretend to buy a miniature from an antique dealer, just in case the government should ask her what she has spent $10,000 on. Like Shahla, the dealer is possessed by his art-objects, "a slave to my relics" (215), which evoke the pre-Islamic past: a jug predating the Mongol invasion, Achaemenian jewels, and silver tables engraved with figures of Cyrus and Darius, "relics of an age long gone but to which people cling like proud but destitute heirs to a dead tycoon" (215). When the dealer produces the miniature, it is described as a

> painting of a palace, one prince slaying another before the eyes of many viziers and courtiers, the scene drenched in sparkling reds, blues, and greens, with gold woven throughout. (216)

The dealer describes it as taken from a book, the Tahmasbi *Shahnameh*, Ferdowski's *Book of Kings*. Ferdowski's epic poem (pre-Islamic), written in the tenth century in classical Persian, became Iran's national epic, with many different illustrated versions. The Tahmasbi is a particularly fine example with some 250 miniatures, painted by the best artists of the period. Like all Iranian miniatures, they are marked by extreme subtlety of colour, using colour clusters to lead the eye, with perhaps a dozen hues of the same colour in a single picture.[16] In the Pahlavi era the *Shahnameh* was exploited to promote a nationalistic agenda; Farnaz remembers her son Parviz performing scenes from it at school, though under the Islamic regime it is no longer taught. The miniature also carries a further nationalistic charge. As the dealer explains, in 1962 an American collector bought it and ripped out the pages to sell them individually, some to a New York museum and some to collectors. The particular book evoked here is known as the *Houghton Shahnameh*, sold by Edmond de Rothschild to Arthur Houghton, the president of the Corning glass works, who promptly began dismantling and selling it.[17] Some pages were displayed at the Metropolitan Museum of Art in New York, to which he donated, to reduce his tax liability. Houghton offered others unsuccessfully to the Shah in 1976 for $20 million, and then auctioned them. In 2006 one page made $1.7million.[18] When the Metropolitan Museum published a book reproducing some of the illustrations, in 1972, the *Shahnameh* was exploited for propaganda purposes. In the foreword, the Iranian ambassador to the United States claimed that, by publishing it, the Metropolitan had honoured the 2,500th anniversary of the founding of the Persian Empire by Cyrus the Great, and thus also the first declaration of human rights.

> Such books assist greatly in bringing about an even closer relationship between the people of Iran and the United States, two peoples dedicated to the principles of freedom, morality, and tolerance set forth by Cyrus the Great so many years ago.[19]

It was Cyrus who restored the shrines and allowed the Jews to return from Babylon to Jerusalem, after their expulsion by Nebuchadnezzar, and thus to rebuild their temple. Cyrus is an Iranian hero — but also a Jewish one.

For Farnaz, contemplating "the orphaned leaf, its counterparts spread around the globe" (217) the miniature becomes "the embodiment of loss" (218). When she flees in her turn she takes it with her, thinking of it as "a lost child" (322). The leaves of the book have been spread around the globe in a manuscript diaspora, some to museums, others, as she imagines, reposing in the cabinet of some European or American collector, "his acquisition filling him with pride not unlike that of a nineteenth century colonialist in search of a piece of the Orient" (217). The miniature offers an image of American materialism, despoiling a culture of its treasures, in an imperial or orientalist-inflected greed, which converts the art object into dollars, dismantling and destroying it. Without American petrodollars, the family, the book and the culture would not have been torn apart. It is a neat analogy — but there is more to the picture than that. It also indicts the Islamic regime.

Farnaz describes the picture in some detail:

> the thin, precise lines, the red and gold of a courtesan's robe, the indigo mosaic of the floor, where the slain king sits, his sword and shield by his side. (217)

The description is precise enough to identify the image as folio 36 verso of the *Houghton Shahnameh*, which depicts the hero Faridun striking down Zahhak with an ox-headed mace. This is the climax of the first cycle of the *Shahnameh*, the moment when Iran is delivered from 1,000 years of tyranny suffered under Zahhak, whose name conjures up the idea of tyranny to any Iranian. Zahhak oppressed the people because Iblis (Satan) had kissed him on the shoulders, causing a serpent to spring from each demanding a daily diet of human brains. Thus Iblis planned to exterminate mankind.[20] The Shahnameh has as one of its core themes the tribulations which Iran endures over the millennia at the hands of both wicked kings and foreign foes. Zahhak is an Arab not a Persian. Transferred from its original book to Sofer's novel the painting suggests that the modern Islamic regime is just one more foreign-inspired force hijacking Iran.

Farnaz is powerfully drawn to the picture as a deeply moving visual experience, an image of a heroic Iranian past, in which the richness and the courtly setting appeal to her nostalgia for the glories of the Shah's court, and also perhaps for tolerance and the freedom of women. The painting shows the daughters of Jamshid freed from tyranny by Faridun, and also depicts a courtesan. Indeed, in the midst of smiting Zahhak, Faridun's eye has wandered towards a woman at the side of the picture.[21] In 1996 Sothebys in London sold this picture for £419,500.[22] The painting, then, can be read in diametrically opposed ways — as an image of a culture torn apart and scattered, the people of the book who are now in exile, as the result of Western materialism and greed; or as an image of the continuity of Arab domination of Iran. At the dealer's, Farnaz mentions Isaac's collection of antique daggers and his favourite, a Mongol sword with a gold-leaf handle. When Isaac finally buys his way out of prison with his entire life savings, the revolutionary guards seize upon the sword. Isaac remarks on its aesthetic values and engraved workmanship. "The workmanship? How about the functionality?" (254) counters the guard, resting the tip on Farnaz's neck. When he carries off the extorted savings, the sword goes too, placing the guard as one more in a line of tyrants wielding the sword over Iran, and forcing the state of property onto the images of Iranian greatness. Terror seems to take little account of art.

So much for the glories of the past. In contrast to the lavish colour of the *Shahnameh*, contemporary Iran majors on monochrome, notoriously in the domination in the western press of images of the black veil.[23] Iran's most celebrated photographer, Abbas, chose to work in black and white, and is openly acknowledged by Sofer as an inspiration for the novel (340), which evokes his images at several points. His book *Iran Diary*, subtitled "Terre des poètes" (Land of Poets), also opens with images of the tomb of Hāfez though in monochrome.[24] Throughout the novel, black and white photographs are evoked and it is tempting to see Sofer as lamenting an inclusive, colourful past which has been replaced by monochrome, at least for women, veiled, devoid of makeup and denied full access to culture. In the streets, for example, shampoo ads and movie posters have given way to murals of clerics. On the other hand, these images appear to offer a corrective to the spectacular and extravagant Pahlavi past. Monochrome is often seen as a kind of resistance to the saturation of the world by colour, in a crowded modern visual marketplace. As Paul Grainge notes,

> The visuality of monochrome seemed to efface its own relation to the sphere of capitalist simulations, sustaining the illusion that it was somehow removed from the market culture in which it was necessarily produced.[25]

As a young man, Isaac had been a keen photographer and had always used black and white, preferring the mystery of grey scale to the nakedness of colour, believing it to be "more archival, better suited to memory" (237). Arguably he likes it because it seems less implicated in the life in which he is making a fortune. As he gets wealthier, and loses some of the affective connection to his family, he changes to colour, "his prints, unlike his life, become more and more saturated, filled like a canvas with splashes of longing" (237). As the *Shahnameh* demonstrates, cultural memory is a central part of how a nation is defined. Black and white can be seen as legitimating certain sorts of experience, converting the past from news to history and from surface spectacle to truth, bringing in associations with the archival, documentary realism, veracity and permanence. Paul Grainge notes that in the 1980s monochrome became a fashionable media choice (*Schindler's List*, *Forrest Gump*, Armani advertisements). But in Iran, black and white is no longer a style choice. In jail Isaac feels that his world has actually become black and white, consisting of filthy snow, grey cement walls and the ashen tinge of his own skin. He comes to think of colour as something fantastic (236). Ironically too, the apparent archival permanence of his photos is an illusion. The photographs become a danger to his family. In a memorable scene, Farnaz and Shirin have already ripped up every photo which shows anything remotely incriminating — sunbathers, ice-skaters, a woman in a skimpy dress, friends who have been executed.

Abbas's photos of Iran chronicle the transformation of revolution into Islamic Republic. Several of his photos (which appeared on the front covers of *Time* and *Stern* among others) became iconic, notably that of Ayatollah Khomeini, strikingly photographed to exploit the high contrast between white beard and black shawl, the left eye partly hidden in the shadows.[26] As one commentator wondered,

> What is this eye hiding? What is going to happen next? Is he in the dark like everybody else as to what is to come, or does he have an inkling of it which he withholds?[27]

Abbas also believed in the archival quality of monochrome; he describes his photographs as "fixés pour toujours — images suspendues dans le temps". In contrast words are seen as fluid: "le verbe n'est jamais figé".[28] When threatened by mobs, he always said that he was photographing "just for history", a ploy which was surprisingly successful.[29] None the less, as a result of his first book, the photo-essay *Iran, la révolution confisquée* Abbas became *camera non grata* in Iran and went into exile for seventeen years.[30] His photos often operate by ironic juxtaposition; a shantytown followed by the Shah celebrating Persepolis,[31] or a lone veiled woman on the edges of an all-male demonstration, excluded already from the revolution.[32] Others juxtapose tradition and modernity: two men at prayer with an oil refinery standing in the direction of Mecca, for example.[33] As we shall see, juxtapositions of this type also inform Sofer's narrative method. Three photos by Abbas are explicitly evoked in the novel. At one point Farnaz remembers her son's history lesson, on the French Revolution and the Terror, with images of heads on poles, and reflects that this is a story now coming to life around her.

> For hadn't she witnessed, only months ago, the charred body of a prostitute placed on a stretcher and paraded down the street, surrounded by a chanting, euphoric mob. (69)

Having set the woman's body on fire the mob appears oblivious to the fact that pieces are falling off her. Farnaz continues:

> And had she not seen photographs of the Shah's ministers in a morgue, naked,
> like mice in a testing laboratory, an experiment gone bad. (69)

Both images feature in *Iran Diary*. The first is the result of a mob, supposedly
inspired by "the purifying fire of Islam", burning down the brothel area of
Tehran.[34] The burned prostitute stands in strong contrast to the red and gold
courtesan of the miniature, and offers an unambiguous image of a woman punished
for sexual freedom. The image of the ministers (who include Abbas Ali Khalatbari,
former Minister of Foreign Affairs, and General Hassan Pakhravan, former Deputy
Prime Minister and the head of SAVAK) suggests a social experiment which has
backfired as an imposed, premature modernisation creates a traditionalist backlash.
There are also unhappy associations with the infliction of pain on living beings
in the pursuit of truth: scientific or interrogatory.[35] At another point in the novel
Farnaz notes her in-laws' doorknocker, the hand of Fatimah, an Islamic talisman
which was a gift from their neighbours. Immediately afterwards she is confronted
with an image of bloody handprints on walls — again an Abbas image, signifying
willingness for martyrdom. The caption reads "blood calls out for revenge".[36]
The image migrates from the Islamic sphere to the Judaic and the revolutionary,
demonstrating how previous cooperation between different religious groups has
given way to violence. Where the Shahnameh, torn apart by its purchaser, is only
a metaphor for a dismembered people, the Abbas images focus upon actual bodily
damage — the dismembered prostitute, the corpses, the hands.

Illustrations may be black and white but Sofer's narrative is anything but. One
memory explores how images mean, what they can tell us about our lives, and how
they may be read in different ways, in this case in relation not to the past but the
future. In Seville, on holiday, Isaac forces Farnaz to attend a bullfight, overriding
her protests about the brutality of the spectacle. Like any good tourist he intends to
see the sights, ticking off the traditions of the past, even the brutal ones. In return,
she insists that he visit a fortune-teller where he is alarmed to see that the cards
he draws depict a stooped man dressed in black, and a figure in medieval armour
on a white horse, along with a magician. The cards described include the five of
cups, traditionally the card of loss, and number thirteen, the death card, which
appear to indicate a "black future" (237). The clairvoyant, however, argues that the
meanings of the images are not so obvious. Traditionally, the five of cups suggests
that although the cup of happiness has been overturned, the presence of two full
cups in the background implies a need for a major restructuring of one's life, and
future happiness. The death card may merely indicate the death of the old life, and
the magician (sometimes shown as the cobbler) the danger of taking possession of
the world but losing the soul.[37] In the preceding episode Farnaz had been accosted
by a cobbler, returning Isaac's shoes to her. The implication is that damage may be
repaired, images re-read, just as Isaac's lashed feet will eventually fit back into the
shoes, and the brutality of the past need not go on into the future.

Sofer's method is to complicate any easy condemnation of any one side —
Jewish or Muslim, Americanised or traditional — by a series of juxtaposed iconic
images. But what of the narrative method? Like the miniature, Abbas's photos were

once part of a book but have now been placed in a different book, which makes its own analysis of events, neither glorifying the past nor condoning its abuses. The dismembered images of different Iranian pasts have been put back together, reconnected by language. By placing the images in a different narrative context, Sofer's technique taps into the essential dynamic of ekphrasis — where the image is always dominated in the end by the word. The poetry of Hāfez is quoted in the novel by Jews, Muslims, Royalists and revolutionaries, capping each other's quotations, united by the power of language (101). In the novel the story is told in 47 short snapshot episodes, from four different viewpoints: Isaac, Farnaz, Shirin and Parviz, a student in America lodged with a Hassidic family in Crown Heights in Brooklyn. These alternating narrative sections cast an ironic light on the claims of any one culture, often by means of subtle juxtapositions and parallels. Sofer's strategy is in some ways a risky one in relation to the Hassidic group, emphasising features common to both Jewish and Muslim fundamentalists. As a young man Isaac identified America with freedom and indulgence. He remembers how in September 1942 he lost his virginity with an American woman, whom he met with a group of American soldiers, stationed with other Allies in Iran to transport supplies to Russia. "Neutral" but pro-German Iran had been invaded. Singing Sinatra songs, drunk on arrack, Isaac succumbs to the charms of Irene McKinley from Galveston, though the night of passion is followed by summary dismissal; no men are allowed in her army quarters. Isaac does not protest. She "was helping the global force against the Reich" (34). The image of American seductive power is clearly foregrounded; America is identified with political and sexual liberation, but it is also an occupying force.

The following scene moves to Parviz, also a young man, in America. In his architecture class Parviz is looking at photographic slides, "bright images of Californian homes" (37) with atriums, and vast expanses of glass. To him they seem "simple and sunny and cheerful, carrying within their uncomplicated lines the promise of docile decades" spent in the same town, street and house (37). His fellow students, spellbound by the images, are the products of just such homes. Parviz, however, is not exactly living the dream. His parental allowance interrupted, he is lodging in the damp, cockroach-ridden basement of Zalman Mendelson. It is a world of greyness; his television has such poor reception that there are often no images at all, or at best figures horribly distorted as in an amusement park mirror-maze. All he can see of the world is feet passing in the street above. Desperately lonely, Parviz in America shares the solitude of his jailed father, also in a cockroach-ridden basement, also surrounded by horribly twisted bodies, also with a view only of passing feet in the corridor above (193). In the prison Isaac has a false family thrust upon him. In Iran everyone has to be addressed as father, brother, sister and so on. "The revolution, like all others, wished to turn the citizens into one big family" (12). In America Parviz had answered an advertisement: "Kind, loving family renting basement room" (41). The Mendelsons are in fact a kind family "but they are not his" (41), and the sound of their children running about overhead merely intensifies his loneliness — just as Isaac hears the torturer's child running overhead in the prison.

Sofer's exploration of the ways in which religion can bring comfort or be divisive is steeped in irony. Isaac is imprisoned by the regime because of his religion, though Isaac has always been a secular Jew, observing few holidays and dismissing Hassids as "beardies" (41). Parviz, on the other hand, is not Jewish enough in America for the Mendelsons, who police his friendship with their daughter Rachel very closely. While quite clearly the ultra-orthodox Mendelsons are not the equivalent of the torturers in Iran, they function to complicate any clear-cut condemnation of religious orthodoxy and to undermine any easy dichotomy between Iran and America as regarding religious tolerance and inclusiveness. Zalman is treated sympathetically; his community have already got one Iranian refugee back on his feet (Broukhim, the florist), and are subsidising Parviz in exchange for a few hours' work in a hat shop. Yet they are also ultra-orthodox, sexually repressive and proselytising. When a customer comes into Broukhim's shop and is advised to buy a peace lily, on the grounds that "like a lover, it's easy to please" (326), the angry reaction by the pious woman to this harmless joke speaks volumes for the possibility of peaceful coexistence with others. The Mendelsons regularly host Hassidic "emissaries", Jews who travel to other locations (often at some risk) to support a beleaguered Jewish community.[38] Unlike other Hassidic groups which advise members to separate themselves from worldly temptations, the Chabad form of Judaism, located in Crown Heights, emphasises outreach to non-religious Jews. Sofer takes a satiric view of one such, whose mother enters the hat shop to equip her son, "this accomplished boy of 18 who has already found himself a wife and is on his way to save the Jews of Los Angeles" (273). Predictably a normal hat size is inadequate for this young man. Zalman's father, like Isaac, had also been imprisoned just for being Jewish (in Leningrad) and is captured in a grim photograph, unsmiling, because all his teeth were knocked out in prison. In his youth Zalman had been an emissary to Morocco. Parviz discovers in the basement a photograph of a Muslim girl, and a letter from Zalman's father, angrily calling him home. As Zalman later says, he gave up the girl he loved because "I look at myself not as an individual, but as a piece of a whole" (313). Though he sacrificed a temporary happiness, he now has eight children and confidently expects that in three generations he will have brought a thousand observant Jews into the world: "That's the only way for us to make up for the extermination of our people" (313). As a result, Zalman sees no future for Parviz with Rachel. Parviz objects, "You can't force spirituality on someone." "You can. I am proof of it", counters Zalman (312).

Rachel, almost as modestly dressed as an Iranian woman, and forbidden any physical contact with the male, is persistently identified with nature, not with culture. She works in the florists and would like to study botany, but her roots in Hassidism will prevent this. The closest the young couple get to culture is a walk to Shakespeare's tree (supposedly a graft from his garden). While Parviz has lost his roots and cannot be grafted back into flourishing orthodoxy, Rachel's roots tie her to a future as a mother. In the following section, Isaac thinks of his children as proof of his faith in the world, "like a landscaper who plants an oak tree knowing that it will not be fully grown in his lifetime — but that it will grow" (197). The reflection is occasioned by the sound of the torturer's child upstairs. Mohsen had been tortured under the Shah, and did not think he could ever have children. His child is "his miracle child, the badge of his faith" (210). His orthodoxy, like the Mendelsons', is the product of suffering, pain and death. In Brooklyn Parviz attends the circumcision party for the Mendelson twins and remembers a photo of himself similarly displayed on a pillow (311), an image of a group identity forged out of pain and loss: "each generation welcoming the next with an irreversible scar — a covenant with God, yes, but perhaps also a covenant with pain" (311). The parallels draw the three different "families" — Islamic, Hassidic, secular — together. Spatial and chronological synchronicity and intercultural syncretism bring together Iran and America, Muslim and Jew, modernity and tradition.

In some senses the parallels seem to work in favour of the Hassidic group rather than the secular groups. In Iran Isaac buries his father, the last of the family to be interred in the family tomb, and prepares for exile, while in Brooklyn the Mendelsons are celebrating new life, the birth of male twins. Iran is marked by death, America apparently by life. The collective also has its points; individualism is a lonely affair. Even before he was imprisoned, Isaac was "a specialist in solitary confinement" (199), allowing distance to grow between himself and his family. The alternating sections of the novel reinforce the sense of a fractured nuclear family, a group of four individuals rather than a collective entity, as the Muslims and Hassids seem to be. The bridges between the family members are subliminal, unexpressed, tenuous. Parviz likes to walk on Brooklyn Bridge, because there he can exist "with no connection to any land — or any person — but with the reassurance that connection is possible" (111). Sofer's narrative method works in ironic terms to undermine certainties, but also to indicate the possibility of connection, as the reader draws the parallels across different locations and groups.

Significantly, when the Amins escape, they do embrace a group identity. Earlier in the novel Shirin had been horrified by the erasure of individual identity involved when her mother sets to work to tear up all the family photographs. She could hardly bring herself to start ripping apart her own image. Where should she begin, she wonders, should she tear through the eye or the hair? (119) She recalls her detestation of magic tricks and magicians' assistants. "What kind of person volunteers to be erased?" (115). Her father has already disappeared, and now his life also seems to be being torn up. But when the family set off for exile, they realise that their only unconfiscated passport is Shirin's from which, by removing her photograph and erasing the details of her identity, Isaac is able to forge a family passport. The individual image is erased in favour of a strengthened group identity.

One final image draws a tentative moral. At the same time as the Mendelsons are celebrating, the Amins also come together in a fragile image of Jewish survival. A lamb is sacrificed to celebrate Isaac's release. Just as Parviz reflected on the pain of the circumcision, so Shirin wonders why people "thank God with blood" (266). There is a power-outage, "the lights go out, the city going black" (266), and the Amins light their table with candles, using the only ones they have left, usually reserved for commemorating the dead on holidays. At this point, Isaac enters the room, the white of his beard stark in the light of the candles. For a moment we are back in a black-and-white world. But for Shirin her father suddenly recalls Rembrandt's painting, *Old Jew Seated*.

A poster of the painting once hung over her father's desk, and Shirin had seen the figure's gaunt, aged hands and downcast eyes, as the epitome of sadness. Now she suddenly understands the painting and sees its beauty. In its sepia tones the painting is somewhere between the blackness of Islamified Tehran and the highly coloured nationalist past; it is almost all in shades of brown. Her father now looks old, like the painting, but he has survived. The scene ends with the candles guttering, supposedly a sign of the unquiet spirit of the person commemorated, with Shirin wondering if there are enough candles to account for all those who have not left the earth peacefully. This is a scene which indicates the numbers lost, and the continuity across the ages, linking the Amins with their Jewish heritage and ancestors, but also, importantly, with other groups. The meat from the sacrificed lamb has been shared with their Muslim neighbours; the painting evokes a past age of tolerance. As H. W. Janson notes,

> Rembrandt had a special sympathy for the Jews, as the heirs of the biblical past and as the patient victims of suffering.[39]

Rembrandt, proverbially known as the friend of Jews, lived in the Jewish quarter of Amsterdam where many of his neighbours were refugees from the Spanish Inquisition, given shelter in tolerant Amsterdam.[40] The old Jew, painted in 1654, wears a tattered robe and large flat beret, typical garb for an Ashkenazi Jew, at this date, and was probably a penniless refugee from Poland, paid to serve as a model.[41] So the picture is an image of the possibility of survival, continuity and tolerance.

Sofer puts all the pictures into a different book, her own ekphrastic photo-essay on the revolution, and by her words makes for a more subtle and nuanced understanding of the past. Reframing the pictures, she indicates that neither the highly coloured nationalist image, the Eurocentric view, or the monochrome photograph express the whole truth of Iran. As W. J. T. Mitchell argues, in his analysis of ekphrasis, the visual is always in some sense "other" to the verbal.[42] The alien visual object of verbal reproduction can emphasise separation and distance between reader and object, historical distance in the case of Keats' urn, or exotic distance, in the case of orientalism. Sofer's novel, however, indicates the problems of distances — but also operates to build bridges across them.

Notes to Chapter 20

1. Dalia Sofer, *The Septembers of Shiraz* (London: Picador, 2008, first published New York: HarperCollins, 2007).
2. *Encyclopaedia Iranica*. "Judeo-Persian Communities VI. The Pahlavi Era (1925–1929)," <http://www.iranica.com/articles/judeo-persian-vi-the-pahlavi-era-1925–1929> [accessed 8 September 2010].
3. Marla Harris, "Consuming Words: Memoirs by Iranian Jewish Women," *Nashim: A Journal of Jewish Women's Studies and Gender Issues*, 15 (5769, 2008), 149.
4. Deborah Solomon, "Tales from Tehran," *New York Times*, 26 August 2007. <http://www.nytimes.com/2007/08/26magazine> [accessed 18 August 2010].

5. Harris, 148.

6. Until the recent translated and abridged version. See Habib Levy, *Comprehensive History of the Jews of Iran: The Outset of the Diaspora*, ed. and abridged by Hooshang Ebrami, trans. by George W. Maschke (Costa Mesa, CA: Mazda, 1998).

7. Houman Sarshar (ed.), *Esther's Children: A Portrait of Iranian Jews*. (Los Angeles: Center for Iranian Jewish Oral history/The Jewish Publication Society, 2002).

8. Anna Free, "Moonlit Revelations: The Discourse of the End in Gina B. Nahai's *Moonlight on the Avenue of Faith*," *Papers: Explorations into Children's Literature*, 16, 2 (2006), 35–39.

9. Azar Nafisi, *Reading Lolita in Tehran. A Memoir in Books* (London: I. B. Tauris, 2003) is the most notorious. See Jennifer Worth, "Unveiling *Persepolis* as Embodied Performance," *Theatre Research International*, 32, 2 (2007), 143–60. See also Gina Nahai, "So What's With All the Iranian Memoirs," *Publishers Weekly*, 26 November 2007, 5810.

10. Gillian Whitlock, *Soft Weapons: Autobiography in Transit* (Chicago and London: University of Chicago Press, 2007), 13.

11. Seyed Mohammed Marandi, "Reading Azar Nafisi in Tehran," *Comparative American Studies*, 6, 2 (2008), 179–89.

12. Robert Graham, *Iran: the Illusion of Power* (London: Croom Helm, 1978).

13. Soli Shahvar, "The Islamic Regime in Iran and its Attitude towards the Jews: The Religious and Political Dimensions," *Immigrants and Minorities* 27, 1 (March 2009), 82–117.

14. Dalia Sofer, "Of These, Solitude," in Danya Ruttenberg (ed.), *Yentl's Revenge: The Next Wave of Jewish Feminism* (New York: Seal Press, 2001), 211.

15. Sara Ivry, "Stolen Gems," *Tablet Magazine*, 20 August 2007. (Audio interview). www.tabletmag.com/podcasts/3202/stolen-gems/ [18 August 2010].

16. Stuart Cary Welch, *A King's Book of Kings: The Shah-nameh of Shah Tamasp*. (New York and London: Thames and Hudson in association with the Metropolitan Museum, 1972), 112–13.

17. Souren Melikian, "Destroying a Treasure: The Sad Story of a Manuscript," *International Herald Tribune*, 27 April 1996. <http://.caissoas/CAIS/Art/manuscript.htm> [accessed 8 September 2010].

18. Ibid.

19. Stuart Cary Welch and Martin Bernard Dickson, *The Houghton Shahnameh* (Cambridge, MA: Harvard University Press, 1981), 7.

20. See Robert Hillenbrand (ed.), *Shahnama: The Visual Language of the Persian Book of Kings* (Aldershot: Ashgate, 2001). I am enormously grateful for an explanation of the miniature from Robert Hillenbrand, personal email, 8 September 2010.

21. Welch, *A King's Book of Kings*, 13.

22. Melikian.

23. Elli Lester Roushanzamir, "Chimera Veil of 'Iranian Woman' and Processes of U. S. Textual Commodification. How U.S. Print Media Represent Iran," *Journal of Communication Inquiry*, 28, 1 (2004), 9–28.

24. Abbas, *Iran Diary, 1971–2002* (Paris: Éditions Autrement, 2002), 18.

25. Paul Grainge, *Monochrome Memories. Nostalgia and Style in Retro America* (Westport, CT: Praeger, 2002), 3.

26. Abbas, 133.

27. Babak Ebrahimian, "Pictures from a Revolution: The 1979 Iranian Uprising," *PAJ: A Journal of Performance and Art*, 25, 2 (2003), 27.

28. Abbas, 135.

29. Ibid., 140.

30. Shiva Balaghi, "Abbas's Photographs of Iran," *Middle East Report*, 233 (2004), 28–33.

31. Abbas, 32, 34.

32. Ibid., 115.

33. Ibid., 112.

34. Ibid., 58.

35. Ibid., 78.

36. Ibid., 55.

37. Alfred Douglas, *The Tarot: The Origins, Meanings and Uses of the Cards* (London: Penguin, 1973).

38. William Lobdell, "A Booming Sect Sends Jewish Emissaries Abroad," *Los Angeles Times*, 11 September 2006. <http://www.rickross.com/reference/lubavitch/lubavitch41.html> [accessed 8 September 2010].

39. H. W. Janson, *History of Art* (Englewood Cliffs, NJ: Prentice-Hall, 1974).

40. Steven Nadler, *Rembrandt's Jews* (Chicago and London: University of Chicago Press, 2003).

41. Michael Zell, *Reframing Rembrandt: Jews and the Christian Image in Seventeenth Century Amsterdam* (Berkeley: Ahmanson, 2002).

42. W. J. T. Mitchell, *Picture Theory* (Chicago and London: University of Chicago Press, 1994).

CHAPTER 21

Trotskyism in the Early Work of Saul Bellow

Bellow's enthusiasm for Trotskyism tends to be summarily dismissed as a youthful peccadillo, or as just one among many of the weltering ideas which populate his fiction. As Edward Shils commented, "If there's a bad idea out there — Trotskyism, Reichism, Steinerism — leave it to our friend Saul to swallow it."[1] Arguably, however, the later Bellow's reputation as a neoconservative has obscured the importance to his life and writings of his early enthusiasm for Trotskyism. The 2010 publication of a selection of his letters opens with Bellow aged 17 writing to Yetta Barshevsky, a fellow high school student who introduced him to Trotskyism. In the letter the callow Bellow, disappointed in love, writes "I sever relations with you", conceding only that "We may still be casual friends."[2] In fact they stayed friends for more than sixty years. When she died, Bellow wrote her eulogy, describing how she had introduced him to world politics when they were at high school, and had given him Trotsky's pamphlet on the German question.[3] Yetta first married his friend Nathan Goldstein (aka Natie Gould) and later Max Shachtman, the American Trotskyist leader who became Trotsky's sole literary representative. Bellow was still thinking about Trotsky in the 1990s in his correspondence with Albert Glotzer (his lifelong friend and at one point Trotsky's secretary).[4] Bellow's involvement in radical left-wing politics, at Tuley High School and at university, produced his first publications (political pieces) in left-wing journals (*The Beacon* and *Soapbox*) and his first published short story, an antifascist fable. Although critics have tended to see Bellow's Trotskyism as a product of his involvement with the *Partisan Review* group, during that journal's Trotskyist phase, he appears to have been recruited to the journal because of his established political reputation rather than for his as yet unproven literary talent. Writing to F. W. Dupee in 1941, the editor Philip Rahv described Bellow as one of "the apprentice writers" he had met in Chicago.[5] In fact, *Partisan Review* was the least radical of the journals to which the young Bellow contributed. Between the 1930s and the 1950s Bellow's literary output centred on the political specificities of the time, most notably in "The Mexican General" (1942), based on Bellow's visit to Trotsky in Mexico, where he arrived within hours of the assassination.

In some respects, Bellow's enthusiasm for Trotsky is unsurprising. Writing in 1993 Bellow pointed out that when the Russian revolution took place in 1917, he was two years old and his parents, who had emigrated from Saint Petersburg to Montreal in 1913, followed subsequent events in Russia very keenly: "at the dinner table the Tsar, the war, the front, Lenin, Trotsky were mentioned as often as parents, sisters and brothers in the old country."[6] Grandfather Bellow had taken refuge in the Winter Palace during the Revolution; his mother's relatives were famous Mensheviks. While the older generation assumed that the Bolsheviks would soon be suppressed, their children were keen to join the revolution, including the son of Bellow's Hebrew teacher: "he went off to build a new order under Lenin and Trotsky. And he disappeared."[7] Despite embracing Americanisation Bellow's friends believed that "they were also somehow Russian" and read Tolstoy and Dostoevsky, going on to Lenin's *State and Revolution* and the pamphlets of Trotsky.[8] The Tuley High School debating society discussed *The Communist Manifesto*. Bellow read it and described himself as "swept away by the power of the analysis".[9] When a Commission of Inquiry was set up in Mexico in 1937, to consider the charges made against Trotsky in the Moscow Show Trials (in which he was alleged to be a fascist collaborator, and condemned to death in his absence) Bellow and his Trotskyist friends "followed the proceedings bitterly, passionately, for we were of course the Outs; the Stalinists were the Ins."[10] Even much later in his life Bellow still admired Trotsky, both for his politics and his culture.

> How could I forget that Trotsky had created the Red Army, that he had read French novels at the front while defeating Denikin? That great crowds had been swayed by his coruscating speeches?[11]

Bellow's political education began in earnest at "The Forum", a church hall on California Avenue which hosted debates between socialists, communists and anarchists. He read Marx and Engels, "Blasting away at *Value, Price and Profit* while the police raided a brothel across the street".[12] When the Young Communist League attempted to recruit him in the late 1930s, they were far, far too late. "I had already read Trotsky's pamphlet on the German question and was convinced that Stalin's errors had brought Hitler to power."[13] Trotsky wrote two major pamphlets on the German question. The first, in 1930, to which Bellow is referring, argued that the ideological error of the Comintern (Stalin) consisted in always seeing the main enemy as Social Democracy, and therefore not standing up to Hitler. Trotsky called instead for a united struggle against fascism, to include democratic forces as well as socialists, not an enticing prospect for the purists of the Communist party. In the second pamphlet, written in 1932, Trotsky foresaw the radicalisation of the American working class once the country began to emerge from its economic crisis.[14] Reflecting his Trotskyist beliefs, Bellow's early short stories, much more political than his novels, are marked by a profound ambivalence to war, distrust of democratic reforms, and a belief that capitalism had failed.

For Bellow, 1933 marked graduation from Tuley and entry into the University of Chicago, where he and Isaac Rosenfeld organised "Cell Number Five" of the Trotskyist Youth Group. As Alan Wald records, the Socialist Club of the University of Chicago published *Soapbox*, a sixteen-page magazine with a quotation on its masthead from William Randolph Hearst: "Red Radicalism has planted a soapbox on every campus of America."[15] Under the leadership of Nathan Gould, *Soapbox* made no secret of its political allegiances. It hailed Trotsky's 57th birthday enthusiastically, and attracted endorsements from Max Shachtman, James T. Farrell, Sidney Hook and Meyer Shapiro, among others. Bellow published political commentary, including "This Is The Way We Go To School" in December 1936, under the pseudonym John Paul.[16] Bellow had moved to Northwestern University in Evanston, in 1935, and may have used a pseudonym to deflect undue attention from his instructors.[17] The piece attacked a local resident of Evanston who had published a "handbook" for patriots, giving an exposé of Communist activity in the United States. Bellow was scathing about bourgeois Evanston and Northwestern, which he described as "intellectually flat-chested", and supplied details of the poor working conditions and pay of the ground and building staff.[18] In 1934 the general strikes had produced a new mood of activism in America, and Bellow rode the rails with his friend Herb Passin to see for himself, cheering on the sit-in strikers at the Studebaker plant from a boxcar. "Of course, I sympathized with the strikers."[19] When his old friend Sydney J. Harris founded a journal, *The Beacon*, which featured articles about local political disputes and union activities, he appointed Bellow as associate editor. For the young Bellow, however, Harris was not nearly radical enough, and he was incensed when Harris allowed the Stalinist Young Communist League to advertise in the journal. In 1936 "Saul Gordon Bellow" had reviewed J. T. Farrell's *A World I Never Made* in *The Beacon*, applauding its left-wing politics. Writing to Farrell in 1937 he complained that

> Editorially I can't push the magazine to the left because Harris is a shrewd opportunistic bastard who won't permit it. However, if we load the magazine with Bolshevik writers of national reputation, we can have Harris hanging on a ledge before long.[20]

In this however he was sadly mistaken; it was Bellow who left *The Beacon*.

Bellow also published pieces for the radical student newspaper, *The Daily Northwestern*. "Pets on the North Shore" (1936) again targeted the Evanston bourgeoisie via their pampered pooches. More importantly Bellow's first published story, "The Hell It Can't", appeared there in 1936. The story takes its title from the response of a character in Sinclair Lewis's novel, *It Can't Happen Here* (1935), to the suggestion that America could never turn Fascist.[21] In the novel "Buzz" Windrip, the populist leader of a "patriotic" movement in America, creates his own militia (the Minute Men or "MM", modeled on Hitler's "SS"), seizes power, and sets up a fascist dictatorship with martial law and concentration camps. The hero writes for a radical paper and survives to see Windrip's power waning. Lewis's novel was more optimistic than Bellow's story, in which Henry Howland is seized in the night by a group of paramilitary "patriots" and taken away for a brutal whipping which is still in progress as the story ends. Set in Chicago (the hero recalls friendly neighborhood exchanges about the Cubs) the story draws its horror from the absolute familiarity of the surroundings, emphasising that militarism and fascism could be right at home in America. As the story opens the enemy is already within the door. Henry hears a bell ringing, a hinge creaking, boots on the stairs, and the door of his room flying open. The action then consists entirely of the walk along the familiar street, past everyday landmarks, with Henry longing for a familiar face to appear, to witness his fate, "Now they were about to end him" (5). The story ends "he was five blocks from home."[22] The street teems with military activity, including young soldiers fresh from "some high school camp", who ignore Henry's plight, their faces "young, hard and unforgiving." "They were getting them young now, and well-trained" (5). The walls are plastered with propaganda posters, "Fight. Don't Be An Enemy At Home" (5) runs the caption to the face of a soldier with a bayonet, in front of a girl holding bandages. In the background men sing war-songs in saloons, chorusing "it won't be long till we're there" (5), with "there" meaning London, Lisbon or Rome. Whereas in Lewis's novel Windrip decides to invade Mexico and introduces the draft, Bellow's emphasis is on the European theatre of war. Henry recalls newsreels of Austrian troops on the run, and French troops leaving a fortress. Henry's crime is to have opposed American involvement in European war. Despite its early date the story resonates powerfully with *Dangling Man* (1944) and *The Victim* (1947) each in their different ways engaging with Bellow's doubts about the war, the one reflecting his opposition to it, the other, in its theme of anti-semitic persecution, his post-war remorse. Confronted with the Holocaust, Bellow viewed his earlier position with horror.[23] "Not only did I feel that my Jewish Marxist friends were wrong in theory, but I was horrified by the positions they — we — had taken."[24] In *Dangling Man* the deradicalised Joseph eventually succumbs to the social regimentation of war, though his final statement was described by Bellow as ironic.[25]

> Hurray for regular hours!
> And for the supervision of the spirit!
> Long live regimentation![26]

Bellow's distaste for war was typical of the left in the period. In interview in 1999 Bellow described his visit to Mexico where he had an appointment to meet Trotsky, with whom he wanted especially to discuss the problem of Finland and the issue of the war.[27] Trotsky had refused to dissociate himself from Stalin's invasion of Finland, in 1939, in the belief that it would advance the cause of socialism by nationalising land and by setting up cooperatives and workers' councils. As Bellow notes, he had his first doubts about Trotsky over Finland, but dismissed them.

> The Trotsky line was that a worker's state, no matter how degenerate, could not wage an imperialist war.[28]

As a result, Bellow stood by the party line, "the main enemy is at home, it's an imperialist war."[29] Later his doubts grew. While the Socialist Workers Party stood by the USSR, a minority led by James Burnham and Max Shachtman described the USSR as no longer a workers' state, but a new form of bureaucratic collectivism, and eventually in 1940 split to form the Workers' Party, taking forty per cent of the membership with them, including eventually Bellow. Writing to Oscar Tarcov in 1940 he describes his alienation from the factional fight, deploring Trotsky's "attempt to knife Burnham and cast him out of the movement", the hysteria of the old-timers and the stupidity of the polemics.[30] He was unwilling, however, at first to leave, "just when it is becoming dangerous".[31] More importantly he saw the split as a disaster. "It's a goddam shame that at the time that the war is on us the only revolutionary party in the country falls to pieces."[32] Trotsky's own advice, when asked in 1940 what an American Trotskyist should do if drafted, was "let him be drafted. ... he must go with his generation and participate in its life."[33] Eventually (after delays as a result of his Canadian citizenship and a hernia operation) Bellow joined the Merchant Marine in the last months of the war. Tellingly, in the early manuscript of *The Adventures of Augie March*, Augie is not the eager recruit to the war of the published novel, but chooses the Merchant Marine because it offers greater independence and an easier discharge.[34]

Hindsight always offers twenty-twenty vision, but it is important to underline that even after the outbreak of war, the Left in the 1940s did not prioritise the need to fight fascism, but rather the creation of an international brotherhood of the working class that would make war obsolete. The Workers' Party started its own journal, *Labor Action* in 1940. Even as late as 20 May 1940 it ran the headline "Let Bankers Fight on the Maginot line; Labor's Fight is at Home on the Picket Line", subheaded "Against the Allies and the Axis". On its front page on 5th August it argued that the Nazis feared too swift a British collapse lest the disintegration of the Empire lead to world revolution. ("The air raids are more for show than serious attempts to kick at the enemy.") One article was headed "40 Hour Week will be the first War Victim" which, as Edward Alexander remarks, conveniently ignored the casualties at Pearl Harbor.[35] *Partisan Review* was altogether more measured. On 15 November 1939 its editors advertised in *New Republic* that they had "consistently exposed the imperialist nature of this war, after as well as before it began."[36] They argued that although the Allies were preferable to the Nazis, their differences would be eliminated by an all-out war, with its erosion of individual liberties. The overthrow of the Chamberlain–Churchill and Roosevelt administrations was likely to be the only way to stave off the intellectual repression and regimentation required by war. A 1939 statement signed by *Partisan Review's* editors ran:

> This war must give birth to military dictatorship and to forms of intellectual repression far more violent than those evoked by the last war.[37]

The war eventually divided them, however. *Partisan Review* published Dwight Macdonald and Clement Greenberg's anti-war essay "10 Propositions on the War" proclaiming that "All support of whatever kind must be withheld from Churchill and Roosevelt."[38] Later however the editors themselves attacked Macdonald and he left to form his own anti-war periodical.[39] The introduction of the Voorhis Act in 1940 also complicated matters for writers and publishers. *Labor Action* described it (26 August 1940) as a huge threat to civil liberties since it required an organisation to hand over every scrap of information about itself and its membership if it was directly or indirectly affiliated with a political party in a foreign country or an international political organisation, thus implicating any labour organisation with international affiliations. Concerned that *Partisan Review* could be suppressed if it seemed to be publishing anti-war propaganda, Rahv and Phillips became increasingly reluctant to condemn the war, even more so when a financial crisis in 1943 almost closed the journal, which was rescued only by the financial support of Mrs Norton, the wife of a high-ranking army officer, who asked them not to embarrass her husband by political statements as long as the war lasted.[40]

If the Trotskyist position on war finds expression in Bellow's first story and in *Dangling Man*, the Trotskyist view of the Depression was also influential. For Bellow, "the beginning of the Great Depression was also the beginning of my mental life".[41] The depression saw a widespread conviction that capitalism had failed and that only the most radical social change could restore social and economic order. In 1937 the second great slump of the Depression looked even more promising for the growth of Labor movements but in fact 1938 was a disaster for them, as the working-class movement split between the CIO and AFL. Quite apart from the additional split in 1940 of the Trotskyist movement, it became almost impossible for American intellectuals to sustain their Marxism in the absence of any effective connection to the working class.[42] Bellow's "Two Morning Monologues" (1941) centres on the failure of the system, and the illusion that prosperity can be restored by orthodox methods. As Bellow noted, "the depression was the first time capitalism was under direct attack for its failures".[43]

Reminiscing about the period ("In the days of Mr Roosevelt") Bellow remembered his algebra teacher singing "Happy Days Are Here Again". (She was not being paid; City Hall had gone bust.) Bellow, however, did not share her enthusiasm for rescue by Roosevelt. As a socialist, he believed that Roosevelt's reforms were merely saving the country for capitalism. Radical orthodoxy in the Thirties held that parliamentary European reformism had failed and that "the real choice was between the hateful dictatorship of the Right and the temporary and therefore enlightened dictatorship of the Left".[44] Wryly the later Bellow noted how the masses actually fell in behind Roosevelt, a thoroughly patrician figure. "They did not call for a proletarian President."[45] "Two Morning Monologues" (1941), contrasts different reactions to the imminent demise of Capitalism. In the first "9.A.M. Without Work" the educated Mandelbaum complains that his workman father cannot see that the system has failed, and therefore remains wedded to the American dream. His father has invested money in Mandelbaum's education and in good capitalist fashion he expects a return. "Pride and Investment. I take those words to supply the whole meaning of his attitude."[46] To Mandelbaum's consternation, he advertises his son's capacities in the paper, as if he were selling a product. Mandelbaum spends long hours killing time, reading the papers and "following the fight between the bookies and the courts" (233). The latter phrase links the first monologue to the second, "11.30 A.M. the Gambler". In the depression there had been a crackdown on illegal gambling and 1940 saw the Chicago Crime Commission's fight against Frank "the Enforcer" Nitti, and his control of bookies' establishments, a by-product of his efforts to control the Bartenders' Union. If capitalism had failed, organised labor did not appear to be offering a solution. Unions found it difficult to resist "The Outfit" in Chicago where labor racketeering (the illicit use of unions by criminal groups) was a speciality. Importantly the gambler never lays eyes on the horses on whom the bets are placed. He dreams about one day seeing them run, far away from "the book in the tobacco shop, beyond the room where the smooth billiards run" (234). He is part of an illegal operation and has no connection with the labouring masses, "the sucker scraping the griddle "(234) and the girls he hears pushing laundry carts with their twelve-hour days, "eight on the books and four around the block" (235). The gambler's comment that "System is nothing" (234) extends beyond the story from the naïve beliefs of other gamblers that there is a magical "system" to winning, to the political system. The capitalist system and the unions are rackets.

The point was reinforced in a 1942 story set in mid-October 1922, a period of full prosperity. "Mr Katz, Mr Cohen and Cosmology" appeared (credited to "S. G. Bellow") in the first issue of *Retort*, an anarchist-pacifist literary journal, edited by Holley R. Cantine from a cabin in Bearsville, near Woodstock. Cantine also published an anthology compiled by war resisters.[47] Again Bellow employed the device of contrasting characters, and again the story centres on two men spending a day without work, though in this case only because it is Sunday. Mr Katz is a clothing cutter and Mr Cohen a tailor. Katz and Cohen are both immigrants, Katz from Warsaw via Amsterdam, Cohen a fugitive from Russia under the Tsar. As he tells Katz "I was in Kishinev in the days of Stolypin. I served in the Kavkaz."[48] Stolypin, Minister of the Interior and then Prime Minister (1906–11), was notorious for his ruthlessly repressive measures against revolutionaries; Kishinev was the site of a pogrom which shocked the world; the Caucasus region was a hive of revolutionary activity, where Stolypin used the army to put down disturbances.[49] As their leisurely Sunday indicates, in contrast to their pasts, Katz and Cohen are now enjoying peace and prosperity, unworried by political conflict. (Significantly the setting is Canada not America.) Yet the story does not endorse any nostalgic vision of the Twenties. Mr Katz, self-educated and keenly interested in cosmology, takes a walk with Mr Cohen, a flat-earther with no intellectual curiosity whatsoever. Intellectual and social gifts appear to be at odds. Katz is a frightening figure to his landlady's children whereas Cohen benevolently funds their movie attendance. Katz's lectures on the universe are repeatedly interrupted by Mr Cohen's sociable encounters, "Mr Katz standing aside, alone" (17). On the Esplanade "everyone Mr Cohen knows in the city seems to be promenading" (17). In response to Katz's lengthy account of the aeons of time before life existed, Cohen comments merely that he is more than sixty years old and that a year is now not a lot of time for him. "Sneeze and wipe your nose and it's a year already" (19). It strikes Mr Katz that he has never thought personally about time and that he is only some thirty "sneezes" behind his companion. "What have my thirty-three years meant?" he asks himself, saddened (19). The wind has risen, dusk is falling, and the day has turned more autumnal. The pair separate, Cohen to visit friends, Katz to return alone to his rooming house, still wondering "why he never thought of Time in a more personal sense" (19). Contemplating the stars from his window, setting his alarm for 6 a.m. and yet another week of work,

> He sees his life as pieces of cloth fed under the falling and again falling needle of a machine. (20)

A distant train, the sound of his clock, a whistle in the street, all appear to form "one apparatus", one system:

> all are stitching shut long seams, drawing in — to close it forever — all of past life. (20)

The story closes with the image of human subjection to mechanical labour, as if work were stitching Mr Katz's own shroud.

Like "Two Morning Monologues" and "Mr Katz and Mr Cohen", "The Mexican General" also focuses on two opposed characters, the idealist intellectual (Trotsky) and a petty opportunist, the General, a Mexican police chief, who stage-manages the exhibition of Trotsky's body to the press, to milk publicity for his own political career in the forthcoming election in Jalisco. He poses in photos in Trotsky's study, with the ice pick, with the body of Trotsky, with his widow, and is partly based on General José Manuel Nuñez, the chief of police in Mexico City, who was pictured posing in similar photographs in the press.[50] Again, the action of the story covers one day, following the General and his three "nieces" (paid women) on a tourist excursion around Patzcuaro, while Citrón describes the aftermath of Trotsky's death, two weeks ago, to his fellow bodyguard, Paco. Trotsky had visited Patzcuaro in 1938 where he, André Breton and Diego Rivera drew up the "Manifesto for an Independent Revolutionary Art". Patzcuaro was a haunt of bohemians and artists, part of the world of the avant-garde. But the Patzcuaro of the story has no affiliations with avant-garde art or revolutionary fervour. Rather it is designed to suggest that revolution did not transform Mexican culture. The contrast between Trotsky and Felipe is part of a generalised disillusionment. Mexico may embody a successful revolutionary past, but the General, who is following in his father's footsteps in seeking political office, is not the man his father was (181) and serves to illustrate the decadence of the revolutionary spirit, in a state which, like the USSR, now has opportunist heirs looking out only for their own interests.[51] In Patzcuaro, the group note with amusement the old-fashioned cinema. The film showing is *Rosa De Xochimilco*. This is not a stray detail. This is one of a small group of Mexican films in the late 1930s which focus on Indians and invoke ideas of a primitive paradise. (Think Gauguin's Tahiti.) Characters tend to be stereotypical Indians, marked by dignity, silence, inscrutability.[52] In the story the General is cast in the Indian role in his impassivity and concern for his own dignity, and is described as "austere" (183), "expressionless" (185) and "like a film star" (181). "Maybe it's the Indian part of him", jokes Paco (184). *Rosa de Xochimilco* (1939) is primarily notable for the views of Xochimilco, the pre-Hispanic settlement where floating gardens of flowers and vegetables are surrounded by canals, as in the days of the Aztecs. The film promulgates a timeless, museumised image of pre-revolutionary Mexico. Patzcuaro, famed for its indigenous peoples and their "butterfly" fishing nets, sells the same image to tourists. These films also tended to celebrate local religious or popular ceremonies, such as the choice of the most beautiful local woman.[53] Bellow's story makes much of the rivalry between the three nieces (with comments on their differing charms from the bodyguards) and effectively follows a similar scenario, closing as the General summons one of the three to his bed, leaving Citrón and Paco guessing which is the chosen one. The film carries an ironic charge using the museumised image to undercut any revolutionary content.

In *The Adventures of Augie March*, Augie makes a vigorous defence of directness, Augie plans to make the record freestyle,

> first to knock, first admitted; sometimes an innocent knock, sometimes a not so innocent.[54]

In his view there is no fineness or accuracy of suppression: "if you hold down one thing, you hold down the adjoining", and no way of camouflaging the nature of the knock "by acoustical work on the door or gloving the knuckles". In contrast Bellow's story is ruled by indirection and suppression, structured around a series of doors and thresholds, its action split into passages of prose which are carefully separated from each other by typographic spaces.[55] Citrón recounts how the General had managed the press, as Trotsky lay on his deathbed, letting them into his room in twos and threes. What the story suppresses is the fact that one of those admitted, posing as a reporter, was Saul Bellow. Bellow had set off to visit Trotsky with his friend Herb Passin, and arrived in Mexico City shortly after Trotsky had died.

> We had an appointment with Trotsky and we came to the door of the house: an unusual amount of excitement.[56]

Bellow and Passin "said we were newspapermen" and were directed to the hospital. The shock of the event resonates through his account with its repeated emphasis on blood.

> We asked to see Trotsky and they opened the door and said, he's in there, so we went in and there was Trotsky. He had just died. ... He was covered in blood and bloody bandages and his white beard was full of blood.[57]

Bellow stayed for Trotsky's funeral, and as the story demonstrates was clearly aware of the way Trotsky's body was treated, exhibited in a public autopsy to which the police admitted crowds of "the curious" (193), while Trotsky was turned around like a slab of beef, his brain extracted and weighed. As Citrón says, "The curio hunters would have got his heart if we had let them" (193). He makes this comment as the party are themselves buying tourist curios, in one of many parallels between the frame tale and the inset tale. Citrón acknowledges that his own role in the aftermath of the assassination was quite minor. He is one of

> "the others" who crowd in at the doors and are never thought the issue of the struggle but who are nevertheless those whom leaders lead, oppressors oppress, and saviours save. (188)

"The Mexican General" is a threshold story, between Bellow's earlier enthusiasm for Trotsky and a more realistic assessment, a form of self-criticism in best Marxist style on the part of Bellow, a horrified spectator at the deathbed of his hero. The inset story of Trotsky's assassination emerges only slowly. The opening mimes the difficulty of entering into the story proper, with a convergence between story theme and narrative environment: it opens with a door which will not open. Maria cannot get her hotel room door to open and there is a violent struggle on the threshold.

The doors are like "the doors of a church" (178), and the walls covered with images of Quiroga, a figure whom the ignorant visitors assume to be a king or a saint. Imagistically therefore sex and violence combine to gain entry to a sacred space, in a subtextual image of desecration. Vasco de Quiroga (*c.* 1470–1565) was a social reformer, influenced by More's *Utopia*, who built schools and hospitals, encouraged trades and crafts, and protected indigenous peoples.[58] The story therefore opens with an image of progressive political Utopianism, which is closed off at the end, as the door shuts on the woman. The second scene occurs in the general's room, when the clerk "rapped lightly at the door" (179), and in the third the General knocks at the door of his "nieces", who leave him irritated on the threshold. Despite the passive resistance of Maria who tends to hold things up, the General insists on being admitted: "I'll wait inside; I don't want to loiter in the passage" (182), just as he will gain sexual admittance at the close. The fourth scene moves the group to the dining room, where the bodyguards' meal is cut short: "The girls were already at the door". When they set off on a tour of the sights, the General sets the pace, with the bodyguards in the rear. Thereafter the stages of Citrón's story follow the stages of the tour. Describing Trotsky's wife, he says:

> The old woman had gone to the hospital and that was our next stop. They had reached the top of the street. (189)

The group enter a church, pausing on the threshold to cross themselves, and the story pauses. Then Citrón continues.

> "Where was I? ... That digression threw me off. Had we come to the hospital?"
> "You were just arriving." (189)

At the hospital the General comes out of Trotsky's room with a portentous air. "He shut the door carefully and waited till he had everyone around him. And then he announced, 'He is dead'." (191)[59] At this point in the present the group leave the church. "The tour is over" (191), as is the account of Trotsky's death. Back at the hotel the two guards rest in their room (they may be called upon later to take the party to see *Rosa de Xochimilco*) and hear the three taps from the General, on the wall of the women's room. "They listened to the swift steps at the General's door" (194). The door opens and closes, and the guards are left grinning as the story ends in darkness. A woman has entered but which one? All we know (and they know) is that a door has opened and closed.

What is striking in this structure is that effectively it is the General who controls the pace of the story. It is almost as if Bellow ceded control of the text, which is opened and closed by the General's control of access. To enter the story, we have to push through that first door; when the door closes, the story ends. Citrón's narrative can only proceed at the General's pace. When he calls on the guards, the inset story hangs fire, giving the impatient reader a feeling that nothing much is happening. The embedded narrative is the real action, but it is subject to the control of the frame tale (the door to the story) and runs at the pace of the General. Throughout, Trotsky is never named, and is merely the "russo", the "Viejo". Though it is tempting to see here a prudent awareness of the Voorhis Act (America was now at war) nobody in the *Partisan Review* readership would have had the slightest doubt of the identity of the "Old Man", Trotsky's usual sobriquet. Rather, the indirection underlines the extent to which the story cannot go directly at its own pace, its progress is repeatedly halted. In the background soldiers are drilling in the mud; they "stumbled heavily and out of rhythm" (185), just as Eulalia stumbles on the road in her fashionable shoes. Access to the narrative space is controlled, just as the masses who pushed in at the doors were eventually controlled by the General, just as he regulates access to rooms (and sexual access to their occupants) in the present of the story. Bellow makes the reader share his own frustration. As readers we are like the masses, under control, with no longer any easy access to progress or Utopian possibilities.

As a result, Trotsky remains in some ways unsullied. The story is infused with irony but not lost to idealism. In focussing on the General, Bellow may have taken his cue from the opposition developed in other memoirs of Trotsky. Dwight Macdonald contrasted the principled Trotsky and the opportunist Churchill in his memoir.[60] James T. Farrell remarked on the absence in any of his letters of a single cynical statement about the methods necessary to achieve power, unlike "genuine Machiavellians" like Napoleon.[61] Whatever anyone thought of Trotsky he was no opportunist. As Citrón says, everything about him was based "on principle, principle. I remember him expounding the principle when they chopped up his room with bullets" (188). Trotsky's reputation will live on, as Quiroga's does. But the point is also made that he can no longer set the pace and draw his followers behind him. Nor is it possible now to envisage peaceful change or to hold to pacifist principles. None the less Bellow did not give up lightly on his lost hero. In *The Adventures of Augie March* (1953), Augie glimpses Trotsky and has a sense of

> navigation by the great stars, of the highest considerations, of being fit to speak the most important human words and universal terms. (435)

When Augie leaves Mexico, Trotsky is still alive, as if Bellow had somehow resuscitated him in all his glory.

Bellow's politics now evolved away from Trotskyism and *Partisan Review* towards the more socially democratic position of Max Shachtman, rejecting party and national politics in favour of the creation of an internationalist third force on the democratic Left.[62] It is a change which is clearly envisaged in the evolution of *The Adventures of Augie March*, which Bellow thought of originally as a political novel, with Augie a much more studious and serious character than his later, larky incarnation. In the published version the political theme is almost non-existent and the original activist Augie March becomes the ingénu hero of a boisterously comic novel.[63] In contrast, in the earlier version, Augie is involved with a group called "The Committee for a Reconstituted Europe", run by Frazer and Robey, both much more serious political figures than their later versions. The CRE is designed to combat the idea of the world as regimented and homogenised, a universal ant-heap. It aims to preserve the individuality of ancient cultures — Basque, Catalan, Piedmontese, Welsh, Bohemian — so that the dominant states can be met with effective passive resistance, and a new European federation formed. (The plan also involves land distribution and socialist practices in industry.) Augie becomes their man in Spain, swayed by Robey's theory of gigantism, the idea that great states become tyrants. Similar "Third Camp" positions were common from the late 1930s onwards, as the rise of a bipolar international order left the independent European Left demoralised.[64] The CRE bears some resemblance to Dwight Macdonald's 1948 plan to create an organisation called "Europe-America Groups", to create a new force on the democratic Left. (Supporters included Bellow's friends Isaac Rosenfeld, Philip Rahv, William Phillips and Delmore Schwarz). Even during the war, Max Shachtman and the Workers' Party supported the idea that the best hope for democracy and lasting peace would be movements independent of the Allied governments. Shachtman's was an internationalist vision of the warring empires' common defeat by popular resistance movements independent of British, Russian, or American governments. Shachtman identified the Yugoslavian partisans as the most promising example.[65]

As did another of Bellow's protagonists. Bellow's last fictional word on his political past is "Mosby's Memoirs", written on his return to Mexico in 1968. Bellow now looked back on his political views as naive.

> Our own movement ... was often foolish, even comically absurd. During the Spanish civil war, the issue of material aid for the Spanish Republic was furiously debated by comrades who didn't have a dime to contribute.[66]

In "Mosby's Memoirs" Bellow ascribes his own political errors satirically to Lustgarten, and allows him to expiate them. Importantly, Jewish Lustgarten suffers from the same political naivety as the younger Bellow, the same recondite examinations of the same issues:

> Whether the American working class should give *material* aid to the Loyalist government of Spain. ... There was, of course, no material aid to give. But *had* there been any, *should* it have been given?[67]

Lustgarten also displays an agonised ability to split hairs over the issue of Finland.

> Technically, Stalinism could not be Imperialism by definition. What then should a revolutionary party say to the Finns? (156)

Jewish Lustgarten remains in America throughout the war "just sitting around" (163), but arrives in Europe immediately after its end, and gives Trotskyism one more chance. In the internationalist belief in the theory of permanent revolution ("you don't build socialism in one country", 165), he sets off for Yugoslavia, for what he assumes is a "V.I.P. deal" (165) as a foreign observer, declaring, "I really believe Tito may redeem Marxism by actually transforming the dictatorship of the proletariat" (165). He returns emaciated, sun-blackened and embittered from what has turned out to be a forced labour brigade. As a member of a chain gang in Dalmatia, Lustgarten has been thoroughly punished for his political errors. But the right, in the shape of his chronicler, Mosby, comes off worse.[68] For all his clever political-historical pronouncements, Mosby has no connection to society at all. Unmarried, friendless, childless, Mosby has suppressed all human ties — unlike Lustgarten, a keen father and uxorious husband. Mosby and Lustgarten are alter egos, doubles, the one conservative and the other socialist, allowing Bellow to satirise both sides of the political spectrum, but in the end the socialist still comes off best in the comparison. As Bellow said in 1993,

> What you invest your energy and enthusiasm in when you are young you can never bring yourself to give up altogether.[69]

Notes to Chapter 21

1. Joseph Epstein, "The Long, Unhappy Life of Saul Bellow," *New Criterion*, 29, 4 (2010), 1.
2. Saul Bellow, *Letters*, ed. Benjamin Taylor (New York: Viking, 2010), 4.
3. Ibid., 528.
4. Ibid., 470–72.
5. Hugh Wilford, *The New York Intellectuals: From Vanguard to Institution* (Manchester: Manchester University Press, 1995), 55.
6. Saul Bellow, "Marx At My Table," *The Guardian*, 10 April 1993, 23.
7. Ibid.
8. Ibid.
9. Saul Bellow, *It All Adds Up: From the Dim Past to the Uncertain Future: A Non-Fiction Collection* (London: Secker and Warburg, 1994), 301.
10. Bellow, "Marx at My Table".
11. Ibid.
12. Ibid.
13. Ibid.
14. See Albert Glotzer, *Trotsky: Memoir and Critique* (Buffalo: New York, Prometheus Books, 1989).
15. Alan Wald, *The New York Intellectuals: The Rise and Decline of the Anti-Stalinist Left From the 1930s to the 1980s* (Chapel Hill: University of North Carolina Press, 1987), 246.
16. Richard Peter O'Brien, "The Radical Politics of American Fiction: Saul Bellow and *Partisan Review*, 1941–1953," (PhD Leeds Metropolitan University, 2010). O'Brien's is much the most comprehensive discussion of the topic. He also notes John Paul, "Northwestern is a Prison, "*The Beacon*, 1, 1 (1937), 8–9.
17. It is also common for Trotskyists to use pseudonyms. See those listed by Peter Drucker, *Max Shachtman and His Left: A Socialist's Odyssey Through the "American Century"* (Atlantic Highlands, NJ: Humanities Press, 1994), xv.
18. John Paul, "This is the Way We Go To School," *Soapbox*, 2, 2 (December 1936), 7.
19. Saul Bellow, *It All Adds Up*, 24.
20. Bellow, *Letters*, 5.
21. Sinclair Lewis, *It Can't Happen Here* (London: Jonathan Cape, 1935), 26.
22. Saul Bellow, "The Hell It Can't," *Daily Northwestern*, 19 Feb. 1936, 8. Subsequent references follow citations in parentheses.
23. See Judie Newman, "Bellow's Ransom Tale: The Holocaust, *The Victim*, and *The Double*," *Saul Bellow Journal*, 14, 1 (1996), 3–18.
24. Saul Bellow, *It All Adds Up*, 310.
25. Bellow, *Letters*, 36.
26. Saul Bellow, *Dangling Man* (London: Penguin, 1963), 159.
27. Saul Bellow, "Before I Go: A Conversation with Norman Manea," *Salmagundi*, 155/156 (Summer 2007), 152. According to Gregory Bellow (email 11 April 2011) the meeting was arranged by Albert Glotzer.
28. Saul Bellow, *It All Adds Up*, 307.
29. Ibid., 306.
30. Bellow, *Letters*, 15.
31. Ibid.
32. Ibid.

33. Nicolas Mosley, *The Assassination of Trotsky* (London: Michael Joseph, 1972), 14.
34. Daniel Fuchs, *Saul Bellow: Vision and Revision* (Durham, NC: Duke University Press, 1984), 65.
35. Edward Alexander, "Irving Howe and the Holocaust: Dilemmas of a Radical Jewish Intellectual," *American Jewish History*, 88, 1 (2000), 96.
36. S. A. Longstaff, "*Partisan Review* and the Second World War," *Salmagundi*, 43 (Winter 1979), 111.
37. Ibid., 112.
38. William Phillips and Philip Rahv, "10 Propositions and 8 Errors," *Partisan Review*, 8, 6 (1941), 449–508.
39. Longstaff, 118–19.
40. Ibid., 123.
41. Saul Bellow, "In the Days of Mr Roosevelt," *Esquire* (December 1983), 533.
42. See Christopher Phelps, *Young Sidney Hook: Marxist and Pragmatist* (Ann Arbor: University of Michigan Press, 2005), ch. 4; and Mike Davis, *Prisoners of the American Dream: Politics and Economy in the History of the U.S. Working Class* (New York: Verso, 1986), 67–69.
43. Saul Bellow, *It All Adds Up*, 297.
44. Saul Bellow, "In the Days," 536.
45. Ibid., 532. Subsequent references follow citations in parentheses.
46. Saul Bellow, "Two Morning Monologues," *Partisan Review*, 8, 3 (1941), 230. Subsequent references follow citations in parentheses.
47. *Retort: An Anarchist Review*, vols 1–5, Bearsville 1942–51 (Santa Barbara: Greenwood Reprint, 1968).
48. S. G. Bellow, "Mr Katz, Mr Cohen and Cosmology," *Retort: A Quarterly of Social Philosophy and the Arts*, 1 (1942), 18. Subsequent references follow citations in parentheses.
49. Abraham Ascher, *P. A. Stolypin: The Search for Stability in Late Imperial Russia* (Stanford: Stanford University Press, 2001).
50. Photographs of him appear in *Life*, "Bloody Murder in Mexico Ends Great Revolutionary Career of Trotsky," 2 September 1940, 17–21; and in Alain Dugrand, *Trotsky in Mexico* (Manchester: Carcanet, 1992).
51. Saul Bellow, "The Mexican General," *Partisan Review*, 9, 3 (1942), 186. Subsequent references follow citations in parentheses.
52. I am greatly indebted to Minister Ignacio Duran Loera, John King and Andrea Noble, for their assistance in tracing details of these films.
53. See Jorge Ayala Blanco, *La Aventura del Cine Mexicano* (Mexico City: Ediciones Era, 1968); Anne T. Doremus, *Culture, Politics and National Identity in Mexican Literature and Film, 1929–1952* (New York: Peter Lang, 2001); Emilio García Riera, *Historia Documental del Cine Mexicano*, vol. 2 (Mexico: Universidad de Guadalajara, 1992).
54. Saul Bellow, *The Adventures of Augie March* (London: Penguin, 1966), 7.
55. The typographical spaces are maintained in the reprinted version. Saul Bellow, "The Mexican General," in Nicholas Moore and Douglas Newton (eds), *Atlantic Anthology* (London: Fortune, 1945), 22–34.
56. Bellow, "Before I Go," 151.
57. Ibid., 152.
58. Thomas Walsh, "Heroism in Bellow's "The Mexican General," *Saul Bellow Journal*, 1, 2 (1982), 31–33.
59. Bellow derives this scene from a different police chief: L. A. Salazar, chief of the Mexican secret police who made the announcement, in just these terms. See Leandro A. Sanchez Salazar and Julian Gorkin, *Murder in Mexico* (London: Secker and Warburg, 1950); and Judie Newman, "Saul Bellow and Trotsky," *Saul Bellow Journal*, 1, 1 (1981), 26–31.
60. Dwight Macdonald, "Trotsky is Dead: An Attempt at an Appreciation," *Partisan Review*, 7, 5 (1940), 339–53.
61. James T. Farrell, "The Cultural Front: Leon Trotsky," *Partisan Review*, 7.5 (1940), 389.
62. O'Brien, "The Radical Politics of American Fiction," 195.
63. Fuchs, *Saul Bellow: Vision and Revision*, 43–49.
64. Wilford, *The New York Intellectuals*.

65. Drucker, 147; Max Shachtman, *The Bureaucratic Revolution: The Rise of the Stalinist State* (New York: The Donald Press, 1962).
66. Saul Bellow, *It All Adds Up*, 100–01.
67. Saul Bellow, *Mosby's Memoirs and Other Stories*. (London: Penguin, 1971), 155. Subsequent references follow citations in parentheses.
68. See Judie Newman, "Zapotec Man and the Torajan Granny: *Mosby's Memoirs* and the Sacrifice of the Heart," in Gerhard Bach and Gloria Cronin (eds), *Small Planets: Saul Bellow as Short Fiction Writer* (East Lansing: Michigan State University Press, 2000), 113–26 (Chapter 12 in this volume).
69. Bellow, "Marx at My Table".

CHAPTER 22

Updike's *Terrorist*:
Rewriting the Domestic Myth

After 9/11 the commonest reaction among writers was to argue that the event could not be written about, resisted language, or lay outside literary paradigms. Jay McInerney and Bret Easton Ellis agreed on 9/11 that they could not go back to the novels they had been writing.[1] Martin Amis wrote that "After a couple of hours at their desks on September 12, 2001, all the writers on earth were reluctantly considering a change of occupation."[2] There was a general assumption that the old paradigms were not sufficient to encompass the event, the old stories would not serve, and personal or domestic narratives came in for particular criticism. In his analysis of 9/11 fiction, in *After the Fall*, Richard Gray categorises all those novels which employ the domestic or the sentimental as inadequate responses to the 9/11 attacks.[3] In his view retreating into domestic detail allows the unforeseen and the unknowable to be assimilated into familiar tropes and domestic structures. Gray cites DeLillo's *Falling Man*, Ken Kalfus's *A Disorder Peculiar to the Country*, even in part Cormac McCarthy's *The Road*, with its wished-for domesticity. Gayle Brandeis's *Self Storage* is dismissed as sentimental; Leila Halaby's *Once in a Promised Land* fails because it has a happy ending. In *The Writing on the Wall* by Lynne Sharon Schwartz, the reader is told that "There is a connection between the public and the private" but the heroine also knows that this connection "is merely a distraction" from her personal concerns.[4] In Reynolds Price's *The Good Priest's Son* September 11 becomes the occasion for a journey back home, to return to the father, while in Jonathan Safran Foer's *Extremely Loud & Incredibly Close*, it is the catalyst for Oskar Shell's attempt to unlock the secrets of his life and also get closer to his lost father. More shockingly, perhaps, in *A Disorder Peculiar to the Country*, Joyce is elated as the towers fall, since she assumes the husband with whom she has fallen out has died in the South Tower, and promptly embarks on a series of terror-sex liaisons. The domestic emphasis is not limited to Anglophone fiction; it is also European. Petra Fachinger has observed a tendency in 9/11 fiction to pair domestic stress with trauma on the world stage and lists a number of American novels that link 9/11 to family crises, together with parallel examples of recent German novels and short stories.[5] Similarly Michael Rothberg argues that the domestification of 9/11 is a means of avoiding the outward movement of American power, the ways in which

American foreign policy is entangled in global networks. Rothberg maintains that American writers have suffered from a failure of imagination.

> The most difficult things for citizens of the U.S. Empire to grasp is not the internal difference of their motley multiculture, but the prosthetic reach of that empire into other worlds.[6]

Rothberg also offers Schwartz's *The Writing on the Wall*, as a classic example of depoliticising discourse. A rather more measured assessment was taken by Catherine Morley, who took a longer view, placing 9/11 novels in the tradition of American fiction, and arguing that, rather than exemplifying a domestic turn, they merely continued the domination in American fiction of the late 1990s of the domestic and individual narrative.[7] Indeed, critics of 9/11 novels might well benefit from an even longer perspective as a corrective. Just why the domestic, even the sentimental, should not offer an adequate response to 9/11 is never fully explained by them. The suspicion lingers that the world of women and children is not envisaged as a positive place for literary responses. By these criteria *Uncle Tom's Cabin* would have been judged a failure as a response to the crisis of the Fugitive Slave Law.

The dangers of the domestic as an ideology were certainly well delineated in the aftermath of the attacks. In an argument which bears careful consideration, Susan Faludi has argued that the reaction of the United States to 9/11 involved a resanctification of the conventionally domestic, and a reversion to an original terror dream of vulnerable womanhood threatened by racial others, and in need of rescue by white males.[8] Some of the earliest reactions of this type appeared in graphic form. In Beau Smith's comic story "Soldiers" a unit of male U.S. soldiers helps police, fire-fighters and rescue workers (all male) to rescue two women and a little girl at Ground Zero.[9] In Sam Glanzman's four-page comic, *There Were Tears in her Eyes*, a male witness to the attacks comments "it's as if they raped the Statue of Liberty".[10] The last image in the comic depicts a highly feminised Statue of Liberty, weeping as she watches the towers burn.[11] In *The Terror Dream* Faludi describes her surprise shortly after 9/11 when she was approached by interviewers about the so-called end of feminism. The irony of responding to a terrorist attack by heralding feminism's demise, given the Islamic terrorists' conservative views on the place of women, was not lost on her. Yet reaction to 9/11 did appear to exacerbate anti-feminist trends, with feminism almost envisaged as treasonable by right-wing commentators. John O'Sullivan (writing on October 15 2001 in the *National Review*) accused feminists of taking the side of medieval Islamists as opposed to ordinary American men.[12] The suggestion was also advanced in the media that a feminised nation had gone soft, and that radical Islamists had exploited a perceived weakness in American manhood. Jerry Falwell, for example, claimed that by altering traditional roles, feminists had

> caused God to lift the veil of protection which has allowed no one to attack America on our soil since 1812.[13]

Although most of the victims of 9/11 (by a ratio of three to one) were male, orphaned girls and "9/11 widows" became a major media focus, along with an emphasis on a restored "femininity". The return to domesticity and to the shelter of the protective male was loudly, if erroneously, trumpeted in the media. Lipstick sales were gleefully reported as up by twelve per cent after 9/11, single women were supposedly rushing to the altar, "security moms" were giving up work to stay home with their children. After 9/11 Faludi also noted a recursus in American culture to images of the Western, and a resurgence of a John Wayne type of masculinity, particularly evoking his role as Ethan Edwards in *The Searchers,* rescuing his abducted niece, Debbie, from the Comanches. When Hollywood was called upon to support the war on terror Chuck Workman's film *The Spirit of America* (airing in mid-December 2001) began and ended with the opening scenes from *The Searchers.* Workman saw Wayne as a quintessential U.S. hero because

> He's a rescuer. When he rescues the girl, that's what the movie is all about.[14]

In short, what was an attack on an urban workplace representative of global capitalism was rewritten as an attack on the domestic circle, and on vulnerable women.[15]

So, does Updike suffer from a similar failure of imagination, peddling a domestic ideology in his fictional treatment of terror? At first, it might seem so. Updike described watching the fall of the towers in September 2001, in a piece written for the *Talk of the Town* in the *New Yorker.* He reported that he had been visiting "some kin" (gender unspecified) in Brooklyn Heights, and saw the south tower fall "straight down like an elevator, with a tinkling shiver and a groan of concussion".[16] In contrast, his first fictional treatment of 9/11, "Varieties of Religious Experience" (originally published in the *Atlantic Monthly* in 2002), echoes the developing domestic and female emphasis. The central character, Dan Kellogg, witnesses the fate of the tower not in terms of a falling man but as that of a fallen woman:

> as abruptly as a girl letting fall her silken gown, the entire skyscraper dropped its sheath and vanished with a silvery rippling noise.[17]

Imagistically a young woman (a girl in a timeless silk gown) has been disrobed, lost her protective covering, and been plucked from sight. The cast list of the story is also overwhelmingly female. Dan is watching from his daughter's apartment, in company with a nanny and one of his two little granddaughters, the embodiments of innocence and the need for protection. Emily is absent; a single mom, she is "slim and hard and professional" (87) and works in finance in New York. Until she arrives home, he sees himself as "the leader of this defenceless, isolated trio" (86). He had previously planned to visit an exhibition of works by Wayne Thiebaud, noted for his parody pop-art depictions of cakes, in Disneyesque candy colours. Instead he engages in cookie-baking to distract his granddaughter. (Baking is now a serious business.) When he and the family subsequently go to church, even the pastor is female. The second section of the story depicts the threat to these women in the shape of a 9/11 hijacker, apparently entirely motivated by an anti-feminine animus, situating him in a strip club where the naked women are repeatedly described by him as sluts (90, 91), and where he is aggressively nasty to the waitress. Mohamed has been raised with two sisters in Cairo, just like his 9/11 original, Mohamed Atta. Atta's sisters were older than him and successful professionals, one a medical doctor and the other a professor of zoology. Updike, however, casts them as women in need of protection: "it was to keep them from ending as sluts that he had dedicated himself to the holy jihad" (93). Mohamed sees his sisters as "too light-headed to know that the temptations twittering at them from television and radio were from Satan, designed to lure them into eternal flame" (93). In the third section, Jim Finch, high up in the World Trade Center, makes repeated attempts on his cell phone to explain what is happening to his wife Marcy, all of which founder, as she keeps interrupting him to rehearse a catalogue of domestic minutiae and shopping. When Jim tells her to shut up and tell him what she can see of the towers from her windows, her voice trembles "like a child scared she has done wrong and will be punished" (97). When Jim realises there is no escape, he can think only of the image of his plump little daughter "in soccer shorts, scared and pink in the face" (99), not his son. In the fourth section Carolyn, an elderly widow, quivers in helpless terror as the American males on board United Airlines Flight 93 vote to storm the cockpit of the hijacked plane. There seem to be no stewardesses involved, and nobody asks Carolyn to vote or to participate in the action. Only the male passengers vote. Watching the "stampeding American men" (107), repeatedly characterised as hefty football players forming a scrum, Carolyn realises that "her parents and husband and all the protectors of her long protected life" (108) have deserted her. The story closes with Dan back at his daughter's apartment six months later, recalling how 9/11 had initially destroyed his faith in God, and how "news events had tended to corroborate his revelation" (108). The reports include a woman drowning her five children, Catholic priests committing child abuse, and fathers murdering wives and children. Child protection clearly remains his overriding concern, and in the story women are assimilated to the helpless child image. As a result the story resonates with a retrograde myth of weak womanhood, childish innocence, and the threat to the domestic world, rather than engaging with political and economic causes.

But to his credit Updike did not leave things there. His subsequent novel, *Terrorist* (2006), focusses deliberately upon domestic terrorism, centring, not upon 9/11 and its foreign terrorists, but on an American would-be suicide bomber, Ahmad, a young Muslim of partly Egyptian extraction. The plot is based upon events prior to 9/11, a planned attempt to blow up the Lincoln and Hudson tunnels using car bombs, a conspiracy which was thwarted in June 1993 by the presence of an informant on the inside.[18] As in the novel, the terrorist group, inspired by a local imam, had been under investigation for some time. As a result, the international dimension is decidedly muted. Indeed, the action is largely driven by Charlie Chehab, a CIA informant who uses Ahmad simply to flush out the terrorists. Updike's Islamic terrorist is therefore the hapless victim of manipulation (both by the jihadists and by the CIA sting); the attack would have been prevented, had Charlie's cover not been blown; Ahmad is motivated largely by distaste for American materialism, rather than by global issues. The strength of the novel, however, consists in Updike's revision of his previous fiction. In *Terrorist*, Updike offers a radical critique of the domestic myth, in a succession of interiors which offer a vision of the stultifying paralysis of the traditional homemaker (Jack Levy's massively corpulent, almost immobilised wife), grotesquely exaggerated evocations of the domestic dream (the furniture warehouse in which Ahmad works), and a model of an alternative domesticity (the terrorist's home with his single mom), which is unconventional but creative and life-affirming. In addition, the rhetoric of home and homeland is comprehensively undermined in a set-piece sermon in an African American church, which juxtaposes Israelite, American and Palestinian versions of home.

Updike makes furniture a symbol of the worn-out American domestic myth, and its dangers. When Ahmad is offered a job as a truck driver, he points out that as an eighteen-year-old he holds a licence which precludes transporting hazardous materials. His imam reassures him that the firm don't want him to carry anything hazardous; he will be transporting used furniture for Excellency Home Furnishings.[19] There is nothing complicated to the job. Charlie reassures him that "Furniture isn't like a car, it doesn't have a lot of secrets. What you see is what you get" (150). In the event however what Ahmad sees reveals the very real dangers and secrets of domestic furnishings. When he has to deliver an (aptly named) ottoman to an address in a rundown beach resort, the Americans on the streets are characterised as childish; children and adults are wearing huge Dr Seuss hats, the obese grandparents are dressed "as toddlers" (191) in playsuits. In contrast the Arabic-speaker who opens the door to Ahmad is lean, wiry, flat of stomach, and once Ahmad has left, far from putting his feet up on the ottoman he draws a small sharp knife, slits the stitches and extracts a huge sum of money, the finance for the explosives.

In interview Updike once referred to America as "a couch potato of a country."[20] He also reflected on the work of Raymond Carver as presenting

> domestic life as curiously packed and sinister, as somehow dangerous, as if its meagre scuffed decors were about to trip into darkness.[21]

In Carver's world objects are dominant and relationships form around them, memorably in "Why don't you dance?" where furniture set out on a lawn attracts occupants and structures relationships.[22] Here, the depiction of Beth Levy in her La-Z-Boy armchair bears out the moral that the armchair can kill you. Massively obese, Beth is stuffing herself with cookies in front of the daytime soaps, which are much more dramatic than her own life. It takes her some eight pages to extricate herself from the chair when the phone rings, pages replete with details of her vacuum cleaner, the celadon green carpet, her yearning for an Oriental rug, her domestic appliances, and finally the Shaker chair by the phone which is now far too narrow for comfort. The Shakers were clearly less well-upholstered than Beth and evoke an image of a leaner, idealistic past from which America has declined. The "echoing three-sided rooms" (126) of the soaps offer a parallel to her own hollow existence. Her lengthy internal monologue conveys a sense of an inward-looking, confined life, with everything happening inside her own head. Like her declawed cat Carmela, who can't go outside, but dreams every night of feral activities (22), Beth watches soaps full of sex, jealousy and murder, from all of which she is protected:

insulated against the passion and danger that crackle wherever people truly rub against one another. (126)

Carmela is of course also a name drawn from a television series, that of the materialistic homemaker-wife of mafia boss Tony Soprano, in *The Sopranos*, a man with such doubts about his killings that he regularly visits a psychiatrist. It is not just the woman who is the target here. The scene reflects on the softness and lack of vigour of men, both in the brand name La-Z-Boy and in the soaps where the actors are immature "men-boys" (126). Men have gone boyish and soft. (The novel makes much of the TV ads for products to correct erectile dysfunction (171).) Beth's husband, Jack, has his tongue firmly in his cheek when he quips that

> We should all go back to being hunter-gatherers, with a hundred-percent employment rate and a healthy amount of starvation. (136)

But the suspicion lingers that cave man was better at protecting his dependents than the new man of the present. Certainly, as a high-school counsellor, Jack sees through the myths of American domesticity, regularly encountering children who "appear to have no flesh and blood parents" at all. (34)

The connection between Beth's domesticity and the official, civil ideology (women need to be protected) is made explicit in a phone call from her sister, warning her that there is an increased terrorist risk. Hermione, a spinster, works for the Secretary of Homeland Security. Her long exposition of the external threats to America (cyber-attacks, insecure ports, indefensible malls) falls on deaf ears; for Beth it is time to go shopping for "basics" (137), "Cookies and snacks" (137), though first she flops back into the La-Z-Boy and raises the foot rest. What this scene establishes is that the domestic myth is dangerous in itself, that America has moved into ever more confined spaces, and that public, civic life has shrunk. Beth herself comments on the general decline of civility in America, which she ascribes to the fact that "television has made people at home now everywhere" (124). But her husband Jack seems to be at home nowhere. Jack has already described his home as stifling; "the room's black air has become hard to breathe" (22), as if the smoke of 9/11 still lingered. He has a sense that "houses have compressed into housing" (26), squeezed closer by rising costs. What were once roomy homes have turned into commercial assets, their gardens gone, their trees threatened. He jokes that the whole neighbourhood could do with a bomb (32), as if the United States had invited destruction by allowing its ideals to fail. A once expansive America is typified in the rundown town of New Prospect, its school, once a castle in appearance, progressively reduced by the demands of highways. Spaces for public and civic engagement have been reduced to the domestic interior, with its sinister, entrapping La-Z-Boy. The scene reads as an exaggerated parody of the post-9/11 argument that America has gone soft and flabby, careless of danger, its men too enfeebled to protect its dependent women.

In the furniture warehouse Updike also situates his terrorist in an apparently domestic scene, though it is in fact a commercial location where that dream is sold to customers. The warehouse offers a grotesquely exaggerated embodiment of domesticity, in a mass accumulation of used furniture:

> a nightmare room containing chairs, end tables, coffee tables, table lamps, standing lamps, sofas, easy chairs, dining tables and chairs, footstools, sideboards, chandeliers hanging thick as jungle vines, wall sconces in various enamelled or metallic finishes, and large and small mirrors from stark to ornate, their frames gilded or silvered amalgams of leaves and chunky flowers and carved ribbons and eagles in profile, with lifted wings and clasping talons; American eagles stare back above Ahmad's startled reflection. (149–50)

The catalogue moves seamlessly from the mundane domestic (chairs) to the glorification and magnification of domestic space (in mirrors) as a patriotic statement (American eagles). The showroom building itself imitates the arrangement of domestic housing, with the catalogue repeated upstairs, in a second massive inventory of beds, bedside tables, bureaus, dressing tables, armoires, chaises longues, upholstered side chairs , stools and "little table lamps softer ... to go with what should happen in a bedroom" (150). For Ahmad the desperate variety of styles and textures merely masks "the wear and boredom of it, the closed spaces, the floors and ceilings constantly measuring finitude, the silent stuffiness and hopelessness of lives without God" (151). Through Ahmad's eyes Updike emphasises furniture as an example of secular American consumerism, functioning as a defence against death: "Hurry, buy now, since the afterlife's pure and plain joys are an empty fable" (152). Where at first in the showroom Ahmad feels excited, "about to be enlisted in the armies of trade" (152), his enthusiasm soon gives way to an awareness of the pervasive consumerism all around him. En route to a delivery, Charlie comments that advertising pushes sex,

> "because it means consumption. First the liquor and flowers that go with dating, and then the breeding and the buying that goes with that, baby food and SUVs and — " "Dinette sets," Ahmad supplies. (213)

Sure enough, when they deliver the dinette set with cinnamon finish, they are met by a housewife with two small children who react "as if another set of siblings is being delivered" (214). Furniture seems to have taken on a life of its own.

An alternative image of domesticity is offered by Ahmad's home, a small apartment shared with his single-mom Teresa. This domestic space is quite unorthodox. Teresa uses her bedroom as her studio; it smells of paint and turpentine and has harsh fluorescent lighting, and hardly any furniture. It seems a bigger space as a result. Teresa plays different gender roles. She deliberately signs her paintings "Terry", because male painters get better prices. For Jack, Terry is "a wild one, a rule-breaker, terri-ble. A holy Terror" (164). Nobody is engaging in terror-sex here. The conflation of terror and woman in her name implies that she is not in any need of protection. She laughs at the idea that single-moms are downtrodden and undervalued (89), and cheerfully dons an Islamic headscarf for her son's commencement purely to please him. Jack concedes that in fact the house has a "homier" (88) feeling than he had imagined. Ahmad acknowledges that she has brought him up well and (unlike the characters of Foer or Price) he shows no desire to go in quest of his absent father. The unorthodox domestic space thus opens outwards into a broader area of art, freedom and love. Despite the inevitable sex scenes, Terry's real passion is for art (190). Her domestic arrangements may not fit the conventional image but they seem a sight healthier than Beth's. The apparently dysfunctional and polluted domestic space works better than the supposed ideal.

So far so good. The domestic has been comprehensively parodied, even pilloried, in a grotesque exaggeration of its plenitude, hollowing out its meaningfulness, and a less ideologically restrictive version has potentially been substituted. It might none the less be argued that the novel still lacks any broader international dimension, remaining at the level of the individual story of Ahmad's religious crisis and coming of age. Furniture, however, also forms the link to Updike's unpicking of the rhetoric of home and homelands in a wider historic and religious sense. When Charlie offers Ahmad a surprise, he assumes it will be another ottoman, or at least a hassock, containing money, an end-of-summer bonus, but to his astonishment he is provided with a hooker, Joryleen, who is waiting for him upstairs amidst the serried lines of beds. Joryleen, thoroughly bamboozled by her pain of a boyfriend Tylenol, who is adept at exploiting the domestic myth, is selling her body just until she and her boyfriend "can have a house of our own" (218). Incongruously, the Islamic terrorist promptly attempts to rescue her from her life of shame and turn her back into the choirgirl he used to know: Ahmad refuses to have penetrative sex with her, settles her on an Oriental rug, with an oasis pattern, and pays her to sing "What a friend we have in Jesus", as she did in her gospel choir. Ahmad, in short, figures as a would-be rescuer, not a threat to women at all, creating a little oasis in the desert of beds and furnishings. The Oriental rug (rather like a magic carpet) takes the pair back in time to a more innocent moment in their lives, and opens a vista into the past in broader and national and international terms.

The scene refers back explicitly to Ahmad's visit to Joryleen's African-American church, where the pastor's sermon underlines the ambiguity of all notions of home and homeland. In the sermon the Middle East becomes America, with the Egyptian pharaoh as the slave owner, and the Israelites seizing the homes of the Canaanites, in a fairly pointed reference to Arab–Israeli conflicts in the present. The pastor bases his jeremiad on events narrated in the second book of the Hebrew Bible, Exodus, concerning the Hebrews' deliverance from slavery in Egypt to freedom in the Promised Land of Canaan, where they form the new Israelite nation. The Exodus narrative is, of course, a very old story, of special resonance in American culture. Few Christian communities have identified more closely with the children of Israel than America's founding fathers, notably John Winthrop, who emphasised the idea that the Puritans had inherited the divine covenant first given to the Hebrews, making America a New Israel. In this founding myth the Puritans identified their political struggle against England with that of the ancient Hebrews against the persecutions of (variously) the Pharaoh and/or the king of Babylon. The Exodus narrative has also been central to African-American counter-discourse, with its imagery employed to evoke deliverance from the Egypt of American slavery. For American Jews it also has links to the founding of the state of Israel, in the example of the *SS Exodus*, a ship carrying Jewish refugees who were then refused entry to Palestine, which inspired Leon Uris's Novel, *Exodus* (1958) and the subsequent film. In the novel, New Prospect, with its Moorish City Hall and long history of Middle Eastern immigration, was itself once seen as the land of milk and honey, but its people have now opted for the golden calf of materialism, re-enslaved to possessions. The multivalence of this metaphor, with America as New Canaan or old Egypt, allows Updike to question the notion of America as homeland and the ways in which the rhetoric of home is deployed to political purposes. As Anna Hartnell has argued,

> America's desire to be a "light unto the nations" has frequently been narrated in terms that explicitly reference the book of Exodus and its typological readings in the New Testament.[23]

In Hartnell's analysis the idea that America serves as an example of freedom around the globe is completely displaced by the African-American evocation of the same story, which highlights America itself as a place of slavery and persecution. It is important to emphasise also that Updike chooses as his Biblical text the moment of *failure* to enter the Promised Land, knocking away the supports from the ideology of America as New Canaan in an image of the unrealised nature of the Israelite mission. In the sermon, drawing primarily upon Numbers 14, and associated texts, the pastor focusses on the point at which the Hebrews' nerve failed on the very borders of Canaan, and the fact that Moses was denied admission to the Promised Land. As Kristaan Versluys notes, hailing the sermon scene as a tour de force, religious instruction depends upon the explication of holy texts, "how to apply old stories and timeworn texts to present day situations".[24] Exodus is an old story about a homeland and its foundation, but it is reconfigured by Updike to undermine American ideological assumptions. In Numbers 14 the Israelites send out scouts to spy out the land of the Canaanites, subsequently take fright at the account of the giants supposedly living there, waver in their faith in Moses and Aaron, and decide to go back to Egypt. "Would God that we had died in the land of Egypt! Or would God we had died in this wilderness" (Numbers 14, 2). The modern pastor uses the text to conflate his present-day backsliders with their Biblical precedents, linking back to the days of slavery and then the Civil Rights struggle, and ironically assuming the voice of the waverer.

> That Pharaoh, he wasn't so bad. He fed us, though not much. He gave us cabins to sleep in, down by the marsh with all the mosquitoes. He sent us welfare checks, pretty regular. He gave us jobs dishing up fries in McDonalds, for the minimum wage. (55)

As the preacher pictures it, the Israelites still had "a soft spot for that golden calf" (56) and were quite prepared to give up their civil rights.

> They wanted to forget their sorrows in dope and disgraceful behavior on Saturday nights. (57)

The point of the sermon is to extol the absolute primacy and necessity of faith. Because the Israelites lacked faith in God, he showed them no mercy and excluded almost all of them from the Promised Land. (The scouts are killed, the others condemned to forty years in the wilderness.) Despite Moses's pleas the Lord refuses to relent:

> I'm tired of all this forgiving I'm supposed to do. I want some glory for a change. I want your carcasses. (57)

Nor is this harsh god the product of poetic license on the part of the preacher. The Bible itself reads "Your carcasses shall fall in the wilderness" (Numbers 14:29). Updike had prepared for *Terrorist* by reading the Quran and commented in interview that he was surprised by the anger and hatred in it, but that as a seventh-century text, it was perhaps not so surprising that it was harsh.[25] In choosing this particular text, from the Old Testament, he draws the different deities together. As Ahmad reflects, recognising the names in the story, there is a kinship between Islam and the Judeo-Christian faiths. "These people around him are too in their fashion People of the Book" (62).

For the pastor, religious faith is firmly linked to American freedom: "Martin Luther King had faith on the Mall in Washington" (59), "Rosa Parks had faith in that bus in Montgomery, Alabama" (60). But, as Hartnell also argues, the nature of American freedom is problematised in the use of the Exodus story, in the attitude displayed towards the Canaanites, and the fact that the Promised Land is based upon the exclusion of its native population. The Biblical Canaan is essentially the land west of the Jordan, now modern-day Israel, Lebanon and the Palestinian territory. Charlie Chehab and his Lebanese family are descendants of the Biblical Canaanites, who also serve here as an allegory for the position of the Palestinians today in the present state of Israel. In the Biblical story only Caleb has faith (Numbers 14:6–8) urging the Israelites on towards the land of milk and honey. The pastor gives voice to Caleb in rather militaristic terms: "Caleb said, 'Let's go, let us go up at once and possess it. We can take 'em, giants or not. Let's go do it!'" (55). The shifting nature of the Exodus metaphor makes this a risky strategy on Updike's part, as the African Americans morph from victims of past oppression to perpetrators in their turn, part of an American Empire convinced of its sacred mission and its own innocence. America was not the homeland of the European colonists, but a place of conquest, and the line blurs today between American Israelite and dispossessed Canaanite, as one group's homeland is obtained at the expense of another's.

One dimension of this sermon scene, however, has attracted no critical comment: the role of women. The pastor's rhetoric is very much part of the dominant American consensus. He caters unashamedly to misogynism, making jokes about female garrulity and weakness.

> Mercy, our beloved sisters do know how to *speak*. God didn't give Eve our strength of arm or shoulder, but he gave her double our strength of tongue. (53)

He also mocks his wife's shopping habits, teasingly recalling the French toast she makes to mollify him "after she's bought herself a new dress ... or some fancy alligator purse she feels the teeniest bit guilty about" (53). In the sermon women feature only as potential victims along with their children. The Israelites fear that "our wives and our children should be a prey" (55). With the sole exception of Rosa Parks, women are weak and vulnerable and their men are failing to protect them. In the preacher's account, the men could also have claimed a seat at the front, but preferred the back of the bus because it was "cosy" (60).

We have a little game of craps going, we have our little pint of Four Roses
to pass around, we have our little crack pipe, and heroin needle, we have our
underage crackhead girlfriends. (60)

Ahmad, however, sees things differently. The scene modulates from an all-male
misogynistic event to an occasion which puts women at the centre of the stage
and (in the person of the little girl sitting next to him) right in his lap. For him,
"The mosque was a domain of men; here women in their spring-shimmer, their
expansive soft flesh, dominate" (50). He is seated amidst a whole brood of little
girls, and picks out Joryleen in the choir, "a mass of mostly women, massive
women" (52). Women respond to the preacher and at the close of the sermon their
voices are raised as equals with the men, hailing "The Lord of Mary", "The Lord
of Bathsheba", "The Lord of Zipporah". As the choir crash into song, their voices
have "a stately, frontal quality, like an army advancing without fear of attack" (63).
Women, notably Joryleen, her voice "young and pure" (64) and two other soloists
dominate in the final performance of "What a friend we have in Jesus", a familiar
hymn. The congregation "know this song, they like it" (62). In the performance,
however, the women improvise upon it, harmonise, call and respond to each other,
displaying female mastery, inventiveness, and the ability to take an old well-known
piece and make it new. The thinner woman begins in a voice that sounds "like a
man's, a mellow man's" (64), while the organist appears to be going his own way,
and Joryleen's voice rises "in sudden freedom to a shriek" (64). The congregation
murmur approval "of these liberties" (64), as the third member of the trio chimes
in, and Joryleen tries a few off notes, harmonising. "The song is shedding the
clothing of its words" (64), changing and evolving with the singers who are ad
libbing freely, so that the hymn "can be accessed at any point" (65). Jesus has been
shortened to "Jeez, Jeez, Jeez" (66) and his name slapped across the beat "as if
another song is leaking in" (66), though everyone comes back together for the last
notes. In little, the scene gives us a model of Updike's own fictional strategy; an old
story, a domestic story, is revised and altered to meet new circumstances, its known
elements defamiliarised and made afresh, freely interpreted and recreated.

The denouement of the novel bears out the revisionary message. The CIA plot
founders largely because of the American desire to be a hero. Charlie Chehab
has waited too long to spring his trap, and his cover is blown. As the Secretary
of Homeland Security complains, "He wasn't following procedure. He had some
vision of a great revelation and round-up, like in the movies, starring guess who?
Him" (259). For him, Charlie, whose beheaded corpse reveals clear signs of torture,
is merely a commodity. "I *hate* losing an asset", (259) he whines. In the terrorist
plot, although Ahmad is intercepted and dissuaded from pressing the detonator
by Jack, the chain of causation leads back to women. Because of his affair with
Terry, Jack has mentioned Ahmad to Beth, who mentions him to Hermione. In
the upshot, therefore, the day is saved by the combined forces of a single, childless,
career-woman, Hermione, and an ageing adulterer. John Wayne is nowhere in
sight. Critics of *Terrorist* have tended to focus on issues of ethnicity and race to the
exclusion of other concerns. Representative examples include important essays by

Mita Banerjee, Anna Hartnell and Pamela Mansutti. Banerjee argues that when under extreme psychological duress, any culture tends to activate the particular manifestation of difference which is most genuine to it — in her argument, race.[26] But as Faludi demonstrates, it was gender which leapt onto the centre of the stage following 9/11, and it is gendered relations which are at the heart of 9/11 fiction. As a result, Updike's focus on the domestic is just what a novel about terrorism should be offering. In its parodic version of the domestic myth, *Terrorist* revises gendered readings of 9/11; argues that America is not an innocent victim; and empties the domestic space of its ideological power.

Notes to Chapter 22

1. Sonia Baelo-Allué, "The Depiction of 9/11 in Literature: The Role of Images and Intermedial References," *Radical History Review*, 111 (Fall 2011), 184–93.
2. Martin Amis, "The Voice of the Lonely Crowd," *Guardian*, 12 June 2002, 4.
3. Richard Gray, *After the Fall: American Literature Since 9/11* (Chichester: Wiley-Blackwell, 2011).
4. Lynne Sharon Schwartz, *The Writing on the Wall* (New York: Counterpoint, 2005), 294.
5. Petra Fachinger, "The Making of a "Terrorist": John Updike's *Terrorist* and Christoph Peters's *Ein Zimmer im Haus des Krieges*," *Canadian Review of Comparative literature/Revue canadienne de littérature compare*, 34, 4 (2007), 410–22.
6. Michael Rothberg, "A Failure of the Imagination: A Response to Richard Gray," *American Literary History*, 21, 1 (2009), 152–58.
7. Catherine Morley, "How Do We Write About This? The Domestic and the Global in the Post 9/11 Novel," *Journal of American Studies*, 45, 4 (2011), 717–31.
8. Susan Faludi, *The Terror Dream: Fear and Fantasy in Post-9/11 America* (New York: Henry Holt, 2007).
9. Beau Smith, "Soldiers," in Paul Levitz (ed.), *9/11: The World's Finest Comic Book Writers and Artists Tell Stories to Remember*, vol. 2 (New York: DC Comics, 2002) 89–94.
10. Sam Glanzman, "There Were Tears in Her Eyes," in Paul Levitz (ed.), *9/11: The World's Finest Comic Book Writers and Artists Tell Stories to Remember*, vol. 2 (New York: DC Comics, 2002), 207–10.
11. See Juanjo Bermúdez de Castro, *Rewriting Terror: The 9/11 Terrorists in American Fiction* (Madrid: Universidad de Alcalá, 2012) for discussion of graphic works.
12. Faludi, 23.
13. Ibid., 22.
14. Ibid., 7.
15. For more extensive discussion of Faludi's argument and another example of a novel which challenges the domestic myth, André Dubus III, *The Garden of Last Days* (New York: W. W. Norton, 2008), see Judie Newman, *Utopia and Terror in Contemporary American Fiction* (New York and London: Routledge, 2013).
16. John Updike, "September 11, 2001," in *Due Considerations: Essays and Criticism* (London: Hamish Hamilton, 2007), 117–18.
17. John Updike, "Varieties of Religious Experience," in *My Father's Tears and Other Stories* (New York: Alfred A. Knopf, 2009), 82. Page references follow subsequent quotations in parentheses.
18. Jörg Thomas Richter, "John Updike, *Terrorist*," in Susanne Peters, Klaus Stierstorfer, Laurenz Volkmann (ed.), *Novels: Part II* (Trier: WVT, 2008), 481–93.
19. John Updike, *Terrorist* (New York: Alfred A. Knopf, 2006). Page references follow subsequent quotations in parentheses.
20. Tom Ashbrook, "John Updike's *Terrorist*," *On Point*, 13 June 2006. (Audio) <http://onpoint. wbur.org/2006/06/13/john-updikes-terrorist/> [accessed 4 January 2013].
21. John Updike, "Raymond Carver, 1938–1988," *Higher Gossip: Essays and Criticism* (New York: Random House, 2012), 79.

22. Raymond Carver, "Why Don't You Dance?," in *The Stories of Raymond Carver* (London: Picador, 1985) 187–91.

23. Anna Hartnell, "Violence and the Faithful in Post 9/11 America: Updike's Terrorist, Islam and the Specter of Exceptionalism," *Modern Fiction Studies*, 57, 3 (2011), 494.

24. Kristiaan Versluys, *Out of the Blue: September 11 and the Novel* (New York: Columbia University Press, 2009), 178.

25. Ashbrook.

26. Mita Banerjee, "'Whiteness of a Different Color'? Racial Profiling in John Updike's *Terrorist*," *Neohelicon: Acta Comparationis Litterarum Universarum*, 35, 2 (2008), 15. See also Pamela Mansutti, "Ethno-religious Identities and Cosmopolitan Echoes in John Updike's *Terrorist* (2006) and Joseph O'Neill's *Netherland* (2008)," *Altre Modernità* (Università degli Studi di Milano), 9 September 2011, 105–23. <http://riviste.unimi.it/index.php/AMonline/article/view/1297/1520> [accessed 1 July 2013].

CHAPTER 23

Saul Bellow and the
Theory of Comedy

In 2014 New Perspectives Theatre Company staged the first theatre adaptation of a short story by Saul Bellow, "Him with His Foot in His Mouth", adapted and directed by Jack McNamara, and starring Stephen Chance as Harry Shawmut. McNamara came across the story by accident in a junk shop in South London. Several pages later, and still in the shop, he decided that this was a work that he would one day turn into a show. New Perspectives has an ambitious remit of international and national touring, and a mission to bring theatre to rural villages. The company's previous British production, David Rudkin's *The Love Song of Alfred J. Hitchcock*, transferred to the *Brits on Broadway* festival in New York for three weeks in May 2014. Their work is made to tour, to fit into unlikely spaces in order to make high-quality theatre accessible to all. As a monologue, the story lent itself to the creation of a one-man show, with screen projection of images to illustrate settings and subsidiary characters, and a minority of props. *Him with His Foot in His Mouth* opened in London at the Greenwich Theatre for five nights, and then toured until April, taking in theatres in Exeter, Mansfield and Leeds, plus a dozen villages, and the Lakeside Arts Theatre, Nottingham, on 3 April 2014. Approached by the Director just before the tour began, I did a publicity interview about Bellow, wrote the programme notes, attended a rehearsal and a performance, and chaired a post-performance discussion with members of the Nottingham audience, who were highly appreciative.[1] Throughout the tour audience reaction was generally positive.[2] Brian Harvey, who saw the play in the Create Theatre in Mansfield, said "For me it had everything — comic, moving and above all stimulating. The language was a delight. A gem of a piece in conception and execution." For Pati Smith, the same production was "A tour de force. A very engaging and witty play with an incredible performance by the sole actor." In Coddington (population 972) an audience member described it as "Fascinating! A very talented performer who held my attention throughout. I loved the way in which the story built in layers in such an enriching way." In Sutton Cum Lound, an even tinier village (population 687), Barry Gillson saw it in the Village Hall and appreciated a "Deep and profound play." In the metropolitan press the reviews were rather more mixed, though the suitability of the story for adaptation was immediately recognised. The reviewer for the *Guardian* commented that "Saul Bellow wrote exquisite prose and memorable characters, many of whom address us directly. So why hasn't his work been adapted for the stage more often?"[3] This play had the added advantage that it was essentially a dramatised rehearsal as Harry Shawmut rehearses what he will say to Miss Rose. Even so the reviewer felt that the play lacked the quiet comedy and messy warmth of Bellow's work, and went on for far too long. Other reviewers commented approvingly on Chance's ability to draw in the audience by using them to help rehearse his apology for an unprovoked wisecrack made against Miss Rose thirty-five years before. As one critic wrote, "The apology may be a rehearsal but this accomplished performance is anything but."[4] *The Stage* gave the play a good review, but highlighted its comedy as confusing, and not at all straightforward in its effects. Some members of the London audience laughed right through; others seemed baffled, even though Chance was an engaging storyteller.[5]

Arguably the responses to the dramatic production inform our understanding of Bellow's comic practice in this story, which draws upon warring concepts of the function of comedy. It should be noted that, although remarkably faithful to the original, the production makes important changes from page to stage. Firstly, from the beginning, the sense of Shawmut writing a letter is replaced by a monologue, in which he prepares for a meeting with Miss Rose. The story opens with a frame, an epistolary salutation signalling a letter, "DEAR MISS ROSE".[6] The action of the play, however, opens with the actor emerging from behind a screen and rehearsing various ways of addressing her.

> He tries out each of the following greetings, as if an imaginary person has just walked in.
> Miss Rose!
> He goes back behind the screen and returns.
> Dear Miss Rose
> Not right. He goes back and returns.
> Well, Carla Rose
> Not right. He goes back and returns.
> It's you!!
> Too exclamatory. He leaves and returns.
> Softly.
> Carla, my dear child.
> He likes this.[7]

From this point on he addresses the imagined Carla Rose, directly engaging the audience, and rehearsing what he plans to say when they meet. In the story, even though it is a first-person narrative, the title is "Him with His Foot in His Mouth", not "Me with My Foot in My Mouth". It is also a letter, even if in draft, interrupted by asides in which Shawmut comments on his text. It is not being framed as a spontaneous, sincere outpouring of Shawmut's inner consciousness, unrepressed and sincere, as it is on stage. The little framing device of the letter takes us one step further away from Shawmut, and suggests that he is to some degree at least, playing a role, an impression strengthened by his italicised, personal self-interruptions: *"should I say that?"* (5) *"I will say it all and then revise, send Miss Rose only the suitable parts"* (4). On the page readers trust Shawmut rather less than on stage, aware that we are dealing with two people, the self and the writer of the letter, whereas in the play we tend to empathise more with the actor, if only for his endurance over two hours of monologue.

Secondly, the play offers a more upbeat ending. In the story Shawmut closes

> There isn't much time left. The federal marshal, any day now, will be setting out from Seattle. (59)

Shawmut's sojourn in British Columbia is about to be put to a forcible end, as the powers of the state take control of him, and return him to America to face fraud charges for mis-sale of bonds. Shawmut emphasises his Swedenborgian friend's concept that man remains a divine being, even in an apparently God-forsaken world, and that it is up to men to bring back the divine light.

> The body, she says is subject to the forces of gravity. But the soul is ruled by levity, pure. (59)

In both story and play Shawmut makes a valiant attempt at levity with a series of one-liners and witticisms from Clemenceau, Churchill and Disraeli, among others. The stage production made incidental changes, replacing particular witticisms with similar utterances from Dr Johnson, Oscar Wilde, Mark Twain, Leonard Cohen and, memorably Bette Midler to Princess Anne: "How delightful that you love nature, in spite of what it did to you."[8] In production most companies would tailor the jokes to the location and this one went down particularly well with a British audience. But the play closes quite differently from the story. Shawmut reads the audience a letter from Belle Rose, Carla's sister, informing him that "Sadly, Carla passed away last summer".[9] He then admits that

> I needed to find myself an ending.
> So I experimented by writing myself this letter from the imagined Belle Rose.
> But I found it dissatisfying
> And a poor choice of name.
> Too exotic to be related to the features I saw in dear Carla.
> But I wrote the letter to put a cap on a story with no end.[10]

As a result, the final glorious insult appears to have been dealt by Miss Rose herself, by never responding to his request to meet. Shawmut is none the less upbeat. "I opened my mouth to make a coarse joke and thirty five years later the result is a communion."[11] At the close it turns out that all is not lost after all. The play ends as follows:

> **Suddenly we hear footsteps from behind the audience. Harry is shocked.**
> **He hides behind the screen. The footsteps come closer and then stop.**
> **Harry emerges. He looks at someone behind us.**
> **With affection**
> Carla Rose![12]

And the lights go out. Miss Rose has come back; human bonds have replaced financial ones; Shawmut is not under arrest; the comedy is affirmative. The joke against Miss Rose is defused, loses its aggressive charge, and in a sense Shawmut is exonerated.

The two endings exemplify the dynamic in the story between two different concepts of comedy — as a means of reforming society, or as merely the expression of an aggressive, materialistic society. The dramatic setting for the joke on Miss Rose will be a familiar one to any theatregoer; it exemplifies the comedy of the green world. Thirty-five years previously Shawmut took up his first teaching post at Ribier College, in Massachusetts, "where so much of the nineteenth century still stands" (5). Shawmut is bowled over by the beautiful New England setting. As a Midwesterner, he has never seen birches, roadside ferns, or deep pinewoods before, and feels awkwardly out of place, "a camel on the village green" (7). Shawmut has no experience of a progressive college, nor has he come into contact with the Eastern establishment (7). In fact, Ribier is not typical of New England; it is a Bohemian college, a refuge and enclave for disturbed rich kids. The college is set in deep woods and features a Greek revival library building with green reading lamps (10), where "the light in the porch is mossy and sunny — bright green moss, leafy sunlight, lichen on the columns" (7). When Miss Rose emerges, a woman characterised as the "under priestess of this temple" (11), her pallor makes her look "green" (11). She leans against a Greek column and says "Oh, Dr Shawmut, in that cap you look like an archaeologist" (8). Shawmut replies, apparently gratuitously, "And you look like something I just dug up" (8). Is Shawmut merely demonstrating aggression and misogyny? Or does that Arcadian setting, the privileged green world, apart from society, tell us something more? Aristotle argued that comedy springs from a perceived defect, yet one which is not so painful as to arouse compassion. For comedy to work, we must feel pleasure at a lack of fellow feeling. Shawmut's insult none the less appears to be exceptionally cruel and quite unprovoked. Arguably, however, Shawmut lashes out because he is Jewish, not "establishment". He sees Miss Rose as in "another sphere" (5), for example, comparing her to a nun or shepherdess. He is already socially uneasy and is then singled out by Miss Rose, whose comment implies that his only relation to the classical tradition is that of an outsider. He has no real place, as a Jew, in the midst of these sacred Greek monuments. At most he can curate them. Shawmut overreacts, but more against the setting than against Miss Rose. Bellow's own unease with the dominant WASP elite shines through here in the character of Shawmut, and the various references to Jewishness in his letter to Carla. (He assumes she will find his humour alien, for example, since she is Scottish-Irish.) The target is as much the fake antiquity of his surroundings as Miss Rose herself. The joke functions by condensation, conflating Miss Rose and the triumphalist Greek revival architecture, establishing both as ruins or relics. The scene is recognisably that of the library at Bard College, an Ionic temple built in 1893, with stone columns, where Bellow reportedly made this remark to the librarian.[13] Triumphalist architecture of this type promotes the idea that American society is like that of the Greeks, a paradise where democracy can take root and flourish. Shawmut's quip represents a different freedom from that evoked by the Greek revival architecture. The joke punctures WASP pretensions, attacking American democracy as being in ruins, needing to be saved from oblivion by a new immigrant. In this respect the green setting is highly significant.

Discussing the drama of the green world in *The Anatomy of Criticism*, Northrop Frye argued that the theme of comedy is social integration and renewal, associated with a temporary escape from society (often represented by a repressive court) into an idyllic and simplified life in pastoral or bohemian surroundings.[14] In the action of such a play, obstructions which get in the way of the formation of a new society are swept away, whether they are represented by unjust laws (*A Midsummer Night's Dream*), authoritarian parents (*All's Well that Ends Well*) or despotic rulers (*Measure for Measure*). The hero's society rebels against an older model (often represented by the *senex*, or old man) and he escapes to a temporary new world where distinctions of rank, gender and even species are fluid, a world characterised by fantasy, licence, androgyny, the presence of fairies or animals, women dressed as men, and an absence of social distinctions. Examples would include *Love's Labour's Lost*, with its plot of educational retreat from the world, *The Winter's Tale* (set on the sea coast of Bohemia), and a whole succession of plays set in wooded locations: *As You Like It* (the Forest of Arden), *The Merry Wives of Windsor* (Windsor forest), *A Midsummer Night's Dream* (a Greek forest) and *Two Gentlemen of Verona*, where Valentine leads a band of forest outlaws. *Two Gentlemen of Verona* revolves around infidelity. In *Herzog* (set in a green retreat in the Berkshires) the limping friend who makes a fool of Herzog by seducing his wife is called Valentine, though the latter's wife is named Phoebe (the innocent shepherdess in *As You Like It*). Comedies of the green type generally feature a licensed fool, exposing characters to mockery: Feste in *Twelfth Night*, or Touchstone in *As You Like It*. In addition, a classically identified woman is often the trigger producing rebirth: Helena in *All's Well That Ends Well*, Hermia in *The Winter's Tale*, Hero in *Much Ado About Nothing*. The feminine is the Other which challenges the social allegiances of the masculine self, just as Miss Rose emerges from the green shadows, to provoke Shawmut. Frye associated green comedy with the victory of summer and youth over winter and age. In green comedy we go to a realm where authority is in abeyance, people can really be themselves and make fools of themselves in different ways. The comedy can be cruel, as is the treatment of the lovers in *A Midsummer Night's Dream*. At the close of the play, however, even after savage and chaotic events, order is usually re-established, with a return to the social norm, though a regenerated one. Happy marriages tend to assert the power of love and human bonds over legal or financial ones. Over–repressive societies are reformed; wildness is tamed and feeds the new settlement. Bellow's story deploys these elements quite knowingly. The story looks back to a green world of liberated wit and ponders whether comedy is a force for social renewal or whether it is merely aggressive. Interviewed in the *New York Times* in 1984 on the topic of the story and its one-liners, Bellow argued that the story attracted him because

> it is written on a theme, the legitimate irresponsibility of comedy. The life of Shawmut developed out of that. It's an interesting problem; things just pop out of your mouth. They come from comic inspiration, and that is one of the prominent forms of freedom.[15]

Bellow's comment reflects Jean Paul Richter's aphorism that "Freedom gives wit and wit gives freedom". John Paul was Bellow's pseudonym at the start of his writing career.[16]

Northrop Frye was an archetypal critic, strongly influenced by the work of Carl Jung, as was Bellow at this stage of his career as he subliminally acknowledges in Carla Rose's name.[17] Frye portrays the green world as akin to a dream world where we can recognise and indulge our own desires, illustrating

> the archetypal function of literature ... in visualising the world of desire, not as an escape from "reality" but as the genuine form of the world that human life tries to imitate.[18]

Frye's image here of a true world in art as opposed to a lower, material world of confusion chimes with Shawmut's newly found enthusiasm for Swedenborg, whose theory of correspondences held that everything in the physical world corresponds to a spiritual value, and that after death there would be a period of self-discovery in which the social masks would dissolve away and the true self be revealed.[19] The contemporary equivalent of the green world is brought to life on the one occasion where Shawmut is himself the butt of a joke. At a conference, Shawmut imposes himself on an eminent musicologist, Kippenberg, and bores him by reading his conference paper to him. When he asks him if he's keeping him from sleep, Kippenberg responds "No, no — on the contrary, you're keeping me awake" (18). The location is the Villa Serbelloni, a retreat for artists and scholars on Lake Como, lavishly designed and decorated, and with famous gardens. Shawmut dwells on its eighteenth-century décor, taffeta sofas, silk lamps and statuary, all presided over by the enormous Kippenberg "all swelled out in green" (18), clad in velvet dinner clothes, "a copious costume, kelly green in color" (17). Importantly Shawmut does not resent the putdown; quite the contrary: "It was a privilege to have provoked it" (18). Shawmut is happily tolerant of the joke, because it is set in the artistic enclave of the villa, a green world of artistic freedom and wit, a world at one remove from normal social conventions.

Whatever one thinks of Shawmut's joke against Miss Rose, the other wisecracks mentioned in the story appear to be examples of comedy of a corrective nature, offering a healthy critique of social behaviour, especially as concerns the relation of art to money. At a dinner, a Professor at the University of British Columbia observes that he agrees with Alexander Pope about the ultimate unreality of evil, as seen from the highest point of metaphysics, "To a rational mind, nothing bad ever happens" (17). Shawmut is outraged and responds "Oh? Do you mean that every gas chamber has a silver lining?" (17). From his Jewish viewpoint — indeed from any moral perspective — Shawmut is making a valid point. Rationality can lead the thinker into immoral positions, whereas in its very essence a joke depends upon the circumvention of the rational mind. Shawmut describes his witticisms as spontaneous, almost akin to divine possession. Freud's analysis of this type of "tendentious" joke (as we shall see below) also underlines the way in which it represents a moment of liberation from reason and convention. In another example, Shawmut hears at the dinner table that Professor Schulteiss, a bragging polymath who thinks he knows everything about everything, is concerned that there will be nobody erudite enough to write his obituary when he dies, and he promptly quips "I don't know if I'm qualified, but I'd be happy to do the job" (25). Surely Schulteiss was altogether too full of himself and deserved to be brought back to earth? Though Shawmut makes amends at his wife's behest, he maintains that "When I said things I said them for art's sake, i.e., without perversity or malice" (26), and argues that he should follow through rather than apologise. Shawmut underlines the fact that his wisecracks are completely unconscious, spontaneous, as astonishing to him as they are to others, and compares them to seizures, hysterical symptoms, moments of divine possession involving convulsions of the earth:

> what happens when I am provoked happens because the earth heaves up underfoot, and then from opposite ends of the heavens I get a simultaneous shock to both ears. I am deafened and I have to open my mouth. (26)

Another example of the wisecrack is the rejoinder made to Mrs Pergamon, an extremely rich patron of the arts who bores Shawmut throughout a dinner by expatiating on financial affairs. The dinner looks like a social occasion but is in fact designed to extract a hefty donation from her, money which will pass into the hands of a group whom Shawmut mistrusts. "They were a bad lot, and a big grant would have given them more power than was good for anyone" (27). Shawmut is fresh from a performance of sacred music, Pergolesi's *Stabat Mater*, and is in a sublime and spiritual state, in which the warring values of money and music are apparent to him. Mrs Pergamon's fortune is so enormous that it "was almost a sacred attribute. And also I had conducted sacred music, so it was sacred against sacred" (27–28). Dripping with diamonds, Mrs Pergamon spends the dinner explaining financial matters, particularly how the great philanthropic foundations (Carnegie, Rockefeller, Mellon and Ford) divide up their patronage of the different fields of art. "The Pergamons did music, mainly" (28). When she tells him she is writing her memoirs, his social mask slips and he jibes, "Will you use a typewriter or an adding machine?" (28), a joke which Bellow himself made.[20] Like the preceding quip, pretensions are punctured, and in this case the subordination of the arts to the world of finance is targeted. The joke itself is not calculated; it is actually music that has been taken over by calculation. The scene explicitly dramatises art and money as warring values. Money dominates Shawmut's society. His name derives from that of a Jewish pauper, a shamus, a synagogue hanger-on, but in Massachusetts he finds he shares it with a bank.

For Shawmut the jokes illustrate "The intellect of man declaring its independence from worldly power" (31). One joke draws out these implications. Shawmut loses his bullying lawyer Klaussen, after a lunch in the latter's club dining room, "filled with bullies, a scene from Daumier" (31). It is a location where federal judges, machine politicians, paving contractors, and chairmen of boards confer. When Shawmut learns that the club is being rewired because of failures of power, he quips that "While they're at it they might arrange to have people electrocuted in the dining room" (31). For Shawmut power is in the wrong hands, there has been a failure of power in American society. Bellow himself commented in relation to the story that the only emphasis in American society now was on "making it", and that people had "surrendered their personal moral objectives to government and schools and psychologists."[21] He gave as an example the response to a recent FBI sting operation to uncover corruption among Chicago judges, in which all the lawyers in town were terribly indignant, not about the fraud, but about the fact that members of their own profession had cooperated with the FBI. Even Shawmut's final witticism has a moral edge. Again, the setting is a dinner supposedly sociable but designed for ulterior purposes, to influence Babette, a rich widow from an old moneyed family, whom his former brother-in-law Hansl is courting. Since her family is "musical and artistic" (54) Hansl wants Shawmut to impress her with his "cultural clout" (54). But after a perfunctory mention of Monteverdi, Babette goes on for hours about the politics surrounding cable-TV franchises in Chicago, and developments in the film industry, paying scant attention to Shawmut's complete lack of interest in these areas of popular art. Finally, as they reach the cloakroom, on the way out, she apologises for monopolising the conversation. "That's all right," responds Shawmut, "You didn't say a thing" (55). Again, the target is a world in which art has no real place, and human bonds are subordinate to financial ones. (Hansl does not care for Babette; he is only after her money.) Shawmut may be rude, but his jokes have a social function. All those he humiliates are located in a more moneyed and powerful world of overblown egos, deflated by jokes which reassert moral or aesthetic values. The world of art is being championed both explicitly and implicitly; Shawmut uses the art of the joke to remind them of its power.

So far so green. On stage the return of Miss Rose at the end of the play suggests a positive vision of comedy. The green world is validated. Harmony is re-established, sins forgiven and the world renewed. On the page, however, the return of social authority is imaged in its most repressive form, its punitive laws, in the shape of the federal marshal. Shawmut has fled from the repressive state to the edge of a forested wilderness in Canada, escaping from the courts, but he is no Arcadian youth. His green days are emphatically over. He compares himself ruefully to quite a different Shakespearean character, the aging Polonius (4). Bellow's is a winter's tale, with Shawmut now an old man, suffering from haemorrhoids, hypertension and cardiac disease, isolated in wintry British Columbia, a long way from the Forest of Arden. The tone is sombre, an elegy for a world that has passed, a world which held out the prospect of social renewal, but failed to realise it. The last image of the green enclave is parodic, in the shape of the property belonging to Shawmut's brother Philip, an enormous estate in Texas, as big as Douglas Park in Chicago, with "fragrant plantation gardens" (34). Here the pastoral world is long gone, replaced by nature red in tooth and claw, mere savagery. Philip's wife breeds ferocious pit bulldogs, designed to fight and kill. Shawmut says that he can't joke at all about the pit-bulls (36). The image draws upon Swedenborg's view that "Mere nature is hell."[22] Philip has cut all ties with the past, forgotten his sisters' names, abandoned his mother, and eventually swindles Shawmut out of all his money. He has left his immigrant self behind and is now "an all-American production" (40) intent only on making it. Shawmut's relatives all see him as unworldly, unrealistic, and they argue that you have to be tough to make money; that's what life is all about. They use that belief to encourage him to invest with them and lose everything. In this respect "Him with His Foot in His Mouth" anticipates Bellow's comprehensive attack on this kind of cynicism in *More Die of Heartbreak*, which Faye Kuzna has read persuasively as the account of its hero Benn Crader's seduction by exploitative forces disguised as fashionable cynicism.[23]

In the latter part of the story, the emphasis shifts towards a darker, more overtly Freudian approach to comedy, emphasising aggression and economics. Eddie Walish, for example, argues that Shawmut had raised himself by painful efforts from immigrant to middle-class status, and therefore avenges himself with his jokes for the falsifications of his healthy instincts, the deformities imposed upon him in his social ascent. He sees Shawmut as having "rebellious fits" (10), in reaction to the conformity forced upon him. Shawmut himself believes for a time that he can't get on in life until he has "a false self like everybody else" (10). Walish's theory accords to some extent with that of Freud in *The Joke and Its Relation to the Unconscious*. Freud argued that jokes are pleasurable because of the saving of psychic energy; essentially the saving of the effort spent maintaining our inhibitions. His was a calculating and monetary theory of comedy, in which far from being an avenue to a freer society, jokes confirmed the primarily economic nature of the human being, the belief espoused by Philip and the swindling relatives. Freud did see jokes as involving freedom of a kind. In a joke, dangerous feelings of hostility, aggression or cynicism can be expressed and enjoyed, bypassing the censor. "Tendentious jokes" (jokes which involve a listener who does not want to hear them) satisfy our instincts in the face of an obstacle that stands in our way: repression. They tend to operate to undermine authority, creeds and institutions, or to attack people in high places who are protected from direct disparagement by either internal inhibitions or external circumstances. As Eddie Tafoya notes "a good joke pierces the bubble of social tension", allowing listeners entry into a world liberated from the social restraints that Freud says weigh so heavily upon us.[24] Society likes political caricature for this reason: cartoons, court jesters, or satirical prints. Bellow's story exploits this quality of caricature in its humour in the portrayal of Walish as hairy eared, and madly grinning like Alfred E. Neuman in *Mad* magazine (12). Walish vigorously rebuffs any trace of compassion for his twisted spine and limping gait. Shawmut's brother Philip is so fat he resembles a dugong; Babette has a Habsburg jaw and hulking physique; Shawmut's finger is curled like a snail; Kippenberg has caterpillar eyebrows. In Freud's account, the joke gets past the obstacle of power, allowing us to pay back a slur in the same coin, for example, despite the powerful position of the target; or it gets us past an internal obstacle, an inhibition. Freud highlights the principle of economising, in his examples of using as few or as similar words as possible (puns, wordplay, homonyms, *double entendre*), or bringing two different spheres together, in a short circuit, as in the joke against Miss Rose. (And perhaps more literally in the joke at Klaussen's club about electrical power.) For him "pleasure in a joke comes from savings in expenditure".[25] He notes that pleasure in nonsense is often concealed or suppressed in our rational, logical lives; the joke restores old freedoms and disburdens us of the compulsions of our intellectual education.

Much, however, depends on the artistic quality of the joke. Freud outlines the process, emphasising the necessary artistry involved in the joke:

> We have an impulse to insult a certain person; but our sense of propriety, our aesthetic cultivation, is such a barrier to it that the insult cannot take place.[26]

If it did, then in retrospect we would have highly unpleasurable feelings — just like Shawmut. But, if we turn the insult into a good joke or witticism we release pleasure from other sources not obstructed by the same suppression. Jokes use auxiliary devices, artistic tricks, to catch us on the hop and get round our defences. The technique of the joke is thus a form of envelope, circumventing the inhibitions and allowing the message to be delivered. Technique diverts our attention and allows the censorship function to relax so that the forbidden thought is abruptly expressed. The energy that had been directed to censoring the forbidden thought has become superfluous and is discharged in laughter. As Elliot Oring argues, joking is the most social of mental functions.[27] It requires a teller, a target and a listener. Nobody laughs at their own jokes. Importantly Freud saw parallels between jokes and dreams but later scholars have been less convinced, despite the apparent irrationality, or the nonsense elements present in both. After all, dreams have nothing to communicate to anyone except the dreamer. In contrast, although it may be the invention of an individual, the joke will always be swiftly and repeatedly retold. In "Him with His Foot in His Mouth", the joke against Miss Rose is immediately relayed around the campus by Eddie Walish (10). Bellow emphasises the social nature of the joke in his revised version of the story. In its first appearance in the *Atlantic*, the joke about Miss Rose "probably" got around the campus; in the collected version it "certainly" did (10).[28] Similarly Professor Schulteiss is not at the dinner and his wife may not have heard the quip, but Shawmut realises immediately that

> whether she had actually heard me didn't matter, for five or six guests immediately repeated what I had said. (25)

Shawmut's individual performance is not endorsed officially by his society; yet its members spread the joke in all directions.

Inevitably, in a post-Freudian culture sensitive to the diagnostic value of an individual's favourite jokes, Freud's own jokes have come in for analysis. Elliott Oring, for example, considers the ways in which his jokes often betray intensely conflicted feelings about his individual financial indebtedness, the state of his marriage, and his Jewish identity. At different points in his career, Freud depended heavily on patrons. John Carey has also underlined the nature of Freud's society in relation to his theories, and has drawn attention to the way that the jokes which Freud analyses reflect the Vienna of his time, a culture obsessed by money, a ruthless exploitative society dominated by materialism.[29] Freud's whole theory of comedy depends upon ideas of economy, saving, profiting and spending. He explicitly compares the economy of the psyche to that of a business.[30] It is a theory (unlike that of the green world) tainted by its social context and point of origin. "Him with His Foot in His Mouth" introduces us to a similar society, in which, tellingly, wisecracks are targeted at wealthy patrons or those who pretend to an interest in art merely as a strategy in social climbing. The locations of the jokes also often reflect the kind of setting which Freud might have recognised in Vienna: lavish dinners, exclusive clubs and restaurants, displays of wealth and privilege. Shawmut, on the other hand, is quite clear that "My ineptness with money was part of the same hysterical syndrome that caused me to put my foot in my mouth" (20). He expends psychical energy rather than saving it. His unconscious is aligned with an inner self of a spiritual, possessed nature, rather than with repressed animal instinct.

As far as defending comedy is concerned, Shawmut also has a highly representative role. As an expert on Pergolesi he is aligned with the defence of comedy as a social and even as a sacred good. Pergolesi's *Stabat Mater* (which Shawmut conducts in the story) was criticised as too light in style to deliver the necessary pathos of its religious message, too much like his opera, *La Serva Padrona*. Levity was not considered suitable for a religious subject. Bellow, however, has argued that music escapes definition. "There is a dimension of music that prohibits final comprehension and parries or fends off the cognitive habits we respect or revere."[31] Pergolesi was known as the composer of comic operas (*opera buffa*). Indeed, *La Serva Padrona* caused the famous *Querelle des Bouffons* (quarrel of the comic actors) in Paris in 1752, between supporters of serious French opera and those who preferred the new Italian comic style. (Unsurprisingly, given his libertarian views, Rousseau was on the comic side of the argument.) In Shawmut's society money and art are at odds. Avant-garde Tony, a fellow teacher at Ribier, for example, marries a millionairess, gains a lavish studio, and never produces anything serious again. In his jokes, therefore, Shawmut turns the joke back upon the money-obsessed society, expending rather than saving, and targeting the norms of economy and calculation which were the basis of Freud's theory.

Nothing is funnier than people being solemn about comedy. But Bellow's story uses comedy to highly serious ends, as a tool of social correction, and as offering a glimpse of an unconscious world which may be less aligned with the Freudian unconscious of lust and greed and instinct than with an unconscious spiritual impulse, a better self than American society will permit. The stage adaptation, returning to the norms of green comedy in its alternative ending, also developed the spiritual emphasis of the story. The play used lighting to good effect at the close, as Shawmut spoke of the Divine Spirit, holding a lighted candle, which exaggerated his shadow into an immense being on the back wall, awe-inspiring in its grandeur. It made for a much more overtly spiritual ending which did seem to open out into a different, larger world, a world in which Shawmut's inner consciousness could have free expansion, unconstrained by the limitations of conventional society.

Notes to Chapter 23

1. Ellen Hart, "Him with His Foot in his Mouth. An Interview with Judie Newman for New Perspectives," 4 February 2014. <http://yourperspectives.wordpress.com/2014/02/04/him-with-his-foot-in-his-mouth-an-interview-with-judie-newman-for-new-perspectives/>. [accessed 9 February 2014]. (Includes programme notes for production.)

2. Comments by audience members are accessible at <http://www.newperspectives.co.uk/> [accessed 8 April 2014].

3. Lyn. Gardner, "Him with His Foot in His Mouth," *The Guardian*. 19 February 2014. <http://

www.theguardian.com/stage/2014/feb/19/him-with-his-foot-in-his-mouth-review> [accessed 8 April 2014].

4. "Him with His Foot in His Mouth," Greenwich Theatre, London. *The Public Reviews*, 11 February 2014. <http://www.thepublicreviews.com/him-with-his-foot-in-his-mouth-greenwich-theatre-london/> [accessed 8 April 2014].

5. Catherine Usher, "Him with His foot in His Mouth," *The Stage*, 10 February 2014. <http://thestage.co.uk/reviews/review.php/39555/him-with-his-foot-in-his-mouth> [accessed 8 April 2014].

6. Saul Bellow, "Him with His Foot in His Mouth," in *Him with His Foot in His Mouth and Other Stories* (London: Secker and Warburg), 3. Subsequent page references follow quotations in parentheses. The story was first published in the *Atlantic* (November 1982, 114–44).

7. Jack McNamara, *Him with His Foot in His Mouth*, by Saul Bellow. Adapted for the stage by Jack McNamara. December 2013 (typescript). Stage directions are in bold type in the original.

8. Ibid., 31.

9. Ibid..

10. Ibid..

11. Ibid., 32.

12. Ibid., 33.

13. James Atlas, *Bellow: A Biography* (New York: Random House, 2000), 507.

14. Northrop Frye, *The Anatomy of Criticism: Four Essays* (Princeton: Princeton University Press, 1957).

15. D. J. Brucker, "A Candid Talk with Saul Bellow," *New York Times Magazine*, 15 April 1984, 60.

16. Sigmund Freud, *The Joke and its Relation to the Unconscious* (London: Penguin, 2002), 5. Saul Bellow used the pseudonym in two short pieces: John Paul, "This is the Way We Go To School," *Soapbox*, 2, 2 (1936), 7; and "Northwestern is a Prison," *The Beacon*, 1, 1 (1937), 8–9.

17. See Judie Newman, "Bellow and Nihilism: *The Dean's December*," *Studies in the Literary Imagination*, Special Issue: The Philosophical Dimension of Saul Bellow's Novels," 17, 2 (1984), 111–22.

18. Frye, 184.

19. Ernst Benz, *Emanuel Swedenborg: Visionary Savant in the Age of Reason* (West Chester, Pennsylvania: Swedenborg Foundation, 2002).

20. Brucker, 60.

21. Ibid., 57.

22. Saul Bellow, *More Die of Heartbreak* (New York: William Morrow, 1987), 89.

23. Faye Kuzna, "The Demonic Hegemonic; Exploitative Voices in Saul Bellow's *More Die of Heartbreak*," *Critique: Studies in Contemporary Fiction*, 39, 4 (1998), 306–23.

24. Eddie Tafoya, *The Legacy of the Wisecrack* (Boca Raton: Brown Walker Press 2009), 73.

25. Freud, 228.

26. Ibid., 137.

27. Elliott Oring, *The Jokes of Sigmund Freud: A Study in Humor and Jewish Identity* (Philadelphia: University of Pennsylvania Press, 1984).

28. Saul Bellow, "Him with His Foot in His Mouth," *Atlantic* (November 1982), 117.

29. John Carey, "Introduction," in Sigmund Freud, *The Joke and its Relation to the Unconscious* (London: Penguin: 2002), vii–xviii.

30. Freud, 152.

31. Saul Bellow, "Mozart: An Overture," in Saul Bellow, *It All Adds Up. From the Dim Past to the Uncertain Future: A Non-Fiction Collection* (New York: Secker and Warburg, 1995), 5.

CHAPTER 24

Intertextual Updike:
Gertrude and Claudius

Gertrude and Claudius (2000), Updike's only novel set entirely in Europe, is prefaced with a dedication to his second wife, Martha, and a phrase in Occitan:

> De dezir mos cors no fina
> vas selha ren qu'ieu pus am

which translates as "the desire of my heart is endless and only devoted to her, beloved among all others". In the poem, the troubadour poet Jaufré Rudel (*c.* 1150–1200) addresses his lady as his "Amors de terra londana", love from a distant land. Rudel was considered to offer the most extreme example of the courtly love ideal of "amor de lonh", a love that depends upon distance and upon not possessing the beloved, reputedly having fallen in love with the Countess of Tripoli purely from reports of her virtues, without laying eyes upon her. He set off for Tripoli, only to fall ill *en route*, and died in her arms immediately upon arrival.[1] Within the frame of Updike's novel, only Feng (later Claudius), the adulterous lover of Hamlet's mother, and then her second husband, quotes from the troubadours. In the classic exposition of courtly love, love cannot exist in marriage; it depends upon obstacles, whether distance, a husband, or, in Updike's modern updating of the story of Tristan and Isolde, in *Brazil* (1994), the barriers of race and class. Feng deliberately absents himself from the Danish court for some thirty years, unable to bear the sight of his beloved's marriage to his brother Horwendil, but remains devoted to his entirely virtuous lady, Gerutha (Gertrude), until she finally succumbs to his advances at the age of forty-eight.

The sudden appearance of the cult of courtly love has been variously understood as a revolution of the Western psyche, a validation of the female principle, a product of Arabic mysticism, or the result of the reappearance in the West of eastern influences. Critics of Updike have related his interest in courtly love to Denis de Rougemont's influential thesis in *Love in the Western World* and its sequel *Love Declared*, the latter reviewed by Updike, who returned to its ideas at several reprises.[2] De Rougemont emphasised the way in which the love relations of men and women depended upon a particular historical moment, so that their affective life was conditioned by social circumstances.

> "Everything changes except the human heart", say the old sages, but they are wrong. Metaphorically speaking the human heart is strangely sensitive to variations in time and place.[3]

De Rougemont argued that the courtly lover deliberately created obstacles to his happiness, and that his love was essentially love for himself, for the state of being in love, in an individualistic concern for self-validation. The lovers do not need one another's presence, but one another's absence. For him, the influence of courtly love persists in the contemporary cult of romantic love, and in the validation of suffering, a subsidiary effect of which is the acceptance of violence and war. "Happy love has no history — *in European literature*."[4] De Rougemont's influence has continued into the present century in Slavoj Žižek's delineation of the Western *femme fatale* as the heiress of the cruel mistress of courtly love. Updike, however, had reservations. Discussing de Rougemont, Updike agreed that love offered individual validation:

> Only in being loved do we find external corroboration of the supremely high valuation each ego secretly assigns itself.[5]

He was, however, less convinced that courtly love necessarily remained unconsummated. De Rougemont's attribution of its origins to the heresies of the Cathars also gave him pause, and he roundly rejected the implicit Manichaeanism involved in the separation of the realms of spirit and matter, which in denying the Christian doctrines of the Divine Creation and the Incarnation appeared to leave Man caught in the darkness of the flesh, in an evil natural world.[6] In this theorisation love became not a way of entering and accepting the world, but of defying and escaping from it.

In De Rougemont's thesis courtly love becomes toxic to society, as a deeply individualistic enterprise, and he extended his thesis to ascribe most of the ills of modern society to romantic love. Erich Koehler, however, offers a very different understanding of the relation of courtly love to society, in an influential argument summarised in Frederick Goldin's anthology of troubadour poetry, which Updike cites as his source.[7] In the novel Feng is a second son, lacking lands or wealth, his manor modest and his mews small. In addition to Rudel, he quotes from two other troubadours, Arnaut Daniel (1150–1200) and Bertran de Born (b. *c.* 1140), both of whom were immortalised by Dante. Like Feng, de Born exemplifies Koehler's class-inflected reading of the troubadours. As a minor noble whose fortunes depend upon war, he is typical of a class of petty fief-holders for whom mercenary activity was the only means of livelihood. Koehler argued that this inferior segment of courtly society formed the ethical and sociological basis of the courtly love lyric. The relations in the love songs reflect these aspiring young men who wanted to find a dignified place in the social structure in the various courts of Italy, Champagne and Provence.

> The longing for love is now more than a sexual instinct: it is the courtly expression of the longing to be a recognized identity, to be part of a society in which one has some significance.[8]

Representing true courtliness as an ethical state that transcended material conditions was intended to legitimise the position of these newcomers, and foster their integration into privileged society. Essentially the lyric mediated tensions between different sections of the nobility, with love serving as a metaphor for other desires or drives. The lyrics create parallels between the service of love and the homage of the vassal to his sovereign lord. (Chivalry underwrites both love and war.) The state of tension between the lower nobility and the higher courts is thus neutralised by a common ideal, a sublimation of the material and social situation of the *basse noblesse*. In the songs there is much debate about whether the rich and powerful are capable of *fin' amor*, and the consensus is that their power disqualifies them as courtly lovers, since they expect all fortresses to fall before them — whether military or feminine. Gaining immediate erotic satisfaction is entirely foreign to courtly love, which depends upon a lengthy waiting period, and repeated supplications, during which the lover becomes nobler and more refined (in character, manners and potentially in social status). In this analysis, therefore, the lower nobility are the champions of the real values of the chivalric class. Courtly love is a useful form of social glue.

In *Gertrude and Claudius* Updike's exploration of courtly love focusses on two questions. Firstly, can love survive marriage? In courtly love, famously in the judgment of the love court of the Countess of Champagne in 1174, which is cited by Updike, it cannot, given that no obstacle exists between husband and wife.[9] Gertrude's first marriage is unfulfilling, whereas her relationship with Feng restores her to a full sense of self. But will that love survive once the obstacle, her husband, is removed, and she becomes a wife? Secondly, which model of love is healthiest for the state? If we accept Koehler's views, the love ideal of the troubadours was an ordering factor in society, reinforcing community interests, as opposed to de Rougemont's vision of it as disastrously egoistic. *Gertrude and Claudius* opens with a demonstration of aristocratic male power, when Rorik instructs his daughter Gerutha to marry Horwendil the Jute, the conqueror of King Koll, of Norway. In the process, Horwendil (despite, as we later learn, pleas for mercy from Feng) had also slaughtered Sela, Koll's warrior sister, though not before raping her in public. Rorik views him as "a thoroughly modern man" who defeated his enemies, brought appropriate plunder to his lord, and followed the correct social procedures in the ship-burial of Koll.[10] It is no surprise that Horwendil gets Gerutha's hand in marriage. Rorik's own wife, Ona, was a captive slave who fought tooth and nail against him for the first six months of their marriage, and he assumes that love will grow between Gerutha and Horwendil, as it eventually did in his own case. Rather than the romantic love formula of "boy meets girl — boy falls in love — boy marries girl", Rorik espouses the feudal pattern of "boy marries girl — boy meets girl — boy falls in love with girl". Gerutha's descent from Rorik strengthens Horwendil's claim on the throne and assures national stability.

Famously, however, in Shakespeare's *Hamlet*, the love of Gertrude and Claudius is characterised as rank and gross in nature, its consequence being that "something is rotten in the state of Denmark" (*Hamlet* 1.4), a dictum buttressed by references to the kingdom as an unweeded garden (*Hamlet* 1.2), and to the love of its King and Queen as "stewed in corruption" (*Hamlet* 3.4). The death of Hamlet's father instantly threatens Danish sovereignty, in the shape of potential invasion from Norway, and the play culminates in the deaths of the entire royal family in a general bloodbath, and the loss of Danish independence to Fortinbras. As a courtly lover, Feng also has ominous precedents. Dante located Arnaut Daniel in Purgatory (doing penance for lust), but he reserved a place for Bertran de Born in the eighth circle of hell carrying his severed head, as a punishment for having fomented schism between royal brothers.[11] De Born, like Feng, was a co-seigneur of his fiefdom, with his brother Constantine, against whom he fought in battle, and he was also part of a revolt against the alliance of Henry II and Richard the Lion Heart by Henry, Richard's brother, a revolt of brother against brother which offers an ominous parallel with the conflict between Gertrude's two husbands.

Updike, however, closes his novel before the action of Hamlet is fully under way. The reader therefore has a choice. In *Hamlet* Gertrude and Claudius's love relationship produces only death and disaster for their society. It is not the sort of love which creates social order. But as Millicent Bell remarked, perhaps we should accept that the play has no authoritative status as a priority narrative.[12] It is merely one among many versions of the story of Hamlet, from its sources in Saxo Grammaticus and Belleforest to its American rewritings, Henry James's "Master Eustace", or James Branch Cabell's *Hamlet Had an Uncle*, in both of which the Claudius figure is loving and decent and Hamlet rather less so.[13]

> Shakespeare's *Hamlet* is a revision of a dramatic treatment (*Ur-Hamlet*) of a retelling (Belleforest), of a literary treatment (Saxo) of a Scandinavian legend.[14]

Shakespeare felt no compunction in picking and choosing among the details of his sources. In Saxo Grammaticus's account, Hamlet does rather well and actually defeats his uncle and becomes King. Shakespeare was also shamelessly anachronistic. The historical Hamlet is dated *c.* 850–900, but convention sets the story of Shakespeare's play in the mid-thirteenth century and Updike follows suit.[15] Updike's extended fictional time scheme of some thirty years historicises the story, changing the characters' names in each of the novel's three "Acts", and transforming them and their relationships in accordance with the evolution of Denmark from the semi-pagan, feudal Middle Ages to the dawn of the Italianate Renaissance. Characters are thus set against the sweep of social change, their choices subtly interrogating whether their society is going forwards or backwards, evolving progressively or declining into decadence. *Gertrude and Claudius* is a prequel, a form to which *Hamlet* lends itself particularly well. As William Kerrigan notes, the peculiar structure of the revenge plot, where a crime has occurred before the play begins, makes *Hamlet* itself seem like the conclusion of a tragedy that is already well under way. Kerrigan imagines a potential play which sounds suspiciously like the action of Updike's novel.

> Hamlet might be a character who appears in Act Four of *The Hystorie of Claudius* to set the catastrophe in motion.[16]

In Updike's novel Hamlet appears in person only on the last page; he has one speaking line.

It is the essence of a prequel that it turns the clock back, but it is also Janus-faced, with an effect upon future readings of its original. *Jane Eyre*, today, cannot be read without an awareness of the postcolonial revisioning of *Wide Sargasso Sea*, for example.[17] Similarly, the reader of *Gertrude and Claudius* may never see *Hamlet* in quite the same light again. While the prequel goes back to a fresh start, the reading experience then goes forwards in a continuous meditation on the worth or otherwise of the European civilising process, and its effects upon the individual. Gerutha is not the same woman as Geruthe or Gertrude; Feng and Fengon evolve into Claudius; Corambis ages into Corambus and the wordy Polonius; Amleth leaves Denmark behind as Hambleth and then returns, once educated, as Hamlet. Each of the three parts focusses upon the love relations of its age — feudal, courtly and then, in the examples of Hamlet and Ophelia, dangerously individualistic.

In each part of the story Updike essentially explores the relation of erotic love to social order, with Gertrude, whom Updike admired, centre stage in each.

> I love Gertrude, and always have. Everything she says is to the point, and much of it is witty.[18]

Updike used lines spoken by Gertrude as the epigraph to *Brazil*: "all that live must die, passing through Nature to eternity" (*Hamlet* 1.2), and as the title of his collection *More Matter*. Although he mounted a spirited defence of her, describing her as "a pawn in the hands of ambitious men" his interest was not primarily in terms of a feminist revisioning.[19] Indeed, he complained that literary analysis had become less interesting in America because "our national notion of a hot literary topic is 'Did Shakespeare favour the oppression of women?'"[20] In *Gertrude and Claudius*, her lover describes her as entirely natural:

> "Nature" was one of her words, which she used as women of other languages spoke of *der Gott, le bon Dieu, Iddio, Dios*. (76)

In the first part of the story Updike assimilates her to nature, critiquing her feudal marriage, by taking his cue from commentators who have understood the story of Hamlet (often quite variously) in relation to fertility myth. Gerutha herself associates her husband's behaviour towards King Koll as typical of "the dark old days, when the deeds of the sagas were being wrought, and men and gods and natural forces were all as one" (4). As early as 1870 Karl Simrock related *Hamlet* to the Norse myth of Odin and Vali, with Odin as a sun god descending to lower regions to warm the frozen earth after the death of Baldur, god of light.[21] The dark quality of the play, with its midnight scenes, ghost, gloom and mourning, suggests a wintry world, quite literally benighted, a point emphasised in Updike's cited sources, William Kerrigan and Sir Israel Gollancz.[22] Gollancz notes that Horwendil was a mythic figure associated with heavenly light, and sees Gerutha as Mother Earth in the forced embraces of cruel winter, longing for the return of her beloved spring. John Fiske (1873) also argued that the story borrowed elements of the ancient Norse myth of the struggle between spring and winter; the sensuous queen thus becomes the epitome of an earth goddess, joined in sacred or regenerative marriage with a divine king.[23] Horwendil, though a good Christian, buys into this myth himself:

> if goodness does not flow from God through the King then the people will
> suffer and sink, all mutual obligations cancelled, and only an animal selfishness
> left, and savage anarchy. The King is the sun which warms the land. If
> something is amiss with him, his beams are bent. Crops fail, and rot infects the
> grain. (141)

In the novel, Gerutha is repeatedly associated with warmth, Horwendil with cold.
"A warmth surrounded her" (6); her red-gold hair flying out around her face is
"the red of copper diluted by the tin of sunlight" (6), and she has a cheerful, sunny
disposition (8). Gerutha herself sees Christianity as obscuring nature. In the chill of
the chapel she feels that her natural warmth is "chastened" (13), as if her body were
a sin, of which she were accused. At mass she thinks that the Eucharist, held up to
the circular window, is "eating sky" (13). She is struck by her groom's candle-pale
skin, and icy blue eyes like minnows (9); his plated scales of mail remind her of a
merman (53). Horwendil is established as something of a cold fish, lacking in animal
warmth. He laments that humanity has been "sent from the abode of angels to live
on this earth among beasts and filth" (18) and considers "love's gratifications as
bordering on the devil's domain" (130). Nature and Christianity appear to be set on
opposed paths by Horwendil's brand of Christian belief. Updike sets the opening
scene in the aptly named "solar", the main living quarters of a medieval lord, where
lozenges of afternoon sunlight pattern the floor (12). Significantly he also invents
the character of Ona, Gerutha's mother, as a pagan Wendish captive, carried off
against her will and forcibly married to Rorik. The Wends, a Slav people, known
for their large pagan temples and shrines, were only subdued to Christianity in the
Northern Crusade of 1147.[24] Now, as Rorik feels his own strength deteriorating,
he sets up a similar marriage to his own for his daughter. As she submits he is
taken aback by her "demurely slavish" (10) demeanour, that of a captive slave — or
perhaps (and etymologically) a Slav, like his own pagan wife. Horwendil presents
his bride-to-be with a pair of caged linnets, describing them as embodying "mated
happiness" (15), but Gerutha wonders if they are singing out a protest against their
captivity, and loses no time in releasing them. Horwendil's proposal comes "out of
a general political will more than a personal desire" (17), fulfilling a pledge from
Rorik and a social contract. Her individual choice is irrelevant. Indeed when she
later looks for a place of her own to fulfil her own individual desires, she meets with
incomprehension from Corambis. Gerutha complains that she has never lived for
herself, but only as daughter, wife and mother. His rejoinder is telling:

> how do any of us define ourselves but in relation to others? There is no
> unattached free-floating self. (94–95)

Throughout the novel Updike underlines the point that the characters are caught in
a social net, through imagery of clothing as embodying social restraints — for both
men and women. Rorik sees state occasions as warranting "all but immobilizing
robes of velvet and ermine" (10). In his embrace, Horwendil leaves the pattern of
his chainmail armour on Gerutha's face, the stamp of the feudal state. Later, he
has to have help to undo the network of latches, knots and thongs of his plated
armour (53). He sees her "as part of a brocade, a bride of silver threads" (18) rather

than an individual. Gerutha recognises herself as "caught in the stillness of a patterned weave" (19), though, "like a tightly swaddled baby" (19), she is secure in her semi-immobilised state. The clothing imagery continues at her wedding, where she is quite literally weighed down by heavy garments. Like the linnets, fed on cloth seeds (flax and hemp) she is secure, but her individuality has been sacrificed to the concept of a united nation all of one cloth, seamlessly interwoven. The wedding takes place in winter (weddings are scheduled outside the season for war) and Updike's description dwells on the freezing sleigh ride across the snow in icy moonlight (20), Horwendil's face bloodless beneath a gibbous moon. When Gerutha steps out of her constraining clothing she is characterised in terms of earth and vegetation

> as white as an onion, as smooth as a root fresh-pulled from the earth. (24)

Bathetically, however, the divine bridegroom cannot stand up to the excessive warmth of the bedroom, and has fallen fast asleep, leaving their marriage unconsummated, a snub which rankles permanently with his bride. Horwendil repairs the omission; he is not lacking in erotic vigour and his sexual activities fit his nickname of the Hammer; Gerutha feels "hammered" into submission (47). Whereas Horwendil reveres Harald Bluetooth, the establisher of Christianity in Denmark, commemorated as such at Jelling, Gerutha prefers the runic inscription left there by Harald's father: "King Gorm erected this memorial to Tyra his wife, glory of Denmark" (27). In her view, Gorm knew how to value a woman, "back before the Cross arrived to dull the Danish spirit" (27). In their hearts, she believes, the Danes still adore "Tyr, god of sport and war and fertility" (27). Christianity is not deeply rooted in Denmark or in Gerutha. When she gives birth, she characterises her agony in pagan terms as a "blood eagle", using the term for the painful execution method of the Sagas, a sacrifice to Odin, in which the condemned prisoner's ribs were severed from the spine and pulled open to resemble wings. Rorik, "slipping back into paganism" (29), also refers to his approaching death as a blood eagle, condemning the hell-preaching churches in anachronistically Nietzschean terms as peddling a religion "of slaves, and then of peasants and then of merchants" (29). Although by her marriage "Denmark had become a province of her body" (26), Gerutha's own fertility is inadequate. After the birth of Hamlet, a sickly infant, there are no more children to assure the succession, a circumstance for which Horwendil blames her, suggesting that her resentment had "curdled her fructifying juices" (54) which lacked no supply of his seed. His wife snaps back,

> Seed sown, it may be, in such coolness of spirit it failed to kindle the willing soil on which it fell. (54)

Horwendil's prudish Christianity is a fatal flaw in their marriage — and potentially a danger to the state of Denmark. Has Christianity been good for the Danish state? Or does it lack the reverence for women and for the fertility of creation, necessary to the health of a society?

The scene is set for the appearance of the representative of courtly love, in the shape of Feng, temporarily returned from his travels. Although he shared the risks of co-governing Jutland equally with his brother, he has gone unrewarded, living by his lance in the service of the Holy Roman Emperor, the King of France, and the Counts of Genoa, in their struggle with Pisa for control of Corsica and Sardinia. Deeply tanned, Feng is of the warm south in every way, and describes visits to Venice, Castile, Aragon and Byzantium, the warmth of the Mediterranean Sea, and the "sunny" disposition of the people who live beyond the Alps (47). He has met eastern potentates, Moors and Arabs, and the stories he tells evoke "a variegated, fabulous Europe" (52) in which he clearly takes a great delight. Feng brings the wonders of Creation vividly alive; he feeds on different cultures, offering an appreciation and knowledge of a broader sphere. When he takes Gerutha on a visit to the mews where he keeps his falcons, she rides out with him into a greatly enlarged world. It is November but unexpectedly warm (55). Until now, she feels that her life has been like a stone passage with many windows but no doors, its entry and exit guarded by her husband and son, with only death as its exit.

> Death, the end of nature and the opening, the priests of the Crucified God claimed, to a far more glorious world. But how could any world be more glorious than this one? (56)

Out in the open air, she revels in the changing light, the countless objects and perceptions, noises and movement. Updike sets up an opposition here between the glory and light of God's creation and the darkness of a repressive culture. Feng characterises the falcons in terms of the subconscious:

> Reason is not their path. In this they are like our deeper selves, over whom the brain would in vain set itself as master. (86)

In the mews Feng offers Gerutha an object lesson on her own condition. Feng's mews is cramped and dark, reflecting his poverty, quite the reverse of the larger brighter world outside, and offering something of the feeling of a visit to the underworld. There is a pungent scent of rotted meat and mutes, a smell of decay, and a background sound of "smothered weeping" (62). To Gerutha the sport represents an "abuse of the wild" (63), a perversion of unfettered nature. The falcons (all female) benefit from the same security that Gerutha enjoys, but in an exaggerated fashion. Once captured they are kept in a sock (64), "as a baby is swaddled" (64), and prevented from taking flight, their wild nature tamed by bribes of food. Above all their eyes are "seeled", sewn shut, to avoid them bating (flying desperately upwards to escape) "frantic with the possibilities of freedom" (64). Imprisoned in darkness, their sight is only gradually returned to them, once they are considered docile. The falconer has to keep the bird in the dark, but with him at all times, sing to her, speak to her, feed her, accustoming her to his voice and presence. In the scene, Gerutha is warned not to look directly at the birds, which associate the human face with capture. "A strange human face is poison to them, until they are thoroughly manned" (68). Similarly Feng avoids her eye, looking at her only "glancingly" (60), and lecturing her softly and at length on the nature of the birds, afraid that he will frighten her off. The two would-be lovers turn away from each other, in a scene evoking repression. The short November day darkens and grows colder, the sun's rays "occluded" (70), the clouds piling up "like ice cakes" (70). Feng had greeted Gerutha in the language of courtly love, referring to his devotion to a certain lady, who must remain unnamed by the rules of love, but now he announces his decision to depart. "There is a safety in distance, and a purity that leaves the loyalty untested" (71), he decides. Though he adores Gerutha and visualises her as a luminous window into a purer world, he does not seek immediate erotic gratification; what he has learned "from the poetry of Provence" (75) is to defer it. "Like a falcon, love was kept best at hunger pitch", he reflects (75). In the scene Updike questions the value of sublimation and repression. Feng quotes again here from the troubadours, in this case Bertran de Born, "Vuolh ses belas dens en dos" ("I want her beautiful teeth as a gift", 76).[25] The poem concerns a lover who puts together an ideal woman from the attributes of many, the teeth from one, the eyes from another, the throat from a third. Feng, for all his passion, remains tied to the code of courtly love in its idealised, sublimated form. It would be treason to bed a still-fertile queen (75); the feudal state appears to be well served by the code of courtly love. The falconry scene establishes a difference therefore between the idealised, sublimated form of courtly love and a mature erotic relationship. It is only when he returns and embarks on an adulterous relationship with Gerutha that their relationship becomes natural and healthy. By then, Feng has in fact become more cultured, more refined and altogether more suitable, and Denmark is catching up with him.

The falconry scene marks a pivotal moment between feudal and renaissance worlds and prefigures Gerutha's liberation. She cannot quite see where Feng is leading her, and has yet to adjust to a brighter, freer world. For Feng the birds represent "a beauty that puts our thoughts of good and evil at the mercy of the real" (61).The scene does not merely link Feng to a better form of relation between love and society; it also establishes that Feng is much more suited to rule in a renaissance world. The scene in the mews may be bookended by references to courtly love but the description of falconry owes everything to Feng's master, the Holy Roman Emperor Frederick II, author of the first zoological treatise in the modern scientific spirit, *The Art of Falconry*.[26] Frederick's court in Sicily was a byword for tolerance and cosmopolitanism, welcoming Jewish and Arab philosophers, and maintaining a harem alongside Christian priests. Aristotle was translated from Greek to Latin there, and the emperor regularly conducted scientific experiments. His account of falconry is thoroughly scientific, based upon minutely observed particulars. On his return Feng's free lance has evolved from war to diplomacy, he speaks half a dozen languages and is at the cutting edge of European culture. He is far better prepared to serve the interests of an early modern state than Horwendil, who knows only war and bigotry. Feng brings good things, both cultural and material, to the table. His gifts to Geruthe include an Arabic incised platter, traded from the Emirate of Granada, a Byzantine cloisonné pendant, a chalice inscribed with both Greek chimeras and Christian imagery, and a gown made from silk, a recent introduction into Northern Europe, and an image in its softness and fluidity of a less constraining social weave. His manor displays astronomical instruments, and Venetian furniture; he explains Aristotle to Geruthe. His is a tolerant culture unlike that of Denmark. Like Thor, Horwendil has a tendency to thunder; in a single booming tirade he manages to inveigh successively against merchants, Jews, Crusaders and Mohammedans (73). Feng, on the other hand, is able to discuss the Byzantine form of Christianity dispassionately, knows something of Islam, and is well acquainted with the cultures of France and Italy. He has a twenty-first-century resonance, as a European in the broadest sense. Where Horwendil sees Hamlet's education in Wittenberg as merely undermining his religious certainties, Feng sympathises with the prince's desire to see more of the world than Denmark. Gerutha points out to her husband that

> there's a ferment going on in cultivated circles to the south, various bits of knowledge the Crusaders brought back, the Arabs and the Byzantine monks ... something about a new way of looking at the world scientifically. (80)

Denmark, however, is not yet ready for the Renaissance. When he departs once more Feng makes Gerutha a present of a falcon, Bathsheba, but she is unable keep her. The social pattern among the captive birds in the royal mews is so firmly established that the other birds will not tolerate any alteration in the pecking order. Rather than see her slaughtered, Geruthe releases her into the forest of Gurre.

   In the second part of the story, Geruthe follows Bathsheba to Gurre, looking for a place "embedded in nature" (95). The potential for a healthier relation between the state and its rulers, fostering cultural growth and development, as opposed to the stagnation of medieval Elsinore, is indicated in the lovers' meeting place. Geruthe prevails upon Corambis to lend her his hunting lodge on the Gurre Sø, a place which she describes as "a foretaste of Paradise" (97). The lakeside lodge includes an old tower, described by Corambis as the remains of some pre-Christian or heretical site, "lakes being regarded as holy" (96), which he has incorporated into the main building, filling the gaps in the archaic structure with new bricks and mortar, rather as Updike incorporates different elements of mythology into his own structure. Picking up on fertility myth, Updike also invents a spring to summer idyll for his lovers. Their courtship begins as winter recedes, with the lodge's single window opening out onto "a curtain of greenery" (103), the trees appearing through the bubbled glass to bend and wave in animistic fashion. A heart-shaped leafy green vine provides a ladder, up which the fifty-nine-year-old Feng climbs, rather unromantically out of breath. Importantly this pastoral realm is not immune to time. Updike evokes Feng's age and establishes the setting as completely up to date.[27] There may be a rugged Norse decor of antlers and bear-skins, but Corambis has also outfitted the tower with a leaded lancet window and a state-of-the-art tiled fireplace, with fitted flue. Birdsong is quickening as the April light signals the approach of the nesting season (104). Feng brings his first gift when the buds have gone from buttons to the leafiness of small cabbages, the second as they unfurl enough to fill the woods with a yellow-green fog (115) and the third when they are "freshly but fully leafed" (123), during a May rainstorm. Like any fertility deity, Feng is appropriately soaking wet when he consummates their relationship. By high summer the vegetation is beginning to snake into the tower in which the lovers meet; the air is filled with the humidity of new growth (132). Nature and culture have come together in what appears to be a fruitful embrace, in which animality is accepted.

In their relationship Geruthe has been transformed from the unaware, darkened captive bird to a luminous peacock, reflecting the image of the cloisonné pendant. The silk gown changes colour "as feathers will" (127), in shimmering peacock hues, its sleeves "wide wings" (127). Feng explains that it is made from worms, but that its patterns "image forth the bejewelled glory of Heaven" (126). The imagery conjoins nature and Christianity, with the peacock as both a bird and (because it sheds and renews its feathers annually) the Byzantine symbol of Christian renewal and resurrection. Similarly the phallic-stemmed chalice represents natural, animal and religious imagery, both Christian and pagan. It is incised with chimeras with Attic bangs, creatures part-woman, part-animal, along with trees and birds but also with grapevines, and a cross. In Byzantine iconography vines suggest the life-giving force of the Eucharist, appropriate to a chalice. Although Geruthe initially sees their love as sin, Feng counters that although there are sins against the Church there are also sins against nature, "Our sin has been these many years one of denying our natures" (90). The lovers discuss whether love is earthen or skyey (112), but the two forms appear to be conjoined in the symbolism of birds and wings. The animal references also coexist with the sense of a divine inspiration in Feng's description of his beloved as his Hagia Sophia or form of light, the feminine principle of divinity. At the same time he rejects both the fleshy excesses and the over-ascetic extremes of Byzantium (108). Geruthe also rejects any over-idealisation ("You would theologize me out of my real existence" (111), she says) and, when she finally offers herself to Feng, describes herself as robed "in the costume of a Mediterranean jade" (128). Although "the cool shadow of forethought" (132), the possibility of discovery, chills their rapture momentarily, the lovers continue to meet right through the crackling October chills (135), and the first appearance of the Northern Lights (135), until on All Saints Day (1 November) the king discovers all. Feng's Calabrian servant Sandro could not stand the cold of the Danish winter and betrayed him in exchange for safe passage to the warm South.

By locating the pair in the lodge at Gurre Sø, Updike also exploits a highly symbolic location, shadowing the greenwood with a darker history. This hunting lodge lies some six kilometres from Elsinore, and originally had several round towers. Updike travelled to Denmark in 1969 and visited the haunts of Kierkegaard, whom he credited with saving him from despair.[28] In his journals Kierkegaard describes the beauty of the lake and its lodge, saying that the landscape "seems to whisper to us, 'it's good to be here.'"[29] He recounts how Good King Valdemar built Gurre on the lake, concealing in the lodge his beloved mistress, little Tove. A keen huntsman, he famously declared, "Let God keep his paradise if I may keep Gurre castle", a phrase echoed by Geruthe (97). The phrase, construed as sacrilegious in preferring Tove's love to God's, became his curse, and he was condemned as a penalty for blasphemy to ride forever madly through the forest, night and day, cracking his whip. The myth of the wild huntsman is generally understood as expressing the opposition between older pagan beliefs (fertility in the lake and forest setting) and the arrival of Christianity.[30] Updike stages a re-enactment. Confronted by the king, and faced with the threat of exile or worse, Feng makes a desperate ride through the forest whipping his horse mercilessly, to reach his manor, procure the poison secreted there, and get back to Elsinore in time to conceal himself in the freezing garden where Horwendil takes his afternoon nap. "Intent upon the hunt, the kill" (157), he accomplishes two rides of two hours each, in less than three. Quite apart from the suggestion of fratricide as original sin, the particulars of the scene indict Feng as a potentially demonic presence. "With a snake's silence" (156) Feng glides into the garden and administers his poison from a vial concealed in a Byzantine jade cross (a present from another Byzantine jade in his past). The garden is a place of death and decay; Feng's feet slide on rotten apples and pears, and he makes his escape by slithering up a garderobe (latrine chute), full of subterranean, sunless, white centipedes, as if he were emerging like Satan from the bowels of the earth. Horwendil's death is ascribed to a serpent's bite, and the poison creates the impression of a sudden frost: Horwendil's body is "frozen" and his skin covered in a "silvery crust" (162). All Saints Day marks the end of the old year and the beginning of the new in the pagan calendar, but the fertile green imagery of the lovers appears to have been replaced with death and decay. Will there be a new beginning for Denmark, from frozen rot to the regeneration of its culture implied in the lovers? Or will rankness and decay remain at the heart of the state?

In the final act of the novel the possibility lingers that Gertrude and Claudius's relationship will not materially alter the social pattern. Like the preceding two parts, it begins "The King was irate" (163), a phrase used first by Rorik admonishing Gerutha, then by Horwendil furious with Hamlet, and now by Claudius demanding that Hamlet return to Denmark. Where Rorik admonished and Horwendil asked, Claudius simply announces commands. Gertrude is taken aback by the speed of his evolution, from Feng into "the imperial dignity of Latin" (164) in his new name. Even in their private moments he now speaks as if there were others about them, courtiers and emissaries (164) and he uses the royal "we", in the belief that "Denmark and I … are now synonymous" (164). Claudius wants things to go smoothly, "the past sealed off" (166), and for that he has the recipe: marriage. Hamlet must be drawn back to Elsinore lest a rival faction begins to form around him, and their wedding will be the lure. The marriage will settle the succession and any residual gossip, and stabilise the country. Gertrude fears that love is behind her and that she is presiding over "the extinction of the adulterous, rapturous couple" (171), as the seducer becomes a public man and his far-off beloved a daily presence, but she is proved wrong in the unbridled passion of their wedding night. Claudius roundly declares his belief that "Without love, we die, or at best live stunted" (196). Contemplating his bride he quotes twice more from the troubadours, from Arnaut Daniel's "L'aura amara": "Tant fo clara ma prima lutz d'eslir lieis don cre crel cors los huoills" (so clear it made me, my first flash of choosing her whose eyes my heart fears), 197).[31] He loves her "del pe tro c'al coma" (207) from her foot to her hair, and still worships her.

> The Creation that has you in it, wife, must hold salvation for the vilest sinner. (202)

Courtly love may have mutated into marriage but it remains a humanist reaction against prudish Christianity, exalting femininity as an ennobling spiritual and moral force. Claudius is very much Updike's own mouthpiece here. In "Lust" he argued that

> if God created the world, He created sex, and one way to construe our inexhaustible sexual interest is as praise of Creation.[32]

Claudius remains a murderer (though no more than Horwendil was, and arguably only in self-defence), but forgiveness and penitence appear to be on the cards. Picking up on Shakespeare (*Hamlet* 4.7), he describes Gertrude as "conjunctive to my soul" (202) and evokes a merciful Christianity. When he remembers Gertrude's first nakedness he thinks of her as looking as she would appear on the day of judgement, "forgiveness being disposed as freely on that day as the loaves and fishes" (207). As Stephen Greenblatt commented, Claudius's religion allows for "a carnality that heals, not imprisons, the soul."[33] The point is reinforced in the symbolism of his wife's embroidery of Mary Magdalen at the feet of the risen Christ. Gertrude is finally able to relax; their passion has survived the removal of its obstacle. Moreover, she is no longer a distant lady, in the sense that she is no longer distant from her true self. Marriage to Claudius "was meeting herself come from afar" (202). Quite clearly the first question raised by the novel — whether love can survive marriage — has been answered in the affirmative.

But will the marriage offer a stable basis for Danish society? Claudius has left war behind, and operates by peaceful diplomacy, dispatching ambassadors to Norway, but Gertrude fears the war which Hamlet brings within himself (200), in the shape of self-division. Updike lays the blame for the disaster of the play squarely on Hamlet, crediting Salvador de Madariaga with helping him to see Hamlet as "the callous, egocentric villain of *Hamlet*".[34] Gertrude expresses a similar view. Hamlet is "too charmed by himself" (177), "the only man in his universe" (177). De Madariaga, whose work Updike quotes affirmatively in the "Afterword" to the novel, understood the central problem of the play as that of the balance between an individual and his society, with the pressure on Hamlet of a far too socialised world driving him into himself and making him over-subjective.[35] Hamlet would like to be an actor on a stage outside his own head, but finds it impossibly difficult. In Updike's novel we move from individuals who are absolutely subordinate to social norms to a complete egotist who cannot find a social role. Worse, Hamlet has a Manichaean vision, in which that which is not wholly divine is utterly sinful. The final part of the novel focusses on Gertrude's audience with Ophelia, and on her hopes to advance Hamlet's marriage, as "the quickest way out of his sterile egotism" (185), a means of tying him into the established order. But Ophelia reveals only the divided nature of the prince, who alternately extols her virtues and expresses disgust at woman's susceptibility to lust (183). Gertrude thinks that the lovers should be "left alone in desire's grip" (189) but, catastrophically, Polonius follows the logic of de Rougemont and decides that setting up some obstacles to their love might fan Hamlet's flame (188), a procedure which (in the play at least) convinces Hamlet of Ophelia's duplicity and engenders disaster. As G. Wilson Knight argues, Hamlet is in despair and only love can rescue him. When Ophelia repels him, he loses his last hope, abandons romantic values and envisages love only in terms of sex, as dirty and unclean.[36] Hamlet is unable to see evil and good, flesh and spirit as coexisting in the same person; he divides woman into Manichaean opposites, ideal or debased. Placing an obstacle between the pair in fact seals Hamlet into his individualism, in conformity with de Rougemont's toxic model. In short, the love of Hamlet and Ophelia appears to bode nothing but ill for their society. Updike steps outside the frame again in the "Afterword" to quote G. Wilson Knight:

> Putting aside the murder being covered up, Claudius seems a capable king, Gertrude a noble queen, Ophelia a treasure of sweetness, Polonius a tedious but not evil counsellor, Laertes a generic young man. Hamlet pulls them all into death. (212)

At the close, Claudius stands in the sunlight that floods the Great Hall, from a sky "clearer than the conscience of a saint" (203). On the edge of Updike's fictional world looms another, far more ominous one, yet the novel proper ends with a triumphant Claudius, confident that "the era of Claudius had dawned. It would shine in Denmark's annals" (210). Updike leaves it to the reader to decide whether he or Shakespeare has the last word.

Notes to Chapter 24

1. Frederick Goldin, *Lyrics of the Troubadours and Trouvères: An Anthology and a History* (New York: Doubleday, 1973).

2. On courtly love see Adam Begley, *Updike* (New York: Harper, 2014), 239–43; Alain Corbellari, "John Updike's Tristanian Passion," *Tristania*, 19 (1999), 115–26; Brian Duffy, "Male Sexuality in John Updike's *Villages*," *John Updike Review*, 4, 1 (2016), 1–26; Joan Tasker Grimbert, "John Updike's *Brazil*," *Tristania*, 23 (2004), 61–73; James Schiff, *John Updike Revisited* (New York: Twayne, 1998).

3. Denis de Rougemont, *Love in the Western World* (Princeton: Princeton University Press, 1983), 3.

4. Ibid., 52.

5. John Updike, "More Love in the Western World," in *Assorted Prose* (New York: Knopf, 1965), 229.

6. Ibid., 230.

7. Erich Koehler, "Observations historiques et sociologiques sur la poésie des troubadours," *Cahiers de Civilisation Médiévale*, 7 (1964), 27–51.

8. Goldin, *Lyrics of the Troubadours and Trouvères*, 11.

9. Updike, "More Love in the Western World," 242.

10. John Updike, *Gertrude and Claudius* (New York: Knopf, 2000), 4. Subsequent page references follow citations in parentheses.

11. Dante Alighieri, *The Divine Comedy* (Oxford: Oxford University Press, 2008), Inferno xxviii, 113–42; Goldin, *Lyrics of the Troubadours and Trouvères*, 224–27.

12. Millicent Bell, "Updike's Shakespeare," *Partisan Review*, 68, 2 (2001), 345–49.

13. See Henry D. Janowitz, "'Master Eustace' and *Gertrude and Claudius*: Henry James and John Updike Rewrite *Hamlet*," *Hamlet Studies*, 25 (2003), 189–99; Henry James, "Master Eustace," *The Galaxy*, 12, 5 (1871), 595–612; James Branch Cabell, *Hamlet Had an Uncle: A Comedy of*

Honor (New York: Farrar and Rinehart, 1940); Martha Tuck Rozett, *Talking Back to Shakespeare* (Newark: University of Delaware Press, 1994).

14. William F. Hansen, *Saxo Grammaticus and the Life of Hamlet: A Translation, History and Commentary* (Lincoln, NB and London: University of Nebraska Press, 1983), 67.

15. John Updike, "A 'Special Message' for the Franklin Library's Signed First Edition Society edition of *Gertrude and Claudius* (2000)," in *Due Considerations: Essays and Criticism* (London: Hamish Hamilton, 2007), 640.

16. William Kerrigan, *Hamlet's Perfection* (Baltimore: Johns Hopkins University Press 1994), 124.

17. See Judie Newman, *The Ballistic Bard: Postcolonial Fictions* (London: Arnold, 1995), 13–28.

18. John Updike, "Letter to Rosemary Herbert, Book Review Editor of the *Boston Herald*, anent *Gertrude and Claudius* (2000)," in Christopher Carduff (ed.), *Higher Gossip: Essays and Criticism* (London: Hamish Hamilton, 2012), 447.

19. Updike, "A 'Special Message'," 639.

20. John Updike "Fairy Tales and Paradigms," in *Due Considerations: Essays and Criticism* (London: Hamish Hamilton, 2007), 307; see however Laura Elena Savu, "In Desire's Grip: Gender, Politics and Intertextual Games in Updike's *Gertrude and Claudius*," *Papers on Language and Literature*, 39, 1 (2003), 22–48.

21. Karl Simrock, *Die Quellen des Shakespeare in Novellen, Märchen und Sagen* (Bonn: A. Marcus, 1870).

22. William Kerrigan, *Hamlet's Perfection* (Baltimore: Johns Hopkins University Press 1994); Sir Israel Gollancz, *The Sources of Hamlet* (Oxford: Oxford University Press, 1926).

23. John Fiske, *Myths and Mythmakers* (Boston: James R. Osgood, 1873); Rajiva Verma, "Conceptions of Myth and Ritual and Criticism of Shakespeare, 1880–1970" (PhD thesis, University of Warwick, 1972).

24. Eric Christiansen, *The Northern Crusades: The Baltic and the Catholic Frontier 1100–1525* (London: Macmillan, 1980).

25. Goldin, *Lyrics of the Troubadours and Trouvères*, 238.

26. Frederick II of Hohenstaufen, *The Art of Falconry (De Arte Venandi Con Avibus)*, trans. Casey A. Wood and F. Marjorie Frye (Stanford: Stanford University Press, 1943).

27. Updike draws for the dates of these innovations upon Joseph and Francis Gies, *Life in a Medieval Castle* (New York: Harper, 1974).

28. Adam Begley, *Updike* (New York: Harper, 2014), 307.

29. Søren Kierkegaard, *Kierkegaard's Journals and Notebooks*, vol. 1: *Journals AA–DD*, ed. Bruce H. Kirmmse, Niels Jørgen Cappelørn, Alastair Hannay, George Pattison, Jon Stewart (Princeton: Princeton University Press, 2007), 6.

30. Alexander Porteous, *The Lore of the Forest* (New York: Cosimo, 2005), 100.

31. Goldin, *Lyrics of the Troubadours and Trouvères*, 209–11.

32. John Updike, "Lust," in *More Matter* (London: Hamish Hamilton, 1999), 46.

33. See Stephen Greenblatt, "With Dirge in Marriage," *New Republic*, 222, 8 (2000), 32–39. <http://search.proquest.com/docview/212939774?accountid=8018> [accessed 15 February 2016]. <http://search.proquest.com/2939774?accountid=8018>

34. Updike, "Letter to Rosemary Herbert," 448.

35. Salvador de Madariaga, *On Hamlet* (London: Hollis and Carter, 1948).

36. G. Wilson Knight, *The Wheel of Fire* (London: Methuen, 1930).

CHAPTER 25

Presidential Politics as Sexual Politics:
Memories of the Ford Administration

In *Memories of the Ford Administration* Alf Clayton, the historian narrator, offers only a scant page directly concerning the presidency of Gerald Ford, and concludes that nothing can really be known about him. Alf dismisses him cursorily as

> the only non-assassinated President whose name ends with "d", the only Nebraska native and Michigan politician to attain the office, and the only skier.[1]

The novel therefore appears to belong to James Buchanan, the fifteenth and only bachelor president, whose biography Alf is struggling to write, an impression strengthened for many readers by Updike's own fascination for the Pennsylvanian president, the topic of his play *Buchanan Dying*. Arguably, however, the real story is as much that of the Ford years, especially of the history and origins of their sexual politics, investigated through Buchanan's and Alf's parallel failures in their love relationships. Updike focusses on the nature of American political freedom, and its relationship to art, taking his cue from a not-uncritical reading of Camille Paglia's post-Nietzschean version of cultural history in *Sexual Personae* (1990). Paglia deploys the opposition between the Apollonian and the Dionysian in culture in order to challenge the Romantic concept of nature as benign, and of sexual relationships as healthily guilt-free. It is Alf's understanding of sexual politics, the product of his experiences in contemporary culture, that informs his portrayal of the Buchanan presidency. In alternating nineteenth- and twentieth-century scenes, the novel restores Paglia's chthonian dimension to sex, as invested with power relationships and aggressive urges, and thus as always, in some senses, political. The inset nineteenth-century story revolves around Buchanan's unsuccessful struggle to prevent the nation yielding to aggression and descending into Civil War, ending as the South secedes. As James Schiff has argued, Buchanan's failure to maintain the political union is prefigured in the failure of his projected marital union with Ann Coleman, and her sudden, violent death.[2] Alf portrays Buchanan, pleading with the South, as a man who is "in love with his raven-haired mistress, yet still has a wife and children ... to consider" (233). Where Buchanan's failure hinges upon a minor breach of convention (taking tea with another lady before calling upon his betrothed), Alf's problem is not repressive convention but the laissez-faire sexual politics of the Ford years. The frame-story of the novel, set in the permissive era of sexual liberation, involves a battle of the sexes. Alf's belief in sexual relations as benign founders on the rocks of male and female rivalries, in the shape of Brent Muller, deconstructionist husband of his mistress Genevieve, and two women, Jennifer and Ann Arthrop, used as bait to discredit Alf. Both women play double roles; both have also been actors in Aristophanes' *Lysistrata*, the original, classic battle of the sexes where women outwit men in the political sphere much as they do in the contemporary plot of this novel. Updike's focus upon the ambiguities of freedom (both personal and political) conditions the twists and turns of the plot. Masks and personae animate the narrative structure, as Alf takes on the role and persona of Buchanan and is taken in by the personae of others, to his ultimate mortification.

Updike and Camille Paglia make strange bedfellows and the argument somewhat baldly stated above will stand some elaboration. In "Freedom and Equality: Two American Bluebirds" (1992) Updike invoked Paglia in a discussion of the relation between freedom and equality. Updike emphasised that the American constitution says little about equality, and is more concerned with balancing unequal entities (state and federal authority, judicial and legislative branches of government) to create a stable structure of power that is also responsive to the voice of the people. He described his own early fiction as focussing upon the elusive nature of freedom, with characters rebelling against a benevolent but confining order (*The Poorhouse Fair*), conforming to it to protect a child (*The Centaur*) and, in *Rabbit Run*, demonstrating that freedom is "running to nowhere" if purchased at the price of other people's suffering.[3] In *Memories of the Ford Administration* Buchanan's legalistic constitutionalism, challenged by Andrew Jackson's populist emphasis upon the passions of the people, is a major strand in the plot, as is the family misery caused by Alf's sexual freedom. For Updike freedom is ambiguous. He cites James M. McPherson's argument that in the Civil War both sides thought that they were fighting for freedom (for slaves, for states' rights) and notes also Jack Thomas's idea that societies die from intensification of their own first principle, in Athens an excess of democracy, and in America, of liberty.[4] Athens was conquered by authoritarian Sparta in the final stages of the Peloponnesian War; the excesses of the liberated Sixties wreak havoc on America. Updike quotes Paglia's "thrillingly Nietzschean" book, *Sexual Personae*, as arguing that freedom is an overrated modern idea, originating in the Romantic rebellion (exemplified by Rousseau) against bourgeois society, whereas in her view it is only in society that one can be an individual.[5] Outside its protection, nature "is waiting at society's gate to dissolve us in her chthonian bosom".[6] As Updike comments, human beings are centaur-like.

> Half animal, half responsible citizen, we each offer up some of our chthonian longings, in exchange for freedom from chthonian chaos.[7]

Reviewing Paglia's *Sex, Art and American Culture* (1992), a collection of previously published essays, Updike underlined the neo-conservative, anti-feminist tenor of Paglia's work, wryly condemning it as highly reassuring for the male reader, given that it applauds the uncontrollable elements of male sexuality. He nonetheless agreed with her argument that the roots of sexual attraction go deeper than our codes of civilised behaviour allow. He describes the first chapter of *Sexual Personae* as "simply magnificent, dense with stark truths and sweeping insights" as Paglia sets forth her cosmology under the title "Sexual Violence, or Nature and Art", opposing the female-Dionysian-chthonian to the male-Apollonian-skyey.[8] For Updike, her awareness of the life-enabling religious impulses moving beneath the quirks of human culture is her most valuable and refreshing trait.[9] Discussing sexual attraction, Updike argued that we are attracted to psyches as well as bodies. Yet he also gives full weight to the Dionysian.

> Not only does the sexual appetite join us to "the beasts of the field" and our chthonian mother ... "the ancient power of fright and lust" — but it calls into activity our most elegant faculties, of self-display, social intercourse, and idealization.[10]

Updike notes Paglia's demonisation of contemporary feminism and of academia, two topics dramatised in *Memories of the Ford Administration* in Jennifer Arthrop's vulgar feminism and in Alf's own experiences as a lecturer at the all-female Wayward College, where deconstruction has effectively dismembered the Humanities, and advanced a view of signification as arbitrary, and history as merely a construction. In contrast, Paglia believes that history has an inherent shape and meaning; she defends the notion of culture as continuous from the Greeks, and holds that there is a person behind every text. Her work is founded on the desire to reinsert emotion into cultural history and to resist the tyranny of the word. Her rejection of Derridean deconstruction is as resounding as Updike's, if not nearly as subtle as his comic portrayal of Brent Muller, a deconstructionist by career, yet in reality a churchgoer and traditional family man. Paglia also insists upon the religious dimension of cultural politics, in a fashion which, for all her supposed post-Catholic paganism, resonates strongly with Updike's own insistence on human guilt and shame, and on the ways in which the legacies of the past inflect the present.

While clearly influenced by Paglia, Updike dramatises her ideas in a variety of ways, to tease out the ambivalences and ambiguities in the connection between the personal and the political. Alf Clayton's historical project draws upon Paglia's stated aims, as described in her "Preface" to *Sexual Personae*: to rethink American cultural history in order to "flesh out intellect with emotion",[11] to clarify the heritage of the Sixties, which heroically broke with the confines of the Fifties but failed in her view to sustain their energies,[12] and to restore a serious understanding of the Dionysian in culture, as the realm of chaos, disorder and darkness. For Paglia, society is a system of inherited forms that constitute a defence against the power of nature, of which sex is a subset. "Without society, we would be storm tossed on the barbarous sea that is nature", she argues, introducing a marine imagery which Updike also adopts.[13] The idea of the ultimate benevolence of nature and God is the most potent of the survival mechanisms, without which culture would revert to fear and despair. The grandeur of culture, the consolation of religion, conceal from us our subordination to nature:

> But let nature shrug, and all is ruin. Fire, flood, lightning, thunder, hurricane, volcano, earthquake — anywhere at any time.[14]

Given that sexuality and emotion are at the intricate intersection of nature and culture, it is therefore an oversimplification for Paglia if sexual relations are reduced to a matter of social convention. Feminism is the heir of Rousseau, pitting nature against corrupt society. But aggression is part of nature; sex involves power struggles and identity forged in conflict.[15] Freedom is not without its darker underside: "Whenever sexual freedom is sought or achieved, sadomasochism will not be far behind. Romanticism always turns into decadence."[16] Paglia understands culture as an uninterrupted continuum from the Greeks to the present, in which Christianity has not defeated paganism, which surfaces repeatedly in the work of art, memorably characterised as a sexual force field distorted by fluctuations in masculinity and femininity.[17] Culture at large is a continual opposition between the Apollonian (order, form, light, symmetry) and the Dionysian (chaos, fluidity, darkness, miasma). The Apollonian Western mind believes that by naming and classifying, nature and archaic night can be pushed back. To name is to control: "Name and person are part of the West's quest for form."[18] The aesthetic sense also involves a swerve from the chthonian as the eye excludes, selects and enhances. Apollo is associated with the golden mean, moderation, a virtue distinctly evident in Buchanan's quest for compromise, negotiation and avoidance of excess. In contrast the Dionysian involves dissolution, earthly depths, waste, muck, and is associated with woman, the oceanic matrix or primal slime. As opposed to the Olympian gods the Dionysian is the realm of the daemonic, spirits of altogether lower levels of deity. In Paglia's distinctly uninviting portrayal, woman is the Dionysian miasma, the world of fluids, the "chthonian swamp" of generation.[19] Woman reeks of the sea.[20] Men may retain the reptilian brain, "killer survivor of the archaic era".[21] But woman's reproductive organs are labyrinthine, "lurid in colour, vagrant in contour, and architecturally incoherent".[22] They evoke an evolutionary revulsion from slime, our site of biologic origins.[23] Women's hair recalls Medusa in its "writhing vegetable growth of nature".[24] In response culture creates personality, recurrent types and masks, in order to give shape and form, to enhance separation and individuation, and as a defence against engulfment or dissolution. (The persona of the *femme fatale* is one such recurrent type.) Yet the process is never secure:

> In the day we are social creatures, but at night we descend to the dream world where nature reigns, where there is no law but sex, cruelty and metamorphosis.[25]

Paglia argues that western personality originates in the idea of masks; society is a place of masks, of ritual theatre. Her notion of the persona draws upon its original Greek meaning as the clay or wooden mask, reverberating to project the voice of the classical actor. Historically, the term broadens out over time to become the actor in the role, the social role or public function, the individual as citizen, and finally to how we understand the term today.[26] Crucially, Updike not only emphasises theatrical metaphors, social roles and deceptive masks, but also inscribes this argument into his narrative structure. In the novel Updike never writes quite for himself but always through the assumed persona of Alf, a fellow writer, who is himself projecting his own views and experiences through the figure of Buchanan. Alf's own disordered life draws him to attempt to create a tightly bounded persona in the shape of Buchanan, while Updike uses Alf as a means to explore the sexual politics of the Sixties and Seventies. In the nineteenth-century plot of the novel, the struggle to maintain an Apollonian order ultimately proves wanting as the country lurches into the Civil War; paradoxically the contemporary plot initially appears to move away from the Dionysian towards a renewed order, though at Alf's expense.

Updike's novel firmly establishes connections with Paglia, notably in relation to Alf's personal sexual attitudes, which influence his predilections as a writer for an understanding of history as the product of the subconscious, disordered impulses of its subjects. Alf's biography of Buchanan is not primarily interested in the historical record or the public deed:

> my tropism was toward the unlit, the underside, the region of shades where his personal demon teased our statesman, visiting embarrassment upon his dignity and violence upon his peacefulness. (178)

In terms of exploring the relation between sexual and national politics Updike could hardly have invented a starker opposition than between James Buchanan, supposedly the only virgin President, and the promiscuous Alf, a creature of his era. "Sex still had a good name during the Ford administration" (6) when one-night stands, bathhouses and sex shops abound. Indeed, "What had been unthinkable under Eisenhower, and racy under Kennedy had become, under Ford, almost compulsory" (6). Alf's freedom is qualified, however, by images of Dionysian dissolution. The novel opens as, newly separated, he watches Nixon's resignation speech in the gathering darkness, viewing the national scandal as a welcome distraction from his domestic one, which sits in the bosom of his family "like a great clammy frog, smelling of the swamp of irrecoverable loss" (4). When his wife Norma, "the Queen of Disorder" (9), aptly named for Bellini's pagan priestess, returns from a date involving sex in the woods with the leader of the local choral society (a comic reference to the Greek chorus) he comments on her "wiggly" (12) hair, the dust and cobwebs of the marital home, a "hairy, fringy nest" (8), her unfinished sentences, and half-done paintings. Form is never complete in Norma's world. Her house, full of cats and dogs, is a realm of such animality that one night there sends Alf to hospital with an asthma attack. In the broader public sphere, Sixties freedoms are also shadowed by images of decadence and degeneration. The town of Adams is in economic decline, and the local movie house has descended quite literally into the Dionysian, evolving from popular blockbusters to a triple X sex cinema. One sexual encounter spells out the problems of the healthy, liberal Sixties ideal. At the beginning of his narrative Alf recalls having engaged in sex with Wendy Wadleigh in complete conformity with the norms of the period. He finds her in some ways unattractive but in the Ford era "it was assumed that any man and woman alone in a room with a lock on the door were duty-bound to fuck" (16). Post-coitally, however, Alf is seized with chthonian distaste, as icy slime drips onto him. Not quite as liberated as he might seem, he dwells upon the female genitalia as "livid, oysterish, scarcely endurable complexity" (15–16). Wendy seems like a primeval swamp in her excessive wetness; Alf keeps slipping "like a man in smooth soled boots on a mudbank" (19). Nonetheless his "reptile brain" (22) takes over, though Wendy is less than enthusiastic at the prospect of oral sex: "I'm all goopy down there" (23). While Updike is known for the abundance of his sexual descriptions, *Memories of the Ford Administration* pays an inordinate amount of attention to slime, bodily fluids, muck, the viscous, and the oozing. Alf is overtaken here by revulsion and resentment, in a scene exposing the clash between the Sixties idea of sex as good, clean fun and the chthonian realm of slime and aggression.

In response Alf adopts the male strategy of imposing a persona on female formlessness, objectifying woman as a means of fixing her form and stabilising nature from flux. Paradoxically Alf's affair with Genevieve represents an attempt to reclaim an orderly life. First encountered by the reader fresh from church on Easter Sunday, in a hound's-tooth jacket and smartly pleated white skirt, she is a black-and-white figure, sharply defined in contrasting tones and geometric forms, her perfectly shaped silhouette and trim, compact body as neat as an artist's image of a "nymph" (53). The emphasis is on separation, contrast, and firmly defined form. At home Genevieve maintains a "European" (54) sense of regularity, involving impeccable housewifery skills, obedient children, and a cool, ordered décor. Even the manicured garden displays her orderliness, with its weed-free beds and mulched plantings. Nature is under firm control. Norma's psychosexual interior, unforgettably characterised as a tidal swamp where a narrow path wound past "giant nodding cattails and hidden egret nests, with a slip into indifference gaping on both sides" (55), contrasts with Genevieve's entrails, "city streets, straight, broad, and zippy" (55). The Dionysian abyss has yielded to civilised form, with untamed nature becoming the city state. When, however, Genevieve confesses to her husband and sets divorce in train, Alf is taken aback at the subsequent cocktail party as Genevieve plays her public role flawlessly with no sign of interest in him, her mask firmly in place. Alf remains uncomfortably aware that Brent and Genevieve have orchestrated the sequence of events. He has been cast in a social role which is not of his own choosing. "My part was all written. I was a character in their play" (56).

As a result, when Alf turns to creating the character of Buchanan he reverses direction, moving from Apollonian ordered forms to a nightmarish story of darkness and dissolution. Just as Alf shows some reluctance to embark on matrimony with Genevieve, Buchanan is introduced explaining to Ann Coleman that their wedding must be postponed on grounds of civic and legal commitments. The couple are imagined in 1819 walking across the city of Lancaster, formerly Hickory Town, but now renamed in a movement from nature towards culture, in imitation of an English city. It has even adopted as its emblem the red rose of Lancaster, historical badge of one side in an English Civil War, the Wars of the Roses. Alf presents the town through a series of European referents, signalling hierarchy and order, its former wildness subjected to naming and control, tamed by European inherited forms. The streets are named for the colonial past and for recurrent historical personae, and inherited titles: King, Queen, Duke and Orange streets. The inn is called after William Pitt, the Earl of Chatham. Wooden merchants' signs depict fixed images of Indian chiefs and European kings. Demuth's tobacco shop still features its 1770 signboard portraying a periwigged dandy with a snuffbox; they pass the house of Jacob Eichholz, a portrait painter who "fixed in paints" (42) the faces of the leading citizens. European forms contain and fix the human body as well; Buchanan wears a tail coat, waistcoat, constricting high collar and well-tied cravat. In its sunshine the city seems to be smiling down on them like the historic carved face of the Eavesdropper on the Bowsman house with its blank stone eyes (40). Despite the abundance of light, Apollonian order seems to demand a degree of optical selection, even blindness. On the one hand Buchanan decries the domination of European ideas in American politics, castigating Madison for his passion for French rationality, and Monroe for creating in Washington a Versailles of empty etiquette (43). For him "This continent was meant to be an escape from Europe, not a provincial imitation of it" (43). On the other he expresses his fear of the common man and his "natural greed and low appetites" (44), implicitly recognising the opposition between the passions of the people and politically restraining forms. As a result, Buchanan remains completely "wedded to the Constitution" (33), but never to Ann.

In Ann's eyes, however, Buchanan shares the thinness of the portraits around them, a shadow looming between her and the sun. To her, Buchanan's dress is not so very different from the bewigged dandy. Indeed his prospective mother-in-law characterises him as a "popinjay" (40); Ann as a "half-man, a chimera" (46) with an "illusionary thinness, like a large occluding emblem of painted tin" (47), not even as thick as the signboards or the slate tombstones of the nearby burial ground. As they enter its shade, Ann recalls lines from Byron, "The bright sun was extinguished" (47). Byron's "Darkness" (1816), written in the fabled year of no summer, the result of a volcanic eruption in Indonesia, tells of an environmental apocalypse in which all natural light is extinguished and mankind becomes extinct. There are no religious references to the Day of Judgment; the world simply disintegrates into the dust and chaos from which it sprung. Ann supplies the final lines:

> The winds were wither'd in the stagnant air,
> And the clouds perish'd; Darkness had no need
> Of aid from them — She was the Universe. (48)

When she had first read the lines she remembers feeling the front parlour falling away dizzyingly, and her terror at the mysterious She, with its Godlike capital letter. In "Freedom and Equality" Updike cited Tocqueville's claim that the loss of the feudal class system and particularly the aristocracy, weakened by revolution, left a yawning void, which was filled by poets, in the absence of their previous heroic themes, with images of nature.[27] Updike's scene is relentlessly textualised, a tissue of names and signs which make Ann fear becoming shut in "the coffin of a book" (47). Her fear appears informed by Tocqueville's argument. In Europe, she thinks, poets may be allowed to frighten young women, but not in America, so recently seized from the Indians and "soaked with their blood" (48), as the autumn leaves supposedly demonstrate. European-inspired inherited forms appear to have yielded in America to a vision of archaic night, and the triumph of the destructive feminine.

When Buchanan appears to slight her, by taking tea with Grace Hubley, she breaks off the engagement, once more quoting Byron, infuriating Buchanan who views him as the acolyte of "the tyrant Napoleon" (92). Democratic Buchanan sees Byron as linked to political despotism, not Romantic freedom. Angrily he decides to give Ann a few days to cool off before winning her over and restoring the status quo. As a result he seriously underestimates the power of both art and nature and the possible magnitude of the disaster at hand.

Significantly Buchanan's weakness for the Apollonian is a major factor in the catastrophe. Calling at the Jenkins house to report on the success of a legal case, Buchanan instinctively flinches at operating the doorknocker, a bare-breasted mermaid, and is relieved to enter an explicitly Apollonian scene, a temple of light brightly illuminated by the best spermaceti candles and smelling of the sea, "an august incense" (62). At its heart sits the enchanting Grace Hubley, on a sofa with a serpentine back, displaying an enticing amount of "siren breast" (62). Light suffuses the scene, from Grace's radiant face to the mirrored sconces and her iridescent, Persian shawl. The fireplace mantle is shaped in the form of a Greek temple, with an entablature, pillars and a carved classical frieze of acanthus leaves. Buchanan's chair is neo-Grecian, with an appropriately Apollonian lyre-shaped splat. Grace is clearly a devotee of order, form and light, and has absolute faith in a benevolent deity (69), a point rather undermined in Alf's view by her agonising later death when her clothing caught fire. The serpentine and marine imagery strikes a warning note, suggesting the persona of the temptress. It is clear that some woman told Ann of the visit; sexual rivalries among women figure at the centre of the causal knot. Like a siren, Grace has an enchanting Southern accent, though she is passionately opposed to slavery (seen as Dionysian, involving the sexual abuse of women and a debasing immorality), and roundly, if classically, consigns all slaveholders to Hades (65). In response, Buchanan reminds Grace that in Ancient Greece the contract between master and slave allowed considerable advantages to the slave. He brushes aside Grace's abolitionism as evidence of excessive passion, as opposed to his own belief in the golden mean, compromise and moderation. The scene suggests that Buchanan is far too swift to discount the passions (abolitionist or otherwise) and lingers too long in an Apollonian illusion. The South and slavery will prove his nemesis in political terms, just as Grace wrecks his personal affairs. In Alf's thesis, Buchanan's loss of Ann made him forever after too cautious and indecisive in action.

In the subsequent dramatisation of the death of Ann Coleman (an artistic tour de force), Updike makes a clear distinction between passion safely contained in art and the actual angry passions of wounded pride, regret and humiliation experienced by the scorned Ann. Alf, still clinging to a mythic order, cheerfully invents for Ann a coach ride to Philadelphia, in a Concorde carriage of the "Tallyho!" type usually featured in British prints, its panels painted with different sanitised renditions of erotic myth: Eros and Psyche, Venus and Mars, Artemis and Actaeon. Such is the movement of the coach however that Ann emerges almost seasick with the motion, and immediately takes to her bed. Her sister Sarah departs for a performance in Philadelphia's New Theatre (splendidly illuminated by gaslight), featuring three

British works, Arthur Murphy's *The Grecian Daughter*, Collins' *Ode to the Passions*, and the comic opera, *The Adopted Child*, which highlight the role of the passions in relation to democracy, and the extent to which art can or cannot contain them. In *The Grecian Daughter* Euphrasia saves her father's life by breastfeeding him in captivity, and then stabs to death the aptly named tyrant, Dionysus I, who destroyed democracy in Syracuse. A popular play in nineteenth-century America, it glorifies democracy, and woman's role as its defender. Samuel Birch's *The Adopted Daughter*, however, involves the restitution of ancestral power to an aristocratic heir. At this point Alf attempts to create an alternative history for Ann and Buchanan, imagining him pursuing her to Philadelphia, reconciliation, a long happy marriage and withdrawal from political life, with the result that Stephen Douglas becomes the fifteenth President, stifles abolitionists and Southern fire-eaters alike, and sees slavery fade away. By the time Douglas defeats Lincoln in 1860, Mr. and Mrs. Buchanan would have forgotten, as if in a dream, their moments of angry passion (121). Alf, however, bookends this fairy tale of sweetness and light with quotations from Collins' "Despair" (117) and "Anger" (121).

Alf has yielded to a desire for Apollonian form and structure, but he cannot stick to it and the narrative turns away towards waste and death instead. Alf's narrative oscillates continuously between the two forces of Apollo and Dionysus. He constructs scenes in order to thrust something into the "void where history leaves off" (112), but the void recurs. Much as he would like to confine passion and aggression within a literary form, he has to recognise their real strength. Ann Coleman died of hysterical convulsions, in some accounts by an excess of laudanum, even perhaps by her own hand. In the novel, responsibility for her fatal hysteria is firmly laid at the door of her oppressive father. Squeezed on all sides by patriarchal prohibitions, Ann becomes fevered, breathless and delirious. Hysteria (meaning frenzy) involves the conversion of psychological states into physical symptoms. (Alf's asthma is rather similar.) The term originates in the Greek for uterus, seen by the Greeks as liable to wander around the body. Ann's symptoms include a strange weakness, a feeling of floating off "below the waist" (123). In the 1980s feminists (notably Catherine Clément and Hélène Cixous) reclaimed the term and argued that oppressive social roles lay behind the (now discredited) diagnosis.[28] In her decline Ann feels as if "sunk into a shame of chaos, *mad disquietude*", recalling "Darkness" with its images of volcanoes and cannibalism, "a turbulent muddy reality just beneath the glitter and comfort of afternoon tea" (121), a "muck of disgrace" (122). Her head echoes with formless images which she cannot organise or control, while outside the evening darkens, and the garden of frozen forms steeped in Philadelphian "miasma" (122) becomes colourless and disappears. Ann is cold as a "Greek slave of marble" (131) in a sunless world, like Byron's, in which form disappears and dissolves, her mouth fills with slime, her urine smells like a horse's stale, and she descends into a dream world ruled by terror. When she administers the fatal dose of laudanum, it is overtly presented as a yielding to the Dionysian. The opium floats like gold flecks in a "muddy-bottomed spring" (126), offering death as dissolution into slime and viscidity (133). The doctor describes laudanum as holding a demon, and it is contained in a small vial, shaped like a homunculus. As Paglia notes, Goethe's *Faust*, a Dionysian drama, features Homunculus, a fabricated being hovering in a glass retort.[29] Ann sinks into image-filled dreams, as if yielding to decadent Romanticism and its idea of being snatched away in full bloom, of "emptying some dull opiate to the drains and sinking Lethe-wards"(127). Throughout this dark night of the soul Ann's thoughts oscillate between an opium-led illusion of divine love and the notion of god as an absence. Men may have tried "to believe in eternal light" but since the rise of the revolutionary spirit, darkness has become "our element, our punishment for wanting to be free" (132).

So far, so chthonian. In the sequence of scenes involving Buchanan and Ann, Updike engages overtly with the Apollonian and Dionysian, and it is a fair judgement to say that the latter has been more in evidence than the former. Apollonian forms have not provided Alf with enough defence against a nature which seems almost monstrous. The cultural forms of America do not appear to be robust enough to protect Ann Coleman. Or, indeed, its citizenry. The interview which Alf imagines between Buchanan and Andrew Jackson in 1824 reinforces the impression that in America savagery and violence are only lightly contained. Jackson, the representative of "backwoods America" (183), is both violent and sadistic. While Buchanan is attempting a political negotiation (later the basis of the "bargain and sale" controversy) Jackson refuses any compromise whatsoever. Everything about him signals aggression, from frontier background to military record, scars, and the musket ball still carried from a duel in which he deliberately took aim at his opponent in his manly parts, ensuring an agonising death. Equally delighted by his massacres of the Seminoles, British, French and Spanish he decries George Washington's softness. America, for him, is characterised as "a contention of free wills and selfish interests, set loose in a wilderness to survive" (187). The conversation takes place in the open air (where Jackson's rancid stink is marginally less offensive) against a background of architecturally incomplete forms, "ill-financed starts at marmoreal grandeur" (180), the half-built Capitol, and a White House lacking its Grecian portico, all pervaded by a miasmic mist from the surrounding swamps. Washington is a raw city, its classical designs unrealised. It is against this background that Jackson offers the moral that in America, power lies in the passions of the people (188). Despite its architectural pretensions, American democracy has yet to equal that of the Greeks, though it mirrors their deficiencies. Both men ignore a drunken, ragged black man lying in a stupor nearby. The Athenian *demos* did not include slaves, and neither, as yet, does America.

Nor did Athens include women. Updike, however, remedies the omission. Just as Buchanan's relationships foundered on female rivalry, so Alf is faced with temptation in the shape of Jennifer Arthrop and her mother, in scenes in which national politics are shadowed by the role of the *demos*, the people, evoking the oldest democracy, that of Athens. America seems to have deteriorated since Jackson's time. Alf's apartment, in an area of Adams in decline from the 1830s when Jackson constructed it as an ideal industrialopolis and workers' paradise (79), contains a monument to Presidents Washington and Adams, with statues of Liberty and Equality (79), now decorated with obscene graffiti and painted pudenda. It is in this apartment that he is pursued by Jennifer Arthrop, a student ostensibly consulting him about her work, while getting ever closer to her prey. In her term paper Updike provides a wickedly funny parody (*contra* Paglia) of the notion that sexual politics dictates national politics. Entitled *Protestant-Christian Mythmaking as an Enforcer of Male-Aggressive Foreign Policy in the Administrations of William McKinley and Theodore Roosevelt*, this magnum opus dwells upon McKinley on his knees in prayer before possessing the Philippines ("sexual significance of going down on one's knees", 81), the Philippines as a lightly clad maiden in cartoons, the vaginal innuendo of Dewy Bay, feminised images of Samoa, Roosevelt's big stick policy, the reluctance of Colombia to cede canal rights (virginity) and the sexual symbolism of dredging the canal (81). Intellectually, however, Alf now rejects the Sixties idea that sex has a political heft: "all the screwing in the world will not rattle bank foundations or bring down the walls of the Pentagon" (82). Cunningly he quizzes his student on the non-annexation of Cuba by Buchanan, drawing attention to the Ostend Manifesto of 1854. "Who was James Buchanan?" asks Jennifer, a revelation of ignorance which quite quells her "siren's song" (84). Back on firm ground, Alf bests her in the battle with her own rhetoric, calling attention to the phallic shape of Cuba, and the large cigars made there, big sticks all its own. When he discovers that she got his address from Brent Muller, his suspicions are confirmed. Jennifer is a honey trap, deployed to disgrace him with Genevieve. With his apartment transformed into "a moral arena, a theatre of combat" (150) he fights back, taking his cue from Paglia's contention that liberalism "defines government as tyrant father but demands it behave as nurturant mother", providing for its citizens, describing McKinley as nurturing and vulnerable, and declaring that his own pet project is to write about effeminacy in the Presidency, the President "as natural mother" (86).[30]

Mothers, however, may be less than nurturant. While Alf outwits the first attack on him, he meets his match in Jennifer's mother, a mistress of the mask. Alf's memory moves to Mrs Arthrop when he recalls a performance of a play about Emily Dickinson, *The Belle of Amherst*. At the theatre he had carried Genevieve, who had fainted in the interval, to the ladies' room where a crowd of women took over, dragging her into a silken foyer faintly redolent of female urine. His mind moves to Wayward, which also has a theatre, and to its student centre, a similar "gynous concentration" (194) with a subliminal scent that bombards his pheromone receptors with the aroma of a hundred young female students, sharpening his memory: "The senses are Mnemosyne's handmaidens" (195). Alf certainly puts the senses back into history, Paglia-fashion, but there is a price to pay. In *Sexual Personae* Paglia characterises Emily Dickinson's poetry as sadomasochistic, replete with images of violence and horror. "The brutality of the Belle of Amherst would stop a truck."[31] She gives a representative example, quoting the phrase "A Small Leech on the Vitals" (from "One Anguish –in a Crowd"), a line suggesting chronic gnawing doubt, as "an invisible haemorrhaging wound like a stress ulcer".[32] Genevieve's faint is the result of a duodenal ulcer caused by the stress of her relation with Alf (193). So much for sex as healthy and benign. Genevieve's faint also recreates her Apollonian, defensive mask. In Paglia's view Dickinson exploited a series of sexual personae in her poems, performances which reveal the Dionysian disorderings of stable social structures, the violence and aggression of nature, and apocalyptic visions of cataclysm.[33] Where a conventional feminist critique would see Dickinson as hemmed in by patriarchy, an impediment to her genius, Paglia argues that she uses personae in order to deal with the absence of limits, the excess of freedom in the Romantic solipsism of her imagination.[34] Paglia also draws attention to Dickinson's fondness for deaths and especially corpses: "She values corpses as artefacts; personality has passed from Dionysian mutability into Apollonian perfection."[35] Similarly, when Genevieve swoons, she resembles an effigy "in glossy, colorless wax" with "precise, decisively marked features" (193). Where Ann Coleman's death was ascribed to both stifling patriarchy and Romantic imaginative freedom, Genevieve's sexual objectification as a tightly formed persona appears to be a form of death-in-life. The female artist (Dickinson, as projected in the play by Julie Harris, the actress who played the role) has felled her into immobility.

Mrs Arthrop, however, knows how to exploit the mask in a suppler manner. In the novel the battle between Apollonian and Dionysian is always essentially the same battle, between similar personae, wearing the same masks and expressing the same aggressive rivalry, Grace versus Ann, Genevieve versus Norma, and then Ann versus Jennifer. Importantly Alf meets Mrs Arthrop when she attends the dress rehearsal of *Lysistrata*. Aristophanes designed his comic battle of the sexes around a conjugal strike. United, the women of Athens deny their husbands sexual relations in a successful bid to end the Peloponnesian War. "Screwing" (82) may not be a winning political strategy, but abstinence is. Appropriately, Brent's tool, Jennifer, plays the male role of Cinesias, a small, male part, but with a big scene with "this real cock teaser" (200). In the play Cinesias pursues his wife, the evasive Myrrhine, just as Jennifer had pursued Alf around his desk. In the novel, Jennifer, a woman, pursues a man, acting a role on behalf of Brent. In the play she plays a man pursuing a woman. Myrrhine finds endless reasons for delay, eventually disappearing into the female-occupied Acropolis, leaving Cinesias cursing in sexual frustration.[36] *Lysistrata*, one of the first portrayals of women onstage, was performed entirely by men in masks; it offers an inversion of the real world, calling into question conventional gender boundaries. In like fashion, Jennifer finds Myrrhine sadistic and feels like raping her (200). Jennifer is for the first time questioning the conventional binaries of male/female, sadist/masochist, desire/anger and war/love. Sex roles are not as simple or as biologically determined as Paglia's theory would suggest.

Lysistrata was produced as part of the Greater Dionysia, a festival both religious and civic, honouring Dionysus, and sponsored by the *demos* as a showcase for Athenian democratic ideology. The plays tend to advocate positions held by minorities, though they also show a consistent bias against populist politicians and the manipulation of democratic freedoms. Andrew Jackson would have got short shrift on the Athenian stage. Whereas in Greek tragedy women tend to be seen as wild, with gender strife often ending in disaster, in comedy harmony is normally restored. *Lysistrata* was produced in 411 BC, twenty years into the Peloponnesian War, at the end of which in 404 Athens had lost her navy, empire and for a time even her democratic freedoms. In the play the women win their point (beating the old politicians, the Magistrates) and the Spartan and Athenian ambassadors negotiate a peace. Jennifer sees this as a return for women to the role of sex slaves, reading the classic work in terms of Muller's deconstructionism, but in fact Lysistrata champions both her own sex and the civic values of all the Greeks. As an example of inherited cultural forms, the play may seem to work against Brent's anti-canonical position, yet it does him a favour in the shape of Mrs Arthrop, who reveals to Alf that she had played the role in her youth. Although today the play is often seen as feminist, Mrs Arthrop underlines the fact that Lysistrata only gained her education by eavesdropping on men's talk. In Mrs Arthrop's youth that point caused no offence; the play, staged during the Korean War, was controversial only for its anti-war theme. (It was acceptable to be against war in the abstract, but not when America was actually fighting.)

Unlike the play, the novel emphasises aggressive female rivalry. Mrs Arthrop had the star role, while her daughter has only a bit part. Alf realises that she is upstaging her daughter; this is "Women against women. Women at war" (252). Mrs Arthrop is under the impression that Alf has slept with Jennifer, and competitive jealousy is her motivation for sleeping with him. Alf's projected biography of Buchanan had been partly inspired by the deconstructionist view, propagated by Brent, that history is only texts (35). Ironically, deeply enmeshed in the story of Ann Coleman, he sleeps with Mrs Arthrop purely because she shares her name, allowing the word (Ann) to lead him, and to determine the course of his actions. Alf justifies the sexual encounter with the reflection that, as Tocqueville pointed out, "Americans prize freedom above all other goods" (217), but in fact the sexual encounter involves power struggles and conflicting identities. In essence, both Alf and Ann are masked. Although wearing her hair in a Grecian "Psyche" knot, Mrs Arthrop's face of "Olmec passivity" (221) suggests a more impenetrable American persona. Alf's value to her was the fantasy of sharing a man erotically with her daughter; hers to him "a chance to rescue lonely Ann" (222). Alf was adopting the role of Buchanan, finally getting the girl. But when Brent reveals Alf's adultery to Genevieve, she ends their relationship. Civil War in Ancient Greece was ended (at least onstage) by women, a force for peace. Restriction on sexuality brought an end to violence. Buchanan's unfulfilled relationship with Ann Coleman, however, leaves him forever a pacificator, unable to appreciate the feelings of either North or South, dismissive of abolitionist fervour and unable to maintain the peace. In nineteenth-century America, the full horror of war is unleashed. In the Seventies plot Alf's unrestrained sexuality cooks his goose. But what pulled the strings of disaster? Male desire or women's rivalries? Sexual freedom, or sexual conflicts? How secure are the categories of male and female? And how does art relate to politics? The example of the classical play suggests that wisdom and truth remain embodied in the literary canon, a touchstone of continuity with the past. But for Alf the two women acting in it have given the deconstructionist his victory.

To sum up: in the frame narrative Updike presides over a movement from Dionysian indulgence to Apollonian order and back, as Alf's sexual desires lead him first to seek a more ordered existence with Genevieve and then return him to Norma, the Queen of Disorder, when Genevieve rejects him. In like fashion, his book on Buchanan remains in incomplete form, dissolving into fragments in the final chapters of the novel. In the inset story Ann Coleman's descent into death is followed by Buchanan's flight from passion and his embrace of political formalities, legalistic pettifogging and diplomatic evasions. Two lengthy episodes focus on European courts and diplomacy. When Andrew Jackson despatches Buchanan (a thorn in his side) on a diplomatic mission to the Russian court, he is plunged into a world of ceremonial ritual, high culture and art. Tsar Nikolai, an apparently cultured man, has a fondness for Romantic prints and a large collection of the Gothic landscapes of Caspar David Friedrich. This does not stop him, however, from setting up the secret police, ruthlessly suppressing the Decembrist revolt and hanging the poet Ryleyev (who died clutching a volume of Byron). Autocratic repression trumps Romantic individualism and the pursuit of democratic freedom.

Buchanan moves on from Russia to London, again as a diplomat. The inset story draws towards a close with an explicit meditation on the relationship of art and politics. *Memories of the Ford Administration* offers a dark vision of American history, and of history itself, as dominated by less than idealistic motives. The point is developed in Alf's portrayal of Buchanan's 1855 meeting with Nathaniel Hawthorne, consul at Liverpool when Buchanan was Ambassador at the Court of St James — the last fully fictionalised scene in his novel before its form breaks down into incomplete notes. Despite the European setting and the emphasis on inherited tradition, nothing could be less Apollonian than Hawthorne's office, up an ill-lit stairway, and dominated by a hideous lithograph of Zachary Taylor, darkly veiled by black coal smoke. An unstable Windsor chair squeaks at Buchanan's every movement, threatening collapse. The emphasis is upon incompletion and formal dissolution. Although busts and portraits line the walls, the effect is not of stability and form, but of shadowy figures which appear to be about to take on life. The sequence of presidents is incomplete, lacking the latest incumbents, and the map of the United States, twenty years out of date, lacks both Texas and California, underlining the vulnerability of the Union to the loss of more Southern states. There is nothing immutable about America. Hawthorne, as much a political compromiser as Buchanan, had gained his lucrative appointment as Consul by writing the campaign biography of the victorious Franklin Pierce. Now, however, he is perfectly clear that the Union is under threat and that the issue of slavery will not go away. It has become "a passion, on both sides, which there will be no quenching but with blood" (265). The passions of the people are in the ascendant; a bust of Jackson, fierce and terrible, presides over them. In conversation, Buchanan argues that politics is all about compromise. Hawthorne, however, draws a line between art and politics, reminding him that despite intense pressure on him to withdraw "The Custom House" from *The Scarlet Letter*, he resisted all such pleas.

> A compromised work of art becomes on the instant worthless, since we look to art for an otherworldly integrity. (269)

Alf has transported Buchanan into the Gothic world of Hawthorne, a world of animated portraits, dark masks and, in the example of *The Scarlet Letter*, America's first fictional portrayal of sexual passion in relation to politics. Buchanan's claims ring hollow, quite literally. The scene ends with his high-pitched laugh, mixed with the shriek of the chair, as Hawthorne feels on his neck "a chill of the uncanny", as if the shriek had arisen in his own "haunted, reverberant skull" (277). Just as the mask formed a hollow resonance chamber for the Greek actor, projecting his character outwards, so Updike translates Hawthorne from the world of the stable, fixed persona to the realms of fluidity and dissolution. The regions of darkness are not so easily excluded, and their presence remains continuous through art across the ages.

Notes to Chapter 25

1. John Updike, *Memories of the Ford Administration: A Novel* (London: Hamish Hamilton, 1992), 367. Subsequent page references follow quotations in parentheses.
2. James Schiff, *John Updike Revisited* (New York: Twayne, 1998), 137.
3. John Updike, "Freedom and Equality: Two American Bluebirds," in *More Matter: Essays and Criticism* (London: Hamish Hamilton, 1999), 10.
4. Ibid., 13.
5. Ibid., 10.
6. Ibid., 11.
7. Ibid.
8. John Updike, "She's Got Personality," in *More Matter: Essays and Criticism* (London: Hamish Hamilton, 1999), 606.
9. Ibid., 608.
10. John Updike, "Lust," in More *Matter: Essays and Criticism* (London: Hamish Hamilton, 1999), 45.
11. Camille Paglia, *Sexual Personae: Art and Decadence from Nefertiti to Emily Dickinson* (New York: Vintage, 1991), xiii.
12. Camille Paglia, *Sex, Art and American Culture: Essays* (London : Penguin, 1992), vii.
13. Paglia, *Sexual Personae*, 1.
14. Ibid.
15. Ibid., 2.
16. Ibid., 3.
17. Paglia, *Sex, Art and American Culture*, 13.
18. Paglia, *Sexual Personae*, 5.
19. Paglia, *Sex, Art and American Culture*, 109.
20. Paglia, *Sexual Personae*, 92.
21. Ibid., 11.
22. Ibid., 17.
23. Ibid.
24. Paglia, *Sexual Personae*, 14.
25. Ibid., 4.
26. Paglia, *Sex, Art and American Culture*, 102.
27. Updike, "Freedom and Equality," 4.
28. Hélène Cixous and Catherine Clément, *The Newly Born Woman*, trans. Betsy Wing (Minneapolis: University of Minnesota Press, 1986).
29. Paglia, *Sexual Personae*, 255–56.
30. Ibid., 3.

31. Ibid., 624.
32. Ibid., 626.
33. Ibid., 652.
34. Ibid.
35. Ibid., 665.
36. Aristophanes, *Three Plays by Aristophanes: Staging Women*, trans. and ed. Jeffrey Henderson (New York and London: Routledge, 1996), lines 845–1025.

FURTHER READING

Contemporary Fiction

Saul Bellow and History (London: Macmillan; New York: Saint Martin's Press, 1984).
John Updike (London: Macmillan; New York: Saint Martin's Press, 1988).
Nadine Gordimer (New York and London: Routledge, 1988, 2014). In Spanish as *Nadine Gordimer: Palabra, Sexo y Consciencia en África* (Buenos Aires: Editorial Almagesto, 1997).
The Ballistic Bard: Postcolonial Fictions (London: Edward Arnold, 1995).
Alison Lurie: A Critical Study (Amsterdam and Atlanta: Rodopi, 2000).
Nadine Gordimer's Burger's Daughter: A Casebook (Oxford University Press, 2003).
Fictions of America: Narratives of Global Empire (New York and London Routledge, 2007).
Utopia and Terror in Contemporary American Fiction (New York and London: Routledge 2013).

Nineteenth-Century Fiction

"Kate Chopin: Short Fiction and the Arts of Subversion," in A. Robert Lee (ed.), *The 19th Century American Short Story* (London: Vision Press, 1985), 150–63.
Dred: A Tale of the Great Dismal Swamp, by Harriet Beecher Stowe (Halifax: Ryburn B.A.A.S. American Library, 1992. Reprinted Edinburgh University Press, 1999, 2014).
"Was Tom White? Stowe's *Dred* and Twain's *Pudd'nhead Wilson*," *Slavery and Abolition*, 20, 2 (1999), 125–36.
"Stowe's Sunny Memories of Highland Slavery," in Janet Beer and Bridget Bennett (eds), *Special Relationships: Anglo-American Affinities and Antagonisms 1854–1936* (Manchester University Press, 2002), 28–41.
"Staging Black Insurrection: *Dred* on Stage," in Cindy Weinstein (ed.), *The Cambridge Companion to Harriet Beecher Stowe* (Cambridge University Press, 2004), 113–30.
"The Afterlife of *Dred* on the British Stage," in Denise Kohn, Sarah Meer and Emily Todd (eds), *Transatlantic Stowe: Harriet Beecher Stowe and European Culture* (Iowa City: University of Iowa Press, 2005), 208–24.
(With Celeste Marie Bernier), "*The Bondwoman's Narrative*: Text, Paratext, Intertext and Hypertext," *Journal of American Studies*, 39, 2 (2005), 147–65.
(Editor with Celeste-Marie Bernier), *Public Art, Memorials, and Atlantic Slavery* (New York and London: Routledge, 2009).
"Writing against slavery: Harriet Beecher Stowe," in Elizabeth Clapp and Julie Roy Jeffrey (eds), *Women, Dissent and Anti-slavery in Britain and America, 1790–1865* (Oxford University Press, 2011), 175–96.
"Harriet Beecher Stowe and the 'Book That Started This Great War'," in Coleman Hutchison (ed.), *Cambridge History of American Civil War Literature* (Cambridge: Cambridge University Press, 2016), 3–16.
"Harriet Beecher Stowe's Cuban characters: *Uncle Tom's Cabin* and Gertrudis Gómez de Avellaneda's *Sab*," in Cristina Herrera and Larissa Mercado-López (eds), *(Re)mapping the Latina/o Literary Landscape: New Works and New Directions* (London: Palgrave Literatures of the Americas, 2016), 21–34.

"Louisa May Alcott's Family Post Box," in Celeste-Marie Bernier, Judie Newman and Matthew Pethers (eds), *Edinburgh Companion to Nineteenth-Century American Letters and Letter-Writing* (Edinburgh University Press, 2016), 642–54.

INDEX

9/11: 1, 282–85, 287, 293, 257, 250–51

Abbas, *Iran Diary* 258–60
Adler, Alfred 7, 235–36
African-American literature, *see* Hurston, neo-slave narratives
Agamben, Giorgio 2
Alcott, Louisa May 339
Alighieri, Dante 308, 310
American Beauty 225–27
Amis, Martin 282
anthropology, social 6, 7
    see also Barley, Bellow, Boas, Douglas, Goldenweiser, Herskovits, Hurston, Leyton, Parsons, Radin
anti-ocular discourse, 218
apartheid and novel, *see* Gordimer
Apter, Emily 199
Aristophanes:
    Lysistrata 323, 333–34
Ardrey, Robert 28, 47, 49–51, 58
artists 74–77, 256, 274, 288, 300, 328
Ashcroft, Bill 202
Atta, Mohamed 284

Baker, Houston 190, 192, 195
Bal, Mieke 1
Barley, Nigel 156–57, 159
Barthes, Roland 75
Barshevsky, Yetta 267
Baym, Nina 98
Bell, Millicent 310
Bellow, Gregory 279 n. 27
Bellow, Saul:
    and anthropology 62–72
    and death 156–67
    and gift exchange 26–32
    and Holocaust 116–277
    and *Partisan Review* 267–77
    pseudonym 269
    and Trotskyism 267–81
    works:
        The Adventures of Augie March 63–64, 124, 271, 275, 277
        "Cousins" 62–72
        Dangling Man 270, 272
        The Dean's December 124, 125
        "The Hell It Can't" 269

Henderson the Rain King 62, 124–25
Herzog 125, 299
"Him With His Foot in His Mouth" 295–306
Humboldt's Gift 26–32, 125
"In the Days of Mr Roosevelt" 272
"The Mexican General" 274–77
More Die of Heartbreak 303
"Mosby's Memoirs" 156–67, 278–79
"Mr Katz, Mr Cohen and Cosmology" 273–74
Mr Sammler's Planet 124, 125
"Pets on the North Shore" 269
Seize the Day 125
"This Is The Way We Go To School" 269
To Jerusalem and Back 63
"Two Morning Monologues" 272
The Victim 116–26
bibis 127, 135
Bigsby, Christopher 132, 133
biography 73–86
Birch, Samuel:
    The Adopted Child 330
birth order, *see* Adler, Sulloway
Blanchot, Maurice 224
Bloom, Harold 188
blowback 239–40
Boas, Franz, 62, 64–65, 71, 189
book-reviewing 6
Bradbury, Malcolm 9
Buchanan, James, *see* Updike, *Memories of the Ford Administration*
Butler, Judith 244
Byron, George Gordon (Lord Byron) 328, 329, 330, 335

Cabell, James Branch:
    Hamlet Had an Uncle, 310
Callaway, Henry:
    The Religious System of the Amazulu, 15–16
Canetti, Elias 17
cannibalism 27–30
canon formation 4, 128–29, 131, 136–37, 140, 334
Carby, Hazel 188
Carey, John 304
Carr, J.L. (Joseph Lloyd) 6
Carroll, Rachel 1, 3
Carver, Raymond:
    "Why don't you dance?" 286
Castells, Manuel 237

Chevigny, Bell Gale 75–76
Cheyfitz, Eric 144–46, 199
Chopin, Kate 338
Chow, Rey 203
Christ, Carol 101
Christianity and paganism, *see* Updike *Gertrude and*
    Claudius, and *Memories of the Ford Administration*
Cixous, Hélène, and Catherine Clément 330
Clifford, James 150, 151
Clinton, Bill 225–26, 227
clothing, 146, 15–154
Coates, Paul 124
Coetzee, J.M. (John Maxwell) 11–12
    Dusklands 10
    Foe 185
    Waiting for the Barbarians 10, 202
collecting 146, 150–54
Collins, William:
    The Passions 333
comedy 5
    and Aristotle 298
    and Bellow 156–57
    and death 159
    and tendentious jokes 300–01
    Freudian theory of 300–05
    green 299–300, 302
    see also Aristophanes, metaphor
Condé, Maryse:
    I Tituba 132
contemporary, notion of 1–3, 12
courtly love 3, 307, 310, 313, 315, 319
counter-discourse 87, 107
Cronin, Gloria 188
cults 9, 18, 33–46, 94, 158

Dabashi, Hamid 240
Dart, Raymond 48–49
Darwin, Charles 235
de Bellis, Jack 215
de Certeau, Michel 218
de Madariaga, Salvador 319
de Quincey, Thomas:
    The Pains of Opium 118–20, 122, 124
de Rougemont, Denis 307–09, 320
de Tocqueville, Alexis 334
Debord, Guy:
    and film 224
    The Society of the Spectacle 218–20, 224
Desai, Anita:
    Baumgartner's Bombay 8
Dickinson, Emily 9, 108, 332–33
Dinesen, Isak (Karen Blixen) 87
Dostoevsky, Fyodor 116, 203, 268
double, the, *see* Rank
Douglas, Mary 7, 203
Dreiser, Theodore 8

Dubus, André III 12
    The Garden of Last Days 250
    House of Sand and Fog 239–52

ekphrasis 253–66
Elias, Norbert 184
Eliot, George 73
Emerson, Ralph Waldo 31, 99, 102, 103, 108
empire, British, *see* J. G. Farrell
empire, American, *see* Dubus, Johnson
English 1–2 course 102
Erdrich, Louise:
    Tracks 125
ethology 48
Evans, Colin 10
Exodus 289–91

Fachinger, Petra 282
Faludi, Susan 283–84, 293
Falwell, Jerry 283

I. G. Farben 123

Farrell, J. G.:
    The Siege of Krishnapur 143–55
Farrell, James T. 269, 277
Ferdowski, *The Shahnameh* 256–58, 259, 260
Ferguson, Niall 239
Festinger, Leon:
    When Prophecy Fails 37
Fetterley, Judith 99
Fielding, Kenneth 5
Fiske, John 311
folk tale, *see* fairy tale, jump story, Lurie
Fool, the 162–63
footbinding, 240
Ford, Ford Madox:
    The Fifth Queen 8
Ford, Gerald 322
Foucault, Michel 100, 174, 218
fraternities 104–07
Freud, Sigmund, 7
    and Bellow 119, 123, 300–05
    and Updike 216
Frye, Joanne 101
Frye, Northrup 7, 299, 300
Fuchs, Dan 164
Fuller, Margaret 75–76
furniture 111, 147, 255, 286–89, 329, 336

gaze 171, 174, 218–19, 225
gift exchange, *see* Bellow, Hurston, Mauss
Gilbert, Sandra and Susan Gubar 9
Glanzman, Sam 283
globalisation 1, 11, 202, 212, 232–34, 237
Glotzer, Albert 267

Goethe, Johann Wolfgang von:
  Der Erlkönig 148
  Faust 331
Goffman, Erving 7, 34–35, 37, 39, 40, 42, 44
Goldenweiser, Alexander 62 65
Goldin, Farideh:
  Wedding Song 254
Goldin, Frederick 308
Gollancz, Sir Israel 311
Googoosh 247
Gordimer, Nadine:
  Burger's Daughter 15, 338
  The Conservationist 10, 15–25, 180
  A Guest of Honour 7
  "Is There Nowhere Else Where We Can Meet?" 180
  Jump 176–87
  "Something Out There" 47–61
Gordon, David 80, 81
Gordon, Mary 11
  Men and Angels 73–86
Gothic:
  and Nathaniel Hawthorne 336
  and Sixties cults 94
  modern 89
  postcolonial 87–98
Gould, Nathan 267, 269
Graham, Robert 242–43
Grainge, Paul 258–59
Gray, Richard 282
Green, Daniel 6
Greene, Graham 6
Greenblatt, Stephen 319
Greenland 12, 198–212

Hāfez 253, 255, 258, 261
Hakakian, Roya:
  Journey from the Land of No 254
Handl, Irene 6
Hardt, Michael and Antonio Negri 239
Hartnell, Anna 290, 291, 293
Hawthorne, Nathaniel 108
  and film 132
  and Franklin Pierce 335
  and historicism 131, 138
  and Salem 130–32, 133
  works:
    The Blithedale Romance 35, 109, 132, 135
    "The Custom House" 133–34, 335
    "Drowne's Wooden Image" 133
    The Marble Faun 132
    "Rappaccini's Daughter" 132, 133
    The Scarlet Letter 127–29
Heath, Stephen 9
Hegel, Georg Wilhelm Friedrich 66–70
Heilbrun, Carolyn 73, 85, 99
Hemenway, Robert 189, 190

Hersh, Seymour 239
Herskovits, Melville 62, 65
Hillenbrand, Robert 265 n. 20
historical novel, *see* Bigsby, Condé, Desai, J. G. Farrell, Ford Madox Ford, Jhabvala *Heat and Dust*, Mukherjee, Updike *Memories of the Ford Administration*
history:
  American, *see* Buchanan, Hawthorne, Salem
  and deconstruction 324, 334
  Danish, *see* Høeg
  Indian 2, 49, 130–33, 136–37, 240
  intellectual 8
  Iranian 12, 239–52, 253–66
  Jewish, *see* Jews
  South African, *see* Gordimer
Høeg, Peter:
  Smilla's Sense of Snow 12, 198–214
Hohenstaufen, Frederick II of 315
Hook, Andrew 4, 7
Howells, William Dean:
  The Undiscovered Country 35
Huggan, Graham 202
human rights imperialism 240
Hume, Kathryn 4
Hungerford, Amy 2
Hurston, Zora Neale:
  and Boas 189
  and gift exchange 189–97
  and oral storytelling 195
  works:
    "The Gilded Six Bits" 197 n. 4
    Their Eyes Were Watching God 2, 7, 188–97
Hutner, Gordon 2
hysteria 330

Iannone, Carol 169
India, *see* History
intercalated stories 110–13
intertextuality 3, 5, 8, 33–46, 97, 108, 170, 215, 222, 307–21
Iran, Jews of, *see* history
Iranian-American novel, *see* Dubus, Nahai, Sofer

Jackson, Andrew 323, 331, 333, 335
Jacobs, Harriet 9
James, Henry:
  "The American Scene" 171
  The Bostonians 35–36
  "Master Eustace" 310
  "Professor Fargo" 35
  Washington Square 171
Jay, Martin 218
Jesup Expedition 12, 62, 65, 67, 70, 71
Jews:
  in Amsterdam 264

Hassidic 261–63
Iranian see Nahai, Sofer
see also Bellow and anthropology, Bellow and Holocaust
Jhabvala, Ruth Prawer:
    and Gothic 87–98
    works:
        "Expiation" 93
        Heat and Dust 8
        The Short Story in England 1700–1753 89
        Three Continents 6, 12, 87–98
Johnson, Chalmers 239–40
jump story 13, 179–87
Jung, Carl 7, 121, 300

Kant, Immanuel 69–70
Karloff, Boris 121
Kerrigan, William 310, 311
Kiely, Robert 101
Kierkegaard, Søren 96, 317
Kiernan, Robert F. 162, 165
Kinzer, Stephen 252 n. 26
Koeberg nuclear power station 57
Koehler, Eric 308–09
Knight, G. Wilson 320
Kristeva, Julia 8, 33
Kumar, Amitava 232
Kuzna, Faye 303
Kwakiutl, see gift exchange

Laclau, Ernesto 113
Lawrence, D.H. 7
Leavis, F.R. 7, 9
Lewis, Sinclair:
    It Can't Happen Here 269, 270
Leyton, Elliott 93
Luedtke, Luther S. 130, 132–33
Lull, James 231
Lurie, Alison 10, 12
    and biography 73–86
    and costume 34
    and folktale 34
    and Transcendentalism 10
    works:
        Clever Gretchen and Other Forgotten Folktales 34
        Imaginary Friends 33–46
        The Language of Clothes 34, 41
        Love and Friendship 99–108, 113
        The Truth About Lorin Jones 73–86
        V. R. Lang: A Memoir 83
Lyotard, Jean-François 100

Macherey, Pierre 137
Mackenthun, Gesa 144, 145
Majeed, Javed 149
Marx, Leo 8
Mason, Mrs Rufus Osgood 189–90

Mather, Cotton 131, 136
Mauss, Marcel 7, 28, 31, 62, 65, 189
Mayer, Ruth 212
Mayo, Elton 37
McNamara, Jack 275
medieval literature, 5
    see also courtly love, Saxo Grammaticus, troubadour
        poets
memoirs 254–55
Messent, Peter 194
metaphor 143–55
Mill, James 149
Miller, Arthur G. 158
mimicry, see Gordimer, Something Out There
Minh-ha, Trin T. 196
Mitchell, W. J. T. 264
Moretti, Franco 6
Morley, Catherine 283
Morrison, Toni 2, Beloved 125
Mukherjee, Bharati 6
    and globalisation 231–38
    and Hawthorne 127–42
    and Sikh terrorism 237
    works:
        Desirable Daughters 12, 231–38
        The Holder of the World 127–42
        Jasmine 87
        The Sorrow and the Terror 237
        The Tree Bride 237
Murphy, Arthur:
    The Grecian Daughter 330

Nafisi, Azar:
    Reading Lolita in Tehran 240–41
Nahai, Gina 12
    and fairy tale 254
    and Iranian history 254
    works:
        Caspian Rain 254
        Cry of the Peacock 254
        Moonlight on the Avenue of Faith 254
narratology 4
Native Americans, see Kwakiutl, Nipmuc, Zapotec
Ndebele, Njabulo 176, 177, 181, 182
neo-historicism 4, 100, 131, 137, 138, 140, 144
neo-slave narratives 9
Nietzsche, Friedrich 2, 313, 322
Nipmuc, see Mukherjee The Holder of the World
Niranjani, Tejaswini 100

O'Donnell, Patrick 137–38
oral storytelling, see folk tale, Hurston, jump story,
    Nahai
Oring, Elliott 304
Osborne, Peter 1, 3
O'Sullivan, John 283

Paglia, Camille 322–33
Paley, Grace 4
    and family politics 168
    and Vietnam 168–75
    works:
        "A Conversation With My Father" 168, 170
        Enormous Changes at the Last Minute 170
        "Faith in a Tree" 168–75
        "Goodbye and Good Luck" 169
        Just As I Thought 168
        Later the Same Day 169
parasitism, *see* Høeg
Parsons, Elsie Clews 158
Paz, Octavio 233
Pergolesi, Giovanni Battista 301
Poe, Edgar Allan 108
pollution, *see* Douglas
postcolonial literature, 2, 8, 10, 12, 13, 128, 129, 137,
        139, 140, 151, 176, 196, 311
postmodernism 73
Prager, Emily 8
primates:
    and evolution 48–49
    as gods of settlement 57
    as sacred baboon 57–58
    see also Ardrey, ethology, Gordimer *Something Out
        There*

Radin, Paul 65
Rafael, Vicente 199
Rank, Otto 117, 119, 120 124, 161
reader 1, 3, 4, 10, 12, 15, 22, 24, 33, 34, 38, 39, 42, 44,
        45, 50, 59, 65, 75, 84–85, 94–99, 101, 111, 113, 124,
        136, 171–74, 178, 180, 182, 190, 196, 204, 207,
        208, 223, 224, 234, 237–38, 244–45, 247, 250, 264,
        276, 277, 296, 310–11, 320, 323
realism 15, 21–24, 73–75, 77, 79, 80, 83, 176, 216, 259
Rembrandt van Rijn 264
Reservoir Dogs 217
revisionings 113, 127
Rhys, Jean:
    Wide Sargasso Sea 10, 87, 128
Richter, Jean Paul 299
Ristoff, Dilvo 217
Robinson, Douglas 199
Robinson. Marilyn:
    and nuclear waste 11
    and Transcendentalism 10
    works:
        Gilead 11
        Home 11
        Housekeeping 11, 99–102, 108–15
        Lila 11
        Mother Country 11
Rosa de Xochimilco 274, 276
Rothberg, Michael 282–83

Rushdie, Salman 47

Sachs, Albie 176–77, 181
Sagan, Eli 26, 27, 29
San Juan, Jr., E. 202, 207
Sanday, Peggy Reeves 105–06
Saxo Grammaticus 310
Shachtman, Max 267, 269, 270, 278
Schama, Simon 9
Schiff, James 322
The Searchers 284
Sedgwick, Eve Kosofsky 88
serial killer 7, 12
    see also Sobhraj
Serres, Michel:
    The Parasite 208–12
sexual politics 9
    and 9/11: 283–84
    and fraternities 104–06
    and land 15–25, 206
    in *Memories of the Ford Administration* 322–37
    and trance maiden 33–46
    and troubadours 307–09
Shakespeare, William:
    and green comedy 299
    head used as ammunition 147
    works:
        Hamlet 302, 307–21
        The Tempest 146
        The Winter's Tale 13
Sick, Gary 239
Simrock, Karl 311
Sitas, Ari 185
    Smith, Beau, "Soldiers" 283
Sobhraj, Charles 12, 87–98
sociobiology 232
Sofer, Dalia, 12
    The Septembers of Shiraz 253–66
solidarity criticism 176
Sollors, Werner 232
    The Spirit of America 284
spirit possession 17, 18
Spivak, Gayatri 240
Stowe, Harriet Beecher 338
Sulloway, Frank J. 235
survival guilt 117, 121, 160, 163
Swedenborg, Emanuel 297, 300, 302

Tafoya, Eddie 308
Tanner, Tony 8
Taylor, Jacqueline 172
Terdiman, Richard, 87, 107
territorial imperative 28, 48, 49, 50, 52, 145
terrorism, 3, 47–48, 237, 240
    and domestic myth 282–94
Thoreau, Henry 2, 99, 102, 108, 112

The Thousand and One Nights 124
Thule, *see* Greenland
e trance maiden 33–46
Transcendentalism 2, 10, 40, 94, 99–115
translation 145–55, 198–214
Trotsky, Leon, assassination of 125, 160, 277, 274–77
Trotskyism, 267–81
troubadour poets 307–09, 315, 318
Turkel, Gerald 245
Twain, Mark (Samuel L. Clemens):
 The Adventures of Huckleberry Finn 100
 Pudd'nhead Wilson 338

Updike, John 7, 9, 11, 12
 and ethnicity, 292–93
 and *Exodus* 289–91
 and film 215–16, 225–27
 and popular song 221–23
 and *The Scarlet Letter* 12, 132
 and terror 282–94
 works:
  Brazil 307, 311
  Buchanan Dying 322
  The Centaur 323
  Couples 12
  "Freedom and Equality" 323, 328
  Gertrude and Claudius 307–21
  In the Beauty of the Lilies 215, 216
  Just Looking 216
  Memories of the Ford Administration 322–37
  "Movie House" 215
  The Poorhouse Fair 215, 323
  Rabbit at Rest 216–24, 225
  Rabbit is Rich 216
  Rabbit Redux 216
  "Rabbit Remembered" 216, 224–27
  Rabbit, Run 11, 215, 221, 323
  "Reflections on Radio" 221, 226

Seek My Face 216
Terrorist 282–94
"Varieties of Religious Experience" 284–85
Widows of Eastwick 13
Witches of Eastwick 13
see also anti-ocular discourse, Christianity, furniture,
 Paglia, sexual politics
utopia 3, 35, 36, 185, 276, 277

Venuti, Lawrence 199, 200
Versluys, Kristiaan 290
Vietnam, *see* Paley
Vincent, Bernard 145
virtual reality 138–40
Viswanathan, Gauri 136

Wallace, David Foster:
 Infinite Jest 2
Wallace, Michele 188
Waugh, Evelyn 5
West Coast offence 234
western 49, 234, 284
Wharton, Edith, *Hudson River Bracketed* 35
White, Allon 9
Whitlock, Gillian 240, 254
Williams, Sherley Anne 190
Wilson, Edward O. 232
Winthrop, John 289
Wirten, Eva Hemmungs 201
Wolfe, Alan 168
Words magazine 6

Yale, Elihu 136–37

Zapotecs, *see* Bellow, "Mosby's Memoirs"
Zulu myth 15–18